**PHILIP'S**

G000294697

STREET ATLAS
Buckinghamshire

First published in 1990 by

Philip's, a division of
Octopus Publishing Group Ltd
2–4 Heron Quays, London E14 4JP

Second colour edition 2001
Third impression with revisions 2003

ISBN 0-540-08016-0 (hardback)
ISBN 0-540-08017-9 (spiral)

© Philip's 2003

OS Ordnance Survey®

This product includes mapping data licensed
from Ordnance Survey® with the permission of
the Controller of Her Majesty's Stationery Office.
© Crown copyright 2003. All rights reserved.
Licence number 100011710

Printed and bound in Spain
by Cayfosa-Quebecor

Contents

III   **Key to map symbols**

IV   **Key to map pages**

VI   **Route planning**

VIII   **Administrative and Postcode boundaries**

1   **Street maps** at 3½ inches to 1 mile

214   **Index** of towns and villages

215   **Index** of streets, hospitals, industrial estates, railway
stations, schools, shopping centres and universities
and places of interest

Digital Data

The exceptionally high-quality mapping found in this atlas is available as digital data in TIFF
format, which is easily convertible to other bitmapped (raster) image formats.

The index is also available in digital form as a standard database table. It contains all the details
found in the printed index together with the National Grid reference for the map square in which
each entry is named.

For further information and to discuss your requirements, please contact Philip's on
020 7531 8438 or james.mann@philips-maps.co.uk

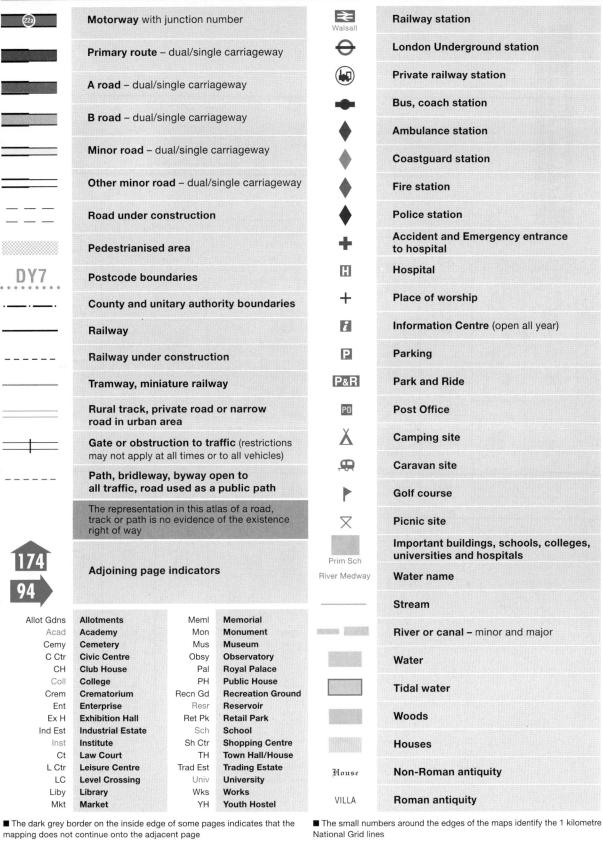

	Motorway with junction number			Railway station
	Primary route – dual/single carriageway			London Underground station
	A road – dual/single carriageway			Private railway station
	B road – dual/single carriageway			Bus, coach station
	Minor road – dual/single carriageway			Ambulance station
	Other minor road – dual/single carriageway			Coastguard station
	Road under construction			Fire station
	Pedestrianised area			Police station
DY7	Postcode boundaries			Accident and Emergency entrance to hospital
	County and unitary authority boundaries		H	Hospital
	Railway		+	Place of worship
	Railway under construction		i	Information Centre (open all year)
	Tramway, miniature railway		P	Parking
	Rural track, private road or narrow road in urban area		P&R	Park and Ride
	Gate or obstruction to traffic (restrictions may not apply at all times or to all vehicles)		PO	Post Office
	Path, bridleway, byway open to all traffic, road used as a public path			Camping site
	The representation in this atlas of a road, track or path is no evidence of the existence right of way			Caravan site
				Golf course
				Picnic site
174 94	Adjoining page indicators	Prim Sch		Important buildings, schools, colleges, universities and hospitals
		River Medway		Water name
				Stream
				River or canal – minor and major
				Water
				Tidal water
				Woods
				Houses
			House	Non-Roman antiquity
			VILLA	Roman antiquity

Allot Gdns	Allotments	Meml	Memorial
Acad	Academy	Mon	Monument
Cemy	Cemetery	Mus	Museum
C Ctr	Civic Centre	Obsy	Observatory
CH	Club House	Pal	Royal Palace
Coll	College	PH	Public House
Crem	Crematorium	Recn Gd	Recreation Ground
Ent	Enterprise	Resr	Reservoir
Ex H	Exhibition Hall	Ret Pk	Retail Park
Ind Est	Industrial Estate	Sch	School
Inst	Institute	Sh Ctr	Shopping Centre
Ct	Law Court	TH	Town Hall/House
L Ctr	Leisure Centre	Trad Est	Trading Estate
LC	Level Crossing	Univ	University
Liby	Library	Wks	Works
Mkt	Market	YH	Youth Hostel

■ The dark grey border on the inside edge of some pages indicates that the mapping does not continue onto the adjacent page

■ The small numbers around the edges of the maps identify the 1 kilometre National Grid lines

The scale of the maps is 5.52 cm to 1 km
3½ inches to 1 mile 1: 18103

0	¼	½	¾	1 mile
0	250m	500m	750m	1 kilometre

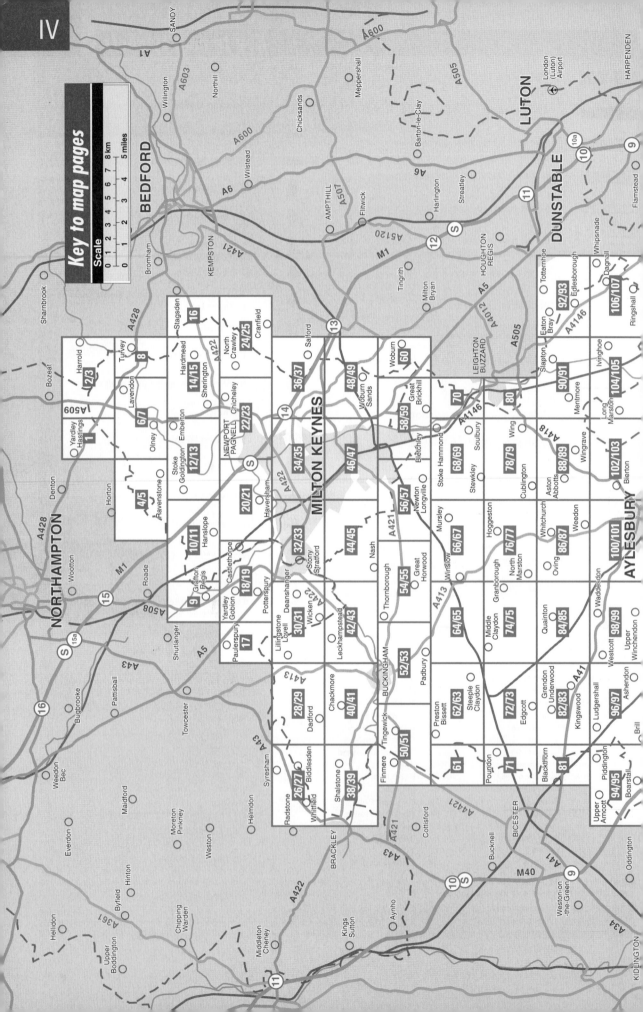

IV

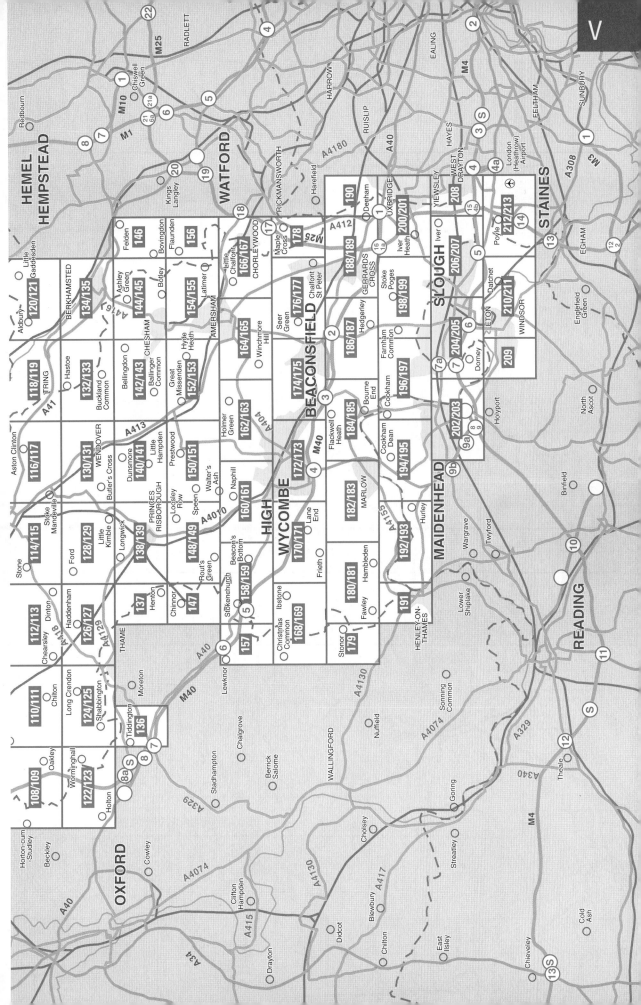

Route planning

Scale

0 1 2 3 4 5 6 7 8 km
0   1   2   3   4   5 miles

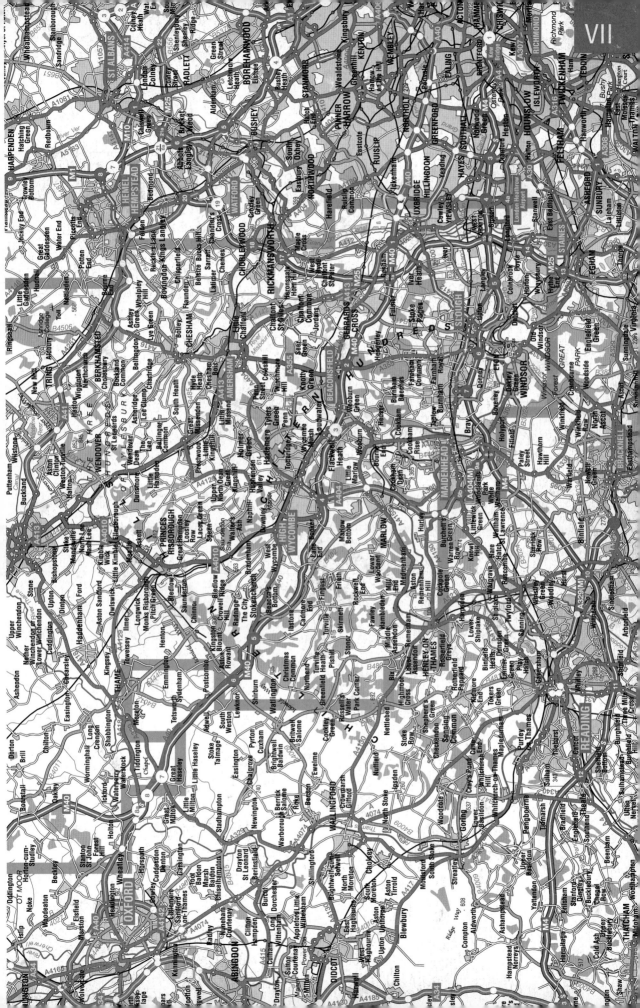

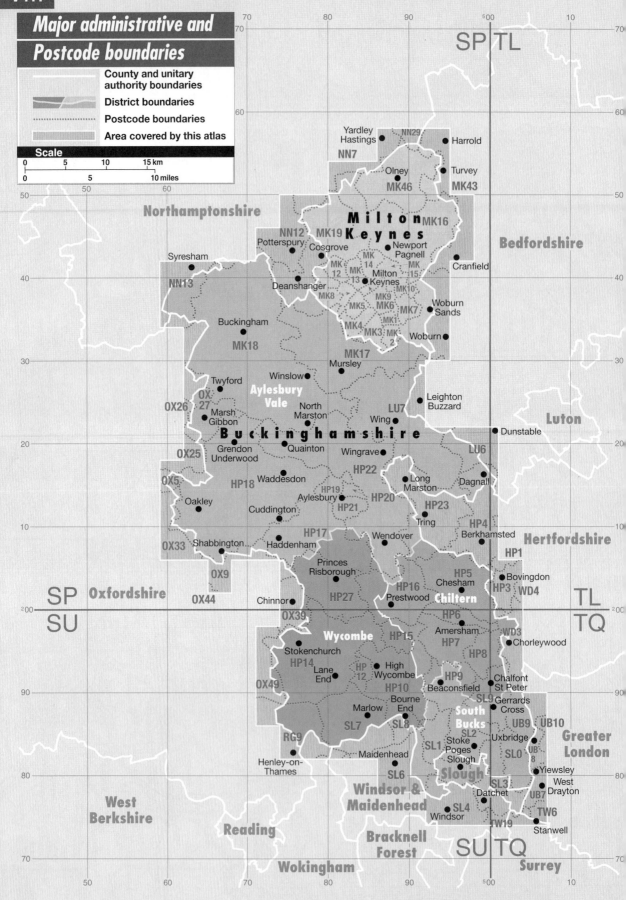

Major administrative and Postcode boundaries

	County and unitary authority boundaries
	District boundaries
	Postcode boundaries
	Area covered by this atlas

Scale

0   5   10   15 km
0   5   10 miles

SP|TL

Northamptonshire

Bedfordshire

Yardley Hastings
NN29
Harrold
NN7
Olney
MK46
Turvey
MK43

Milton Keynes
MK16

NN12
Potterspury
MK19
Newport Pagnell
Cosgrove
Cranfield

Syresham

NN13

MK 12
MK 14
MK 15
Deanshanger
MK 13
Milton Keynes
MK10
MK8
MK9
Woburn Sands
MK5
MK6
MK7
MK1
Woburn
MK4
MK3
MK 2

Buckingham
MK18

MK17
Mursley

Twyford
Winslow

OX 27
Aylesbury Vale
Leighton Buzzard
OX26
Marsh Gibbon
North Marston
LU7
Wing

Luton

Buckinghamshire

Dunstable

OX25
Grendon Underwood
Quainton
Wingrave
LU6

HP22
Long Marston
OX5
HP18
Waddesdon
Dagnall
HP19
Oakley
Aylesbury
HP20
HP23
Cuddington
HP21
Tring
HP4
Berkhamsted
HP17
Wendover
OX33
Shabbington
Haddenham
Hertfordshire
HP1
OX9
Princes Risborough
HP5
Bovingdon
Chesham
HP3
WD4

SP
Oxfordshire
OX44
HP16
Prestwood
Chiltern
TL
Chinnor
HP27
HP6
TQ
SU
Amersham
WD3
Chorleywood

Wycombe
HP15
HP7
HP8

Stokenchurch
HP14
HP 12
High Wycombe
HP9
Chalfont St Peter
Lane End
Beaconsfield
OX49
HP10
SL9
Gerrards Cross
Bourne End
South Bucks
UB9
UB10
Marlow
SL2
Stoke Poges
Uxbridge
Greater London
SL7
SL8
SL1
Slough
SL0
UB 8
RG9
Maidenhead
SL6
Slough
Yiewsley
West Drayton
Henley-on-Thames
SL3
Datchet
UB7
TW6
Windsor & Maidenhead
SL4
Windsor
TW19
Stanwell

West Berkshire

Reading

Bracknell Forest

SU|TQ
Surrey

Wokingham

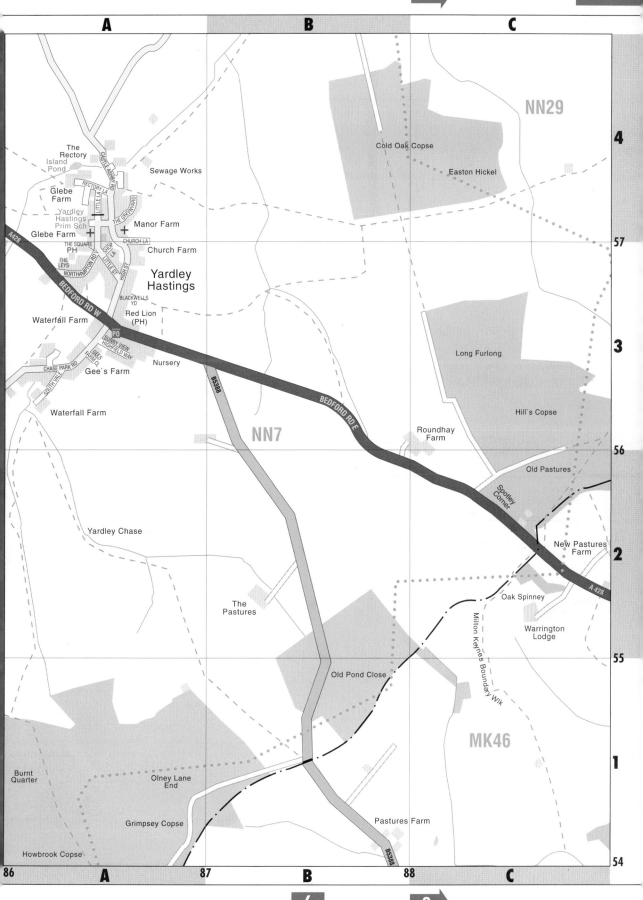

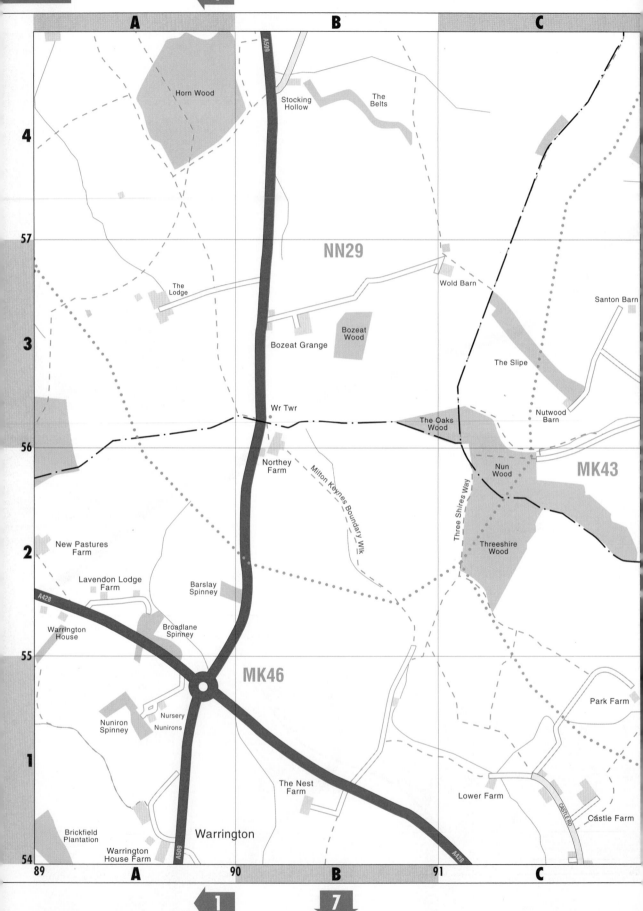

Horn Wood

Stocking Hollow

The Belts

4

57

NN29

The Lodge

Wold Barn

Santon Barn

Bozeat Wood

3

Bozeat Grange

The Slipe

Nutwood Barn

Wr Twr

The Oaks Wood

56

Northey Farm

Nun Wood

MK43

Milton Keynes Boundary Wlk

Three Shires Way

Threeshire Wood

2

New Pastures Farm

Lavendon Lodge Farm

Barslay Spinney

Warrington House

Broadlane Spinney

55

MK46

Park Farm

Nuniron Spinney

Nursery Nunirons

1

The Nest Farm

Lower Farm

Castle Farm

Castle Rd

Brickfield Plantation

Warrington

Warrington House Farm

54

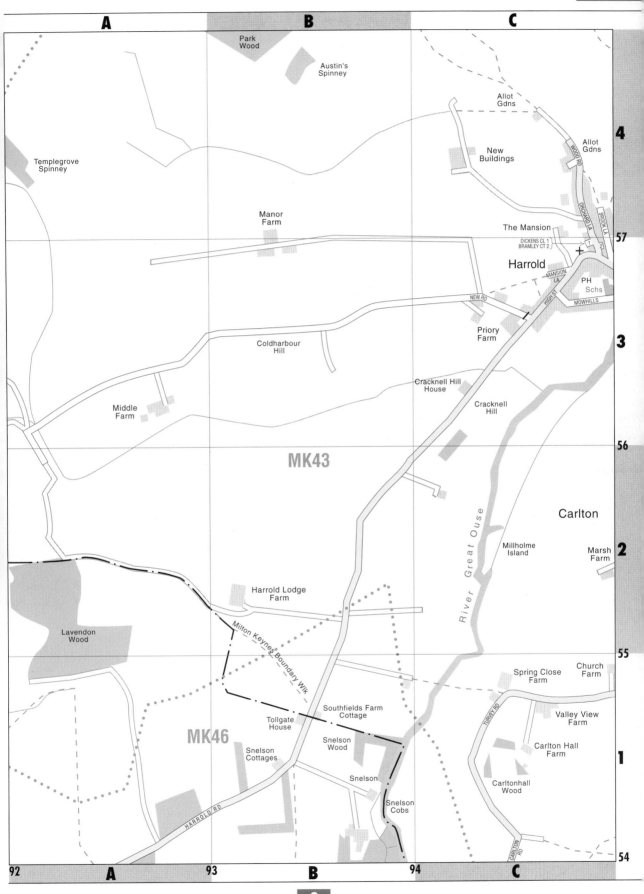

Park
Wood

Austin's
Spinney

Allot
Gdns

Allot
Gdns

New
Buildings

WOOD RD

4

Templegrove
Spinney

ORCHARD LA

BROOK LA

The Mansion

DICKENS CL 1
BRAMLEY CT 2

57

Manor
Farm

Harrold

MANSION LA

PH
Schs

NEW RD

HIGH ST

MOWHILLS

Coldharbour
Hill

Priory
Farm

3

Cracknell Hill
House

Cracknell
Hill

Middle
Farm

56

MK43

Carlton

Millholme
Island

Marsh
Farm

2

River Great Ouse

Lavendon
Wood

Harrold Lodge
Farm

55

Milton Keynes Boundary Wlk

Spring Close
Farm

Church
Farm

TURVEY RD

Southfields Farm
Cottage

Valley View
Farm

MK46

Tollgate
House

Snelson
Wood

Carlton Hall
Farm

1

Snelson
Cottages

Snelson

Carltonhall
Wood

Snelson
Cobs

CARLTON RD

HARROLD RD

54

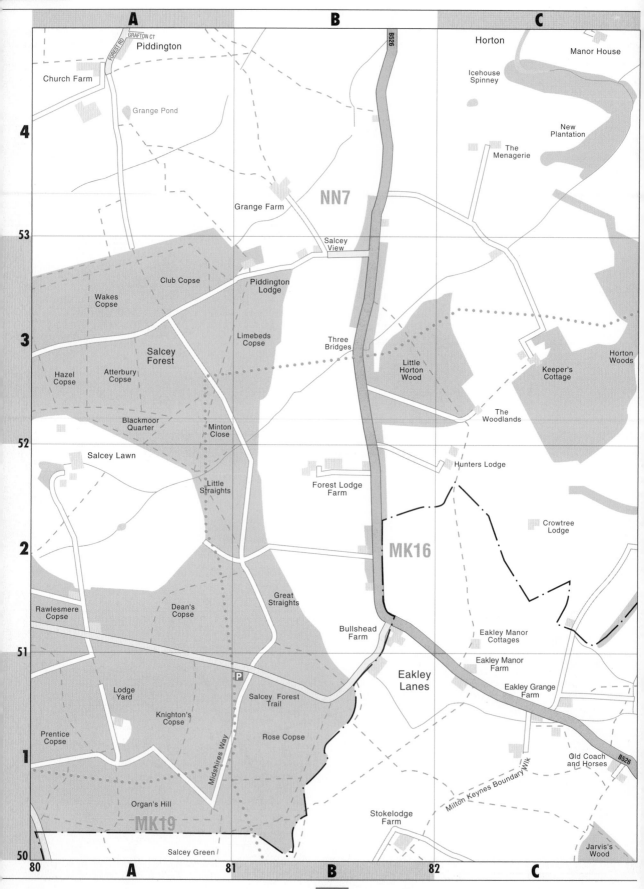

A   **B**   **C**

GRAFTON CT

FOREST RD

Piddington

Church Farm

Grange Pond

Horton

Manor House

Icehouse Spinney

New Plantation

The Menagerie

4

NN7

B526

53

Grange Farm

Salcey View

Club Copse

Piddington Lodge

Wakes Copse

Limebeds Copse

Three Bridges

Little Horton Wood

Horton Woods

3

Salcey Forest

Keeper's Cottage

Hazel Copse

Atterbury Copse

The Woodlands

Blackmoor Quarter

Minton Close

52

Salcey Lawn

Little Straights

Hunters Lodge

Forest Lodge Farm

Crowtree Lodge

2

MK16

Rawlesmere Copse

Dean's Copse

Great Straights

Eakley Manor Cottages

Bullshead Farm

Eakley Manor Farm

51

P

Lodge Yard

Salcey Forest Trail

Eakley Lanes

Eakley Grange Farm

Knighton's Copse

Midshires Way

Prentice Copse

Rose Copse

Old Coach and Horses

B526

1

Organ's Hill

Milton Keynes Boundary Wlk

MK19

Stokelodge Farm

Jarvis's Wood

50

Salcey Green

80   **A**   81   **B**   82   **C**

A

The Paddock

Manor Farm

The Wold

Hay Copse

Yardley Chase

NN7

B

Church Slade

Biggin Lodge

C

4

Ravenstone Road Copse

Barnstaple Wood

Milton Keynes Boundary Wlk

53

Great Wood

Dinglederry

Ash Beds

Roadley's Brake

3

Hanger Spinney

Woodlands

52

MK16

Cheyney Farm

MK46

2

Parkfield Farm

Milton Keynes Boundary Wlk

NORTHEND

Northend Farm

Parkfield Spinney

Cemy

51

Abbey Farm

THE ALMSHOUSES

Horseshoe Farm

PH

BAY LA

THE CLOSE

ABBEY WAY

CHESPORT CL.

Home Farm

Spring Barn

Ravenstone

WESTON RD

1

Yew Tree Farm

COMMON ST

Sheep Dip

B526

Mannings Farm

Lower Farm House

50

A
B
C

A   **B**   **C**

Howbrook Copse

Grimpsey Copse

Yardley Chase

Church Slade

Olney Park Farm

Olney Park Cottages

Milton Keynes Boundary Wlk

B5388

Olney Hyde

4

Smith's Farm

NN7

Court Farm

Yardley Rd

Kilwick Wood

Sewage Works

53

Ind Est

Warrington Road Farm

3

Hungary Hall

Stilebrook Rd

Aspreys

Kippell Hill

Mitchell Hill

Mow Sokod Way

Lilly Hill

Ferrw Long

Furlong

Olney Mid Sch

Short Massey 1
Crab Tree Cl 2

Dickens Spinney

Hawkswood

Long Massey

Dal Bots

Foxhill

Maybush Wlk

Moores Hill

Kensington Pl

Midland Rd

A509

Wellingborough Rd

Dartmouth Rd

East St

52

MK46

Resr

Overhills

Aspreys

Flaggs Mdw

Stocken Cl

Guinea
Fishermans Cl

Rivetts Cl

B5388

Coles La

Dingleberry

Liby

Long Lane

Whitmees Cl

Cherry Orch

West Side

Rise

Long La

Cobbs Gdn

West St

Dickens Spinney

Johnsons Field

Springfield

Dells

Orchard Rise

High St

Pheasants Nest

Anding Cl

Silswood

Olney Fst Sch

Ashlea

Elmlea Dr

Court Oak

Thornlea

Croft

Spring La

Pigtle

Parton

Daffnell Rd

Stanley Ct

Mus

P

The Alcove

Bacon Hill

Hollow

Stone Pit Cl

Spinney Hill Rd

Wood

Beech Ave

Oakdown Cres

Market Pl 1
Osborn's Ct 2
Church St 3

High St

2

Overbrook Spinney

Olney

Weston Park

Flamingo Zoo Park

Weston Rd

Goosey Bridge

Sluice

51

Milton Keynes Boundary Wlk

The Wilderness

Laundry Cottage

Otter Pool

Bridge St

Wood La

Cross La

PH

Manor House

Heron Water

River Great Ouse

Emberton Country Park

1

Church Farm

High St

Compass Orch

Revers La

PO

The Close

Weston Underwood

Grebe Lake

Visitor Ctr

Snipe Pool

Olney Rd

A509

The Willows

50

86   **A**   87   **B**   88   **C**

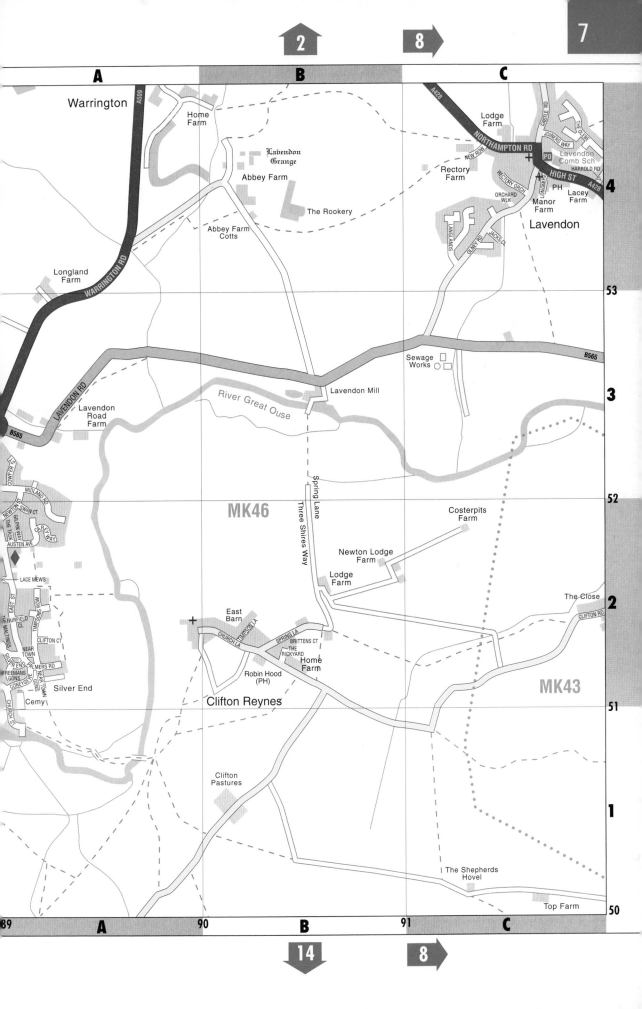

A   B   C

4

Snip Wood

HARROLD RD

THE GLEBE

Uphoe Manor House

A428

Cemy

New Barn

Copymoor

CARLTON RD

New Park

Cricket Ground

Milton Keynes Boundary Wlk

53

MK46

B565

Cemy

New Gains Farm

Turvey Lower Sch

HAWTHORN CL

NORFOLK RD

MAY RD

Turvey House

Chantry Farm

CHURCH TERR

PO

Turvey

MORDAUNT CL

CROFT

BAMFORD

LA

ELMWD

ABBEY SQ

3

BEDFORD RD

Turvey Bridge

CRANES CL

BRIDGE ST

THE GREEN

HIGH ST

A42

BAMFORDS YD

JACK'S LA

Cold Brayfield

Waterfield Farm

Brayfield Farm

The Ye Three Fyshes (PH)

TURVEY MILL LA

MILL GN

LADYBRIDGE TERR

NEWTON RD

Ford

Turvey Abbey

Brayfield House

BAKERS CL

52

MK43

Lodge

Long Belt

Abbey Farm

Newton Blossomville

The Old Mill Burnt Down (PH)

Newton Blossomville CE Fst Sch

BROOK LA

River Great Ouse

Turvey Cottage

Top Lodge

Woodside Cottage

Mossy Bank Wood

2

HARDMEAD RD

Home Farm

Westfields Barn

New Wood

Keepers Cottage

51

Turvey Hall

Newton Park

Milton Keynes Boundary Wlk

1

Clifton Spinney

Gullet Wood

Two Chimneys

Sheepwalks Spinney

Mast

Newton Wood

MK16

Turvey Lodge Farm

50

92   A   93   B   94   C

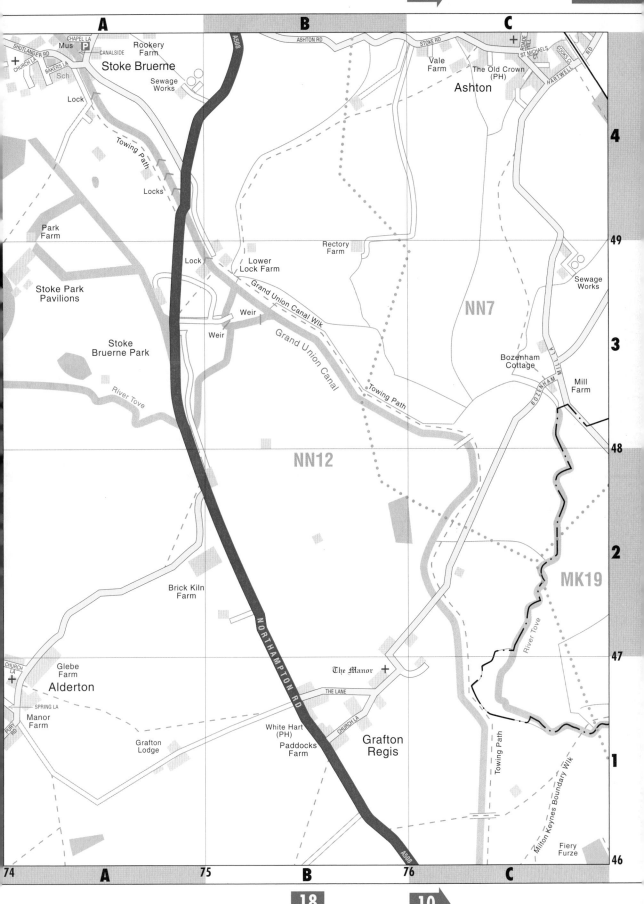

A

SHUTLANGER RD
CHURCH LA
BAKERS LA
CHAPEL LA
Mus
P
CANALSIDE
Rookery Farm
Sch
Stoke Bruerne
Sewage Works
Lock
Towing Path
Locks
Park Farm
Stoke Park Pavilions
Lock
Lower Lock Farm
Stoke Bruerne Park
Weir
Weir
River Tove
Grand Union Canal Wlk
Grand Union Canal
NN12
Brick Kiln Farm
NORTHAMPTON RD
Glebe Farm
CHURCH LA
Alderton
SPRING LA
BURT RD
Manor Farm
Grafton Lodge
White Hart (PH)
Paddocks Farm
THE LANE
The Manor
CHURCH LA
Grafton Regis

B

A508
ASHTON RD
STOKE RD
Vale Farm
The Old Crown (PH)
ST MICHAELS CT
COOKS CL
ROADE HILL
HARTWELL
Ashton
Rectory Farm
NN7
Sewage Works
Towing Path
Bozenham Cottage
BOZENHAM LA
Mill Farm
MK19
River Tove
Towing Path
Milton Keynes Boundary Wlk
Fiery Furze
A508

C

4
49
3
48
2
47
1
46

9

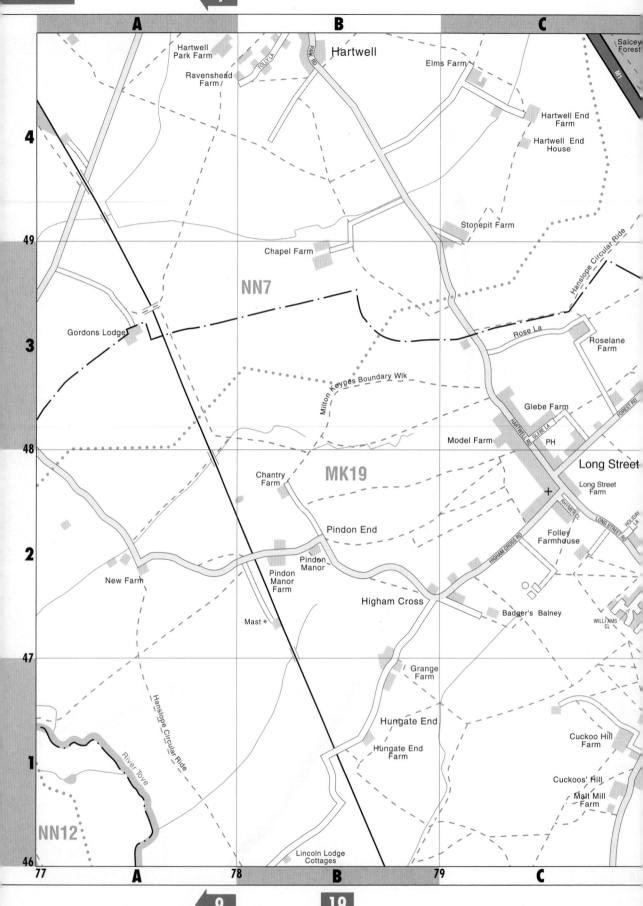

A · B · C

Salcey Forest

Hartwell Park Farm

Ravenshead Farm

Hartwell

Elms Farm

Hartwell End Farm

Hartwell End House

4

Stonepit Farm

49

Chapel Farm

NN7

Hanslope Circular Ride

Rose La

Roselane Farm

3

Gordons Lodge

Milton Keynes Boundary Wlk

Glebe Farm

Model Farm

PH

48

Long Street

MK19

Chantry Farm

Long Street Farm

Pindon End

Folley Farmhouse

2

Pindon Manor

New Farm

Pindon Manor Farm

Higham Cross

Badger's Balney

WILLIAMS CL

Mast

47

Grange Farm

Hungate End

Cuckoo Hill Farm

1

River Tove

Hanslope Circular Ride

Hungate End Farm

Cuckoos' Hill

Malt Mill Farm

NN12

46

Lincoln Lodge Cottages

77 · A · 78 · B · 79 · C

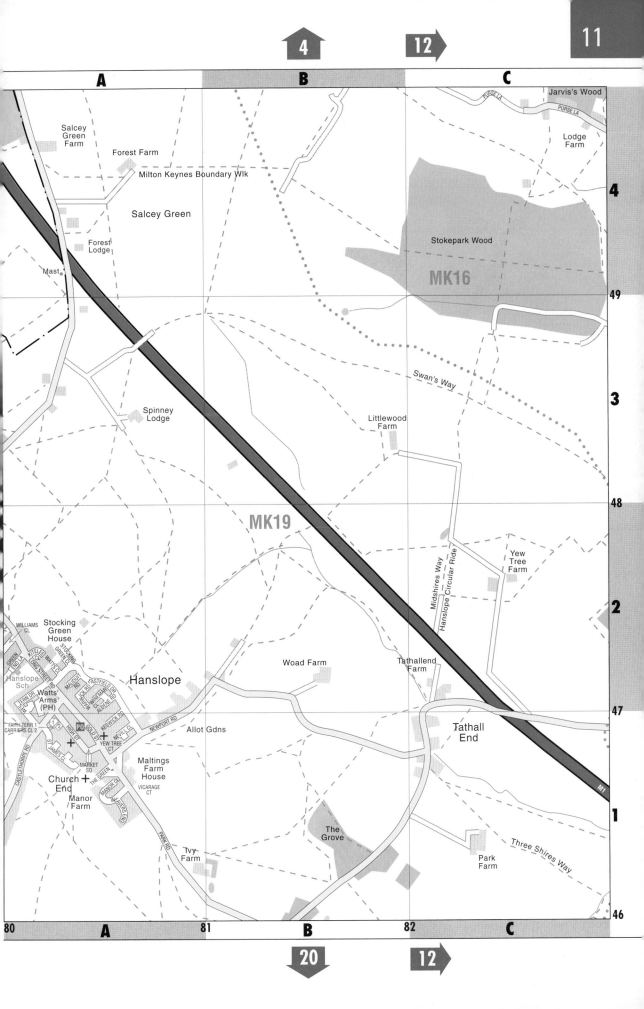

A **B** **C**

Jarvis's Wood

PURSE LA
PURSE LA

Salcey
Green
Farm

Forest Farm

Lodge
Farm

Milton Keynes Boundary Wlk

4

Salcey Green

Stokepark Wood

Forest
Lodge

MK16

Mast

49

Swan's Way

3

Spinney
Lodge

Littlewood
Farm

48

MK19

Midshires Way
Hanslope Circular Ride

Yew
Tree
Farm

2

Stocking
Green
House

WILLIAMS
CL

Tathallend
Farm

Woad Farm

Hanslope
Sch

Hanslope

Watts'
Arms
(PH)

47

FAITH TERR 1
CARRIERS CL 2

PO

Allot Gdns

Tathall
End

KESWICK RD

NEVILL CL

NEWPORT RD

YEW TREE
CT

St JAMES CL

CASTLETHORPE RD

MARKET
SQ

Maltings
Farm
House

VICARAGE
CT

Church
End

Manor
Farm

THE GREEN

WEAVERS END

MANOR CL

PARK RD

Tvy
Farm

The
Grove

Park
Farm

1

Three Shires Way

M1

46

A   **B**   **C**

B526

PURSE LA

4

Church Farm

Mount Pleasant

SPRINGBANK CT

CHURCH LA

DAG LA

ORCHARD WAY

MOUNT PLEASANT

49

Old Park Farm

HIGH ST

DAG LA

MALTING CL

The White Hart (PH)

P

GEORGE INN PL

PO

Stoke Goldington

KINGS LA

BERKELEY CL

LEASIDE

WESTSIDE LA

Stoke Goldington CE Fst Sch

Hotel

RAM ALLEY

BAKERS CL

3

Ram Alley

TOWN END CRES

Ram Alley

Sewage Works

Field Barns

RAVENSTONE MILL RD

MK46

Ravenstone Mill

48

Harley Field Barn

MK16

MK19

Gothurst House

River Great Ouse

Park Farm

2

Longland's Wood

The Wilderness

BACK DR

Bunsty Farm

Bath House

Tyringham Hall

47

Bunsty Wood

Gayhurst Spinney

Tyringham

Gayhurst Wood

Digby's Walk

Gayhurst

Tyringham Bridge

1

M1

New Plantation

Sir Francis Drake (PH)

Gayhurst House

Three Shires Way

B526

46

83   **A**   84   **B**   85   **C**

A
B
C

Caravan
Park

MK46

Emberton

Emberton Fst Sch

HULTON DR
BATTLE CL
OLNEY RD
Manor
Farm

WEST FARM WAY
STONE CT
THE P
SAXON
THE FORGE
L
WESTPITS
WEST LA
HIGH ST
PH
HOME FARM CT
GRAVEL WLK
CHURCH LA
HONEY HILL

A509

NEWPORT RD

4

Woolwich Barn

River Great Ouse

Blackwell
Spinney

49

Sowel
Spinney

NEWPORT RD

Buryorchard
Spinney

3

Filgrave

Rectory
Farm

Manor
Farm

TOWER
CL

Ash
Spinney

Lodge
Spinney

A509

Filgrave
Farm

48

Broadmore
Covert

MK16

Three Shires Way

Baker's
Spinney

Fifty Acre
Spinney

Broadmore
House

GUN LA

2

Blackthorn
Covert

Hill Plantation

Ash
Spinney

Reservoirs

FENCES LA

47

Fences
Farm

Baker's Farm

VILLAGE
CL

River Great Ouse

MARYOT CL

HIGH ST
KNOLL CL
CHURCH RD

End
Farm

WATER LA

PO
PH
CARTERS
CL

1

THE RICK YD
LEYS VIEW

Gallards
Farm

CROFTS
END

Manor
House

SHERINGTON RD
MANOR
CTYD

46

B526

A **B** **C**

Three Shires Way

Rectory Farm

Petsoe Manor Farm

4

Petsoe Manor

Petsoe End

Hill Farm

Clay Farm

Grange Farm

49

MK46

Hollington Wood

3

Mulducks

Wood Farm

Parrages Wood

Seven Acre Covert

Short Wood

48

2

MK16

Thickthorn Woo

Gowle's Farm

47

Perry La

FIELD CL

CHURCH END

GUN LA

PARK RD

CHURCH RD

Sherington

Grange Farm

Brickyard Cottage

BRIGGS ORCH

Sherington CE Fst Sch

SCHOOL LA

1

CARTERS CL

HILLVIEW

Chicheley Brook

Brandon's Wood

CROFTS END

NEWPORT RD

A 422

Crofts End

BEDFORD RD

Bedlam

A 509

BEDLAM LA

A 422

Bedlam Spinney

46

89 **A** **90** **B** **91** **C**

A 509

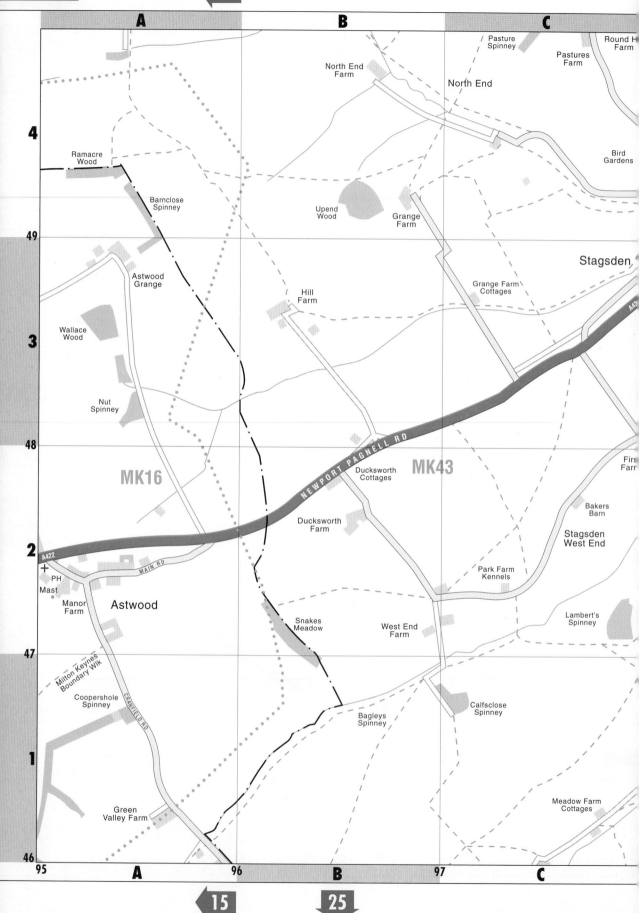

A   **B**   **C**

Pasture Spinney

Round H
Farm

North End Farm

Pastures Farm

North End

Bird Gardens

4

Ramacre Wood

Barnclose Spinney

Upend Wood

Grange Farm

49

Stagsden

Astwood Grange

Hill Farm

Grange Farm Cottages

Wallace Wood

3

Nut Spinney

48

First Farr

MK16

NEWPORT PAGNELL RD

Ducksworth Cottages

MK43

Bakers Barn

Ducksworth Farm

Stagsden West End

2   A422

Park Farm Kennels

MAIN RD

Lambert's Spinney

PH
Mast

Snakes Meadow

West End Farm

Manor Farm

Astwood

47

CRANFIELD RD

Milton Keynes Boundary Wlk

Calfsclose Spinney

Coopershole Spinney

Bagleys Spinney

1

Meadow Farm Cottages

Green Valley Farm

46

95   **A**   **96**   **B**   **97**   **C**

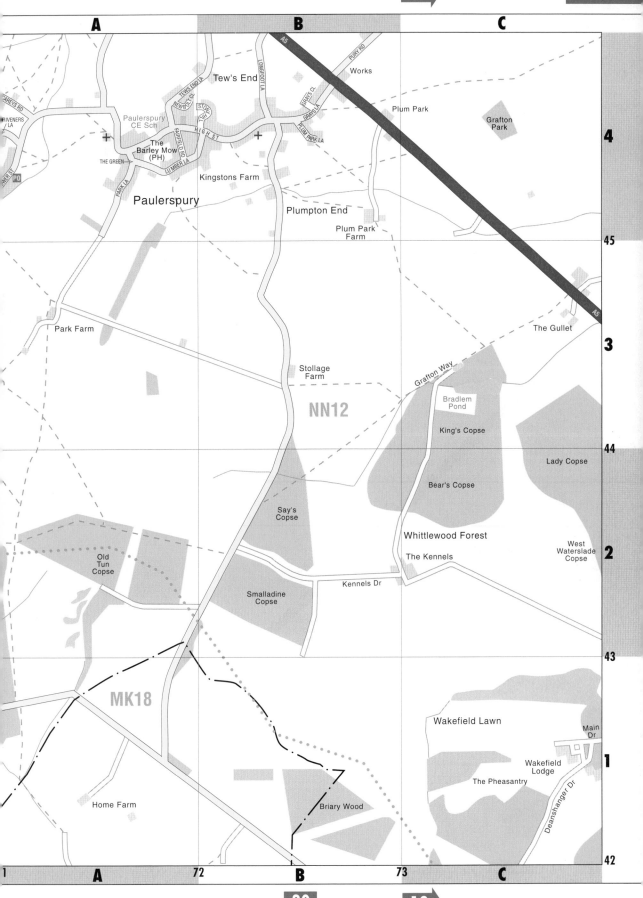

A B C

Tew's End

Works

Plum Park

Grafton Park

Paulerspury CE Sch

4

The Barley Mow (PH)

THE GREEN

PO

Kingstons Farm

Paulerspury

Plumpton End

Plum Park Farm

45

Park Farm

The Gullet

A5

3

Stollage Farm

Grafton Way

NN12

Bradlem Pond

King's Copse

44

Lady Copse

Say's Copse

Bear's Copse

Old Tun Copse

Whittlewood Forest

West Waterslade Copse

2

The Kennels

Smalladine Copse

Kennels Dr

43

MK18

Wakefield Lawn

Main Dr

Home Farm

Briary Wood

Wakefield Lodge

The Pheasantry

Deanshanger Dr

1

42

A **B** **C**

4

Grafton Cottage Farm

Grafton Fields

NORTHAMPTON RD

A508

Grand Union Canal Wlk

Milton Keynes Boundary Wlk

Grand Union Canal

Yardley Wharf

Old Wha Farm

45

Mount Pleasant Farm

Wr Twr

GRAYS LA

Queens Oak Farm

MOOREND RD

GRAFTON RD

HIGHCROFT CL

LIME RD

VICARAGE CL

WOODCK CL

CREST HILL

DRUCE END

BROWNSFIELD

MOUNT PLEASANT

HIGH ST

Manor Farm

Potterspury Lodge Sch

White Rose Farm

Moor End

MANOR WAY

SCHOOL LA

HESKETH RD

ORCHARD

WARREN RD

CHESTNUT RD

PH

3

Brookfields Farm

Castle Barn

Yardley Gobion CE Prim Sch

HORTONSFIELD RD

BUDGE RD

A5

Manor Farm

Yardley Gobion

MALBOROUGH WAY

EASTFIELD

SCHOOL

Oakley Spinney

44

NN12

YARDLEY RD

East Waterslade Copse

Beech House Farm

2

Assart Farm

Sunnyside Farm PH

BLACKWELL END

THE ORCHARD

SANDERS LA

MEADOW VIEW

BEECH HOUSE DR

TOWCESTER DR

WATLING ST

Wakefield Gdns

Nursery

Greystone Lodge

HIGH ST

John Hellins Prim Sch

BROWNSWOOD DR

MEADOW LA

CHURCH LA

CHURCH END

Kennels Dr

ELMFIELD CL

MAYS WAY

HOMESTEAD WAY

CRETLE WAY

FURTHO LA

43

Wakefield Farm

MORPH

POUNDFIELD RD

GRAFTON CL

Dairy Quarter

Main Drive Cottages

Main Dr

Potterspury

Potterspury House

MK19

1

Redmoor Copse

Puxley Farm

Dairy Farm

A5

Cherrytree Lodge

42

74 **A** 75 **B** 76 **C**

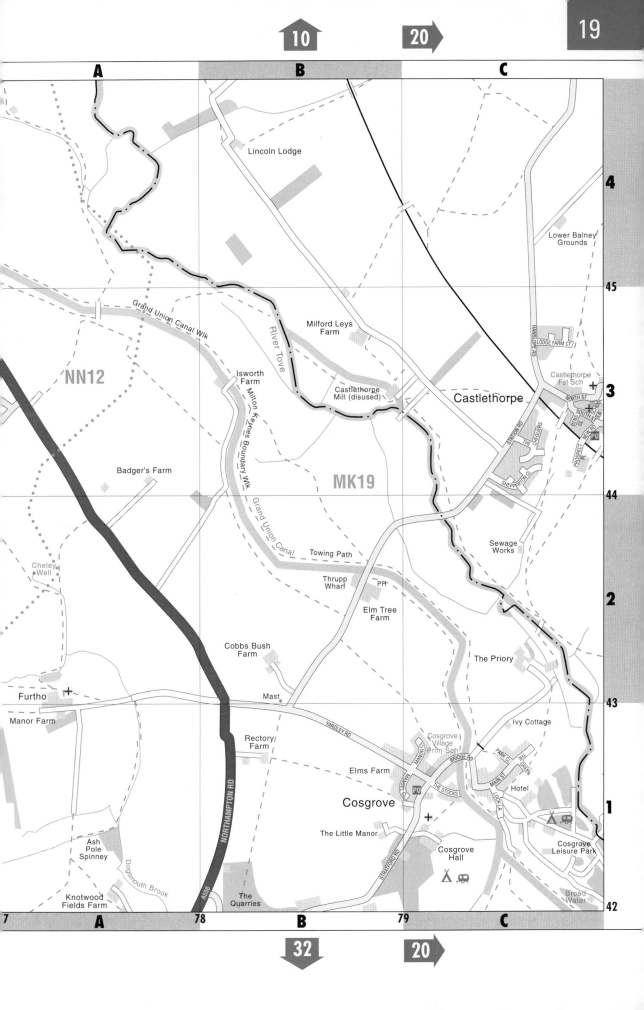

A B C

4

Lincoln Lodge

Lower Balney
Grounds

45

Grand Union Canal Wlk

River Tove

Milford Leys
Farm

HANSLOPE RD

LODGE FARM CT

NN12

Isworth
Farm

Milton Keynes Boundary Wlk

Castlethorpe
Mill (disused)

Castlethorpe

Castlethorpe
Fst Sch

STATION RD

NORTH ST

THE CHEQUERS

BENS CL

SOUTH CL

NEW RD

PROSPECT PL

3

PO

Badger's Farm

MK19

SHEPPERTON CL

44

Grand Union Canal

Towing Path

Sewage
Works

Cheley
Well

Thrupp
Wharf

PH

Elm Tree
Farm

2

The Priory

Cobbs Bush
Farm

Furtho

Mast

43

Manor Farm

YARDLEY RD

Ivy Cottage

Rectory
Farm

Cosgrove
Village
Prim Sch

BRIDGE RD

PARK CL

THE GREEN

MANOR CL

Elms Farm

MANOR CL

PO

THE STOCKS

MAIN ST

LOCK LA

Hotel

Cosgrove

The Little Manor

STRATFORD RD

Cosgrove
Hall

Cosgrove
Leisure Park

1

Ash
Pole
Spinney

NORTHAMPTON RD

A508

Dogsmouth Brook

Knotwood
Fields Farm

The
Quarries

Broad
Water

42

19
11

A   **B**   **C**

PARK RD

Manor
Farm

Upper Balney
Grounds

Long
Plantation

Mast
Park House

Narrow
Leys

4

Hanslope Park

MK16

Hanger
Quarter

Swan's Way
Midshires Way

Bullington End

45

Glenmore Farm

Hanslope
Lodge

New Buildings

BULLINGTON END RD

THRUPP CL

Castlethorpe

NORTH ST

SOUTH ST

3

Leamington
Farm

Maltings
Farm

WOLVERTON RD

Pineham Farm

44

MK19

Pikes
Farm

Field
House
Farm

Water
Tower

Fox
Covert

LODGE FARM

Otley Farm

2

Haythorn Spinney

Crossroads

Pike's Farm

43

Haversham

The Greyhound
(PH)

Haversham
Fst Sch

Haversham
Manor

CHALMERS AVE

RONMIL DR

KEPPEL AVE

BROOKFIELD RD

MANOR DR

THE CRESCENT

HAVERSHAM RD

HIGH

1

River Great Ouse

MK12

P

MK13

Cosgrove
Leisure Park

42

80   **A**   **81**   **B**   **82**   **C**

19
33

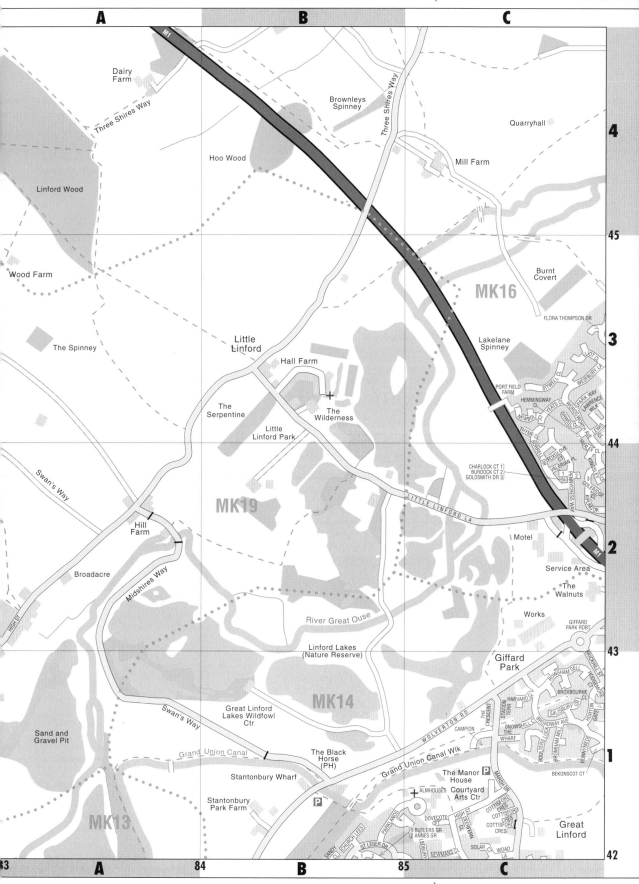

A B C

4
45
3
44
2
43
1
42

Dairy Farm

Three Shires Way

Brownleys Spinney

Three Shires Way

Quarryhall

Hoo Wood

Mill Farm

Linford Wood

MK16

Burnt Covert

Wood Farm

FLORA THOMPSON DR

The Spinney

Little Linford

Lakelane Spinney

Hall Farm

SITWELL CL
ELIOT CL
SPARK WAY
WESTBURY LA
LAWRENCE WLK
HEMMINGWAY CL
YEATS CL
WORDSWORTH AVE
LEWIS
ORWELL CL
KINGSLEY CL
HUXLEY CL

The Serpentine

The Wilderness

NEWBOLT CL

Little Linford Park

THYME CL
FOXGLOVE CT
SORRELL DR
COLERIDGE CL
VALERIAN PL
KIPLING 'OR

PORT FIELD FARM

MK19

CHARLOCK CT 1
BURDOCK CT 2
GOLDSMITH DR 3

1 2

Swan's Way

LITTLE LINFORD LA

PENYCRESS WAY

Hill Farm

Motel

M1

Midshires Way

Broadacre

Service Area

The Walnuts

HIGH ST

Works

GIFFARD PARK RDBT

River Great Ouse

Linford Lakes (Nature Reserve)

Giffard Park

BRICKHILL ST

MK14

ROWSHAM DELL
HORNGREAVE
BROXBOURNE

Swan's Way

Great Linford Lakes Wildfowl Ctr

HARVARD CL

SALISBURY GRT

STATION TERR
SNOWSHILL CT
BROADWAY AVE
MORTON GATE

Sand and Gravel Pit

WOLVERTON RD

CAMPION

THE CRESCENT

THE WHARF

RUNNYMEDE

Grand Union Canal

The Black Horse (PH)

Grand Union Canal Wlk

BOULTERS LOCK
BROMHAM MILL
BEKONSCOT CT

Stantonbury Wharf

MARSH DR

The Manor House

Courtyard Arts Ctr

ALMHOUSES

Stantonbury Park Farm

P

DOVECOTE CT

COTTISFORD CRES
COTTISFORD CRES
COTTISFORD CRES

MK13

PARKLANDS

HIGH ST
DEBEREN CL
SOLAR CT
WOAD LA

Great Linford

SANDY CL
CHURCH LEES
ST LEGER DR
LEDBURY CT
NEWMANS CL

1 BUTLERS GR
2 ANNES GR

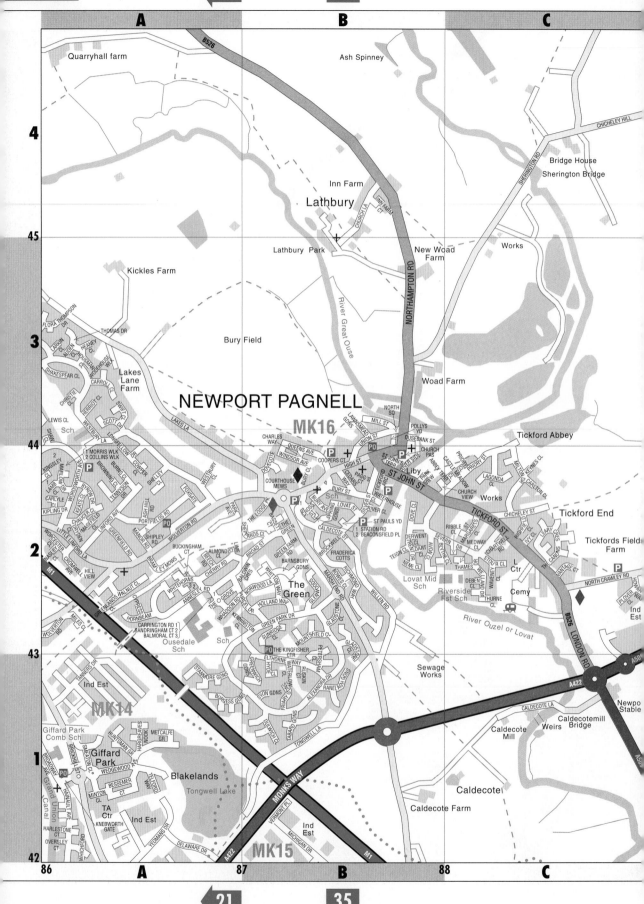

A   B   C

Quarryhall farm

Ash Spinney

B526

4

CHICHELEY HILL

Bridge House
Sheringham Bridge

SHERINGTON RD

Inn Farm

Lathbury

INN FARM CT

CHURCH LA

NORTHAMPTON RD

New Woad
Farm

45

Lathbury Park

Works

Kickles Farm

River Great Ouse

Bury Field

3

Flora Thompson Dr
LARKIN CL
WALDEN CL
HEANEY CL
HOUSMAN CL
WORDSWORTH DR
THOMAS DR
Lakes
Lane
Farm

Woad Farm

SHAKESPEAR CL
CHRISTIE CL
HERRIOT CL
SCOTT DR
CARROLL CL
SWIFT CL
LONGFELLOW DR
WESTBURY LA
LAKES LA

NEWPORT PAGNELL

LEWIS CL
Sch
MK16

NORTH
SQ
MILL ST

Tickford Abbey

44

1 MORRIS WLK
2 COLLINS WLK
KINGSLEY CL
MARLOW DR
BURNS CL
SHELLEY CL
WESTBURY CL
CHARLES WAY
QUEENS AVE
WINDSOR AVE
COOPERS CT
ST JOHNS TERR
ST JOHN ST
POLLYS YD
OUSEBANK ST
CHURCH PAS
Liby
CASTLE MEADOW
PRIORY ST
LAGONDA
MILTON CL
KEYNES CL

2
WORCESTER CL
LAMB CL
LITTLE LINFORD LA
CARLYLE CL
KIPLING DR
CHAUCER DR
MASEFIELD
ASH HILL RD
PORTFIELDS RD
WOLVERTON RD
SHIPLEY RD
MANOR RD
BUCKINGHAM CT
ALMOND CT
CHERRY RD
BRADWELL EY MEWS
HORNBEAM
WHITEHORNS
THE GROVE
BALDWIN CRES
WALTON HIGH
The Green
MARKET HILL
BURY ST
HIGH ST
Sch
Lovat Mid
Sch
CHURCH VIEW
Works
Tickford End

Tickfords Field
Farm

MK14

Giffard Park
Comb Sch

Giffard
Park

Blakelands

Tongwell Lake

MONKS WAY

MK15

86   A   87   B   88   C

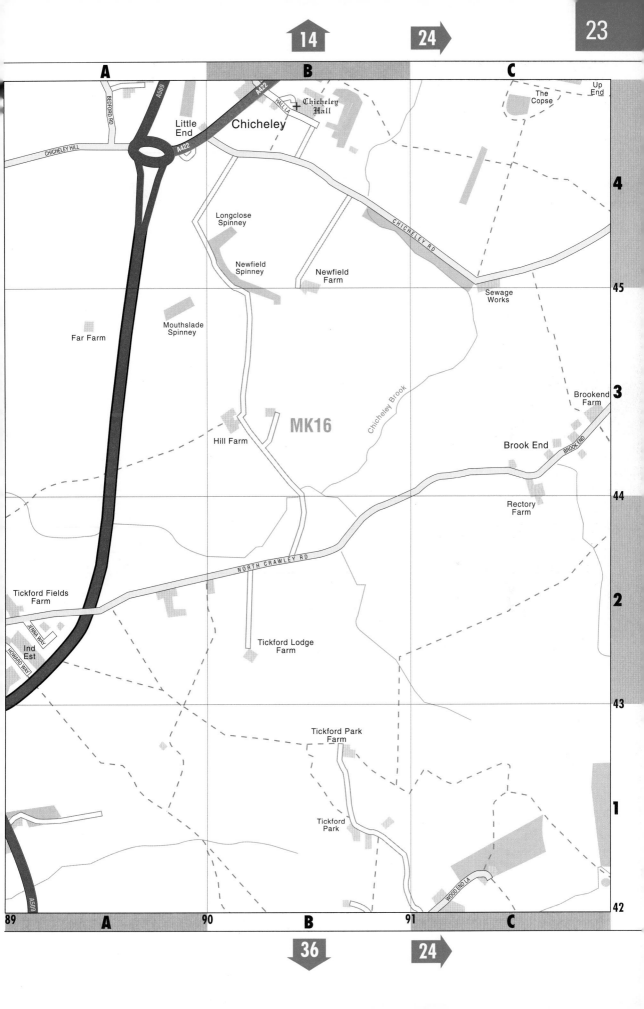

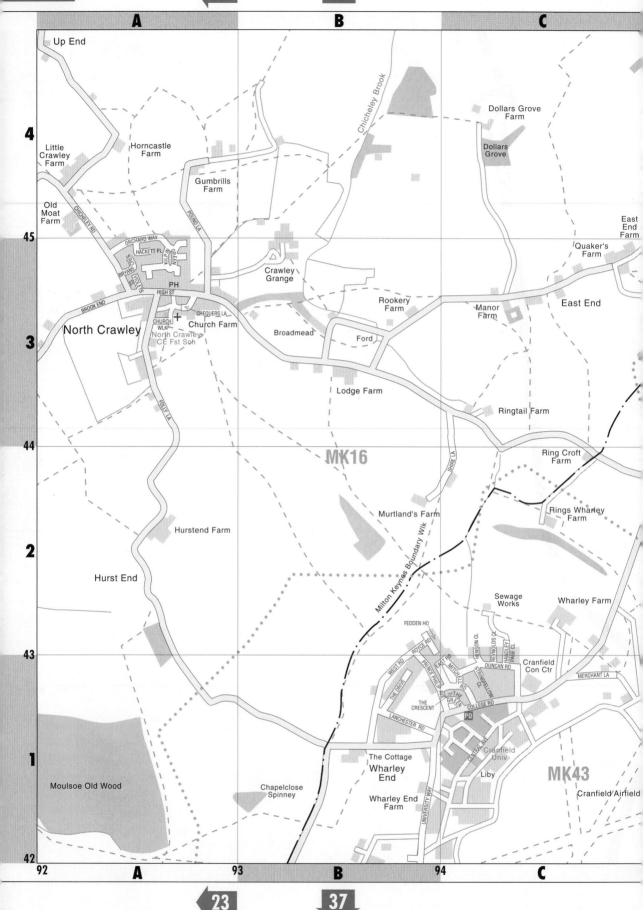

Up End

4

Little
Crawley
Farm

Horncastle
Farm

Chicheley Brook

Dollars Grove
Farm

Dollars
Grove

Gumbrills
Farm

Old
Moat
Farm

CHICHELEY RD

POUND LA

45

East
End
Farm

ORCHARD WAY

HACKETT PL

KILP... GREEN

Crawley
Grange

Quaker's
Farm

BRYANS
VIOLETS

PH

HIGH ST

Rookery
Farm

Manor
Farm

East End

3

BROOK END

CHURCH
WLK

CHEQUERS LA

Church Farm

North Crawley

North Crawley
CE Fst Sch

Broadmead

Ford

Lodge Farm

Ringtail Farm

FOLLY LA

Ring Croft
Farm

44

MK16

SHIRE LA

Murtland's Farm

Rings Wharley
Farm

Hurstend Farm

2

Milton Keynes Boundary Wlk

Sewage
Works

Wharley Farm

Hurst End

43

FEDDEN HO

ROYCE RD

WEST RD

PRINCE PHILIP AV

EAST RD

MITCHELL
RD

DUNCAN RD

HENSON CL

REYNOLDS CL

HANDLEY CL

PAGE CL

Cranfield
Con Ctr

MERCHANT LA

THE DRIVE

THE
CRESCENT

STRINGFELLOW
CL

THE
GREEN

COLLEGE RD

LANCHESTER RD

PO

1

Moulsoe Old Wood

Chapelclose
Spinney

The Cottage

Wharley
End

CENTRAL AVE

Cranfield
Univ

Liby

MK43

Cranfield Airfield

UNIVERSITY WAY

Wharley End
Farm

42

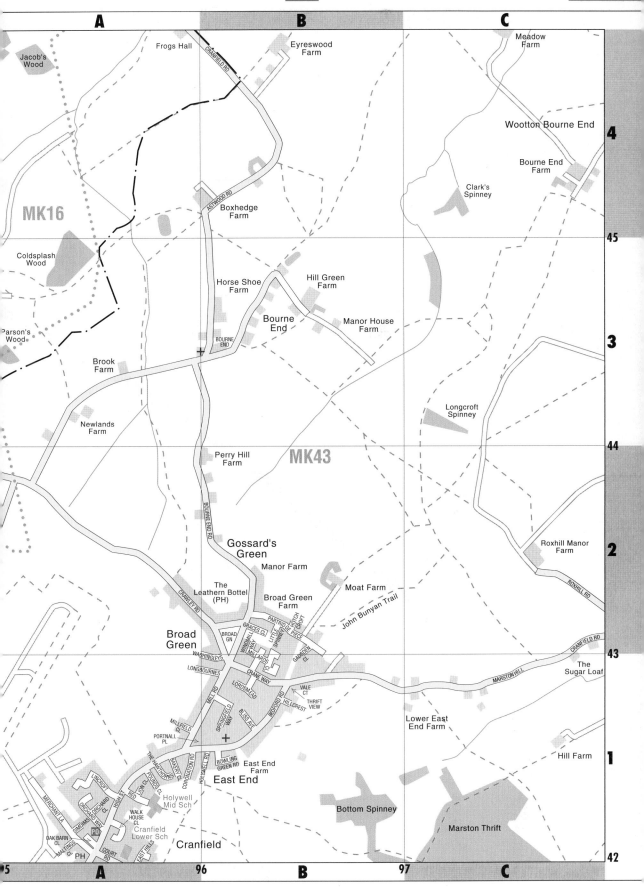

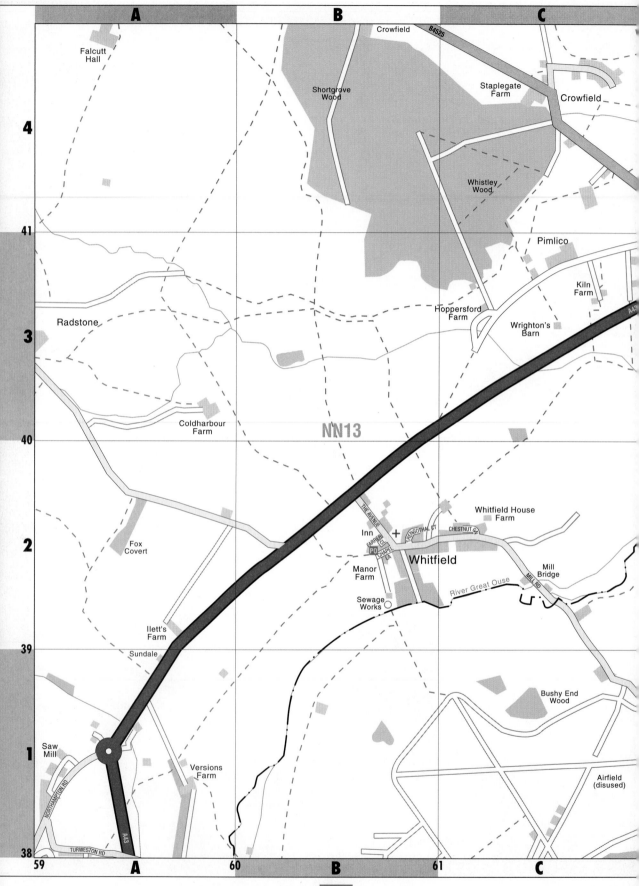

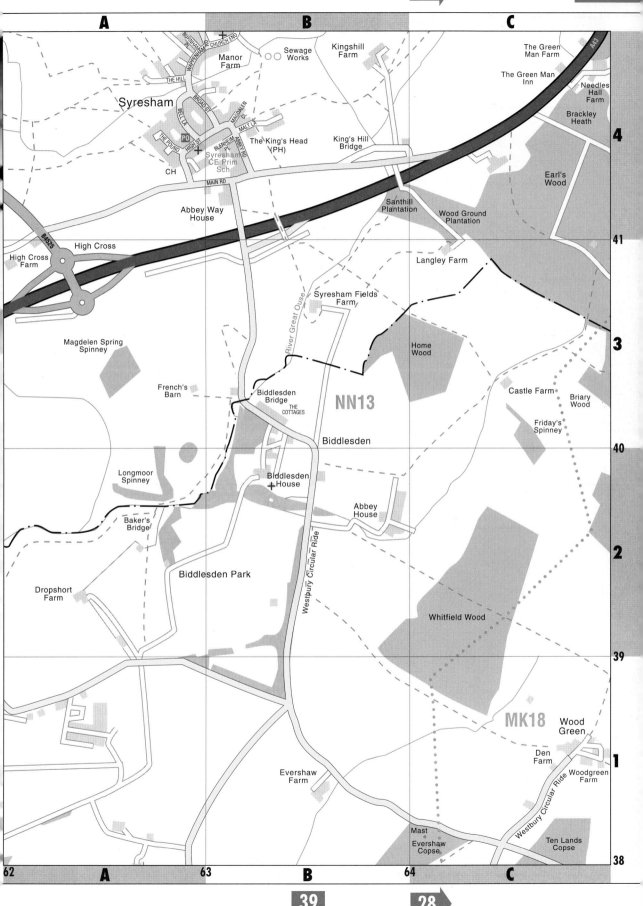

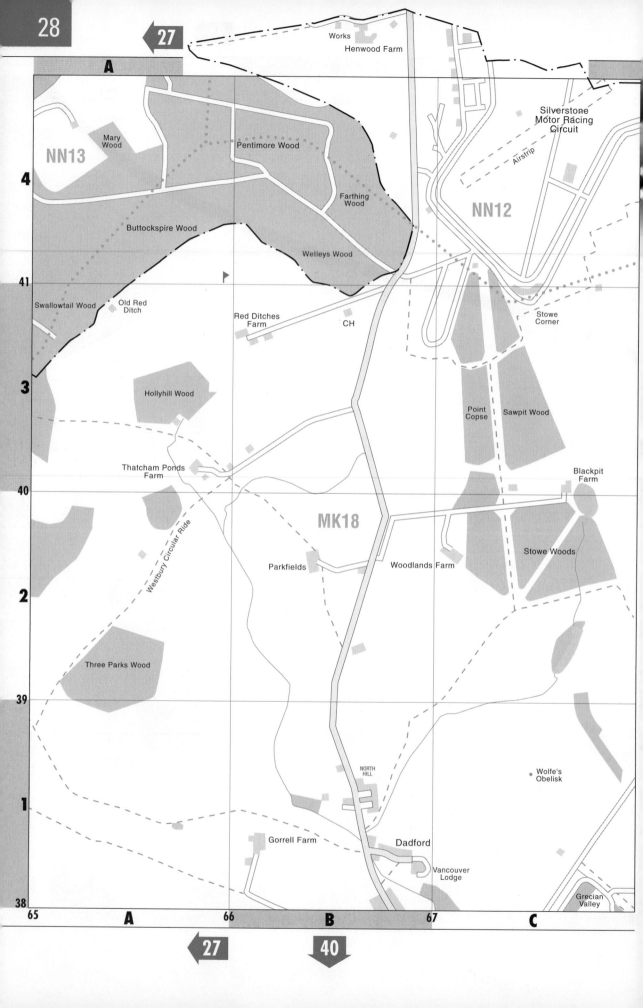

A

NN13

Mary
Wood

Pentimore Wood

4

Farthing
Wood

Buttockspire Wood

Wetleys Wood

Silverstone
Motor Racing
Circuit

Airstrip

NN12

41

Swallowtail Wood
Old Red
Ditch

Red Ditches
Farm

CH

Stowe
Corner

3

Hollyhill Wood

Point
Copse

Sawpit Wood

Thatcham Ponds
Farm

40

Blackpit
Farm

MK18

Westbury Circular Ride

Parkfields

Woodlands Farm

Stowe Woods

2

Three Parks Wood

39

NORTH
HILL

Wolfe's
Obelisk

1

Gorrell Farm

Dadford

Vancouver
Lodge

Grecian
Valley

38

A **B** **C**

NN12

Hill Cops

West Ashalls Copse

Deanshanger Dr

East Ashalls Copse

Long Copse

Briary Wood Farm

Briary Lodge

Forest Farm

4

Manor Cotts

Manor House

The Spinney

Manor Lodge

41

Bradley Fields Farm

Valley Farm

PO

Wicken Wood

Church Farm

CHURCH LA

BROOKSIDE

3

✝

Lillingstone Lovell

Notamore Copse

Lilby Wood

MK19

Glebe Farm

Leckhampstead Wood

40

Hall Farm

MK18

Hill Farm

2

Brook House (Ruin)

39

Wicken Road Farm

1

WICKEN RD

The Shaw

Park Copse

Lodge Farm

Pottery Farm

Leckhampstead House

LONG ROW

Limes End

38
71 **A** 72 **B** 73 **C**

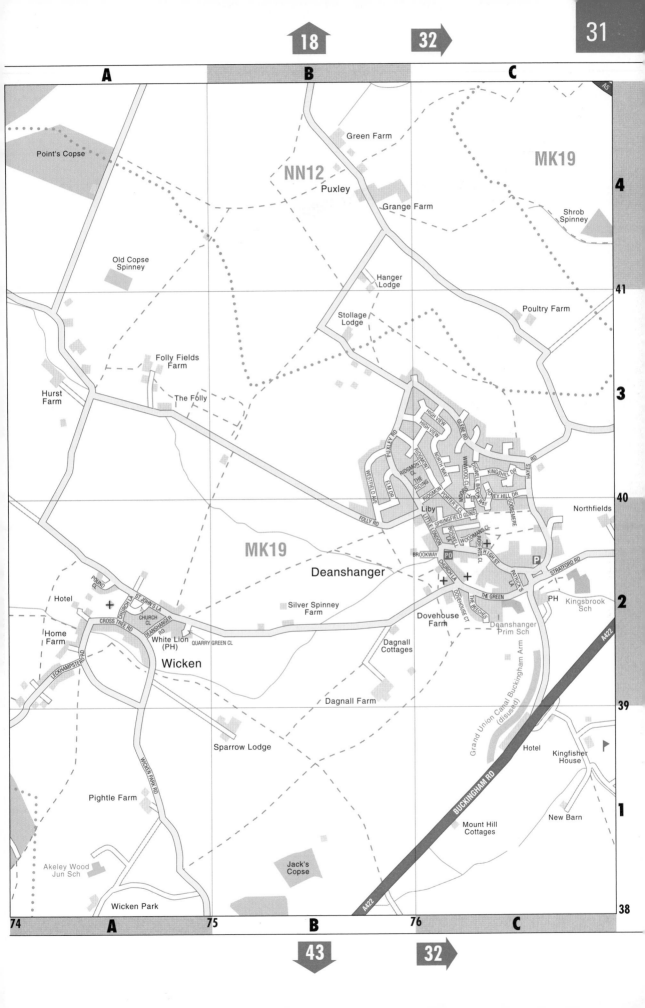

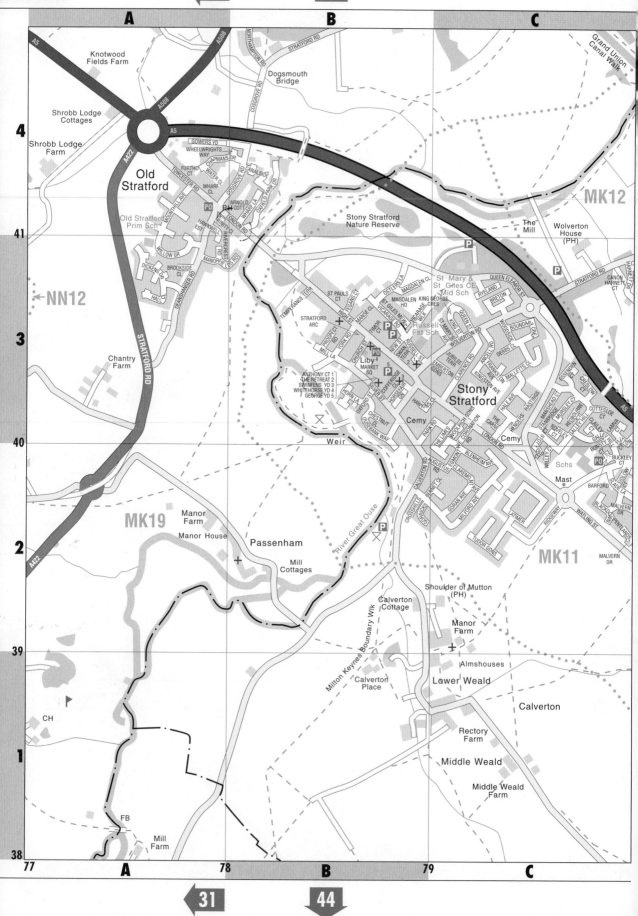

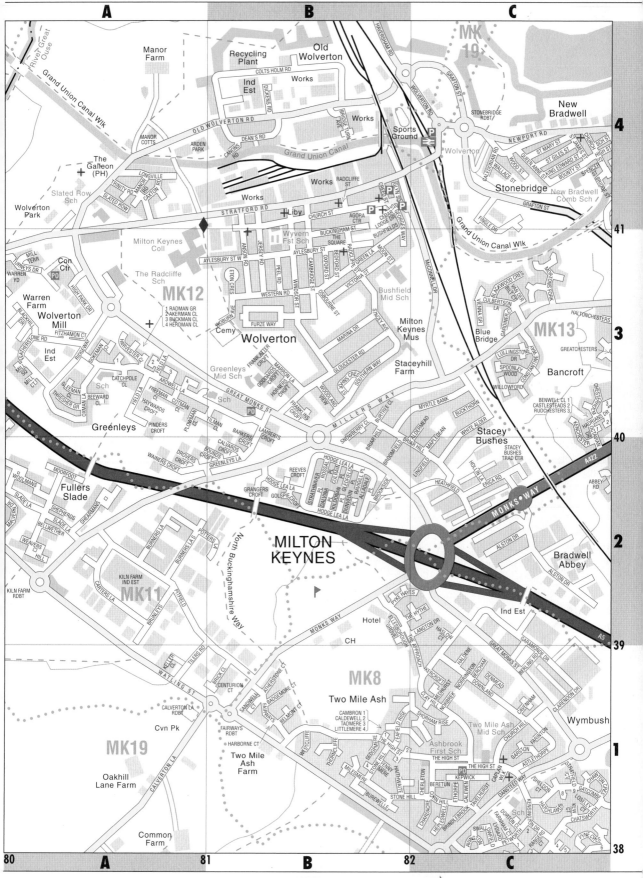

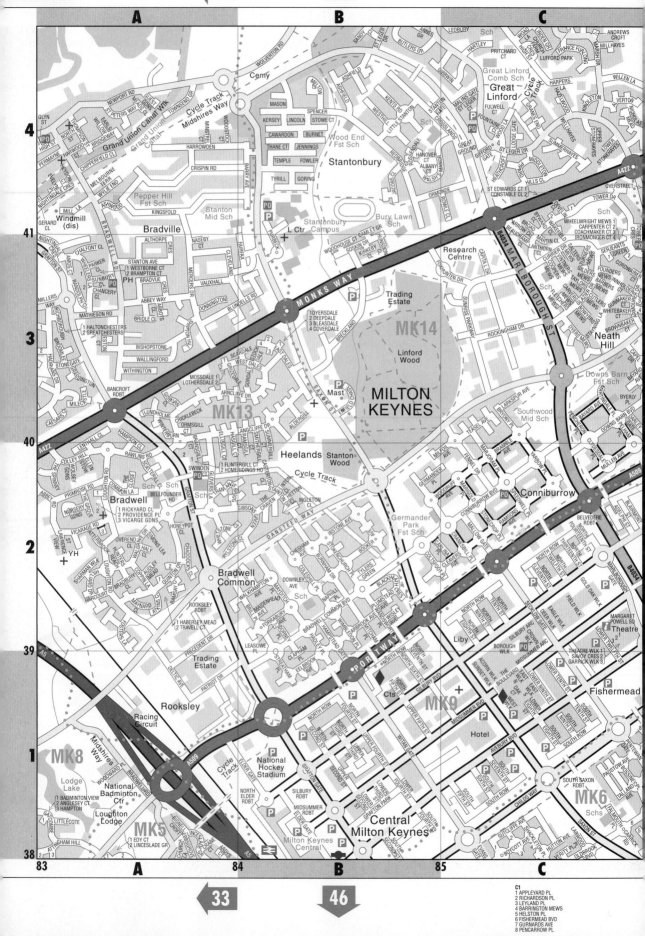

C1
1 APPLEYARD PL
2 RICHARDSON PL
3 LEYLAND PL
4 BARRINGTON MEWS
5 HELSTON PL
6 FISHERMEAD BVD
7 GURNARDS AVE
8 PENCARROW PL

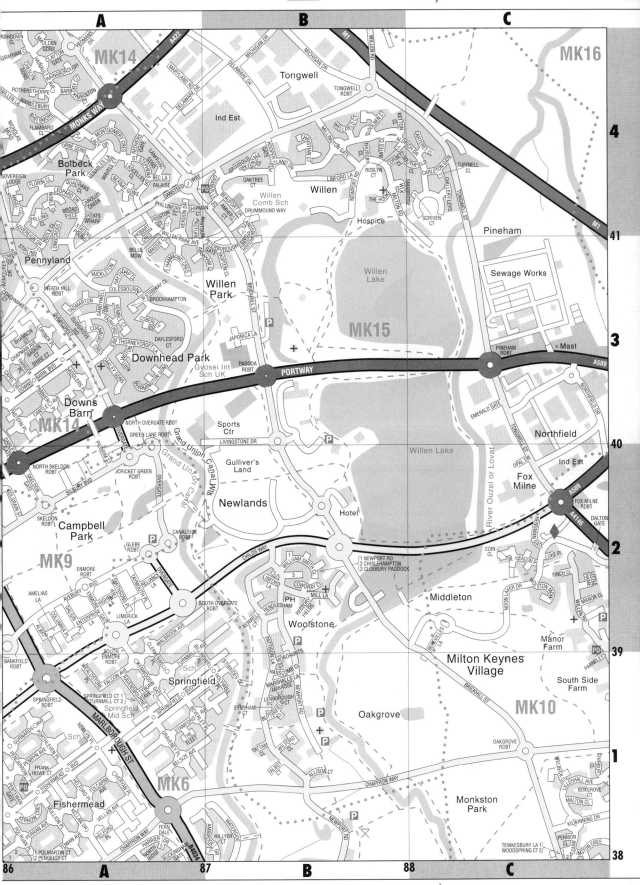

A   **B**   **C**

A509

Hotel

COMPTON CT

Moulsoe

Glebe Farm

Church Farm

NEWPORT RD

4

A509

M1

41

14

P

Hermitage Farm

PORTWAY

MK16

Broughton Grounds Com Woodlands Nature Reserve

3

A5130

NORTHFIELD RDBT

The Manor House

Broughton Barn

Old Covert

CHILDS WAY A509

The Old Rectory

Mast

Broughton Barns Cotts

Roundhill Spinney

40

Brooklands Farm

Atterbury

Hotel

New Covert

BROUGHTON RD

BROUGHTON MANOR BSNS PK

Ravenstone House

2

A4146

Broughton

1 MEADOW LA
2 BABINGTON CL

TANFIELD LA

TONGWELL ST

MK10

MK17

M1

WORRELLE AVE

Kingston Bridge

39

BROUGHTON

GRIFFITH GATE RDBT

GRIFFITH LEYS

HASWELL

CHAFFRON WAY

Fen Farm

HOPKINS CL
PADDOCK CL

KINGSOE HOME

WEBBS HOME

Kingston

MONKSTON RDBT

MAGDVILLE DR

MAIDSTONE RD

Kingston Ind Est

CORMANS RD
WALDON RD
CAMPANIA CL
WINGER

CHAFFRON WAY

BARSETT
CURLEWS CL
CHICKSANDS AVE

NEWMARKET CT

CHIPPENHAM DR

A5130 NEWPORT RD

A421

1

LILLESHALL AVE
NETLEY CT
FLAXLEY GATE
SHREWSBURY

LITTLE DUNMOW
AMPLEFORTH
LINDISFARNE DR

CHETWODE AVE
BEES

WYMONDHAM
HURLEY CROFT
HOPES CROFT

L Ctr

LASBOROUGH RD

WHITEHALL AVE

KINGSTON RDBT

LAUNDE 1
PERSHORE CROFT 2
STAVORDALE 3
ST BOTOLPHS 4

KILWINNING DR
BRIDLINGTON DR
BLANCHLAND CIRC
STANBROOK

ST BARTHOLOMEWS
WITHAM DR
ESSSBY LA

MARGAM CRES
WADHURST LA

WINCHESTER CIRC

BRINKLOW RDBT

BRANSWORTH AVE

MK7

A421

STANDING WAY

ETHERIDGE AVE

38

89   **A**   **90**   **B**   **91**   **C**

A   B   C

Wood End Farm

MK16

Lower Wood

Cranfield Tech Pk

UNIVERSITY WAY

Cranfield Airfield

Stilliters Farm

Mast

MK43

Villa Pk

4

Leys Farm

41

Conn's Farm

Broughton Grounds

3

Salford Wood

Holcotmoors Farm

CRANFIELD RD

Holcotmoors Lodge

Whitsundoles Farm

Milton Keynes Boundary Wlk

40

MK17

2

College Farm

Mill Farm

Rectory Farm

BROUGHTON RD

Rook Tree Farm Ind Est

BRITTONS LA

THE COURT

MILL LA

Salford

MANOR CT.

Rook Tree Farm

Salfordford Bridge

WAVENDON RD

Manor House

The Islands

39

Inn

Waterhall

Church Farm

Hulcote

Water Hall Farm

Fox Covert

Hulcot Manor

1

Aspley Hall

Eagle Farm

CRANFIELD RD

Wavendon Lodge

LOWER END RD

A421

M1

38

92   A   93   B   94   C

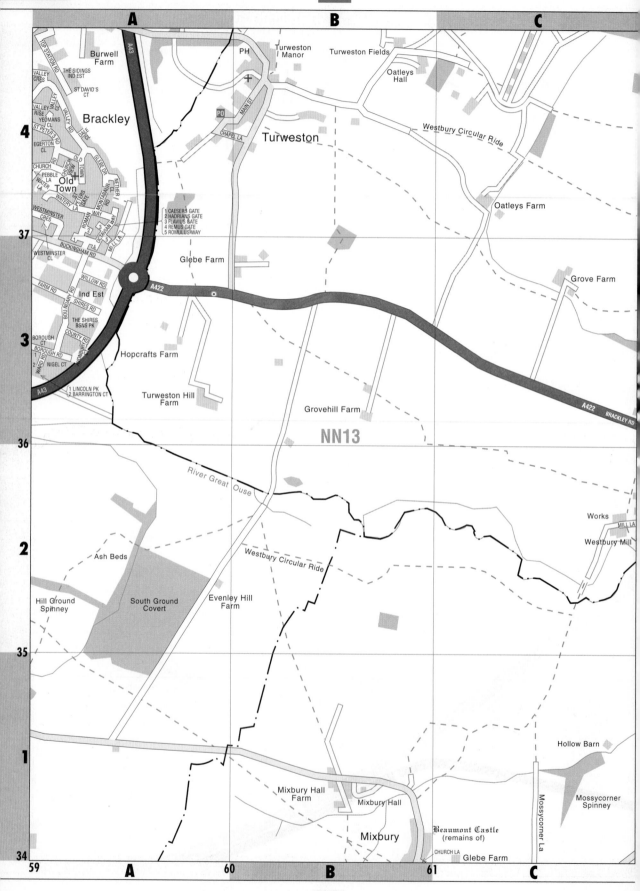

A **B** **C**

Burwell
Farm

THE SIDINGS
IND EST

TOP STATION RD

VALLEY
CRES

St DAVID'S
CT

PH

Turweston
Manor

Turweston Fields

Oatleys
Hall

Westbury Circular Ride

VALLEY
RISE

YEOMANS
CL

St PETERS RD

VALLEY RD

OLD
TOWN

GLEBE DR

HETHER RD

MAIN ST

PO

CHAPEL LA

Turweston

Brackley

EGERTON
CL

CHURCH
VIEW

CHURCH LA

PEBBLE
LA

WATER
LA

**Old
Town**

WATERY LA

St PETERS GATE

MONTABAUR RD

ROMAN WAY

OCTAVIAN WAY

MILL LA

1 CAESER'S GATE
2 HADRIANS GATE
3 FLAVIUS GATE
4 REMUS GATE
5 ROMULUS WAY

Oatleys Farm

4

WESTMINSTER
CRES

37

WESTMINSTER
CL

BUCKINGHAM RD

FARM RD

BOUNDARY RD

WILLOW RD

SHIRES RD

Ind Est

THE SHIRES
BSNS PK

A422

Glebe Farm

Grove Farm

3

BOROUGH
CT

BOROUGH RD

WARD RD

COUNTY RD

NONBURY RD

NIGEL CT

Ind Est

Hopcrafts Farm

Turweston Hill
Farm

Grovehill Farm

A422   BRACKLEY RD

A43

1 LINCOLN PK
2 BARRINGTON CT

36

NN13

River Great Ouse

Works

MILL LA

2

Ash Beds

Westbury Circular Ride

Westbury Mill

Hill Ground
Spinney

South Ground
Covert

Evenley Hill
Farm

35

1

Hollow Barn

Mixbury Hall
Farm

Mixbury Hall

Mossycorner La

Mossycorner
Spinney

Mixbury

Beaumont Castle
(remains of)

CHURCH LA

Glebe Farm

34

59 **A** **60** **B** **61** **C**

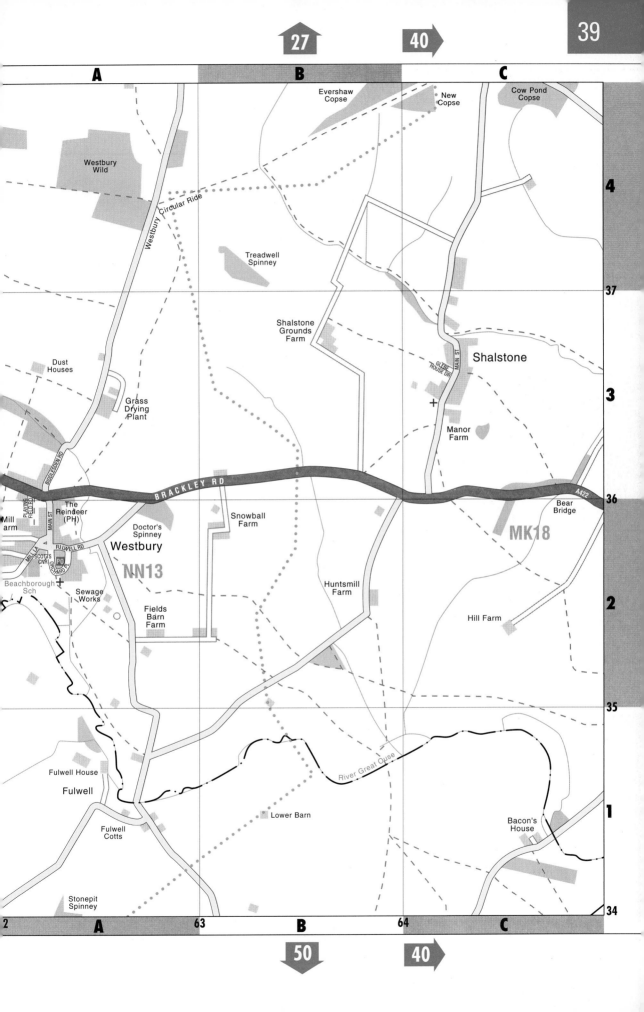

A B C

4

37

3

Evershaw
Copse

New
Copse

Cow Pond
Copse

Westbury
Wild

Westbury Circular Ride

Treadwell
Spinney

Shalstone
Grounds
Farm

Shalstone

GLEBE HOUSE DR

MAIN ST

Manor
Farm

Dust
Houses

Grass
Drying
Plant

BIDDLESDEN RD

BRACKLEY RD

A422

36

Bear
Bridge

Mill
arm

The
Reindeer
(PH)

Doctor's
Spinney

Snowball
Farm

MK18

MAIN ST

Westbury

FULWELL RD

SCOTT'S
CNR

ORCHARD PL

PO

NN13

Huntsmill
Farm

Hill Farm

2

Beachborough
Sch

Sewage
Works

Fields
Barn
Farm

35

Fulwell House

River Great Ouse

Fulwell

Lower Barn

Bacon's
House

1

Fulwell
Cotts

Stonepit
Spinney

34

2 A 63 B 64 C

← 39
28

A   **B**   **C**

Hill Gate Spinney

Boycott Manor Farm

+

Home Farm

Temple

Grecian Valley

Mo

Kiln Spinney

Stowe Sch

+

+

4

Boycott Manor

Stowe Gardens

Shell Bridge

Stowe Park

CH ▶

Temple

37

The Lake

Welsh Lane Farm

Boycott Manor Lodge

Weir

Oxford Water

3

Ashmore Farm

Water Stratford Wood

MK18

36

A422

Boycott Farm

WELSH LA

Park Farm

Grounds Farm

Stonepit Hill Spinney

Ford

Guernsey Hill Spinney

2

Spinney Hill Farm

Buffler's Holt

The Robin Hood (PH)

35

Manor Farm

Manor Farm Buildings

A42

Town Farm

WATER STRATFORD RD

1

Water Stratford

+

▶

Rectory Farm

Tingewick Mill

Radclive Grange

34

65   A   66   B   67   C

← 39
51

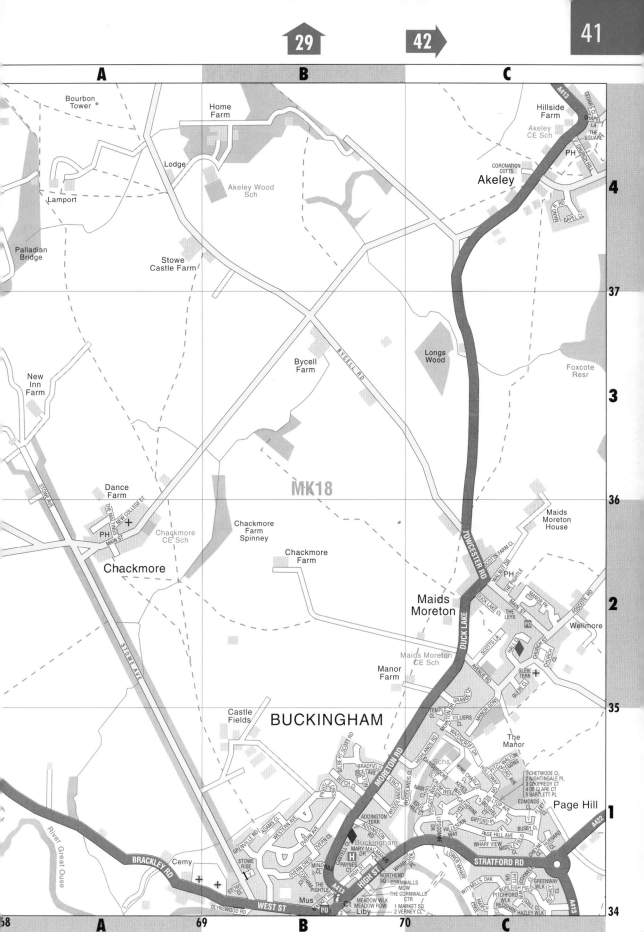

A   B   C

Bourbon
Tower

Home
Farm

Hillside
Farm

Akeley
CE Sch

THE
SQUARE

Lodge

Akeley Wood
Sch

CORONATION
COTTS

Akeley

PH

CHURCH HILL

4

Lamport

MANOR RD

CAPEL CL

Palladian
Bridge

Stowe
Castle Farm

37

Bycell
Farm

BYCELL RD

Longs
Wood

Foxcote
Resr

3

New
Inn
Farm

STOWE AVE

MK18

36

Dance
Farm

NEW COLLEGE CT

THE MALTINGS

Chackmore
CE Sch

Chackmore
Farm
Spinney

Chackmore
Farm

Maids
Moreton
House

SCOTTS FARM CL

TOWCESTER RD

WALNUT DR

THE PIGHTLE

PH

MAIN ST

FOSSCOTE RD

PH
MAIN ST

Chackmore

Maids
Moreton

DUCK LAKE CL

MANOR PK

THE
LEYS

Wellmore

2

PO

STOWE AVE

DUCK LAKE

SCOTTS LA

HALL CL

CHURCH ST

Maids Moreton
CE Sch

AVENUE RD

GLEBE
TERR

CHURCH

Manor
Farm

GLEBE CL

35

Castle
Fields

BUCKINGHAM

TEMPLE
CL

VILLIERS
CL

GRANS

MANOR GDNS

The
Manor

WAGHCROFT DR

GILBERT SCOTT RD

BRADFIELD
AVE

HIGHLANDS RD

MORETON RD

Schs

PITCH MALTON
GDNS

1 CHETWODE CL
2 NIGHTINGALE PL
3 CROPREDY CT
4 DE CLARE CT
5 BARTLETT PL

Page Hill

River Great Ouse

PIGHTLE CRES

BEECH CL

HILTON
AVE

WOODLANDS CL

CARISBROOKE
CL

KING CHARLES
CT

CATHERINE
CT

HOLLYWAY

EDMONDS
CL

BUSBY CL

A422

ADAMS CL

WESTERN AVE

ADDINGTON
TERR

WOODLANDS RD

NASEBY CL

CRAY
CT

CROMWELL

EDGE
HILL CL

HILLTOP AVE

GIFFORD PL

LIPSCOMBE
DR

PAGE HILL AVE

MIDDLEFIELD

CHEYNE CL

GREENWAY
WLK

GRENVILLE RD

OVERN AVE

OVERN CL

CANTELL CL

MARY
MAC

WHARFSIDE
PL

WHARF VIEW

LOWER WHARF

HUBBARD

PITT
CL

A413

BRACKLEY RD

Cemy

STOWE
RISE

OVERN CRES

COBHAM

MINSHULL
CL

THE
PIGHTLE

PAYNES
CT

MAIN ST

HIGH ST

NORTHEND
SQ

CORNWALLS
MDW

STRATFORD RD

WITTMILLS
OAK

BURLEIGH PIECE

PITCHFORD
CTR

REDSHAW
CL

MARCH
EDGE

HAZLEY WLK

GLYNSWOOD RD

WEST ST

Mus

MARKET HILL

PO

Liby

THE CORNWALLS
CTR

1 MARKET SQ
2 VERNEY CL

MEADOW WLK
MEADOW ROW

Buckingham

A38   69   A   B   70   C   34

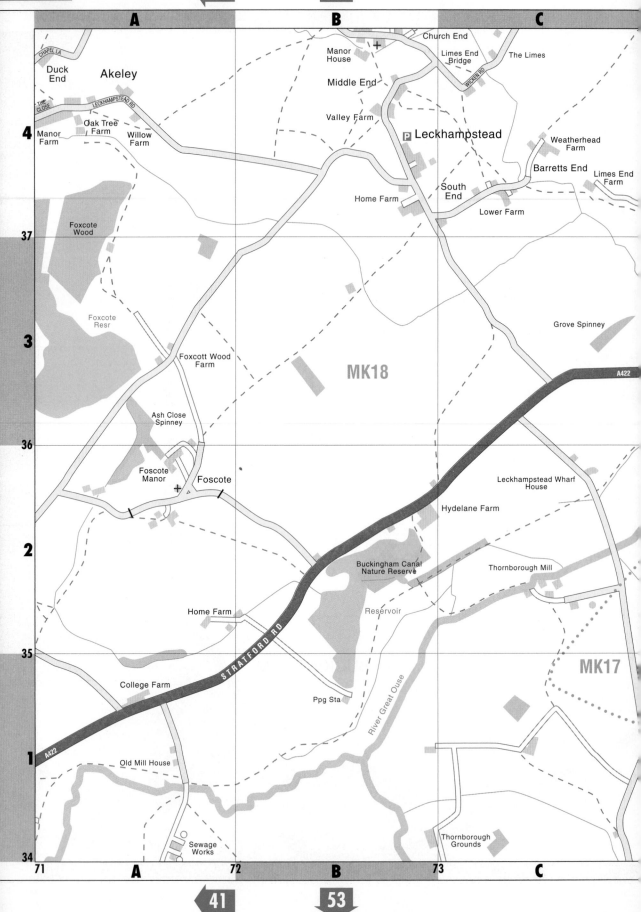

A B C

Chapel La

Duck End

Akeley

Manor House

Church End

Limes End Bridge

The Limes

Middle End

WICKEN RD

The Close

LECKHAMPSTEAD RD

Oak Tree Farm

Valley Farm

P Leckhampstead

Weatherhead Farm

4

Manor Farm

Willow Farm

Barretts End

Limes End Farm

Home Farm

South End

Lower Farm

37

Foxcote Wood

Foxcote Resr

Grove Spinney

3

Foxcott Wood Farm

MK18

A422

Ash Close Spinney

36

Foscote Manor

Foscote

Leckhampstead Wharf House

Hydelane Farm

2

Thornborough Mill

Buckingham Canal Nature Reserve

Home Farm

Reservoir

STRATFORD RD

35

MK17

College Farm

Ppg Sta

River Great Ouse

A422

1

Old Mill House

Thornborough Grounds

Sewage Works

34

71 A 72 B 73 C

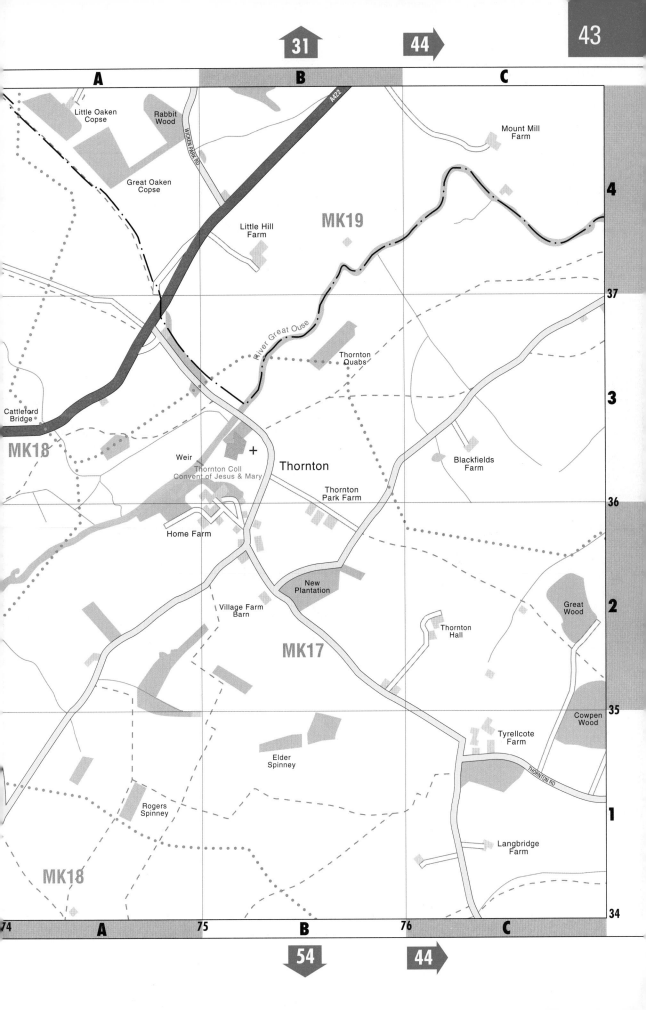

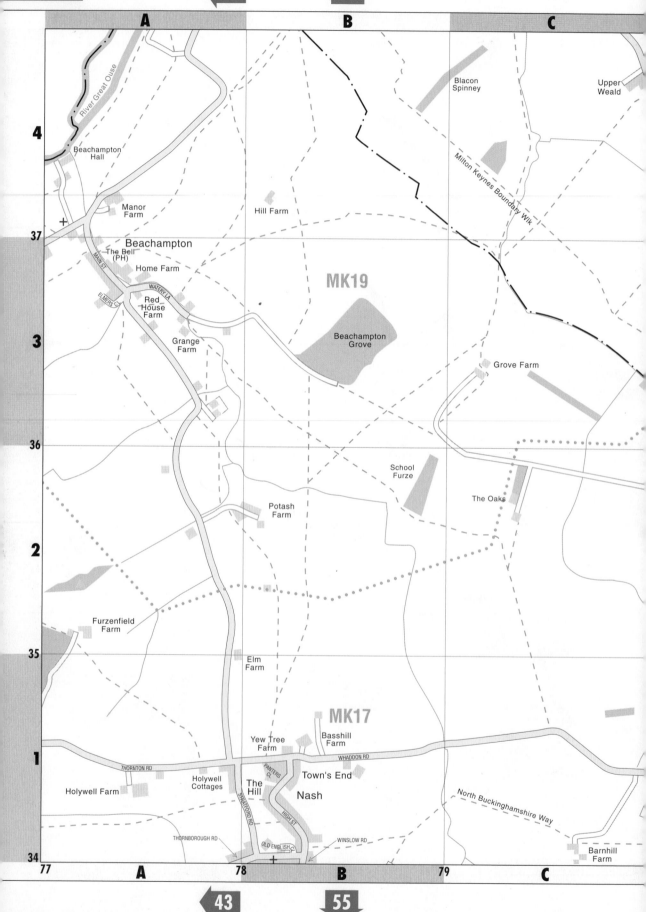

A B C

4

River Great Ouse

Blacon
Spinney

Upper
Weald

Beachampton
Hall

37

Manor
Farm

Hill Farm

Milton Keynes Boundary Wlk

Beachampton

The Bell
(PH)

Home Farm

MK19

MAIN ST

WATERY LA

ELMERS CT

Red
House
Farm

Beachampton
Grove

3

Grange
Farm

Grove Farm

36

School
Furze

Potash
Farm

The Oaks

2

Furzenfield
Farm

35

Elm
Farm

MK17

Yew Tree
Farm

Basshill
Farm

1

THORNTON RD

WHADDON RD

Holywell
Cottages

PANTERS CL

Town's End

North Buckinghamshire Way

Holywell Farm

The
Hill

STRATFORD RD

Nash

HIGH ST

THORNBOROUGH RD

OLD ENGLISH

WINSLOW RD

Barnhill
Farm

34

77

A

78

B

79

C

33
46

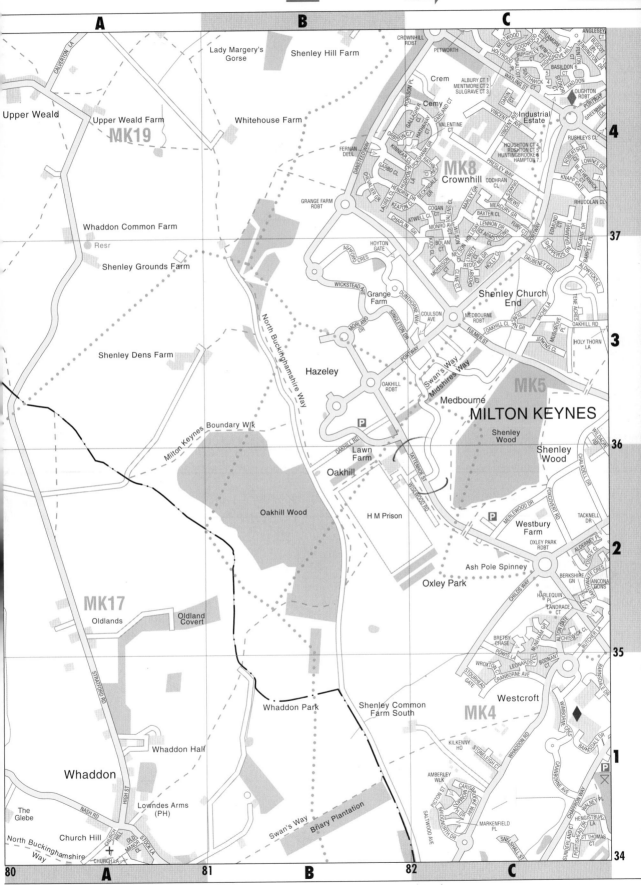

A

B

C

Upper Weald

Lady Margery's Gorse

Shenley Hill Farm

CROWNHILL RDBT

PETWORTH

ANGLESEY CT

WESTWOOD

BREAMORE CT

HOLYROOD

GOODWOOD

AYNSCOMBE

BISSCOTT CT

KENSINGTON CT

FENTON

BURGHLEY

COSGROVE HILL

BASILDON 6

Upper Weald Farm

Whitehouse Farm

Crem

ROBSON PL

GALLEHER

ORBISON CT

KINNEAD CT

CHEVALIER GR

LAUREL CL

HENDRIX DR

KEATON CT

CHAPLIN GR

DANSTEED WAY

HUDSON RD

BECKINSALE CT

HATHAWAY

GARLAND CT

ALBURY CT 1
MENTMORE CT 2
SULGRAVE CT 3

ALBURY

CT

WATLING ST

SOUTHWICK

HAMDON

HOUGHTON RDBT

PORTWAY

GREENHILL

RUSHLEYS CL

ROBERTSON

BLYTHWICK

LOWNES GR

KNAPP GATE

RHUDDLAN CL

MK19

Crem

Cemy

MK8
Crownhill

GARBO CL

VINCENT AVE

VALENTINE
CT

PRESLEY WAY

COGAN

ATWELL CL

MONRO AVE

MARLEY GR

BAXTER CL

MERCURY GR

LENNON DR

WILSON

CL

BOLAN
CT

CROSSLEY

CT

REDDY

CL

HOLLY CT

DAUBENEY GATE

EDMUND CT

GRAMMELL

ENGAINE DR

BARRETT PL

ALDWYCKS CL

Industrial
Estate

4

Whaddon Common Farm

Resr

GRANGE FARM
RDBT

FERNAN
DELL

Shenley Grounds Farm

ASHFORD CRES

WICKSTEAD AVE

HOYTON
GATE

CLINE CT

37

Shenley Dens Farm

North Buckinghamshire Way

Grange
Farm

MORLAND
DR

SINGLETON DR

DURTHORNE WAY

COULSON
AVE

PORTWAY

MEDBOURNE
RDBT

FULMER ST

OAKHILL CL

DON GR

JENKINS CL

Shenley Church
End

HOLY THORN
LA

FINE ACRES
RD

MUSGROVE
PL

OAKHILL RD

3

Hazeley

OAKHILL
RDBT

Swan's Way

Midshires Way

VACHE LA

MK5

Milton Keynes Boundary Wlk

P

Medbourne

Shenley
Wood

MILTON KEYNES

Oakhill Wood

Oakhill Rd

Lawn
Farm

Oakhill

TATTENHOE ST

WESTWOOD RD

Shenley
Wood

CHALKDELL DR

WILDRAKE
RD

36

H M Prison

P

MERLEWOOD DR

FOXCOVERT RD

TACKNELL
DR

Westbury
Farm

OXLEY PARK
RDBT

ALDERNEY PL

JERSEY CT

BERKSHIRE
GN

GATE CRES

ANCONA
GDNS

2

MK17

Oldlands

Oldland
Covert

Ash Pole Spinney

Oxley Park

CHILDS WAY

HARLEQUIN
PL

LANDRACE
CT

ALTON GATE

CHISWICK CL

BUTCHER LA

BARNSDALE DR

BRETBY
CHASE

POWIS LA

MUNGHAM
GR

LEONARDS
GATE

WROXTON
GATE

BOONANT
CT

CRANBORNE AVE

STOURHEAD
GATE

Westcroft

WHADDON RD

35

Whaddon Park

Shenley Common
Farm South

MK4

WIMBORNE CRES

BARNSDALE DR

Whaddon Hall

STRATFORD RD

KILKENNY
HO

STONELEIGH CT

CRANBORNE AVE

CHARMBORN WAY

1

Whaddon

The
Glebe

NASH RD

HIGH ST

Lowndes Arms
(PH)

S STOCK LA

Swan's Way

Briary Plantation

AMBERLEY
WLK

PICTON ST

SALTWOOD AVE

CARISBROOKE WAY

BRIDGNORTH DR

MARKENFIELD
PL

SUNDERLAND CT

PORTISHEAD DR

WALNEY PL

HENGISTBURY
LA

ST THOMAS
CT

SNELSHALL ST

34

North Buckinghamshire
Way

Church Hill

CHURCH HILL

OLD
MANOR CL

CHURCH LA

80

A

81

B

82

C

A2
1 ALSTONEFIELD
2 GILLAMOOR CL
3 FADMOOR PL
4 APPLETON MEWS

B1
1 GREYSTONLEY
2 DENCHWORTH CL
3 MARSHAW PL
4 FERNBOROUGH HAVEN
5 SPARSHOLT CL
6 HUNGERFORD HO
7 ASHBURNHAM CL
8 HOLLINWELL CL

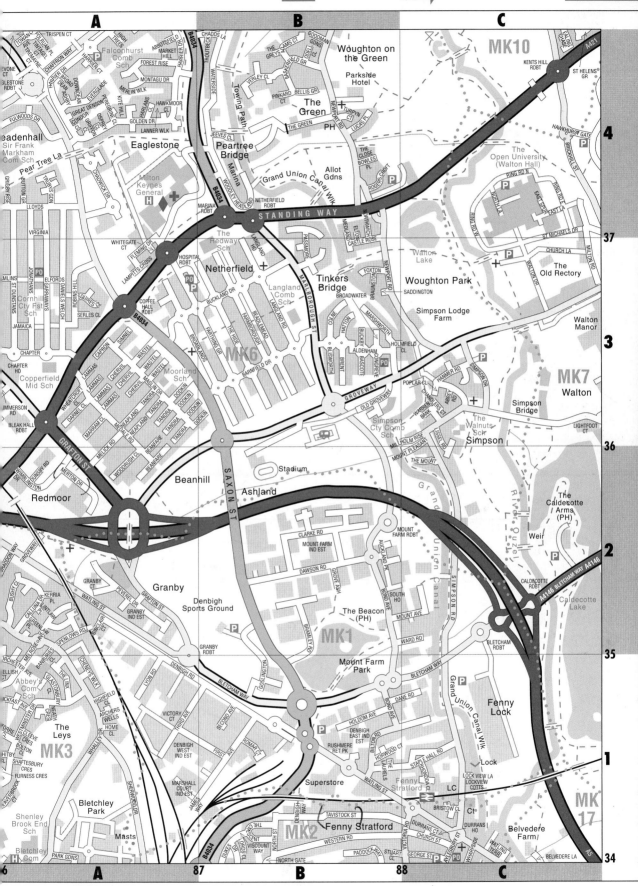

47 36

A B C

A421 STANDING WAY
Training Ctr
BEDGEBURY PL
BIRGATE RD
LAMBERHURST GR
MILLBANK PL
TUNBRIDGE GR
HOATHLY MEWS
TIMBOLD DR
WADHURST LA 1
BAYNHAM MEAD 2
WILSLEY POUND 3
COPTHORNE PL 4
FORDCOMBE LEA 5.
ERIDGE GN
SMARDEN BELL
SIDLEY MOOR
KNOLE BRIDGE
TUDELEY HALE
PENSHURST
PUNCHGATE
SWEETLANDS CNR
HIGH HALDEN

MILTON
KEYNES
SOUTHBRIDGE GR
Kents Hill
HARTFIELD CL
CROXBOROUGH LA
GOUDHURST CT
HEVER
SPELDHURST
FRITHWOOD
PIPSTON GN
SHERNFOLD
TIMBOLD DR
Kents Hill
Fst Sch
FELBRIDGE
BOGERS OAK

MK10
Ind Est
HARDING RD

Brinklow
BRANSWORTH AVE
BRUDENELL DR

A5130
Glebe Farm

NEWPORT RD
Wavendon
Tower
The Old
Rectory
Leathern Bottel
(PH)
ST MARY'S CL
LOWER END RD
CROSS END
Wavendon
Manor
Wavendon
A5130

37

De Montfort
Univ
HAMMERWOOD
GATE
Hotel
GROOMBRIDGE
BIRDUP
GROVEWAY
Walnut Tree
RDBT
HONITON CT 1
FLAXBOURNE CT 2
ORTENSIA DR
MINERVA GDNS
COGGESHALL
TRIUMPH DR
IKNIELD CL
PASSALEWE LA
WALTON END
Church
Farm
PO
Wavendon
Fst Sch
Wavendon
FIELDS
Nursery
BELLW

Walton
Manor
ROSEMARY CT
TARRAGON CL
SAMPHIRE CT
CALAMUST CT
PIMPEL GR
PINFOLD
WINDHEAD CL
BALSAM
BLACKBERRY
FYFIELD BARROW
The Old
Farm
GREGORIES DR
Scotch
Firs
STEVENS
FIELD
SHUTTLEWORTH GR
GABLE THORNE
Wavendon
Gate
CLUNY CT
SAUNDERS
DIXIE LA
FORTUNA
CT
Wavendon
Gate Com
Sch
BYRD CRES
Old Farm
Park
LC
MK17

3
Walton
CHINNADUN
ANGEL CT
BERBERIS CL
DUNCHURCH CLOSE
Heronshaw
Fst Sch
Heronsgate
Mid Sch
Walnut
Tree
MK7
1 CORIANDER CT
2 TAMARISK CT
3 PAPRIKA CT
4 BERGAMOT GDNS
BROWNS
WOOD RDBT
CAMOMILE
BRAHMS CT
TANGEMAN
LA
ARNE CL
LUTYENS GDNS
KALMAN GDNS
BELLINI
BRITTEN
GOLDMARK
HANDEL GR
Woodley's Farm

36
SEAGRAVE
REDCOTE
MANOR
CHASE AVE
KATHERINE
WILLIAMS
CIRC
BRICKHILL ST
Walton
Park
RDBT
BOURTON LOW
BLETCHAM WAY
DELIUS
GERSHWIN CL
MAHLER CL
ELGAR GR
BOWEN CL
MORLEY CRES
HINDEMITH
GDNS
NOVELLO
BEETHOVEN CL
DREATMEAD DELL

Walton Park
Caldecotte
Lake
A4146
ONSLOW CT
FREDINGTON
SHERBOURNE DR
BRADBOURNE LA
Tilbrook
IND EST
Tilbrook
Browns
Wood
MENDELSSOHN
SCHUMANN CL
WAGNER
MOZART CL
STRAUSS GR
HOLST CRES
IRELAND
BERNSTEIN CL
TIPPET CL
BERWALD CL

2
A4146
CALDECOTTE LA
MAPLEDURHAM
LANGFORD PL
HOME
FIELD
TOP
MDW
THE FORTONS
LONG
LAYERS
Caldecotte
Lake
BRANTHAM
CL
MORELAND
HEYBRIDGE
CRES
BERRYFIELD
GATESWICK
LONG
HEDGE

35
Caldecotte
BACKLEYS
AMOUNTAIN
LC
Tilbrook
Farm
The Wheatsheaf
(PH)
Rectory
Farm
HAYNES
CL
EDWIN CL
Blind Pond
Ind Est
PARKWAY
Brown's Wood
Bow Brickhill
Park

Bow
Brickhill
Bow Brickhill
Crossing
STATION RD
GREENWAYS
DOWNS VIEW
GROVESBROOK
RUSHMERE CL
Bow Brickhill
Fst Sch
CHURCH RD
DRAKEWELL RD
Milton
Keynes
Boundary
Wlk
Bow Brickhill
Heath

1
Bow Brickhill
LONDON END LA
Weeks
Covert
Mast
CH
The
Heath

34
89 A 90 B 91 C

47 59

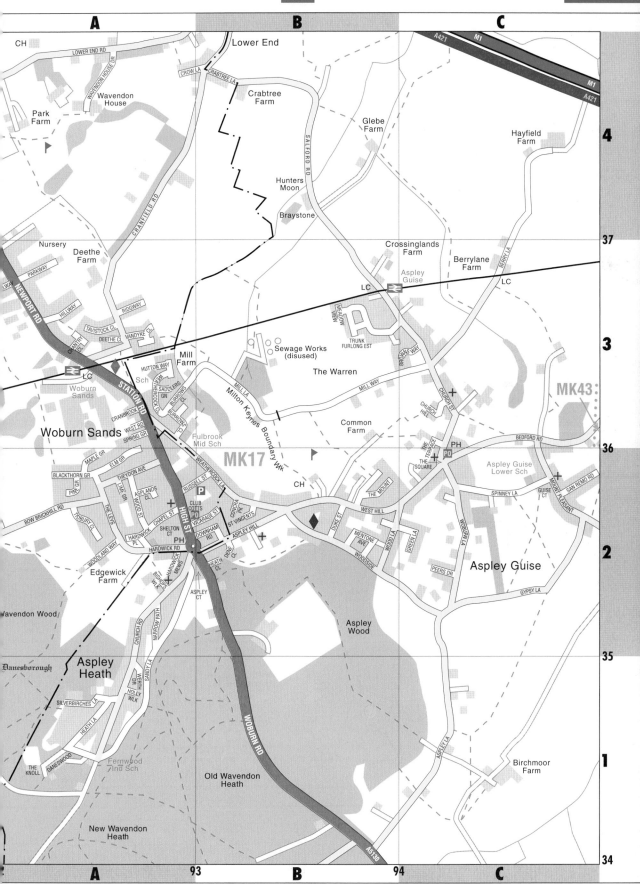

A B C

Radclive
Radclive Manor
River Great Ouse
Grovehill Farm
CH
TINGEWICK RD
A421
4
Rectory Barn
Farm
Dudley Bridge
WATER STRATFORD RD
Tingewick
Manor
Farm
Tingewick
Hall
STOWE VIEW
Cemy
Sewage
Works
33
RADCLIVE RD
Durrants Farm
Royal Oak
(PH)
PO
West Well Cl
HILLSIDE
BUCKINGHAM ST
CHURCH ST
ST MARYS CT
SANDPIT HILL
Woodfield
Nursery
The
Bungalows
STRANGERS LA
WEST WELL LA
MAIN ST
OLD FORGE CL
CROSS LA
N GORRELL CL
HICKMANS
CL
Sch
BACK LA
UPPER ST
STOCKLEYS LA
NEW ST
THE MALTINGS
SION TERR
3
Parsonage
Farm
Windbush
Farm
West Well
Farm
Airfield
(dis)
Primrosehill Farm
MK18
32
Leyland Farm
HILLSIDE
Tingewick
Wood
Gawcott
MAIN ST
THE RISE
COW LA
NEW INN
CHURCH ST
BACK
Eagle's Farm
Gawcott
Inf Sch
2
Wood Farm
Round Wood
Lenborough Wood
31
Plough Farm
1
Dairy
Farm
Park
Spinney
Bushey Lane
Farm
BUSHES LA
HILLESDEN
HAMLET
Old Park Farm
MAIN ST
THE
ELMS
POUND LA
The Laurels
Lockharbour Farm
30
5 A 66 B 67 C

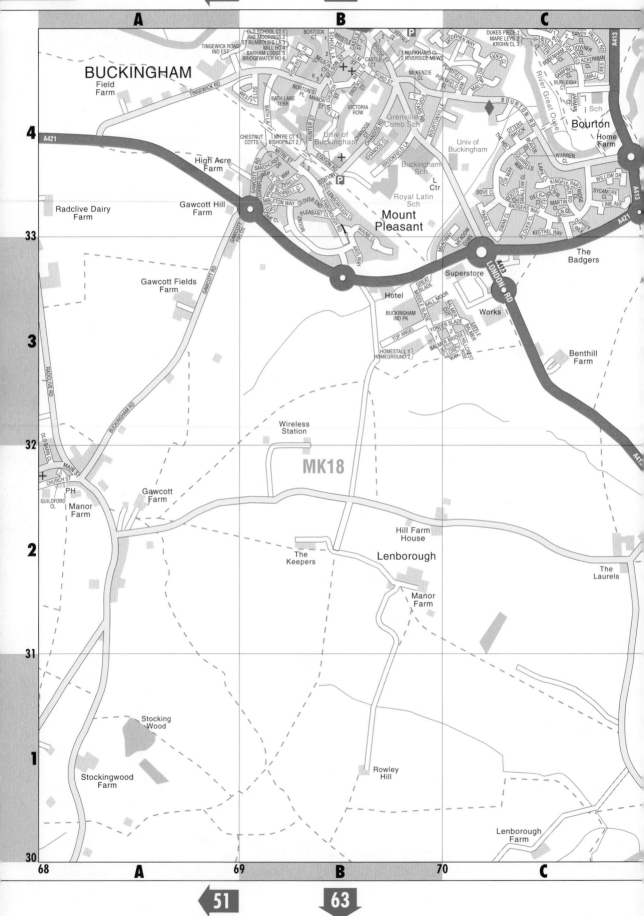

51
41

A **B** **C**

BUCKINGHAM

Field Farm

OLD SCHOOL CT 1
THE MOORINGS 2
ST RUMBOLD'S LA 3
MILL HO 4
BARHAM LODGE 5
BRIDGEWATER HO 6

TINGEWICK ROAD IND EST

BOSTOCK CT 1

1 MARKHAMS CL
2 RIVERSIDE MEWS

DUKES PIECE 1
MARE LEYS 2
KROHN CL 3

Bourton

Home Farm

A421

4

High Acre Farm

Radclive Dairy Farm

Gawcott Hill Farm

Univ of Buckingham

Buckingham Sch

Univ of Buckingham

L Ctr

Royal Latin Sch

Mount Pleasant

The Badgers

33

Gawcott Fields Farm

Superstore

Hotel

Works

Benthill Farm

BUCKINGHAM IND PK

TOP ANGEL

HOMESTALL 1
HOMEGROUND 2

3

Wireless Station

MK18

32

Gawcott Farm

Hill Farm House

Manor Farm

The Keepers

Lenborough

The Laurels

2

Stocking Wood

31

Stockingwood Farm

Rowley Hill

Lenborough Farm

1

30

68 **A** 69 **B** 70 **C**

51
63

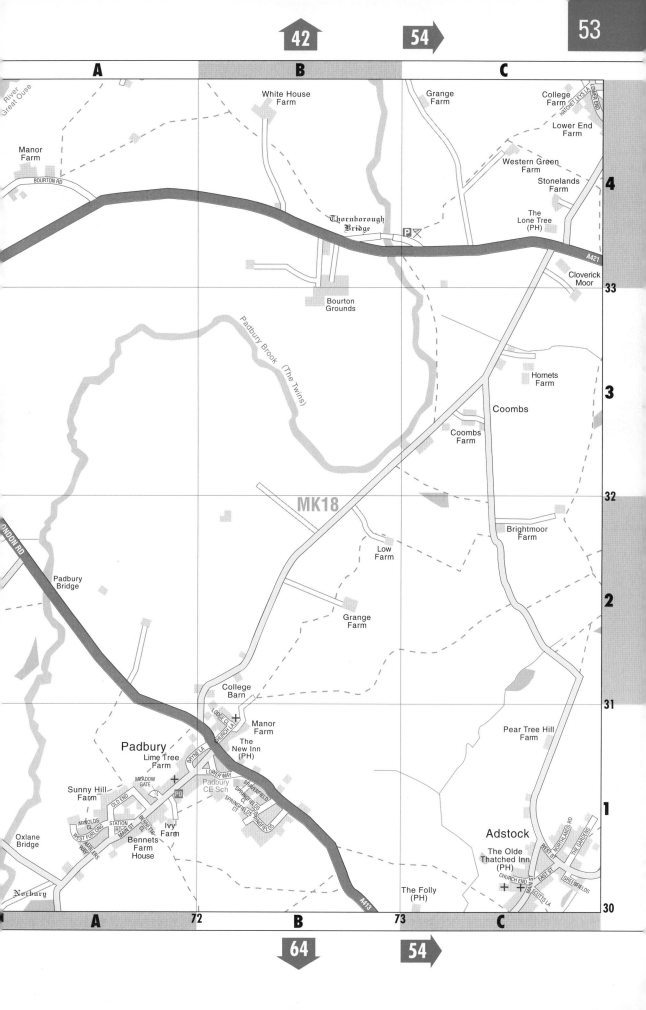

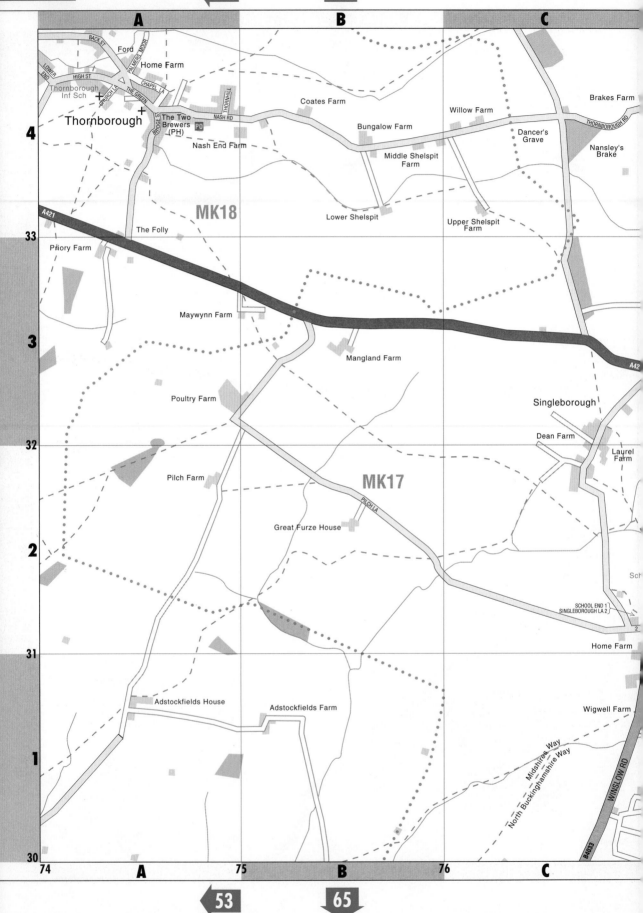

A

B

C

Back St

Ford

Home Farm

Lower End

High St

Thornborough Inf Sch

Pinch La

The Green

Chapel La

Thornborough

The Two Brewers (PH)

PO

Nash Rd

Thornhill

Coates Farm

Bungalow Farm

Willow Farm

Brakes Farm

Thornborough Rd

Dancer's Grave

Nansley's Brake

4

Nash End Farm

Middle Shelspit Farm

Bridge St

Palmers Moor

MK18

A421

The Folly

Lower Shelspit

Upper Shelspit Farm

33

Priory Farm

Maywynn Farm

Mangland Farm

A42

3

Poultry Farm

Singleborough

Dean Farm

32

Laurel Farm

Pilch Farm

MK17

PILCH LA

2

Great Furze House

School End 1
Singleborough La 2

2

Home Farm

31

Adstockfields House

Adstockfields Farm

Wigwell Farm

1

Midshires Way

North Buckinghamshire Way

Winslow Rd

B4033

30

74

A

75

B

76

C

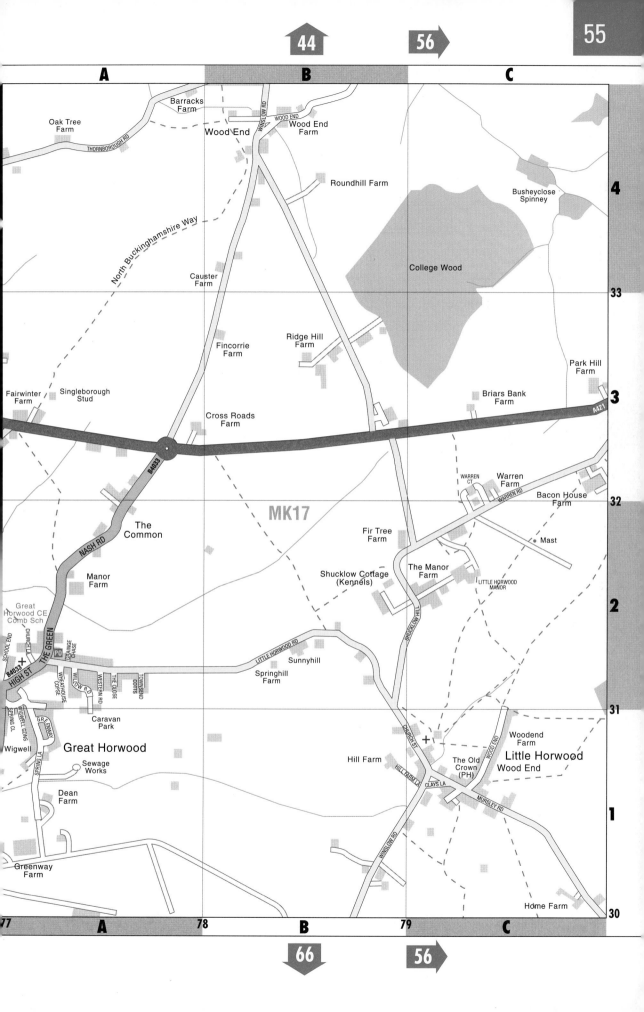

A **B** **C**

Oak Tree Farm

Barracks Farm

THORNBOROUGH RD

Wood End

WINSLOW RD

WOOD END

Wood End Farm

Roundhill Farm

Busheyclose Spinney

4

North Buckinghamshire Way

Causter Farm

College Wood

33

Fincorrie Farm

Ridge Hill Farm

Park Hill Farm

Fairwinter Farm

Singleborough Stud

Cross Roads Farm

Briars Bank Farm

A421

3

B4033

WARREN CT

Warren Farm

WARREN RD

Bacon House Farm

32

MK17

The Common

NASH RD

Fir Tree Farm

SHUCKLOW HILL

The Manor Farm

LITTLE HORWOOD MANOR

• Mast

Manor Farm

Shucklow Cottage (Kennels)

2

Great Horwood CE Comb Sch

CHURCH END

THE GREEN

GRANGE CHASE

LITTLE HORWOOD RD

Springhill Farm

Sunnyhill

SCHOOL END

PO

WHEATHOUSE COPSE

WILLOW RD

WESTERN RD

THE CLOSE

TOWNSEND COTTS

B4033

HIGH ST

31

WIGWELL GDNS

SPRING CL

GREENWAY

SPRING LA

Caravan Park

Wigwell

Great Horwood

CHURCH ST

Hill Farm

HILL FARM LA

+

CLAYS LA

The Old Crown (PH)

WOOD END

Woodend Farm

Little Horwood
Wood End

MURSLEY RD

Dean Farm

Sewage Works

WINSLOW RD

1

Greenway Farm

Home Farm

30

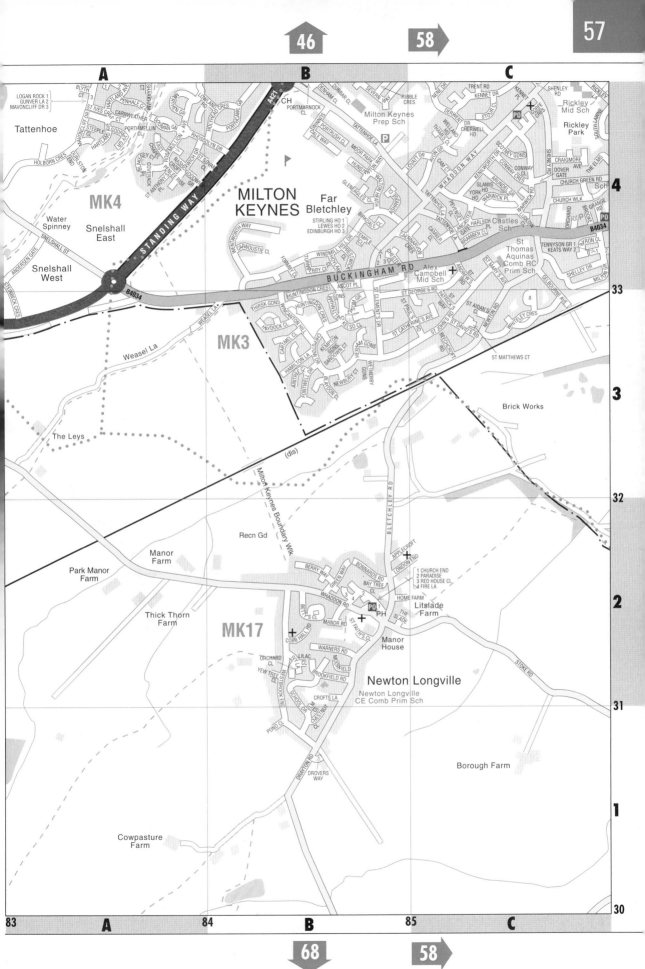

← 57   47 →

B4
1 ALEXANDER HO
2 LEE HO
3 CHRISTINE HO
4 WOODWARD HO
5 WETHERBURN CT
6 STANIER SQ
7 THE CONCOURSE
8 AGORA CTR

A   B   C

MK17

MILTON KEYNES

MK3

MK2   Water Eaton

Bletchley Park Mus
Bletchley
Milton Keynes Coll (Bletchley Ctr)
Old Bletchley Sch
BUCKINGHAM RD
B4034
TA Ctr
Holne Chase Sch
Nature Reserve
Bletchley
Blue Lagoon
Clay Pit
Milton Keynes Boundary Wlk
Old Fox Covert
Slad Farm
Skew Bridge Villa
Chadwell Farm
MK17
Rectory Farm
Burnell Farm

PRINCES WAY RDBT
South Terr
Knowles Schs
Liby
Libry
Eaton Mill Cty Comb Sch
Bishop Parker RC Comb Sch
Drayton Park Sch
Leon Sch
Waterhall Comb Sch
Bramley Grange
STOKE RD

Grand Union Canal Wlk
River Ouzel
Eaton Leys Farm
Galleylane Spinney
Grand Union Canal
Willowbridge Boat Yard
Towing Path
Stoke House
The Old Dairy Farm
MILL LA
Southlands Farm
Sewage Works
A4146

1 GWYNANT CT
2 DIDDINGTON CL

Dropshort Farm
BELVEDERE LA
WATLING ST
Hawthorn Ave
Wharfside

← 57   69 →

86   A   87   B   88   C   30

A   B   C

New Wavendon Heath

WOBURN RD

A5130

Birchmoor
Green

NEWPORT RD

CRAWLEY RD A4012

4

Bells
Copse

Birchmoor
Arms
(PH)

Dolton's
Farm

DRAKELOE L

ELEANOR
CL

ELEANO
WLK

Tollhouse
Grove

Hundreds
Farm

Horsemoor
Farm

A5130

CASWELL L

STAUNTON
HO

MARQUIS CT

BEDFORD ST

Woburn Lower
Sch

HIGH ST

PO

Woburn

MARKET
PL
TH

DUCK LA

GEORGE ST

A4012

33

Little Brickhill
Copse

Charle Wood

Maryland
Coll

HOWLAND
PL

BLOOMSBURY CL

LEIGHTON ST

TIMBER LA

LONDON END

Shire Oak

Wayn Close

Pinfold Pond

Crowholt
Plantation

3

Lowe's Wood

Job's Farm

Greensand Ridge Wlk

Pinfoldpond

Utcoate
Grange

Milton Keynes Boundary Wlk

Circuitt's
Covert

32

Buttermilk
Farm

MK17

Buttermilk Wood

2

A5

Nun Wood

Apesfield
Farm

Sheeplane
Belt

31

Rammamere
Farm

Sheeplane

1

Sand Pit

The
Fox & Hounds
(PH)

Bushycommon
Wood

Hill Farm

Bragenham Wood

King's Wood

WOBURN RD

LU7

A5

Arnold's
Cottages

Rammamere
Heath

30

92   A   93   B   94   C

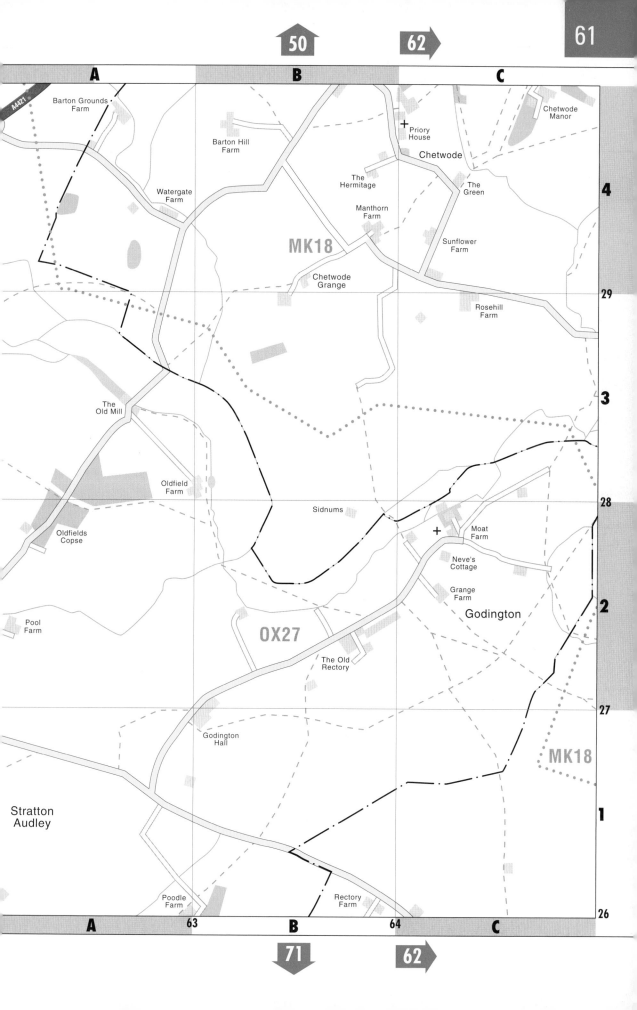

A   B   C

A4421

Barton Grounds
Farm

Barton Hill
Farm

Watergate
Farm

Chetwode
Manor

+ Priory
House

Chetwode

The
Hermitage

The
Green

Manthorn
Farm

MK18

Sunflower
Farm

Chetwode
Grange

Rosehill
Farm

4

29

3

The
Old Mill

Oldfield
Farm

Sidnums

28

Oldfields
Copse

+

Moat
Farm

Neve's
Cottage

Pool
Farm

Grange
Farm

Godington

2

OX27

The Old
Rectory

27

Godington
Hall

MK18

Stratton
Audley

1

Poodle
Farm

Rectory
Farm

26

A   63   B   64   C

A   **B**   **C**

Church
Farm
Old Hat
(PH)
SCHOOL LA
POUND LA
LEYS LA
The Laurels

Preston
Bissett
MAIN ST
THE SQUARE

Thorpes
Farm

Poplars
Farm

College
Farm

Copperhouse
Farm

Fir Tree Cottage

Buryfield Spinney

Jubilee
Farm Hou

Jubilee
Farm

4

29

Casemore
Farm

Westfield
Farm

Manor Farm

3

MK18

Cowley
Farm

28

← OX27

Cowley
Old House

Cowley
Lodge

2

Twyford Mill

Three Bridge
Mill

27

Church View
Farm

Seven Stars
(PH)

Twyford
CE Sch
MILL LA
MAIN ST
CHURCH ST
GRANGE
CL
SCHOOL LA

Home
Farm

1

OX27

Twyford
PO
Hall

Crown
(PH)
BICESTER RD

Portway
Cottages
PORTWAY RD

MANOR
CT

ROSEHILL
CRES

26

65   A   66   B   67   C

A   B   C

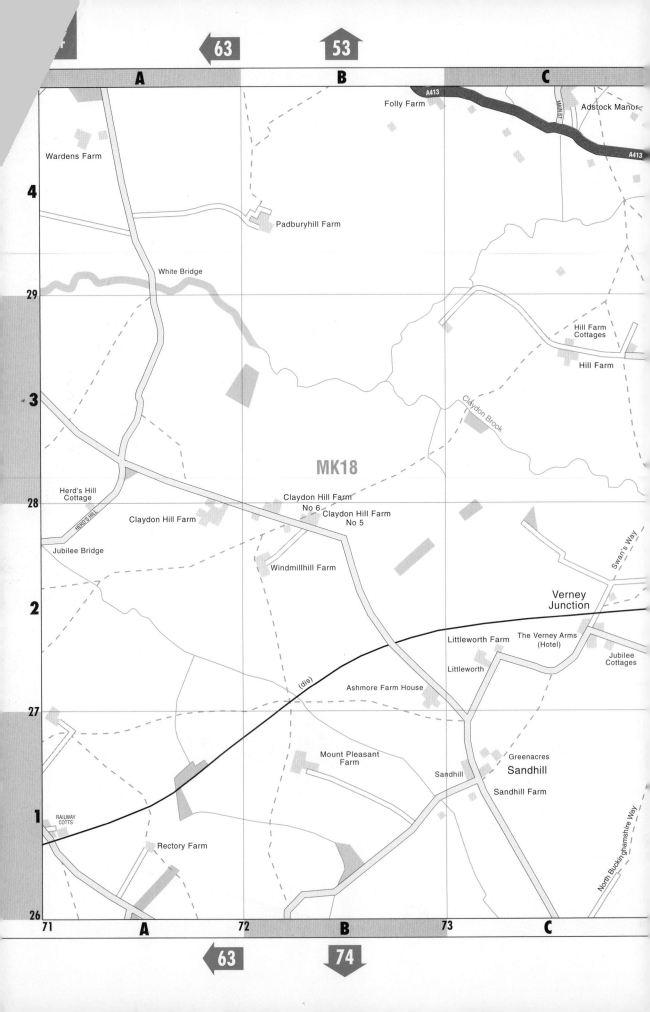

Folly Farm

A413

MAIN ST

Adstock Manor

Wardens Farm

4

Padburyhill Farm

White Bridge

29

Hill Farm
Cottages

Hill Farm

Claydon Brook

3

MK18

Herd's Hill
Cottage

28

Claydon Hill Farm
No 6

Claydon Hill Farm
No 5

Claydon Hill Farm

HERD'S HILL

Swan's Way

Jubilee Bridge

Windmillhill Farm

2

Verney
Junction

Littleworth Farm

The Verney Arms
(Hotel)

Littleworth

Jubilee
Cottages

(dis)

Ashmore Farm House

27

Mount Pleasant
Farm

Greenacres

Sandhill

Sandhill

Sandhill Farm

1

RAILWAY
COTTS

North Buckinghamshire Way

Rectory Farm

26

71   72   73

A   B   C

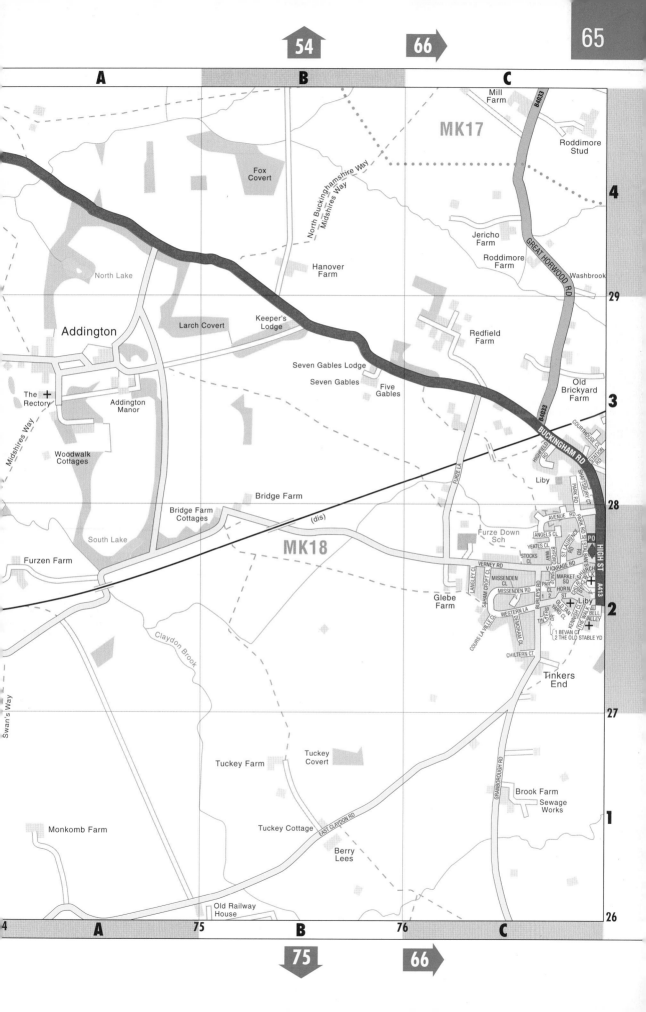

A | B | C

Greenway Farm

Mount Pleasant

4

The Hollows

Horwood House

Osierbed Spinney

Fishpond Spinney

29

The White House

(dis)

Roddimore Covert

Moco Farm

Clare Farm

Canada

Foxhole Farm

MK17

TANK HOUSE RD

COMERFORD WAY

MCLERNON WAY

THE SPINNEY

RUDDS CL

FLEDGELING WLK

MAGPIE LANE CL

LONGWELL LA

Spring Corner

Dodley Hill Farm

3

STATION RD

OLD MILL FURLONG

SCOTT EVANS CT

LOXADES WAY

LONGLANDS CT

LONGLANDS WLK

KEACH CL

LAMBTONS WAY

BEAMISH WAY

MEETING OAK LA

Redhall Farm

Winslow CE Sch

Abovemead Farm

28

P

GN TAMBUS

CRICKETERS ROW

ELMFIELDS GATE

OAK WAY

DOVE HOUSE CL

NORTH CROFT

P

GREYHOUND LA

FAIR MDW

COPSE

MK18

Midshires Way

Winslow

SHEPHERDS ROW

ELMSIDE

EXCHEQUERS

ROW END

Ivy Farm

GATE

COPSE

Duck End

OLD END

CHARLTO CL

2

A413

SHEEP ST

Hotel

CLAYCUTTERS

TENNIS LA

GLEBE CL

Shipton Mead Farm

SMITH

B4032

WINSLOW RD

B4032

Jubilee Cottages

Rands Farm

Shipton

Shipton Farm

27

Swanbourne House Sch

Shipton Bridge

Claydon Brook

1

Haybush Farm

Midshires Way

Swan's Way

Bennett's Hill

26

North Hill Farm

A413

77 | A | 78 | B | 79 | C

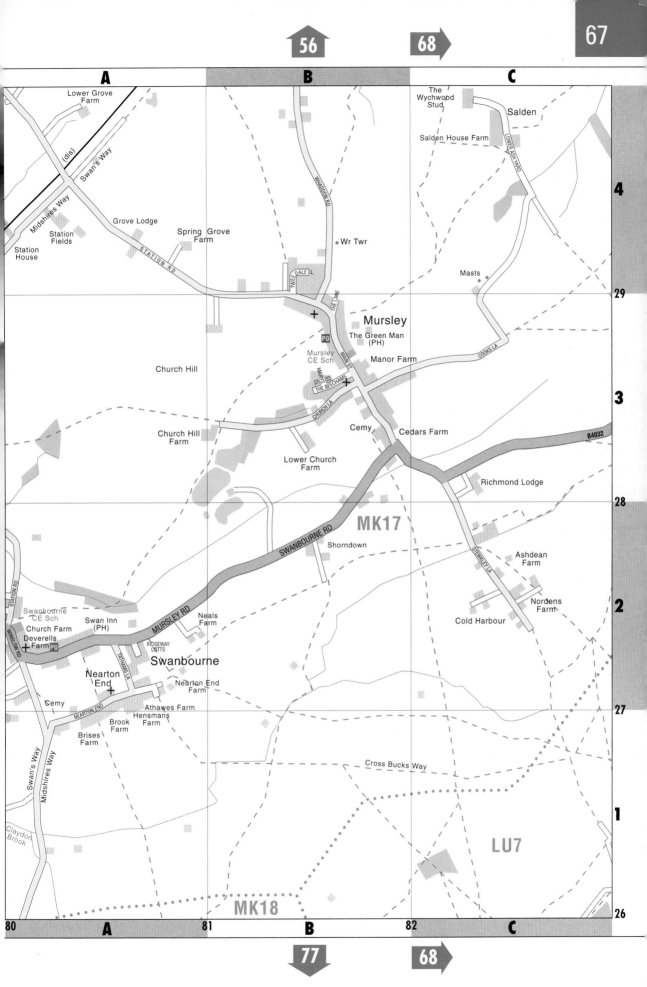

A   B   C

Lower Grove Farm

The Wychwood Stud

Salden

Salden House Farm

LOWER ASH YARD

4

(dis)

Swan's Way

Midshires Way

Grove Lodge

Station Fields

Station House

STATION RD

Spring Grove Farm

WHADDON RD

Wr Twr

Masts

29

TWEEDALE CL

THE LANE

PO

Mursley

The Green Man (PH)

Mursley CE Sch

Manor Farm

COOKS LA

Church Hill

MAIN ST

THE BEECHAMS

MARTS CL

CHURCH LA

Cemy

Cedars Farm

B4032

3

Church Hill Farm

Lower Church Farm

Richmond Lodge

28

MK17

SWANBOURNE RD

Shorndown

Ashdean Farm

STEWKLEY LA

Nordens Farm

STATION RD

Swanbourne CE Sch

Swan Inn (PH)

Neals Farm

Cold Harbour

2

Church Farm

Deverells Farm

WINSLOW RD

PO

RIDGEWAY COTTS

Swanbourne

Nearton End

Cemy

FATHAMS LA

Nearton End Farm

NEARTON END

Athawes Farm

Hensmans Farm

27

Brook Farm

Brises Farm

Cross Bucks Way

1

Swan's Way

Midshires Way

Claydon Brook

LU7

MK18

26

80   A   81   B   82   C

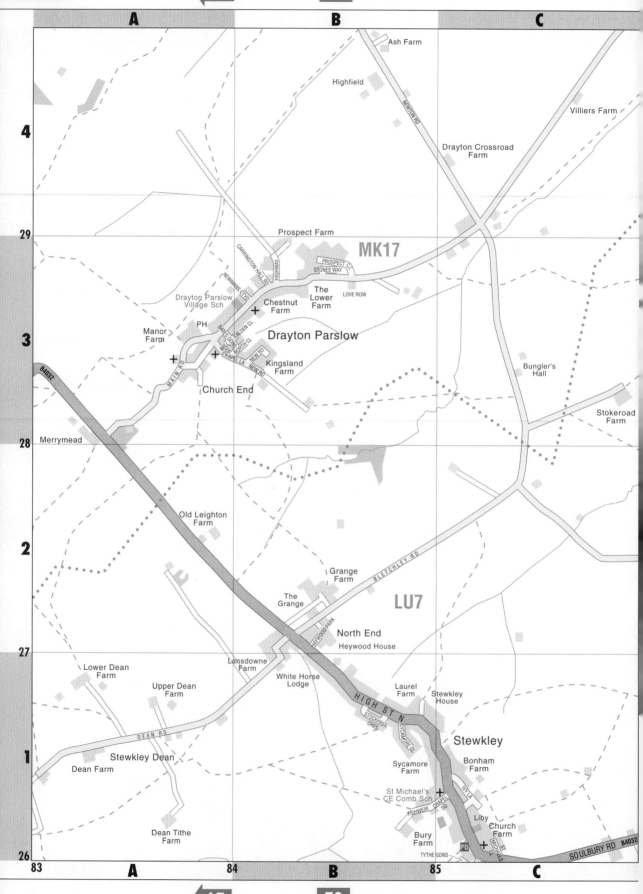

A B C

4

29

MK17

Ash Farm

Highfield

Villiers Farm

Drayton Crossroad Farm

Prospect Farm

CARRINGTON HALL RD

HIGHWAY

NEWMANS CTYD

Drayton Parslow Village Sch

PROSPECT CL

STONES WAY

The Lower Farm

LOVE ROW

Chestnut Farm

3

Manor Farm

PH

Drayton Parslow

Bungler's Hall

BATES GDN

GOLDEN CL

BELL CL

NORTH CL

CHAPEL LA

NEW RD

NEW RD

Kingsland Farm

Church End

Stokeroad Farm

28

Merrymead

B4032

MAIN RD

Old Leighton Farm

2

Grange Farm

BLETCHLEY RD

LU7

The Grange

HAYWOOD PARK

North End

Heywood House

27

Lower Dean Farm

Lansdowne Farm

White Horse Lodge

Upper Dean Farm

Laurel Farm

Stewkley House

HIGH ST N

STOCKHALL CRES

SYCAMORE CL

Stewkley

DEAN RD

Stewkley Dean

1

Dean Farm

Sycamore Farm

Bonham Farm

St Michael's CE Comb Sch

IVY LA

FISHWEIR

CHAPEL SQ

Liby

Church Farm

Dean Tithe Farm

Bury Farm

PO

ST MICHAELS CL

TYTHE GDNS

SOULBURY RD B4032

26

83 A 84 B 85 C

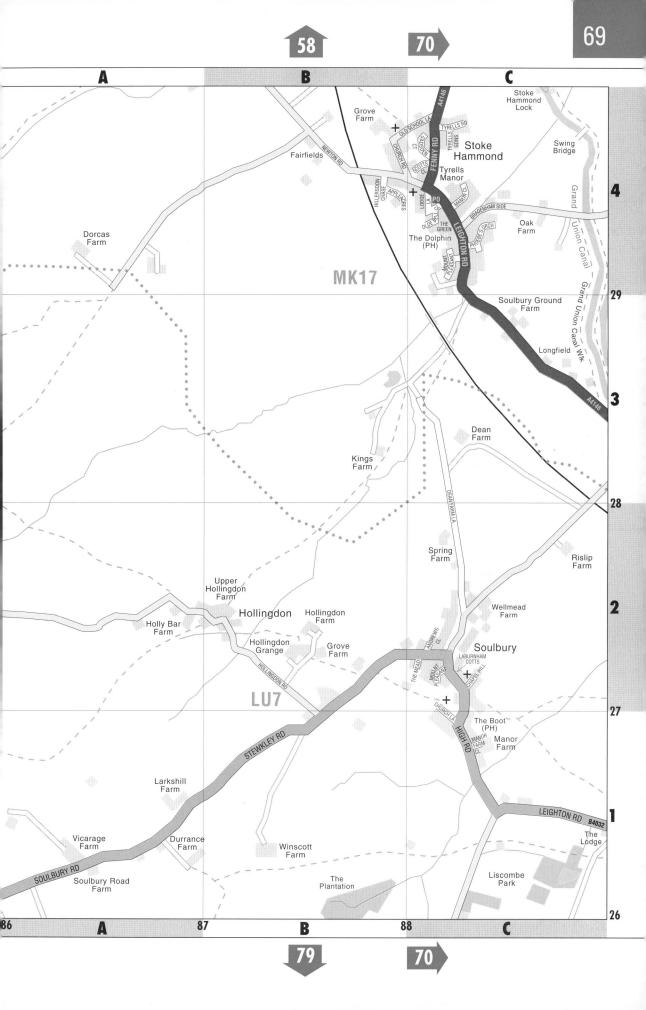

Grove
Farm

Stoke
Hammond
Lock

Stoke
Hammond

Swing
Bridge

TYRELLS RD

TYRELLS
GDNS

Tyrells
Manor

Fairfields

NEWTON RD

A4146

OLD SCHOOL LA

CHURCH RD

SCOTTS CL

CL

LINDSAY CL

FENNY RD

HILLERSDON CHASE

APPLEACRES

LODGE LA

PO

OLDE BELL CL

MANOR CL

THE GREEN

MOUNT PLEASANT

The Dolphin
(PH)

BRAGENHAM SIDE

PHOEBE'S ORCH

LEIGHTON RD

Oak
Farm

Grand Union Canal

MK17

Dorcas
Farm

4

29

Soulbury Ground
Farm

Longfield

Grand Union Canal Wlk

A4146

3

Dean
Farm

Kings
Farm

DEAN FARM LA

28

Spring
Farm

Rislip
Farm

Upper
Hollingdon
Farm

Hollingdon

Hollingdon
Farm

Wellmead
Farm

2

Holly Bar
Farm

Hollingdon
Grange

Grove
Farm

HOLLINGDON RD

THE MEAD

ANDREWS CL

MOUNT PLEASANT

LABURNHAM
COTTS

Soulbury

CHAPEL HILL

LU7

CHURCH LA

27

STEWKLEY RD

HIGH RD

The Boot
(PH)

MANOR
FARM CL

Manor
Farm

Larkshill
Farm

Winscott
Farm

LEIGHTON RD

B4032

1

Vicarage
Farm

Durrance
Farm

The
Lodge

SOULBURY RD

Soulbury Road
Farm

The
Plantation

Liscombe
Park

26

69
59

A   **B**   **C**

4

River Ouzel

Paper Mill

MK17

STOKE LA

Ivy Lane Farm

IV LA

Sewage Works

Stockgrove Farm

Greensand Ridge Wlk

P

Stockgrove Country Park

Partridge Hill

Furze Hill

Alders Farm

Oak Wood

29

Partridge House

CH

Upper Kiln Farm

Kiln Farm

Shire Oak

Rushmere Park

Three Locks (PH)

Red Bridge

Bragenham Farm

Bragenham

BRAGENHAM LA

3

A4146

Stapleford Mill

Stapleford Farm

Ludley Cottage

28

Grand Union Canal

River Ouzel

LU7

Grand Union Canal Wlk

Nares Gadley Farm

LINSLADE RD

Rushmere

THE HEATH

CH

2

Chelmscote Manor Farm

Broad Oak

Grange Mill

OLD LINSLADE RD

HEATH DUKES RIDE

SANDY LA

REDWOOD GLADE

PLANTATION RD

REDWOOD GLADE

27

MANOR CT

P

Old Linslade

Old Linslade Manor

TALL PINES

OXENDON CT

TAYLOR'S RIDE

ROBINSWOOD CL

DINGLE DEL

WOODLAND AVE

Corbettshill Farm

1

B4032

Dollar Farm

LEIGHTON RD

The Globe (PH)

STOKE RD

GLOBE LA

A4146

Sewage Works

BOSSINGTON LA

THE MARTINS

DR

B4032

Linslade Wood

26

89   **A**   90   **B**   91   **C**

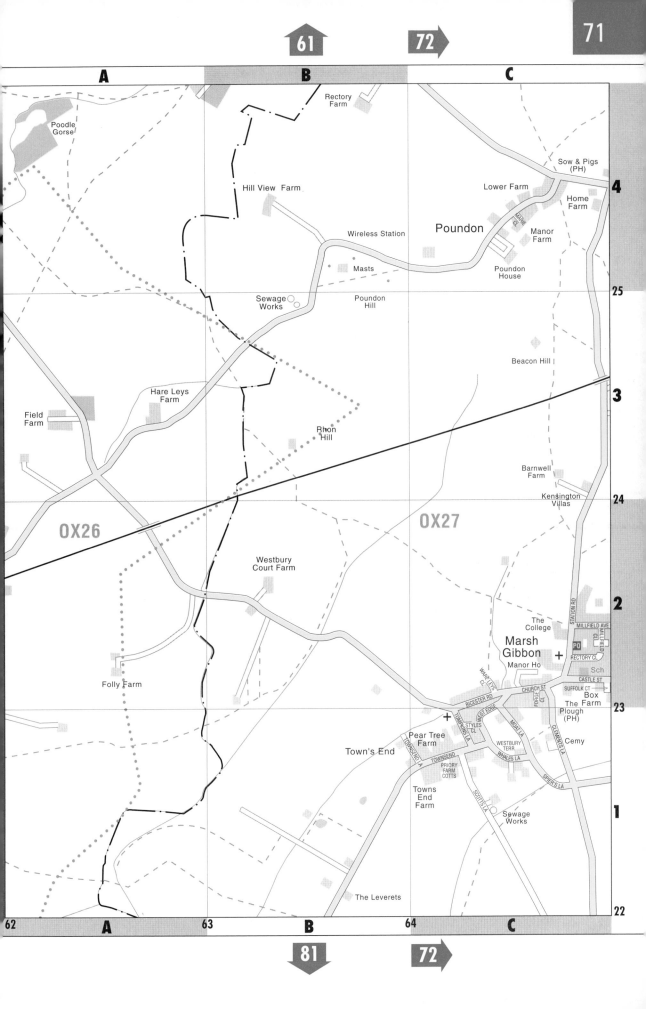

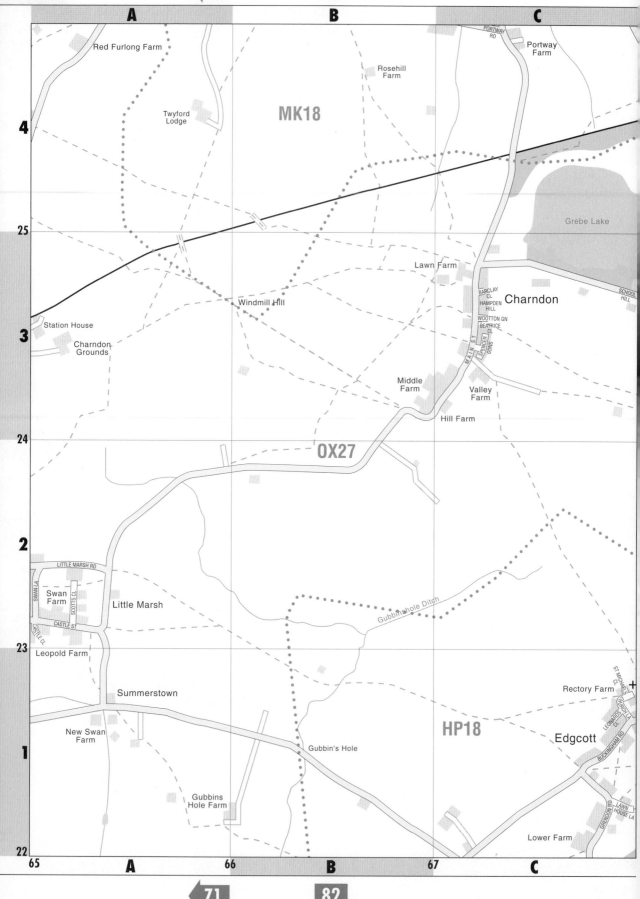

71
62

A

B

C

Red Furlong Farm

Rosehill Farm

PORTWAY RD

Portway Farm

Twyford Lodge

MK18

4

Grebe Lake

25

Lawn Farm

SCHOOL HILL

BARCLAY CL

HAMPDEN HILL

Charndon

Windmill Hill

WOOTTON GN

BEATRICE CL

MAIN ST

SPENCER GDNS

Station House

3

Charndon Grounds

Middle Farm

Valley Farm

Hill Farm

24

OX27

2

LITTLE MARSH RD

SWAN LA

Swan Farm

SCOTTS CL

Little Marsh

Gubbinshole Ditch

CASTLE ST

CASTLE CL

23

Leopold Farm

St MICHAELS CL

CHURCH LA

Rectory Farm

Summerstown

HP18

LEONARDS CL

Edgcott

New Swan Farm

Gubbin's Hole

1

BUCKINGHAM RD

GRENDON RD

LAWN HOUSE LA

Gubbins Hole Farm

Lower Farm

22

65

A

66

B

67

C

(dis)

Rose Hill
Farm

Blackmoorhill

Shepherd's
Furze Farm

4

Calvert Jubilee
Nature Reserve

Blackmorehill
Farm

25

SCHOOL
HILL

WERNER TERR

BRACKLEY LA

Great
Pond
Farm

MK18

Shrubs
Wood

Calvert

Knowl Hill

3

Decoypond
Wood

24

OX27

THREEPOINTS LA

Knowlhill
Farm

Dunstyhill
Farm

Sheephouse
Wood

2

Dunsty Hill

23

PERRY HILL

Lawn Hill
Farm

Manor
Farm

BUCKINGHAM RD

LAWN HILL

HP18

Moor
Farm

1

Rosall
Farm

Prune
Farm

Greatmoor

Springhill
(HM Prison)

HM Young
Offender Inst
(Grendon)

22

73
64

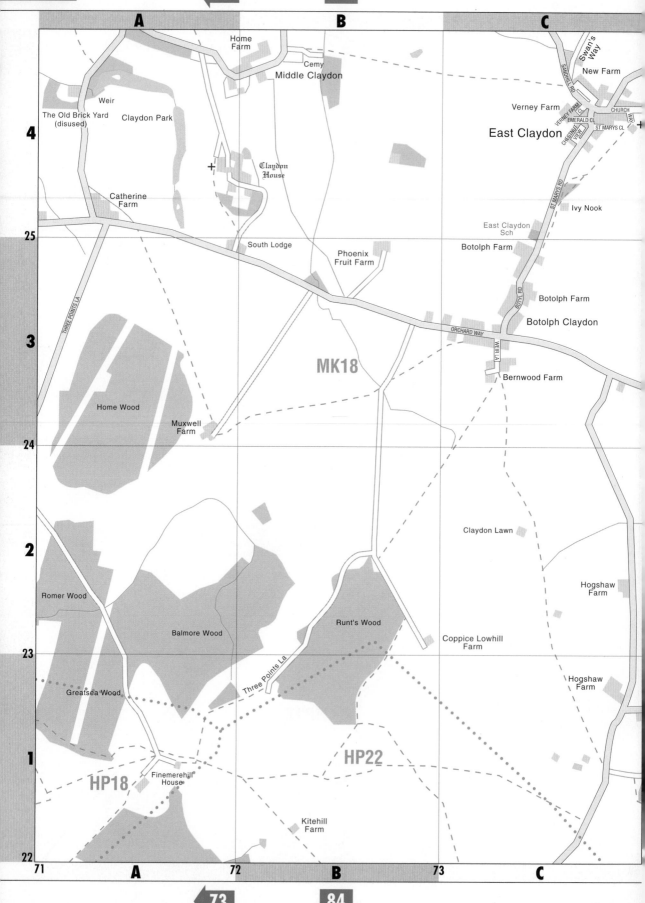

A B C

Home Farm

Cemy
Middle Claydon

Swan's Way

SANDHILL RD

New Farm

Weir

The Old Brick Yard
(disused)

Claydon Park

VERNEY FARM
EMERALD CL
VERNEY FARM CL

Verney Farm

CHURCH WAY

CHESTNUT VIEW
ST MARYS CL

East Claydon

4

Claydon House

Catherine Farm

ST MARYS RD

Ivy Nook

25

South Lodge

Phoenix
Fruit Farm

East Claydon
Sch

Botolph Farm

BOTYL RD

Botolph Farm

3

ORCHARD WAY

Botolph Claydon

MK18

WEIR LA

Home Wood

Muxwell
Farm

Bernwood Farm

24

Claydon Lawn

2

Romer Wood

Hogshaw
Farm

Balmore Wood

Runt's Wood

Coppice Lowhill
Farm

23

Three Points La

Greatsea Wood

Hogshaw
Farm

1

HP22

HP18

Finemerehill
House

Kitehill
Farm

22

71 A 72 B 73 C

A
B
C

Electricity
Sub-Station

Millknob
Hill

4

Granborough

Sion Hill
Farm

Rookery
Farm

Ley House
Farm

HOLLOW HILL

WINDMILL RD

BATES CL

MARKS ORCH

SOVEREIGN CL

PH

GREEN END

25

CHURCH LA

CHELTENHAM VIEW

PARK RD

MARSTON RD

North Buckinghamshire Way

HOGSHAW RD

Hogshaw Road
Farm

3

Wings
Farm

24

Lower
Farm

MK18

Middle
Farm

2

Sewage
Works

23

Brook
Farm

QUAINTON RD

Hill End
Farm

Fulbrook
House

Midshires Way

Carters Lane
Farm

CARTER'S LA

Fulbrook
Farm

SWAN'S WAY

1

Hogshaw Hill
Farm

Quainton Hill

Stonehill
Farm

Manor
Farm

22

4
A
75
B
76
C

← 75
↑ 66

A   B   C

A413

BENNETT'S HILL

North Hill Farm

Swan's Way

MK17

4

Oakham Farm

Holcombe Cottages

Christmas Gorse

Buxlow Farm

Green End

Lower Green End Farm

GREEN END

The Neptune Farm

Grange Farm

25

Green End Farm

Lathwells Farm

3

MK18

Midshires Way

Maynes Hill Farm

24

Marstonfields Farm

The Bungalow

Crandon Farm

Buttermilkhall Farm

2

Swan's Way

Guy's Thorns

Stevens Farm

GRANBOROUGH RD

GIBBINGS CL

ELMERS MDW

HP22

23

QUAINTON RD

HILL FARM

North Marston CE Sch

MARSTONFIELDS RD

CARTERS MDW

DUDLEY CL

SHEPPERDS CL

The Bell (PH)

Manor Farm

HIGH ST

SCHOOL HILL

CHURCH ST

Townsend

Glebe Farm

Ramhill Farm

North Marston

MORTON CL

SOUTH LA

Burnaby Farm

1

PORTWAY

PULPIT LA

MEADWAY

22

← 75
↓ 86

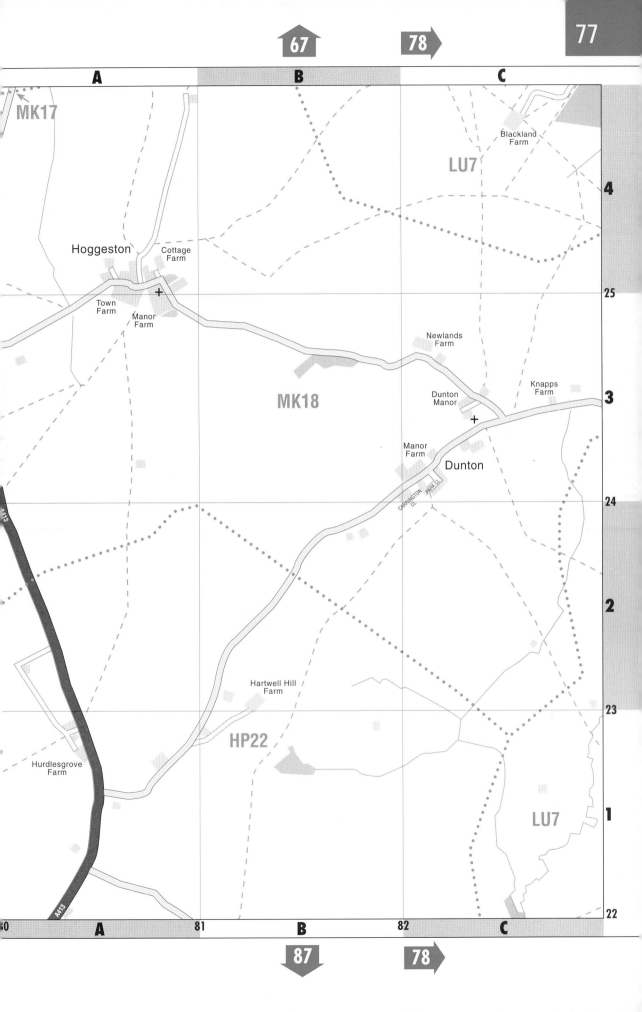

A   B   C

MK17

Blackland
Farm

LU7

4

Hoggeston   Cottage
Farm

25

Town
Farm   Manor
Farm

Newlands
Farm

MK18

Knapps
Farm

Dunton
Manor

3

Manor
Farm

Dunton

CARRINGTON CL   PARK CL

24

2

Hartwell Hill
Farm

23

HP22

Hurdlesgrove
Farm

LU7

1

A413

22

77
68

A **B** **C**

4

TYTHE GDNS

PARSONS CL

SOULBURY RD

B4032

Red Barn Farm

TYTHE CL

FOLDING

OLD MANOR CL

DOVE ST

ORKNEY CL

MANOR CL

WALDUCKS CL

Manor House

LOVETTS END

HIGH ST

MALTINGS CL

South End

COURTHEDGE CL

ORCHARD LA

Breach Farm

Carpenters' Arms (PH)

FARM CL

KINGS ST

Wing Road Farm

North Farm

SOUTH LA

25

Kiln Farm

WING RD

MK18

DUNTON RD

Sewage Works

Forge Farm

3

Littlecote

Littlecote Dairy Farm

Penton Farm

Warren Farm

Littlecote Farm

Mount Pleasant Farm

Kingsbridge Farm

24

LU7

Poultry Farm

2

Steart Farm

New Dairy Farm

Cedars Farm

23

South Tinkers Hole Farm

Lockharts

1

Cublington

READS LA

Neales Farm

Poultry Farm

ST NICHOLAS CL 1
CHENEY CL 2
MEADOW CL 3

STEWKLEY RD

SILVER ST

The Olde Manor

Old Manor Farm

ACORN BSNS CTR

Old House Farm

HIGH ST

BELL CL

WING RD

Manor Farm

RIDING'S WAY

WHITCHURCH RD

PH

ASTON ABBOTTS RD

Southend Farm

ROSES CL

22

83 **A** 84 **B** 85 **C**

A B C

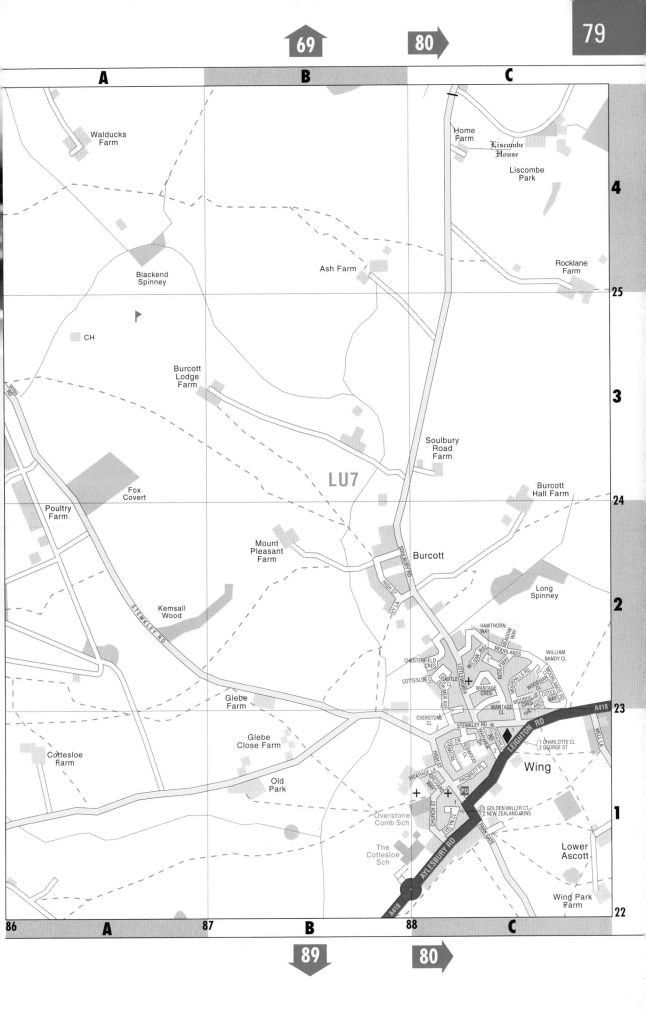

Walducks
Farm

Home
Farm

Liscombe
House

Liscombe
Park

4

Blackend
Spinney

Ash Farm

Rocklane
Farm

25

CH

Burcott
Lodge
Farm

3

WING RD

Soulbury
Road
Farm

LU7

Fox
Covert

Burcott
Hall Farm

24

Poultry
Farm

Mount
Pleasant
Farm

Burcott

Long
Spinney

SOULBURY RD

HIGH ST

SMITH LA

2

Hawthorn
Way

Meadow Way

William
Bandy Cl

Chesterfield
Cres

Willow Way

Moorlands

Moorlands Rd

Moorhills Rd

Kemsall
Wood

STEWKLEY RD

Cottesloe Cl

Castle
Cl

Wantage
Cres

Moorhills
Cres

Woodman
Cl

Cotes
Way

The Lands

A418

LITTLEWORTH

CROMER AVE

Glebe
Farm

Wantage
Cl

Overstone
Cl

Stewkley Rd

23

Cottesloe
Farm

Glebe
Close Farm

Old
Park

HIGH ST

DOD DR

WARWICK RD

REDWOOD CL

PROSPECT PL

ROTHSCHILD RD

LEIGHTON RD

1 CHARLOTTE CL
2 GEORGE ST

WELL LA

Wing

VICARAGE LA

ORCHARD WAY

PO

1
2

1 GOLDEN MILLER CT
2 NEW ZEALAND GDNS

1

Overstone
Comb Sch

CHURCH ST

EVELYN CL

PARK GATE

AYLESBURY RD

Lower
Ascott

The
Cottesloe
Sch

A418

Wing Park
Farm

22

86 A 87 B 88 C

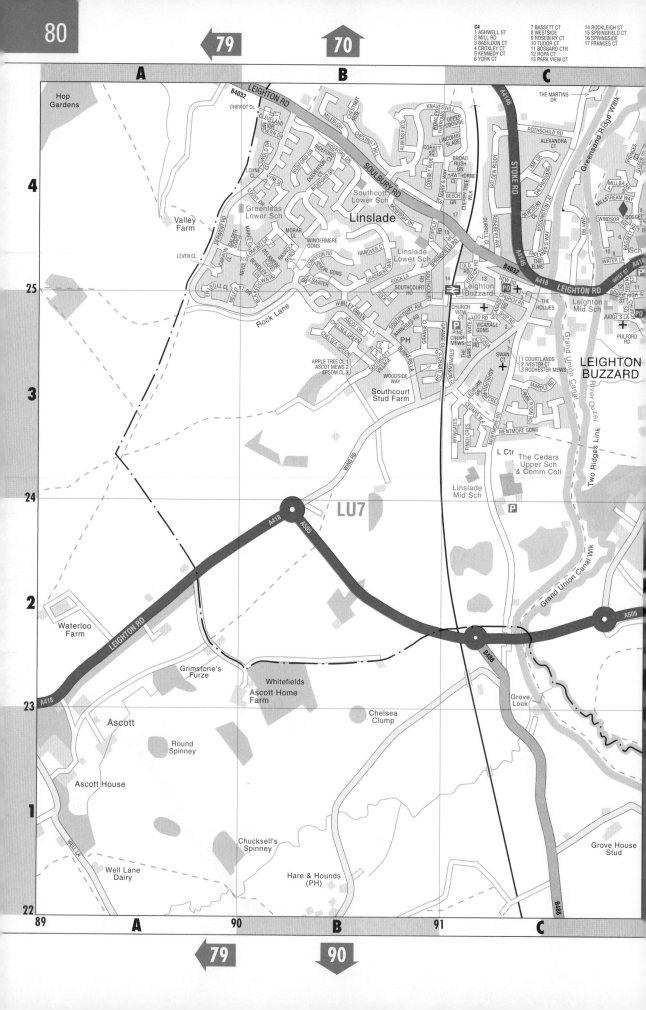

79
70

C4
1 ASHWELL ST
2 MILL RD
3 BASILDON CT
4 CROXLEY CT
5 KENNEDY CT
6 YORK CT
7 BASSETT CT
8 WESTSIDE
9 ROSEBERY CT
10 TUDOR CT
11 BOSSARD CTR
12 ROPA CT
13 PARK VIEW CT
14 ROCKLEIGH CT
15 SPRINGFIELD CT
16 SPRINGSIDE
17 FRANCES CT

A
B
C

Hop Gardens

THE MARTINS DR

B4032

LEIGHTON RD

CHEVIOT CL

SOULBURY RD

KNAVES HILL

ROTHSCHILD RD

ALEXANDRA CT

Greensand Ridge Walk

4

Valley Farm

Greenleas Lower Sch

Linslade

Southcott Lower Sch

STOKE RD

A4146

MILLBANK

WINDSOR AVE

DOGGET

LEVEN CL

Linslade Lower Sch

A418

B4032

Sch

WATER LA

A418

25

Rock Lane

Southcourt Ho

Leighton Buzzard

Leighton Mid Sch

LEIGHTON RD

HIMLEY GREEN

CHELSEA GREEN

ASCOT DR

PH

CHURCH VIEW CT

PINE CREST MEWS

THE HOLLIES

PULFORD RD

LEIGHTON BUZZARD

APPLE TREE CL 1
ASCOT MEWS 2
EPSOM CL 3

SOUTHCOTT VILLAGE

WOODSIDE WAY

SWAN CT

1 COURTLANDS
2 IVESTER CT
3 ROCHESTER MEWS

3

Southcourt Stud Farm

Grand Union Canal

River Ouzel

Two Ridges Link

L Ctr

The Cedars Upper Sch & Comm Coll

WING RD

24

Linslade Mid Sch

LU7

A418

A505

Grand Union Canal Wlk

2

Waterloo Farm

LEIGHTON RD

A505

Grimstone's Furze

Whitefields Ascott Home Farm

B488

Grove Lock

23

A418

Ascott

Chelsea Clump

Round Spinney

Ascott House

1

WELL LA

Chucksell's Spinney

Grove House Stud

Well Lane Dairy

Hare & Hounds (PH)

22

89
A
90
B
91
C

B488

79
90

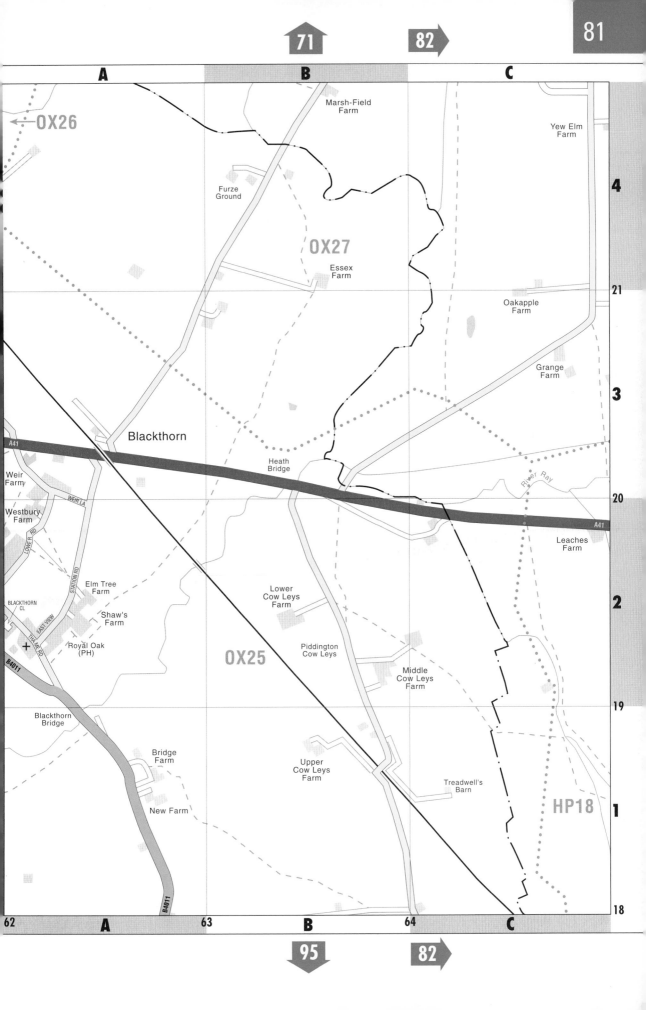

71 82

A B C

OX26

Marsh-Field Farm

Yew Elm Farm

Furze Ground

4

OX27

Essex Farm

Oakapple Farm

21

Grange Farm

3

Blackthorn

Heath Bridge

River Ray

A41

Weir Farm

Leaches Farm

Westbury Farm

WEIR LA

20

A41

LOWER RD

STATION RD

Elm Tree Farm

Lower Cow Leys Farm

BLACKTHORN CL

Shaw's Farm

2

EAST VIEW

Piddington Cow Leys

Middle Cow Leys Farm

+

Royal Oak (PH)

THAME RD

OX25

B4011

Blackthorn Bridge

19

Bridge Farm

Upper Cow Leys Farm

Treadwell's Barn

HP18

1

New Farm

B4011

18

62 63 64

A B C

A B C

4

OX27

Yew Elm
Farm

Gubbinshole Ditch

Marsh Gibbon Rd

Park Rd

Springhi Rd

Tudor Farm

Dunmead Farm

Hall Clo

21

River Ray

Manor Farm

Corbecott Rd

The Broadway

Rivlptons Paddocks

Millers Cln

Main Rd

Shakespeare
Farm

Shakespeare Orch

Save & Se Clo

3

Three Points

20

HP18

Winding Brook

White House
Farm

A41

Tetchwick Brook

Cub Pond

Gallow's Bridge

2

A41

Tetchwick Farm

Tetchwick

19

New Barn
Farm

1

Sewage
Works

Tittershall Wood

18

65 A 66 B 67 C

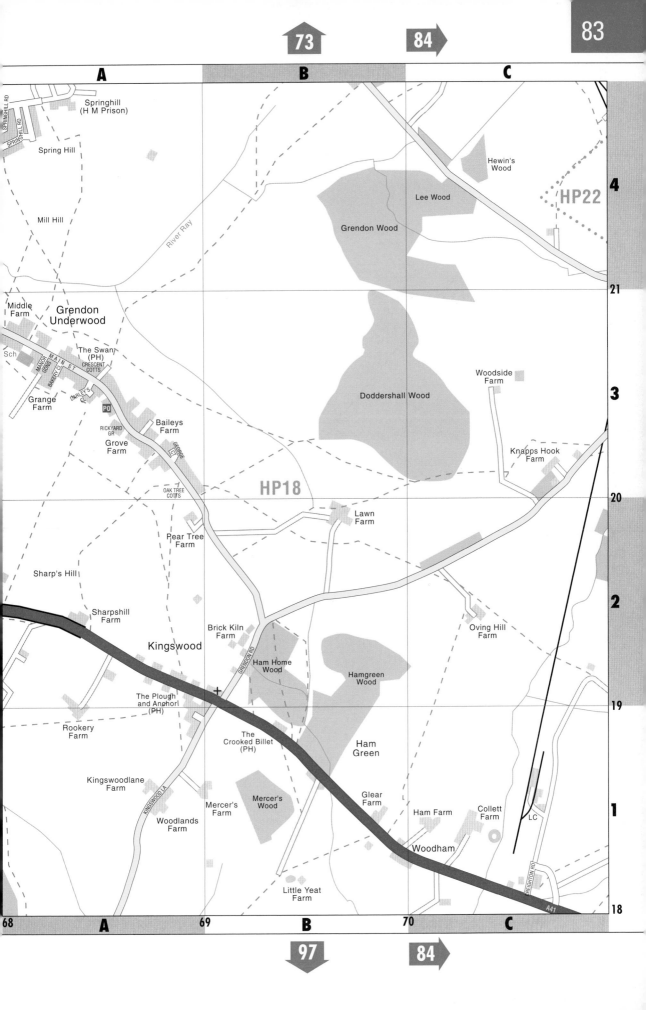

A

B

C

Springhill
(H M Prison)

SPRINGHILL RD

Spring Hill

Mill Hill

River Ray

Hewin's
Wood

Lee Wood

HP22

4

Grendon Wood

21

Middle
Farm

Grendon
Underwood

Sch

MANOR
GDNS

MAIN ST

BAKERY CL

CHARLEY'S CL

The Swan
(PH)

CRESCENT
COTTS

PO

Grange
Farm

RICKYARD
GR

Grove
Farm

GEORGE CL

Baileys
Farm

Doddershall Wood

Woodside
Farm

3

Knapps Hook
Farm

OAK TREE
COTTS

HP18

Lawn
Farm

20

Pear Tree
Farm

Sharp's Hill

Sharpshill
Farm

Oving Hill
Farm

2

Kingswood

Brick Kiln
Farm

GRENDON RD

Ham Home
Wood

Hamgreen
Wood

+

The Plough
and Anchor
(PH)

19

Rookery
Farm

The Crooked Billet
(PH)

Ham
Green

Kingswoodlane
Farm

KINGSWOOD LA

Mercer's
Farm

Mercer's
Wood

Glear
Farm

Ham Farm

Collett
Farm

LC

1

Woodlands
Farm

Woodham

CREIGHTON RD

Little Yeat
Farm

A41

18

A
B
C

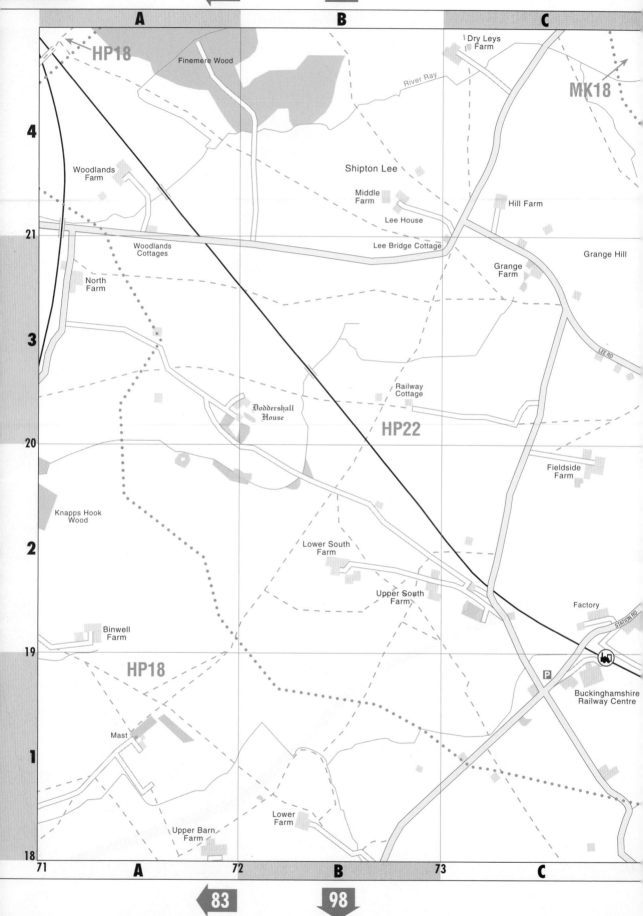

A   **B**   **C**

HP18

Finemere Wood

River Ray

Dry Leys Farm

MK18

4

Shipton Lee

Woodlands Farm

Middle Farm

Hill Farm

Lee House

21

Woodlands Cottages

Lee Bridge Cottage

Grange Hill

Grange Farm

North Farm

3

Railway Cottage

Doddershall House

HP22

20

Fieldside Farm

Knapps Hook Wood

2

Lower South Farm

Upper South Farm

Factory

Binwell Farm

STATION RD

19

HP18

P

Buckinghamshire Railway Centre

Mast

1

Lower Farm

Upper Barn Farm

18
71   **A**   72   **B**   73   **C**

LEE RD

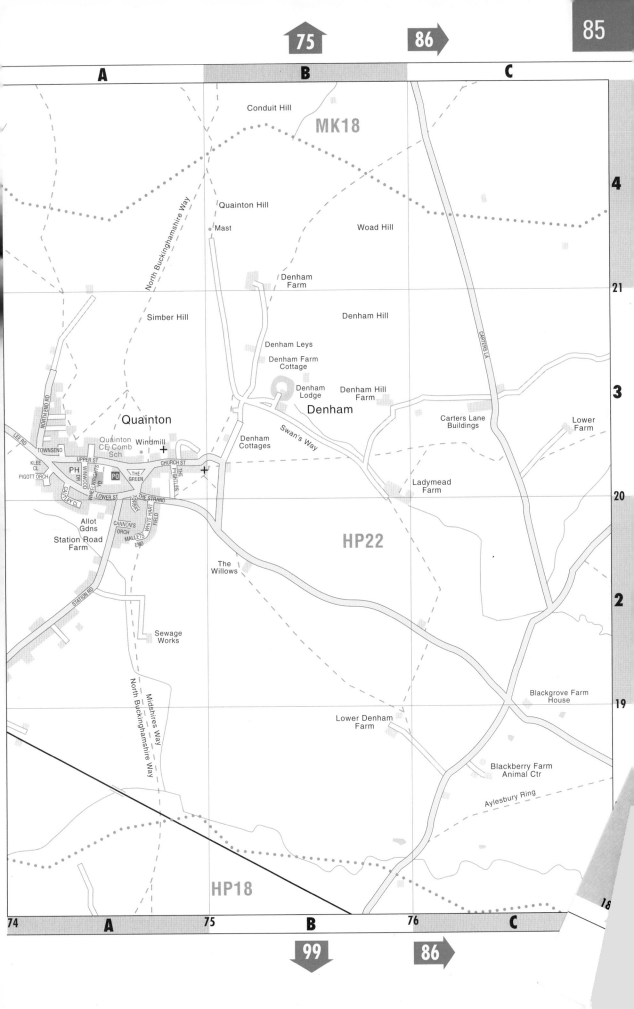

A   **B**   **C**

Conduit Hill

MK18

4

Quainton Hill

Mast   Woad Hill

North Buckinghamshire Way

Denham Farm

21

Simber Hill   Denham Hill

Denham Leys

Denham Farm Cottage

Denham Lodge   Denham Hill Farm

Denham   3

Quainton   Carters Lane Buildings

Lower Farm

CARTERS LA

Windmill   Denham Cottages   Swan's Way

Quainton CE Comb Sch

NORTH END RD

LEE RD   TOWNSEND   UPPER ST

KLEE CL   PH   PO   THE GREEN   CHURCH ST   THE PIGHTLES

PIGOTT ORCH   COLUMNW   WHEELWRIGHTS YD

Ladymead Farm

CAUZEY CL   LOWER ST   THE STRAND

20

Allot Gdns   CANNON'S ORCH   MALLETS END

Station Road Farm   WHITE HART FIELD

HP22

STATION RD   The Willows

2

Sewage Works

Midshires Way

North Buckinghamshire Way

Blackgrove Farm House

19

Lower Denham Farm

Blackberry Farm Animal Ctr

Aylesbury Ring

HP18

18

85
76

A **B** **C**

MK18

4

Marston Hill

Bushy Farm

PULPIT LA

MEADWAY

Home Farm

Crossroads Farm

WHITCHURCH LA

Oving

P

THE PIGHTLE

BOWLING ALLEY

Recn Gd

Church Farm

Black Boy (PH)

CHURCH LA

STONE VIEW

Whitchurch Comb Sch

NORTH MARSTON LA

ASHGROVE GDNS

ASHGROVE GDNS

THE MEADOWS

MANOR RD

DARK LA

Oving House

GREEN ACRES CL

ASHGROVE GDNS

A413

21

PITCHCOTT RD

Bunshill

OVING RD

CRABS GR

MT. PLEASANT
RICKYARD

MARKET HILL

Pitchcott Hill

WEIR LA

CASTLE LA

3

Pitchcott Hill Farm

Pitchcott

Holbornhill Farm

Scotshill Farm

Dunn Mill

Manor Farm

20

HP22

2

19

Aylesbury Ring

Folly Farm

1

Upper Blackgrove Farm

Middle Blackgrove Farm

Whitesfield Farm

Cow Ground Buildings

Whitesfield Farm Cottages

7 **A** **78** **B** **79** **C**

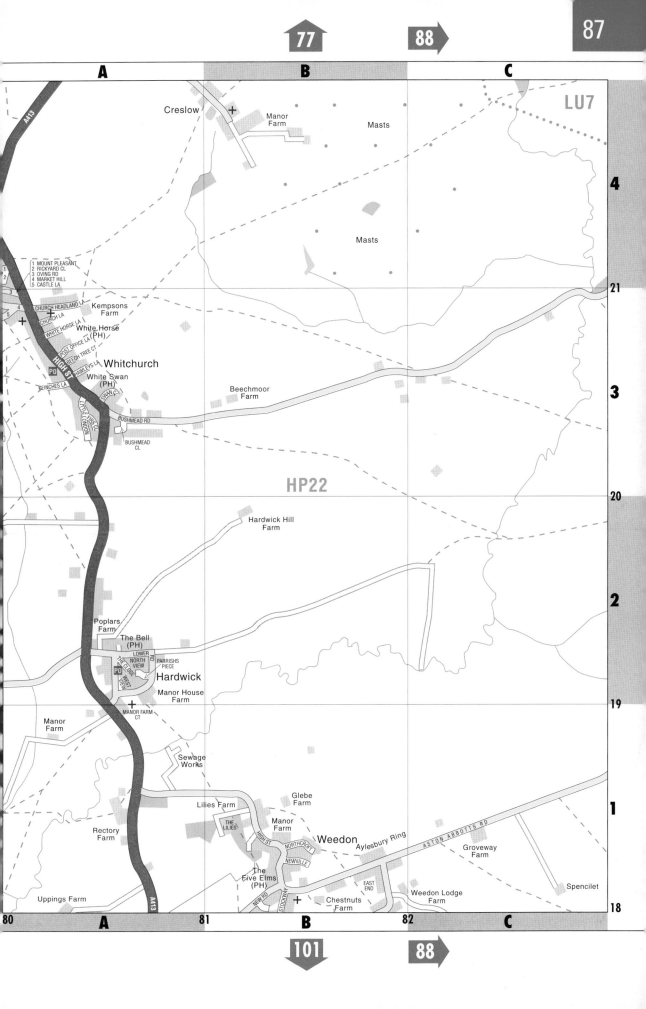

A   B   C

4

Sewage Works

LU7

Red Barn

21

Willow Brook Farm

Red Barn Farm

Vicarage Farm

THE HAY BARN BSNS PK

Longmoor Farm

CURLINGTON RD

Works

3

Freemasons Wood

Church Farm

Aston Abbotts

Home Farm

The Abbey

ROSS RD

Bull & Butcher (PH)

Norduck Farm

20

MOAT LA

THE GREEN

NASHS FARM

BRICSTOCK

New Zealand

WINGRAVE RD

Wingrave Crossroads

Winslow Rd

Windmill Hill Farm

THE LINES

HP22

2

LINES HILL

Windmill Hill

Fox Covert

Barns Farm

A418

19

Lower Burston Farm

Burston Hill Farm

1

Burston Hill

Manor Farm

A418

BREWHOUSE LA

Hale Farm

18

Aylesbury Ring

83   A   84   B   85   C

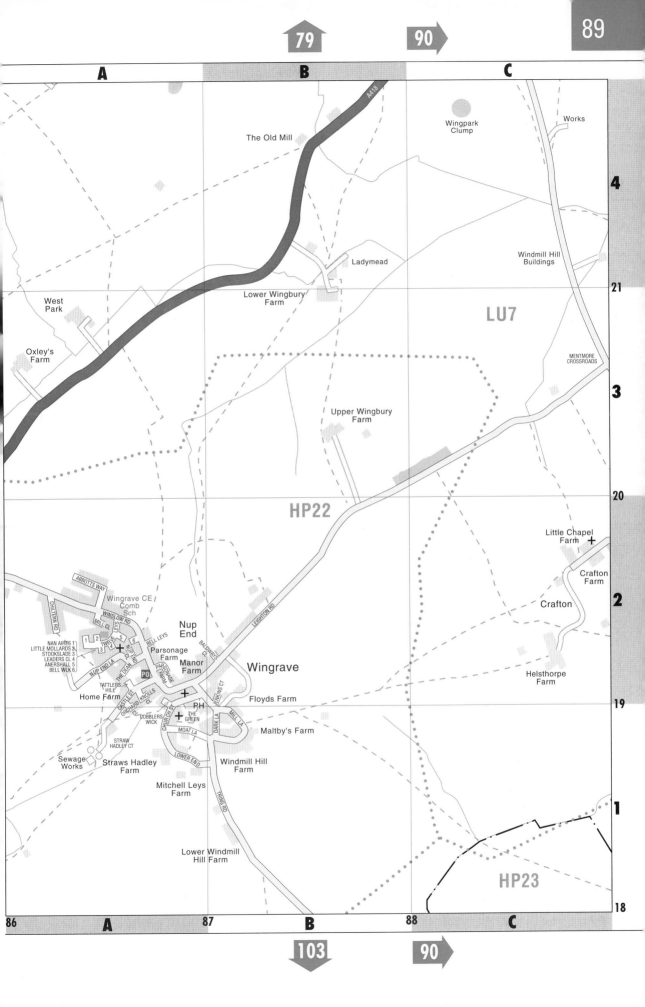

A
B
C

4

Works

Wingpark
Clump

The Old Mill

Windmill Hill
Buildings

21

Ladymead

Lower Wingbury
Farm

LU7

West
Park

MENTMORE
CROSSROADS

Oxley's
Farm

3

Upper Wingbury
Farm

20

HP22

Little Chapel
Farm

Crafton
Farm

ABBOTTS WAY

Crafton

2

Wingrave CE
Comb
Sch

CHILTERN RD

WINSLOW RD

MILL CL

Nup
End

LEIGHTON RD

NAN AIRES 1
LITTLE MOLLARDS 2
STOOKSLADE 3
LEADERS CL 4
ANERSHALL 5
BELL WLK 6.

BELL LEYS

Parsonage
Farm

Helsthorpe
Farm

NUP END LA

PO

Manor
Farm

Wingrave

TATTLERS
HILL

THE DEAN

PARSONAGE
FARM

KNOLLS
CL

JENKINS CT

Home Farm

CASTLE ST

ORCHARD
CL

Floyds Farm

19

PH

COBBLERS
WICK

CHURCH ST

THE
GREEN

DARK LA

MILL LA

Maltby's Farm

MOAT LA

STRAW
HADLEY CT

Sewage
Works

LOWER END

Windmill Hill
Farm

Straws Hadley
Farm

Mitchell Leys
Farm

THING RD

1

Lower Windmill
Hill Farm

HP23

18

86
A
87
B
88
C

89
80

A   B   C

Manor Farm

Ledburn

MANOR FARM LA

WELL LA

LETBURNE CT

LAKE'S COTTS

Ledburn Farm

The Lodge

4

Windmill Hill

Rowden Farm

21

B488

Mentmore Crossroads

3

Mentmore Stud Farm

The Belt

LU7

Mentmore

HOWELL HILL CL

20

Wing Lodge

THE GREEN

The Stag Inn (PH)

Crafton Stud Farm

Big Wood

Mentmore

Mentmore Park

ROSEBERY MEWS

Home Farm

Mansom

2

New Spinney

Crafton Lodge

Mentmore Park Farm

19

The Belt

CH

Cheddington Lodge

1

HP23

18

89   A   90   B   91   C

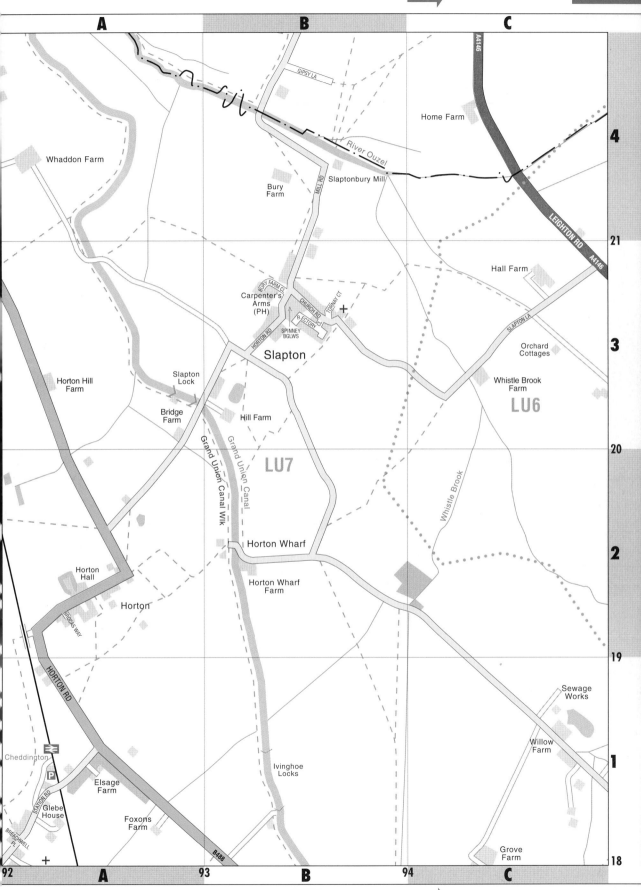

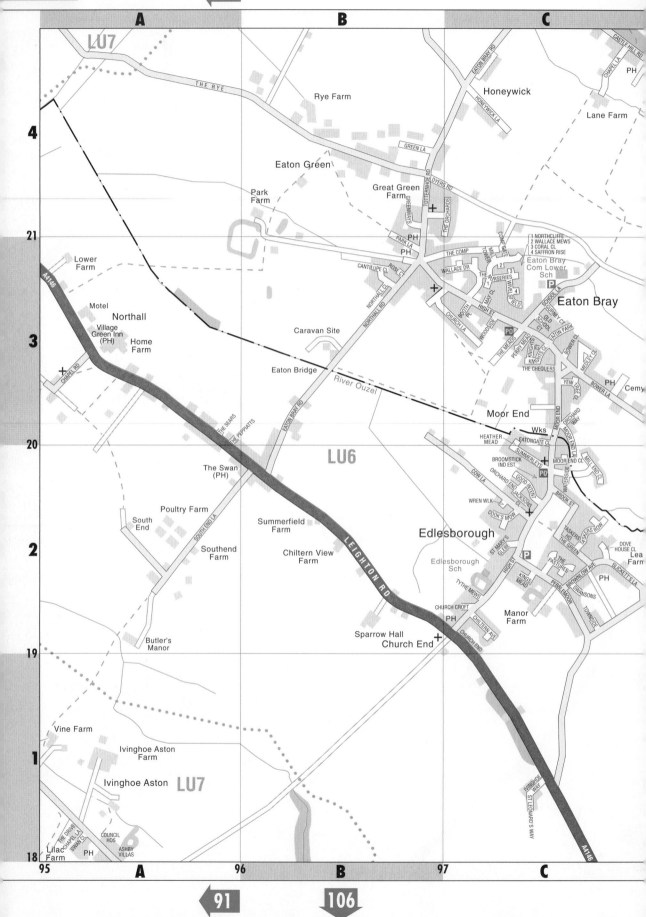

A B C

LU7

THE RYE

Rye Farm

Honeywick

CASTLE HILL RD

CHAPEL LA

PH

EATON BRAY RD

Lane Farm

GREEN LA

4

Eaton Green

HONEYWICK LA

TOTTERNHOE RD

DYERS RD

Great Green Farm

Park Farm

GREENWAYS

THE ORCHARDS

21

PARK LA

PH

PH

THE COMP

COMP SITE

1 NORTHCLIFFE
2 WALLACE MEWS
3 CORAL CL
4 SAFFRON RISE

Lower Farm

CANTILUPE CL

ROSE CT

WALLACE DR

THE NURSERIES

WIVELSFIELD

Eaton Bray
Com Lower
Sch

P

Eaton Bray

A4146

NORTHALL RD

NORTHALL RD

Motel

Northall

BOOTH RD

HIGH ST

SCHOOL LA

OLD SCHOOL CL

EATON PARK

BOWER CL

MEGLEY CT

3

Village Green Inn (PH)

Home Farm

CHAPEL RD

Caravan Site

EATON BRAY RD

CHURCH LA

PO

THE MEADS

PERY MEAD

KNIGHTS CL

WOODSIDE

KIN

BOWER LA

PH

Cemy

Eaton Bridge

River Ouzel

THE CHEQUERS

YEW TREE RD

MOOR END

ORCHARD WAY

Moor End

Wks

20

THE SEARS

THE PEPPIATTS

HEATHER MEAD

EATONGATE CL

SUMMERLEYS

BROOMSTICK IND EST

MOOR END CL

MILL END CL

PO

The Swan (PH)

LU6

ORCHARD END

GOOD INTENT

JACKSONS CL

WATERSIDE

BROOK ST

Poultry Farm

South End

SOUTH END LA

COW LA

WREN WLK

COOK'S MDW

Edlesborough

PASKERS HO

SEAS ROW

TH

THE GREEN

DOVE HOUSE CL

Lea Farm

2

Southend Farm

Summerfield Farm

Chiltern View Farm

LEIGHTON RD

St MARY'S GLEBE

Edlesborough Sch

HIGH ST

P

THE PASTURES

BROWNLOW AVE

SWANSONS

PH

SLICKETT'S LA

TOWNSIDE

KINGS MEAD

PEBBLEMOOR

TYTHE MEWS

Manor Farm

Butler's Manor

CHURCH CROFT

CHILTERN AVE

PH

19

Sparrow Hall

Church End

CHURCH END

Vine Farm

1

Ivinghoe Aston Farm

IVINGHOE WAY

St LEONARD'S WAY

Ivinghoe Aston

LU7

A4146

THE DRIVE

CHAPEL LA

SWAN CL

Council Hos

18

Lilac Farm

PH

ASHBY VILLAS

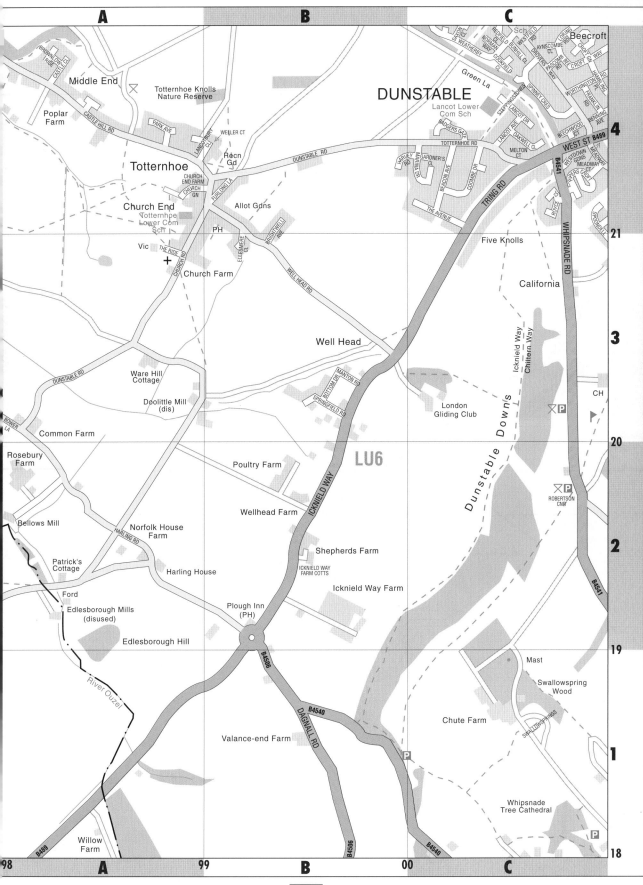

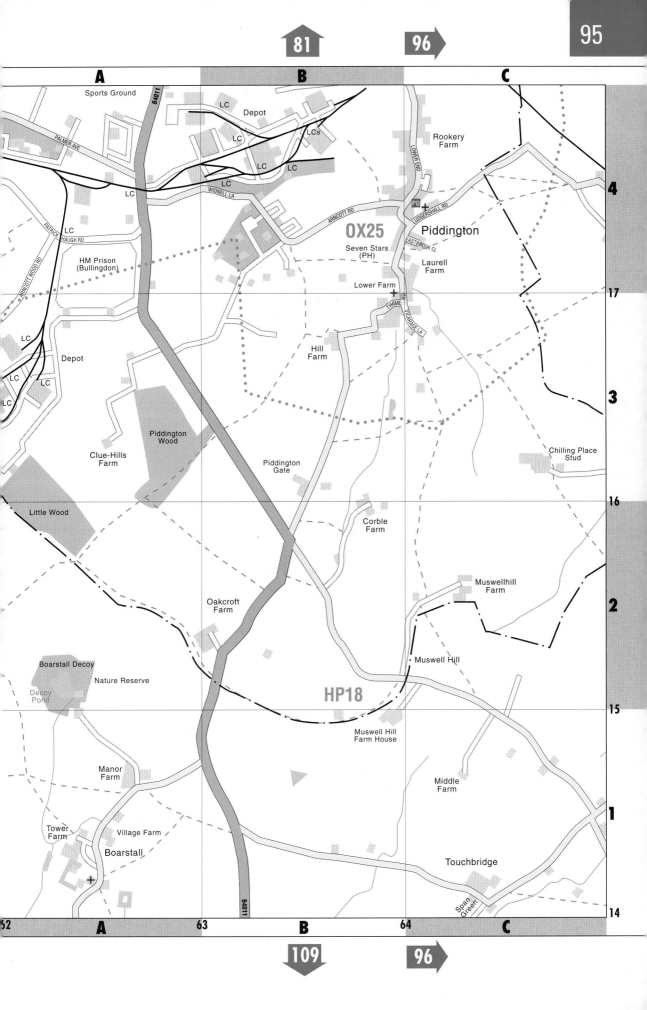

A
B
C

Nursery

Kings Farm

D'Oyley's Farm

Rookery Farm

The Green

PIDDINGTON RD

BICESTER RD

Bridge Farm

DUCK LA

Ludgershall

Bull & Butcher (PH)

SOLTERS

CL

Glebe Farm

WHITE HART

HIGH ST

BROOK CL

SALTERS LA

4

Manor Farm

Eastfield Farm

BRILL RD

CHURCH LA

Ludgershall Farm

+

WOTTON END

17

KINGSWOOD LA

The Lake

Clearfields Farm

3

Long Wood

Tittershall Wood

HP18

Poletrees Farm

Lapland Farm

The Warrells

16

Fivearch Bridge

Fivearch Wood

Rushbeds Wood Nature Reserve

Grenville's Wood

2

Lawn Farm

Tramway Farm

Rid's Hill

15

Brillbury Hall Farm

Coldharbour Farm

TRAM HILL

1

Brill Common

Dorton Park Farm

NORCOTTS KILN COTTS

Chinkwell Wood

Dorton

Brill

NORTH HILL

Windmill

WINDMILL ST

THE LAWNS

TEMPLE ST

GODFREYS CL

Brook Farm

SOUTH HILLS

PH

BRAE HILL

HIGH LAND CL

Ct

Brill CE Comb Sch

14

65
66
67

A
B
C

A **B** **C**

A41

Newhouse
Farm

South View
Farm

Littleton Middle
Farm

Hall
Farm

4

Westcott
CE Sch

The
White Swan
(PH)

Westcott

Waddesdon
Gardens

Waddesdon
Farm

A41 HIGH ST

17

PO

BURNHAM RD

HIGH ST

WHITCHURCH RD

LOWER GREEN

QUEEN ST

Waddesdon
Dairy

Works

Westcott
Farm

ASHENDON RD

RALPH CRES

Lodge Hill

Westcott
Field
Farm

Waddesdon
Manor
(National Trust)

3

Windmill
Plantation

16

HP18

Gypsy
Bottom

Windmill Hill
Farm

2

Watbridge
Farm
Cottages

15

Grassy
Dell

Decoy
Farm

1

Watbridge
Farm

Decoy
Wood

14

71 **A** 72 **B** 73 **C**

A   B   C

Lower
Farm

HP22

Lower Fleetmarston
Farm

4

17

Fleet Marston
Cottages

Fleet Marston
Farm

3 A41

Berryfield

Berryfield
House

Berryfield
Farm

16

Fleet
Marston

HP18

Quarrendon House
Farm

Putlowes
Cottages

PUTLOWES DR

2

Billingsfield
Cottages

READING RD 1
NAPPIN CL 2
ROBINSON CL 3

HAYWOOD WAY

GRIMMER CL

FLETCHER CL

DICKS WAY

Fleet Marston
Spinney

Putlowes

BICESTER RD

GAINSBOROUGH PL

BELGRAVE RD

15

Haydon
Hill

A41

River Thame

Sewage
Works

MULLINS WAY 1
CONSTABLE PL 2

REMBRANDT PL

GOYA PL

LAUTREC WAY

MONET END

BROWN CL

PICASSO PL

DICKENS WAY

RUBENS CL

DANSWOATH WAY

MEREDITH DR

BARRIE RD

AUSTEN CL

SEWELL CL

SCOTT DR

DAHL WAY

MARY RD

HP19

Sheepcote Hill
Farm

RABANS CL

EDISON RD

BESSEMER CRES

RABANS LA

TOMPION RD

BRUNEL RD

TELFORD CL

SMEATON CL

1

Ind Est

COLDHARBOUR
WAY

Eythrope

Bear Brook

Haydon Mill
Farm

14

77   A   78   B   79   C

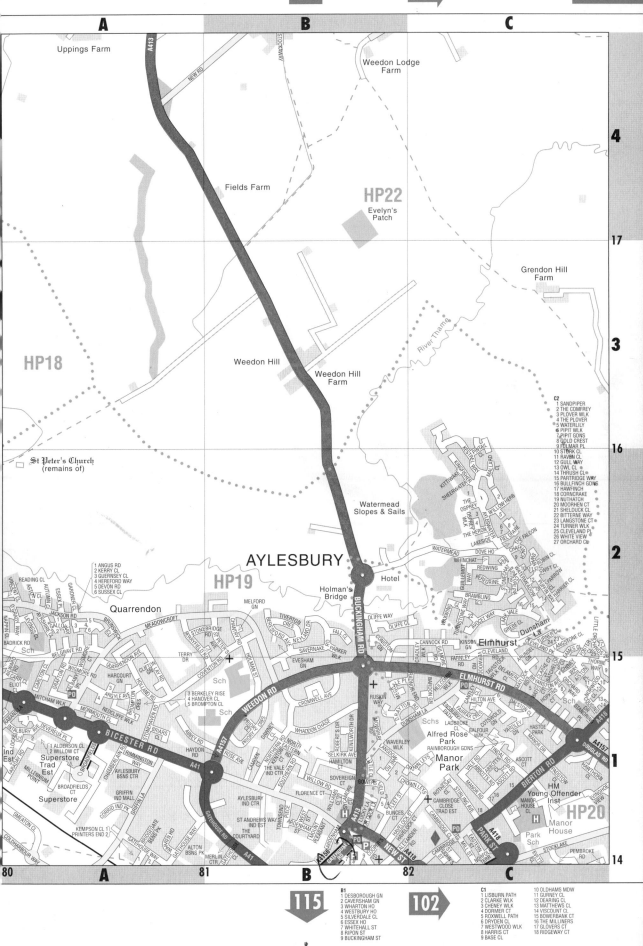

87

102

Uppings Farm

New Rd

A413

Weedon Lodge Farm

Fields Farm

HP22

Evelyn's Patch

4

17

HP18

Grendon Hill Farm

River Thame

3

St Peter's Church (remains of)

Weedon Hill

Weedon Hill Farm

C2
1 SANDPIPER
2 THE COMFREY
3 PLOVER WLK
4 THE PLOVER
5 WATERLILY
6 PIPIT WLK
7 PIPIT GDNS
8 GOLD CREST
9 FOLMAR PL
10 STORK CL
11 RAVEN CL
12 GULL WAY
13 OWL CL
14 THRUSH CL
15 PARTRIDGE WAY
16 BULLFINCH GDNS
17 HAWFINCH
18 CORNCRAKE
19 NUTHATCH
20 MOORHEN CT
21 SHELDUCK CL
22 BITTERNE WAY
23 LANGSTONE CT
24 TURNER WLK
25 CLEVELAND PL
26 WHITE VIEW
27 ORCHARD CL

16

Watermead Slopes & Sails

2

AYLESBURY

HP19

Holman's Bridge

Hotel

Watermead

Elmhurst

Dunsham La

Quarrendon

Melford Gn

BUCKINGHAM RD

15

1 ANGUS RD
2 KERRY CL
3 GUERNSEY CL
4 HEREFORD WAY
5 DEVON RD
6 SUSSEX CL

READING CL

3 BERKELEY RISE
4 HANOVER CL
5 BROMPTON CL

ELMHURST RD

Sch

WEEDON RD

CROMWELL AVE

RUSKIN WAY

Alfred Rose Park

Manor Park

BICESTER RD

A41

A4157

1 ALDERSON CL
2 WILLOW CT

Superstore Trad Est

Aylesbury BSNS CTR

BIERTON RD

A418

DOUGLAS RD

1

Broadfields Superstore

Millennium Point

Aylesbury Ind Est

St Andrews Ind Est

The Courtyard

NEW ST

A413

A418

HM Young Offender Inst

Manor House

Park Sch

HP20

Manor House

KEMPSON CL
1 PRINTERS END 2

Alton BSNS Pk

Merlin Ctr

A41

GATEHOUSE RD

PARK ST

Pembroke Rd

80   A   81   B   82   C   14

115

102

B1
1 DESBOROUGH GN
2 CAVERSHAM GN
3 WHARTON HO
4 WESTBURY HO
5 SILVERDALE CL
6 ESSEX HO
7 WHITEHALL ST
8 RIPON ST
9 BUCKINGHAM ST

C1
1 LISBURN PATH
2 CLARKE WLK
3 CHENEY CT
4 DORMER CT
5 ROXWELL PATH
6 DRYDEN CL
7 WESTWOOD WLK
8 HARRIS CT
9 BASE CL
10 OLDHAMS MDW
11 GURNEY CL
12 DEARING CL
13 MATTHEWS CL
14 VISCOUNT CL
15 BOWERBANK CT
16 THE MILLINERS
17 GLOVERS CT
18 RIDGEWAY CT

101 88

A B C

Aylesbury Ring

Home Farm
Rowsham
MANOR RD
A418
BENNETTS LA
Hale Farm
Ridgeway
Baileys Farm
Seabrook Farm

4

Rowsham Bridge

17

Crane End Farm
Aylesbury Ring

CANE END LA

3
Church Farm
Hulcott
Manor Farm

Grove Farm

New Covert

16
GROVE CT
CH

HOODS FARM CL
BROOK-A-LN LA
THE FIRS
READ DR
THE FIRS CL
HP22
GIB LA

BARNETT WAY
KINGS MDW
OLD FORGE GDNS
WILLIAM HILL
BURCOTT LA

2
THE CLOSE
GREAT LA
GRENDON WAY
OLD ORCHARDS
Badricks Farm
MOAT END
COWLEY CL
Burcott

Bierton
PH
BEECH CL
AYLESBURY RD
St JAMES WAY
PARSONS CL
BURCOTT CL
BROUGHTON CL
MARSHALLS LEA

Church Farm
BISHOPS MDW
CHURCH FARM

Bierton CE Comb Sch

15
THORNE WAY
HILL DR
A418
1 OLDHAMS MDW
2 HONDUR CL
3 BIERTON RD
4 LAWRENCE CL
5 SHEPHERD CL

COPPICE CL
ASPEN CL
POPLAR CL
POPLAR
FIELD CLO
GREEN VIEW
FIELD WAY
BROUGHTON CROSSING
PH

PHIPPS
ARCHER
WESLEY CL
LARCH
CEDAR CL
COPSE
THE HILL
THE PASTURES
MEADOW WAY

1
A4157
DOUGLAS RD
AYLESBURY
GRASSLANDS
HP20

IVINGHOE VIEW
ASHLEY CL
ROW CL
HADDINGTON WAY
STOCKLAKE
STOCKLAKE
STOCKLAKE

OAKFIELD RD
NORTHFIELD RD

Grand Union Canal Aylesbury Arm
BROUGHTON LA
P
Grand Union Canal Wlk
Towing Path

HAMBROUGH
PARK STREET IND EST
WINGATE WAY
A4157
Bear Brook
Brook Farm
IVY LA

14
83 A 84 B 85 C

A **B** **C**

Thistlebrook
Farm

Boarscroft
Farm

4

ALNWICK RD

Whitwell Farm

17

Thistle Brook

Marstongate
Station

3

HP22

Aylesbury Ring

HP23

Folly
Farm

POTASH
LA

Red House
Farm

16

Fox
Covert

2

15

Manor
Farm

Potash
Farm

+

Grange Farm

Rectory
Farm

Puttenham

1

Draytonmead
Farm

Works

COLLEGE RD

Monks Court

Merrymead Farm

Grand Union Canal

Grand Union Canal Wlk

Aylesbury Arm

14

86 **A** 87 **B** 88 **C**

A   **B**   **C**

Broadmead
Farm

Alnwick
Farm

4

Betlow
Farm

Mast

17

Cheddington

BLENHEIM
CL

STATION RD

MENTMORE RD

CHURCH
HILL

LU7

LONG MARSTON LA

WEST END RD

Manor
House

West End
Farm

BARKHAM CL

MANOR RD

NEW ST

THE BALK

BERRYFIELD

SUNNY BANK

HILL SIDE

GOOSE ACRE

Westend
Hill

Southend
Hill

3

Camp
(dis)

CHEDDINGTON LA

Long Leys
Farm

POTASH LA

16

Old
Toms
Farm

BROOM LEY

CHURCH VIEW

STATION RD

CHAPEL LA

+ Central
Farm

The Boot
(PH)

PO

HP23

MARSTON RD

THE
OLD FORGE

Long Marston
CE Prim Sch

Old Church
Farm

2

+

Long
Marston

TRING RD

Great
Farm

Camp Site
(dis)

Sewage
Works

Church
Farm

CHURCH FARM LA

ASTROPE LA

Millfield

LUKES LA

Lower
End

Astrope

Gubblecote

15

LONG MARSTON RD

Astrope
Farm

College
Farm

Gubblecote
Farm

Grand Union Canal

VICARAGE RD

PH

+

Dover
Castle

Moat
Farm

Gurney's
Farm

Aylesbury Ring

Locks

1

Aylesbury Arm

WINGRAVE RD

Dixon's Gap
Bridge

WATERY LA

CHURCH RD

Grand Union Canal

Locks

Wilstone
Bridge

GRANGE RD

Startop's
End

Anglers
Retreat
(PH)

Grand Union Canal Wlk

Half Moon
(PH)

SANDBROOK LA

ROSEBARN LA

PO

+

Wilstone

LOWER ICKNIELD WAY

Startop
Farm

B489

P

14

89   **A**   90   **B**   91   **C**

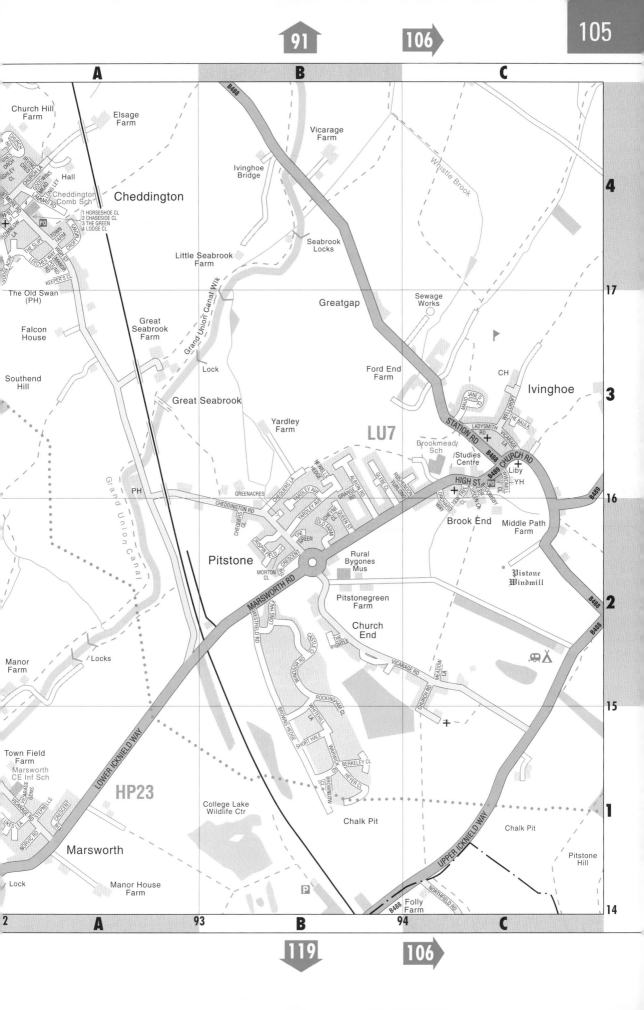

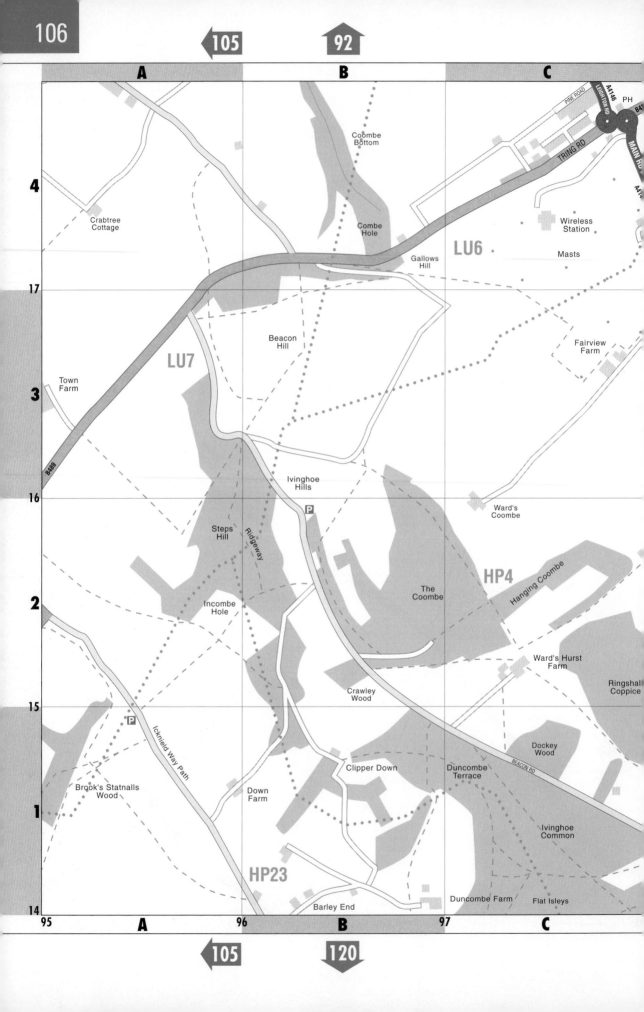

A   B   C

4

Crabtree
Cottage

Coombe
Bottom

Combe
Hole

Gallows
Hill

LU6

Wireless
Station

Masts

PINE ROAD
LEIGHTON RD
PH
A4146
TRING RD
MAIN Rd
B4
A41

17

Beacon
Hill

LU7

Fairview
Farm

3

Town
Farm

B489

Ivinghoe
Hills

P

16

Steps
Hill

Ridgeway

Ward's
Coombe

HP4

The
Coombe

Hanging Coombe

2

Incombe
Hole

Ward's Hurst
Farm

Ringshall
Coppice

Crawley
Wood

15

P

Icknield Way Path

Dockey
Wood

Duncombe
Terrace

BEACON RD

1

Brook's Statnalls
Wood

Down
Farm

Clipper Down

Ivinghoe
Common

HP23

Duncombe Farm

Flat Isleys

14

95   A   96   B   97   C

Barley End

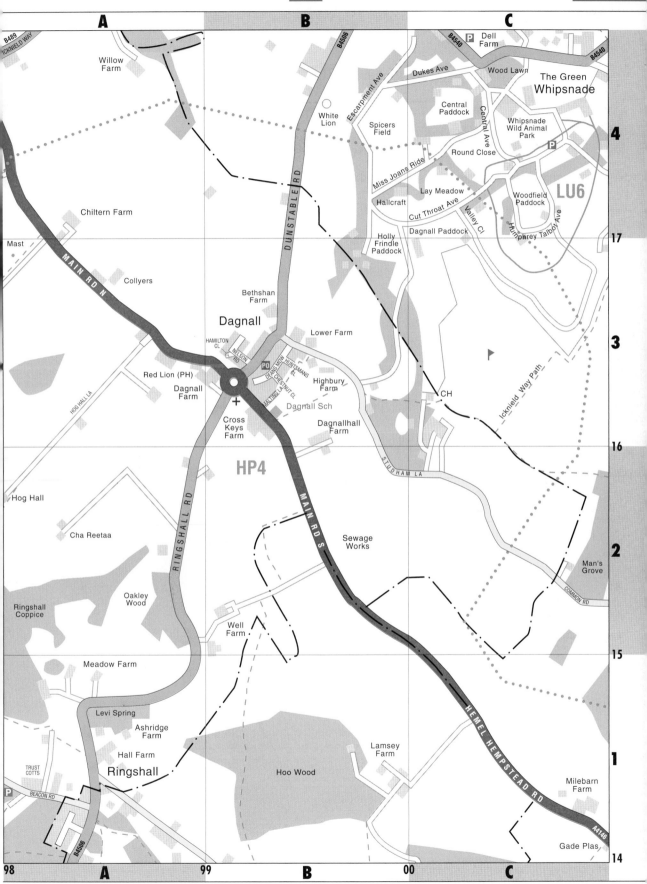

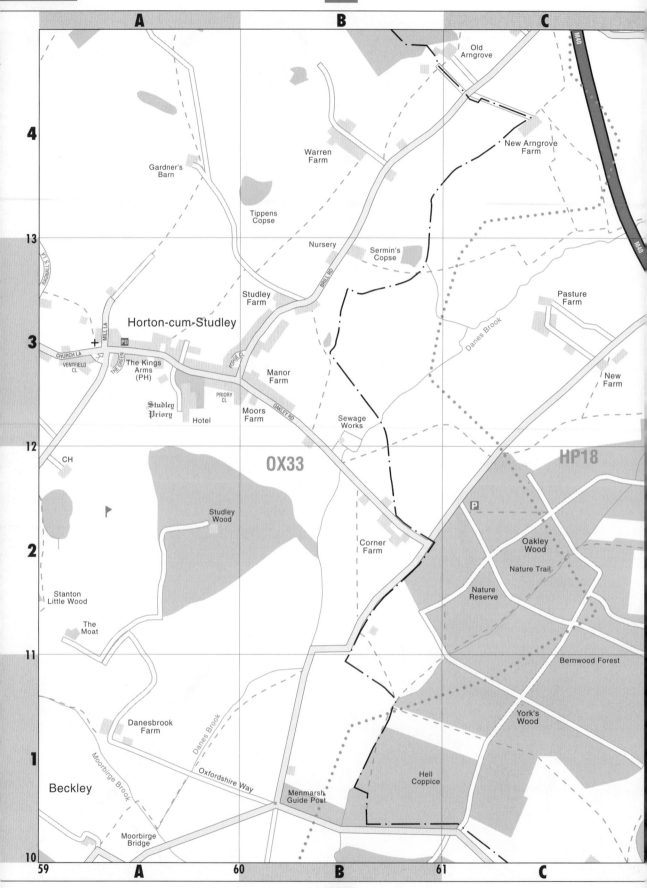

109
96

A

B

C

Spa
Farm

Dorton
House

Ashfold
Prep Sch

Spa
Wood

Dorton Park

BRAE HILL CL
PRIMROSE
TERR
TEMPLE
ST
HIGH ST
PO
HARRIS
CL
Brill
THE FIRS
CHURCH ST
SPA CL
CHURCH ST
THE
SQUARE
Brill
House
CLARKES FIELD
CL

4

Manor
Farm

THAME RD

Parkpale
Farm

Chiltonpark
Farm

13

3

Leatherslade
Farm

Ryman's
Farm

Leap
Hill

Chilton
Grove

Buttermilk
Hall

12

B4011

HP18

Grove
Spinney

2

Addingrove
Farm

Hornage
Farm

11

Meads
Farm

Ixhill

1

Hornage
Copse

B4011

10

65

A

66

B

67

C

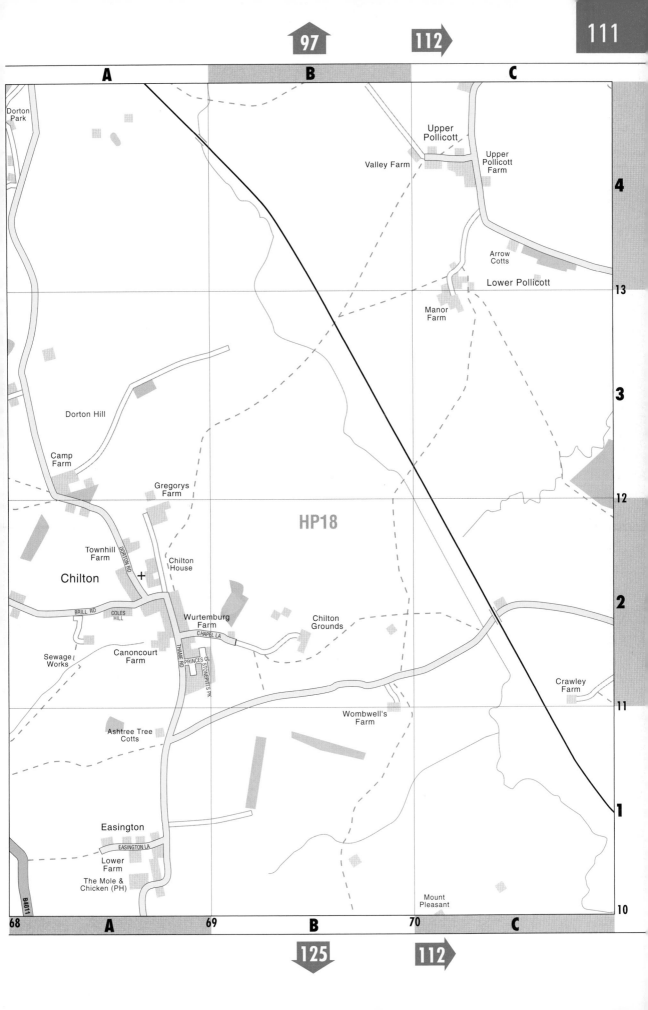

97
112
125
112

A B C

Dorton Park

Upper Pollicott

Valley Farm

Upper Pollicott Farm

4

Arrow Cotts

Lower Pollicott

13

Manor Farm

Dorton Hill

3

Camp Farm

Gregorys Farm

12

HP18

Townhill Farm

DORTON RD

Chilton House

Chilton

Chilton Grounds

2

Chilton Grounds

BRILL RD

COLES HILL

Wurtemburg Farm

CHAPEL LA

Sewage Works

Canoncourt Farm

THAME RD

PRINCES CL

STONEPITS PK

Crawley Farm

Wombwell's Farm

11

Ashtree Tree Cotts

1

Easington

EASINGTON LA

Lower Farm

The Mole & Chicken (PH)

Mount Pleasant

10

B4011

68 69 70

A B C

← 111
98

A   **B**   **C**

4

Marsh Farm

Musk Hill
Farm

Cedarwood
Bungalow

Obsy

13

Winchendon Hill
Farm

3

BARRACK HILL

Hall

Nether Winchendon
or
Lower Winchendon

Brackwell
Farm

Manor Farm

Old Mill

Chearsley Furze

CANNON'S HILL

HP18

12

Whaddonfield
Farm

The Villas

Nether
Winchendon
House

Sewage Works

Thame Valley Wlk

Lower
Farm

2

Holyman's
Farm

FROG LA

River Thame

Cuddington
Bridges

CUDDINGTON
CT

LOWER
GN

GREAT
STONE

LOW'R
MO'

BR'S LA

LOWERCHURCH ST

UPPER CHURCH ST

SPURT'S HILL

Cuddington
CE Sch

PH

THE
GREEN

AYLESBURY RD

SWAN HILL
COTTS

Cuddington Mill
Farm

BRIDGEWAY

WELFORD
WAY

BERNARD
CL

11

CHALTON RD

WINCHENDON RD

1 COUSINS PIECE
2 EVANS CL
3 CHURCH PIECE

CUDDINGTON HILL

HILLSIDE
COTTS

Furze Farm

LAMMAS
PATH

AYLESBURY RD

DADBROOK CL 1
DADFIELD CL 2

DADBROOK

Chestnut
View

LAMMAS LA

Chearsley Hill
House

OLD PLOUGH CL

Dadbrook
House

SCHOOL LA

Bell
Inn

THE BERNARD'S

THE GREEN

TURNIP CL

DARK LA

LOWER GREEN LA

Chearsley

PO

WATTS GN

STUPP'S LA

ELM BROOK
CL

Lower Green
Farm

1

Manor Farm

CHURCH LA

BOTTOM
ORCH

CRENDON RD

Grove
Farm

CHEARSLEY RD

Arch Bridge

Dad Brook

HP17

Bettymoor
Plantation

A418

AYLESBURY RD

10

71   **A**   72   **B**   73   **C**

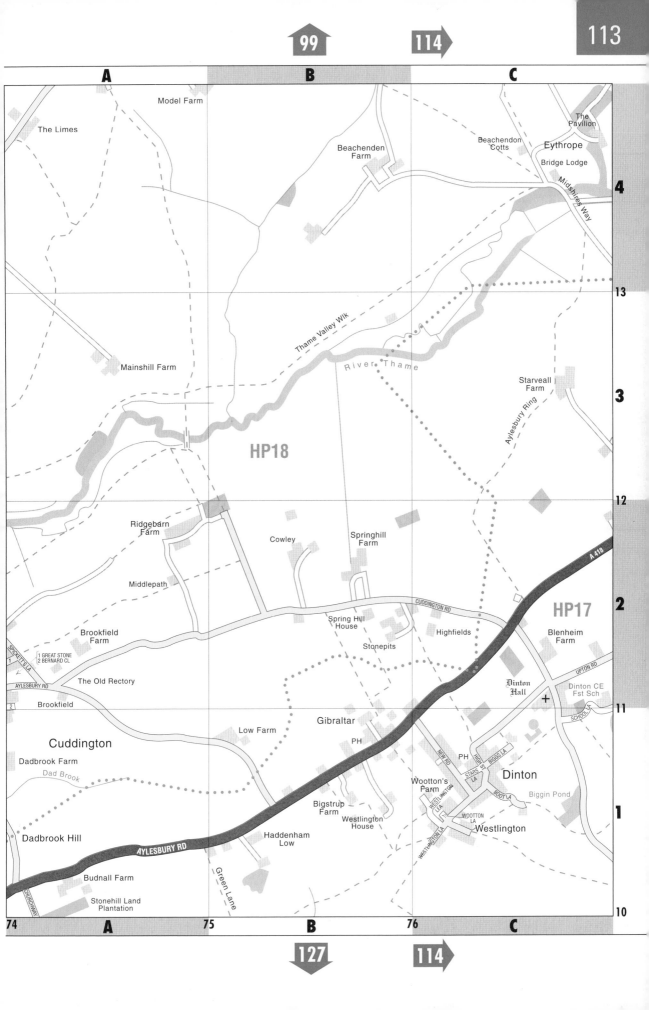

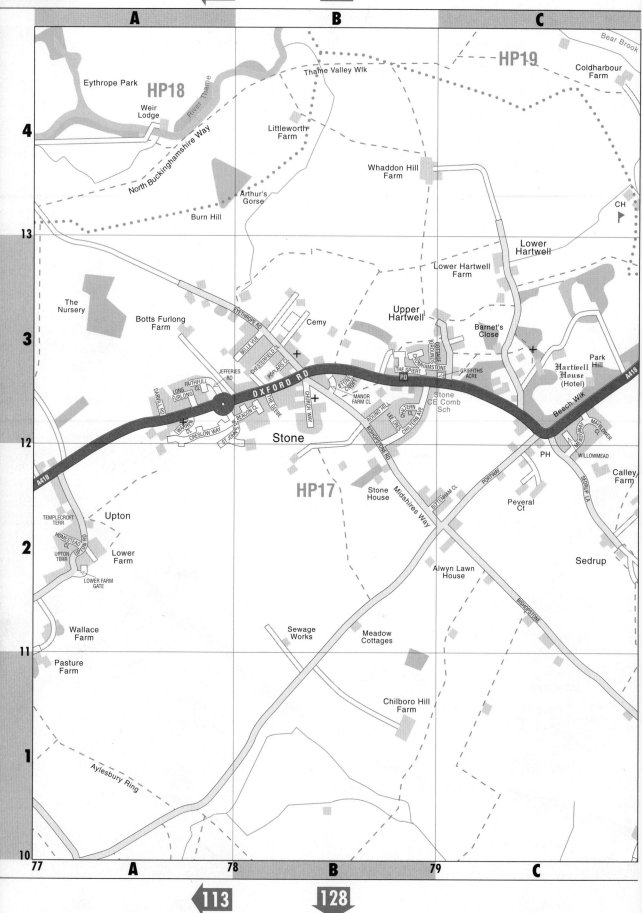

A B C

HP19

Bear Brook

Coldharbour Farm

Eythrope Park

HP18

Weir Lodge

River Thame

Thame Valley Wlk

North Buckinghamshire Way

Littleworth Farm

Whaddon Hill Farm

CH

4

Arthur's Gorse

Burn Hill

Lower Hartwell

13

Lower Hartwell Farm

The Nursery

Botts Furlong Farm

EYTHROPE RD

Cemy

Upper Hartwell

Barnet's Close

Park Hill

Hartwell House (Hotel)

A418

3

BELLE VUE

CHESTERFIELD CL

POPLARS CL

COTTAGE GROUNDS

CROMHAMSTONE

GRIFFITHS ACRE

Beech WIK

JEFFERIES RD

THE SPIERT

PO

FAITHFULL CL

LONG FURLONG

DARVILL RD

BEACON CL

OXFORD RD

THE GLEBE

CHURCH WAY

S. STONE CROFT

MANOR FARM CL

Stone CE Comb Sch

CHILTERN AVE

CHILTERN CL

LEE CRES

ROUND HILL

MAYFLOWER CT

MEADOW WAY

SEDRUP LA

WARR'S CL

CRESLOW WAY

ST JOHN'S ST

Stone

BISHOPSTONE RD

PH

WILLOWMEAD

12

Calley Farm

A418

Peveral Ct

TEMPLECROFT TERR

Upton

HP17

Stone House

Midshires Way

PORTWAY

Sedrup

HOMESTEAD CL

UPTON RD

Lower Farm

BITTENHAM CL

2

UPTON TERR

LOWER FARM GATE

Alwyn Lawn House

BISHOPSTONE

Wallace Farm

Sewage Works

Meadow Cottages

11

Pasture Farm

Chilboro Hill Farm

1

Aylesbury Ring

10

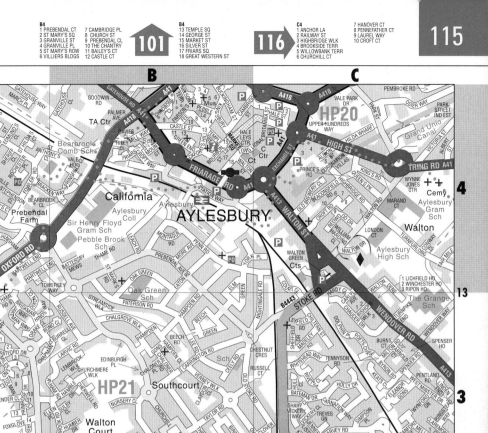

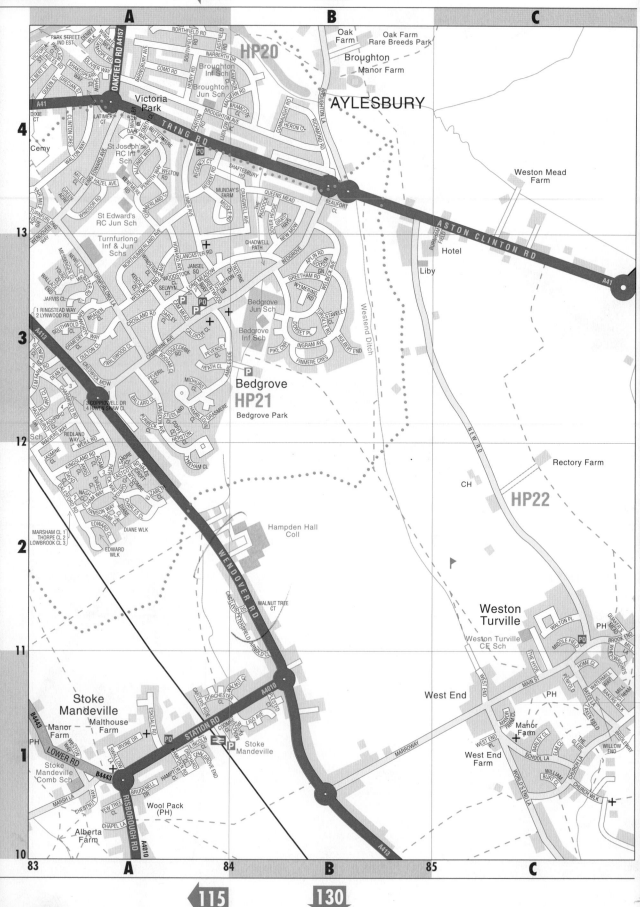

Grand Union Canal Wlk
Grand Union Canal
(Aylesbury Arm)
HP23
College
Farm
Dropshort
Farm
Cherry
Farm
A41
COLLEGE RD
Works
Lower
Farm
ASTON CLINTON
RD
Sunny Brook
Farm
MODEL
ROW
Vatche's
Farm
Buckland
NORMILL
TERR
Aston Clinton
HP22
Moat
Farm
Church
Farm
PEGGS LA
AYLESBURY RD
THE GREENWOOD 1
BROOK CL 2
SUNNYBROOK
CL
Manor
Farm
Brook
Farm
BROOK ST
LONG PLOUGH
CHAPEL
DR
GREEN END
THE ORCHARD
NEW RD
Nield's
Farm
2
CHURCH CL
ARCHIVE
CL
PLEASANCE
WAY
THE BEECHWOOD
GARLAND
WAY
BEECHWOOD WK
Rothschild
Arms
(PH)
PARSLEY CL
PO
PITMANS DR
GINGERS CL
TWITCHELL LA
TALBOT RD
Sch
WARWICK
CL
YORKE
CL
ROTHSCHILD
AVE
OVERSTREET
LONGCROFT
MILTON CL
CHESTNUT CL
ROSEBERY RD
BEECHWOOD
HO
WESTON
CT
WESTON RD
CHURCH
CL
Park
Farm
CHURCH LA
PH
TURVEY
CL
MOUNT CL
ORCHARD
DR
LOWER ICKNIELD WAY
BEACONSFIELD RD
DEAN WAY
Rookery
Farm House
LONDON RD
PH
TOMKINS CL
DENNIS CL
BROOKFIELD
FARM
Aston Clinton
Park
Old Rectory
Farm
Splash
Covert
Green
Park
Wellonhead
Bridge
STABLEBRIDGE RD
P
Bye
Green
Airfield
BYE GN
BROOK END
ANSTEY
BROOK
Brook End
LOWER
GN
B4009
CHILTERN WAY
Brook Farm
Sewage
Works
Grand Union Canal Wlk
MILL LA
BROOKSIDE
Mill
Farm
Rosemead
Covert
UPPER ICKNIELD WAY
CH
Church
Farm
Halton
Camp
Grand Union Canal
Wendover Arm
Marl
Copse
Wendover
Woods
Lower
Farm
THE
LEYS
BROOKSIDE
OLD
SCHOOL
CL
MCEWEN RIDE
RUSHMERE
Aston
Hill
CHESTNUT END
CHURCH
VIEW
ST MICHAEL'S
CL
Halton
Halton
House
B4009
MANSION HILL

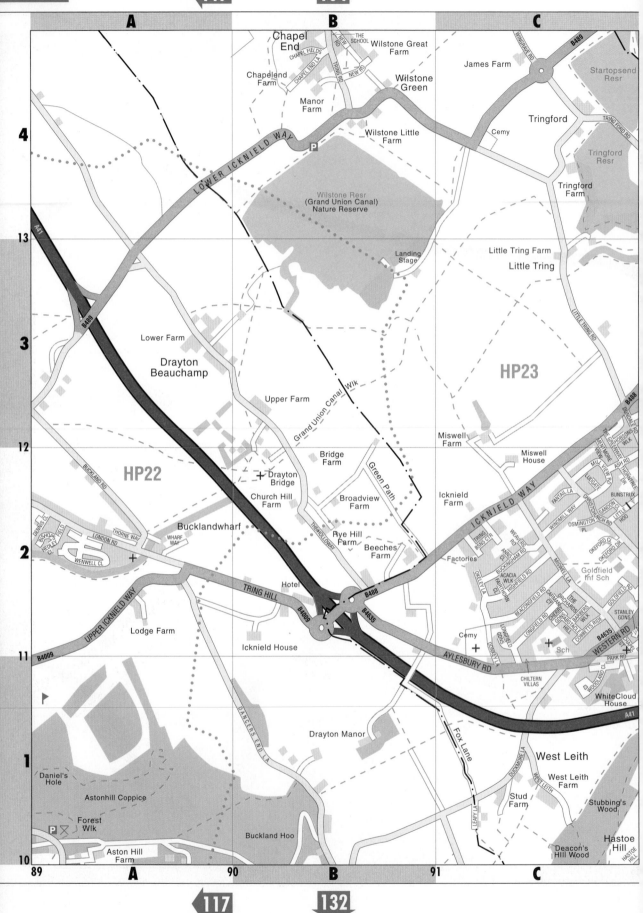

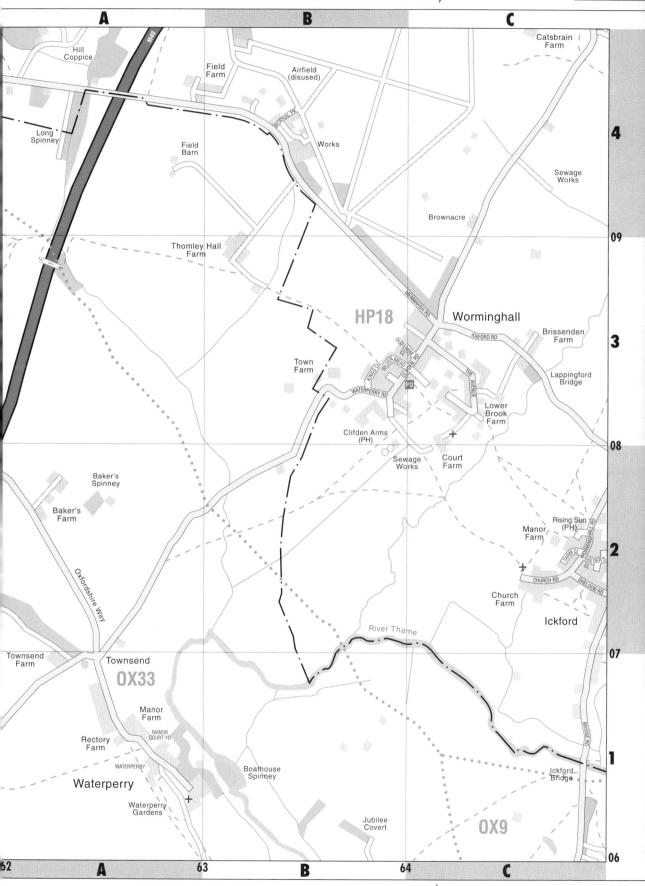

A

B

C

Woodway Farm

4

Westfield Farm

Lower
Peppershill Farm

09

Peppershill

Crendon
House

Hill
Farm

Peppershill Farm

3

HP18

08

Peacehaven
Farm

Lower
Farm

Upper
Farm

2

Ickford

GOLDER'S CL

SCHOOL CL

FIELD CL

TURNFIELDS

PO

SHELDON RD

Ickford
Comb Sch

BULL'S LA

Little
Ickford

Marsh
Farm

Sewage
Works

Lower
Farm
CL

THE BURNHAMS

MARSH RD

LONG CRENDON RD

HOME CL

MORTON KING
CL

Shabbington

Thame Valley Wlk

Rookery
Farm

THE VINE

Village
Farm

LIMES WAY

SCHOOL LA

07

ICKFORD RD

PO

KIMBELLS CL

River Thame

DUKES CL

Franklins
Farm

Old
Fisherman
(PH)

1

OX9

River Thame

OX9

Manor Farm

North
Weston

06

65

A

66

B

67

C

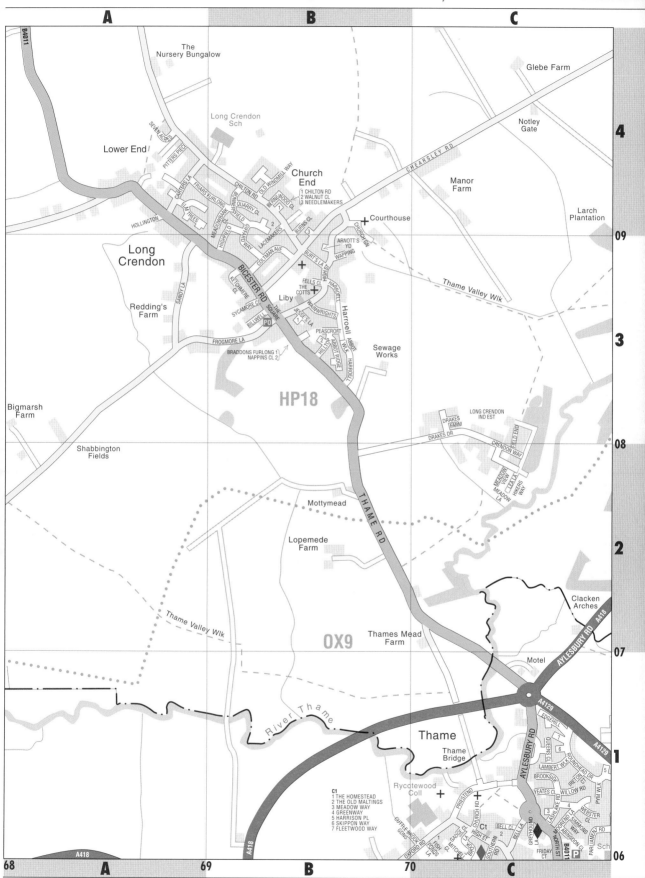

A B C

The Nursery Bungalow

Glebe Farm

Notley Gate

Long Crendon Sch

4

Lower End

Chearsley Rd

Manor Farm

Larch Plantation

Church End

1 CHILTON RD
2 WALNUT CL
3 NEEDLEMAKERS

SEVEN ACRES
PITTERS PIECE
CARTERS LA
TRIARS FURLONG
CHILTON RD
OLD WINDMILL WAY
BENNEWOOD CL
WALNUT CL

Courthouse

09

QUARRY CL
MEADOWBANK
HIGHFIELD
GIFFORD WAY
COLTMAN AVE
BURNS CL
HIGH ST
CHURCH ON

ARNOTT'S YD
WAPPING

Long Crendon

ELM TREES
HOLLINGTON

SUMMERSFIELD
LACEMAKERS

BURT'S LA

Thame Valley Wlk

Redding's Farm

SANDY LA

BICESTER RD
KETCHMERE CL
SYCAMORE CL
BILLWELL
THE SQUARE
PO

Liby

FELLS CL
THE COTTS

WAINWRIGHTS
JESSE'S LA
HILTS
ABBOT RIDGE

HARROELL
ABBOT WLK
HARROELL

3

FROGMORE LA

PEASCROFT

Sewage Works

BRADDONS FURLONG 1
NAPPINS CL 2

HP18

Bigmarsh Farm

DRAKES FARM

LONG CRENDON IND EST

FIELD END

Shabbington Fields

DRAKES DR

CRENDON WAY

08

MEADOW VIEW
MEADOW LA
VILLA CL
HICKERS WAY

Mottymead

2

Lopemede Farm

Clacken Arches

A418

AYLESBURY RD

Thame Valley Wlk

OX9

Thames Mead Farm

Motel

07

A4129

River Thame

Thame

AYLESBURY RD

EDGEHILL
QUEENS CL
ROUNDHEAD DR
LAMBERT WY
BROOKSIDE
YEATES CL
IRETON CL
WILLOW RD
PYM WLK
WEBSTER CL

1

Thame Bridge

Rycotewood Coll

C1
1 THE HOMESTEAD
2 THE OLD MALTINGS
3 MEADOW WAY
4 GREENWAY
5 HARRISON PL
6 SKIPPON WAY
7 FLEETWOOD WAY

GUTTLE BROOK GDNS
OXFORD RD
PRIESTEND
CHURCH RD
BELL LA

LASHLAKE RD
GAOGE RD
HIGH ST
BELL CL
MITCHE
BSO

GREYHOUND LA
FRIDAY CT

DOBBINS LA
SIMMONS WAY
ABINGDON CL
PARLIAMENT RD
NORTH ST
B4011
P
Sch

A418

SOUTHERN RD

06

68 A 69 B 70 C

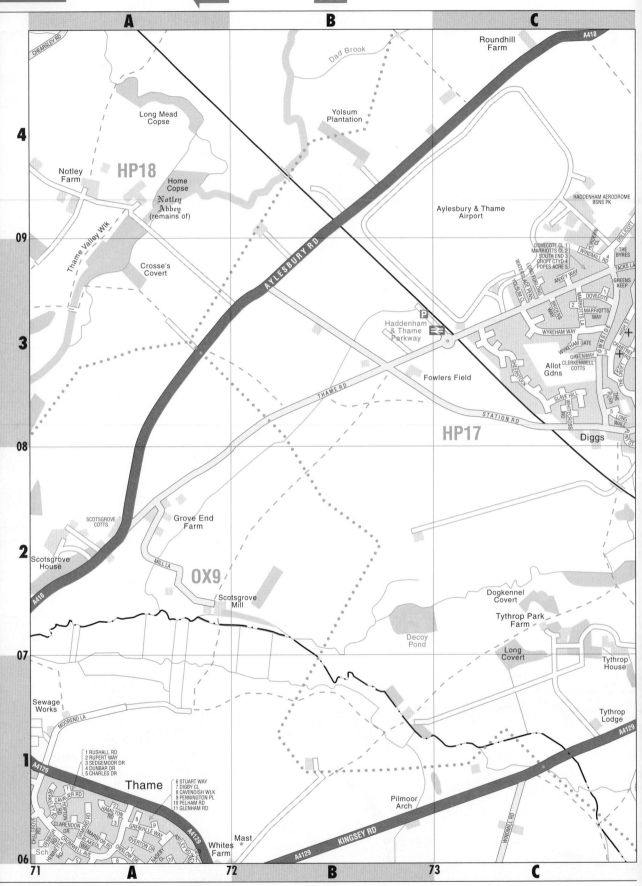

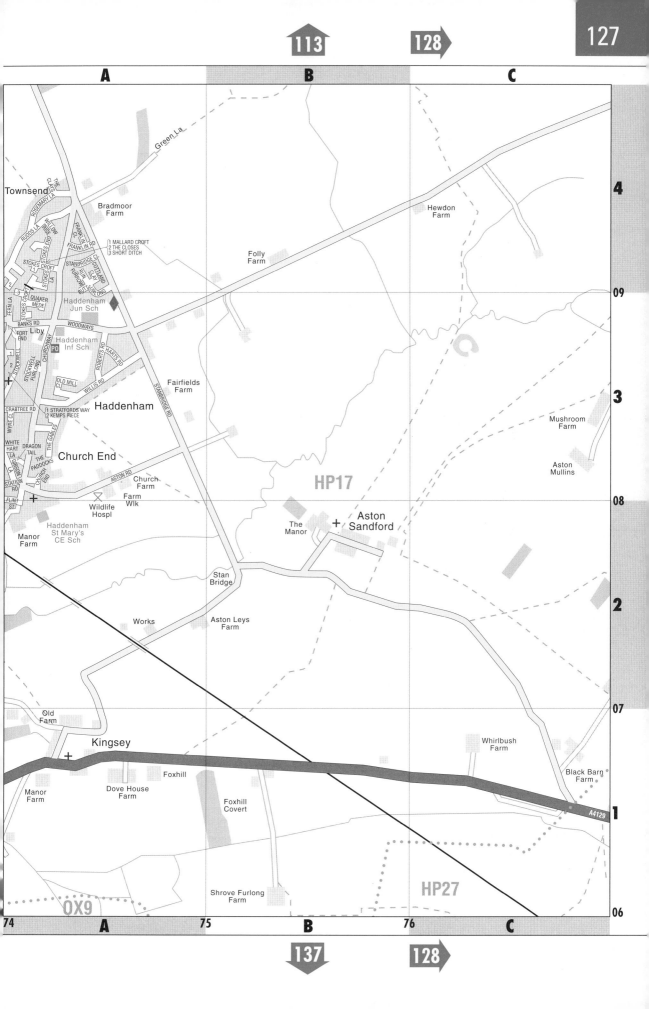

A
B
C

Green La

Townsend

Bradmoor Farm

Hewdon Farm

4

THE CLAYS LA
ROSEMARY LA
WILLOW
RISE
RUDDS LA
STOKES END
FRANKLIN CL
FRANKLIN RD
STANBRIDGE CL
SCOTLAND
CLAY
RUN
FURROW
STOKES CROFT
STOKES LA

1 MALLARD CROFT
2 THE CLOSES
3 SHORT DITCH

Folly Farm

FERN LA
QUAKER MEDE
Haddenham Jun Sch

09

BANKS RD
FORT END
Liby
WOODWAYS

CHURCHWAY
STOCKWELL FURLONG
PO
Haddenham Inf Sch

ROBERTS RD
HARTS RD

OLD MILL CL
WILLIS RD
STANBRIDGE RD

Fairfields Farm

3

CRABTREE RD
WYRE CL
WHITE HART LA
DRAGON TAIL
GIBSON LA
THE GABLES
THE PADDOCKS
CHURCH END
STATION RD
FLINT ST

Haddenham

1 STRATFORDS WAY
2 KEMPS PIECE

Mushroom Farm

Aston Mullins

Church End

ASTON RD
Church Farm
Farm Wlk

Wildlife Hospl

HP17

08

Manor Farm

Haddenham St Mary's CE Sch

The Manor

Aston Sandford

Stan Bridge

2

Works

Aston Leys Farm

07

Old Farm

Kingsey

Whirlbush Farm

Manor Farm

Dove House Farm

Foxhill

Black Barn Farm

A4129

1

Foxhill Covert

Shrove Furlong Farm

HP27

06

OX9

74
A
75
B
76
C

127
114

A　　　　　　　　　B　　　　　　　　　C

BRIDGE FARM
BLDGS

Moat
Farm

Moreton
Village

Dinton
Hermit
(PH)

WATER LA

Ford

Moreton
Farm

4

Manor
Farm

BURGESS LA

Ford
Farm

CHAPEL RD

LINDEN WAY

FRAUCUP CL

09

Aylesbury Ring

North Buckinghamshire Way

Midshires Way

HP17

3

Lower Waldridge
Farm

Fox
Covert

Pollard
Farm

08

Poplar
Farm

Waldridge
Manor

2

Waldridge
Village

Black
Barn

07

Pasture
Farm

Stockwell Lane
Farm

Hill
Ground
Farm

HP27

Owlswick
Farm

1

A 4129

Green Lane
Farm

GREEN LA

Midshires Way

STOCKWELL LA

Little Acre
Farm

Owlswick

Ray
Farm

A 4129

Manor
Farm

06

77　　　　　　A　　　　78　　　　　　B　　　　79　　　　　　C

127
138

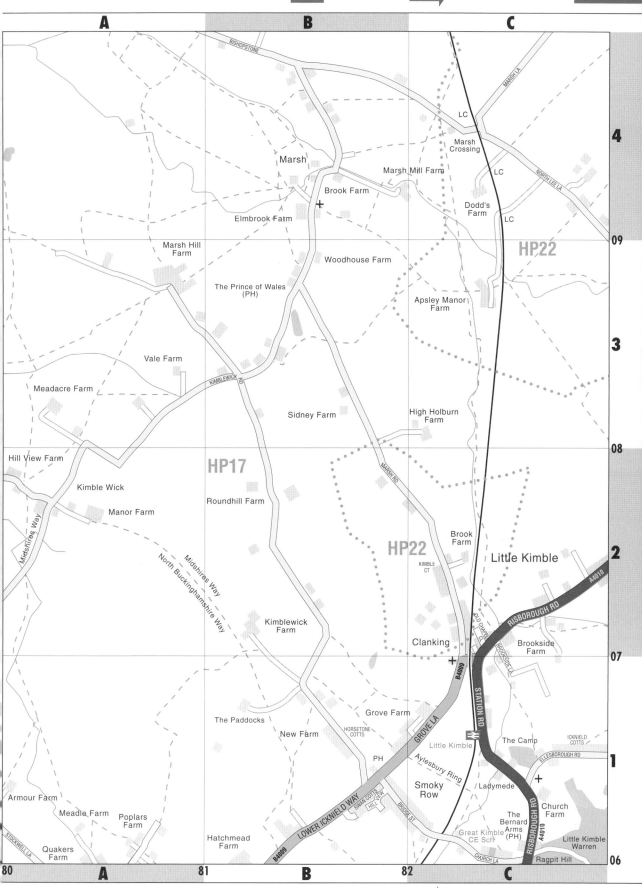

129
116

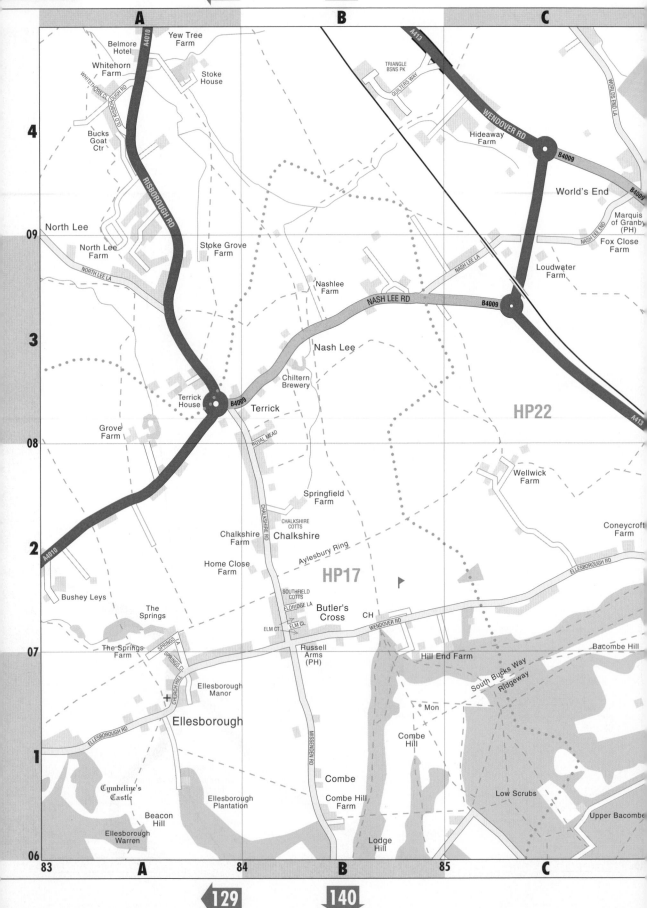

129
140

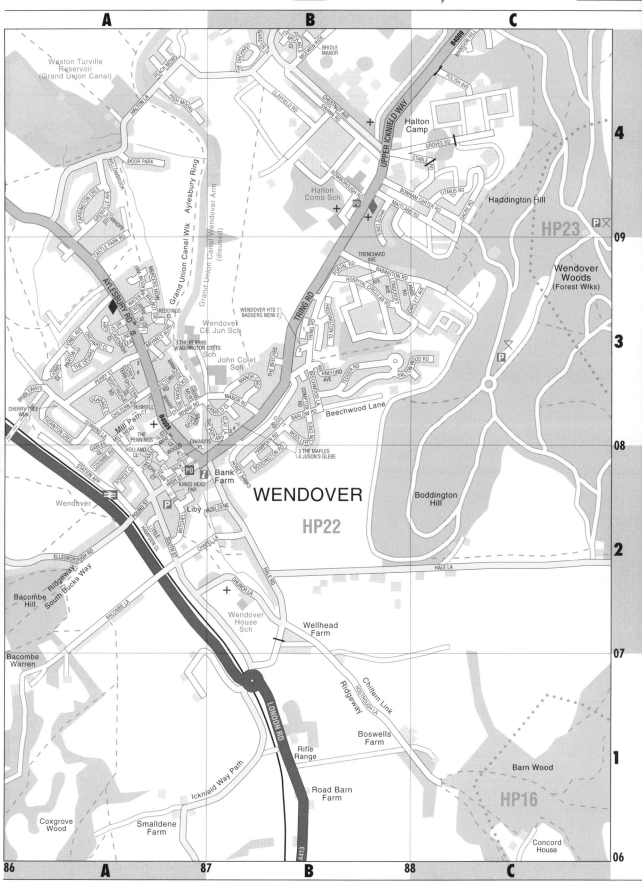

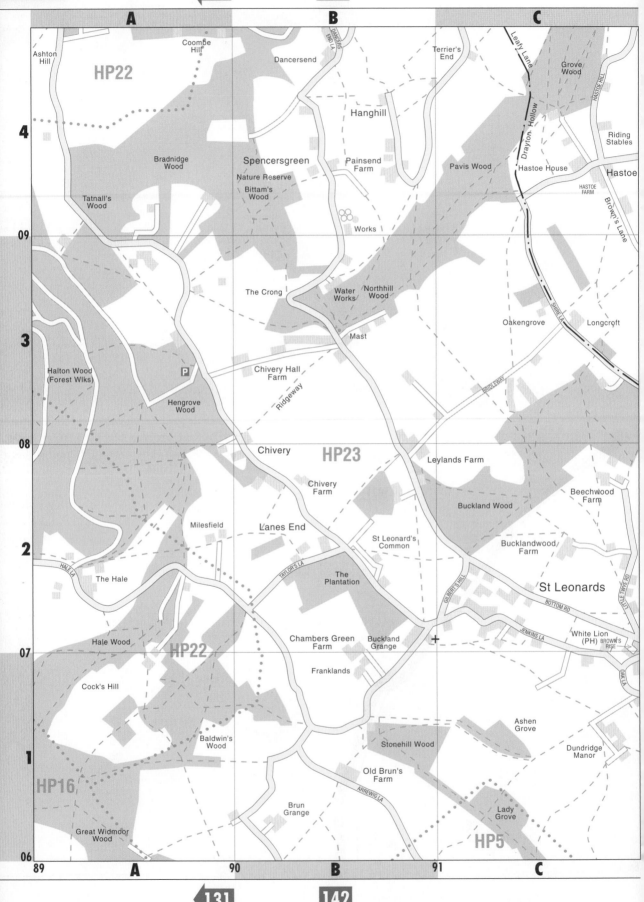

131
118

A **B** **C**

Ashton
Hill

Coombe
Hill

HP22

Dancersend

Terrier's
End

Leafy Lane

Grove
Wood

HASTOE HILL

4

Bradnidge
Wood

Spencersgreen

Hanghill

Painsend
Farm

Pavis Wood

Drayton Hollow

Hastoe House

Riding
Stables

Hastoe

Tatnall's
Wood

Nature Reserve

Bittam's
Wood

HASTOE
FARM

Brown's Lane

Works

09

The Crong

Water
Works

Northhill
Wood

Oakengrove

Longcroft

SHIRE LA

3

Halton Wood
(Forest Wlks)

P

Mast

Chivery Hall
Farm

Ridgeway

BRIDLEWAY

Hengrove
Wood

08

Chivery

HP23

Leylands Farm

Beechwood
Farm

Chivery
Farm

Buckland Wood

Milesfield

Lanes End

St Leonard's
Common

Bucklandwood
Farm

2

TAYLOR'S LA

The Hale

HALE LA

The
Plantation

GILBERT'S HILL

St Leonards

BOTTOM RD

LITTLE TWYE RD

Hale Wood

HP22

Chambers Green
Farm

Buckland
Grange

+

JENKINS LA

White Lion
(PH)

BROWN'S
RISE

07

Cock's Hill

Franklands

OAK LA

Ashen
Grove

Baldwin's
Wood

Stonehill Wood

Dundridge
Manor

1

HP16

Old Brun's
Farm

ARREWIG LA

Brun
Grange

Lady
Grove

Great Widmoor
Wood

HP5

06

89   90   91

A **B** **C**

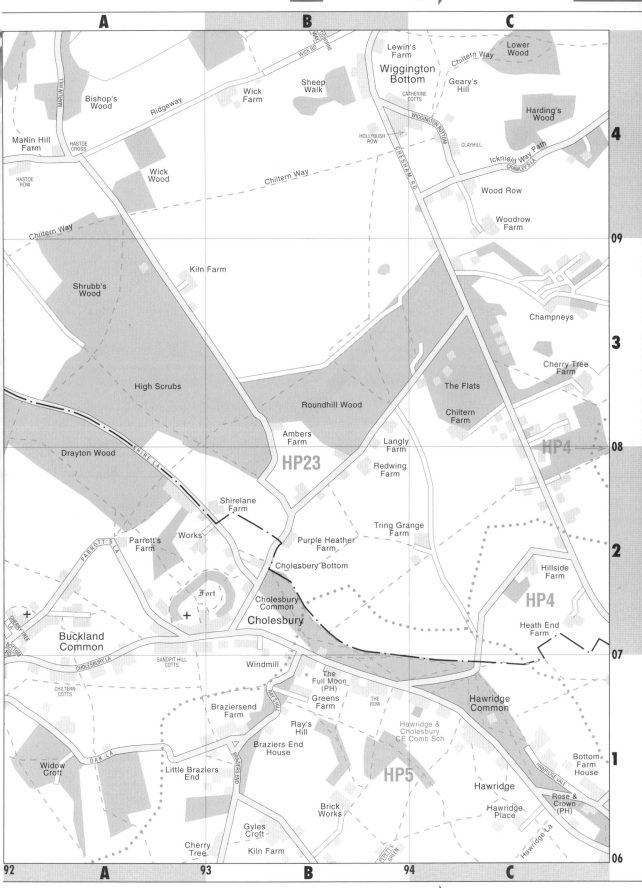

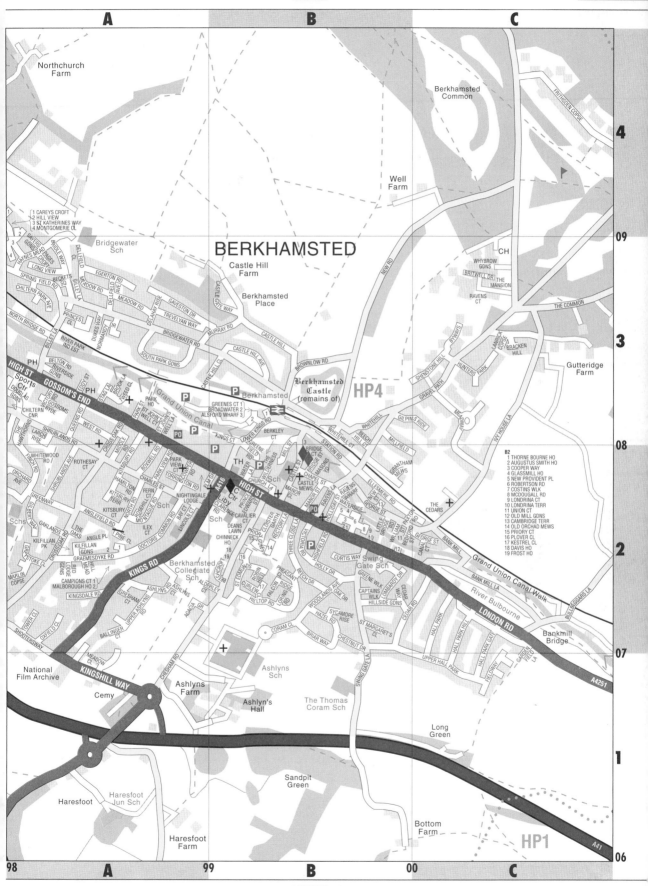

BERKHAMSTED

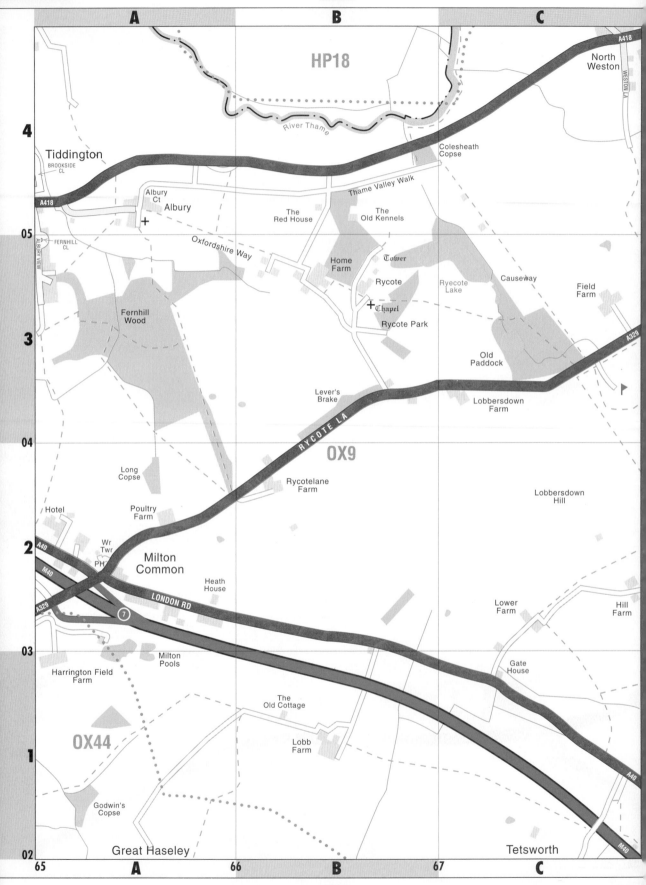

124

A   B   C

HP18

North Weston

A418

WESTON LA

River Thame

4

Tiddington

Colesheath Copse

BROOKSIDE CL

A418

Albury Ct   Albury

Thame Valley Walk

The Red House   The Old Kennels

05

ALBURY VIEW

FERNHILL CL

Oxfordshire Way

Home Farm

Tower

Rycote

Ryecote Lake

Causeway

Field Farm

Fernhill Wood

Chapel

Rycote Park

3

Old Paddock

A329

Lever's Brake

Lobbersdown Farm

RYCOTE LA

04

OX9

Rycotelane Farm

Lobbersdown Hill

Long Copse

Hotel

Poultry Farm

A40

Wr Twr

PH

Milton Common

2

M40

Heath House

A329

LONDON RD

Lower Farm

Hill Farm

7

03

Milton Pools

Gate House

Harrington Field Farm

OX44

The Old Cottage

Lobb Farm

1

Godwin's Copse

A40

Great Haseley

Tetsworth

M40

02
65   A   66   B   67   C

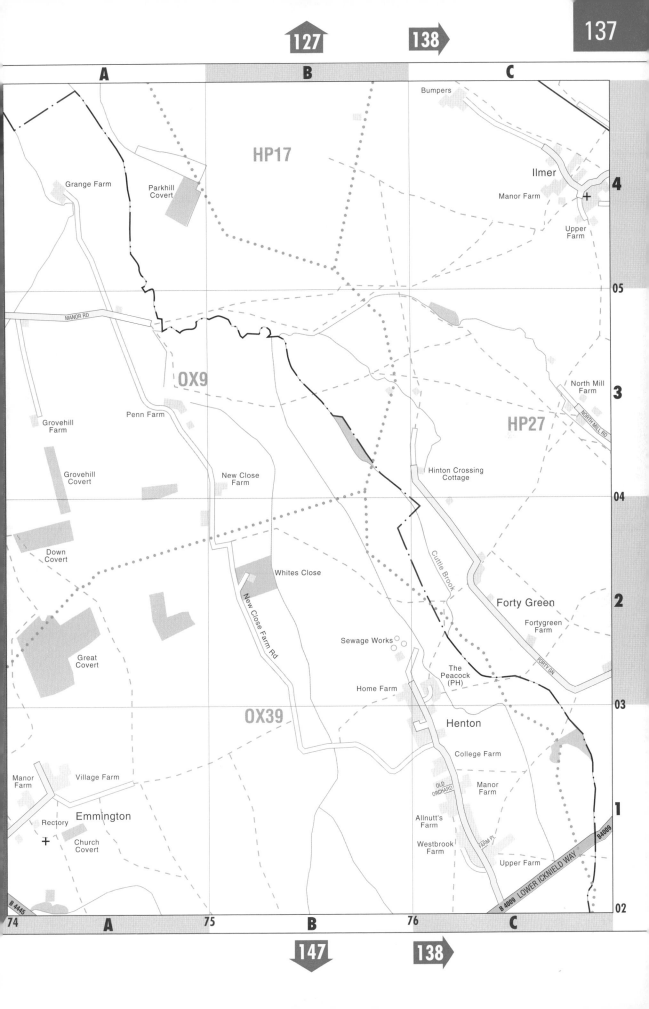

A   **B**   **C**

4

Lower
Farm

Anderdons
Farm

Tifnams

Buntings

Redhouse
Farm

A4129

Chadwell Hill
Cottage

Longwick

Chadwell
Hill

Rose
Farm

SAWMILL RD
BLACKSMITHS RD
WHEELWRIGHT RD
SAWPIT WAY

CENTENARY
COTTS

BAR LA

05

Swan's Way

ORCHARD CL
WALNUT TREE CL
SWALNUT CRES
DODRELLS RD

CLAYDONS
PL

PH

B4009

Longwick CE
Comb Sch

MEADOW DR

PO

Laurels
Farm

BLENHEIM CL 1
THE GREEN 2

PH

Midshires Way

BOXER RD

B4444

WILLIAMS WAY

BARN RD

BELL CRES

THE WILLOWS

CHESTNUT WAY

IVY CL

LITTLE
ORCHARD CL

LONGWICK RD

A4129

3

WOODBINE CL

Works

NORTH MILL RD

Longwick
Mill

04

HP27

B4444

The
Ford

Little
Horsenden
Farm

Sewage
Works

Sandpit
Farm

SUMMERLEYS RD

Waltons
Farm

Holly
Green
Farm

LOWER ICKNIELD WAY

Summerleys

Park
Mill

SANDPIT LA

Sandpit
Lane
Farm

 Icknield Line

NORTH MILL

2

Holly
Green

Pitch
Green
Farm

LC

PRINCES EST

Skittle
Green

CHAPEL LA

Pitch
Green

Brew House
Farm

03

SKITTLE GN

RIDGEWAY MEADS

Manor
Farm

Mast

Princes
Risborough

CHINNOR RD

THE
VINEYARDS

HORSENDEN LA

B4009

CROSS
LANES

Horsenden

P

1

WEST LA

Westfield
Farm

PERRY LA

Cemy

BLEDLOW
COTTS

Bledlow

PICTS LA 1
SHOOTACRE LA 2

LYDE
END

Bledlow
House

BLEDLOW RIDGE RD

1
2

P

CHURCH END

Saunderton

BLEDLOW RD

02

77   **A**   **78**   **B**   **79**   **C**

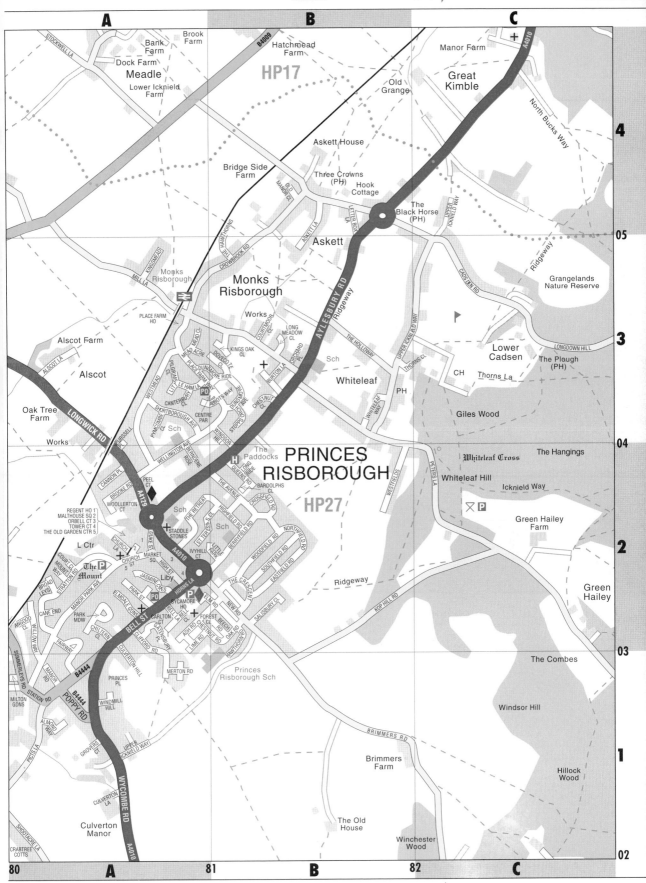

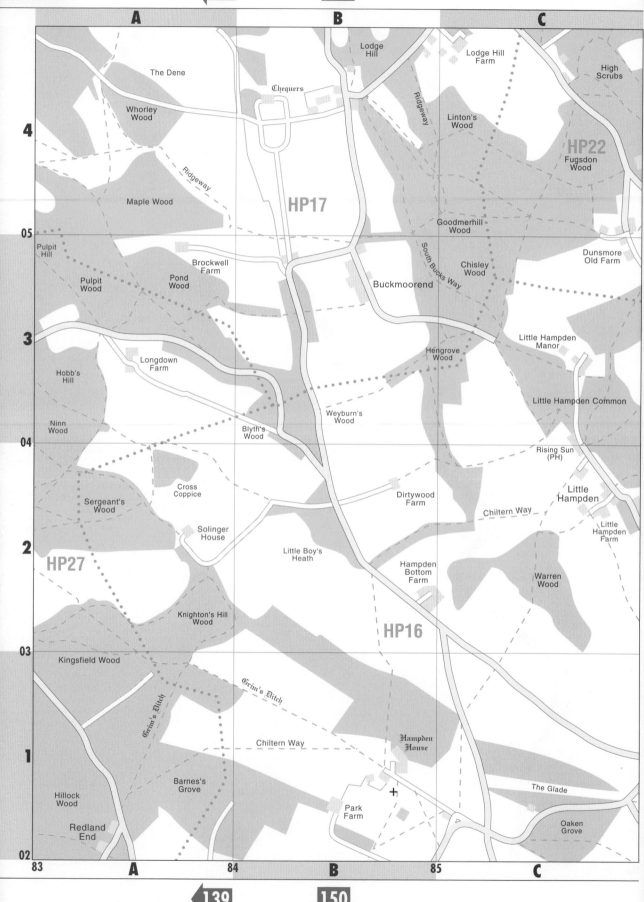

139
130

A B C

4

The Dene

Chequers

Lodge Hill

Lodge Hill Farm

High Scrubs

Whorley Wood

Ridgeway

Linton's Wood

HP22

Fugsdon Wood

HP17

Ridgeway

Maple Wood

Goodmerhill Wood

05

Pulpit Hill

Brockwell Farm

South Bucks Way

Chisley Wood

Dunsmore Old Farm

Pulpit Wood

Pond Wood

Buckmoorend

3

Hobb's Hill

Longdown Farm

Hengrove Wood

Little Hampden Manor

Ninn Wood

Blyth's Wood

Weyburn's Wood

Little Hampden Common

04

Rising Sun (PH)

Cross Coppice

Dirtywood Farm

Little Hampden

Sergeant's Wood

Chiltern Way

Little Hampden Farm

Solinger House

Little Boy's Heath

2

HP27

Hampden Bottom Farm

Warren Wood

Knighton's Hill Wood

HP16

03

Kingsfield Wood

Grim's Ditch

Grim's Ditch

1

Chiltern Way

Hampden House

Hillock Wood

Barnes's Grove

The Glade

Redland End

Park Farm

Oaken Grove

02

83 A 84 B 85 C

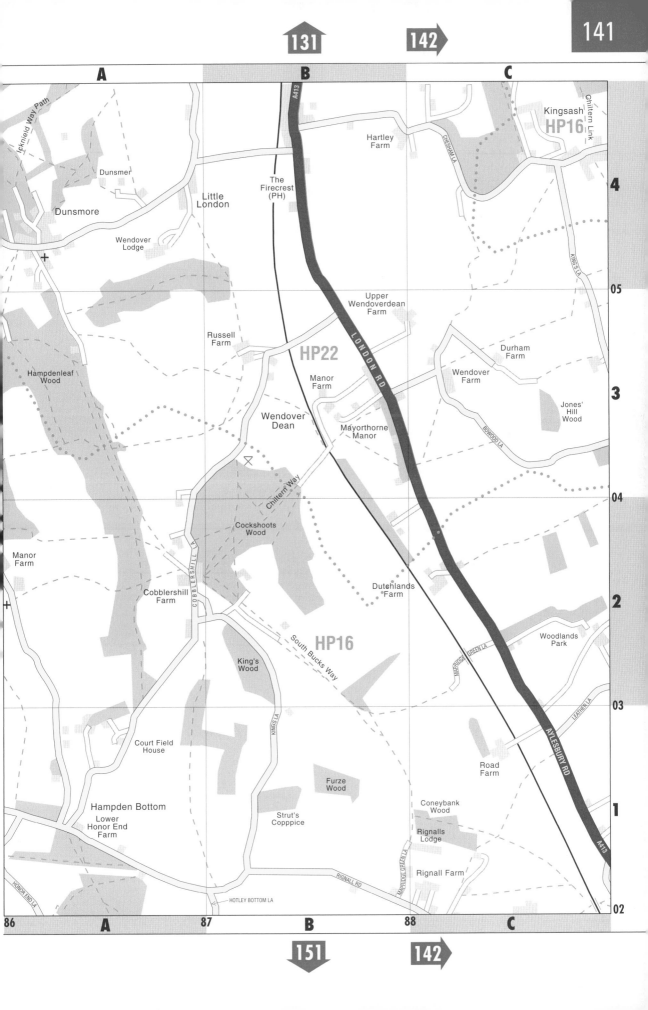

A
B
C

HP23

Timberley La

Lordling Wood

HP23

Old Swan
(PH)

Furze Field

Chiltern Way

Kingswood

ARREWIG LA

Erriwig Farm

HP5

4

The Gate
(PH)

Lee Gate

Kingsgate
Farm

Swan Bottom

Three Gates
Farm

05

Gwenfa
Farm

Bray's Wood

HP22

Chiltern Link

Lee Clump

Lownde's Wood

3

Church
Farm

The Lee

Home
Farm

Leeclump
Farm

PRINCES LA

The Bugle
(PH)

Bassibones
Farm

Church
(restored)

Lee Common
CE Sch

OXFORD ST

ST MARY'S LA

CROCKETTS LA

Cock and Rabbit
(PH)

Hawthorn Farm

HP16

Lower Bassibones
Farm

Lee Common

Rushmoor
Wood

MARTIN DELL
COTTS

CHERRY TREE LA

04

King's La

Pipers

SLY CNR

Hunt's Green

Field End
Grange

Ballinger Bottom

Chiltern Link

2

Hunt's Green
Farm

CHILTERN RD

BLACK THORNE LA

Ballinger
Row

Ballinger Common

LEATHER LA

BLACKFIELD LA

03

Hammondshall Farm

Springfield Farm

Ballinger Farm

BALLINGER
GRANGE

Wr Twr

Ballinger Grove

1

Havenfields

POTTER ROW

HERBERTS HOLE

Park Farm

Ballinger Bottom
(South)

PO

A413

AYLESBURY RD

MEADOW
LA

BALLINGER RD

MARRIOTTS AVE

MARRIOTTS AVE

02

Bury Farm

89

A

90

B

91

C

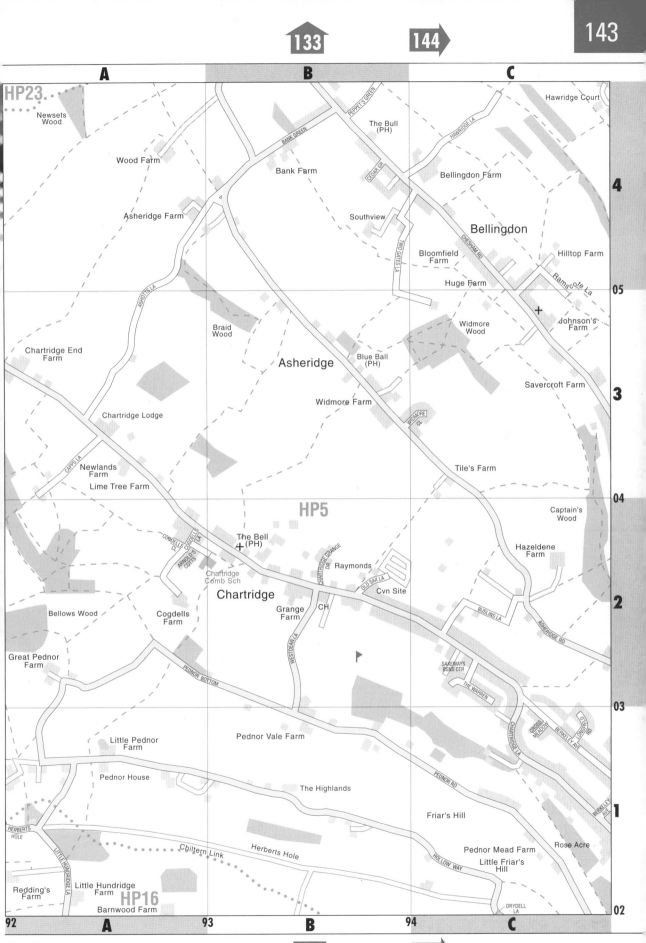

HP23

Newsets Wood

Wood Farm

Asheridge Farm

ASHOTTS LA

Chartridge End Farm

Chartridge Lodge

CAPPS LA

Newlands Farm

Lime Tree Farm

Braid Wood

BANK GREEN

Bank Farm

PEPPET'S GREEN

The Bull (PH)

CEDAR GR

Southview

TWO GATES LA

Asheridge

Blue Ball (PH)

Widmore Farm

WIDMORE CL

HAWRIDGE LA

Bellingdon Farm

Bellingdon

CHESHAM RD

Bloomfield Farm

Huge Farm

Widmore Wood

Tile's Farm

Hawridge Court

Hilltop Farm

Ramscote La

Johnson's Farm

Savercroft Farm

05

04

HP5

Bellows Wood

Great Pednor Farm

COGDELLS CL

COGDELLS LA

ARNOLD'S COTTS

Cogdells Farm

The Bell (PH)

Chartridge Comb Sch

Chartridge

Grange Farm

CH

WESTDEAN LA

PEDNOR BOTTOM

CHARTRIDGE GRANGE DR

Raymonds

OLD SAX LA

Cvn Site

Captain's Wood

Hazeldene Farm

BUSLINS LA

ASHERIDGE RD

SAXEWAYS BSNS CTR

THE WARREN

CHARTRIDGE LA

CROSS MEADOW

BERKELEY AVE

LONGDELL RD

03

Little Pednor Farm

Pednor House

HERBERTS HOLE

LITTLE HUNDRIDGE LA

Redding's Farm

Little Hundridge Farm

HP16

Barnwood Farm

Pednor Vale Farm

Chiltern Link

The Highlands

Herberts Hole

PEDNOR RD

Friar's Hill

HOLLOW WAY

Pednor Mead Farm

Little Friar's Hill

DRYDELL LA

Rose Acre

BERKELEY AVE

02

92 93 94

A B C

153 144

4

3

2

1

A B C

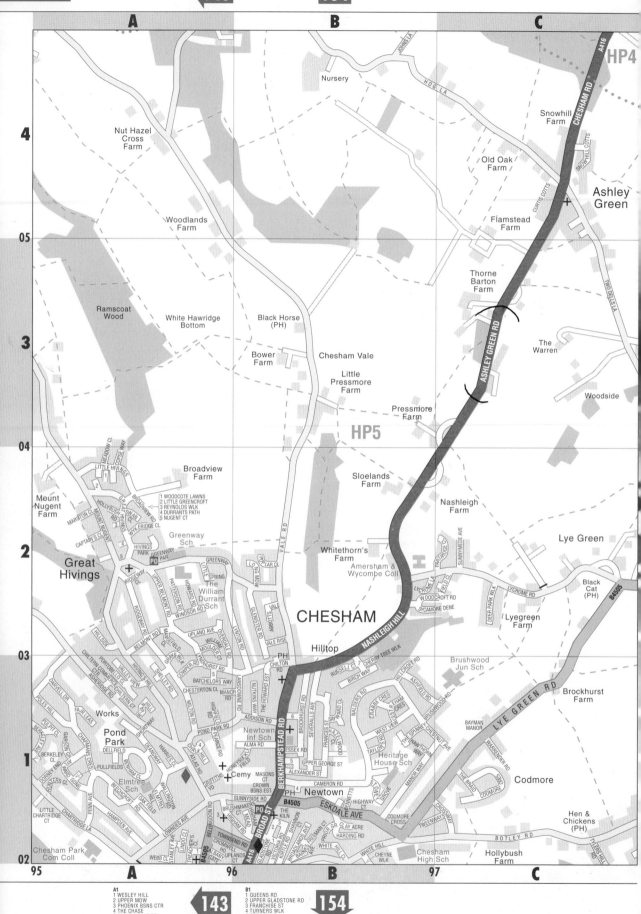

A B C

4

Nut Hazel
Cross
Farm

Nursery

HOG LA

JOHN'S LA

Snowhill
Farm

CHESHAM RD

A416

HP4

Old Oak
Farm

Curtis Cotts

Ashley
Green

SNOWHILL COTTS

Woodlands
Farm

Flamstead
Farm

05

Ramscoat
Wood

White Hawridge
Bottom

Black Horse
(PH)

Thorne
Barton
Farm

TWO DELLS LA

3

Bower
Farm

Chesham Vale

Little
Pressmore
Farm

ASHLEY GREEN RD

The
Warren

Woodside

Pressmore
Farm

HP5

04

Broadview
Farm

1 WOODCOTE LAWNS
2 LITTLE GREENCROFT
3 REYNOLDS WLK
4 DURRANTS PATH
5 NUGENT CT

Sloelands
Farm

Nashleigh
Farm

Lye Green

Mount
Nugent
Farm

Greenway
Sch

Whitethorn's
Farm

Amersham &
Wycombe Coll

SUNNYMEDE AVE

PARTRIDGE CL

LYCROME LA

RED CL

Black
Cat
(PH)

B4505

2

Great
Hivings

PO

Greenway
Par

The
William
Durrant
Sch

VALE RD

WOODCROFT RD

LYCROME RD

DEER PARK WLK

Lyegreen
Farm

CHESHAM

NASHLEIGH HILL

SYCAMORE DENE

Brushwood
Jun Sch

Brockhurst
Farm

03

PH

Hilltop

Chilton
Rd

CHERRY TREE WLK

RUSSELL CT

BIRCH WAY

HILLCROFT RD

ASHFIELD RD

LYE GREEN RD

Works

Pond
Park

BERKHAMPSTEAD RD

Newtown
Inf Sch

ALMA RD

ESSEX RD

CRABBE CRES

WEST VIEW

R HEAD CRES

BRUSHWOOD RD

BAYMAN
MANOR

Codmore

1

Elmtree
Sch

Cemy

MASONS
CT
CROWN
BSNS EST

UPPER GEORGE ST

ALEXANDER ST

CAMERON RD

Newtown

Heritage
House Sch

MANOR WAY

CODMORE

THE BRAID

Hen &
Chickens
(PH)

Chesham
High Sch

Hollybush
Farm

BROAD ST

B4505

ESKDALE AVE

CODMORE
CROSS

BOTLEY RD

WHITE HILL

Chesham Park
Com Coll

A416

A1
1 WESLEY HILL
2 UPPER MDW
3 PHOENIX BSNS CTR
4 THE CHASE
5 NIGHTINGALE RD

B1
1 QUEENS RD
2 UPPER GLADSTONE RD
3 FRANCHISE ST
4 TURNERS WLK
5 GEORGE ST
6 BRITANNIA RD
7 PRESTON HILL

143 154

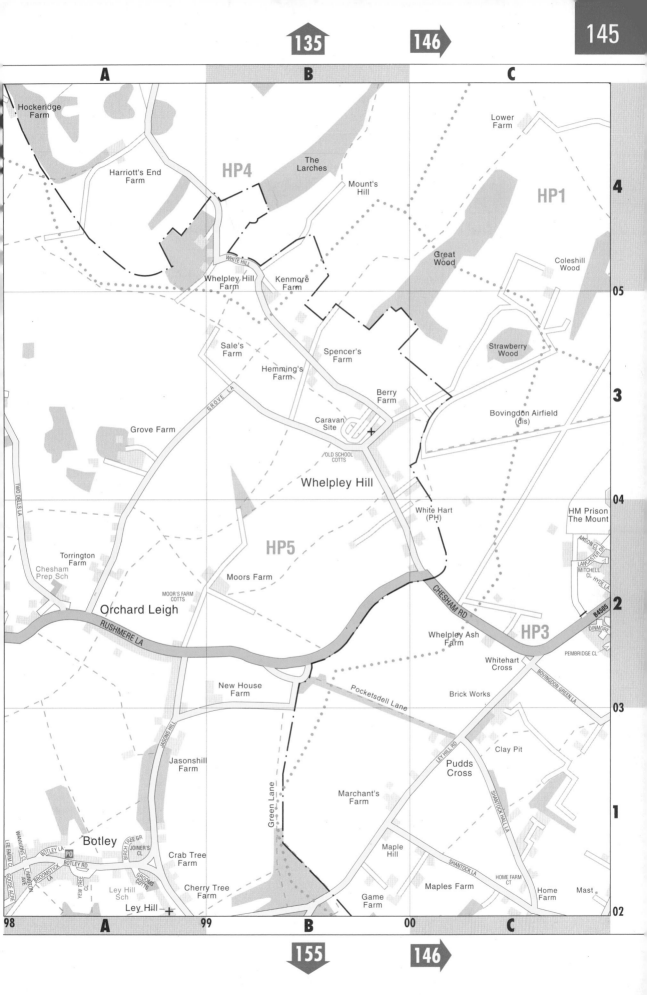

A B C

Hockeridge
Farm

Harriott's End
Farm

HP4

The
Larches

Mount's
Hill

Lower
Farm

HP1

4

Great
Wood

Coleshill
Wood

WHITE HILL

Whelpley Hill
Farm

Kenmore
Farm

05

Sale's
Farm

Spencer's
Farm

Strawberry
Wood

GROVE LA

Hemming's
Farm

Berry
Farm

3

Grove Farm

Caravan
Site

Bovingdon Airfield
(dis)

OLD SCHOOL
COTTS

Whelpley Hill

04

White Hart
(PH)

HM Prison
The Mount

TWO DELLS LA

HP5

ANSON CL DR

LANCASTER
CL
MITCHELL
CL HYDE LA

Torrington
Farm

Chesham
Prep Sch

Moors Farm

2

Orchard Leigh

MOOR'S FARM
COTTS

RUSHMERE LA

CHESHAM RD

Whelpley Ash
Farm

HP3

B4505

DINMORE

PEMBRIDGE CL

Whitehart
Cross

BOVINGDON GREEN LA

New House
Farm

Pocketsdell Lane

Brick Works

03

JASONS HILL

Jasonshill
Farm

LEY HILL RD

Clay Pit

Pudds
Cross

SHANTOCK HALL LA

1

Green Lane

Marchant's
Farm

Botley

BIRCH TREE GR

JOINER'S
CL

Crab Tree
Farm

Maple
Hill

Maples Farm

SHANTOCK LA

HOME FARM
CT

Home
Farm

Mast

LEE FARM CL
WANNIONS CL
GOOSE ACRE
LINNINGTON
AVE
BOTLEY LA
PO
BROOMSTICK
LA
BOTLEY RD
YEW TREE
CL
GROOMS
COTTS

Ley Hill
Sch

Cherry Tree
Farm

Ley Hill

Game
Farm

02

98 A 99 B 00 C 02

145

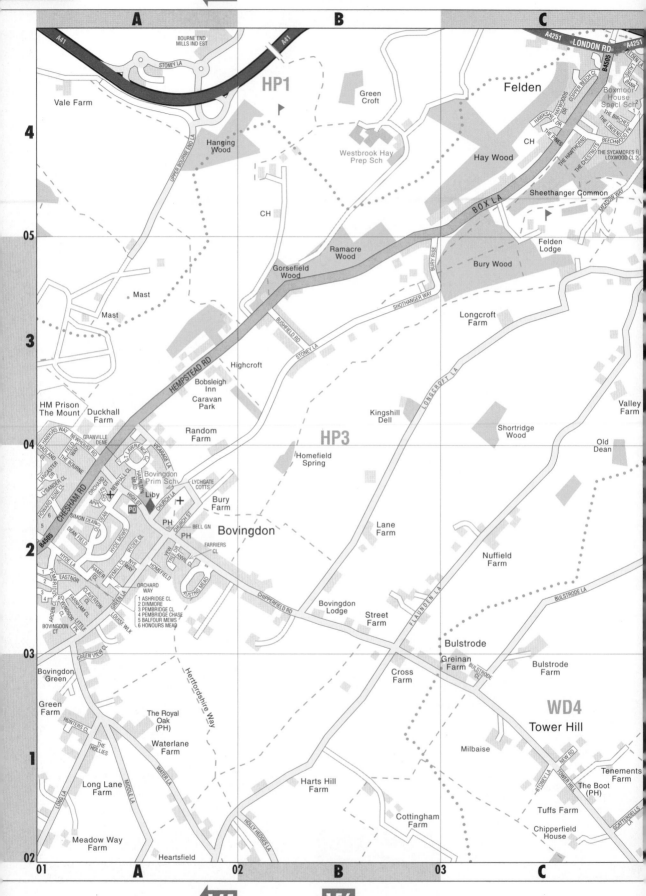

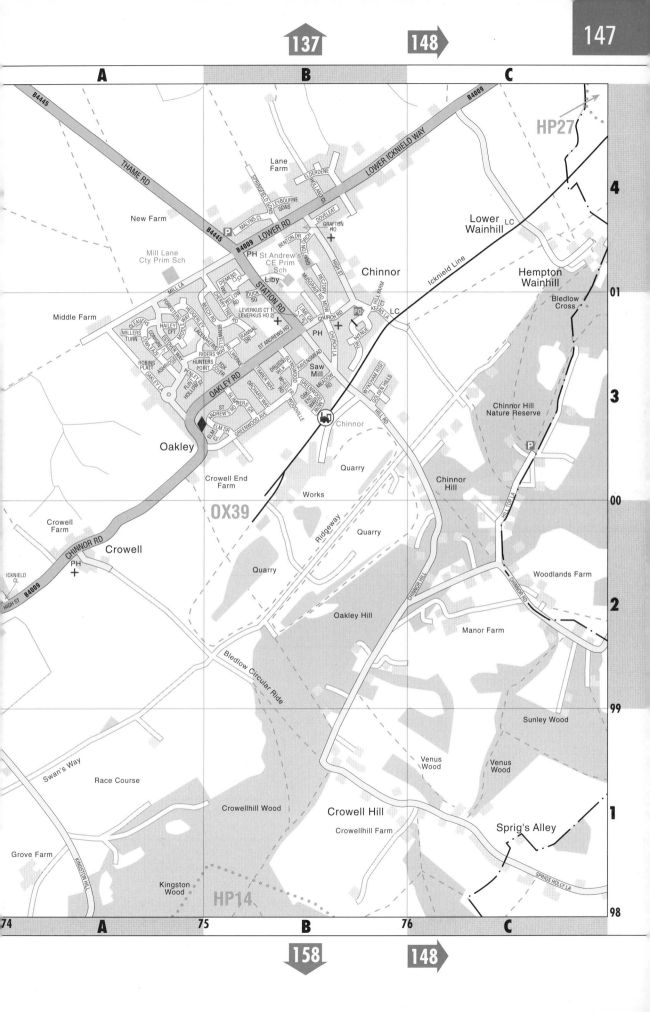

147
138

A **B** **C**

Icknield Line

Midshires Way

4

The Warren

The Cop

Thickthorne Wood

Dean Plantation

Frogmore Farm

ODDLEY LA

BLEDLOW RIDGE RD

BLEDLOW RD

Chiltern Way

Church Farm

Icknield Way Path

Home Farm

HP27

01

Ridgeway

WIGAN'S LA

LEE RD

Parsonage Farm

CH

Keeper's House

3

Bledlow Great Wood

Lodge Hill

Shimmell's Farm

00

Bledlow Circular Ride

Callow Down Farm

Chiltern Way

HP14

Home Wood

OX39

Frenche's Wood

2

Wigan's Farm

Beechgrove Farm

CHINNOR RD

Harper's Farm

99

Lodge Hill Farm

Hedgerley Wood

Bledlow Ridge

Rout's Green

RETREAT LA

CHAPEL LA

Radnage Bottom Farm

RADNAGE LA

1

Daws Hill Farm

The Boot (PH)

SPRIGS HOLLY LA

CHURCH LA

Studmore Farm

98

77 **A** **78** **B** **79** **C**

147
159

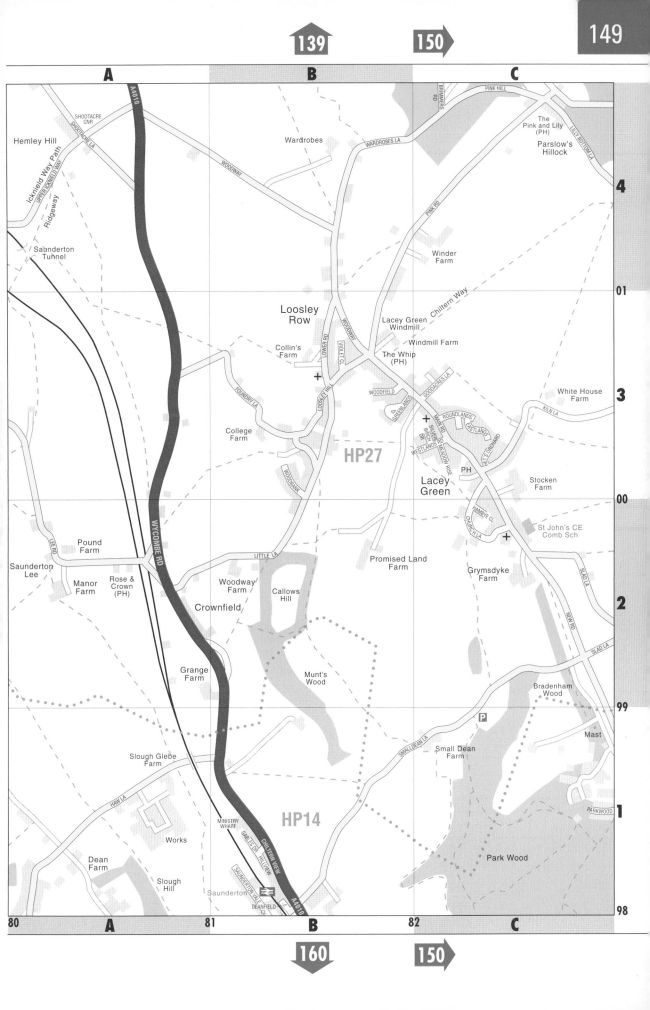

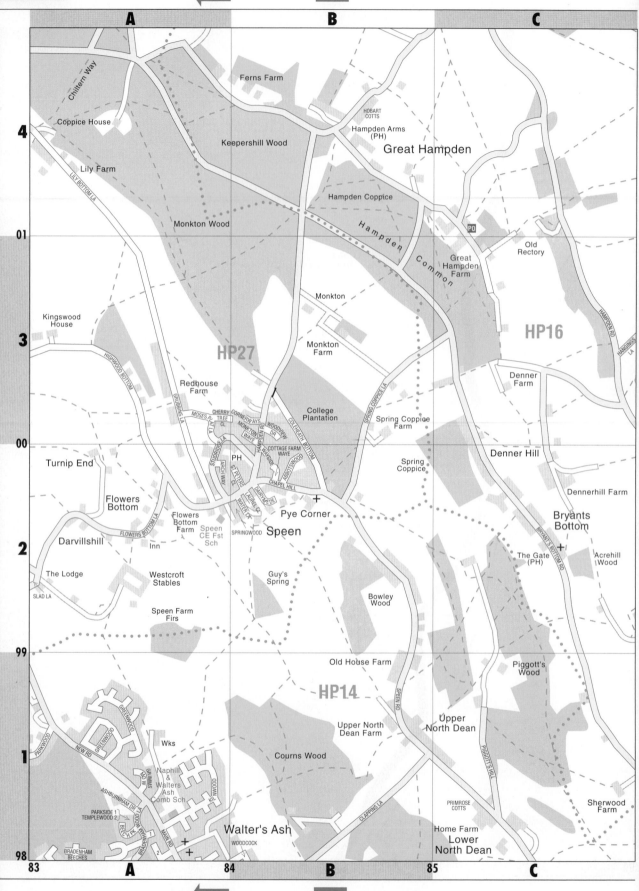

A B C

Chiltern Way

Ferns Farm

HOBART COTTS

Hampden Arms (PH)

Great Hampden

Coppice House

4

Keepershill Wood

Lily Farm

LILY BOTTOM LA

Hampden Coppice

Monkton Wood

01

Hampden Common

Great Hampden Farm

PO

Old Rectory

Kingswood House

Monkton

HP16

HP27

3

Monkton Farm

HIGHWOOD BOTTOM

Denner Farm

HAMPDEN RD

HANGINGS LA

GRUBBINS LA

Redhouse Farm

CHERRY CORNERWAYS TREE CL

MOSES PLAT LA

WOODVIEW DR

College Plantation

SPRING COPPICE LA

Spring Coppice Farm

00

MONKTON WAYE

HAMPDEN RD

WAYSIDE

COLEHEATH BOTTOM

Spring Coppice

Denner Hill

Turnip End

PH

STUDRIDGE LA

ARCH WAY

ST PETERS CL

Cottage Farm Waye

ABBOTSWOOD

Dennerhill Farm

Flowers Bottom

LAUREL CT

DURMEDE

Chapel Hill

Bryants Bottom

Darvillshill

FLOWERS BOTTOM LA

Flowers Bottom Farm

WATER LK

Speen CE Fst Sch

SPRINGWOOD

Pye Corner

Speen

BRYANT'S BOTTOM RD

The Gate (PH)

Acrehill Wood

2

The Lodge

Inn

Westcroft Stables

Guy's Spring

Bowley Wood

SLAD LA

Speen Farm Firs

99

Old House Farm

Piggott's Wood

SPEEN RD

HP14

PARKWOOD

NEW RD

GREENWOOD

GREENWOOD

Wks

Upper North Dean Farm

Upper North Dean

PIGGOTT'S HILL

1

GRIMMS MD W

ASHBURNHAM DR

ODDMN

ODDMN KIL

Naphill & Walters Ash Comb Sch

Courns Wood

Sherwood Farm

PRIMROSE COTTS

WHRBROTGH

PARKSIDE 1 TEMPLEWOOD 2

BEECH PK

CLAPPINS LA

Home Farm

Lower North Dean

BRADENHAM BEECHES

Walter's Ash

WOODCOCK

98

83 A 84 B 85 C

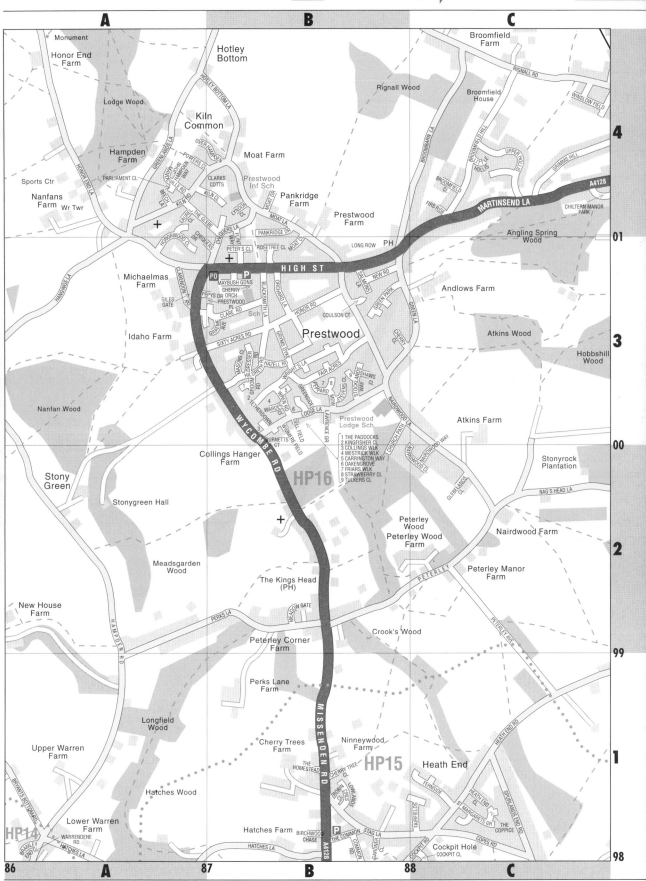

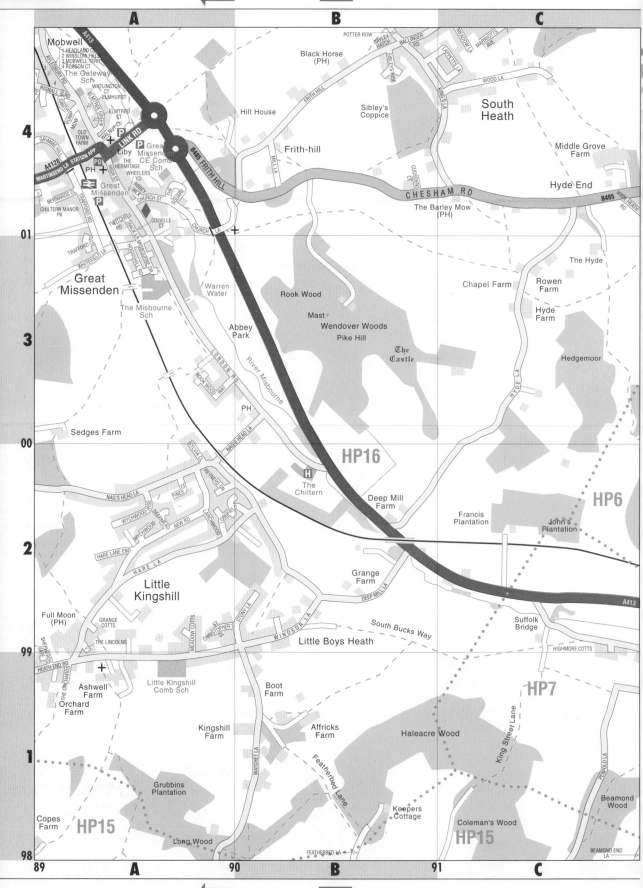

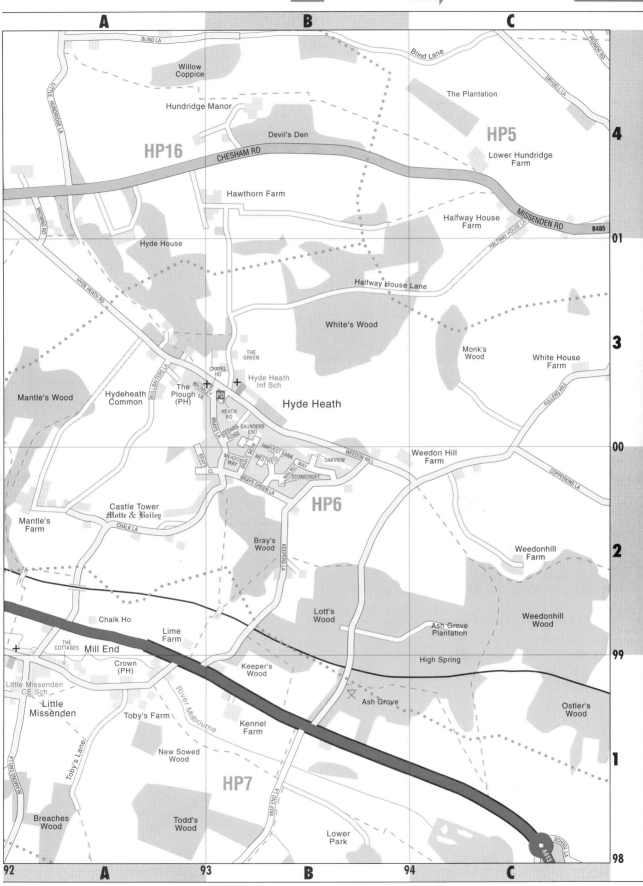

A B C

BLIND LA
BLIND LANE
PENFOLD RD
DRYDELL LA

Willow
Coppice

The Plantation

Hundridge Manor

HP5

4

Devil's Den

HP16

Lower Hundridge
Farm

CHESHAM RD

Hawthorn Farm

Halfway House
Farm

MISSENDEN RD
B485

Hyde House

01

HYDE HEATH RD

Halfway House Lane

HALFWAY HOUSE LA

White's Wood

Monk's
Wood

White House
Farm

3

THE
GREEN

Mantle's Wood

CHAPEL
HO

Hyde Heath
Inf Sch

FULLERS HILL

Hydeheath
Common

BROMLEY LA

The Plough
(PH)

PO

Hyde Heath

BULL BAITERS LA

HEATH
RD

CEDARS
RIDGE

SAUNDERS
END

BRAYS LA

HARVEST BANK

Weedon Hill
Farm

00

MEADOW
WAY

BRAYS MDW

WESTREO

WEEDON HILL

OAKVIEW

WALNUT WAY

STONECROFT

COPPERKINS LA

BRAYS
CL

BRAYS GREEN LA

HP6

Castle Tower
Motte & Bailey

CHALK LA

Mantle's
Farm

Bray's
Wood

KEEPERS LA

Weedonhill
Farm

2

Lott's
Wood

Weedonhill
Wood

Chalk Ho

Ash Grove
Plantation

Lime
Farm

THE
COTTAGES

Mill End

High Spring

99

Crown
(PH)

Keeper's
Wood

Little Missenden
CE Sch

Ash Grove

Ostler's
Wood

Little
Missenden

Toby's Farm

River Misbourne

Kennel
Farm

BEAMOND END LA

TOBY'S LANE

New Sowed
Wood

MOP END LA

HP7

1

Breaches
Wood

Todd's
Wood

Lower
Park

A413

SCHOOL LA

98

92 A 93 B 94 C

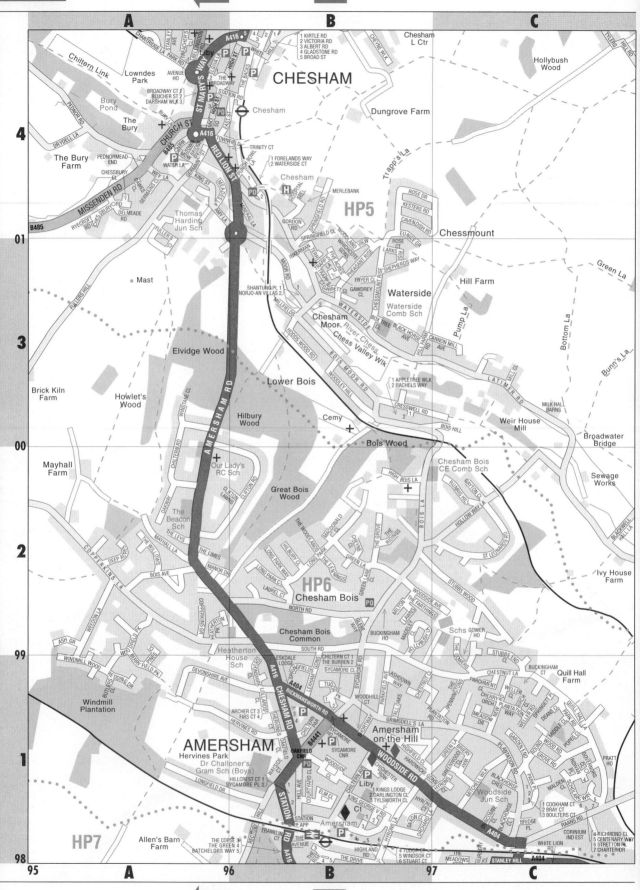

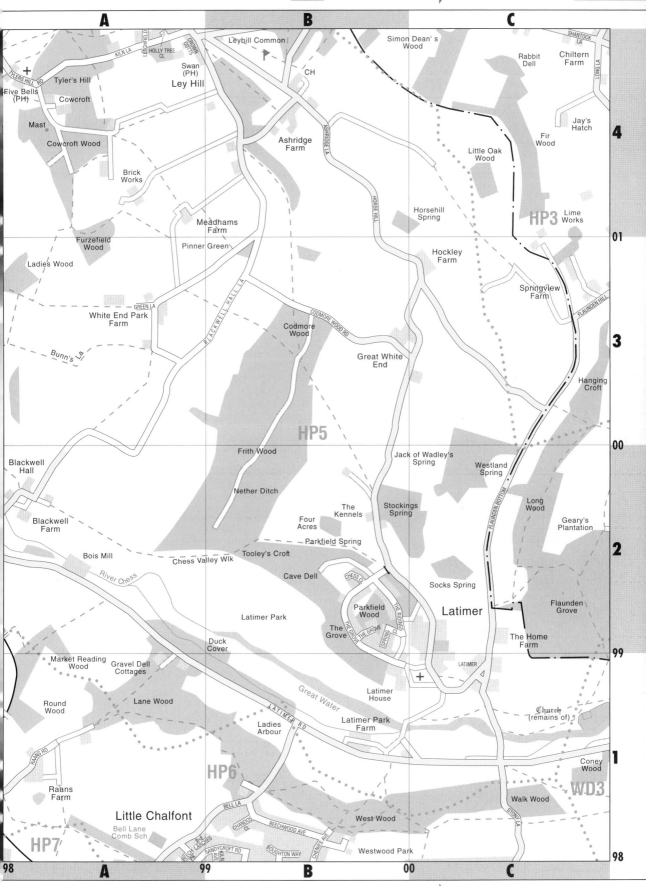

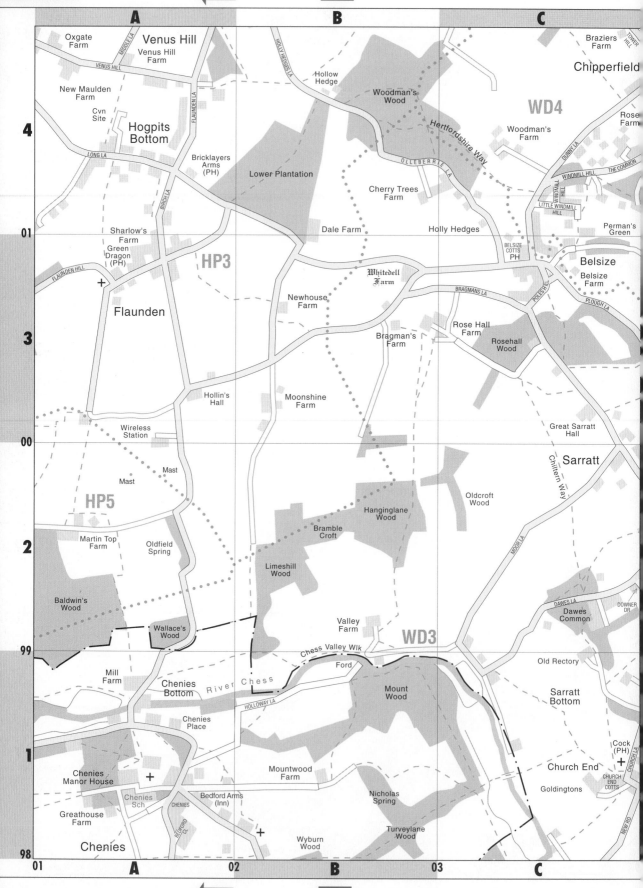

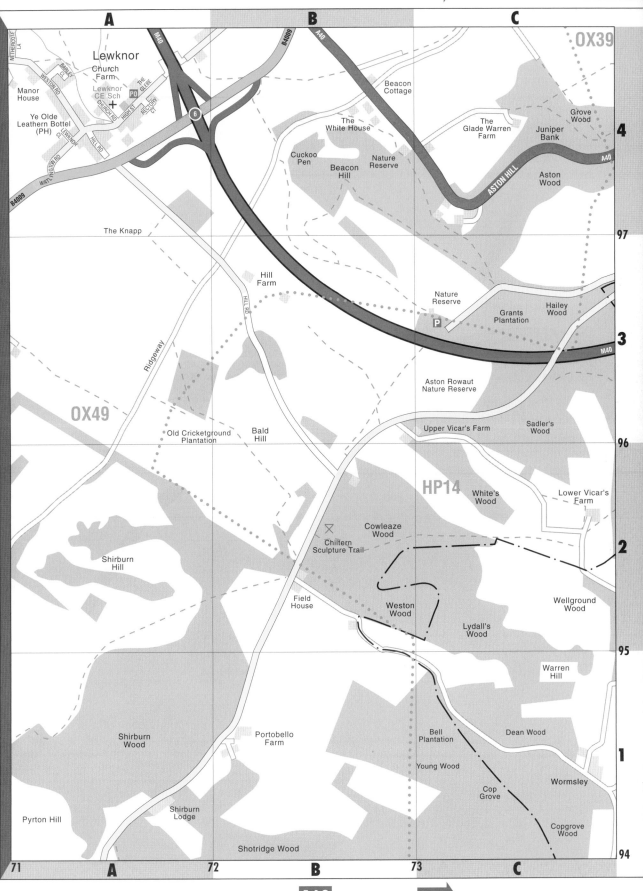

OX39

A

B

C

Lewknor
Church
Farm
Lewknor
CE Sch
PO
Manor
House
Ye Olde
Leathern Bottel
(PH)
NETHERCOTE LA
WESTON RD
BARLEY CL
THE GLEBE
HIGH ST
CHURCH RD
RECTORY CT
WATLINGTON RD
LEWKNOR CL
HILL RD
B4009
B4009
M40
A40
6

Beacon
Cottage

The
White House

Cuckoo
Pen

Beacon
Hill

Nature
Reserve

The
Glade Warren
Farm

Grove
Wood

Juniper
Bank

Aston
Wood

ASTON HILL

A40

4

The Knapp

97

Hill
Farm

Nature
Reserve

Grants
Plantation

Hailey
Wood

P

M40

3

Ridgeway

HILL RD

Aston Rowaut
Nature Reserve

OX49

Old Cricketground
Plantation

Bald
Hill

Upper Vicar's Farm

Sadler's
Wood

96

HP14

White's
Wood

Lower Vicar's
Farm

Shirburn
Hill

Cowleaze
Wood

Chiltern
Sculpture Trail

Wellground
Wood

2

Field
House

Weston
Wood

Lydall's
Wood

95

Warren
Hill

Shirburn
Wood

Portobello
Farm

Bell
Plantation

Dean Wood

Young Wood

1

Pyrton Hill

Shirburn
Lodge

Cop
Grove

Wormsley

Copgrove
Wood

Shotridge Wood

94

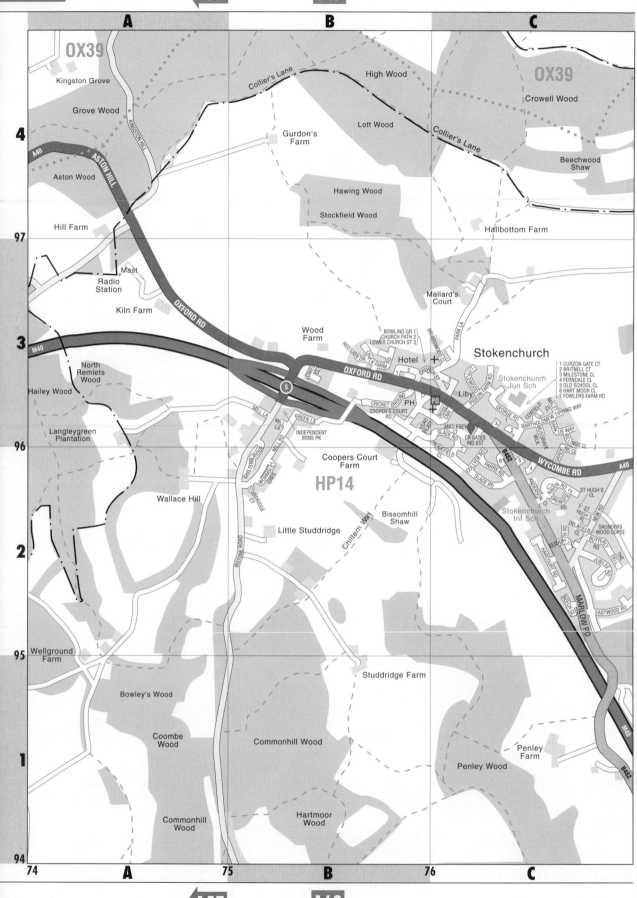

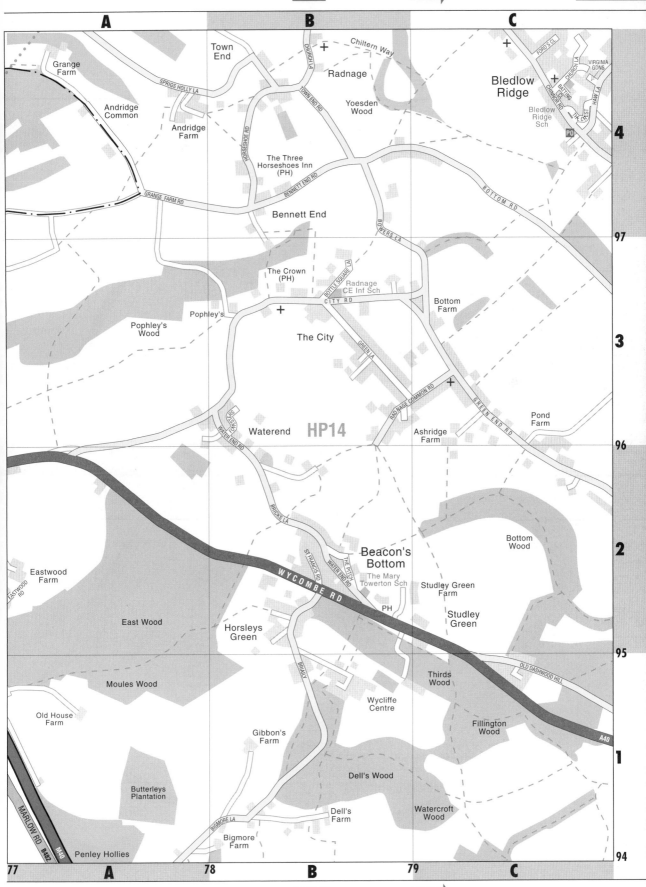

A **B** **C**

Grange
Farm

Town
End

Chiltern Way

Ford's Cl.

Radnage

Virginia
Gdns

Bledlow
Ridge

Andridge
Common

SPRIGS HOLLY LA

Yoesden
Wood

CHURCH LA

BALTING

THE CREST

CHIMNOR RD

HAW LA

Andridge
Farm

Bledlow
Ridge
Sch

HORSESHOE RD

TOWNEND RD

PO

4

The Three
Horseshoes Inn
(PH)

BOTTOM RD

BENNETT END RD

Bennett End

GRANGE FARM RD

BOWERS LA

97

The Crown
(PH)

Radnage
CE Inf Sch

BOTTLE SQUARE LA

Bottom
Farm

Pophley's Wood

Pophley's

CITY RD

The City

GREEN LA

3

RADNAGE COMMON RD

GREEN END RD

Pond
Farm

Waterend

WATER END RD

HP14

Ashridge
Farm

96

BRICKS LA

Bottom
Wood

Eastwood
Farm

ST FRANCIS RD

WATER END RD

THE PITCH

Beacon's
Bottom

2

EASTWOOD RD

WYCOMBE RD

The Mary
Towerton Sch

Studley Green
Farm

East Wood

Horsleys
Green

PH

Studley
Green

A40

95

OLD DASHWOOD HILL

Moules Wood

BRIARLY

Thirds
Wood

Wycliffe
Centre

Old House
Farm

Fillington
Wood

MARLOW RD

B482

M40

Gibbon's
Farm

Dell's
Wood

Watercroft
Wood

1

Butterleys
Plantation

Dell's
Farm

BIGMORE LA

Bigmore
Farm

Penley Hollies

94

77 **A** **78** **B** **79** **C**

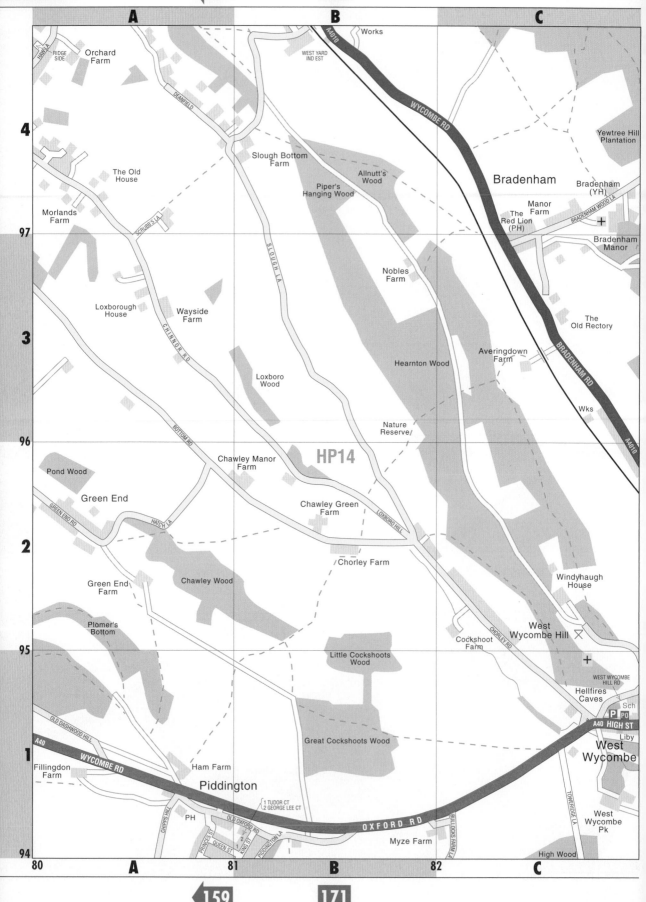

A   B   C

4

Orchard
Farm
RIDGE
SIDE
HAM LA

DEANFIELD

Works
WEST YARD
IND EST

WYCOMBE RD
A4010

Bradenham

Yewtree Hill
Plantation

Bradenham
(YH)

The Old
House

Slough Bottom
Farm

Allnutt's
Wood

Piper's
Hanging Wood

Manor
Farm

BRADENHAM WOOD LA

97

Morlands
Farm

SCRUBB'S LA

Nobles
Farm

The
Red Lion
(PH)

Bradenham
Manor

3

Loxborough
House

Wayside
Farm

CHINNOR RD

SLOUGH LA

Loxboro
Wood

Hearnton Wood

Averingdown
Farm

BRADENHAM RD

The
Old Rectory

Wks

A4010

96

Pond Wood

BOTTOM RD

Chawley Manor
Farm

HP14

Nature
Reserve

Green End

GREEN END RD

HATCH LA

Chawley Green
Farm

LOXBORO HILL

2

Green End
Farm

Chawley Wood

Chorley Farm

Windyhaugh
House

West
Wycombe Hill

Plomer's
Bottom

Cockshoot
Farm

CHORLEY RD

95

Little Cockshoots
Wood

WEST WYCOMBE
HILL RD

Hellfires
Caves

P   PO

Sch

A40   HIGH ST

Liby

1

Fillingdon
Farm

A40

OLD DASHWOOD HILL

WYCOMBE RD

Ham Farm

Piddington

Great Cockshoots Wood

West
Wycombe

West
Wycombe
Pk

CHIPPS HILL

PH

PRINCES ST

QUEEN ST

KING ST

OLD OXFORD RD

PIDDINGTON LA

1 TUDOR CT
2 GEORGE LEE CT

OXFORD RD

BULLOCKS FARM LA

Myze Farm

TOWERIDGE LA

WEST
WYCOMBE LA

High Wood

94

80   A   81   B   82   C

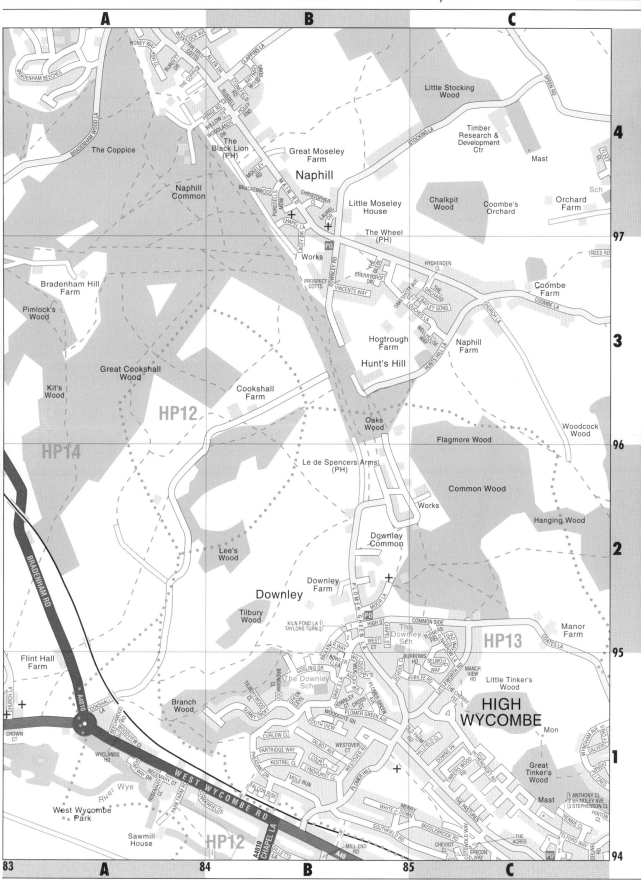

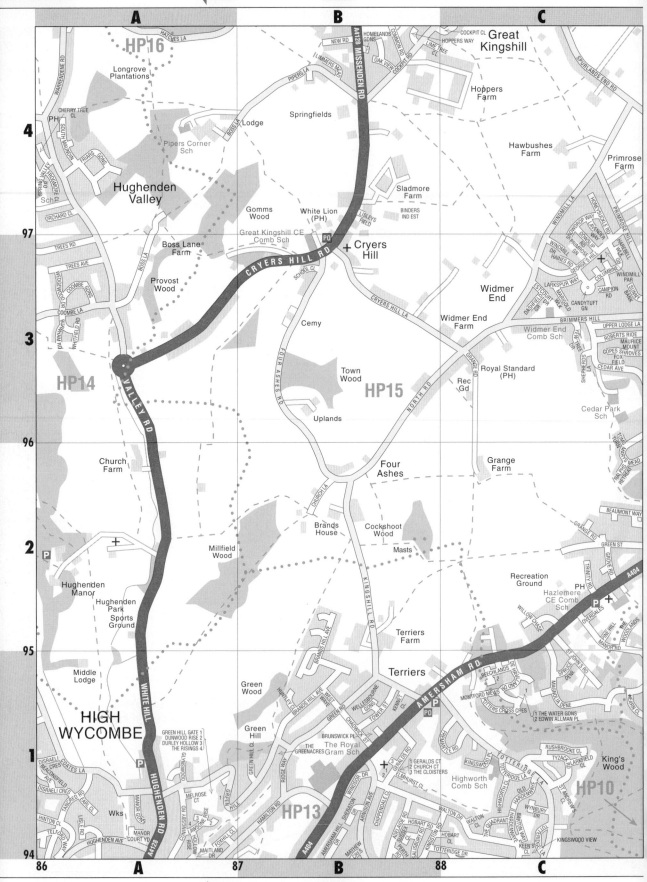

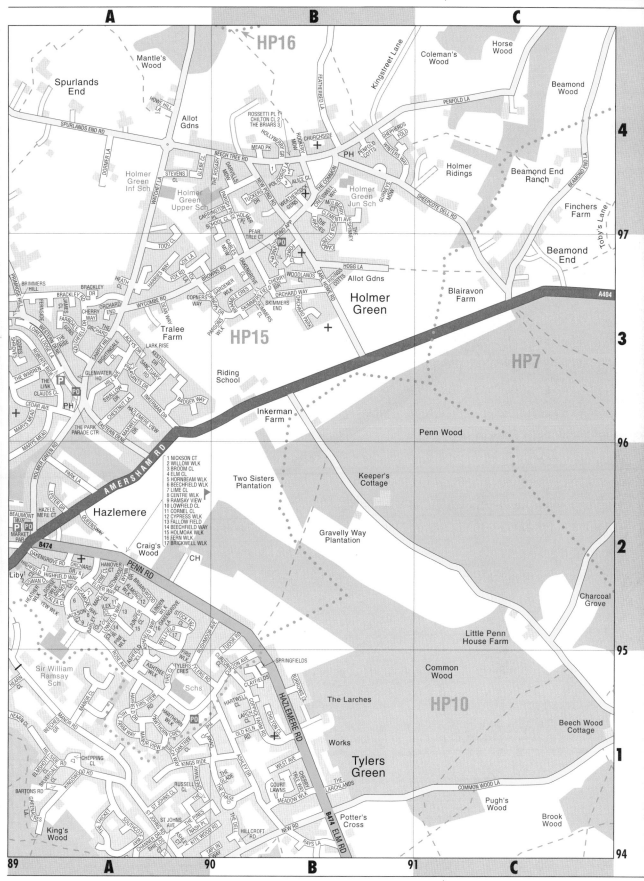

A
B
C

HP16

Spurlands End
Mantle's Wood

Allot Gdns

ROSSETTI PL 1
CHILTON CL 2
THE BRIARS 3

Kingstreet Lane

Coleman's Wood

Horse Wood

Beamond Wood

4

SPURLANDS END RD

HOWE HILL LA

DORMER LA

WATCHET LA

Holmer Green Inf Sch

STEVENS CL

GLEBE CL

THE ROSARY

BEECH TREE RD

DARRELLS

MEAD PK

HOLLYBERRY GR

CHURCHSIDE

NEW POND RD

PARISH PIECE

SCHOOL LA

Holmer Green Upper Sch

TUCKERS DR

CARRINGTON

HIGH RD

HOLMER

ALICE CL

WEATHERBROOK GDNS

CRESSWELL

MULBERRY

PEAR TREE CT

POND APP

GABLES

OAKENGROVE

CHERRY GR

WOODLANDS

THE LARCHES

CLEMENTI AVE

THE SPINNEY

GUINEAS MDW

SHEEPCOTE DELL RD

PH

PENFOLD COTTS

WINTERS WAY

SHEPHERDS FOLD

Holmer Green Jun Sch

97

Holmer Ridings

Beamond End Ranch

Finchers Farm

Toby's Lane

Beamond End

A404

Holmer Green

Blairavon Farm

HP15

TODD CL

FOX RD

FOX LA

BROWNS RD

GARDENER WLK

BRAMBLE CRES

SKIMMERS CL

SKIMMERS END

ORCHARD PARK

ORCHARD WAY

EARL HOWE RD

RIDINGS COTTS

HOGG LA

Allot Gdns

HARRIES WAY

COPNERS WAY

WYCOMBE RD

COPNERS DR

PARSONS CR

CAMP

HP7

Tralee Farm

LARK RISE

Riding School

Inkerman Farm

Penn Wood

96

HEATH CL

BRACKLEY DR

ORCHARD END

CHERRY WAY

THE ORCHARD

LACEYS DR

SANCTUARY

KESTREL

PHEASANTS DR

HILL AVE

SWALLOW DR

BADGER WAY

INKERMAN DR

CHESTNUT LA

BRIMMERS HILL

BRACKLEY RD

FERNSIDE

JAMES CL

FARNDALE GDNS

SOUTHFIELD

GAWDT HILL

GLENWATER HO

NIGHTINGALE CL

MAXWELL DENE

HAZLEMERE VIEW

EASTERN DENE

PRIMROSE HILL

COPES RD

THE SHRUBS

THE WARREN

WESTERN DENE

ROBERTS RIDE

TOWER LODGE LA

MARYS MEAD

CEDAR AVE

CLAUDS CL

THE LINK

P

PO

PH

THE PARK PARADE CTR

Keeper's Cottage

1 NICKSON CT
2 WILLOW WLK
3 BROOM CL
4 ELM CL
5 HORNBEAM WLK
6 BEECHFIELD WLK
7 LIME CL
8 CENTRE WLK
9 RAMSAY VIEW
10 LOWFIELD CL
11 CORNEL CL
12 CYPRESS WLK
13 FALLOW FIELD
14 BEECHFIELD WAY
15 HOLMOAK WLK
16 FERN WLK
17 BRICKWELL WLK

Two Sisters Plantation

Gravelly Way Plantation

AMERSHAM RD

Hazlemere

HOLMER GREEN RD

PARK LA

LESTER GR

QUEENSWAY

HAZEL MERE CT

BEAUMONT WAY

P

PO

MARKET PAR

B474

Lib/

DAKENGROVE LA

HIGHFIELD DR

HIGHFIELD WAY

PENN RD

HANOVER CT

CEDARWOOD

BRIARSWOOD

RICHMONDS

Craig's Wood

CH

Little Penn House Farm

Charcoal Grove

2

ROWAN CL

HEATHER CL

AZALEA CL

SYCAMORE WAY

BARLEY

JACKSON LA

YEW WLK

MAPLE CL

ILEX CL

LABURNUM WAY

OAKENGROVE CL

LINDEN CL

WELFIELD

STOCK PL

PINE WLK

ROSE AVE

LOWFIELD WAY

ASHFIELD

FIRS CL

ASHTREE WLK

TUDOR RD

RUSHMOOR AVE

JUNIPER CL

Common Wood

HP10

Sir William Ramsay Sch

HEARN CL

HEARN CL

MANOR CL

BEECHES DR

MANOR RD

MANOR VIEW

FIRS VIEW

HAYFIELD RD

TYLERS CRES

TYLERS RD

PLYERS CL

CURZON AVE

SPRINGFIELDS

CLAYFIELDS

BURROWS CL

HARTWELL

LARCH CL

COPPICE FARM RD

CHILTON

The Larches

95

1

KING'S WOOD

BARTONS RD

GREENACRES LA

HILLSIDE RD

SILVERDALE RD

KINGSWOOD RD

CHEPPING CL

THE THICKET

SOUTHCOTE

CHANNELS DR

KITE WOOD RD

HAWTHORN WLK

HAWTHORN CRES

FARM WAY

BIRCH

OAKTREE

KINGS RIDE

HAWTHORN DR

THE GLADE

THE CHASE

MEADOW WLK

RUSSELL CL

THE PINES

ST JOHNS CL

ST JOHNS AVE

MASH PL

ASHER

HILLCROFT RD

TAPLIN

RAYS LA

WEST AVE

COURT LAWNS

CHERRY TREE WAY

NEW RD

HAZLEMERE RD

THE LARCHLANDS

Works

Tylers Green

Potter's Cross

B474 ELM RD

COMMON WOOD LA

Pugh's Wood

Beech Wood Cottage

Brook Wood

94

89
A
90
B
91
C

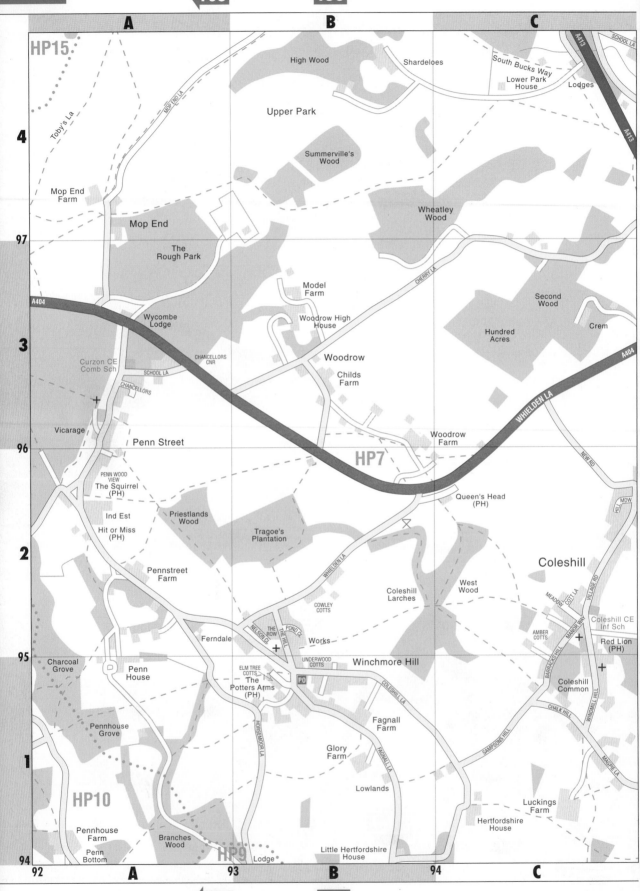

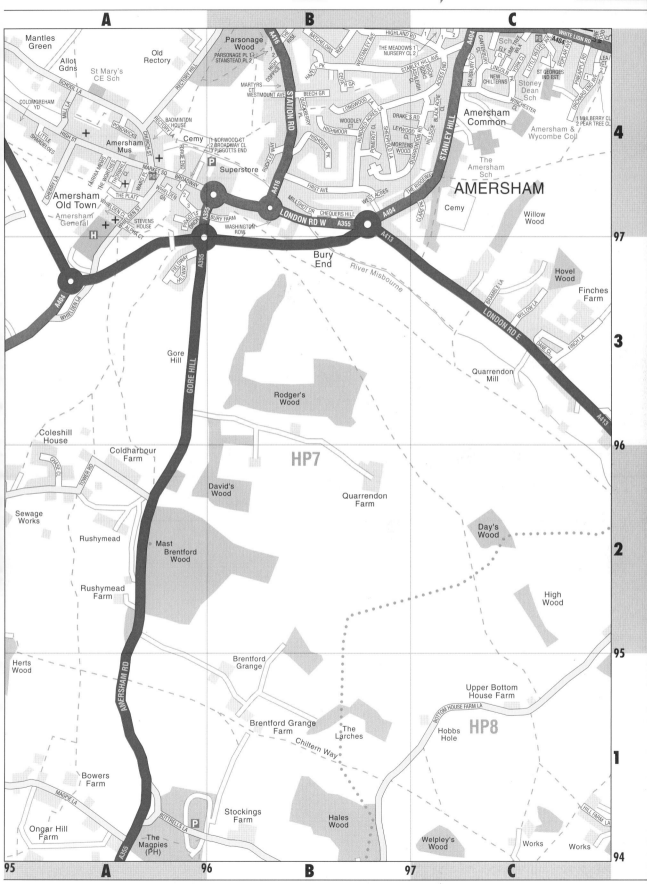

Mantles Green
Allot Gdns
Old Rectory
St Mary's CE Sch
COLDMOREHAM YD
SCHOOL LA
MILL LA
HIGH ST
LITTLE SHARDELOES
CHERRY LA
PONDWICKS
RECTORY HILL
CHURCH ST
RECTORY LA
BADMINTON HOUSE
Cemy
Amersham Mus
Amersham Old Town
Amersham General
H
FAIRFAX MEWS
THE WORTHIES
THE DRILL
MARKET SQ
PO
WARD PL
FORGE END
WHIELDEN GN
WHIELDEN CL
WHIELDEN ST
THE PLATT
Stevens House
ALPHA CT
PIGGOTTS ORCH
BROADWAY
BURY FARM
A355
P
Washington Row
FELLWAY
ALLWAY

Parsonage Wood
STATION RD
A416
THE RISE
PARSONAGE PL 1
STANSTEAD PL 2
HIGH COPPICE
MARTYRS CT
WESTMOUNT AVE
WOODLEY CT
HUNDRED ACRES LA
HIGHMOOR
HIGHOVER PK
QUICKBERRY
BEECH GR
HAZEL PK
CEDA
GR GR
LONGWOOD
FIRST AVE
CHEQUERS HILL
MILLSHOT DR
BUCKLEY WAY
1 NORWOOD CT
2 BROADWAY CL
3 PIGGOTTS END
Superstore
LONDON RD W
A355
1 2

BATCHELORS WAY
HIGHLAND RD
WESTANLEY AVE
THE MEADOWS 1
NURSERY CL 2
STANLEY HILL AVE
ASHLEIGH GDNS
ACRES END
DRAKES RD
POMEROY CL
SHEPPARDS LA
LEYWOOD CL
MORTENS WOOD
QUARRENDON RD
THE RIDGEWAY
CLARE PK
WEST ACRES
A404
A413

Sch
CANTERBURY CT
SALISBURY CT
ELY CL
LINCOLN
YORK CL
WINCHESTER
LIME TREE WLK
LITTLE REEVES AVE
NEW CHILTERNS
ST GEORGES IND EST
WHITE LION RD
PO
A404
PINEAPPLE RD
POPLAR AVE
ORCHARD END AVE
1 MULBERRY CL
2 PEAR TREE CL
LEA CT
Stoney Dean Sch
Amersham Common
Amersham & Wycombe Coll
The Amersham Sch
AMERSHAM
Cemy
Willow Wood

4

A404
WHIELDEN LA
A355
GORE HILL

97

Bury End
River Misbourne
LONDON RD E
Hovel Wood
Finches Farm
BRAMBLE LA
WILLOW LA
DANE CL
FINCH LA
Quarrendon Mill
A413

Gore Hill

3

Coleshill House
Coldharbour Farm
CHASE CL
TOWER RD
Sewage Works
Rushymead
Mast Brentford Wood
Rushymead Farm
Rodger's Wood
David's Wood
HP7
Quarrendon Farm
Day's Wood
High Wood

96

2

Herts Wood
AMERSHAM RD
A355
Brentford Grange
Brentford Grange Farm
The Larches
Chiltern Way
Upper Bottom House Farm
BOTTOM HOUSE FARM LA
Hobbs Hole
HP8

95

Bowers Farm
MAGPIE LA
BOTTRELLS LA
P
The Magpies (PH)
Stockings Farm
Hales Wood
Welpley's Wood
Works
Works
HILL FARM LA

1

Ongar Hill Farm
A355

94

165
155

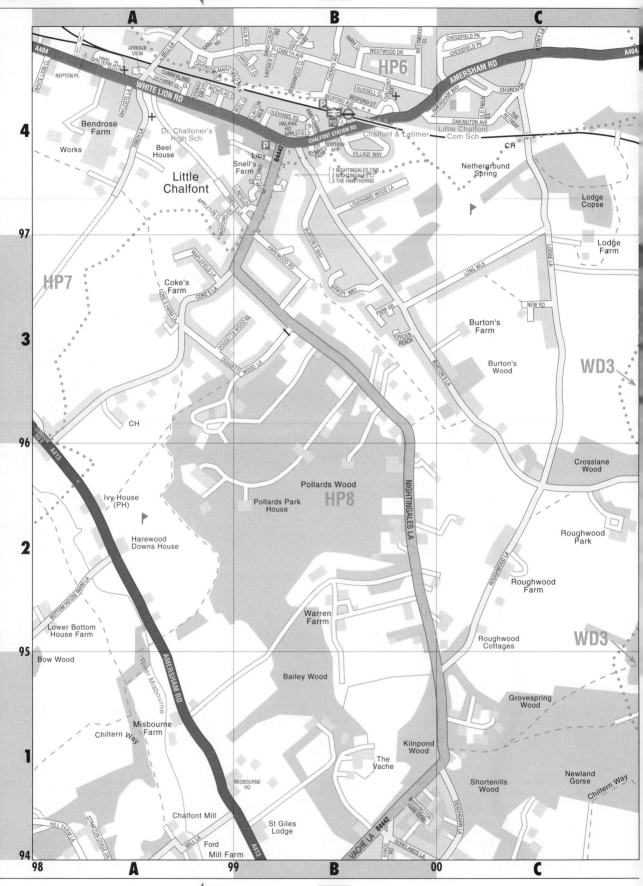

165
177

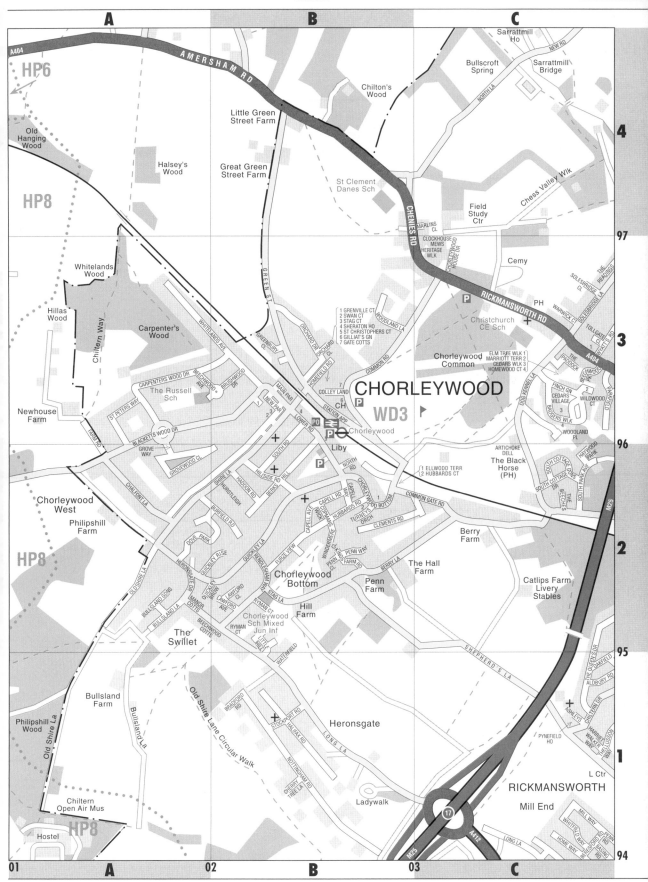

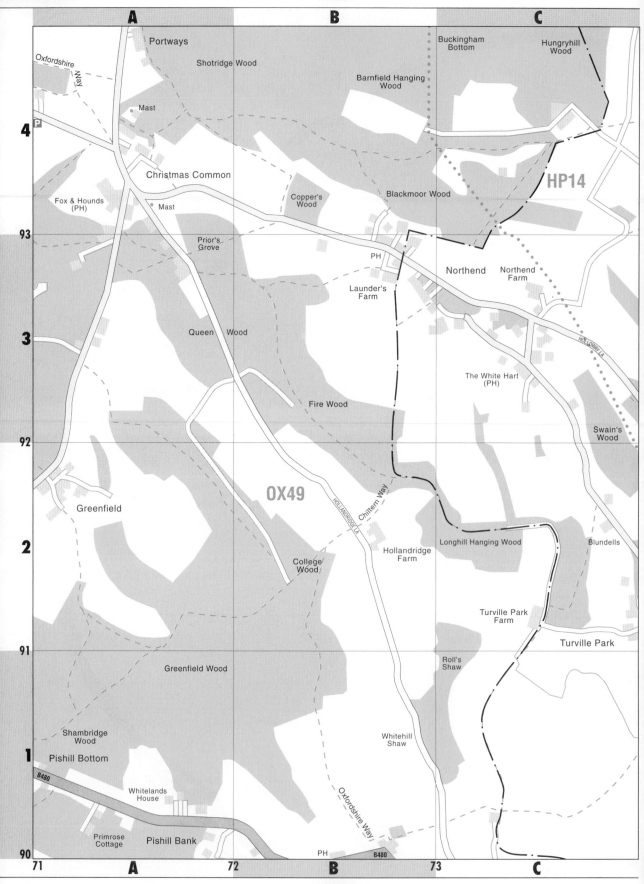

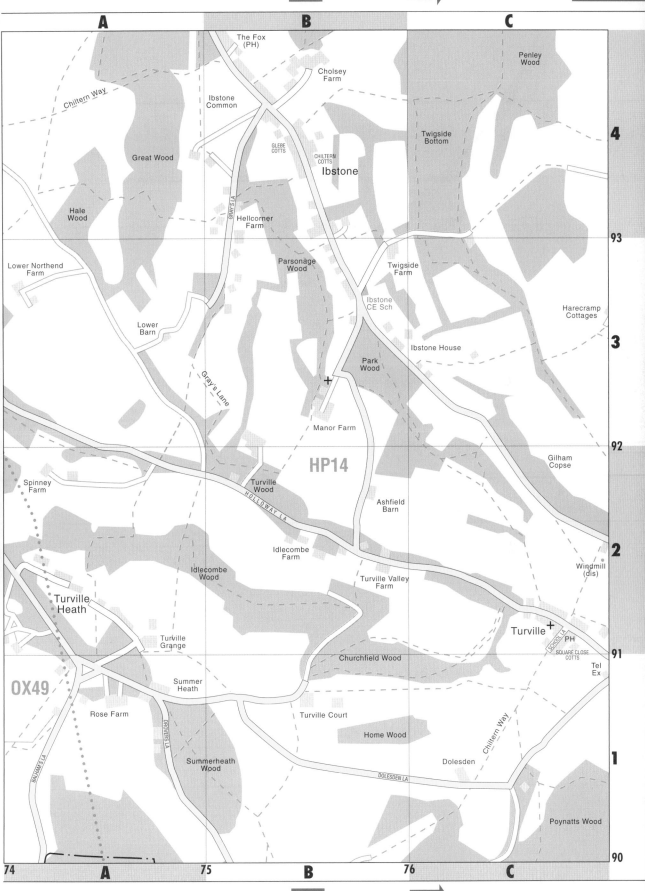

169
159

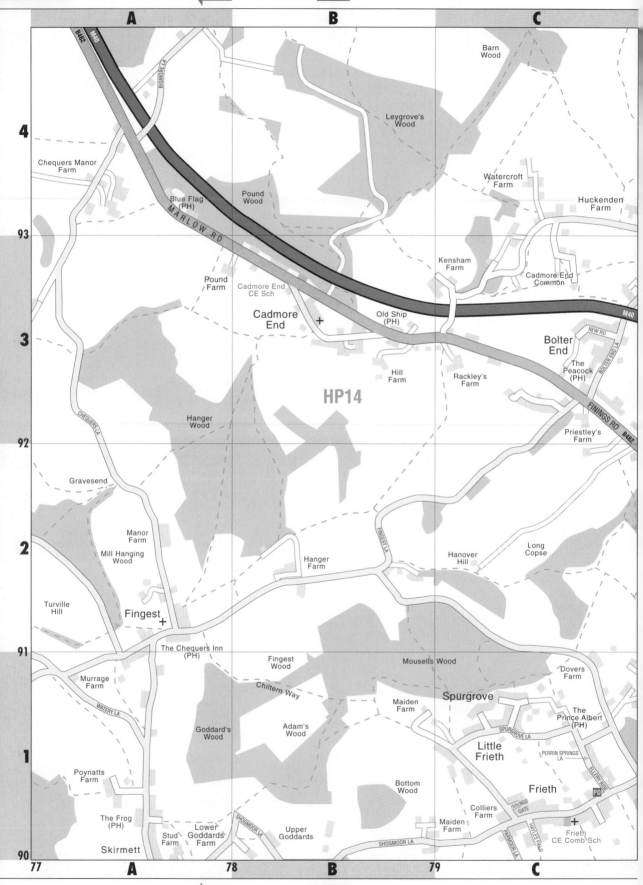

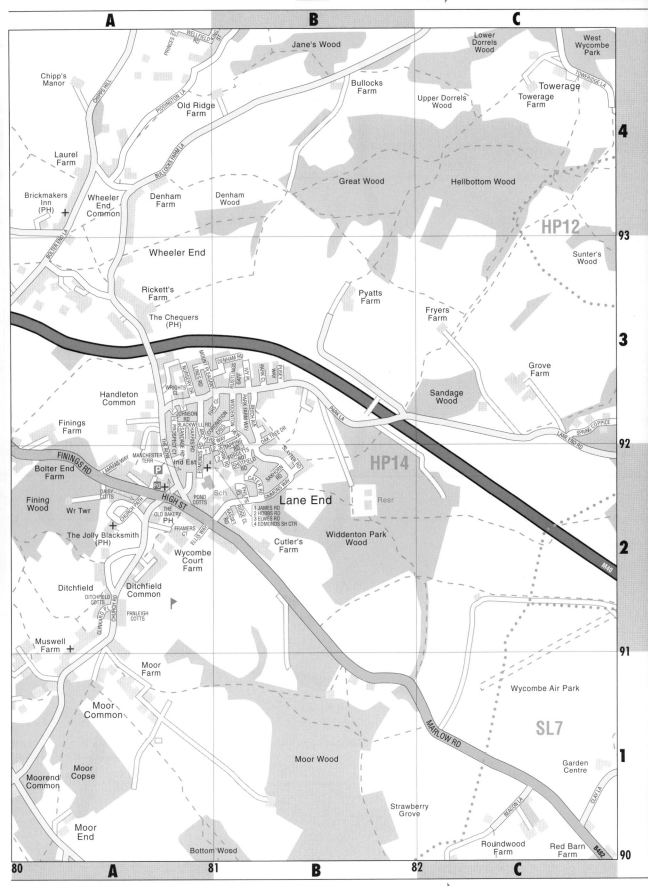

A · B · C

Chipp's
Manor

Jane's Wood

Lower
Dorrels
Wood

West
Wycombe
Park

TOWERIDGE LA

Towerage

Bullocks
Farm

Towerage
Farm

Upper Dorrels
Wood

Old Ridge
Farm

PIDDINGTON LA

BULLOCKS FARM LA

CHIPPS HILL

Laurel
Farm

4

Great Wood

Hellbottom Wood

93

Brickmakers
Inn
(PH)

Wheeler
End
Common

Denham
Farm

Denham
Wood

HP12

Sunter's
Wood

BOLTER END LA

Wheeler End

Rickett's
Farm

Pyatts
Farm

Fryers
Farm

3

The Chequers
(PH)

Grove
Farm

Handleton
Common

DENHAM RD

MOUNT PLEASANT

NURSERY DR

LINES RD

IVY PL

PARK CL

PUSEY WAY

Sandage
Wood

Finings
Farm

WRIGHTS CL

JOHNSON RD

FRS CL

WIDDENTON

PARK FARM WAY

BEECH AVE

PARK LA

92

FININGS RD

PROSPECT CL

BLACKWELL RD

HARRIS RD

EDMONDS RD

RYERS WAY

CORONATION CRES

TAPPING RD

THORNE RD

FORGETTS RD

OAK TREE DR

HP14

Bolter End
Farm

THE ROW

LAMMAS WAY

MANCHESTER
TERR

Ind Est

SHOTFIELD RD

SLATER RD

SAXRON RD

Fining
Wood

DAISY
COTTS

P

PO

HIGH ST

SCH

Sch

PHIL PS

CATER RD

SIMMONS WAY

Lane End

Resr

Wr Twr

CHURCH PATH

CHURCH RD

THE
OLD BAKERY
PH

POND
COTTS

RIDGE CL

BASSET

1 JAMES RD
2 HOBBS RD
3 ELWES RD
4 EDMONDS SH CTR

Widdenton Park
Wood

The Jolly Blacksmith
(PH)

FRAMERS
CT

ELLIS WAY

Cutler's
Farm

2

Ditchfield

Wycombe
Court
Farm

DITCHFIELD
COTTS

Ditchfield
Common

Muswell
Farm

CLINKARD PL

PANLEIGH
COTTS

91

Moor
Farm

Wycombe Air Park

SL7

Moor
Common

MARLOW RD

Moor
Copse

Moor Wood

Garden
Centre

1

Moorend
Common

BEACON LA

Strawberry
Grove

CLAY LA

B492

Moor
End

Bottom Wood

Roundwood
Farm

Red Barn
Farm

90

80 · A · 81 · B · 82 · C

171 161

C4
1 COTSWOLD CT
2 VICTORIA CT
3 ELLIOTT HO
4 DILWYN CT
5 PENDRILL HO
6 BARCLAY CT
7 GILBERT HO
8 CHILTERN CT
9 CUTLER'S CT
10 CARRINGTON CT
11 RIVERSIDE BSNS CTR
12 HAYDEN HO

A   B   C

HP13

WEST WYCOMBE RD

Park Farm

Millbrook Comb Sch

River Wye

Toweridge Lane   Mast

Sands Wood   Sands

Desborough Castle

Castlefield Wood

Adams Park

Sunter's Wood

Round Wood

Rowliff Wood

Liby

Oakridge Sch

ARCHDALE

BRIDLE GATE

High Barber's Wood

HP14

Spring Coppice

Booker Hill Sch

Castlefield Sch

Five Acre Wood

HP12

HIGH WYCOMBE

HP11
Wycombe High Sch

Booker Common

Booker

Recn Gd

Cressex

Chiltern Gate Sch

Verney Ave Sch

Blenheim

John Hampden Gram Sch

Sports Ctr

TA Ctr

Cressex Com Sch

Holmers Farm

JOHN HALL WAY

Hotel

Superstore

Blue Max Mus

Wycombe Air Park

Clay Lane Farm

The Blacksmiths Arms (PH)

Handy Cross Farm

SL7

Reading Shaw

Hill Green

Old House Farm

Ragman's Castle

HP10

Redhouse Farm

Hillgreen Wood

Hollyhill Wood

Refuse Destructor

Monkton Cottage

83   A   84   B   85   C

171 183

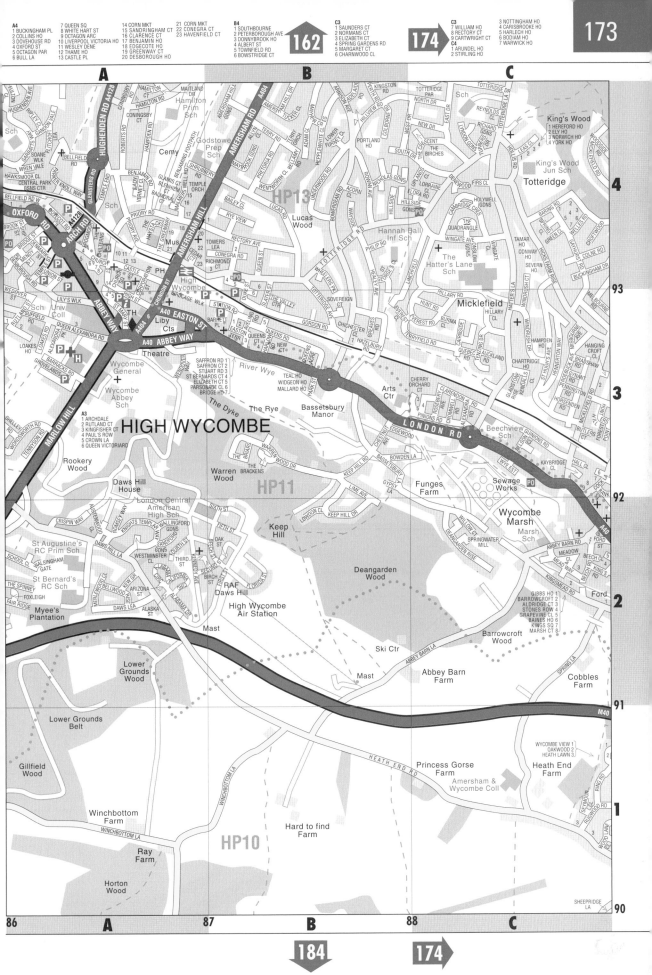

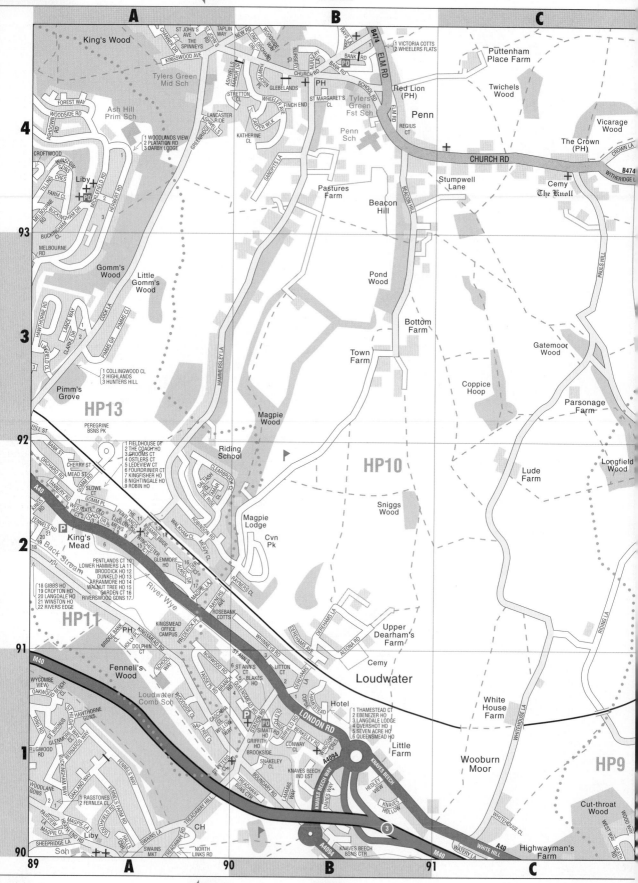

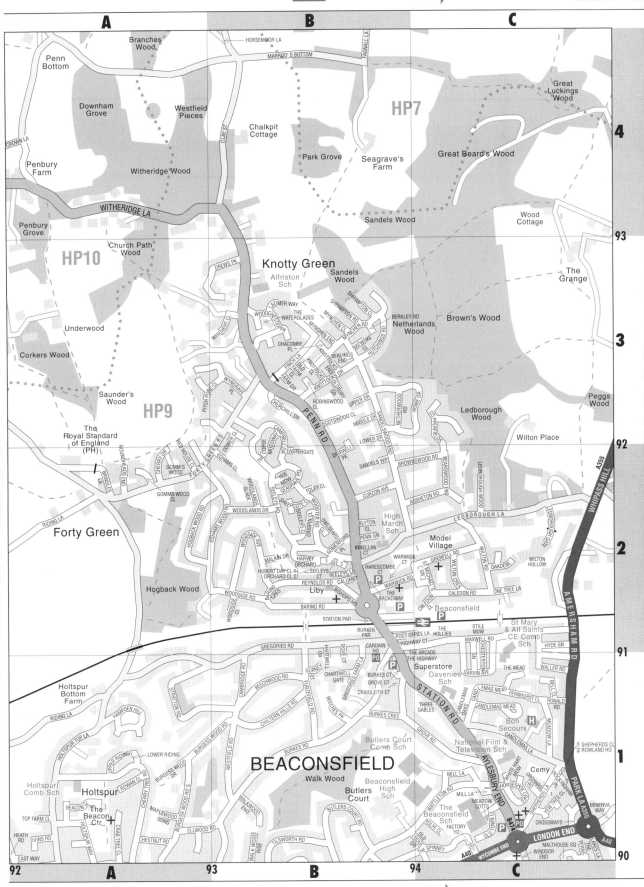

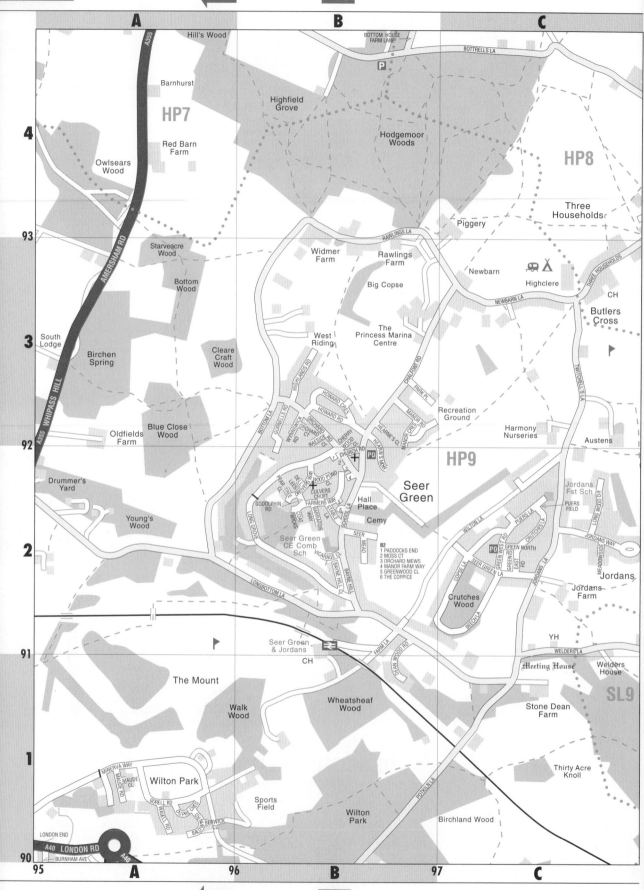

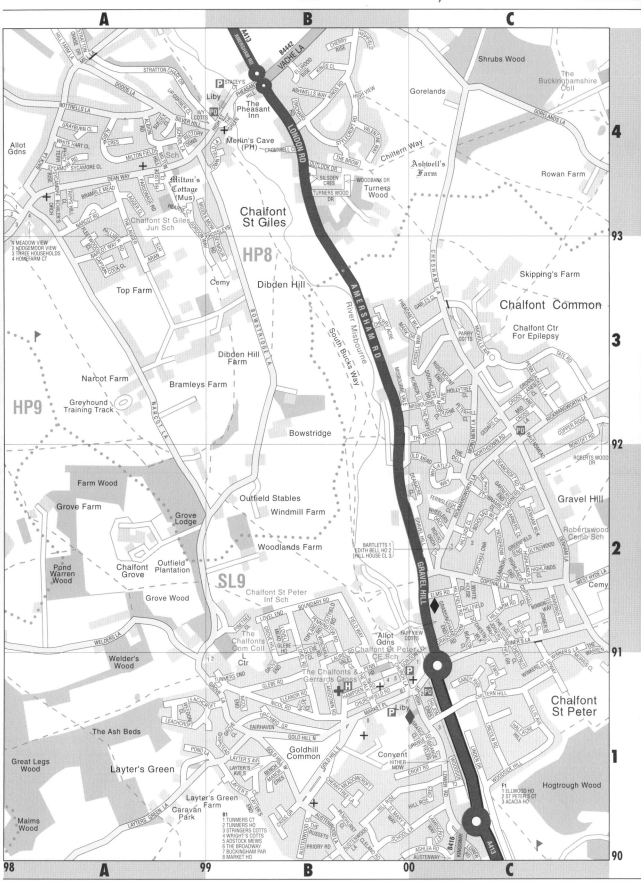

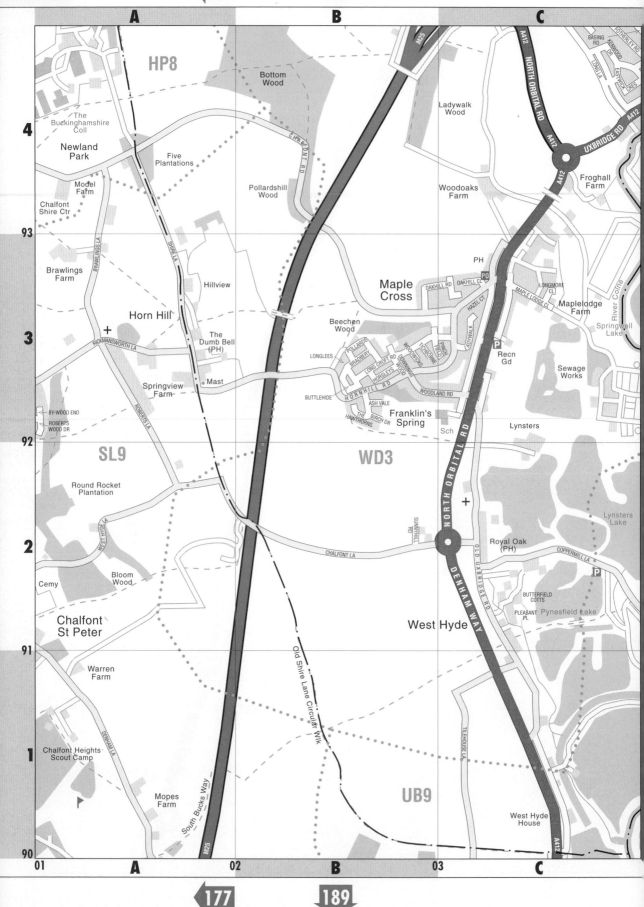

A

B

C

Pishill Bank

Bank Farm

Pishill

Long Wood

Pishill House

B480

B480

CHURCH HILL

HOLLANDRIDGE LA

BALHAMS LA

Balhams' Farmhouse

OX49

The Warren

4

Nuttall's Farm

Doyley Wood

Pishillbury Wood

Whitepond Farm

89

Upper Maidensgrove

Russell's Water Common

Maidensgrove Farm

The Round Clump

Stonor

Five Horseshoes (PH)

Little Cookley Hill

PARK LA

Oak Farm

Park Wood

Stonor Arms (Hotel)

3

Maidensgrove

Chiltern Way

Almshill Wood

Hatch Lane

Big Ashes Plantation

Lodge Farm

Rowdow

Upper Assendon Farm

Nature Trail

Warburg Nature Reserve

Great Hill

88

Pages Bottom

Maidensgrove Scrubs

Kitesgrove Wood

Pages Farm

P

Stockings Plantation

RG9

Soundess Wood

Freedom Wood

The Firfields

2

Oxfordshire Way

Soundess House

Warmscombe La

Bix Bottom

87

St Jame's Church (remains of)

Crocker End

Wellgrove Wood

Valley Farm

Bix Bottom

Paradise Wood

Halfridge Wood

1

A4130

RECTORY LA

Halfridge Gate

Coney Burrow

Bix

Little Bixbottom Farm

B480

86

1

A

72

B

73

C

A

B

C

4

Balhams's Wood

Chiltern Way

Drovers

DROVERS LA

Southend

Southend Farm

Binfield Bottom

Great Wood

HP14

Stonor House

OX49

Kildridge Wood

Kimble Farm

Old Luxters Farm Brewery

DUDLEY LA

89

Stonor Park (Deer Park)

Gussetts Wood

Jubilee Plantation

Henleyhill Wood

3

Coxlease Farm

Upper Woodend Farm

Woodcocks Bill

88

Bosmore Farm

Hanging Wood

Lower Woodend Farm

2

Jubilee Plantation

RG9

Roundhouse Farm

Highfield Plantation

The Walnut Tree (PH)

Great Wood Ho

Great Wood

87

Jackson's Farm

Fawley Bottom

Fawley Green Farm

Red Hill

Fawley Bottom Farm House

Fawley

1

Kitchener's Firs

FAWLEY BOTTOM LA

DOBSON'S LA

BENHAMS LA

Pallbach Hill

Eversdown

Benhams

Brackenhill Stud Farm

86

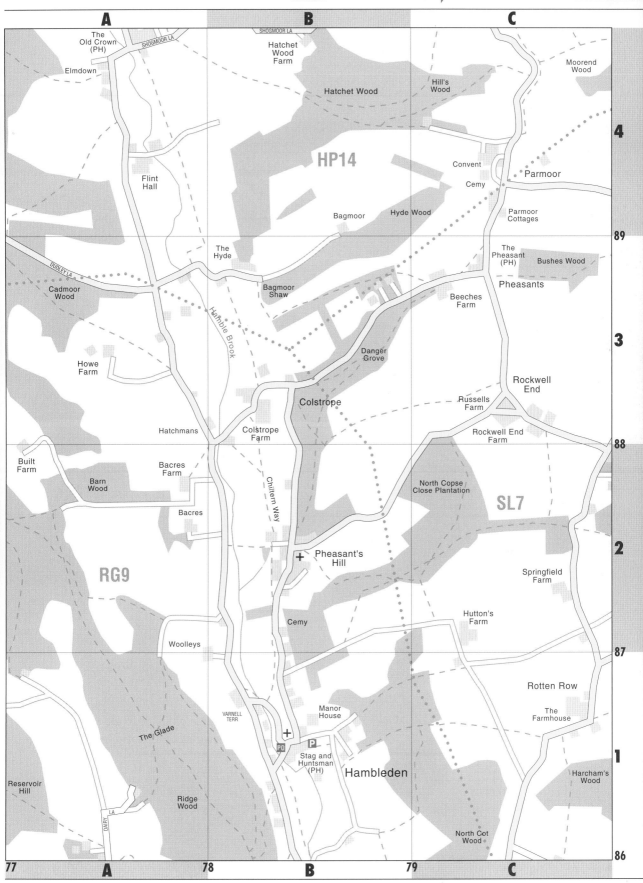

A **B** **C**

The
Old Crown
(PH)
SHOGMOOR LA
SHOGMOOR LA

Elmdown

Hatchet
Wood
Farm

Moorend
Wood

Hill's
Wood

Hatchet Wood

4

Flint
Hall

HP14

Convent

Parmoor

Cemy

Parmoor
Cottages

Bagmoor

Hyde Wood

89

The
Hyde

The
Pheasant
(PH)

Bushes Wood

DUDLEY LA

Cadmoor
Wood

Bagmoor
Shaw

Pheasants

Beeches
Farm

3

Hamble Brook

Danger
Grove

Howe
Farm

Rockwell
End

Colstrope

Russells
Farm

Hatchmans

Colstrope
Farm

Rockwell End
Farm

88

Built
Farm

Bacres
Farm

North Copse
Close Plantation

SL7

Barn
Wood

Bacres

Chiltern Way

2

RG9

+ Pheasant's
Hill

Springfield
Farm

Woolleys

Cemy

Hutton's
Farm

87

Rotten Row

VARNELL
TERR

Manor
House

The
Farmhouse

The Glade

+
PO

P

1

Reservoir
Hill

Stag and
Huntsman
(PH)

Hambleden

Harcham's
Wood

DAIRY LA

Ridge
Wood

North Cot
Wood

86

77 **A** **78** **B** **79** **C**

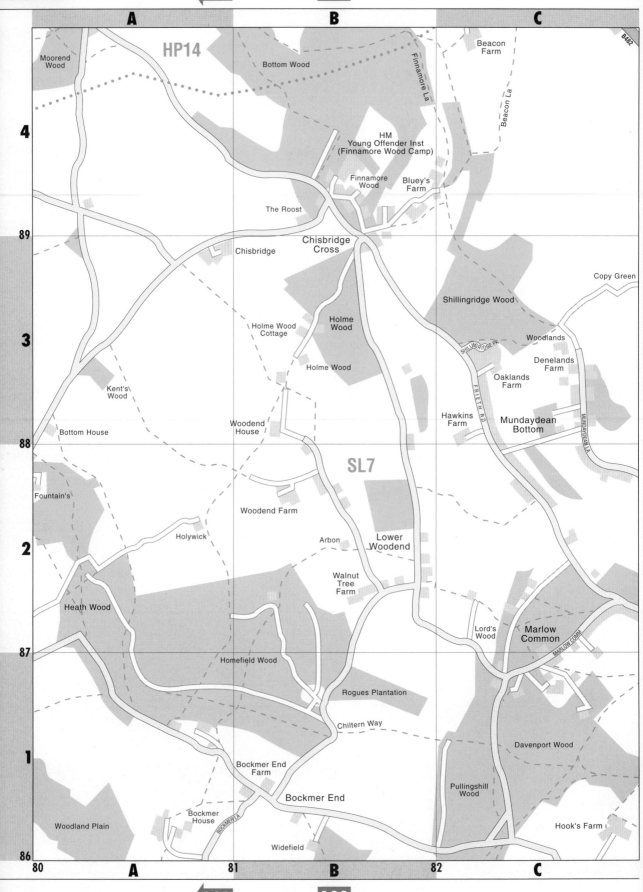

HP14

Moorend Wood

Bottom Wood

Finnamore La

Beacon Farm

Beacon La

B482

HM
Young Offender Inst
(Finnamore Wood Camp)

Finnamore Wood

Bluey's Farm

The Roost

4

Chisbridge Cross

89

Chisbridge

Copy Green

Shillingridge Wood

Holme Wood Cottage

Holme Wood

Woodlands

SHILLINGRIDGE PK

Denelands Farm

3

Holme Wood

Oaklands Farm

Kent's Wood

FRIETH RD

MUNDAYDEAN LA

Bottom House

Woodend House

Hawkins Farm

Mundaydean Bottom

88

Fountain's

SL7

Woodend Farm

Holywick

Arbon

Lower Woodend

2

Walnut Tree Farm

Heath Wood

Lord's Wood

Marlow Common

MARLOW COMM

87

Homefield Wood

Rogues Plantation

Chiltern Way

Davenport Wood

1

Bockmer End Farm

Pullingshill Wood

Hook's Farm

Bockmer End

Bockmer House

BOCKMER LA

Woodland Plain

Widefield

86

80   **A**   81   **B**   82   **C**

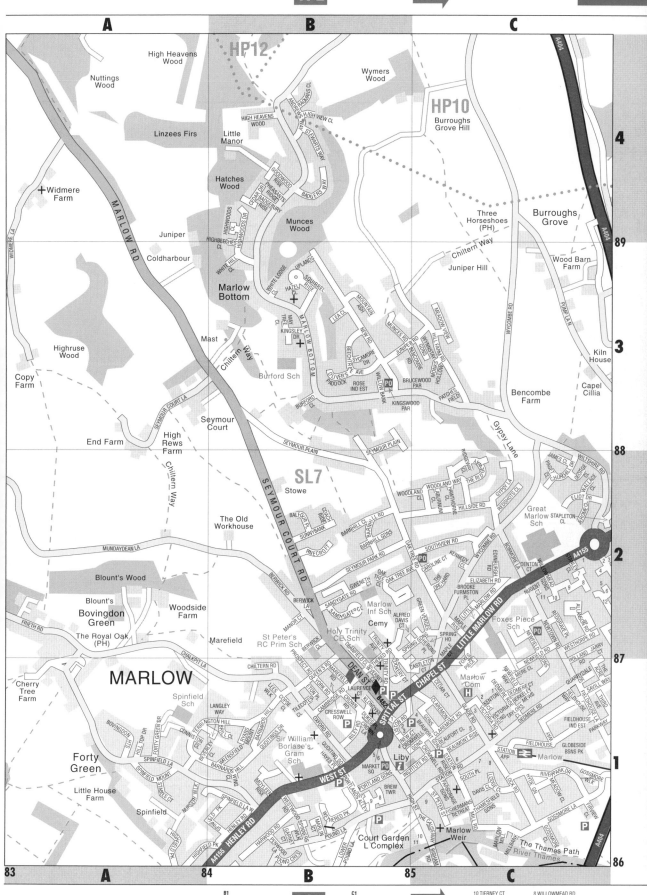

172 184

A B C

HP12

HP10

4

89

3

88

2

87

1

SL7

MARLOW

194 184

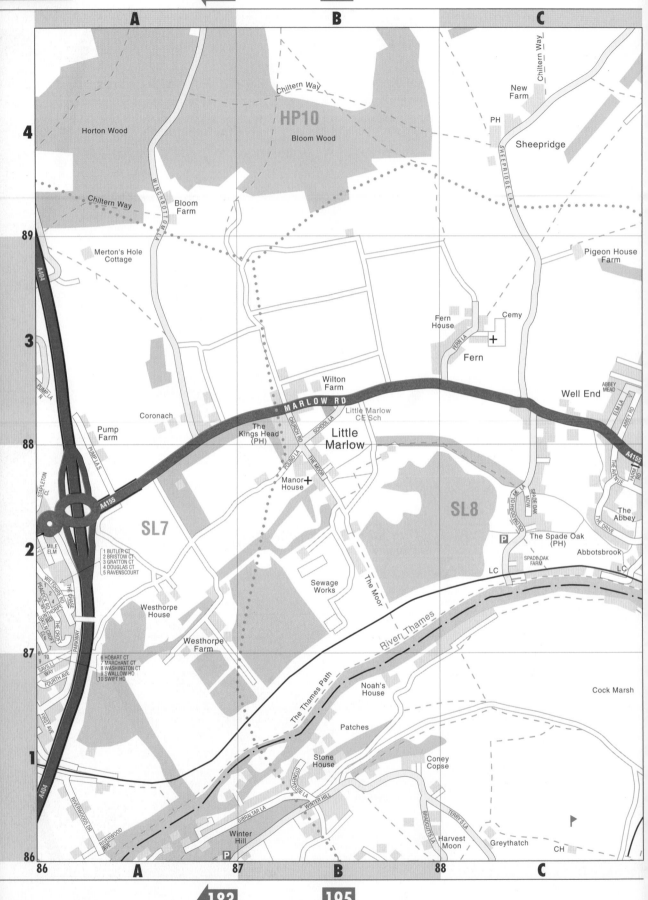

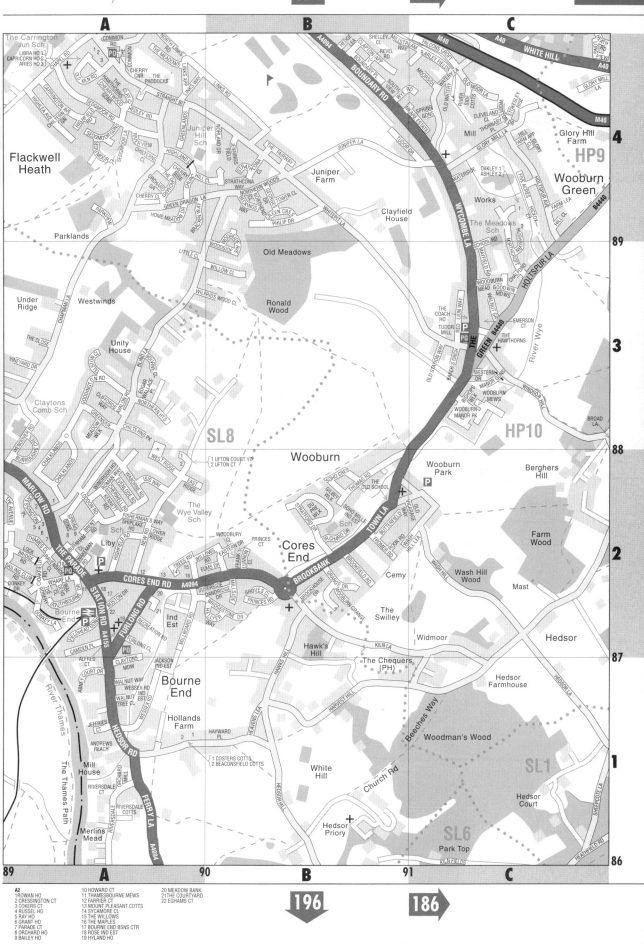

A2
1 ROWAN HO
2 CRESSINGTON CT
3 COKERS CT
4 RUSSEL HO
5 RAY HO
6 GRANT HO
7 PARADE CT
8 ORCHARD HO
9 BAILEY HO
10 HOWARD CT
11 THAMESBOURNE MEWS
12 FARRIER CT
13 MOUNT PLEASANT COTTS
14 SYCAMORE CL
15 THE WILLOWS
16 THE MAPLES
17 BOURNE END BSNS CTR
18 ROSE IND EST
19 HYLAND HO
20 MEADOW BANK
21 THE COURTYARD
22 EGHAMS CT

176
188

A
B
C

BURNHAM AVE

A355
A40

HEDGERLEY LA

LONDON RD

PYEBUSH LA

POTKIL N LA

Birchland Wood

Stampwell Farm

Lower Pyebushes

Pyebushes

OXFORD RD

Birch Wood

4

Hyde Farm

Hotel

HP9

Wapsey's Wood

Further Warren Wood

SL9

89

Green Broom

Works

A40

Burtley Wood

Bower Wood Cotts

Cave Wood

HEDGERLEY LA

3

Hillmotts Farm

Birchen Spring Coppice

Moat Farm

Slade Wood

Slade Farm

WAPSEYS LA

M40

88

BEACONSFIELD COMMON LA

Bower Wood

Hillmotts Furze

Manor Farm

Hedgerley Green

Dorney Bottom

SL1

DORNEY HILL S

Mount Pleasant Farm

Sutton's Wood

VILLAGE LA

Nature Reserve

Leith Grove

2

Pennlands Wood

Hedgerley

White Horse (PH)

THE CHURCH HOLT

Church Wood

Pennlands Farm

SL2

ANDREW HILL LA

KILN LA

Court Farm

HAREMATCH LA

87

Summerlins Wood

The Yew Tree (PH)

Kiln Wood

Brick Mould (PH)

Kiln Wood

STEVENSON RD

GREGORY RD

ROBERT RD

ELKINS RD

JONES WAY

GYPSY WAY

COTTAGE PARK RD

HEDGERLEY HILL

PO

Hanging Wood

Hedgerley Hill

Hedgerley Park

OLD NURSERY CT

COLINSWOOD RD

Egypt Woods

Heathfield Wood

EGYPT LA

HOLLYBUSH CNR

PARISH LA

One Pin Farm

LONGFIELD

1

EGYPT WOOD COTTS

COLINSWOOD

CHRISTMAS LA

School Wood

The One Pin (PH)

ONE PIN LA

WOOD END CL

COLLUM GREEN RD

GYPSY LA

Hedgerley Park Farm

COLLEY HILL LA

WOODLANDS GLADE

HEATHERSIDE GDNS

ROMSEY DR

STOKE WOOD

A355

86

95
96
97

A
B
C

198
188

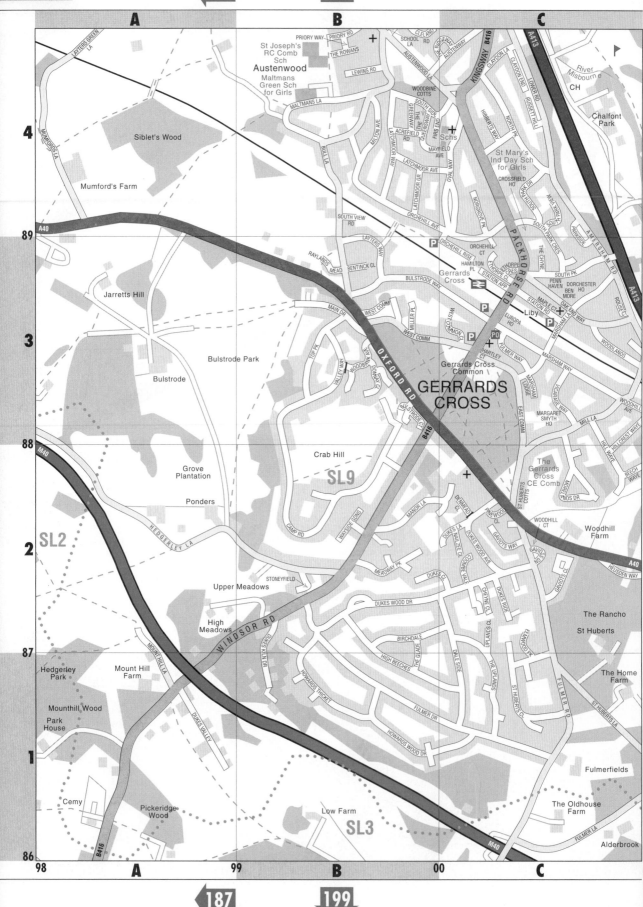

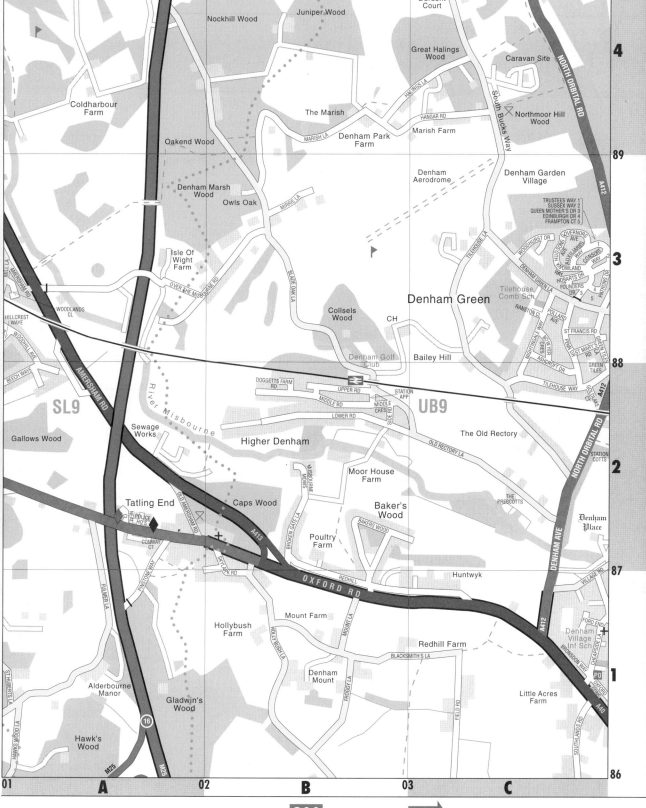

A
B
C

Chalfont Lodge

Denham La

Nockhill Wood

Juniper Wood

Tile House

Durdent Court

Great Halings Wood

Caravan Site

M25

Coldharbour Farm

The Marish

Halings La

Hangar Rd

Marish Farm

South Bucks Way

Northmoor Hill Wood

NORTH ORBITAL RD

A412

Oakend Wood

Marish La

Denham Park Farm

Denham Aerodrome

Denham Garden Village

Denham Marsh Wood

Owls Oak

Mirrie La

TRUSTEES WAY 1
SUSSEX WAY 2
QUEEN MOTHER'S DR 3
EDINBURGH DR 4
FRAMPTON CT 5

Isle Of Wight Farm

Over The Misbourne Rd

Slade Oak La

Tilehouse La

Woodhurst Dr

Governors Ave

Hudsons Ave

Vaux Ways

Knowland

Congord Way

Denham Green La

Hobarts Dr

Founders Dr

Patrons Dr

Amersham Rd

Collsels Wood

Denham Green

Tilehouse Comb Sch

Ranston Cl

Pollard Ave

St Francis Rd

Nightingale Way

Bowyer Cres

First Mary's La

Green Tiles

Ashcroft Dr

Green Tiles

HILLCREST WAYE

WOODLANDS CL

CH

Denham Golf Club

Bailey Hill

Tilehouse Way

Oaklake

WOOHILL AVE

BEECH WAYE

River Misbourne

DOGGETTS FARM RD

UPPER RD

STATION APP

MIDDLE RD

MIDDLE CRES

SIDE RD

UB9

SL9

Gallows Wood

Sewage Works

Higher Denham

LOWER RD

The Old Rectory

Old Rectory La

STATION COTTS

Tatling End

Caps Wood

Misbourne Mdws

Moor House Farm

THE PRESCOTTS

Denham Place

POLICE NR HQ'S

CONWAY CT

Baker's Wood

BAKERS WOOD

DENHAM AVE

A413

BROKEN GATE LA

Poultry Farm

Huntwyk

VILLAGE RD

PINSTONE WAY

OXFORD RD

REDHILL

FILMER LA

Hollybush Farm

HOLLY BUSH LA

Mount Farm

MOUNT LA

Redhill Farm

BLACKSMITH'S LA

FIELD RD

FORD END

CHEAPSIDE LA

Denham Village Inf Sch

BRONSDON WAY

Alderbourne Manor

Gladwin's Wood

Denham Mount

FROGGY LA

Little Acres Farm

PO

OXFORD RD

A40

16

Hawk's Wood

M25

ST HUBERTS LA

HAWKS WOOD LA

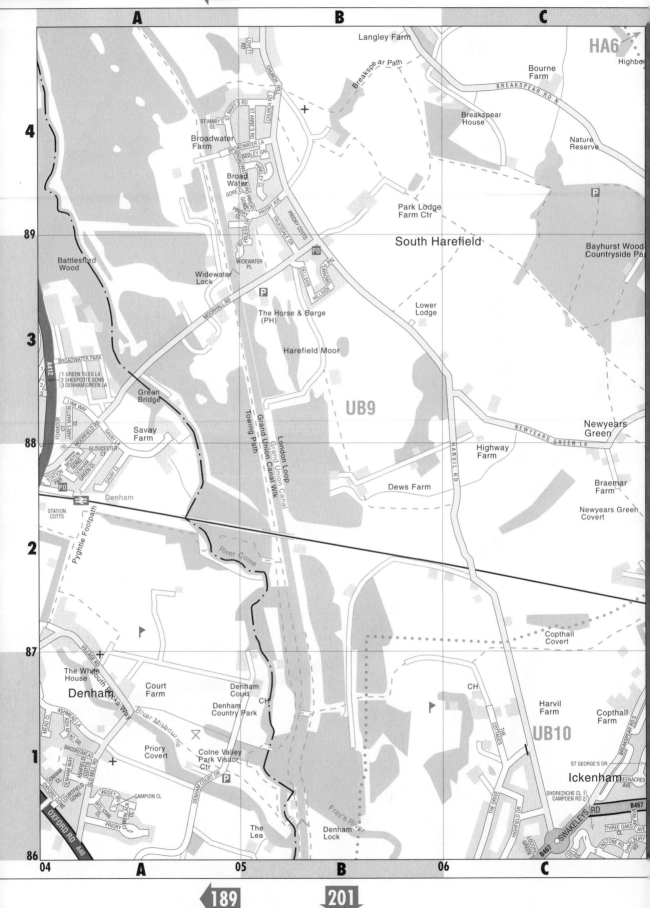

A   B   C

HA6

Highbor

4

89

3

88

2

87

1

86

04   A   05   B   06   C

Langley Farm

Breakspear Path

Bourne Farm

BREAKSPEAR RD N

Breakspear House

Nature Reserve

St Mary's Rd

CH HIGH RD

ST MARY'S CL

ST ANNE'S RD

Broadwater Farm

BROADWATER LA

SEDLEY GRI

SWKLEY CL

Broad Water

GORE CL

PRIORY GDNS

PRIORY AVE

PRIORY COTTS

TRUESDALE DR

Park Lodge Farm Ctr

P

South Harefield

Bayhurst Wood Countryside Par

Battlesford Wood

Widewater Lock

Widewater PL

PO

P

DELLSIDE

THE NARROWS

HILLSIDE

Lower Lodge

MOORHALL RD

The Horse & Barge (PH)

Harefield Moor

UB9

A412

Broadwater Park

1 GREEN TILES LA
2 SHEEPCOTE GDNS
3 DENHAM GREEN LA

Green Bridge

London Loop
Grand Union Canal Wlk

Grand Union Canal

Towing Path

NEWYEARS GREEN LA

Newyears Green

LINK WAY

JAMES MARTIN CL

FOXMOOR

MOORFIELD RD

SAVAY LA

Savay Farm

Highway Farm

HARVIL RD

Braemar Farm

MORTEN GDNS

GLOUCESTER CT

DENHAM GREEN CL

SAVAY CL

88

Dews Farm

Newyears Green Covert

Station Park

PO

Denham

STATION COTTS

Pyghtle Footpath

River Colne

Copthall Covert

2

87

Village Rd

The White House

SOUTH BUCKS WAY

Court Farm

River Misbourne

Denham

Denham Court

Denham Country Park

CH

CH

Harvil Farm

THE COTTAGES

Copthall Farm

UB10

ASHMEAD LA

ASH MEAD DR

Priory Covert

Colne Valley Park Visitor Ctr

DENHAM COURT DR

P

THE DRIVE

HIGHFIELD DR

Ickenham

St George's Dr

GREENACRES AVE

MEAD CL

ASHMEAD WAY

ASHFIELD CT

BACONSMEAD

FERNHAM CT

DENHAM WAY

OLD MILL RD

Campion Cl

LINDSEY RD

WOLSTAN CL

NEWLICK CL

Fray's River

SHOREDICHE CL 1
CAMPDEN RD 2

LOUDEL GREEN

SWAKELEYS RD

B467

B467

THREE OAKS CL

WINLATE CL

CHARLBURY RD

FENSTONE RD

OXFORD RD

A40

PRIORY CL

The Lea

Denham Lock

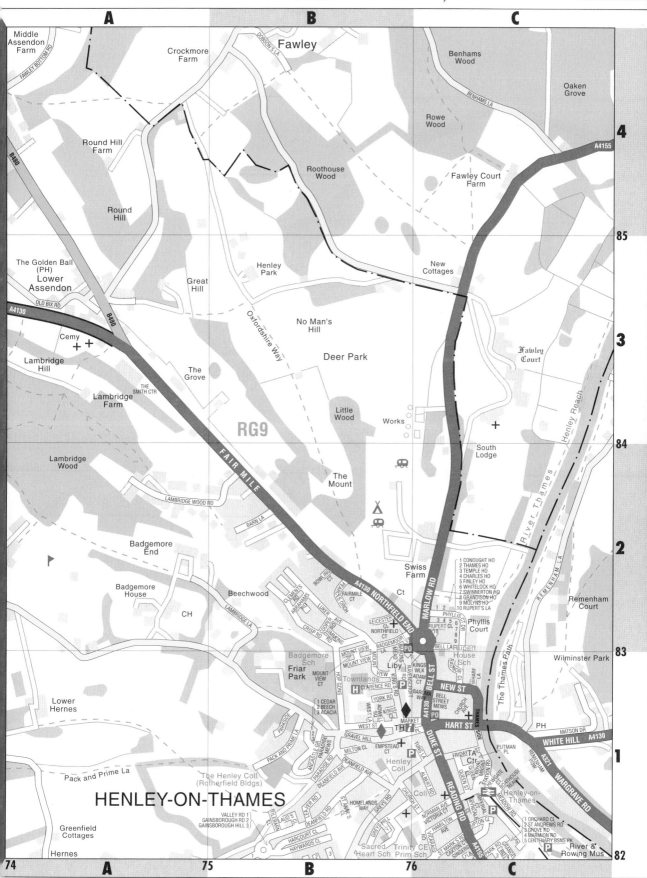

180
192
192

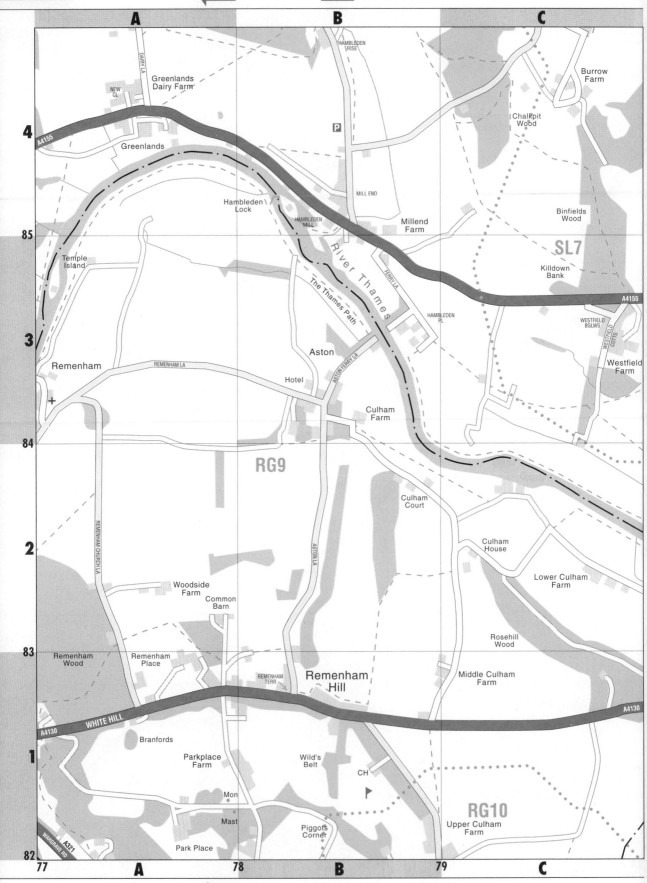

A B C

4

85

3

84

2

83

1

82

77 A 78 B 79 C

A4155

Greenlands
Dairy Farm

NEW
CL

DAIRY LA

Greenlands

HAMBLEDEN
RISE

P

MILL END

Hambleden
Lock

HAMBLEDEN
MILL

Millend
Farm

River Thames

FERRY LA

Temple
Island

The Thames Path

HAMBLEDEN
PL

Remenham

REMENHAM LA

Aston

ASTON FERRY LA

Hotel

Culham
Farm

SL7

Killdown
Bank

A4155

WESTFIELD
BGLWS

WESTFIELD
COTTS

Westfield
Farm

Burrow
Farm

Chalkpit
Wood

Binfields
Wood

RG9

Culham
Court

REMENHAM CHURCH LA

Woodside
Farm

Common
Barn

ASTON LA

Culham
House

Lower Culham
Farm

Remenham
Wood

Remenham
Place

REMENHAM
TERR

Remenham
Hill

Middle Culham
Farm

Rosehill
Wood

A4130

WHITE HILL

A4130

A4130

Branfords

Parkplace
Farm

Wild's
Belt

CH

RG10

Upper Culham
Farm

Mon

Mast

Piggots
Corner

Park Place

WARGRAVE RD

A321

182
194

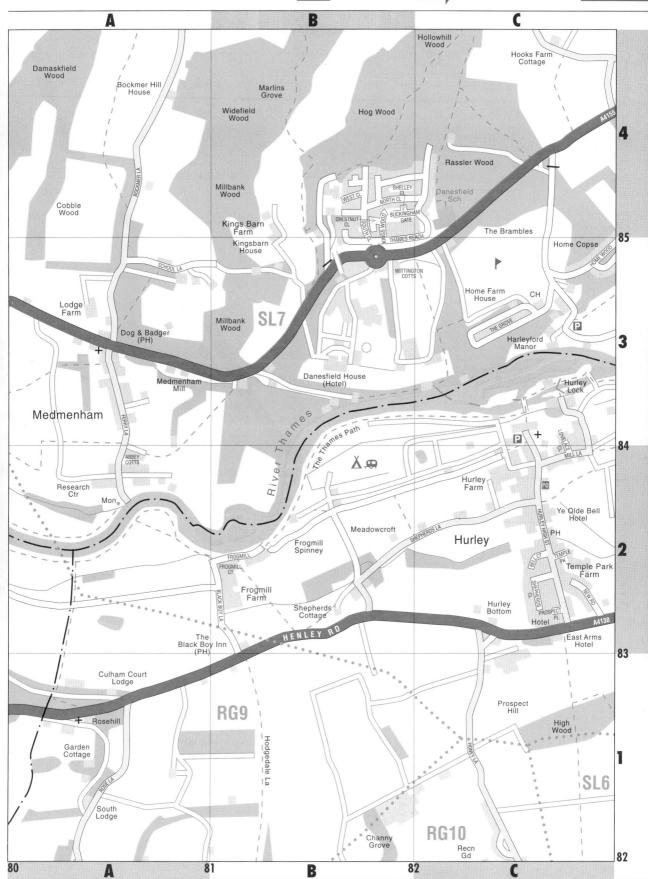

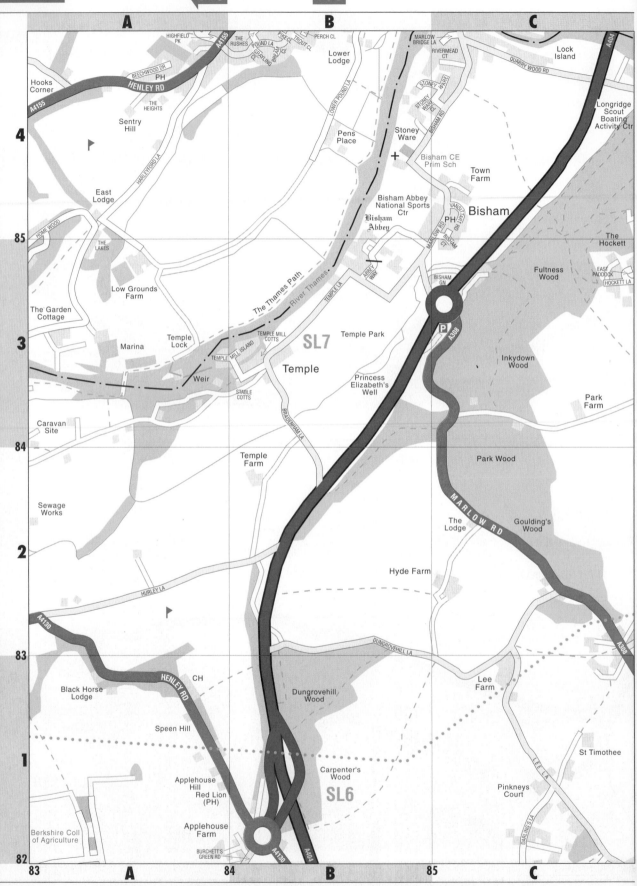

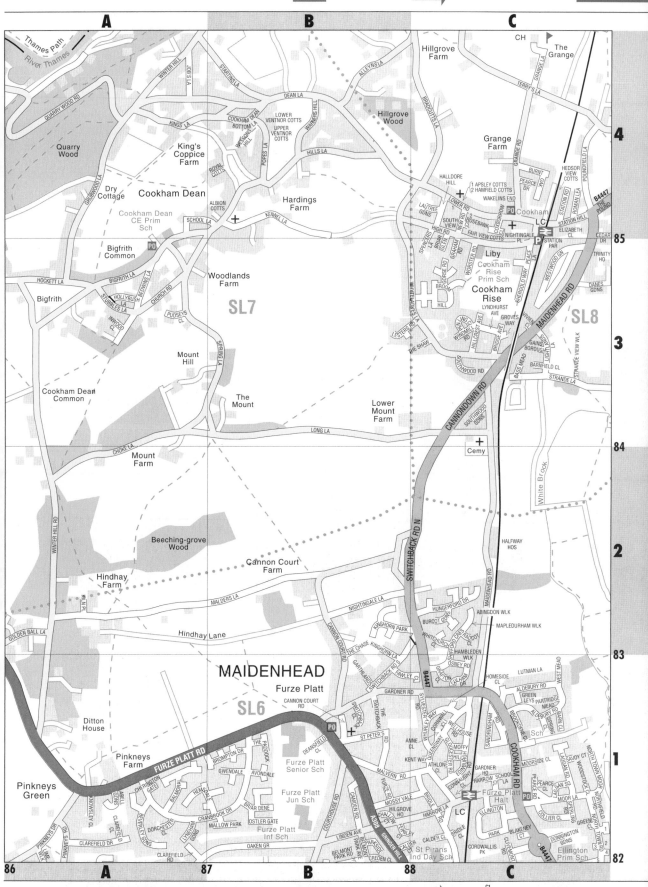

C1
1 NORTH TOWN CL
2 ALYSON CT
3 NORTH GN
4 NORTH TOWN MEAD
5 NORTHDEAN

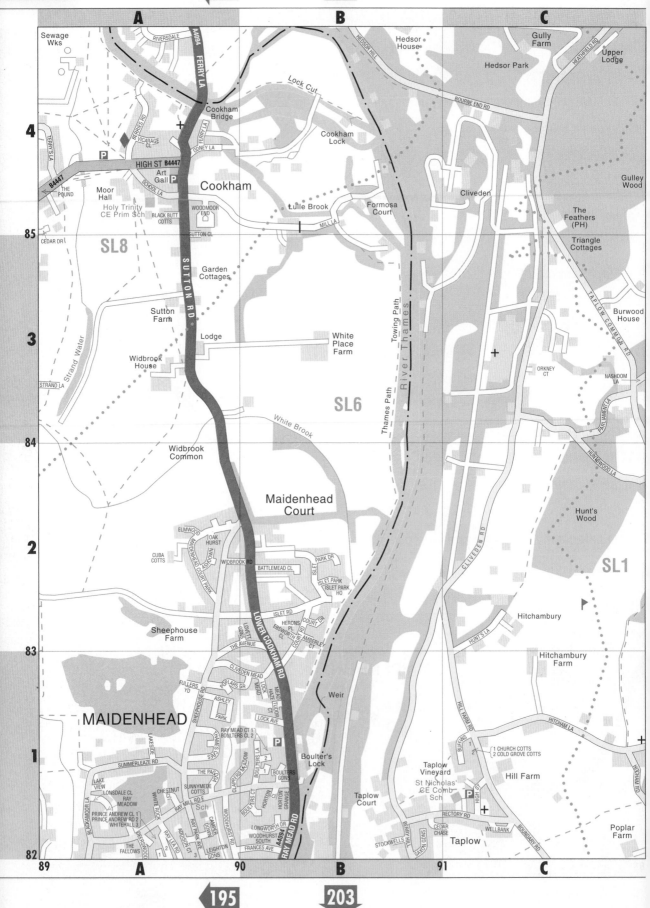

195
185
195
203

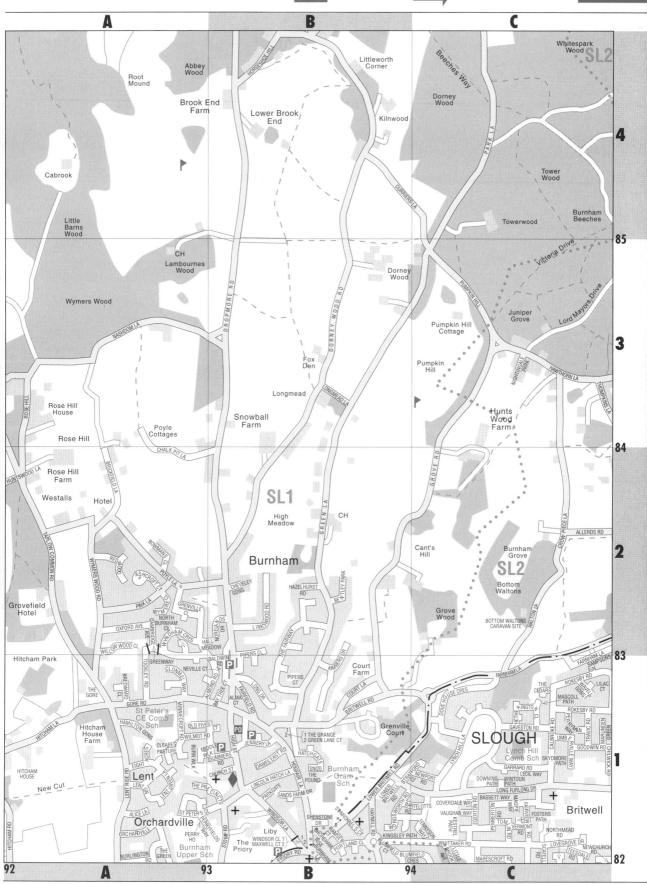

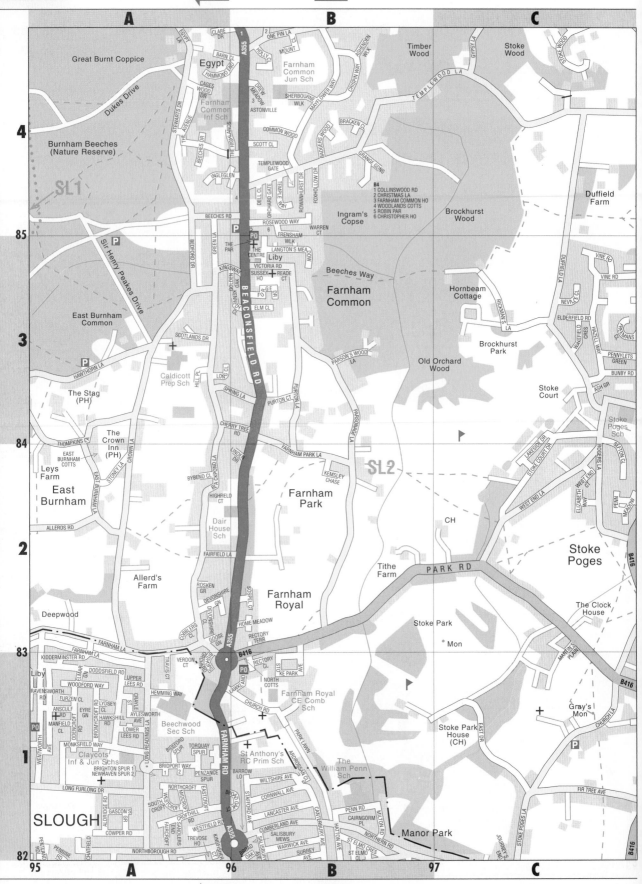

199
189

A   B   C

HAWKSWOOD LA

M40

M25

1a
16

SOUTHLANDS RD

M40

FIELD RD

HOLLYBUSH LA

Rush Green

New House Farm

WILLETTS LA

4

Alderbourne Arches

SL9

Brown's Wood

Ways Farm

Gossams Wood

Oldhouse Wood

UB9

WILLETTS LA

Kingcup Farm

M412

Alderbourne Farm

Blanchards Farm

85

ALDERBOURNE LA

Belle Farm

Sevenhills Farm

Long Coppice

Alder Bourne

Southlands Manor

FULMER COMMON RD

SEVENHILLS RD

LADY YORKE PK

3

Strawberry Wood

The Clump

Dromenagh Farm

DENHAM RD

Round Coppice Farm

Pinewood Film Studios

SL0

LAUREL CT

PINEWOOD GN

FIRS CL

CEDAR CL

ASHFORD RD

THORNBRIDGE RD

COPSE WOOD

Mansfield Farm

84

PINEWOOD RD

PINEWOOD CL

Black Park Country Park

Peace Road

Park Lodge Farm

HEATHERDEN GREEN

Iver Heath

M25

Peace Road

Park Lodge

THE PARKWAY

LONGSTD NE

ST DAVID'S CL

ST DAVID'S

Recn Gd

BIRCH CL

BANGORS RD N

Chandlers Hill

A4007

2

SL3

CHURCH RD

FOSTREVOR GDNS

ANSLOW GDNS

TREWARDEN AVE

HEATH WAY

ST MARGARET'S RD

LAURELS RD

KERNSACRE

1 ST MARGARET'S GATE
2 ST MARGARETS CT

ROWAN GDNS

WARREN WAY

ALDER RD

GLAISER HO

BODLEY HO

Liby

1 2

PO

Iver Heath Jun Sch

SLOUGH RD

Moorwards Farm

83

A412

Warren House

HAWTHORN CL

WHITEHOUSE WAY

Sch

MEAD HO

LOWER MEAD

MEAD

POST

POTTERS CROSS

Beeches Way

A4007

FIVE POINTS

THE CLOSE

HARDINGS CL

SWALLOW ST

Home Cottage Farm

CROSSMOOR

BANGORS RD S

UXBRIDGE RD

PLEASANT COTTS

PH

WOOD LANE CL

White Lodge

HARDINGS ROW

1

A412

WOOD LA

COOPERS ROW

BILLET LA

Langley Park Country Park

Bangors Park Farm

NORWOOD LA

82

MARTINDALE

COPPINS LA

01   A   02   B   03   C

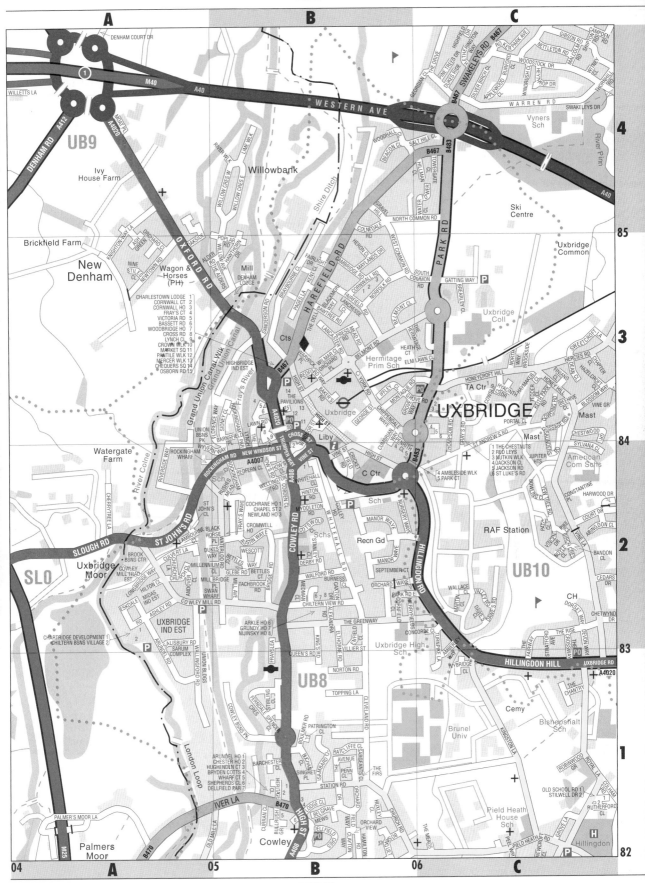

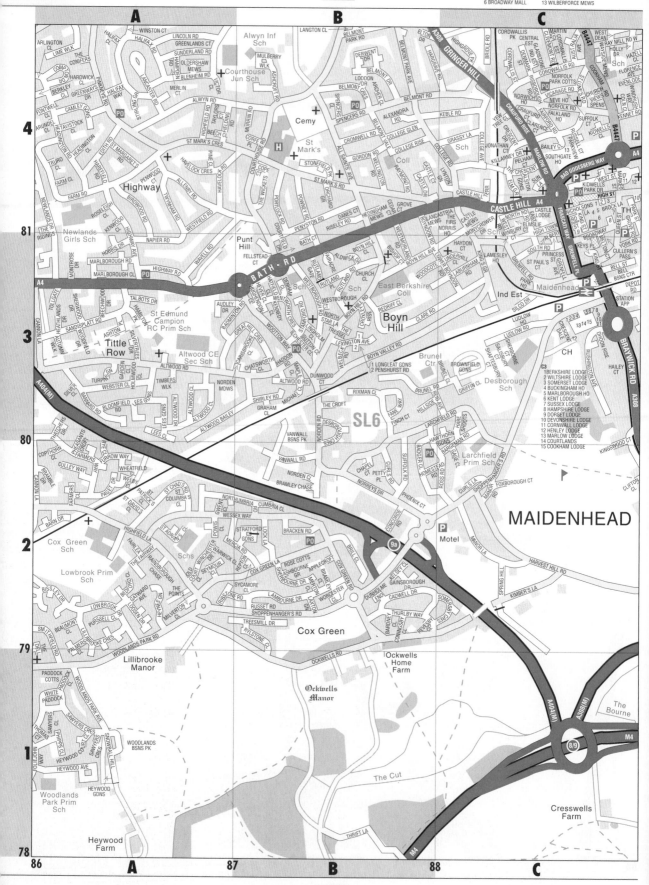

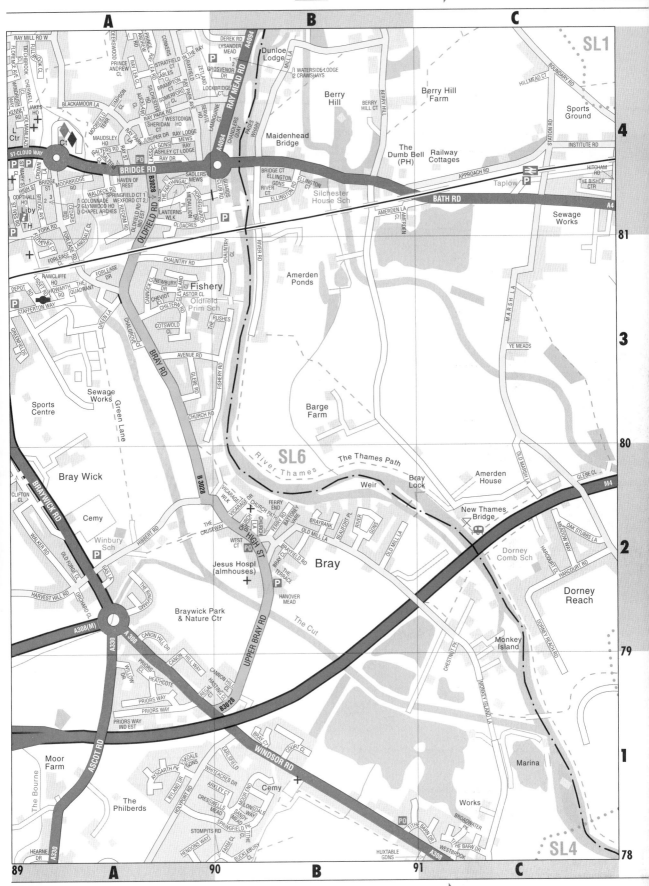

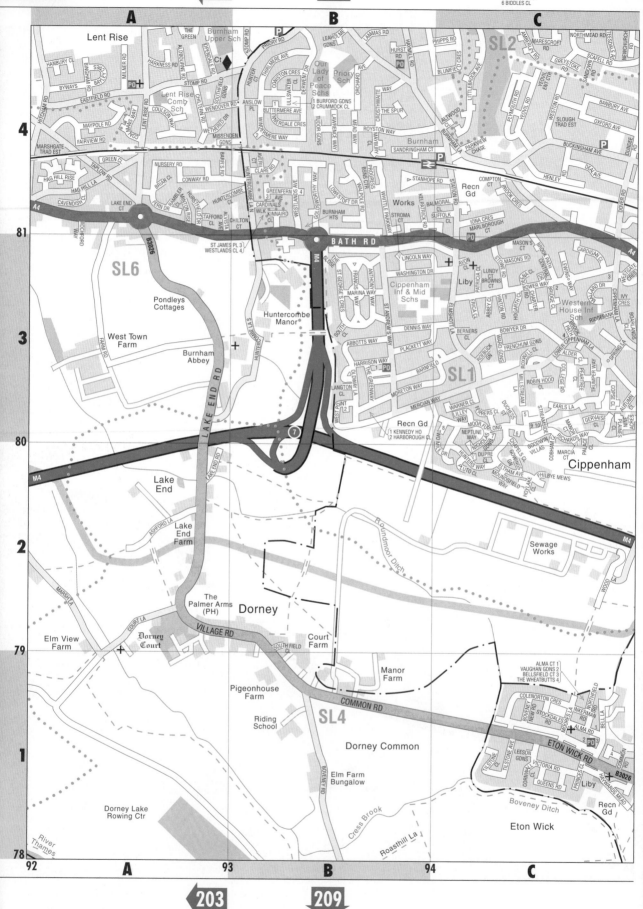

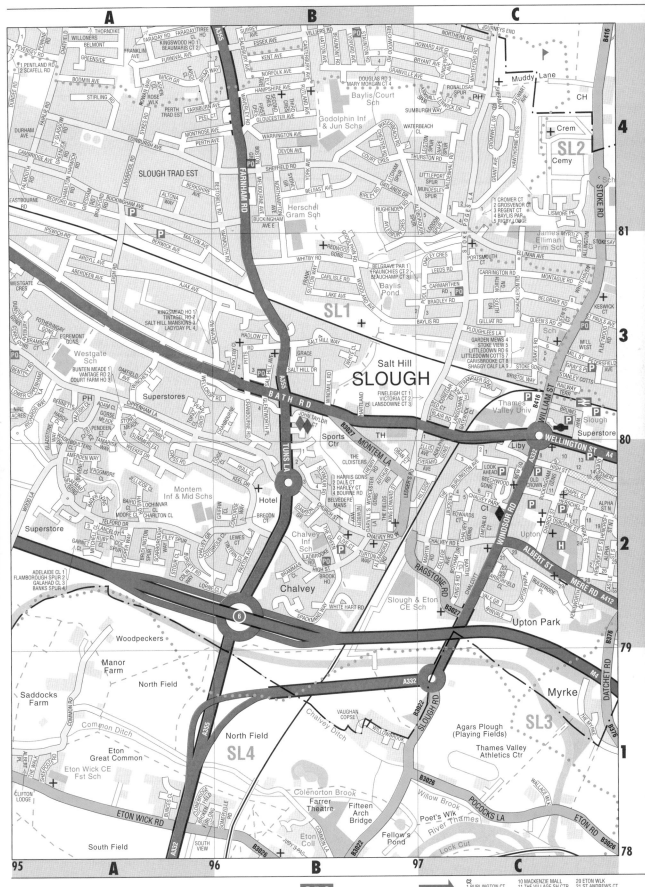

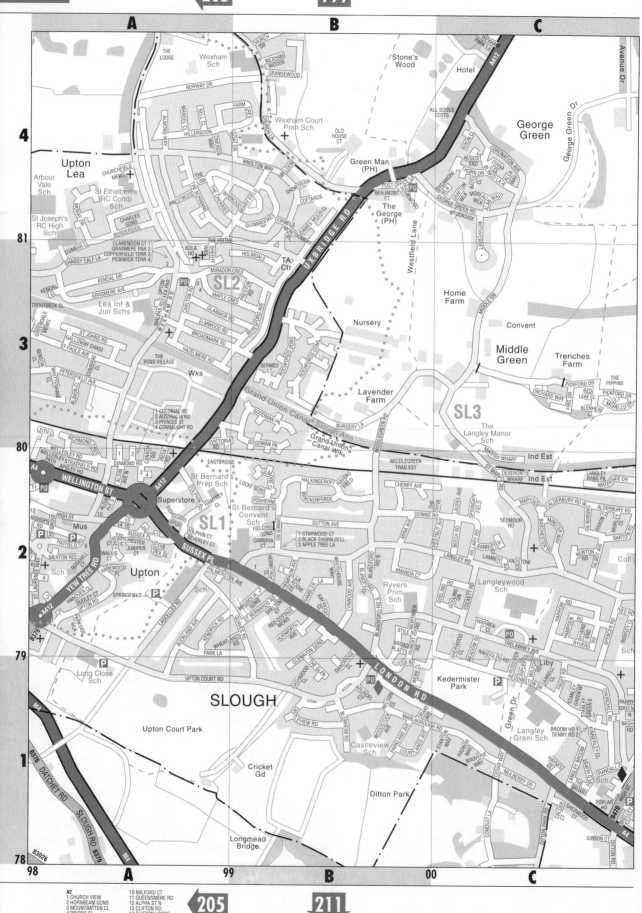

205
199

A   B   C

4

81

3

80

2

79

1

78

98   99   00

205
211

A2
1 CHURCH VIEW
2 HORNBEAM GDNS
3 MOUNTBATTEN CL
4 PRIORS CL
5 EASTFIELD CL
6 CHATHAM CT
7 GROVE CL
8 RYE CT
9 ELIZABETH CT
10 MILFORD CT
11 QUEENSMERE RD
12 ALPHA ST N
13 CLIFTON RD
14 CLIFTON LODGE
15 LASCELLES HO
16 CLEMENT CL
17 CHESHIRE CT
18 SUSSEX KEEP

THE LODGE
Wexham Sch
Upton Lea
Arbour Vale Sch
St Ethelbert's RC Comb Sch
St Joseph's RC High Sch
NORWAY DR
CHURCHFIELD MEWS
FARM CRES
Wexham Court Prim Sch
OLD HOUSE CT
Stone's Wood
Hotel
ALL SOULS COTTS
George Green
GEORGE GREEN DR
AVENUE DR
Green Man (PH)
POST OFFICE
The George (PH)
Westfield Lane
Home Farm
Convent
Middle Green
Trenches Farm
THE PIPPINS
The Langley Manor Sch
SL3
SL2
Lea Inf & Jun Schs
THE BSNS VILLAGE
Wks
Grand Union Canal Slough Arm
Lavender Farm
Nursery
Grand Union Canal Wlk
Goodman Pk
Goodman Pk
VICTORIA RD
Ind Est
MIDDLEGREEN TRAD EST
DESERONTO WHARF Ind Est
WELLINGTON ST
Superstore
St Bernard's Prep Sch
St Bernard's Convent Sch
SL1
CHERRY AVE
Langleywood Sch
Langley Gram Sch
Liby
Ryvers Prim Sch
Mus
Sch
Upton
SUSSEX PL
YEW TREE RD
Sch
Springfield
Upton Court Rd
Long Close Sch
SLOUGH
Kedermister Park
Castleview Sch
LONDON RD
Upton Court Park
Cricket Gd
Ditton Park
DATCHET RD
SLOUGH RD
Longmead Bridge
B3026
Coll
Green Dr

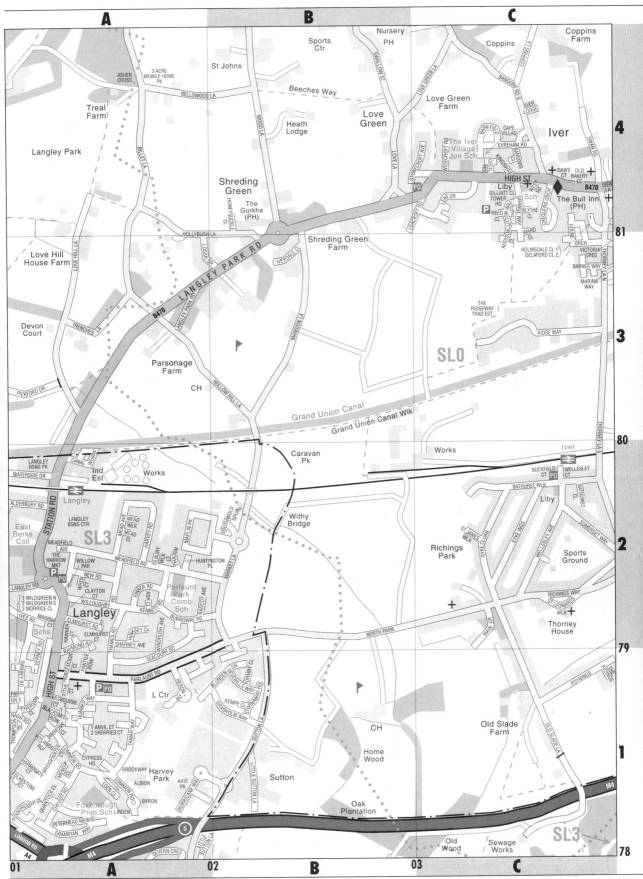

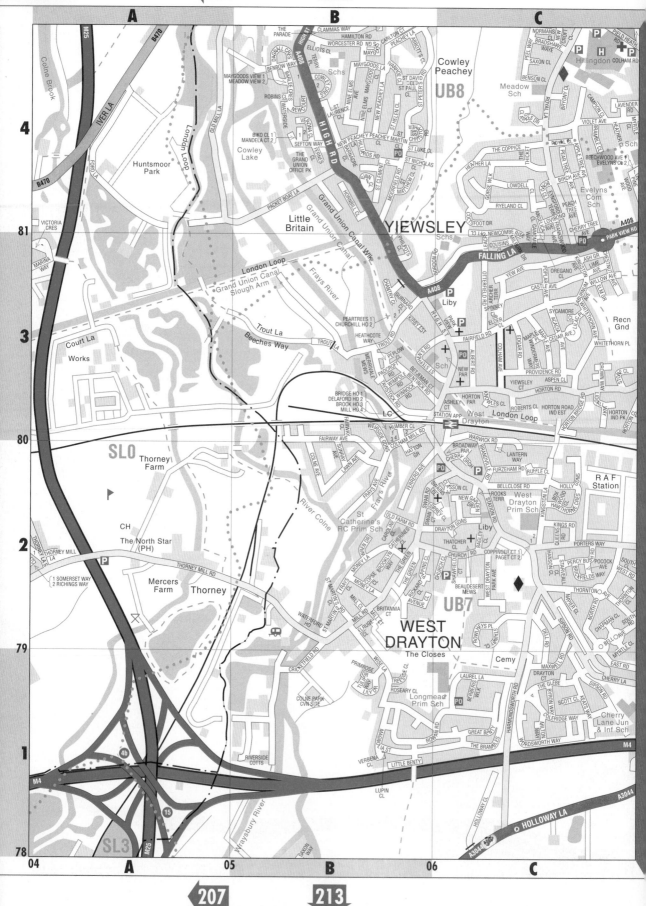

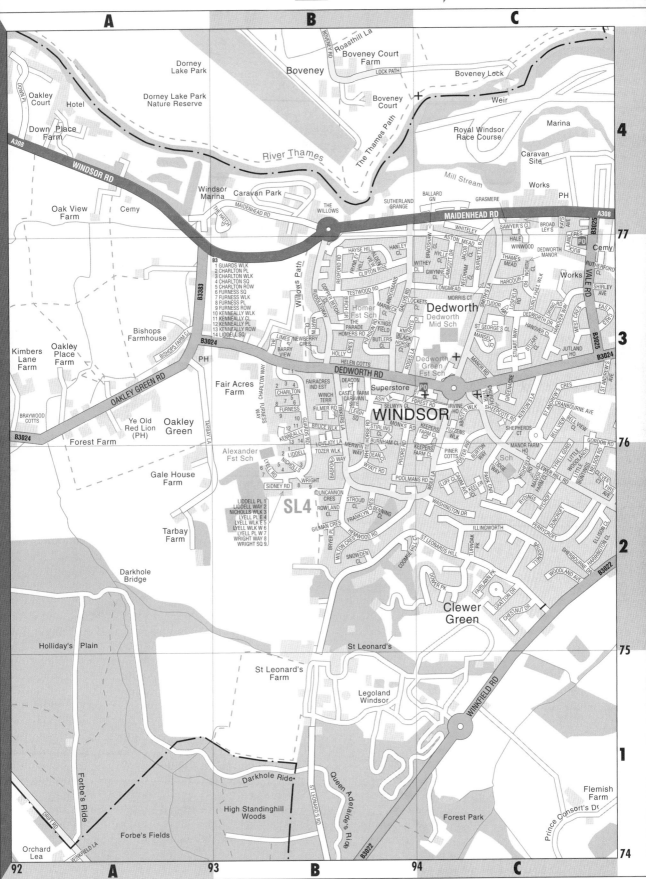

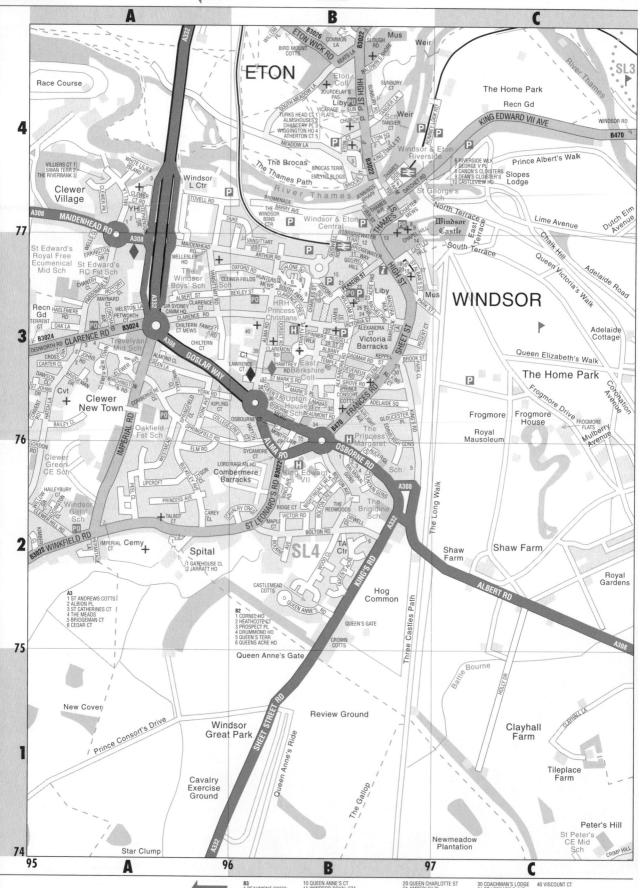

B3
1 BEAUMONT COTTS
2 CAMBRIDGE HO
3 WARD ROYAL PAR
4 CHRISTIAN SQ
5 CRESCENT VILLAS
6 WARD ROYAL
7 BOWES-LYON CL
8 MOUNTBATTEN SQ
9 CHARLES HO

10 QUEEN ANNE'S CT
11 WINDSOR ROYAL STA
12 THE CURFEW YD
13 HORSESHOE CLOISTERS
14 LODGINGS OF THE MILITARY KNIGHTS
15 KING EDWARD CT
16 CHURCH ST
17 ST ALBANS CL
18 CHURCH LA
19 MARKET ST

20 QUEEN CHARLOTTE ST
21 AMBERLEY PL
22 PEASCOD PL
23 ROYAL FREE HO
24 ELLISON HO
25 SUN PAS
26 HIBBERT'S ALLEY
27 WESSEX CT
28 GARFIELD PL
29 KING'S ROAD HO

30 COACHMAN'S LODGE
31 ST LEONARD'S AVE
32 LAMMAS AVE
33 ELIZABETH CT
34 CROSSWAYS CT
35 KNIGHTS PL
36 HOUSTON CT
37 WARWICK CT
38 CHELMSFORD CT
39 CAMPERDOWN HO

40 VISCOUNT CT

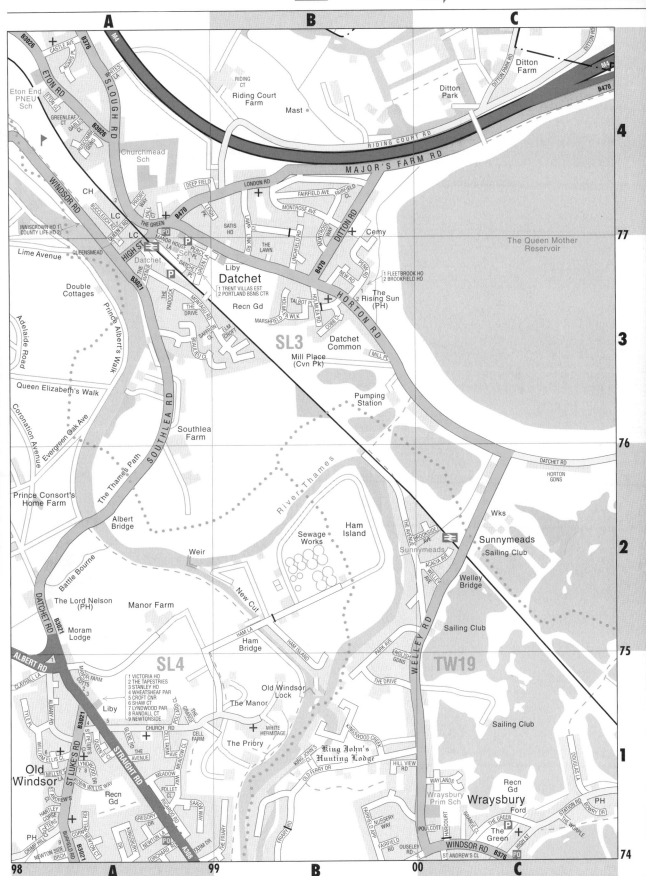

A   B   C

4

77

3

76

2

75

1

74

98   A   99   B   00   C

M4

B3026

CASTLE AVE

B3026

AGARS PL

Eton End
PNEU Sch

ETON RD

GREENLEAF
CT

SLOUGH RD

GARLE'S
RD

WHITES

B3026

PRISCOMBE
GDNS

Churchmead
Sch

INNISCROWN HO 1
COUNTY LIFE HO 2

WINDSOR RD

CH

LC

BUCCLEUCH RD

QUEEN'S RD

PRIORY
WAY

HALL
CT

THE GREEN

LC

LC

MANOR HOUSE
LA

PO

PERCY
PL

SCH
PL

B470

P

B470

Riding
Ct

Riding Court
Farm

Mast

DEEP FIELD

LONDON RD

FAIRFIELD AVE

FAIRFIELD
CL

MONTROSE AVE

SATIS
HO

LAWN
CL

LINK RD

THE
LAWN

LINCHFIELD RD

MONTROSE
WAY

DITTON RD

Cemy

PENN RD

NEW RD

RIDING COURT RD

MAJOR'S FARM RD

M4

Ditton
Farm

DITTON PARK RD

Ditton
Park

B470

DITTON RD

The Queen Mother
Reservoir

1 FLEETBROOK HO
2 BROOKFIELD HO

The
Rising Sun
(PH)

HORTON RD

Queensmead

HIGH ST

Datchet

Liby
Datchet

1 TRENT VILLAS EST
2 PORTLAND BSNS CTR

Recn Gd

THE
DRIVE

THE
PADDOCK

B3021

P

THE AVENUE

1 DATCHET
PL

2 DATCHET
PL

MONTAGU RD

THE
DRIVE

SAFFRON
CL

BEAULEU CL

ELM
CROFT

MARSHFIELD

HOLMEA PK WALK

TALBOT PL

HOLMEA RD

HOLMEA RD

CORB CL

Datchet
Common

MILL PL

SL3

Mill Place
(Cvn Pk)

Pumping
Station

DATCHET RD

HORTON
GDNS

Lime Avenue

Double
Cottages

Adelaide Road

Queen Elizabeth's Walk

Coronation Avenue

Prince Albert's Walk

SOUTHLEA RD

Evergreen Oak Ave

The Thames Path

Southlea
Farm

River Thames

Sewage
Works

Ham
Island

Wks

Sunnymeads

Sunnymeads
Sailing Club

Prince Consort's
Home Farm

Albert
Bridge

Weir

Battle Bourne

DATCHET RD

B3021

The Lord Nelson
(PH)

Moram
Lodge

Manor Farm

New Cut

HAM LA

Ham
Bridge

HAM ISLAND

THE AVENUE

BROOKSIDE
AVE

ACACIA AVE

WELLEY
AVE

THE AVENUE

WELLEY RD

Welley
Bridge

Sailing Club

ALBERT RD

CLAYHALL LA

MANOR FARM
COTTS

Libby

SL4

1 VICTORIA HO
2 THE TAPESTRIES
3 STANLEY HO
4 WHEATSHEAF PAR
5 CROFT CNR
6 SHAW CT
7 LYNDWOOD PAR
8 RANDALL CT
9 NEWTONSIDE

CELL
FARM

CHURCH RD

The Grange

The Manor

Old Windsor
Lock

WHITE
HERMITAGE

The Priory

KINGSWOOD CREEK

King John's
Hunting Lodge

PARK AVE

ENGLISH
GDNS

THE DRIVE

HILL VIEW
RD

TW19

Sailing Club

ALBANY RD

TYLER'S

B3021

WILLIAM ELLIS CL

ST PETER'S

ST LUKE'S RD

QUEEN'S

STRAIGHT RD

GLEBE RD

LYNDWOOD
RD

PO

TELLERS
AVE

MEADOW
LA

THE AVENUE

MEADOW
CL

FOLLET
CL

SAXON WAY

RINGFLD RD

THE FRIARY

FARM DR

A308

FRIARY RD

OLD FERRY DR

King John's
Hunting Lodge

NURSERY
WAY

FAIRFIELD
APP

FAIRFIELD
RD

OUSELEY
RD

ST ANDREW'S CL

POULCOTT

HARCOURT

WINDSOR RD

B376

PO

WAYLANDS

Wraysbury
Prim Sch

GRANGE CL

HIGH ST

Recn
Gd

Wraysbury

The Green

The
Green

STATION RD

DOUGLAS LA

THE WORPLE

BOWRY DR

PH

P

Old
Windsor

MILLER'S
LA

ROBIN WILLIS WAY

Recn
Gd

PH

HARTLEY
COPSE

ST PETERS

GREGORY
DR

KINGSBURY

NEWTON LA

CORNWELL RD

ORCHARD RD

B3021

NEWTON SIDE
ORCH

CRUMP HILLS

ALBANY RD

ST ANDREW'S

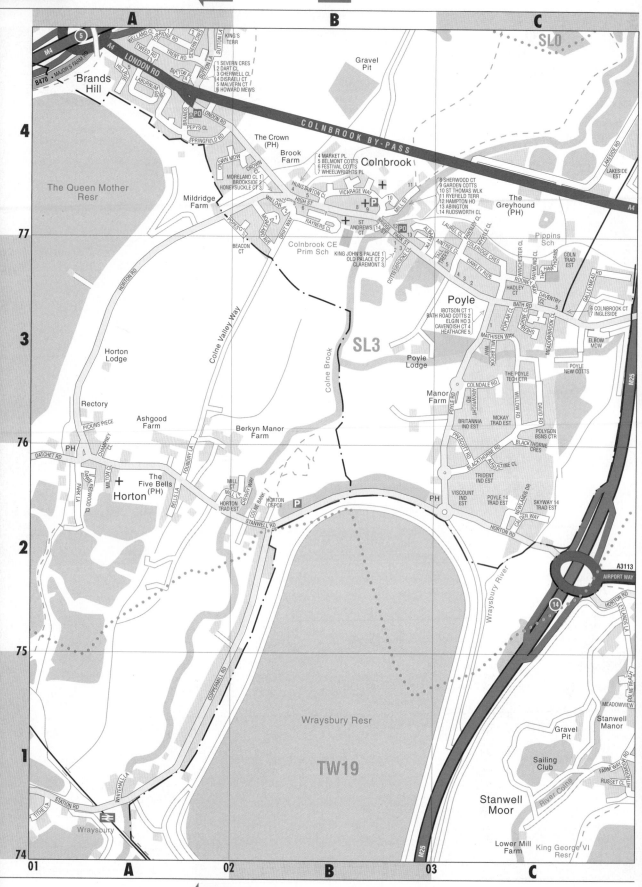

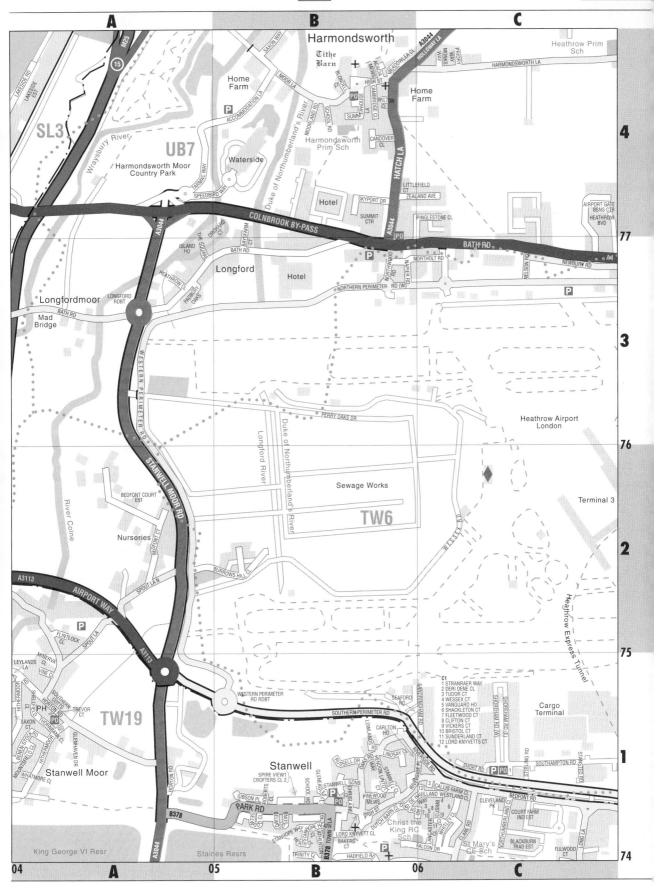

Harmondsworth

Tithe
Barn

Home Farm

Heathrow Prim
Sch

HARMONDSWORTH LA

Home
Farm

SL3

UB7

Harmondsworth Moor
Country Park

Waterside

Harmondsworth
Prim Sch

4

HATCH LA

Hotel

SKYPORT DR

SUMMIT
CTR

AIRPORT GATE
BSNS CTR

HEATHROW
BVD

COLNBROOK BY-PASS

BATH RD

77

ISLAND
HO

Longford

Hotel

NORTHERN PERIMETER RD (W)

Longfordmoor

Longford
RDBT

Mad
Bridge

BATH RD

NORTHERN PERIMETER

3

River Colne

WESTERN PERIMETER RD

STANWELL MOOR RD

PERRY OAKS DR

Duke of Northumberland's River

Heathrow Airport
London

76

BEDFONT COURT
EST

Longford River

Sewage Works

TW6

Terminal 3

Nurseries

SPOUT LAN

BURROWS HILL CL

2

WESSEX RD

A3113

AIRPORT WAY

FLINTLOCK
CL

SPOUT LA

A3113

75

LEYLANDS
LA

MINERVA
CL

VINE CL

WESTERN PERIMETER
RD RDBT

SEAFORD
CL

SANDRINGHAM RD

C1
1 STRANRAER WAY
2 DERI DENE CL
3 TUDOR CT
4 WESSEX CT
5 VANGUARD HO
6 SHACKLETON CT
7 FLEETWOOD CT
8 CLIFTON CT
9 VICKERS CT
10 BRISTOL CT
11 SUNDERLAND CT
12 LORD KNYVETTS CT

Cargo
Terminal

SOUTHERN PERIMETER RD

Heathrow Express Tunnel

PH

TW19

TREVOR
CT

CARLTON
HO

LINDSAY CL

SHOREHAM RD (W)

SHORT RD

SOUTHAMPTON RD

STIRLING RD

STANSTED RD

1

Stanwell Moor

SPIRE VIEW 1
CROFTERS CL 2

SCHOOL RD

STANWELL GDNS

PINEWOOD
MEWS

Cleveland
PK

COURT FARM
IND EST

PARK RD

Stanwell

Christ the
King RC
Sch

BEDFONT RD

BLACKBURN
TRAD EST

King George VI Resr

Staines Resrs

B378 TOWN LA

St Mary's
CE Sch

74

Index

Buckingham St 🄉 Aylesbury HP20..........101 B1

Place name	Location number	Locality, town or village	Postcode district	Page and grid square
May be abbreviated on the map	Present when a number indicates the place's position in a crowded area of mapping	Shown when more than one place has the same name	District for the indexed place	Page number and grid reference for the standard mapping

Public and commercial buildings are highlighted in magenta　　**Places of interest** are highlighted in blue with a star ★

Abbreviations used in the index

App	Approach	Cl	Close	Espl	Esplanade	Orch	Orchard	Sq	Square
Arc	Arcade	Comm	Common	Est	Estate	Par	Parade	Strs	Stairs
Ave	Avenue	Cnr	Corner	Gdns	Gardens	Pk	Park	Stps	Steps
Bvd	Boulevard	Cotts	Cottages	Gn	Green	Pas	Passage	St	Street, Saint
Bldgs	Buildings	Ct	Court	Gr	Grove	Pl	Place	Terr	Terrace
Bglws	Bungalows	Ctyd	Courtyard	Hts	Heights	Prec	Precinct	Trad	Trading Est
Bsns Ctr	Business Centre	Cres	Crescent	Ind Est	Industrial Estate	Prom	Promenade	Wlk	Walk
Bsns Pk	Business Park	Dr	Drive	Intc	Interchange	Ret Pk	Retail Park	W	West
Cswy	Causeway	Dro	Drove	Junc	Junction	Rd	Road	Yd	Yard
Ctr	Centre	E	East	La	Lane	Rdbt	Roundabout		
Cir	Circus	Emb	Embankment	N	North	S	South		

Index of localities, towns and villages

Adstock 53 C1	Colnbrook 212 B4	Haversham 20 C1	Moulsoe 36 B4	Stokenchurch 158 C3
Akeley 41 C4	Cookham 196 A4	Hazelmere 163 A2	Murcott 94 A2	Stone 114 B3
Aldbury 120 B3	Cosgrove 19 B1	Hedgerley 187 B2	Mursley 67 B3	Stonor 179 C3
Alderton 9 A1	Cranfield 25 A1	Henley-on-T 191 A1	Nash 44 B1	Stony Stratford 32 C3
Amersham 154 A1	Cublington 78 A1	Heronsgate 167 B1	New Denham 201 A3	Swanbourne 67 A2
Ashendon 97 C1	Cuddington 113 A1	High Wycombe 173 A3	Newport Pagnell 22 B3	Syresham 27 A4
Ashley Green 144 C4	Dadford 28 B1	Hoggeston 77 A4	Newton Blossomville 8 A2	Taplow 196 C1
Ashton 9 C4	Dagnall 107 B3	Holmer Green 163 B3	Newton Longville 57 B2	Thame 125 C1
Aspley Guise 49 C2	Datchet 211 B3	Holton 122 B1	North Crawley 24 A3	Thornborough 54 A4
Aspley Heath 49 A1	Deanshanger 31 B2	Horton 212 A2	North Marston 76 A1	Tiddington 136 A4
Aston Abbots 88 B3	Denham 190 A1	Horton-cum-S 108 A3	Oakley 109 B3	Tingewick 51 A4
Aston Clinton 117 B3	Denham Green 189 C3	Hughenden Valley 162 A4	Oakley Green 209 A3	Totternhoe 93 A4
Astwood 16 A2	Dinton 113 C1	Hurley 193 C2	Old Stratford 32 A4	Tring 119 B2
Aylesbury 115 B4	Dorney 204 B2	Hyde Heath 153 B3	Old Windsor 211 A1	Turvey 8 C3
Beachampton 44 A3	Dorton 96 C1	Ibstone 169 B4	Olney 6 B2	Turweston 38 B4
Beacon's Bottom 159 B2	Drayton Beauchamp 118 A3	Ickenham 190 C1	Oving 86 B4	Twyford 62 B1
Beaconsfield 175 B1	Drayton Parslow 68 B3	Ickford 124 A2	Padbury 53 A1	Tylers Green 163 B1
Berkhamsted 135 B3	Dunstable 93 C4	Iver 207 C4	Paulerspury 17 A4	Upper Arncott 94 C4
Bierton 102 A2	Eakley Lanes 4 B1	Iver Heath 200 B2	Penn 95 C4	Uxbridge 201 C3
Bisham 194 C4	East Claydon 74 C4	Ivinghoe 105 C3	Piddington 95 C4	Waddesdon 99 A4
Bix 179 B1	Eaton Bray 92 C3	Lacey Green 149 C3	Piddington (Northants)..4 A4	Walter's Ash 150 B1
Blackthorn 81 A3	Edgcott 72 C1	Lane End 171 B4	Pitstone 105 B2	Walton 48 A3
Bledlow 138 A1	Edlesborough 92 C2	Lathbury 22 B4	Pitstone 105 B2	Warrington 7 A4
Bledlow Ridge 159 C4	Ellesborough 130 A1	Latimer 155 C2	Potterspury 18 B1	Water Stratford 40 A1
Botley 145 A1	Emberton 13 C4	Lavendon 7 C4	Poundon 71 C4	Waterperry 123 A1
Bourne End 185 A1	Eton 210 B4	Leckhampstead 42 C4	Poyle 212 C3	Wavendon 48 C4
Bovingdon 146 A2	Farnham Common 198 B3	Lee Common 142 B3	Preston Bissett 62 A4	Weedon 87 B1
Bow Brickhill 48 B1	Fawley 191 B4	Leighton Buzzard 80 C3	Prestwood 151 B3	Wendover 131 B2
Brackley 38 A4	Felden 146 C4	Lewknor 157 A3	Princes Risborough 139 B2	West Drayton 208 B2
Brill 96 A1	Finmere 50 B4	Lillingstone Lovell 30 A3	Quainton 85 A3	Westbury 39 A2
Buckingham 41 B1	Flackwell Heath 185 A4	Little Brickhill 59 C3	Ravenstone 5 B1	Westcott 98 B4
Buckland Common ...133 A2	Frieth 170 C1	Little Chalfont 155 A1	Remenham Hill 192 B1	Weston Turville 116 C2
Burnham 197 B2	Fulmer 199 B4	Little Gaddesden 121 B4	Rickmansworth 167 C1	Weston Underwood 6 A1
Carlton 3 C2	Gawcott 51 C2	Little Horwood 55 C1	Ringshall 107 A1	Whaddon 45 A1
Castlethorpe 19 C3	Gerrards Cross 188 C3	Little Kingshill 152 A2	Salford 37 B2	Wheatley 122 A1
Chackmore 41 A2	Grafton Regis 9 B1	Little Marlow 184 B3	Sarratt 156 C2	Whipsnade 107 C4
Chalfont St Giles 177 B4	Granborough 75 C4	Long Crendon 125 A3	Seer Green 176 B2	Whitchurch 87 A3
Chalfont St Peter 177 C1	Great Brickhill 59 B1	Long Marston 104 A2	Shabbington 124 B2	Whitfield 26 B2
Charndon 72 C3	Great Haseley 136 A1	Longwick 138 B4	Shalstone 39 C3	Wicken 31 A2
Chartridge 143 B2	Great Horwood 55 A1	Loudwater 174 B1	Sheeplane 60 B1	Wigginton 119 B1
Chearsley 112 A1	Great Kimble 139 A1	Ludgershall 96 B4	Sherington 14 A1	Wilstone 104 B1
Cheddington 105 A4	Great Kingshill 162 C4	Maidenhead 202 C2	Slapton 91 B3	Windsor 210 C3
Chenies 156 A1	Great Missenden 152 A3	Maids Moreton 41 C2	Slough 205 B3	Wing 79 C1
Chesham 154 B4	Grendon Underwood 83 A3	Maple Cross 178 B3	Soulbury 69 C2	Wingrave 89 B2
Chicheley 23 B4	Haddenham 127 A3	Marlow 183 A1	South Harefield 190 B3	Winslow 66 A2
Chilton 111 A2	Halton 117 B1	Marlow Bottom 183 B3	South Heath 152 C4	Woburn 60 C3
Chinnor 147 B4	Hambleden 181 B1	Marsh Gibbon 71 C2	Stagsden 16 C3	Woburn Sands 49 A3
Chipperfield 156 C4	Hanslope 11 A2	Marsworth 105 A1	Stanwell 213 B1	Wooburn Green 185 C4
Cholesbury 133 B2	Hardwick 87 A2	Medmenham 193 A3	Steeple Claydon 63 B2	Worminghall 123 C3
Chorleywood 167 B3	Harmondsworth 213 B4	Mentmore 90 B2	Stewkley 68 C1	Wraysbury 211 C1
Clifton Reynes 7 B2	Harrold 3 C3	Milton Keynes 34 B3	Stoke Bruerne 9 A4	Yardley Gobion 18 C3
Cold Brayfield 8 A3	Hartwell 10 B4	Milton Keynes Village 35 C1	Stoke Goldington 12 A3	Yardley Hastings 1 A3
Coleshill 164 C2	Hastoe 133 C4	Mixbury 38 B1	Stoke Hammond 69 C4	
			Stoke Mandeville 116 A1	
			Stoke Poges 198 C2	

3

3 Acre Mobile Home Pk SL0 207 A4

A

Abbey Barn La HP10, HP11 173 C2
Abbey Barn Rd HP11 173 C2
Abbey Cl SL1 204 C3
Abbey Cotts SL7 193 A2
Abbey Mead SL8 184 C3
Abbey Park La SL1 186 C1
Abbey Rd Aylesbury HP19 101 A1
 Bourne End SL8 184 C3
 Milton Keynes, Bradwell MK13 34 A2
 Milton Keynes, Simpson MK6 47 C3
 Syresham NN13 27 B4
Abbey Sq MK43 8 C3
Abbey Terr MK16 22 B2
Abbey Way Bisham SL7 194 B3
 High Wycombe HP11 173 A3
 Milton Keynes MK13 34 A3
 Ravenstone MK46 5 C1
Abbey Wlk HP16 152 A4
Abbey's Com Comb Sch MK3 47 A1
Abbot Ridge HP18 125 B3
Abbot Wlk HP18 125 B3
Abbot's Wlk SL4 209 C3
Abbots Cl MK13 34 A3
Abbots Way
 Little Marlow HP12 172 B2
 Princes Risborough HP27 139 B3
Abbotsfield MK6 47 A4
Abbotswood HP27 150 B2
Abbott's Cl UB8 208 B4
Abbotts Cl HP20 101 C1
Abbotts Rd HP20 101 C1
Abbotts Vale HP5 144 B2
Abbotts Way Slough SL1 204 B3
 Wingrave HP22 89 A2
Abell Gdns SL6 195 A1
Abercromby Ave HP12 172 C4
Abercromby Ct HP12 172 B4
Aberdeen Ave SL1 205 A3
Aberdeen Cl MK3 46 C1
Abingdon Cl Thame OX9 125 C1
 Uxbridge UB10 201 C2
Abingdon Wlk SL6 195 C2
Abington SL3 212 B4
Abney Court Dr SL8 185 A1
Abraham Cl MK15 35 B3
Abrahams Rd RG9 191 B2
Abstacle Hill HP23 118 C2
Acacia RG9 191 B1
Acacia Ave
 West Drayton UB7 208 C3
 Wraysbury TW19 211 C2
Acacia Gr HP4 135 A2
Acacia Ho 3 SL9 177 C1
Acacia Mews UB7 213 B4
Acacia Wlk HP23 118 C2
Accommodation La UB7 213 B4
Ackerman Cl MK18 52 C4
Ackroyd Pl MK5 46 A3
Acorn Bsns Ctr LU7 78 C1
Acorn Cl HP13 173 B4
Acorn Gdns HP12 172 C2
Acorn Wlk MK9 34 C1
Acre Pas SL4 210 B3
Acre The SL7 183 C1
Acrefield Rd SL9 188 B4
Acres End HP7 165 C4
Acres The HP13 161 C1
Adam Cl Aylesbury HP21 116 A2
 High Wycombe HP13 173 B4
 Slough SL1 205 A3
Adams Cl MK18 41 B1
Adams Ct MK6 47 B4
Adams Pk HP12 172 A4
Adams Way HP23 119 A3
Addington Cl SL4 210 A2
Addington Cotts HP22 131 A3
Addington Rd MK18 41 B1
Addington Terr MK18 41 B1
Addison Cl SL0 207 C3
Addison Ct SL6 196 A1
Addison Rd
 Chesham HP5 144 B1
 Steeple Claydon MK18 63 B1
Adelaide Cl SL1 205 A2
Adelaide Rd HP13 162 B1
Adelaide Sq SL4 210 B3
Adelphi Gdns SL1 205 C2
Adelphi St MK9 34 C2
Adkins Cl HP19 100 C2
Admiral Way HP4 134 C3
Adstock Mews 5 SL9 177 B1
Adwell Sq RG9 191 B1
Agars Pl SL3 211 A4
Agora Ctr
 8 Milton Keynes MK2 58 B4
 Milton Keynes, Wolverton MK12 33 B4
Ailward Rd HP19 101 A1
Ainsdale Cl MK3 46 B1
Aintree Cl
 Milton Keynes MK3 57 B3
 Poyle SL3 212 C3
Airport Gate Bsns Ctr UB7 213 C4
Airport Way TW19 213 A2
Aiston Pl HP20 101 C1
Ajax Ave SL1 205 A3
Akeley CE Sch MK18 41 C4
Akeley Wood Jun Sch MK19 31 A1
Akeley Wood Sch MK18 41 B4
Akeman St HP23 119 A2
Akerman Cl MK12 33 A3
Akister Cl MK18 52 C4
Alabama Circ HP11 173 A2
Alabama Dr HP11 173 A2
Alan Wlk SL3 206 C4
Alaska St HP11 173 A2
Albany Ct MK14 34 B4
Albany Gate HP5 144 A1
Albany Pk SL3 212 B4
Albany Pl HP19 101 A1
Albany Rd
 Old Windsor SL4 211 A1
 Windsor SL4 210 B3
Albany Terr HP23 119 A3
Albert Cl 26 SL1 205 C2
Albert Pl SL4 205 A1
Albert Rd Chesham HP5 154 B4
 Henley-on-T RG9 191 C1
 Old Windsor SL4 211 A1
 West Drayton UB7 208 C3
 Windsor SL4 210 C2
Albert St Aylesbury HP20 116 A4
 4 High Wycombe HP13 173 B4
 Maidenhead SL6 202 C4
 Milton Keynes MK2 58 B4
 Slough SL1 205 C2
 Tring HP23 119 A2
 Windsor SL4 210 A3
Albion SL3 207 A1
Albion Cl SL2 206 A3
Albion Cotts SL7 195 B4
Albion Cres HP8 177 A4
Albion Ho HP12 172 B3
Albion Pl
 Milton Keynes MK9 35 A2
 2 Windsor SL4 210 A3
Albion Rd
 Chalfont St Giles HP8 177 A4
 High Wycombe HP12 172 B3
 Pitstone LU7 105 B3
Albion St HP20 115 C4
Albury Ct 3 MK8 33 C1
Albury View OX9 136 A3
Aldborough Spur SL1 205 C4
Aldbourne Rd SL1 204 A4
Aldbury Gdns HP23 119 A3
Aldbury Prim Sch HP23 120 B3
Aldbury Rd WD3 167 C1
Aldebury Rd SL6 195 C1
Alden View SL4 209 B3
Aldene Rd MK19 11 A2
Aldenham MK6 47 B3
Alder Cl SL1 204 C3
Alder Rd Iver Heath SL0 200 B2
 New Denham UB9 201 B3
Alderbourne La
 Fulmer SL3 199 C4
 Iver Heath SL0 200 A4
Alderbury Rd SL3 206 C2
Alderbury Rd W SL3 206 C2
Aldergill MK13 34 B3
Alderley Ct HP4 135 B2
Aldermead MK12 33 C3
Alderney Pl MK5 45 C2
Alders The UB9 201 B3
Alderson Cl HP19 101 A1
Alderton Dr HP4 121 A4
Aldin Ave N SL1 206 A2
Aldin Ave S SL1 206 A2
Aldrich Dr MK15 35 C4
Aldridge Ct HP11 173 C2
Aldridge Rd SL2 198 A1
Aldwick Dr SL6 202 B3
Aldwycks Cl MK5 45 C3
Alex Campbell Cty Mid Sch MK3 57 C4
Alexander Ct HP12 172 C4
Alexander Fst Sch SL4 209 B2
Alexander Ho 1 MK2 58 B4
Alexander Rd HP20 101 B1
Alexander St HP5 144 B1
Alexandra Ct
 Leighton Buzzard LU7 80 C4
 Windsor SL4 210 B3
Alexandra Dr MK16 22 B1
Alexandra Pk HP11 173 A3
Alexandra Rd
 High Wycombe HP13 173 C3
 Maidenhead SL6 202 B4
 Slough SL1 205 B2
 Uxbridge UB8 201 B2
 Windsor SL4 210 B3
Alford Rd HP12 172 B2
Alfred Ct SL8 185 A2
Alfred Davis Ct SL7 183 B2
Alfriston Sch HP9 175 B3
Alham Rd HP21 115 B3
Alice Cl HP15 163 B4
Alice La SL1 197 A1
All Saints CE Jun Sch SL6 202 B3
All Saints View MK5 46 A4
All Saints' Ave SL6 202 B4
All Souls Cotts SL3 206 C4
Alladale Pl MK12 33 B2
Allan Shaw Comb Sch MK18 63 C2
Allanson Rd SL7 183 C2
Allen Cl MK2 58 B3
Allen Dr HP14 161 B4
Allenby Rd SL6 202 A4
Allerds Rd SL2 198 A2
Allerford Ct MK4 46 B2
Alleyns La SL6 195 B4
Allhusen Gdns SL3 199 C4
Allington Ct SL2 205 C3
Allison Ct MK15 35 B1
Allkins Ct SL4 210 B3
Allonby Way HP21 116 A4
Allyn Cl HP13 173 B4
Alma Ct Burnham SL1 197 B1
 Eton SL4 204 C1
Alma Rd
 Berkhamsted HP4 134 C3
 Chesham HP5 144 B1
 Eton SL4 204 C1
 Windsor SL4 210 B3
Almhouses MK14 21 C1
Almond Cl
 Newport Pagnell MK16 22 A2
 Windsor SL4 210 A3
Almond Rd SL1 197 B1
Almond Way HP27 139 A1
Almond Wlk HP15 163 A2
Almons Way SL2 206 A4
Almshouses SL4 210 B4
Almshouses The MK46 5 C1
Alnwick Rd HP23 103 C4
Alpha Ct HP7 165 A4
Alpha St N 12 SL1 206 A2
Alpha St S SL1 205 C2
Alpine Croft MK5 46 A2
Alscot La HP27 139 A3
Alsford Wharf HP4 135 B3
Alston Dr MK13 33 C2
Alston Gdns SL6 202 C4
Alstonefield 1 MK4 46 A2
Althorpe Cres MK13 34 A3
Alton Bsns Pk HP19 101 A1
Alton Gate MK4,MK5 45 C2
Altona Rd HP10 174 B2
Altona Way SL1 205 A4
Altwood Bailey SL6 202 A3
Altwood CE Sec Sch SL6 202 A3
Altwood Cl
 Maidenhead SL6 202 A3
 Slough SL1 204 C4
Altwood Dr SL6 202 A3
Altwood Rd SL6 202 A3
Alverton MK14 34 C4
Alvista Ave SL6 204 A4
Alwin Cl HP21 115 B2
Alwins Field LU7 80 B4
Alwyn Inf Sch SL6 202 B4
Alwyn Rd SL6 202 A4
Alyngton HP4 134 C4
Alyson Ct 2 SL6 195 C1
Amanda Ct SL3 206 B2
Amber Cotts HP7 164 C2
Amberley Ct SL6 196 B2
Amberley Pl 21 SL4 210 B3
Amberley Rd SL2 204 C4
Amberley Way UB10 201 C1
Amberley Wlk MK4 45 C1
Amblers Way MK18 53 A1
Ambleside HP21 116 A3
Ambleside Wlk UB8 201 B2
Ambridge Gr MK6 35 B1
Ambrose Ct MK15 35 B1
Amelias La MK9 35 A2
Amerden Cl SL6 203 B4
Amerden La SL6 203 B4
Amerden Way SL1 205 A2
American Com Schs UB10 201 C2
Amersham & Wycombe Coll Amersham HP7 165 C4
 Chesham HP5 144 B2
 Flackwell Heath HP10 173 C1
Amersham General Hospl HP7 165 A4
Amersham Hill HP13 173 A4
Amersham Hill Dr HP13 173 B4
Amersham Hill Gdns HP13 173 B4
Amersham Mus* HP7 165 A4
Amersham Pl HP7 166 B4
Amersham Rd
 Beaconsfield HP9 176 A3
 Chalfont St Giles HP8 166 A1
 Chalfont St Peter HP8,SL9 177 B3
 Chesham HP5 154 A3
 Chesham HP5 154 B3
 Chorleywood WD3 167 B4
 Denham Green SL9 189 A2
 Hazelmere HP15 163 A2
 Little Chalfont HP6 166 C4
Amersham Sch The HP7 165 C4
Amersham Way HP6 166 C4
Amherst Ct MK15 35 B4
Amos Ct MK13 34 A3
Ampleforth MK10 36 A1
Amy La HP5 154 A4
Ancastle Gr RG9 191 B1
Ancell Rd MK11 32 C3
Anchor La 1 HP20 115 C4
Ancona Gdns MK5 45 C2
Andermans SL4 209 B3
Andersen Gate MK4 57 A4
Anderson Cl HP14 158 C2
Anding Cl MK46 6 C2
Andover Cl UB8 201 A2
Andrew Hill La SL2 187 B2
Andrews Cl LU7 69 C2
Andrews Croft MK14 34 C4
Andrews Reach SL8 185 A1
Andrews Way
 Aylesbury HP19 115 A4
 Marlow Bottom SL7,HP10 183 B4
Anershall HP22 89 A2
Angel Cl MK15 35 A4
Angelica Cl UB7 208 C4
Angelica Ct MK7 48 A3
Angels Cl MK18 65 C2
Angle Pl HP4 135 A2
Anglefield Rd HP4 135 A2
Anglesey Ct
 Milton Keynes MK8 46 A4
 Stokenchurch HP14 158 C3
Angood Cl HP27 139 A2
Angstrom Cl MK5 46 A3
Angus Dr MK3 46 C1
Angus Rd HP19 101 A2
Anne Cl SL6 195 C1
Annes Gr MK14 21 B1
Annesley Rd MK16 22 A2
Anns Cl Aylesbury HP21 116 A2
 Tring HP23 118 C2
Ansculf Rd SL2 198 A1
Anslow Gdns SL0 200 B2
Anslow Pl SL1 204 B4
Anson Cl Aylesbury HP21 115 C2
 Bovingdon HP1 145 C2
Anson Rd MK12 33 B3
Anstey Brook HP22 117 A2
Anstey Cl HP18 99 A3
Anstey Ct HP18 99 A4
Anthony Cl HP13 161 C1
Anthony Ct MK11 32 B3
Anthony Way SL1 204 B3
Anton Way HP21 115 B2
Anvil Cl HP3 146 A2
Anvil Ct SL3 207 A1
Anxey Way HP17 126 C3
Aplin Rd HP21 116 B3
Apple Cotts HP3 146 A2
Apple Tree Ave UB8 208 C4
Apple Tree Cl LU7 80 B3
Appleacres MK17 69 B4
Appleby Heath MK2 58 B3
Applecroft
 Berkhamsted HP4 134 C3
 Maidenhead SL6 202 B2
 Newton Longville MK17 57 B2
Applefield HP7 166 B4
Appleton Cl HP7 166 A4
Appleton Mews 4 MK4 46 A2
Appletree La SL3 206 B2
Appletree Wlk HP5 154 B3
Applewick La HP12 172 B4
Applewood Cl UB8 201 C4
Appleyard Pl 1 MK6 34 C1
Approach Rd SL6 203 C4
Approach The MK8 33 C1
Apsley Cotts SL8 195 C4
Apsley Ho SL1 206 A2
Aran Hts HP8 177 A3
Arborfield Cl SL1 205 C2
Arbour Vale Sch SL2 205 C4
Arbour View HP7 166 A4
Arbroath Cl MK3 46 C2
Arbrook Ave MK13 34 B2
Arcade The HP9 175 C2
Arcadia La MK9 35 A2
Arch Way
 High Wycombe HP13 173 A4
 Lacey Green HP27 150 A2
Archdale 1 HP11 173 A3
Archer Cl SL6 202 B4
Archer Ct HP6 154 B1
Archer Dr HP20 102 A1
Archer Terr UB7 208 C3
Archers Way HP14 171 A3
Archers Wells MK3 47 A1
Archford Croft MK4 46 B2
Archive Cl HP22 117 B3
Arden Cl HP3 146 A2
Arden Pk MK12 33 A4
Ardenham La HP19 101 B1
Ardenham St HP19 101 B1
Ardrossan Cl SL2 198 B1
Ardwell La MK12 33 A3
Ardys Ct MK5 46 A4
Argyle Ave HP19 101 A1
Argyll Ave SL1 205 A3
Aries Ho HP10 185 A4
Aris Way MK18 52 B3
Arizona St HP11 173 A2
Arkle Ho UB8 201 B2
Arkley Ct SL6 203 B1
Arkwright Rd SL3 212 C3
Arlington Cl SL6 202 A4
Arlington Ct MK4 46 C2
Arlott Cres MK6 46 C4
Armourer Dr MK14 34 C3
Armstrong Cl MK8 45 C3
Arncliffe Dr MK13 34 A3
Arncott Rd OX25 95 B4
Arncott Wood Rd OX25 94 C3
Arne La MK7 48 B3
Arnison Ave HP13 162 B1
Arnold Cl HP22 116 B1
Arnold Cott MK19 32 A4
Arnold Ct HP21 115 C3
Arnold's Cotts HP5 143 A2
Arnolds Cl MK18 53 A1
Arnott's Yd HP18 125 B3
Arranmore Ho HP11 174 A2
Arrewig La
 Buckland Common HP23 132 B1
 Lee Common HP5 142 C4
Arrow Pl MK2 58 B2
Arthur Rd Slough SL1 205 B2
 Windsor SL4 210 B3
Artichoke Dell WD3 167 C2
Arts Educational Sch HP23 119 A2
Arundel Cl SL6 202 A4
Arundel Ct SL3 206 B1
Arundel Gn HP20 101 C1
Arundel Gr MK3 57 C4
Arundel Ho
 1 High Wycombe HP13 173 C4
 Uxbridge UB8 201 B1
Arundel Rd
 High Wycombe HP12 172 A3
 Uxbridge UB8 201 A1
Ascot Dr LU7 80 B3
Ascot Mews LU7 80 B3
Ascot Rd SL6 203 A1
Ascott Ct HP20 101 C1
Ascott Ho* LU7 80 A1
Ascott Rd HP20 101 C1
Ash Cl Aylesbury HP20 102 A1
 Slough SL3 207 A2
 Walter's Ash HP14 161 A4
Ash Gn UB9 201 A3
Ash Gr Amersham HP6 154 A2
 Aylesbury HP21 116 A4
 Stoke Poges SL2 198 C3
 West Drayton UB8 208 C3
Ash Hill Prim Sch HP13 174 A4
Ash Hill Rd MK16 22 A2
Ash La SL4 209 B3
Ash Mead Dr UB9 190 A1
Ash Rd
 High Wycombe HP12 172 B2
 Princes Risborough HP27 139 A2
 Tring HP23 118 C2
Ash Tree Ho HP12 172 B2
Ash Vale WD3 178 B3
Ashbourne End HP21 115 B2
Ashbourne Gr SL6 202 B2
Ashbourne Ho 5 SL1 205 C2
Ashbrook Fst Sch MK8 33 C1
Ashburnham Cl 7 MK3 46 B1
Ashburnham Cres LU7 80 C3
Ashburnham Dr HP14 150 A1
Ashby MK6 47 A4
Ashby Rd HP4 134 B4
Ashby Villas LU7 92 A1
Ashcroft Ct SL1 197 A2
Ashcroft Dr UB9 189 C2
Ashcroft Rd SL6 202 B4
Ashcroft Terr HP23 119 A3
Ashdown SL6 196 A2
Ashdown Cl MK14 35 A4
Ashdown Rd HP13 174 A4
Ashdown Way HP6 154 B1
Ashen Cross SL3 207 A4
Ashenden Wlk SL2 198 B4
Ashendon Rd HP18 98 B3
Asheridge Rd HP5 144 A1
Ashfield MK14 34 B4
Ashfield Cl HP15 163 A1
Ashfield Cotts UB9 190 A1
Ashfield Gr MK2 58 B4
Ashfield Rd HP5 144 B1
Ashfield Rise HP18 109 B3
Ashfield Way HP15 163 A2
Ashfold Prep Sch HP18 110 C4
Ashford Cl HP21 116 A3
Ashford Cres MK8 45 B3
Ashford La SL4 204 A2
Ashford Rd SL0 200 B2
Ashgrove MK18 63 B1
Ashgrove Gdns HP22 86 C4
Ashlea MK46 6 C2
Ashlea Rd SL9 177 C1
Ashleigh Cl HP7 165 C4
Ashley HP10 185 C4
Ashley Cl LU7 105 A4
Ashley Ct Aylesbury HP19 115 A4
 Maidenhead SL6 203 A4
 Tylers Green HP10 163 A1
 West Drayton UB7 208 C3
Ashley Dr HP10 163 B1
Ashley Green Rd HP5 144 C3
Ashley Pk SL6 196 A1
Ashley Rd UB8 201 A2
Ashley Row HP20 102 A1
Ashleys WD3 167 C1
Ashlyns Ct HP4 135 A2
Ashlyns Rd HP4 135 A2
Ashlyns Sch HP4 135 B1
Ashmead Comb Sch HP21 115 B3
Ashmead La UB9 190 A1
Ashotts La HP5 143 A3
Ashpole Furlong MK5 46 A4
Ashridge OX39 147 A3
Ashridge Cl
 Bovingdon HP3 146 A2
 Milton Keynes MK3 57 B4
Ashridge Coll Gdns* HP4 121 B3
Ashridge Cotts HP4 121 C3
Ashridge La HP5 155 B4
Ashridge Man Coll HP4 121 B3
Ashridge Rise HP4 134 C3
Ashton Pl SL6 202 A3
Ashton Rd NN12 9 B4
Ashtree Wlk HP15 163 A1
Ashwell St 1 LU7 80 C4
Ashwells HP10 174 A4
Ashwells Manor Dr HP10 174 B4
Ashwells Way HP8 177 B4
Ashwood MK13 34 A4

Askett La HP27 . . . .**139** B4
Aspen Cl Aylesbury HP20 .**102** A1
Slough SL2 . . . .**205** A4
West Drayton UB7 . . . . . .**208** C3
Asplands Cl MK17 . . . .**49** A2
Aspley Ct MK17 . . . .**49** B2
Aspley Guise Lower Sch
MK17 . . . .**49** C2
Aspley Guise Sta MK17 . .**49** B3
Aspley Hill MK17 . . . .**49** B3
Aspley La MK17 . . . .**49** C1
Aspreys MK46 . . . .**6** C2
Assheton Rd HP9 . . . . . .**175** C2
Astlethorpe MK8 . . . .**33** C1
Astley Rd OX9 . . . .**126** A1
Aston Abbotts Rd
Cublington LU7 . . . .**78** B1
Weedon HP7 . . . .**87** C1
Aston Cl Aylesbury HP19 .**101** A2
Milton Keynes MK5 . . . . . .**46** A3
Aston Clinton Rd HP22 .**116** C3
Aston Clinton Sch HP22 **117** B3
Aston Ferry La RG9 . . . .**192** B3
Aston Hill OX49 . . . .**157** C4
Aston La RG9 . . . .**192** B2
Aston Mead SL4 . . . .**209** C4
Aston Rd HP17 . . . .**127** A3
Aston Rowant Nature
Reserve★ HP14 . . . .**157** C3
Astonville SL2 . . . .**198** B4
Astor Cl SL6 . . . .**203** A4
Astronomy Way HP19 . .**115** A4
Astrope La HP23 . . . .**104** A2
Astwood Rd MK43 . . . .**25** B4
Atherstone Ct MK8 . . . .**33** B1
Atherton Ct TW19 . . . . . .**213** B1
Atherton Ct SL4 . . . .**210** B4
Athlone Cl SL6 . . . .**195** C4
Athlone Sq SL4 . . . .**210** B3
Atkins Cl MK13 . . . .**34** A2
Atlas Ho HP3 . . . .**144** A1
Atterbrook MK13 . . . .**34** A2
Attingham Hill MK8 . . . . . .**34** A1
Atwell Cl MK8 . . . .**45** C4
Auckland Cl SL6 . . . .**203** A4
Auckland Pk MK1 . . . .**47** B2
Auckland Rd HP13 . . . . .**173** C4
Auden Cl MK16 . . . .**22** A3
Audley Dr SL6 . . . .**202** A3
Audley Mead MK13 . . . . . .**34** A2
August End SL3 . . . .**206** C4
Augustine Cl SL3 . . . . . .**212** C2
Augustus Rd MK11 . . . . . .**32** B2
Augustus Smith Ho 2
HP4 . . . .**135** B2
Austen Ave MK46 . . . .**7** A2
Austen Pl HP19 . . . .**100** C1
Austenway SL9 . . . .**188** C4
Austenwood Cl
Gerrards Cross SL9 . . . . .**177** B1
High Wycombe HP11 . . . .**173** A3
Austenwood La SL9 . . . .**188** B4
Austin Wray UB8 . . . .**201** B3
Austins Mead HP3 . . . . .**146** A2
Australia Ave SL6 . . . . . .**202** C4
Australia Rd SL1 . . . .**206** C4
Austwick La MK4 . . . .**46** A1
Autumn Cl
Aylesbury HP19 . . . .**101** A2
Slough SL1 . . . .**204** C3
Autumn Wlk SL6 . . . .**202** A3
Auxiliaries Way UB9 . . . .**189** C3
Avalon Rd SL8 . . . .**185** A3
Avebury SL1 . . . .**205** A3
Avebury Bvd MK6,MK9 . . .**34** C1
Aveling Rd HP13 . . . .**173** B3
Avenue Cl UB7 . . . .**208** B2
Avenue Ho HP5 . . . .**154** A4
Avenue Rd
Buckingham MK18 . . . . . .**41** C2
Maidenhead SL6 . . . .**203** A3
Winslow MK18 . . . .**65** C2
Avenue The
Amersham HP7 . . . .**154** B1
Bourne End SL8 . . . .**185** A2
Chinnor OX39 . . . .**147** B3
Datchet SL3 . . . .**211** A3
Dunstable LU6 . . . .**93** C4
Farnham Common SL2 . .**198** A4
Maidenhead SL6 . . . .**196** B2
Old Windsor SL4 . . . .**211** A1
Princes Risborough HP27 .**139** B2
Uxbridge UB8 . . . .**201** B1
Whitfield NN13 . . . .**26** B2
Worminghall HP18 . . . . . .**123** C3
Wraysbury TW19 . . . .**211** B3
Averil Cl SL6 . . . .**204** B4
Avery Ave HP13 . . . .**161** B1
Avington MK8 . . . .**33** C1
Avocet Way HP20 . . . . . .**101** C2
Avon Cl
Newport Pagnell MK16 . . .**22** B2
Slough SL1 . . . .**204** C3
Avon Gr MK3 . . . .**57** C4
Avon Pl HP21 . . . .**115** C2
Avonbury Ct NN13 . . . . . .**38** A3
Avondale SL6 . . . .**195** B1
Axis Pk SL3 . . . .**207** C4
Aylesbury & Thame
Airport HP17 . . . .**126** C4
Aylesbury Bsns Ctr
HP19 . . . .**101** A1
Aylesbury Coll HP21 . . . .**115** B4
Aylesbury Cres SL1 . . . .**205** B4
Aylesbury End HP9 . . . . .**175** C1

Aylesbury Gram Sch
HP21 . . . .**115** C4
Aylesbury High Sch
HP21 . . . .**115** C4
Aylesbury Ind Ctr HP19 .**101** B1
Aylesbury Rd
Aston Clinton HP22 . . . . .**117** A3
Bierton HP22 . . . .**102** A2
Chearsley HP18 . . . .**112** A1
Cuddington HP18 . . . .**113** A2
Great Missenden HP16 . . .**141** C1
Haddenham HP17,HP18 . .**126** B3
Princes Risborough HP27 .**139** B3
Thame OX9 . . . .**126** B3
Tring HP23 . . . .**118** C1
Wendover HP22 . . . .**131** A3
Wing LU7 . . . .**79** C1
Aylesbury St
Milton Keynes, Bletchley
MK2 . . . .**58** C4
Milton Keynes, Wolverton
MK12 . . . .**33** A3
Aylesbury St W MK12 . . .**33** B3
Aylesbury Sta HP20 . . . .**115** B4
Aylewater HP20 . . . .**101** C2
Aylesworth Ave SL2 . . . .**198** A1
Aylward Gdns HP5 . . . . .**144** A1
Aynho Ct MK8 . . . .**45** C4
Aynscombe Cl LU6 . . . . . .**93** C4
Ayr Way MK3 . . . .**46** C1
Ayres Ct HP21 . . . .**115** A3
Ayrshire Cl HP19 . . . .**101** A2
Aysgarth Pk SL6 . . . .**203** A1
Azalea Cl HP15 . . . .**163** A2
Azalea Way SL3 . . . .**206** C4

B

Babington Cl MK10 . . . . . .**36** A2
Babington Rd HP22 . . . . .**131** B3
Baccara Gr MK2 . . . .**58** B4
Bachelors Acre SL4 . . . . .**210** B3
Back Dr MK16 . . . .**12** C2
Back La
Chalfont St Giles HP8 . . . .**177** A4
South Heath HP16 . . . . . .**152** A4
Tingewick MK18 . . . .**51** B3
Back St Gawcott MK18 . . . .**51** C2
Thornborough MK18 . . . . .**54** A4
Wendover HP22 . . . .**131** A3
Backleys MK7 . . . .**48** A1
Backs The HP5 . . . .**154** A4
Bacombe La HP22 . . . . . .**131** A2
Bacon Hill MK46 . . . .**6** C2
Baconsmead UB9 . . . . . .**190** A1
Bad Godesberg Way
SL6 . . . .**202** C3
Bader Gdns SL1 . . . .**205** A4
Badgebury Rise SL7 . . . .**183** B4
Badgemoor La RG9 . . . . .**191** B2
Badgemore Ct MK8 . . . . . .**33** B1
Badgemore Cty Prim Sch
RG9 . . . .**191** B1
Badger Cl SL6 . . . .**202** B2
Badger Way HP15 . . . . . .**163** A3
Badgers Gate LU6 . . . .**93** C4
Badgers Mdw HP22 . . . . .**131** B3
Badgers Oak MK7 . . . .**48** A4
Badgers Way
Buckingham MK18 . . . . . .**52** C4
Marlow Bottom SL7 . . . . .**183** B4
Badgers Wlk WD3 . . . . . .**167** C3
Badgers Wood SL2 . . . . .**198** B4
Badminton Ho HP7 . . . . .**165** A4
Badminton Rd SL6 . . . . . .**202** A3
Badminton View MK8 . . . .**34** A1
Badrick Rd HP19 . . . .**100** C1
Bagley Cl UB7 . . . .**208** C2
Bailey Cl
High Wycombe HP13 . . . .**173** B4
Maidenhead SL6 . . . .**202** C4
Windsor SL4 . . . .**210** A3
Bailey Ho 9 SL8 . . . .**185** A2
Bailey's Ct 11 HP20 . . . . .**115** B4
Baily Ct MK5 . . . .**46** A3
Baines Ho HP11 . . . .**173** C2
Baird Cl SL1 . . . .**205** A2
Baker St
High Wycombe HP11 . . . .**172** C4
Waddesdon HP18 . . . .**99** A3
Baker's Orch HP10 . . . . .**185** C3
Baker's Rd UB8 . . . .**201** B3
Bakers Cl
Stoke Goldington MK16 . . .**12** A3
Turvey MK43 . . . .**8** C3
Bakers Ct HP18 . . . .**99** A3
Bakers La NN12 . . . .**9** A4
Bakers Wlk HP22 . . . .**116** C1
Bakers Wood UB9 . . . . . .**189** B2
Bakery Cl Cranfield MK43 .**25** A1
Grendon Underwood HP18 .**83** A3
Bala Cl MK3 . . . .**58** B3
Bala Way MK2 . . . .**58** B3
Balcary Gdns HP4 . . . . . .**134** C2
Baldways Cl HP22 . . . .**89** B2
Baldwin Cres MK16 . . . . . .**22** A2
Baldwin Rd
Beaconsfield HP9 . . . . . .**176** A1
Burnham SL1 . . . .**197** B1
Baldwin's Shore SL4 . . . .**210** B4
Balfe Mews MK7 . . . .**48** B2
Balfour Mews HP1 . . . . . .**146** A2
Balfour Pl SL7 . . . .**183** B2
Balfour Way HP20 . . . . . .**101** C1
Balham's La
Ibstone OX49 . . . .**179** C4
Stonor OX49 . . . .**179** C4

Ball Moor MK18 . . . .**52** B3
Ballard Cl HP21 . . . .**116** A3
Ballard Gn SL4 . . . .**209** C4
Ballinger Cl HP4 . . . .**135** A2
Ballinger Grange HP16 .**142** C1
Ballinger Rd HP16 . . . . . .**142** C1
Ballinger Row HP16 . . . . .**142** B2
Balmer Bridge MK18 . . . . .**52** C3
Balmer Cut MK18 . . . .**52** C3
Balmerino MK10 . . . .**36** A1
Balmoral SL6 . . . .**195** A1
Balmoral Cl SL1 . . . .**204** C4
Balmoral Ct
High Wycombe HP13 . . . .**173** A4
Newport Pagnell MK16 . . .**22** A2
Balmoral Gdns SL4 . . . . .**210** B2
Balsam Cl MK7 . . . .**48** A3
Bampton Cl MK4 . . . .**46** C1
Banburies SL3 . . . .**47** A1
Banbury Ave SL1 . . . .**204** C4
Bancroft Rdbt MK13 . . . . .**34** A3
Bandon Cl UB10 . . . .**201** C2
Bangors Cl SL0 . . . .**207** C4
Bangors Rd N SL0 . . . . . .**200** B2
Bangors Rd S Iver SL0 . . .**207** C4
Uxbridge SL0 . . . .**200** C1
Bank Gn HP5 . . . .**143** B4
Bank Mill HP4 . . . .**135** C2
Bank Mill La HP4 . . . .**135** C2
Bank Rd HP10 . . . .**174** B4
Bank St HP13 . . . .**174** A2
Bankfield Rdbt MK9 . . . . . .**35** A2
Banks Rd HP17 . . . .**127** A3
Banks Spur SL1 . . . .**205** A2
Bankside HP22 . . . .**131** A3
Banktop Pl MK4 . . . .**46** B2
Banner Ct HP12 . . . .**172** B4
Bannister Cl SL3 . . . .**206** C2
Bantock Cl MK7 . . . .**48** B3
Bar La HP27 . . . .**138** C4
Barbers Mews MK14 . . . . .**34** C3
Barbers Wlk HP23 . . . . . .**118** C2
Barbers Wood HP12 . . . .**172** A2
Barbers Wood Rd HP12 . .**172** A2
Barbury Ct MK14 . . . .**35** A4
Barchester Cl UB8 . . . . . .**201** B1
Barchester Rd SL3 . . . . . .**206** C2
Barclay Cl OX27 . . . .**72** C3
Barclay Ct 6 HP12 . . . . . .**172** C4
Bardney Cl SL6 . . . .**202** B2
Bardolphs Cl HP27 . . . . . .**139** B2
Bardsey Ct MK10 . . . .**36** A1
Barford MK11 . . . .**32** C2
Bargeman Rd SL6 . . . . . .**202** C3
Barham Lodge MK18 . . . . .**52** B4
Baring Cres HP9 . . . .**175** B2
Baring Rd
Beaconsfield HP9 . . . . . .**175** B2
High Wycombe HP13 . . . .**173** C4
Barkers Croft MK12 . . . . . .**33** B2
Barkestone Cl MK4 . . . . . .**46** B1
Barkham Cl LU7 . . . .**104** C4
Barkus Way MK14 . . . . . .**158** C3
Barlee Cres UB8 . . . .**208** B4
Barley Cl
Hazelmere HP15 . . . .**163** A2
Lewknor OX49 . . . .**157** A4
Weston Turville HP22 . . . .**116** C1
Barley Cres HP21 . . . .**115** B2
Barley Fields HP10 . . . . . .**185** C4
Barley Hill Cty Prim Sch
OX9 . . . .**126** A1
Barley Way 8 SL3 . . . . . .**183** B1
Barleycroft MK4 . . . .**46** C2
Barlow Rd HP22 . . . .**131** B3
Barn Cl
Farnham Common SL2 . . .**198** A4
Maidenhead SL6 . . . .**195** C1
Barn Ct HP12 . . . .**172** B4
Barn Dr SL6 . . . .**202** A2
Barn Field SL0 . . . .**207** C4
Barn La RG9 . . . .**191** B2
Barn Rd HP27 . . . .**138** C3
Barnabas Rd LU7 . . . .**80** B3
Barnacre Cl UB8 . . . .**208** B4
Barnard Cres HP21 . . . . . .**115** C3
Barnards Hill SL7 . . . .**183** B1
Barncroft MK43 . . . .**8** C3
Barncroft Rd HP4 . . . .**134** C2
Barnes Ave HP5 . . . .**144** B1
Barnes Pl MK6 . . . .**46** C4
Barnes Wallis Ct HP12 . .**172** C4
Barnes Way SL0 . . . .**207** C3
Barnett Way HP22 . . . . . .**102** A2
Barnfield SL1 . . . .**204** B3
Barnfield Cl SL8 . . . .**195** C3
Barnfield Dr MK6 . . . .**47** B3
Barnhill Cl SL7 . . . .**183** B2
Barnhill Gdns SL7 . . . . . .**183** B2
Barnhill Rd SL7 . . . .**183** B2
Barns Cl OX33 . . . .**122** A1
Barnsbury Ave HP20 . . . .**116** A4
Barnsbury Gdns MK16 . . .**22** B2
Barnsdale Dr MK4 . . . .**46** A1
Barnsfield Pl UB8 . . . .**201** B3
Barnstable Ct MK4 . . . .**46** B1
Baroma Way RG9 . . . .**191** C1
Barons Cl MK2 . . . .**58** B4
Barons Mead RG9 . . . . . .**191** B1
Baronsmead Rd HP12 . . .**172** C2
Barr's Rd SL6 . . . .**204** A4
Barrack Hill HP18 . . . .**112** C3
Barrack La SL4 . . . .**210** B3
Barracks Hill HP7 . . . .**164** C1

Barracks Rd HP11 . . . . . .**173** A3
Barrards Way HP9 . . . . . .**176** B2
Barrett Pl
High Wycombe HP11 . . . .**173** B3
Milton Keynes MK5 . . . . . .**45** C3
Barrie Cl HP19 . . . .**100** C1
Barrington Ct NN13 . . . . . .**38** A3
Barrington Mews 4 MK6 .**34** C1
Barrington Park Gdns
HP8 . . . .**166** B3
Barrow Lo SL2 . . . .**198** B1
Barrowcroft HP11 . . . .**173** C2
Barry Cl HP12 . . . .**172** B2
Barry View SL4 . . . .**209** B3
Bartelotts Rd SL2 . . . .**197** C1
Bartholomew Cl MK7 . . . . .**48** A3
Bartholomew Tipping
Way HP14 . . . .**158** C3
Bartlett Pl MK18 . . . .**41** C1
Bartletts SL9 . . . .**177** C2
Barton Rd
Milton Keynes MK2 . . . . . .**58** B3
Slough SL3 . . . .**206** C2
Barton Way HP13 . . . .**162** C1
Bartons Rd HP10 . . . .**163** A1
Bascote MK6 . . . .**47** B3
Base Cl 9 HP20 . . . .**101** C1
Basford Way SL4 . . . .**209** B2
Basildon Ct
3 Leighton Buzzard LU7 . .**80** C4
Milton Keynes MK8 . . . . . .**45** C4
Basing Rd WD3 . . . .**167** C1
Baskerfield Gr MK6 . . . . . .**47** B4
Bass Mead SL8 . . . .**195** C4
Basset Rd HP14 . . . .**171** B2
Bassetsbury La HP11 . . .**173** B3
Bassett Ct
Leighton Buzzard LU7 . . . .**80** C4
Newport Pagnell MK16 . . .**22** B2
Bassett Rd
Leighton Buzzard LU7 . . . .**80** C4
Uxbridge UB8 . . . .**201** B3
Bassett Way SL2 . . . .**197** C1
Batchelor Cl HP20 . . . . . .**101** C1
Batchelors Way
Amersham HP7 . . . .**165** B4
Chesham HP5 . . . .**144** A1
Bateman Dr HP21 . . . . . .**115** C3
Bates Cl
Granborough MK18 . . . . . .**75** C4
Milton Keynes MK15 . . . . .**35** B4
Slough SL3 . . . .**206** C4
Bates Ct HP20 . . . .**101** C1
Bates Gdns MK17 . . . .**68** A3
Bates La HP21 . . . .**116** C1
Bath Ct SL6 . . . .**202** B3
Bath La MK18 . . . .**52** B4
Bath Lane Terr MK18 . . . . .**52** B4
Bath Rd
Harmondsworth TW6,UB7 .**213** B3
Maidenhead SL6 . . . .**202** B3
Poyle SL3 . . . .**212** C3
Slough SL1,SL6 . . . .**204** C3
Bath Road Cotts SL3 . . . .**212** C3
Bathurst Cl SL0 . . . .**207** C2
Bathurst Wlk SL0 . . . .**207** C2
Batt Furlong HP21 . . . . . .**115** C2
Battersby Mews HP21 . . .**115** B4
Batting Cl HP14 . . . .**159** C4
Battings Wood Gdns
HP14 . . . .**161** B4
Battle Cl MK46 . . . .**13** C4
Battlemead Cl SL6 . . . . . .**196** B2
Battoney Vare SL6 . . . . . .**203** B2
Baulk The
Cheddington LU7 . . . .**104** C4
Ivinghoe LU7 . . . .**105** C3
Bawtree Rd UB8 . . . .**201** B3
Baxter Cl
Milton Keynes MK8 . . . . . .**45** C4
Slough SL1 . . . .**205** C2
Bay Ct HP4 . . . .**135** A2
Bay La MK46 . . . .**5** B1
Bay Tree Cl
Loudwater HP11 . . . .**174** A1
Newton Longville MK17 . . .**57** B2
Bay Tree Ct SL1 . . . .**197** B1
Bayard Ave MK14 . . . .**34** C3
Bayhurst Wood
Countryside Pk★ UB9 .**190** C3
Bayley Cres SL1 . . . .**204** A4
Bayley Gdns HP21 . . . . . .**161** C3
Bayley Hatch HP16 . . . . . .**152** B4
Baylis Court Sch SL1 . . . .**205** B4
Baylis Par SL1 . . . .**205** C4
Baylis Rd SL1 . . . .**205** C3
Bayman Manor HP5 . . . . .**144** C1
Bayne Hill HP9 . . . .**176** B2
Bayne Hill Cl HP9 . . . .**176** B2
Baynham Mead MK7 . . . . .**48** A4
Baysfarm Ct SL7 . . . .**213** B3
Beacham Rd HP12 . . . . . .**172** B2
Beachborough Sch NN13 .**39** A2
Beacon Ave LU6 . . . .**93** C4
Beacon Cl
Beaconsfield HP9 . . . . . .**175** A1
Chalfont St Peter SL9 . . . .**177** C2
Stone HP17 . . . .**114** B3
Uxbridge UB8 . . . .**201** B4
Beacon Ct Colnbrook SL3 .**212** B4
Milton Keynes MK4 . . . . . .**46** B1
Beacon Ctr The HP9 . . . .**175** A1
Beacon Hill HP10 . . . .**174** B4
Beacon La SL7 . . . .**171** C1
Beacon Rd Ivinghoe HP4 .**106** C1
Ringshall HP4 . . . .**106** C1

Beacon Sch The HP6 . . .**154** A2
Beacon Way HP23 . . . . . .**119** B3
Beaconsfield Ave HP3 . .**162** A1
Beaconsfield Com La
SL2 . . . .**187** B3
Beaconsfield Cotts SL8 .**185** A1
Beaconsfield High Sch
HP9 . . . .**175** B1
Beaconsfield Mews
HP9 . . . .**186** A6
Beaconsfield Pl MK16 . . .**22** B2
Beaconsfield Rd
Aston Clinton HP22 . . . . .**117** C2
Aylesbury HP21 . . . .**115** C4
Farnham Common SL2 . .**198** B3
Tring HP23 . . . .**118** C2
Beaconsfield Sch The
HP9 . . . .**175** C1
Beaconsfield Sta HP9 . . .**175** C2
Beadlemead MK6 . . . .**47** B3
Beales La MK7 . . . .**48** A3
Bealings End HP9 . . . . . .**175** B3
Beamish Way MK18 . . . . . .**66** A3
Beamond End La
Holmer Green HP7,HP16 .**163** A4
Hyde Heath HP7,HP16 . . .**163** C4
Beanfare MK6 . . . .**47** B2
Bearbrook Cl HP21 . . . . . .**115** B4
Bearsbrook Comb Sch
HP19 . . . .**115** B4
Bearswood End HP9 . . . .**175** C2
Beatrice Cl OX27 . . . .**72** C3
Beauchamp Cl MK14 . . . . .**34** C3
Beauchamp Cl SL1 . . . . . .**205** C3
Beaudesert Mews UB7 . .**208** C2
Beaufort Cl
Aylesbury HP21 . . . .**116** B4
Marlow SL7 . . . .**183** C1
Beaufort Dr MK15 . . . .**35** C4
Beaufort Gdns SL7 . . . . . .**183** C1
Beaufort Pl SL6 . . . .**203** B2
Beaulieu Cl SL3 . . . .**211** A3
Beaumaris Ct SL1 . . . . . .**205** B4
Beaumaris Gr MK5 . . . . . .**46** A3
Beaumont Cl SL6 . . . .**202** A2
Beaumont Cotts 1 SL4 .**210** B4
Beaumont Ct SL3 . . . .**206** B4
Beaumont Rd Slough SL2 **205** B4
Windsor SL4 . . . .**210** B3
Beaumont Rise SL7 . . . . .**183** C1
Beaumont Way HP15 . . .**162** C2
Beaver Cl MK18 . . . .**52** C4
Bec La MK15 . . . .**35** A4
Beckets Sq HP4 . . . .**135** B2
Beckins Way HP10 . . . . . .**185** B4
Beckinsale Gr MK8 . . . . . .**45** C4
Bedder Rd HP12 . . . .**172** B2
Bede Ct HP4 . . . .**121** B4
Bedfont Court Est
TW19 . . . .**213** A2
Bedfont Ct TW19 . . . .**213** A2
Bedfont Rd TW19 . . . .**213** C1
Bedford Ave
Little Chalfont HP6 . . . . . .**166** B4
Slough SL1 . . . .**205** A4
Bedford Cl Chenies WD3 .**156** A1
Maidenhead SL6 . . . .**202** A2
Bedford Ct HP6 . . . .**166** B4
Bedford Dr SL2 . . . .**198** A3
Bedford Rd
Aspley Guise MK17 . . . . . .**49** C3
Cold Brayfield MK46 . . . . . .**8** A3
Cranfield MK43 . . . .**25** B1
Sherington MK16 . . . .**14** A1
Bedford Rd E NN7 . . . .**1** B3
Bedford Rd W NN7 . . . .**1** A3
Bedford St
Berkhamsted HP4 . . . . . .**135** B2
Milton Keynes, Bletchley
MK2 . . . .**58** B4
Milton Keynes, Wolverton
MK12 . . . .**33** B3
Woburn MK17 . . . .**60** C4
Bedgebury Pl MK7 . . . .**48** A3
Bedgrove HP21 . . . .**116** B3
Bedgrove Inf Sch HP21 . .**116** B3
Bedgrove Jun Sch HP21 **116** B3
Bedlam La MK16 . . . .**14** B1
Bedwins La SL7 . . . .**195** A3
Bedwyn Wlk HP21 . . . . . .**115** B2
Beech RG9 . . . .**191** B1
Beech Ave
Lane End HP14 . . . .**171** B4
Olney MK46 . . . .**6** C2
Beech Cl Bierton HP22 . . .**102** A2
Buckingham MK18 . . . . . .**41** B1
Flackwell Heath HP10 . . . .**174** A1
High Wycombe HP11 . . . .**173** C2
Maidenhead SL6 . . . .**202** A4
Stokenchurch HP14 . . . . .**158** C2
Beech Ct 1 SL7 . . . .**183** C1
Beech Dr HP4 . . . .**135** B2
Beech Gn HP21 . . . .**115** B3
Beech Gr Amersham HP7 .**165** B4
Leighton Buzzard LU7 . . . .**80** C4
Tring HP23 . . . .**119** B2
Beech Hill Ct HP4 . . . .**135** C4
Beech House Dr NN12 . . .**18** C2
Beech La
Prestwood HP16 . . . .**151** A4
Seer Green HP9 . . . .**176** C2
Beech Leys MK18 . . . .**63** C2
Beech Pk
Little Chalfont HP6 . . . . . .**155** A1
Walter's Ash HP14 . . . . . .**150** A1
Beech Rd Aylesbury HP21 **115** B3

Beech Rd continued
Chinnor OX39 ...147 B3
High Wycombe HP11 ...173 C2
Newport Pagnell MK16 ...22 A2
Princes Risborough HP27 ...139 B2
Slough SL3 ...206 C2
Beech St HP11 ...173 B2
Beech Tree Ct HP22 ...87 A3
Beech Tree Rd HP15 ...163 B4
Beech Waye SL9 ...189 A2
Beech Wlk HP23 ...119 A2
Beechams The MK17 ...67 B3
Beechcroft HP4 ...135 B2
Beechcroft Rd
Chesham HP5 ...144 A1
Milton Keynes MK3 ...57 C3
Beeches Dr SL2 ...198 A4
Beeches Gr HP10 ...163 A1
Beeches Pk HP9 ...175 B1
Beeches Rd SL2 ...198 A4
Beeches The
Chorleywood WD3 ...167 C2
Deanshanger MK19 ...31 C2
Tring HP23 ...119 B2
Wendover HP22 ...131 B3
Beechfield Way HP15 ...163 A2
Beechfield Wlk HP15 ...163 A2
Beechingstoke [4] SL7 ...183 C2
Beechlands HP15 ...162 C1
Beechtree Ave SL7 ...183 B3
Beechview Sch HP13 ...173 C3
Beechview Ave
Chorleywood WD3 ...167 A3
Little Chalfont HP6 ...155 B1
Uxbridge UB8 ...208 C4
Beechwood Cl HP6 ...166 B4
Beechwood Cotts WD3 ...167 A2
Beechwood Ct LU6 ...93 C4
Beechwood Dr
Aldbury HP23 ...120 B3
Maidenhead SL6 ...202 A4
Marlow SL7 ...194 A4
Beechwood Gdns SL1 ...205 C2
Beechwood Ho HP22 ...117 C3
Beechwood La HP22 ...131 B3
Beechwood Pk
Chorleywood WD3 ...167 C3
Felden HP3 ...146 C4
Beechwood Pl [21] HP13 ...173 A4
Beechwood Rd
Beaconsfield HP9 ...175 B1
High Wycombe HP12 ...161 A4
Slough SL2 ...205 B4
Beechwood Sec Sch
SL2 ...198 A1
Beechwood Way HP22 ...117 C3
Beecroft Lower Com Sch
LU6 ...93 C4
Beecroft Way LU6 ...93 C4
Beehive Cl UB10 ...201 C3
Beel Cl HP7 ...166 B4
Beethoven Cl MK7 ...48 B2
Beeward Cl MK12 ...33 A3
Beggars La HP23 ...119 C2
Bekonscot Ct MK14 ...21 C1
Bekonscot Model Village★
HP9 ...175 C1
Belfast Ave SL1 ...205 B4
Belgrave Mews UB8 ...201 B1
Belgrave Par SL1 ...205 C3
Belgrave Rd
Aylesbury HP19 ...101 A2
Slough SL1 ...205 C3
Bell Alley MK18 ...65 C2
Bell Ave UB7 ...208 C2
Bell Bsns Ctr SL6 ...202 C3
Bell Cl Beaconsfield HP9 ...175 C1
Cublington LU7 ...78 A1
Drayton Parslow MK17 ...68 A3
Princes Risborough HP27 ...139 A2
Slough SL2 ...206 A4
Thame OX9 ...125 C1
Bell Cres HP27 ...138 C3
Bell Ct SL7 ...193 C2
Bell Gn HP3 ...146 A2
Bell La Berkhamsted HP4 ...134 C3
Eton SL4 ...204 C1
Henley-on-T RG9 ...191 C2
Little Chalfont HP6 ...155 B1
Princes Risborough HP27 ...139 A2
Syresham NN13 ...27 A4
Thame OX9 ...125 C1
Bell Lane Comb Sch
HP6 ...155 A1
Bell Leys HP22 ...89 A3
Bell St Henley-on-T RG9 ...191 C1
Maidenhead SL6 ...202 C3
Princes Risborough HP27 ...139 A2
Bell Street Mews RG9 ...191 C1
Bell View SL4 ...209 C3
Bell View Cl SL4 ...209 C3
Bell Wlk HP22 ...89 A2
Bellamy Rd HP13 ...173 B4
Bellclose Rd UB7 ...208 C4
Belle Vue HP17 ...114 C3
Bellfield Cty Mid Sch
HP13 ...173 A4
Bellfield Rd HP13 ...173 A4
Bellini Cl MK7 ...48 B3
Bellis Gr MK6 ...47 B4
Bells Hill SL2 ...199 A2
Bells Hill Gn SL2 ...199 A3
Bells La SL3 ...212 A2
Bells Mdw HP15 ...35 A4
Bellsfield Ct SL4 ...204 C1
Bellswood La SL0 ...207 A4
Bellway MK17 ...49 A3

Bellwether MK11 ...33 A2
Bellwood Rise HP11 ...173 A3
Belmers Rd HP23 ...119 B1
Belmont SL2 ...205 A4
Belmont Cl UB8 ...201 B3
Belmont Cotts SL3 ...212 B4
Belmont Cres SL6 ...202 B4
Belmont Ct MK8 ...33 B1
Belmont Dr SL6 ...202 B4
Belmont Park Ave SL6 ...202 B4
Belmont Park Rd SL6 ...202 B4
Belmont Rd
Chesham HP5 ...144 A2
Maidenhead SL6 ...202 B4
Uxbridge UB8 ...201 B3
Belmont Vale SL6 ...202 B4
Belsize Ave MK6 ...35 A1
Belsize Cotts WD3 ...156 C3
Belton Rd HP4 ...135 A3
Belvedere La MK17 ...58 C4
Belvedere Mans SL1 ...205 B2
Belvedere Rdbt MK9 ...34 C2
Belvoir Ave MK4 ...46 B1
Bembridge [18] SL1 ...205 C2
Ben More SL9 ...188 C3
Benbow Ct MK5 ...46 A4
Benbow Way UB8 ...208 B4
Bench Manor Cres SL9 ...177 B1
Bencombe Rd SL7 ...183 C3
Benen-Stock Rd TW19 ...213 A1
Benham Cl HP5 ...144 A1
Benhams La RG9 ...180 B1
Benjamin Ho [17] HP13 ...173 A4
Benjamin Rd HP13 ...173 A4
Benjamins Footpath
HP13 ...173 A4
Bennet Cl MK11 ...32 A2
Bennett End Rd HP14 ...159 B4
Bennett's Hill MK18 ...76 B4
Bennetts HP5 ...144 B1
Bennetts Cl Padbury MK18 53 A1
Slough SL1 ...205 A3
Bennetts La HP22 ...102 C4
Benning Ave LU6 ...93 C4
Benning Ct SL4 ...209 B2
Bens Cl MK19 ...19 C3
Benson Cl Slough SL2 ...206 A3
Uxbridge UB8 ...208 C4
Bentall Cl MK15 ...35 B4
Bentinck Cl SL9 ...188 B3
Bentinck Rd UB7 ...208 B3
Bentley Pk SL1 ...197 B2
Bentley Rd SL1 ...205 A3
Benton Dr OX39 ...147 B4
Bentons The HP4 ...134 C3
Benwell Cl MK13 ...33 C3
Benwells OX39 ...147 B3
Berberis Cl MK7 ...48 A3
Berberis Wlk UB7 ...208 C1
Bercham MK8 ...33 C1
Beresford Ave
Aylesbury HP19 ...101 B2
Slough SL2 ...206 B3
Beresford Rd MK4 ...46 A2
Beresford Rd WD3 ...167 C1
Beretun MK8 ...33 C1
Berevilles La MK10 ...35 C2
Bergamot Gdns MK7 ...48 A3
Berkeley Ave HP5 ...143 C2
Berkeley Cl
Chesham HP5 ...144 A1
Pitstone LU7 ...105 A2
Stoke Goldington MK16 ...12 A3
Berkeley Mews SL7 ...183 C1
Berkeley Rd
Loudwater HP10 ...174 B1
Thame OX9 ...126 A1
Berkeley Rise HP19 ...101 A1
Berkhampstead Rd HP5 144 B1
Berkhamsted Castle★
HP4 ...135 B3
Berkhamsted Collegiate
Sch (Boys) HP4 ...135 B4
Berkhamsted Collegiate
Sch (Girls) HP4 ...135 A2
Berkhamsted Sports Ctr
HP4 ...135 A3
Berkhamsted Sta HP4 ...135 B3
Berkley Cl SL6 ...202 A4
Berkley Ct HP4 ...135 B2
Berkley Rd HP9 ...175 B3
Berks Hill WD3 ...167 B3
Berkshire Ave SL1 ...205 A4
Berkshire Coll
of Agriculture SL6 ...194 A1
Berkshire Gn MK5 ...45 C2
Berkshire Lodge [1] SL6 202 C3
Berkshire School of Arts
& Design SL6 ...202 B4
Berling Rd MK8 ...33 C1
Bernard Cl HP18 ...112 C1
Bernard's Cl HP18 ...112 A1
Bernards Cl HP16 ...152 A4
Bernards Way HP10 ...174 A1
Bernay Gdns MK15 ...35 A4
Berndene Rise HP27 ...139 A2
Berners Cl SL1 ...204 C3
Bernewood Cl HP18 ...125 B4
Bernstein Cl MK7 ...48 B2
Berries Rd SL8 ...196 A4
Berry Field SL2 ...206 B4
Berry Field Pk HP6 ...154 A1
Berry Hill SL7 ...203 B4
Berry Hill Ct SL6 ...203 B4
Berry La
Aspley Guise MK17 ...49 C3
Chorleywood WD3 ...167 A2
Berry Way MK17 ...57 B2

Berryfield LU7 ...104 C4
Berryfield Rd
Aylesbury HP19 ...101 A2
Princes Risborough HP27 ...139 B2
Berryfield Sch HP27 ...139 B2
Berrystead MK7 ...48 A2
Berwald Cl MK7 ...48 B2
Berwick Ave SL1 ...205 A3
Berwick Cl
Beaconsfield HP9 ...176 A1
Marlow SL7 ...183 B1
Berwick La SL7 ...183 B2
Berwick Rd SL7 ...183 B2
Bessemer Cres HP19 ...100 C1
Bessemer St MK14 ...22 A1
Bestobell Rd SL1 ...205 B4
Betjeman Ct UB7 ...208 B3
Bettina Gr MK2 ...58 B4
Bettles Cl UB8 ...201 B2
Bettles Ct UB8 ...201 B2
Betty's Cl MK17 ...57 B2
Betty's La HP23 ...119 A2
Bevan Ct MK18 ...65 C2
Bevan Hill HP5 ...144 A1
Bevelwood Gdns HP12 ...172 B4
Beverley Cl SL7 ...183 A1
Beverley Ct SL1 ...206 A2
Beverley Gdns SL6 ...195 A1
Beverley Pl MK6 ...35 A1
Bewdley Dr LU7 ...80 B4
Bexley St SL4 ...210 B3
Beyners Gn HP16 ...152 A2
Bicester Rd
Aylesbury HP18,HP19 ...101 A1
Long Crendon HP18 ...125 B3
Ludgershall HP18 ...96 B4
Marsh Gibbon OX27 ...71 C2
Oakley HP18 ...109 B3
Twyford MK18 ...62 B1
Bickleigh Cres MK4 ...46 B2
Biddles Ct [6] SL1 ...204 C3
Biddlesden Rd NN13 ...39 A3
Bideford Cl LU7 ...80 B4
Bideford Gn LU7 ...80 B4
Bideford Spur SL2 ...198 A1
Bierton CE Comb Sch
HP22 ...102 A2
Bierton Rd HP20 ...101 C1
Bigfrith La SL7 ...195 A3
Biggs La HP27 ...113 C1
Bigmore La HP14 ...170 A4
Bignell Croft MK5 ...34 A1
Biko Cl UB8 ...208 B4
Bilbrook La MK4 ...46 B2
Billet La
Berkhamsted HP4 ...135 A3
Iver SL0,SL3 ...207 A4
Billings Cl HP14 ...158 C3
Billingwell Pl MK6 ...35 A1
Billwell HP18 ...125 B4
Bilton Rd HP20 ...101 B1
Binders Ind Est HP15 ...162 B4
Bingham Cl MK4 ...46 B1
Bingham Rd SL1 ...204 A4
Binghams The SL6 ...203 A2
Birch Ave UB8 ...208 C2
Birch Cl Amersham HP6 ...154 C1
Iver Heath SL0 ...200 B2
Birch Cres UB10 ...201 C2
Birch Ct HP21 ...115 B3
Birch Dr WD3 ...178 B3
Birch Gdns HP7 ...165 C4
Birch Gr Slough SL2 ...205 A4
Windsor SL4 ...209 B3
Birch La HP3 ...156 A4
Birch Rd HP4 ...134 B4
Birch St HP11 ...173 A2
Birch Tree Gr HP5 ...145 A1
Birch Way Chesham HP5 ...144 B1
Tylers Green HP10 ...163 A1
Birchdale SL9 ...188 B2
Birchen Lee MK4 ...46 B1
Birches Rise HP12 ...172 C4
Birches The Felden HP3 ...146 C4
High Wycombe HP13 ...173 C4
Birchfield Gr MK2 ...58 B4
Birchington Rd SL4 ...210 A3
Birchwood Chase HP15 ...151 B3
Birchwood Cl HP12 ...172 A3
Bird Mount Cotts SL4 ...210 B4
Birdcage Wlk HP13 ...173 A4
Birdlip La MK7 ...48 A4
Birds La MK16 ...12 A3
Birdwood Rd SL6 ...202 A4
Birfield Rd HP10 ...174 B1
Birinus Ct HP12 ...172 B3
Birkdale Cl MK3 ...57 B4
Birkett Way HP8 ...166 B3
Birley Rd SL1 ...205 B4
Bisham Abbey National
Sports Ctr SL7 ...194 B4
Bisham CE Prim Sch
SL7 ...194 B4
Bisham Ct Bisham SL7 ...194 C3
[17] Slough SL1 ...205 C2
Bisham Gn SL7 ...194 C3
Bisham Rd Bisham SL7 ...194 C4
Marlow SL7 ...183 C1
Bishop Ct SL6 ...202 B4
Bishop Ctr The SL6 ...203 C4
Bishop Parker
RC Comb Sch MK2 ...58 B3
Bishop Wood Jun Sch
HP23 ...119 A2
Bishops Ct MK18 ...52 B4
Bishops Farm Cl SL4 ...209 A4
Bishops Field HP22 ...118 A2
Bishops Ho HP9 ...175 B2

Bishops Mdw HP22 ...102 A2
Bishops Orch SL2 ...198 A1
Bishops Wlk
Aylesbury HP21 ...115 C3
Woburn Sands MK17 ...49 A2
Wooburn Green HP10 ...185 C4
Bishopstone
Milton Keynes MK13 ...34 A3
Stone HP17 ...115 A1
Bishopstone Rd HP17 ...114 B3
Bissley Dr SL6 ...202 A2
Bit The HP23 ...119 B1
Bittenham Cl HP17 ...114 C2
Bitterne Way [22] MK7 ...48 B2
Black Acre Cl HP7 ...165 C4
Black Boy La RG9,SL7 ...193 B2
Black Horse Ave MK5 ...154 B3
Black Horse Cl SL4 ...209 B3
Black Horse Pl UB8 ...201 B4
Black Park Country Park
Visitor Ctr★ SL3 ...199 C1
Black Park Ctry Pk★
SL0,SL3 ...200 A2
Black Park Rd
Fulmer SL3 ...199 C2
Iver Heath SL3 ...199 C2
Blackamoor La SL6 ...203 A4
Blackberry Ct MK7 ...48 A3
Blackburn Trad Est
TW19 ...213 A1
Blackdown MK11 ...32 C2
Blacketts Wood Dr
WD3 ...167 A3
Blackfield La HP16 ...142 C2
Blackham Ct MK6 ...46 C4
Blackheath Cres MK13 ...34 B2
Blackhorse Cl HP6 ...154 C1
Blackhorse Cres HP6 ...154 C1
Blackmoor Gate MK4 ...46 C1
Blackmore Way UB8 ...201 B3
Blackpond La SL2 ...198 A2
Blacksmith La HP16 ...151 B3
Blacksmith Row SL3 ...207 A1
Blacksmith's La HP9 ...189 B1
Blacksmiths Rd HP27 ...138 B4
Blackthorn Cl OX25 ...81 A2
Blackthorn Dell SL3 ...206 B2
Blackthorn Gr MK17 ...49 A2
Blackthorne Cres SL3 ...212 C3
Blackthorne Ind Pk SL3 212 C3
Blackthorne La HP16 ...142 C2
Blackthorne Rd SL3 ...212 C3
Blackwater Dr HP21 ...115 B2
Blackwell End NN12 ...18 B2
Blackwell Hall La HP5 ...155 B3
Blackwell Pl MK5 ...46 A2
Blackwell Rd HP14 ...171 A3
Blackwells Yd NN7 ...1 A3
Blackwood Cres MK13 ...33 C3
Blaine Cl HP23 ...119 A3
Blair Rd SL1 ...205 C3
Blairmont St MK9 ...34 C2
Blake Way OX9 ...126 A1
Blakedown Rd LU7 ...80 B3
Blakeney Ct
Maidenhead SL6 ...195 C1
Milton Keynes MK4 ...57 A4
Blakes Ho HP10 ...174 B1
Blanchland Circ MK10 ...36 A3
Blandford Cl SL3 ...206 B2
Blandford Rd N SL3 ...206 B2
Blandford Rd S SL3 ...206 B2
Blansby Chase MK4 ...46 B2
Blatherwick Ct MK5 ...45 C4
Blaydon Cl MK3 ...57 B4
Bleak Hall Rdbt MK6 ...47 C2
Bleasdale MK13 ...34 B3
Bledlow Cotts HP27 ...138 C1
Bledlow Ridge Rd HP27 148 B4
Bledlow Ridge Sch
HP14 ...159 C4
Bledow Rd HP27 ...148 C4
Blenheim Ave MK11 ...32 C2
Blenheim Cl
Cheddington LU7 ...104 C4
Longwick HP27 ...138 B3
Slough SL3 ...206 C3
Blenheim Ct HP13 ...173 B1
Blenheim Pl
Aylesbury HP21 ...115 C3
Syresham NN13 ...27 B4
Blenheim Rd
High Wycombe HP12 ...172 B2
Maidenhead SL6 ...202 A4
Slough SL3 ...206 B1
Bletcham Rdbt MK1 ...47 C2
Bletcham Way
Bow Brickhill MK7 ...48 A2
Milton Keynes MK1,MK7 ...47 C1
Walton MK7 ...48 A2
Bletchley Com Hospl
MK3 ...47 A1
Bletchley Park Mus★
MK3 ...58 A4
Bletchley Rd
Milton Keynes MK5 ...46 A2
Newton Longville MK17 ...57 B2
Stewkley LU7 ...68 C2
Bletchley Sta MK3 ...58 A4
Blinco La SL3 ...206 C4
Blind La
Bourne End SL8,HP10 ...185 A3
South Heath HP16 ...153 A4
Blind Pond Ind Est MK17 48 B1
Bliss Ave MK43 ...25 B1

Bliss Ct MK7 ...48 B2
Blisworth MK6 ...47 B3
Blondell Cl UB7 ...213 B4
Bloomfield Rd SL6 ...202 A3
Bloomsbury Ct HP11 ...60 C3
Blossom Way UB10 ...201 C3
Blucher St HP5 ...154 A4
Blue Max Mus★ SL7 ...172 A1
Bluebell Cl HP13 ...52 B4
Bluebell Ct MK7 ...48 A3
Blumfield Cres SL1 ...204 C4
Blumfield Ct SL1 ...197 B1
Blundells Rd MK13 ...34 B3
Blunden Dr SL3 ...207 B1
Blyth Cl HP21 ...115 B2
Blyth Ct MK4 ...57 A4
Blythe Cl Iver SL0 ...207 A4
Newport Pagnell MK16 ...22 B2
Blyton Cl HP9 ...175 B2
Boadicea St [8] SL1 ...204 C3
Boarlands Cl SL1 ...205 C4
Boathouse Reach RG9 ...191 C2
Bobmore La SL7 ...183 C2
Bockmer La SL7 ...193 A4
Boddington Rd HP22 ...131 B2
Bodenham MK18 ...52 C4
Bodiam Cl
Aylesbury HP21 ...116 A3
Milton Keynes MK5 ...46 A3
Bodiam Ho [6] HP13 ...173 C4
Bodle Ct SL3 ...35 A3
Bodmin Ave SL2 ...205 A4
Bodnant Ct MK4 ...45 C1
Bois Ave HP6 ...154 A2
Bois Hill HP5 ...154 B2
Bois La HP6 ...154 B2
Bois Moor Rd HP5 ...154 B3
Bolan Ct MK8 ...45 C3
Bold's Ct SL2 ...199 A3
Bolter End La HP14 ...171 A3
Bolton Ave SL4 ...210 B2
Bolton Cl MK3 ...47 A1
Bolton Cres SL4 ...210 B2
Bolton Rd SL4 ...210 B2
Bon Secours Hospl HP9 175 C1
Bond Ave MK1 ...47 B2
Bond Cl Aylesbury HP21 ...115 C3
West Drayton UB7 ...208 C4
Bonham Carter Rd
HP22 ...131 C4
Bonham Ct HP21 ...115 A3
Bonnards Rd MK17 ...57 B2
Bonnersfield HP18 ...125 B4
Booker Ave MK13 ...34 A3
Booker Cl HP12 ...172 A3
Booker La HP12 ...172 A2
Booker Pl HP12 ...172 A2
Bookerhill Rd HP12 ...172 B3
Boot La HP17 ...113 C1
Booth Pl LU6 ...92 C3
Borderside SL2 ...206 A4
Borough Ct NN13 ...38 A3
Borough Rd NN13 ...38 A3
Borough Wlk MK9 ...34 C2
Bosanquet Cl UB8 ...201 B1
Boss La
Great Kingshill HP14 ...162 A4
Hughenden Valley HP14 ...162 A3
Bossard Pl [11] LU7 ...80 C4
Bossiney Pl MK6 ...34 C4
Bossington La LU7 ...80 C4
Bostock La MK18 ...52 B4
Boston Dr SL8 ...185 A2
Boston Gr SL1 ...205 B4
Boswell Ct MK18 ...41 C1
Boswell La MK19 ...31 C2
Boswick La HP4 ...134 B4
Bosworth Cl MK3 ...46 C1
Botham Dr SL1 ...205 C2
Botley La HP5 ...145 A1
Botley Rd HP5 ...144 C1
Bottesford Cl MK4 ...46 B1
Bottle Dump Rdbt MK17 ...56 C3
Bottle Square La HP14 ...159 B3
Bottom Dr LU6 ...93 C4
Bottom House Farm La
HP8 ...165 C1
Bottom House La HP23 ...120 A1
Bottom La HP9 ...176 B3
Bottom Orch HP18 ...112 A1
Bottom Rd
Bledlow Ridge HP14 ...160 A3
Buckland Common HP23 ...132 C2
Buckland Common HP23 ...133 A2
Bottom Waltons
Caravan Site SL2 ...197 C2
Bottrells La HP7,HP8 ...176 C4
Botyl Rd MK18 ...74 C3
Boughton Way HP6 ...155 B1
Boulevard The MK9 ...34 C3
Boulmer Rd UB8 ...201 B1
Boulters Cl
Maidenhead SL6 ...196 B1
Slough SL1 ...205 A4
Boulters Ct
Amersham HP6 ...154 C1
Maidenhead SL6 ...196 B1
Boulters Gdns SL6 ...196 B1
Boulters La SL6 ...196 B1
Boulters Lock MK14 ...21 C1
Boundary Cres MK11 ...32 C3
Boundary Pl HP10 ...185 B4
Boundary Rd
Brackley NN13 ...38 A3

Boundary Rd *continued*
Gerrards Cross SL9 .....177 B2
Taplow SL6 .....203 C4
Wooburn Green HP10 .....185 B4
Boundary The MK6 .....46 C4
Bounds Croft MK12 .....33 B2
Bounty St MK13 .....33 C4
Bourbon St HP20 .....115 B4
Bourne Ave SL4 .....210 B2
Bourne Cl SL8 .....185 A3
Bourne End MK43 .....25 B3
Bourne End Bsns Ctr 17 SL8 .....185 A2
Bourne End Mills Ind Est HP1 .....146 A4
Bourne End Rd
Bourne End SL6 .....196 C4
Cranfield MK43 .....25 B2
Bourne End Sta SL8 .....185 A2
Bourne Rd
Berkhamsted HP4 .....134 C3
Slough SL1 .....205 B2
Bourne The HP1 .....146 A2
Bourton Low MK7 .....48 A3
Bourton Meadow Sch MK18 .....52 C4
Bourton Rd MK18 .....52 C4
Bourtonville MK18 .....52 B4
Bouverie Way SL3 .....206 C1
Boveney Cl SL1 .....205 A2
Boveney New Rd SL4 .....204 C1
Boveney Rd SL4 .....204 B1
Boveney Wood La SL1 .....186 B1
Bovingdon Ct HP3 .....146 A2
Bovingdon Green La HP3 .....145 C2
Bovingdon Hts SL7 .....183 A1
Bovingdon Prim Sch HP3 .....146 A2
Bow Brickhill Fst Sch MK17 .....48 B1
Bow Brickhill Rd MK17 .....48 C2
Bow Brickhill Sta MK7 .....48 A1
Bowden La HP11 .....173 B3
Bowen Cl MK7 .....48 B3
Bower Cl LU6 .....92 C3
Bower Ct 3 SL1 .....204 C3
Bower La LU6 .....92 C3
Bower Way SL1 .....204 C3
Bowerbank Ct 15 HP20 .....101 C1
Bowerdean Rd HP13 .....173 B4
Bowers La HP14 .....159 B4
Bowes Cl MK16 .....22 B2
Bowes-Lyon Cl 7 SL4 .....210 B3
Bowl Rdbt The MK4 .....46 B3
Bowland Dr MK4 .....46 A1
Bowler Lea HP13 .....161 B1
Bowler Rd HP21 .....115 C2
Bowler's Orch HP8 .....177 A4
Bowles Pl MK6 .....47 B4
Bowling Alley HP22 .....86 B4
Bowling Cl UB10 .....201 C2
Bowling Ct RG9 .....191 B2
Bowling Gr HP14 .....158 B3
Bowling Green Rd MK43 .....25 B1
Bowling Leys MK10 .....36 A1
Bowmans Cl SL1 .....197 A2
Bowmont Dr HP21 .....115 B2
Bowood Ct 5 MK8 .....33 C1
Bowood La
Lee Common HP22 .....141 C3
Wendover HP22 .....141 C3
Bowry Dr TW19 .....211 C1
Bowstridge Ct 6 HP13 .....173 B4
Bowstridge La HP8 .....177 B3
Bowyer Cres UB9 .....189 C3
Bowyer Dr SL1 .....204 C3
Bowyers Mews MK14 .....34 C3
Box La HP3 .....146 C4
Box Tree Cl HP5 .....154 B3
Boxberry Gdns MK7 .....48 A3
Boxer Rd HP27 .....138 B3
Boxgrove Ct MK10 .....35 C1
Boxmoor House Special Sch HP3 .....146 C4
Boxwell Rd HP4 .....135 A2
Boxwood Cl UB7 .....208 C2
Boyce Cres MK7 .....48 C3
Boycott Ave MK6 .....34 C1
Boyle Cl UB10 .....201 C2
Boyn Hill Ave SL6 .....202 B3
Boyn Hill Cl SL6 .....202 B3
Boyn Hill Rd SL6 .....202 B3
Boyn Valley Rd SL6 .....202 B3
Boyndon Rd SL6 .....202 B4
Boyne Hill CE Inf Sch SL6 .....202 B3
Bozenham Mill La NN7, NN12 .....9 C3
Bracken Cl SL2 .....198 B4
Bracken Hill HP4 .....135 C3
Bracken Rd SL6 .....202 B2
Bracken Way
Aylesbury HP21 .....115 A4
Flackwell Heath HP10 .....185 A4
Brackenforde SL3 .....206 B2
Brackens The HP11 .....173 B3
Brackenwood HP14 .....161 B4
Brackley Dr HP15 .....163 A3
Brackley La MK18 .....73 A3
Brackley Rd
Buckingham MK18 .....41 A1
Chackmore MK18 .....41 A1
Hazelmere HP15 .....163 A3
Westbury NN13 .....39 A3
Bradbery WD3 .....178 B3
Bradbourne Dr MK7 .....48 A2
Bradbury Cl MK13 .....34 A2
Bradbury Gdns SL3 .....199 B4
Bradcutts La SL8 .....195 C4
Braddenham Wlk HP21 .....115 C2
Braddons Furlong HP18 .....125 B3
Braden Cl HP21 .....116 A3
Bradenham Beeches HP14 .....161 A4
Bradenham La SL7 .....194 B3
Bradenham Rd HP14 .....161 A2
Bradenham Wood La HP14 .....161 A4
Bradfield Ave MK18 .....41 B1
Bradford Gdns MK5 .....46 A2
Bradford Rd
Heronsgate WD3 .....167 B1
Slough SL1 .....205 A4
Bradley Cl HP18 .....109 B3
Bradley Gr MK4 .....46 A1
Bradley Rd SL1 .....205 C3
Bradshaw Cl SL4 .....209 C3
Bradshaw Rd HP13 .....173 C3
Bradshawe Waye UB8 .....208 C4
Bradvue Cres MK13 .....34 A3
Bradwell Common Bvd MK13 .....34 B2
Bradwell Rd
Milton Keynes, Bradville MK13 .....34 A3
Milton Keynes, Loughton MK13,MK5 .....46 A4
Bradwell Village Mid Sch MK13 .....34 A2
Bradwell Village YH* MK13 .....34 A2
Brae Hill HP18 .....110 A4
Brae Hill Cl HP18 .....110 A4
Braemar Ct 2 SL7 .....183 B1
Braemar Gdns SL1 .....205 A2
Bragenham La MK17,LU7 .....70 B3
Bragenham Side MK17 .....69 C4
Bragmans La WD3 .....156 C3
Brahms Cl MK7 .....48 B3
Braid The HP5 .....144 C1
Brakynbery HP4 .....134 C4
Bramber Cl MK3 .....57 C4
Bramber Ct SL1 .....205 A3
Bramble Ave MK14 .....34 C2
Bramble Cl
Chalfont St Peter SL9 .....177 C2
Uxbridge UB8 .....208 C4
Bramble Cres HP15 .....163 B3
Bramble Dr SL6 .....202 A2
Bramble La HP7 .....165 C3
Bramble Mead HP8 .....177 A4
Brambles The UB7 .....208 C1
Brambleside HP11 .....174 A2
Brambling HP20 .....101 C2
Bramcote Cl HP20 .....116 B4
Bramley Chase SL6 .....202 B2
Bramley Cl SL6 .....202 B2
Bramley Ct MK43 .....3 C3
Bramley End HP14 .....151 A1
Bramley Grange MK2 .....58 B2
Bramley Mdws MK16 .....22 A2
Bramley Rd MK1 .....47 B2
Brammas Cl SL1 .....205 B2
Brampton Ct
Maidenhead SL6 .....203 A4
Milton Keynes MK13 .....34 A3
Branch Rd HP10 .....174 A1
Brandon Rd HP12 .....172 A2
Brands Hill Ave HP13 .....162 B1
Brands Rd SL3 .....212 A4
Brandville Rd UB7 .....208 C2
Bransgill Ct MK13 .....34 A2
Bransworth Ave MK7 .....48 B4
Brantham Cl MK7 .....48 A2
Braunston MK6 .....47 B3
Bravenfield MK18 .....53 B1
Brawlings La SL9 .....178 A3
Bray Cl SL6 .....203 B2
Bray Ct Amersham HP6 .....154 C1
Maidenhead SL6 .....203 B1
Bray Rd SL6 .....203 A3
Braybank SL6 .....203 B2
Braybourne Cl UB8 .....201 B1
Braybrooke Dr MK4 .....46 C2
Brayfield Rd SL6 .....203 B2
Brays Cl HP6 .....153 B2
Brays Green La HP6 .....153 B2
Brays La HP6 .....153 B3
Brays Mdw HP6 .....153 B2
Brayton Ct MK5 .....46 B3
Braywick Rd SL6 .....203 A2
Braywood Cotts SL4 .....209 A3
Braziers End HP5 .....133 B1
Breachwell Pl LU7 .....91 A1
Breakspear Rd N UB9 .....190 C4
Breakspear Rd S UB10 .....190 C1
Bream Cl SL7 .....194 B4
Breamore Ct MK8 .....45 C4
Brearley Ave MK6 .....46 C4
Brearley Cl UB8 .....201 C3
Breckland MK14 .....34 B3
Brecon Ct SL1 .....205 B2
Brecon Way HP13 .....172 C4
Bredward Cl SL1 .....197 A1
Bremen Gr MK5 .....46 A2
Brenchwood Cl HP13 .....161 B1
Brendon Ct MK4 .....46 B1
Brent MK6 .....47 B3
Brent Path HP21 .....115 B2
Brent Rd SL8 .....185 A2
Brentwood Way HP21 .....116 A3
Bretby Chase MK4 .....45 C2
Breton MK11 .....32 C3
Brew Twr SL7 .....183 B1
Brewhouse La HP22 .....88 C1
Briaily HP14 .....159 B1
Briar Cl SL6 .....204 A4
Briar Dene SL6 .....195 B1
Briar Glen SL8 .....195 C3
Briar Hill MK12 .....33 C2
Briar Way
Berkhamsted HP4 .....135 B2
Slough SL2 .....205 A4
Briars Cl HP19 .....101 A1
Briars The
High Wycombe HP11 .....173 B3
Holmer Green HP15 .....163 B4
Slough SL3 .....206 C1
Briarswood HP15 .....163 A2
Briarswood Cl HP14 .....158 C3
Briary View MK17 .....56 B4
Brices Mdw MK5 .....46 A2
Brick Cl MK11 .....33 B1
Brick Hill HP18 .....97 C1
Brick Kiln La HP22 .....102 A2
Brickfield La SL1 .....197 A2
Brickfields Way UB7 .....208 C2
Brickhill Manor Ct MK17 .....59 B3
Brickhill St
Bow Brickhill MK7 .....48 A2
Milton Keynes MK15 .....35 B3
Milton Keynes Village MK10, MK15 .....35 C1
Walton MK7 .....48 A2
Bricks La HP14 .....159 B2
Brickwell Wlk HP15 .....163 A2
Bricstock HP22 .....88 B2
Bridens Way HP17 .....126 C3
Bridge Ave Cookham SL8 .....195 C3
Maidenhead SL6 .....203 A4
Bridge Bank Cl HP11 .....174 A2
Bridge Cl SL1 .....204 C3
Bridge Ct
Berkhamsted HP4 .....135 B2
Maidenhead SL6 .....203 B4
Bridge Farm Bldgs HP17 .....128 A4
Bridge Ho
High Wycombe HP13 .....173 B3
West Drayton UB7 .....208 B3
Bridge Pl HP6 .....154 C1
Bridge Rd Cosgrove MK19 .....19 C1
Ickford HP18,OX9 .....123 C1
Maidenhead SL6 .....203 A4
Uxbridge UB8 .....201 B2
Bridge St
Berkhamsted HP4 .....135 B2
Buckingham MK18 .....52 B4
Colnbrook SL3 .....212 B4
Great Kimble HP17 .....129 B1
High Wycombe HP11 .....173 A4
Leighton Buzzard LU7 .....80 C4
Maidenhead SL6 .....203 B4
Milton Keynes MK13 .....33 C4
Olney MK46 .....6 C2
Thornborough MK18 .....54 A4
Turvey MK43 .....8 B3
Bridge Turn Ave MK12 .....33 B4
Bridgeford Ct MK6 .....46 C4
Bridgegate Bsns Pk HP19 .....101 A1
Bridgeman Ct 5 SL4 .....210 A3
Bridgeman Dr SL4 .....210 A3
Bridgestone Dr SL8 .....185 B2
Bridgewater Ct
Little Gaddesden HP4 .....121 B4
Slough SL3 .....207 A1
Bridgewater Hill HP4 .....134 C4
Bridgewater Ho MK18 .....52 B4
Bridgewater Monument* HP4 .....120 C4
Bridgewater Rd HP4 .....135 A3
Bridgewater Sch HP4 .....135 A3
Bridgewater Terr SL4 .....210 B3
Bridgewater Vistors Ctr* HP4 .....120 C4
Bridgewater Way SL4 .....210 B3
Bridgeway
Cuddington HP18 .....112 C2
Milton Keynes MK13 .....34 A4
Bridle Cl Maidenhead SL6 .....195 C1
Milton Keynes MK13 .....34 A3
Bridle Gate HP11 .....172 C3
Bridle Manor HP22 .....131 B4
Bridle Rd SL6 .....195 C1
Bridle Way HP4 .....135 A3
Bridleway
Buckland Common HP23 .....132 C3
Weston Turville HP22 .....116 C1
Bridleways HP22 .....131 A3
Bridlington Cres MK10 .....36 A1
Bridlington Spur SL1 .....205 A2
Bridport Way SL2 .....198 A1
Briery Way HP6 .....154 C1
Brighton Spur SL2 .....198 A1
Brightwell Ave LU6 .....93 B4
Brigidine Sch The SL4 .....210 B2
Brill CE Comb Sch HP18 .....96 A1
Brill Cl Maidenhead SL6 .....202 B2
Marlow SL7 .....183 B1
Brill Pl MK13 .....34 B2
Brill Rd Chilton HP18 .....111 A2
Horton-cum-S OX33 .....108 B3
Ludgershall HP18 .....96 A4
Oakley HP18 .....109 C3
Brimmers Hill HP15 .....162 C3
Brimmers Rd HP27 .....139 B1
Brimstone Way HP4 .....134 C3
Brindlebrook MK8 .....33 C1
Brindley Ave HP13 .....161 C1
Brinklow Rdbt MK10 .....36 A1
Briskman Way HP21 .....115 A3
Bristle Hill MK18 .....52 B4
Bristol Cl TW19 .....213 C1
Bristol Ct 10 TW19 .....213 C1
Bristol Way SL1 .....205 C3
Bristow Cl MK2 .....47 C1
Bristow Ct SL7 .....184 A2
Britannia Ct UB7 .....208 B2
Britannia Ind Est
High Wycombe HP12 .....172 B4
Poyle SL3 .....212 C3
Britannia Rd 6 HP5 .....144 B1
Britannia St HP20 .....115 C4
Britnell Ct HP14 .....158 C3
Britten Gr MK7 .....48 B3
Brittens Ct MK46 .....7 B2
Brittons La MK17 .....37 B2
Britwell Dr HP4 .....135 C3
Britwell Rd SL1 .....197 B1
Broad Arrow Cl MK14 .....34 C4
Broad Dean MK6 .....47 A4
Broad Gn MK43 .....25 B2
Broad La HP10 .....186 A3
Broad Ley's SL4 .....209 C4
Broad Leys HP27 .....139 A2
Broad Oak SL2 .....198 B1
Broad Oak Ct SL2 .....198 B1
Broad Piece MK15 .....35 A4
Broad Platts SL3 .....206 B2
Broad Rush Gn LU7 .....80 C4
Broad St Chesham HP5 .....144 B1
Newport Pagnell MK16 .....22 B2
Syresham NN13 .....27 A4
Broadfields HP19 .....101 A1
Broadfields Ct HP19 .....101 A1
Broadlands MK6 .....47 A3
Broadlands Ave HP5 .....144 B1
Broadmark Rd SL2 .....206 A3
Broadview Rd HP5 .....144 A2
Broadwater
Berkhamsted HP4 .....135 B3
Milton Keynes MK6 .....47 B3
Broadwater Gdns UB9 .....190 B4
Broadwater La UB9 .....190 B4
Broadwater Pk
Denham Green UB9 .....190 A3
Maidenhead SL6 .....203 C1
Broadway
Amersham HP7 .....165 A4
Maidenhead SL6 .....202 C4
Broadway Ave MK14 .....21 C1
Broadway Cl HP7 .....165 A4
Broadway Ct HP5 .....154 A4
Broadway Mall 6 SL6 .....202 C4
Broadway Par UB7 .....208 C2
Broadway The
Beaconsfield HP9 .....175 B2
Chesham HP5 .....154 A4
6 Gerrards Cross SL9 .....177 B1
Grendon Underwood HP18 .....82 C3
Brocas St SL4 .....210 B4
Brocas Terr SL4 .....210 B4
Brocas Way LU7 .....91 A2
Brock La SL6 .....202 C4
Brock La Mall 7 SL6 .....202 C4
Brockhampton MK15 .....35 A3
Brockhurst Rd HP5 .....144 B1
Brockway SL3 .....207 A1
Brockwell MK16 .....22 B2
Broddick Ho HP11 .....174 A2
Broken Furlong SL4 .....205 A1
Broken Gate La UB9 .....189 B2
Bromham Mill MK14 .....21 C1
Bromley HP23 .....104 A2
Bromley La HP16 .....153 A3
Brompton Cl HP19 .....101 A1
Brompton Cres HP19 .....101 A1
Brompton Dr SL6 .....195 B1
Bromycroft Rd SL2 .....198 A1
Bronsdon Way UB9 .....189 C1
Bronte Cl HP19 .....100 C1
Brook Bsns Ctr UB8 .....201 A2
Brook Cl
Aston Clinton HP22 .....117 B3
Ludgershall HP18 .....96 B4
Brook Cres SL1 .....204 C4
Brook End
North Crawley MK16 .....24 A3
Weston Turville HP22 .....117 A2
Brook Ho Slough SL1 .....205 B2
West Drayton UB7 .....208 B3
Brook La
Berkhamsted HP4 .....135 A3
Harrold MK43 .....3 C4
Newton Blossomville MK43 .....8 A2
Thame OX9 .....125 C1
Brook Path SL1 .....204 C3
Brook St
Aston Clinton HP22 .....117 B3
Edlesborough LU6 .....92 C2
High Wycombe HP11 .....173 A4
Tring HP23 .....119 A2
Windsor SL4 .....210 B3
Brookbank HP10 .....185 B2
Brookdene Cl SL6 .....195 C1
Brooke Cl MK3 .....57 C4
Brooke Furmston Pl SL7 .....183 C2
Brooke Rd HP27 .....139 A2
Brookfield Cl HP23 .....119 A2
Brookfield Farm HP22 .....117 A2
Brookfield Ho SL3 .....211 B3
Brookfield La MK18 .....52 B4
Brookfield Rd
Haversham MK19 .....20 B1
Newton Longville MK17 .....57 B2
Wooburn Green HP10 .....185 B2
Brookhouse Dr HP10 .....185 B2
Brooklands Rd MK2 .....58 B4
Brooklyn Way UB7 .....208 B2
Brookmead Sch LU7 .....105 C3
Brooks Ct MK18 .....52 B4
Brookside Colnbrook SL3 .....212 B4
Halton HP22 .....117 B1
Lillingstone Lovell MK18 .....30 A3
Loudwater HP10 .....174 B1
Milton Keynes MK12 .....33 B2
Oakley HP18 .....109 B3
Slough SL3 .....206 C4
Thame OX9 .....125 C1
Uxbridge UB10 .....201 C3
Weston Turville HP22 .....117 A1
Brookside Ave TW19 .....211 C2
Brookside Cl
Old Stratford MK19 .....32 A3
Tiddington OX9 .....136 A4
Brookside La HP17 .....129 C2
Brookside Terr 4 HP21 .....115 C4
Brooksward Comb Sch MK14 .....34 C4
Brookway MK19 .....31 C2
Broom Cl HP15 .....163 A2
Broom Hill Cookham SL8 .....195 C3
Stoke Poges SL2 .....199 A3
Broom Ho SL3 .....206 C1
Broombarn La HP16 .....151 C4
Broomfield MK12 .....33 B2
Broomfield Cl HP16 .....151 C4
Broomfield Hill HP16 .....151 C4
Broomlee MK13 .....34 A3
Broomstick Ind Est LU6 .....92 C2
Broomstick La HP5 .....145 A1
Brora Cl MK2 .....58 B3
Brotheridge Ct HP21 .....115 A3
Brough Cl MK5 .....46 A3
Broughton Ave HP20 .....116 A4
Broughton Cl HP22 .....102 A2
Broughton Crossing HP22 .....102 B1
Broughton Grounds Com Woodlands* MK16 .....36 C3
Broughton Inf Sch HP20 .....116 A4
Broughton Jun Sch HP20 .....116 A4
Broughton La HP20 .....116 B4
Broughton Manor Bsns Pk MK16 .....36 A2
Broughton Rd
Milton Keynes Village MK10 .....36 A2
Salford MK17 .....37 B2
Brow The HP8 .....177 B4
Brown's Rise HP23 .....132 C2
Brownbaker Ct MK14 .....34 C3
Browne Willis Cl MK2 .....58 B4
Brownfield Gdns SL6 .....202 C3
Browning Cl MK16 .....22 A2
Browning Cres MK3 .....58 A4
Brownlow Ave LU6 .....92 C2
Brownlow Cl LU7 .....105 B1
Brownlow La LU7 .....105 A4
Brownlow Rd HP4 .....135 B3
Brownlow Rise LU6 .....93 A4
Browns Ct SL1 .....204 C3
Browns Hedge LU7,HP23 .....105 B1
Browns Maltings 5 HP23 .....119 A2
Browns Rd
Holmer Green HP15 .....163 B3
South Heath HP16 .....153 A4
Browns Way MK17 .....49 C3
Browns Wood Rdbt MK7 .....48 B3
Brownsfield Rd NN12 .....18 C3
Brownswood Dr NN12 .....18 B2
Brownswood Rd HP9 .....175 C2
Broxbourne Cl MK14 .....21 C1
Bruce Cl SL1 .....205 A3
Bruce Wlk SL4 .....209 B3
Brucewood Par SL7 .....183 C3
Bruckner Gdns MK7 .....48 B3
Brudenell SL4 .....209 C2
Brudenell Dr
Milton Keynes Village MK7, MK10 .....48 B4
Stoke Mandeville HP22 .....116 A1
Brunel Cl SL6 .....202 C3
Brunel Ctr
Maidenhead SL6 .....202 B3
Milton Keynes MK2 .....58 B4
Brunel Rd
Aylesbury HP19 .....100 C1
High Wycombe HP13 .....161 C1
Maidenhead SL6 .....202 B3
Brunel Univ UB8 .....201 C1
Brunel Way SL1 .....205 C3
Brunleys MK11 .....33 A2
Brunswick Cl HP19 .....101 A2
Brunswick Pl HP13 .....162 B1
Brushford Cl MK4 .....46 B2
Brushmakers Ct HP5 .....144 A1
Brushwood Dr WD3 .....167 B3
Brushwood Jun Sch HP5 .....144 C1
Brushwood Rd HP5 .....144 B1
Bryans Cres MK16 .....24 A3
Bryanston Ave HP20 .....101 C1
Bryant Ave SL2 .....205 C4
Bryant's Bottom Rd HP16 .....150 C2
Bryants Acre HP22 .....131 A3
Bryden Cotts UB8 .....201 B1
Bryer Pl SL4 .....209 B2
Bryne La MK18 .....53 A1
Bryony Cl UB8 .....208 C4
Bryony Pl MK14 .....34 C3

Bsns Village The SL2 ...206 A3
Buccleuch Rd SL3 ...211 A4
Buchan Cl UB8 ...201 B1
Buchanan Rd OX25 ...94 C4
Buckby MK6 ...47 B3
Buckfast Ave MK3 ...47 A1
Buckfield Ct SL0 ...207 C2
Buckingham Ave SL1 ...205 A4
Buckingham Ave E SL1 ...205 B4
Buckingham Canal
Nature Reserve★ MK18 ...42 B2
Buckingham Cl HP13 ...174 A4
Buckingham Ct
Amersham HP6 ...154 C1
Newport Pagnell MK16 ...22 A2
Buckingham Dr HP13 ...174 A4
Buckingham Gate
Medmenham SL7 ...193 B4
Milton Keynes MK6 ...35 A1
Buckingham Gdns SL1 ...205 C2
Buckingham Ho
Amersham HP6 ...154 C1
4 Maidenhead SL6 ...202 C3
Buckingham Hospl MK18 41 B1
Buckingham Ind Pk
MK18 ...52 B3
Buckingham Jun Sch
MK18 ...41 C1
Buckingham Par 7 SL9 177 B1
Buckingham Pl 1 HP13 173 A4
Buckingham Rd
Aylesbury HP19,HP20 ...101 B3
Brackley NN13 ...38 A3
Deanshanger MK19 ...31 C1
Edgcott HP18 ...72 C1
Gawcott MK18 ...52 A3
Milton Keynes MK17 ...56 C3
Milton Keynes MK3 ...57 B4
Steeple Claydon MK18 ...63 C2
Tring HP23 ...118 C2
Winslow MK18 ...65 C3
Buckingham Sch MK18 ...52 B4
Buckingham St
9 Aylesbury HP20 ...101 B1
Milton Keynes MK12 ...33 B4
Tingewick MK18 ...51 B3
Buckingham Way HP10 174 A1
Buckinghamshire Coll
The HP8 ...178 A4
Buckinghamshire
Railway Ctr★ HP22 ...84 C1
Buckinghamshire
Univ Coll HP11 ...173 A3
Buckland Ave SL3 ...206 A2
Buckland Cres SL4 ...209 C3
Buckland Dr MK6 ...47 B3
Buckland Gate SL3 ...199 A1
Buckland Rd HP22 ...118 A2
Bucklebury Cl SL6 ...203 B1
Buckley Ct MK11 ...32 C2
Buckman Cl MK12 ...33 A3
Buckmaster Rd HP12 ...172 B2
Bucks County Mus★
HP20 ...115 B4
Bucks Goat Ctr★ HP22 ...130 A4
Buckthorn MK12 ...33 C3
Budge Rd NN12 ...18 C3
Buffins SL6 ...196 C1
Bulbourne Cl HP4 ...134 C3
Bulbourne Ct HP23 ...119 A4
Bulbourne Rd HP23 ...119 B4
Bulkeley Ave SL4 ...210 A2
Bull La
Gerrards Cross SL9 ...188 A3
6 High Wycombe HP11 ...173 A4
Bullbaiters La HP6 ...153 A4
Bullbeggars La HP4 ...135 C2
Bullfinch Gdns 16 HP20 101 C2
Bullocks Farm La HP14 171 A4
Bullrush Gr UB8 ...201 B1
Bulls La HP18 ...124 A2
Bullsland Gdns WD3 ...167 A2
Bullsland La WD3 ...167 A2
Bulstrode Cl WD4 ...146 C1
Bulstrode Ct SL9 ...188 B3
Bulstrode La WD4 ...146 C2
Bulstrode Pl SL1 ...205 C2
Bulstrode Way SL9 ...188 B3
Bunby Rd SL2 ...198 C3
Bunces Cl SL4 ...205 A1
Bunces Ct HP20 ...101 B1
Bungalows The MK18 ...51 B4
Bunhill Cl LU6 ...93 C4
Bunkers La LU7 ...80 B3
Bunstrux HP23 ...119 A2
Bunsty Ct MK11 ...32 C2
Bunten Meade SL1 ...205 A3
Bunyan Cl HP23 ...119 A3
Burano Cl MK7 ...48 B3
Burchard Cres MK5 ...46 A3
Burchett's Green Rd
SL6 ...194 B1
Burcot Gdns SL6 ...195 C2
Burcott Cl HP22 ...102 A2
Burcott La HP22 ...102 B2
Burdeleys La MK5 ...46 A2
Burdett Dr HP14 ...161 A4
Burdock Ct MK16 ...21 C2
Burewelle MK8 ...33 B1
Burfield Rd
Chorleywood WD3 ...167 B2
Old Windsor SL4 ...211 A1
Burford Cl
Ickenham UB10 ...201 C4
Marlow Bottom SL7 ...183 B3
Burford Gdns SL1 ...204 B4
Burford Sch SL7 ...183 B3

Burgess Gdns MK16 ...22 A1
Burgess La HP17 ...128 A4
Burgess Wood Gr HP9 ...175 A1
Burgess Wood Rd HP9 ...175 A1
Burgess Wood Rd S
HP9 ...175 A1
Burgett Rd SL1 ...205 A2
Burghley Ct MK8 ...45 C4
Burholme MK4 ...46 B2
Burkes Cl HP9 ...186 A4
Burkes Cres HP9 ...175 B1
Burkes Ct HP9 ...175 B1
Burkes Par HP9 ...175 B2
Burkes Rd HP9 ...175 B1
Burleigh Ct MK18 ...52 C4
Burleigh Piece MK18 ...52 C4
Burleys Rd MK18 ...65 C2
Burlington Ave SL1 ...205 C2
Burlington Ct 1 SL1 ...205 C2
Burlington Rd
Burnham SL1 ...197 A1
2 Slough SL1 ...205 C2
Burma Cl HP13 ...173 C3
Burn Wlk SL1 ...197 A1
Burners La MK11 ...33 A2
Burners La S MK11 ...33 A2
Burness Cl UB8 ...201 B2
Burnet MK14 ...34 B4
Burnham Ave HP9 ...176 A1
Burnham Beeches (Nature
Reserve)★ SL2 ...198 A4
Burnham Cl
Bourne End SL8 ...185 A2
High Wycombe HP12 ...172 B3
Windsor SL4 ...209 B3
Burnham Dr MK13 ...34 B2
Burnham Field HP22 ...116 A4
Burnham Gram Sch SL1 197 B1
Burnham Hts SL1 ...204 B4
Burnham La SL1 ...204 C4
Burnham Pl NN13 ...27 A4
Burnham Rd
Beaconsfield HP9 ...186 C3
Hughenden Valley HP14 ...162 A3
Westcott HP18 ...98 A4
Burnham Sta SL1 ...204 B4
Burnham Upper Sch
SL1 ...204 A4
Burnhams The HP18 ...124 B2
Burnmoor Cl MK2 ...58 B2
Burns Cl
Long Crendon HP18 ...125 B4
Newport Pagnell MK16 ...22 A2
Burns Ct HP21 ...115 C3
Burns Rd MK3 ...58 A4
Burnt Oak SL8 ...195 C4
Burrell Ct HP21 ...115 B3
Burren The HP6 ...154 B1
Burroughs Cres SL8 ...185 A2
Burroway Rd SL3 ...207 A2
Burrows Cl
Tylers Green HP10 ...163 B1
Woburn Sands MK17 ...49 A3
Burrows Hill Cl TW6 ...213 B2
Burrows Ho SL5 ...161 C1
Burt's La HP18 ...125 B3
Burton La HP27 ...139 B3
Burton Way SL4 ...209 C2
Burtree Cl MK12 ...33 B3
Bury Ave MK16 ...22 B2
Bury Cl MK16 ...22 B2
Bury Farm HP7 ...165 B4
Bury Farm Cl LU7 ...91 B3
Bury Lawn Sch MK8 ...34 B4
Bury Rise HP3 ...146 B3
Bury St MK16 ...22 B2
Buryhook Cnr OX33 ...122 B1
Busby Cl MK18 ...41 C1
Buscot Pl MK8 ...45 C4
Bush The HP17 ...126 C3
Bushel Wharf HP23 ...119 A3
Bushes La MK18 ...51 B1
Bushey Bartrams MK5 ...46 A2
Bushey Cl
Buckingham MK18 ...41 C1
High Wycombe HP12 ...172 C4
Bushfield Mid Sch MK12 ...33 B3
Bushfield Rd HP3 ...146 B3
Bushfields MK12 ...33 B4
Bushmead Rd HP22 ...87 A3
Bushmead Rd HP22 ...87 A3
Bushy Cl MK3 ...47 A2
Buslins La HP5 ...143 C2
Butcher La MK4,MK5 ...45 C2
Bute Brae MK3 ...46 C1
Butler Ct 5 SL7 ...183 C2
Butler Wlk HP14 ...115 A4
Butlers Cl
Amersham HP6 ...154 A1
Windsor SL4 ...209 B3
Butlers Court Comb Sch
HP9 ...175 B1
Butlers Court Rd HP9 ...175 B1
Butlers Ct HP13 ...173 C3
Butlers Gr MK14 ...34 B4
Butterfield HP10 ...185 B3
Butterfield Cl MK15 ...35 B1
Butterfield Cotts WD3 ...178 C2
Butterly Rd HP14 ...158 C2
Buttermere Ave SL1 ...204 B4
Buttermere Cl MK2 ...58 B3
Buttfurlong HP27 ...127 A4

Buttlehide WD3 ...178 B3
Button Gr MK6 ...47 A4
Buzzacott La MK4 ...46 B2
By-Wood End SL9 ...178 A3
Bybend SL2 ...198 A2
Bycell Rd MK18 ...41 B1
Bye Gn HP22 ...117 A2
Byerly Pl MK14 ...34 C3
Byford Way MK18 ...65 C3
Byland Dr SL6 ...203 A1
Byles The HP17 ...126 C3
Byron SL3 ...207 A1
Byron Cl 6 Marlow SL7 ...183 C2
Milton Keynes MK3 ...57 C4
Byron Dr MK16 ...22 A2
Byron Rd HP21 ...115 C3
Byron Way UB7 ...208 C1
Byward Cl MK14 ...34 C4
Byways Berkhamsted HP4 135 C3
Burnham SL1 ...204 A4

C

Cadman Sq MK5 ...46 B3
Cadmore End CE Sch
HP14 ...170 B3
Cadsden Rd HP27 ...139 C3
Cadwell Dr SL6 ...202 B3
Caernarvon Cres MK3 ...57 C4
Caesars Cl MK13 ...34 A3
Caesars Gate NN13 ...38 A3
Cages Wood Dr SL2 ...198 A4
Cairngorm Gate MK6 ...46 B4
Cairngorm Pl SL2 ...198 B1
Cairnside HP13 ...173 C3
Caithness Ct MK3 ...46 C1
Calamus Ct MK7 ...48 A3
Calbroke Rd SL2 ...197 C1
Caldecote La MK16 ...22 C1
Caldecote St MK16 ...22 B2
Caldecotte La MK7 ...48 A2
Caldecotte Lake Dr MK7 ...48 A1
Caldecotte Rdbt MK7 ...47 C2
Calder Cl SL6 ...195 C1
Calder Ct
Maidenhead SL6 ...195 B1
Slough SL3 ...206 C1
Calder Gdns LU7 ...80 A4
Calder Vale MK3 ...46 C1
Calder Way SL3 ...212 C2
Caldewell MK8 ...33 B1
Caldicot Ct MK7 ...48 B2
Caldicott Prep Sch SL2 198 A3
Caledon Cl HP9 ...175 C2
Caledon Rd HP9 ...175 C2
Caledonian Rd MK13 ...33 C4
Calewen MK13 ...33 C1
California Circ HP11 ...173 A2
Callis Rd TW19 ...213 C1
Calluna Dr MK3 ...47 A2
Calumet HP9 ...175 B2
Calvards Croft MK12 ...33 B2
Calverleigh Cres MK4 ...46 B2
Calverley Cres HP13 ...161 C1
Calvert Jubilee Nature
Reserve★ MK18,OX27 ...73 A4
Calverton La MK11 ...33 A1
Calverton La Rdbt MK11 ...33 B1
Calverton Rd MK11 ...32 B2
Calves Cl MK5 ...46 A2
Cam Ct MK3 ...57 C4
Cam Mead HP21 ...116 A3
Camber Cl MK3 ...57 C4
Camberton Rd LU7 ...80 C3
Camborne Ave HP21 ...116 A3
Cambria Ct SL3 ...206 B2
Cambridge Ave
Burnham SL1 ...197 A2
Slough SL1 ...205 A4
Cambridge Cl
Aylesbury HP20 ...101 C1
Harmondsworth UB7 ...213 A1
Cambridge Close
Trad Est HP21 ...101 C1
Cambridge Cres HP13 ...173 C4
Cambridge Ho 2 SL4 ...210 A1
Cambridge Pl 7 HP20 ...115 B4
Cambridge Rd
Beaconsfield HP9 ...175 B1
Marlow SL7 ...183 B1
Uxbridge UB8 ...201 B3
Cambridge St
Aylesbury HP20 ...101 C1
Milton Keynes, Bletchley
MK2 ...58 B4
Milton Keynes, Wolverton
MK12 ...33 B3
Cambridge Terr 18 HP4 ...135 B2
Cambron MK8 ...33 B1
Camden Ct HP19 ...101 C1
Camden Pl SL8 ...185 A2
Camden Rd SL6 ...195 B1
Cameron Rd HP5 ...144 B1
Camlet Gr MK14 ...34 B4
Camley Gdns SL6 ...202 A4
Camm Ave SL4 ...209 C2
Camomile Ct MK7 ...48 B3
Camomile Way UB7 ...208 C3
Camp Rd SL9 ...188 B2
Campania Cl MK10 ...36 A1
Campbell Cl
Buckingham MK18 ...52 C4
High Wycombe HP13 ...172 C4
Campbell Dr HP9 ...175 B3
Campbells Ride HP15 ...163 B4
Campden Rd UB10 ...190 C4

Camperdown SL6 ...196 A1
Camperdown Ho 39 SL4 210 A3
Campion MK14 ...21 C1
Campion Cl
Aylesbury HP20 ...116 A4
Denham UB9 ...190 A1
Uxbridge UB8 ...208 C4
Campion Rd HP15 ...162 C3
Campions HP4 ...135 A4
Canada Rd SL1 ...206 A2
Canal Ct HP4 ...135 C2
Canal Mus★ NN12 ...9 A4
Canal Wharf SL3 ...207 A2
Canalside
Old Stratford MK19 ...32 B4
Stoke Bruerne NN12 ...9 A4
Canalside Rdbt MK9 ...35 A2
Candlemas La HP9 ...175 C1
Candlemas Mead HP9 ...175 C1
Candlemas Oaks HP9 ...175 C1
Candlewicks MK7 ...48 A3
Candover Ct UB7 ...213 B4
Candy La MK5 ...46 A2
Candytuft Gn HP15 ...162 C3
Cane End MK27 ...139 C2
Cane End La HP22 ...102 B3
Canford Ct HP21 ...115 C3
Cannock Cl SL6 ...203 B1
Cannock Rd HP20 ...101 C2
Cannon Court Rd
Cookham SL6 ...195 B2
Maidenhead SL6 ...195 B2
Cannon Hill Cl SL6 ...203 B1
Cannon La SL6 ...202 A3
Cannon Mill Ave HP5 ...154 C3
Cannon Pl HP27 ...139 A2
Cannon's Hill HP18 ...112 B3
Cannon's Orch HP22 ...85 A2
Cannondown Rd SL8 ...195 C3
Canon Harnett Ct MK12 ...32 C3
Canon Hill Dr SL6 ...203 A1
Canon Hill Way SL6 ...203 A1
Canon's Cloisters SL4 ...210 B4
Canons Cl MK12 ...33 A4
Canons The MK16 ...22 C2
Cantell Cl MK18 ...41 B1
Canterbury Ave SL2 ...198 B1
Canterbury Cl
Amersham HP7 ...165 C4
Princes Risborough HP27 ...139 A3
Cantilupe Cl LU6 ...92 B3
Cantle Ave MK14 ...35 A3
Cantley Cl HP20 ...101 C1
Cape Villas SL0 ...207 C4
Capel Cl MK18 ...41 C4
Capel Dr MK14 ...34 C3
Capell Ave WD3 ...167 B2
Capell Rd WD3 ...167 B2
Capell Way WD3 ...167 B2
Capital Dr MK14 ...34 C3
Caplan Wlk MK8 ...33 C1
Capps La MK5 ...46 A2
Capricorn Ho HP10 ...185 A4
Capron MK6 ...47 A3
Captain Cook Cl HP8 ...177 A3
Captain's Cl HP5 ...144 A2
Captains Wlk MK5 ...46 A2
Caraway Cl MK7 ...48 A2
Cardain Ho HP9 ...175 B2
Cardigan Cl
Milton Keynes MK3 ...46 C1
Slough SL1 ...204 C3
Cardinals Wlk SL6 ...204 B4
Cardwell Cl MK4 ...46 B1
Carey Cl Aylesbury HP21 ...115 B2
Windsor SL4 ...210 A2
Carey Way MK46 ...7 A2
Careys Croft HP4 ...135 A4
Careys Rd NN12 ...17 A2
Carhampton Ct MK4 ...46 B2
Carisbrooke Ave HP12 ...172 A3
Carisbrooke Cl SL6 ...202 B3
Carisbrooke Ct
Buckingham MK18 ...41 C1
Slough SL1 ...205 C3
Carisbrooke Ho 4
HP13 ...173 C4
Carisbrooke Way MK4 ...45 C1
Carleton Gate MK15 ...35 C4
Carlina Pl MK14 ...34 B2
Carlisle Rd SL1 ...205 B3
Carlton Cl
Aylesbury HP19 ...101 A1
Newport Pagnell MK16 ...22 C2
Carlton Ct HP27 ...139 A2
Carlton Ho TW19 ...213 B1
Carlton Rd Slough SL2 ...206 A3
Turvey MK43 ...8 C4
Carlyle Ave HP21 ...115 C4
Carlyle Cl MK16 ...22 A2
Carman Ct HP23 ...118 C2
Carmarthen Rd SL1 ...205 C3
Carnation Way HP21 ...115 C3
Carne The MK11 ...32 C3
Carnot Cl MK6 ...46 B2
Carnoustie Cl MK3 ...57 B3
Carnweather Ct MK4 ...57 A4
Caroline Cl UB7 ...208 B2
Caroline Ct SL7 ...183 C2
Carolus Haslett Comb Sch
MK5 ...46 A2
Carolus Creek MK5 ...35 A4
Carpenter Ct MK14 ...34 C4
Carpenters Wood Dr
WD3 ...167 A3
Carpenters Yd HP23 ...119 A2
Carr Cl HP19 ...101 A1
Carrick Rd MK6 ...34 C1

Carriers Cl MK19 ...11 A1
Carrington Ave HP10 ...185 A4
Carrington Cl MK18 ...77 C3
Carrington Cres HP22 ...131 A4
Carrington Ct 10 HP12 ...172 C4
Carrington Hall Rd MK17 68 B3
Carrington Inf Sch
HP10 ...174 A1
Carrington Mid Sch The
HP10 ...185 A4
Carrington Pl
Holmer Green HP15 ...163 B4
Tring HP23 ...119 A3
Carrington Rd
Aylesbury HP21 ...115 B3
High Wycombe HP12 ...172 B3
Newport Pagnell MK16 ...22 A2
Slough SL1 ...205 C3
Carrington Way HP16 ...151 B3
Carroll Cl MK16 ...22 A3
Carron Cl LU7 ...80 A4
Carron Ct MK2 ...58 B2
Carrs Dr HP12 ...172 B4
Carter Cl SL4 ...210 A3
Carter's La HP18 ...75 C1
Carteret Cl MK15 ...35 C4
Carters Cl MK16 ...13 C1
Carters La
Long Crendon HP18 ...125 A4
Milton Keynes MK11 ...33 A2
Quainton HP22 ...85 C3
Carters Mdw MK18 ...76 A1
Carters Ride HP22 ...116 A1
Cartmel Cl MK3 ...57 B3
Cartwright Ct 9 HP13 ...173 C3
Cartwright Pl MK6 ...46 C4
Carver Hill Rd HP11 ...172 C3
Carvers Mews MK14 ...34 C3
Cascadia Cl HP11 ...174 A1
Cashmere Cl MK5 ...46 A2
Casterton Cl MK13 ...34 B2
Castethorpe Fst Sch
MK19 ...19 C3
Castle Ashby Rd NN7 ...1 A4
Castle Ave Datchet SL3 ...211 A4
West Drayton UB7 ...208 A4
Castle Cl
Marsh Gibbon OX27 ...72 A2
Pitstone LU7 ...105 B2
Totternhoe LU6 ...93 A4
Wing LU7 ...79 C2
Castle Ct
12 Aylesbury HP20 ...115 B4
Buckingham MK18 ...52 B4
Maidenhead SL6 ...202 B4
Castle Dr SL6 ...202 B4
Castle Est HP12 ...172 B2
Castle Farm
Caravan Site SL4 ...209 B3
Castle Gate Way HP4 ...135 B3
Castle Hill
Berkhamsted HP4 ...135 B3
Maidenhead SL6 ...202 B4
Windsor SL4 ...210 B3
Castle Hill Ave HP4 ...135 B3
Castle Hill Cl HP4 ...135 B3
Castle Hill Rd LU6 ...93 A4
Castle Hill Terr SL6 ...202 C4
Castle La HP22 ...86 C3
Castle Lodge SL6 ...202 C4
Castle Meadow Cl MK16 ...22 C2
Castle Mews
Berkhamsted HP4 ...135 B2
Maidenhead SL6 ...202 B2
Castle Park Rd HP22 ...131 A3
Castle Pl 13 HP13 ...173 A4
Castle Rd MK46 ...7 C4
Castle Rose MK6 ...47 B3
Castle St Aylesbury HP20 ...115 B4
Berkhamsted HP4 ...135 B2
Buckingham MK18 ...52 B4
High Wycombe HP13 ...173 A4
Marsh Gibbon OX27 ...72 A2
Slough SL1 ...205 C2
Wingrave HP22 ...89 A2
Castle View Gdns HP12 ...172 B4
Castlefield Sch HP12 ...172 B4
Castlefields HP22 ...116 B2
Castlemead Cotts SL4 ...210 B2
Castles Sch MK5 ...57 C4
Castlesteads MK13 ...33 C3
Castlethorpe Fst Sch
MK19 ...19 C3
Castleton Cl SL7 ...183 C3
Castleview Ho SL4 ...210 B4
Castleview Rd SL3 ...206 B1
Castleview Sch SL3 ...206 B1
Caswell La MK17 ...60 C4
Catchpole Cl MK12 ...33 A3
Cater Rd HP14 ...171 B2
Catesby Cl MK5 ...46 B4
Cathay Cl MK3 ...46 B4
Catherine Cotts HP23 ...133 B4
Catherine Ct MK18 ...41 C1
Catherines Cl UB7 ...208 B2
Catkin Cl HP12 ...172 A2
Causeway The
Maidenhead SL6 ...203 B2
Marlow SL7 ...183 C1
Cautley Cl HP22 ...85 A3
Cavalier Ct HP4 ...135 B2
Cavalier Rd OX9 ...126 A1
Cavalry Cres SL4 ...210 B2
Cavendish Cl
Burnham SL6 ...204 A4

Cavendish Cl continued
Little Chalfont HP6 ......166 A4
Wendover HP22 ......131 A3
Cavendish Ct
Milton Keynes MK5 ....46 A4
Poyle SL3 ......212 C3
Cavendish Rd HP5 ....154 B4
Cavendish Wlk OX9 ...126 A1
Cavenham MK3 ......33 C1
Caversham Gn 2 HP20 .101 A3
Cawardon MK14 ......34 B4
Cawcott Dr SL4 ......209 C3
Caxton Ct RG9 ......191 C1
Caxton Dr SL8 ......201 B2
Caxton Rd MK12 ......33 A4
Ceadar Rd HP4 ......135 C2
Cecil Rd SL0 ......207 C4
Cecil Way SL2 ......197 C1
Cecily Ct MK5 ......46 A3
Cedar RG9 ......191 B1
Cedar Ave
Hazelmere HP15 ......163 A3
West Drayton UB7 ....208 C3
Cedar Chase SL6 ......196 B5
Cedar Cl Aylesbury HP20 .102 A1
Iver Heath SL0 ......200 B2
Cedar Ct
High Wycombe HP13 ...173 A4
Maidenhead SL6 ......202 B4
Marlow SL7 ......183 C1
6 Windsor SL4 ......210 A3
Cedar Gr Cookham SL8 .195 C4
Marlow Bottom SL7 ...183 A4
Cedar Gr Amersham HP7 .165 B4
Chartridge HP5 ......143 B4
Cedar Lodge Dr MK12 ..33 B4
Cedar Park HP15 ......162 C3
Cedar Terr HP11 ......172 C4
Cedar Way
Berkhamsted HP4 ....135 B2
Slough SL3 ......206 C1
Cedars Cl Akeley MK18 ...41 C4
Chalfont St Peter SL9 ...177 C3
Cedars Comb Sch MK16 .22 B2
Cedars Dr UB10 ......201 C2
Cedars Rd SL6 ......203 A4
Cedars Ridge HP6 ....153 B3
Cedars The
Berkhamsted HP4 ....135 C2
Slough SL2 ......197 C1
Wendover HP22 ......131 A3
Cedars Upper Sch
& Comm Coll The LU7 ..80 C3
Cedars Village WD3 ...167 C3
Cedars Way
Leighton Buzzard LU7 ..80 C3
Newport Pagnell MK16 ..22 B2
Cedars Wlk WD3 ......167 C3
Ceely Rd HP21 ......115 B3
Celandine CM7 ......48 A3
Celina Cl MK2 ......58 B4
Cell Farm SL4 ......211 A1
Cell Farm Ave SL4 ....211 A1
Centenary Bsns Pk RG9 191 C1
Centenary Cotts HP27 .138 B4
Centenary Way HP6 ...154 C1
Central Ave MK43 ....24 C1
Central Dr SL1 ......204 C3
Central Est SL6 ......202 C4
Central Park Bsns Ctr
HP13 ......173 A4
Centre Par HP27 ......139 A3
Centre The SL2 ......198 B3
Centre Wlk HP15 ......163 A4
Centurion Ct MK11 ...33 B1
Century Ave MK6 ......46 C4
Century Point HP12 ...172 B2
Cestreham Cres HP5 ..144 B1
Chackmore CE Sch MK18 41 A2
Chacombe Pl HP9 ....175 B4
Chadbone Cl HP19 ...115 B4
Chadds La MK6 ......47 B4
Chadwell Path HP21 ..116 B3
Chadwick Dr MK6 ....47 A4
Chadwick St HP13 ....162 B1
Chaffinch HP20 ......101 C2
Chaffron Way
Milton Keynes MK4,MK5,
MK6 ......46 B3
Milton Keynes Village MK6,
MK10,MK15 ......35 B1
Chairborough Rd HP12 .172 B3
Chalcot Pl MK8 ......45 C4
Chalcott SL1 ......205 C2
Chalet Cl HP4 ......134 C2
Chalfont & Latimer Sta
HP7 ......166 B4
Chalfont Cl HP6 ......166 B4
Chalfont Cl MK13 ....34 A3
Chalfont La
Chorleywood WD3 ...167 A2
Maple Cross WD3 ....178 B3
Chalfont Rd
Maple Cross HP8,SL9,WD3 178 B4
Seer Green HP9 ......176 B3
Chalfont Shire Ctr★
HP8 ......178 A4
Chalfont St Giles Inf Sch
HP8 ......177 A4
Chalfont St Giles Jun Sch
HP8 ......177 A4
Chalfont St Peter CE Sch
SL9 ......177 B1
Chalfont St Peter Inf Sch
SL9 ......177 B2

Chalfont Station Rd
HP7 ......166 B4
Chalfont Way HP12 ...172 B2
Chalfonts & Gerrards
Cross Hospl The SL9 .177 B1
Chalfonts Com Coll The
SL9 ......177 B2
Chalford HP10 ......185 C3
Chalgrove Cl SL6 ....203 A3
Chalgrove End HP22 ..116 A1
Chalgrove Rd OX9 ...126 A1
Chalgrove Wlk HP21 .115 B3
Chalk Farm Rd HP14 .158 B4
Chalk Hill Chesham HP5 .144 A1
Coleshill HP7 ......164 C1
Chalk La HP6 ......153 C2
Chalk Pit La SL1 ......197 A2
Chalkdell Dr MK5 ....45 C2
Chalklands SL8 ......185 A2
Chalkpit La SL7 ......183 A2
Chalkshire Cotts HP17 .130 B2
Chalkshire Rd HP17 ..130 B2
Challacombe MK4 ....46 B1
Challener Rd HP12 ...172 B2
Challow Ct SL6 ......195 B1
Chalmers Ave MK19 ...20 B1
Chaloner Cl HP21 ....115 B3
Chaloner Rd HP21 ...115 B3
Chaloners Hill MK18 ..63 B2
Chalvey Gdns SL1 ....205 C2
Chalvey Gr SL1 ......205 A2
Chalvey Pk SL1 ......205 C2
Chalvey Rd E SL1 ....205 C2
Chalvey Rd W SL1 ...205 B2
Chalwell Ridge MK5 ..46 A2
Chamberlain Rd HP19 .101 A1
Champflower MK4 ...46 B2
Champney Cl SL3 ....212 A2
Chancellors HP7 ......164 A3
Chancellors Cnr HP7 .164 A3
Chancery Cl MK13 ...34 A3
Chancery Pl SL4 ......210 B4
Chandlers Ct MK6 ...47 C3
Chandlers Quay SL6 .203 B4
Chandos Cl
Buckingham MK18 ...52 B4
Little Chalfont HP6 ...155 B1
Chandos Ct MK18 ....52 B4
Chandos Mall 14 SL1 .205 C2
Chandos Pl
Milton Keynes MK2 ...58 A4
Wendover HP22 ......131 A3
Chandos Rd MK18 ....52 B4
Channer Dr HP10 ....163 A1
Channory Cl MK4 ....46 A1
Chantry Cl
West Drayton UB7 ...208 B3
Windsor SL4 ......210 A3
Woburn Sands MK17 ..49 A3
Chantry Rd HP19 ....101 B2
Chantry Specl Sch UB7 .208 C3
Chantry The
10 Aylesbury HP20 ...115 B4
Uxbridge UB8 ......201 C1
Chapel Arches SL6 ..203 A4
Chapel Cl HP4 ......121 B3
Chapel Crofts HP4 ...134 C3
Chapel Ct SL6 ......202 B2
Chapel Dr HP22 ......117 C3
Chapel End La HP23 ..118 A4
Chapel Fields HP23 ..118 A4
Chapel Hill
Lacey Green HP27 ...150 A2
Soulbury LU7 ......69 C2
Windsor SL4 ......210 B3
Chapel Ho HP6 ......153 B3
Chapel La Akeley MK18 .41 C4
Bledlow MK27 ......138 A2
Bledlow Ridge HP14 ..148 C1
Chilton HP18 ......111 A2
Drayton Parslow MK17 ..68 A3
High Wycombe HP12 ..172 B4
Ivinghoe LU7 ......92 A1
Long Marston HP23 ..104 A2
Stoke Bruerne NN12 ...9 A4
Stoke Mandeville HP22 .116 A1
Stoke Poges SL2 ....199 A3
Thornborough MK18 ...54 A4
Totternhoe LU6 ......92 C4
Turweston NN13 ......38 A4
Walter's Ash HP14 ...161 B4
Wendover HP22 ......131 A2
Whitfield NN13 ......26 B2
Chapel Rd Dinton HP17 .128 A4
Edlesborough LU6 ....92 A3
Flackwell Heath HP10 .185 A4
Chapel Sq LU7 ......68 C1
Chapel St
Berkhamsted HP4 ...135 B2
High Wycombe HP13 ..161 B2
Marlow SL7 ......183 C1
Slough SL1 ......205 C2
Tring HP23 ......118 C2
Uxbridge UB8 ......201 B2
Woburn Sands MK17 ..49 A2
Chapels Cl SL1 ......204 C3
Chaplin Gr MK8 ......45 B4
Chapman Ave MK14 ..35 A3
Chapman Cl
Aylesbury HP21 ......115 A3
West Drayton UB7 ...208 C2
Chapman La SL8,HP10 .185 A3
Chapmans Cres HP5 .144 A1
Chapmans Dr MK19 ...32 A4
Chappel Mdw HP23 ..119 A3
Chapter MK6 ......47 A2
Chapter Cl UB10 ....201 C3

Chapter Ho MK6 ......47 A3
Chapter Mews SL4 ...210 B4
Charbray Cres MK5 ...46 A2
Chardacre MK8 ......33 C1
Charlbury Rd UB10 ...190 C1
Charles Cl HP21 ......116 A2
Charles Dr OX9 ......126 A1
Charles Gdns SL2 ...206 A4
Charles Ho
Henley-on-T RG9 ...191 C2
9 Windsor SL4 ......210 B3
Charles St
Berkhamsted HP4 ...135 A2
Tring HP23 ......119 A2
Windsor SL4 ......210 B3
Charles Way MK16 ...22 B2
Charlestown Lodge
UB8 ......201 B3
Charlock St SL1 ......21 C2
Charlotte Cl LU7 ....79 C1
Charlton SL4 ......209 B3
Charlton Cl Slough SL1 .205 A2
Swanbourne MK17 ...66 C2
Charlton Pl 2 SL4 ...209 B3
Charlton Row 5 SL4 .209 B3
Charlton Sq 4 SL4 ...209 B3
Charlton Way SL4 ...209 B3
Charlton Wlk 3 SL4 .209 B3
Charmandean Sch MK18 .29 A2
Charmfield Rd HP21 .116 A3
Charnwood Cl 6 HP13 .173 C3
Charsley Cl HP6 ......166 B4
Charter 27 SL1 ......205 C2
Charter Dr HP6 ......154 C1
Charter Rd SL1 ......204 C3
Chartley Ct MK5 ......46 A2
Chartridge Comb Sch
HP5 ......143 B2
Chartridge Development
UB8 ......201 A2
Chartridge Grange Dr
HP5 ......143 B2
Chartridge Ho HP13 .173 C3
Chartridge La HP5 ...143 C1
Chartwell Gate HP9 .175 B1
Chartwell Rd MK16 ...22 C2
Chase Ave MK7 ......48 A2
Chase Cl HP7 ......165 A2
Chase Park Rd NN7 ...1 A3
Chase The Chesham HP5 .144 A1
Maidenhead SL6 ....195 B2
Marlow SL7 ......184 A2
Tylers Green HP10 ...163 B1
Chaseport Cl MK46 ...5 B1
Chaseside Cl LU7 ...105 A4
Chatfield SL2 ......205 A4
Chatham Ct 6 SL1 ...206 A2
Chatsworth MK8 ......33 C1
Chatsworth Cl SL6 ..202 B3
Chaucer Cl
Berkhamsted HP4 ...134 C3
Newport Pagnell MK16 ..22 A2
Windsor SL4 ......210 B2
Chaucer Dr HP21 ....115 C3
Chaucer Rd MK3 ....58 A4
Chauntry Cl SL6 ......203 A3
Chauntry Rd SL6 ....203 A3
Chawton Cres MK8 ...33 C1
Cheapside La UB9 ...189 C1
Cheddington Comb Sch
LU7 ......105 A4
Cheddington La HP23 .104 B3
Cheddington Rd LU7 .105 C2
Cheddington Sta LU7 .91 A1
Chelmsford Ct 38 SL4 .210 B3
Chelsea Gn LU7 ......80 B3
Cheltenham Gdns MK3 .57 B3
Cheney Cl LU7 ......78 A1
Cheney Way HP20 ...101 C1
Cheney Wlk 3 HP20 .101 C1
Cheneys Wlk MK3 ...47 A1
Chenies WD3 ......156 A1
Chenies Ave HP6 ....166 B4
Chenies Manor Ho★
WD3 ......156 A1
Chenies Par HP7 ....166 B4
Chenies Rd WD3 ....167 B4
Chenies Sch WD3 ...156 A1
Chepping Cl HP10 ...163 A1
Chepstow Dr MK3 ...57 B3
Chequers Cl LU7 ....105 B2
Chequers Dr HP16 ..151 B3
Chequers End MK18 ..66 A2
Chequers Hill HP7 ...165 B4
Chequers La
Ibstone HP14 ......170 A3
North Crawley MK16 ..24 A3
Pitstone LU7 ......105 B3
Prestwood HP16 ....151 B4
Chequers Orch SL0 ..207 C4
Chequers Sq UB8 ...201 B3
Chequers St HP21 ...115 C2
Chequers The
Castlethorpe MK19 ...19 C3
Eaton Bray LU6 ......92 C3
Cherington Gate SL6 .195 A1
Cheriton MK4 ......46 C2
Cherleton MK8 ......33 C1
Cherries The SL2 ....206 A4
Cherry Acre SL3 ....177 B3
Cherry Cl
Flackwell Heath HP10 .185 A4
Prestwood HP16 ....151 B3
Cherry Cnr HP10 ....185 A4
Cherry Dr HP9 ......175 A2
Cherry Gdns HP23 ..118 C2

Cherry Gr HP15 ......163 B3
Cherry La Amersham HP7 164 B3
West Drayton UB7 ...208 C1
Cherry Lane Jun
& Inf Sch UB7 ......208 C1
Cherry Leys MK18 ...63 C2
Cherry Orch
Amersham HP6 ......154 C1
Olney MK46 ......6 C2
Prestwood HP16 ....151 B3
Stoke Poges SL2 ....199 A3
West Drayton UB7 ...208 C2
Cherry Orchard Ct
HP13 ......173 C3
Cherry Pit The HP13 .161 C1
Cherry Rd MK16 ......22 A2
Cherry Rise
Chalfont St Giles HP8 .177 B4
Flackwell Heath HP10 .185 A4
Cherry St HP13 ......174 A4
Cherry Tree Ave UB8 .208 C4
Cherry Tree Cl
Great Kingshill HP15 .151 B1
Hughenden Valley HP14 .162 A4
Lacey Green HP27 ...150 A3
Cherry Tree La
Buckland Common HP23 .133 A2
Fulmer SL3 ......199 C3
Heronsgate WD3 ....167 A3
Lee Common HP16 ..142 C2
Cherry Tree Rd
Chinnor OX39 ......147 B3
Farnham Common SL2 .198 B3
Cherry Tree Way HP10 .163 B3
Cherry Tree Wlk
Chesham HP5 ......144 B1
Leighton Buzzard LU7 .80 C4
Wendover HP22 ......131 A3
Cherry Way
Hazelmere HP15 ....163 A3
Horton SL3 ......212 B2
Cherrycroft Dr HP14 .161 B3
Cherrytree La
Gerrards Cross SL9 ..177 B1
Iver Heath SL0 ......201 A2
Cherrywood Cl HP9 .176 B3
Cherrywood Gdns HP10 185 A4
Cherwell Cl
Maidenhead SL6 ....203 A4
Slough SL3 ......212 A4
Cherwell Ho MK3 ...57 C4
Cherwell Rd
Aylesbury HP21 ......115 B3
Bourne End SL8 ....185 A2
Chesham Ave MK13 ..34 B2
Chesham Bois
CE Comb Sch HP6 ...154 C2
Chesham High Sch HP5 144 B1
Chesham Hospl HP5 .154 B4
Chesham L Ctr HP5 ..154 B4
Chesham La
Chalfont St Peter SL9 .177 C3
Wendover HP16,HP22 .141 C4
Chesham Park Com Coll
HP5 ......144 A1
Chesham Prep Sch HP5 145 A2
Chesham Rd
Amersham HP6 ......154 B1
Berkhamsted HP4 ...135 A1
Bovingdon HP3,HP5 .145 C4
Chartridge HP5 ......143 C4
Hyde Heath HP5,HP16 .153 B4
Wigginton HP23,HP4 .133 B4
Chesham Sta HP5 ...154 B4
Cheshire Ct 17 SL1 ..206 A2
Cheslyn Gdns MK14 ..35 A4
Chesney Wold MK6 ...46 C3
Chess Cl Latimer HP5 .155 B2
Stoke Mandeville HP21 .115 B2
Chessbury Cl HP5 ...154 A4
Chessbury Rd HP5 ...154 A4
Chessfield Pk HP6 ...166 C4
Chessmount Rise HP5 .154 B3
Chester Cl MK3 ......57 B3
Chester Ho UB8 ....201 B1
Chester Rd SL1 ......205 B4
Chesterfield Cl HP17 .114 B3
Chesterfield Cres LU7 .79 C2
Chesterfield Pl HP19 .115 A4
Chesterholm MK13 ...33 C3
Chesterton Cl HP5 ..144 A1
Chesterton Gn HP9 .175 C2
Chestnut Ave
Chesham HP5 ......144 B1
High Wycombe HP11 .173 B3
Slough SL3 ......206 C2
West Drayton UB8 ...208 C3
Chestnut Cl
Amersham HP6 ......154 B1
Aston Clinton HP22 ..117 C3
Chalfont St Peter SL9 .177 C1
Dagnall HP4 ......107 B3
Maidenhead SL6 ....196 A1
Medmenham SL7 ....193 B4
Milton Keynes MK11 ..32 B3
Newton Longville MK17 .57 B1
Princes Risborough HP27 .139 B3
Waddesdon HP18 ....99 A3
Chestnut Cotts MK18 .52 B4
Chestnut Cres
Aylesbury HP21 ......115 B3
Milton Keynes MK2 ..58 A3
Chestnut Dr
Berkhamsted HP4 ...135 B2
Windsor SL4 ......209 C2
Chestnut End HP22 ..117 B1
Chestnut Gn NN13 ...26 C2
Chestnut Hill LU7 ...80 B4

Chestnut La
Amersham HP6 ......154 C1
Hazelmere HP15 ....163 A3
Chestnut Lane Sch HP6 154 C2
Chestnut Leys MK18 .63 C2
Chestnut Pk SL6 ....203 C2
Chestnut Rd
Beaconsfield HP9 ...175 A4
Princes Risborough HP27 .139 A4
Yardley Gobion NN12 ..18 C3
Chestnut Rise LU7 ...80 B4
Chestnut View
Chearsley HP18 ....112 A1
East Claydon MK18 ..74 C4
Chestnut Way
Halton HP22 ......131 B3
Longwick HP27 ......138 C3
Stoke Mandeville HP22 .116 A1
Chestnut Wlk SL9 ...177 C1
Chestnuts The
Felden HP3 ......146 C4
Uxbridge UB10 ......201 C3
Chestwood Gr UB10 .201 C3
Chettle Pl NN12 ......18 C1
Chetwode Ave MK10 ..36 A1
Chetwode Cl MK18 ...41 C1
Chetwynd Dr UB10 ..201 C2
Chevalier Gr MK8 ....45 B4
Cheveley Gdns SL1 ..197 B2
Cheviot
High Wycombe HP13 .161 C1
Leighton Buzzard LU7 .80 B4
Maidenhead SL6 ....203 A3
Cheviot Rd SL3 ......207 A3
Cheyne Cl
Amersham HP6 ......154 B2
Buckingham MK18 ...41 C1
Gerrards Cross SL9 ..188 C2
Pitstone LU7 ......105 B2
Cheyne Wlk HP5 ....154 B4
Chichele Hill MK16 ...23 C4
Chicheley Rd
Chicheley MK16 ......23 C4
North Crawley MK16 ..23 C3
Chicheley St MK16 ...22 C2
Chichester Cl HP13 ..173 B3
Chichester Ct SL1 ...206 A2
Chichester Row HP6 .154 C1
Chicksands Ave MK10 .36 A1
Chievely Ct MK4 ......46 B1
Chilcote La HP7 ......166 C1
Childs Way MK4,MK5,MK6,
MK10 ......46 B4
Chillery Leys MK15 ...35 C4
Chillingham Ct MK5 ..46 A2
Chiltern Ave
Amersham HP6 ......154 B1
Edlesborough LU6 ...92 C2
High Wycombe HP12 .172 B3
Stone HP17 ......114 B3
Chiltern Brewery★
HP17 ......130 C3
Chiltern Bsns Village
UB8 ......201 B2
Chiltern Cl
Princes Risborough HP27 .139 A2
Stone HP17 ......114 B3
Wendover HP22 ......131 A3
Chiltern Cnr HP4 ....135 A3
Chiltern Commerce Ctr
HP5 ......144 C4
Chiltern Cotts
Buckland Common HP23 .133 A1
Ibstone HP14 ......169 B4
Chiltern Ct
Amersham HP6 ......154 B1
Chesham HP5 ......144 A1
8 High Wycombe HP12 .172 C4
Windsor SL4 ......210 A3
Winslow MK18 ......65 C2
Chiltern Ct Mews SL4 .210 A3
Chiltern Dr WD3 ....167 C1
Chiltern Gate Sch
HP12 ......172 C2
Chiltern Gn HP10 ...185 B4
Chiltern Hill SL9 ....177 C1
Chiltern Hills Rd HP9 .175 B3
Chiltern Hospl The
HP16 ......152 B2
Chiltern Hts HP7 ....166 A4
Chiltern Manor Pk
HP16 ......152 A4
Chiltern Open Air Mus★
HP8 ......167 A1
Chiltern Par HP6 ....154 B1
Chiltern Park Ave HP4 .135 A3
Chiltern Rd
Amersham HP6 ......154 A1
Burnham SL1 ......204 A4
Maidenhead SL6 ....203 A3
Marlow SL7 ......183 B1
South Heath HP16 ..142 C2
Wendover HP22 ......131 A3
Wingrave HP22 ......89 A2
Chiltern Ridge HP14 .158 B2
Chiltern Sculpture Trail★
HP14 ......157 B2
Chiltern St HP15 ....115 C3
Chiltern View HP14 ..149 B3
Chiltern View Rd UB8 .201 B2
Chiltern Villas HP23 .118 C1
Chiltern Way
Aston Clinton HP22 ..117 C3
Tring HP23 ......119 A3
Chilterns MK4 ......134 C3
Chilterns Cl HP10 ...185 A3
Chilterns Pk SL8 ....185 A3
Chilterns The HP13 ..173 A4

Chilton Cl
Holmer Green HP15 ......**163** B4
Tylers Green HP10 .....**163** B1
Chilton Ct SL6 ....**204** B4
Chilton Rd
Chearsley HP18 ....**112** A1
Chesham HP5 ....**144** B1
Long Crendon HP18 ....**125** B4
Chilwick Rd SL2 ......**197** C1
Chimes The HP12 .....**172** C3
Chinalls MK18 ....**50** B3
Chingle Croft MK4 ......**46** B1
Chinneck Ho HP4 ......**135** B2
Chinnor Hill OX39 .....**147** C2
Chinnor Hill
Nature Reserve★ OX39 **147** C3
Chinnor Rd
Bledlow HP27 ....**138** A1
Bledlow Ridge HP14 ....**148** B2
Chinnor OX39 ....**147** A2
Chinnor Sta OX39 ......**147** B3
Chippendale Cl HP13 ...**162** B1
Chippendale Waye UB8 .**201** B4
Chippenham Dr MK10 ..**36** A4
Chipperfield Cl MK13 ...**34** A4
Chipperfield Rd HP3 ...**146** B2
Chipping Vale MK4 ......**46** B1
Chipps Hill HP14 ......**171** A4
Chipstead SL9 ....**177** B1
Chirbury MK10 ....**35** C1
Chislehampton MK15 ...**35** B2
Chiswick Cl MK4,MK5 ...**45** C2
Chiswick Lodge 3 SL7 .**183** B1
Choke La SL7 ....**195** A2
Cholesbury La HP23 ....**133** A1
Chorley Rd HP14 ......**160** C2
Chorleywood Bottom
WD3 ....**167** B2
Chorleywood House Dr
WD3 ....**167** C3
Chorleywood Sch
Mix Jun Inf WD3 ......**167** B2
Chorleywood Sta WD3 .**167** B3
Chrislaine Cl TW19 ....**213** B1
Christ the King RC Sch
TW19 ....**213** C1
Christchurch CE Sch
WD3 ....**167** C3
Christchurch Ho 18
HP23 ....**119** A2
Christchurch Rd HP23 ..**118** C2
Christian Ct MK15 ......**35** B4
Christian Sq 4 SL4 ....**210** B3
Christie Cl MK16 ......**22** B4
Christine Ho 3 MK2 ....**58** B4
Christmas La SL2 ......**187** B1
Christopher Ct HP14 ...**161** B4
Christopher Ho 6 SL2 .**198** B4
Church Ave RG9 ......**191** C1
Church Cl
Aston Clinton HP22 ....**117** B3
Cuddington HP18 ......**112** C2
Eton SL4 ....**210** B4
Maidenhead SL6 ......**202** B3
Maids Moreton MK18 ...**41** C2
Uxbridge UB8 ....**201** A2
West Drayton UB7 .....**208** C2
Wicken MK19 ....**31** A2
Church Cotts SL6 ......**196** C1
Church Croft LU6 ......**92** C2
Church Ct HP13 ......**162** B1
Church Dr SL6 ....**203** B2
Church End Adstock MK18 **53** C1
Bledlow HP27 ....**138** A1
Edlesborough LU6 ......**92** C2
Haddenham HP17 ......**127** A3
Newton Longville MK17 ..**57** B2
Potterspury NN12 ......**18** C2
Sherington MK16 ......**14** A1
Steeple Claydon MK18 ..**63** A3
Syresham NN13 ....**27** B4
Wavendon MK17 ....**48** C4
Church End Cotts WD3 .**156** C1
Church End Farm LU6 ..**93** A4
Church End Rd MK5 ....**46** A2
Church Farm Cl HP22 ..**102** A2
Church Farm Cres MK14 .**34** C4
Church Farm La HP23 ..**104** C1
Church Farm Wlk★
HP17 ....**127** A3
Church Gn
Long Crendon HP18 ....**125** B4
Totternhoe LU6 ....**93** A4
Church Gr
Little Chalfont HP6 .....**166** C1
Slough SL3 ....**206** B4
Church Green Rd MK3 ..**58** A4
Church Headland La
HP22 ....**87** A3
Church Hill Akeley MK18 .**41** C4
Aspley Guise MK17 .....**49** C3
Cheddington LU7 ......**105** A4
Ellesborough HP17 ....**130** A1
Milton Keynes MK8 .....**33** C1
South Harefield UB9 ...**190** B4
Stonor OX49 ....**179** B4
Whaddon MK17 ....**45** A1
Church Holt The SL2 ...**187** B2
Church La Alderton NN12 .**9** A1
Aston Clinton HP22 ....**117** B2
Berkhamsted HP4 .....**135** B2
Bledlow Ridge HP14 ...**159** C4
Bledlow Ridge, Radnage
HP14 ....**159** B4
Bovingdon HP3 ....**146** A2
Chearsley HP18 ....**112** A1
Cheddington LU7 .....**105** A4
Chinnor OX39 ....**147** B3

Church La continued
Clifton Reynes MK46 ......**7** B2
Deanshanger MK19 ......**31** C2
Eaton Bray LU7 ....**92** C3
Edgcott HP18 ....**72** C1
Emberton MK46 ....**13** C4
Gerrards Cross SL9 ....**177** B1
Grafton Regis NN12 ......**9** B1
Granborough MK18 .....**75** C3
Great Horwood MK17 ...**55** A2
Great Kimble HP17 ....**129** C1
Great Kingshill HP15 ...**162** B2
High Wycombe HP14 ...**161** A1
Horton-cum-S OX33 ...**108** A3
Lacey Green HP27 .....**149** C2
Lillingstone Lovell MK18 ..**30** A3
Ludgershall HP18 ......**96** B4
Maidenhead SL6 ......**203** B2
Marsworth HP23 ......**104** C1
Milton Keynes MK5 ....**46** A4
Mixbury NN13 ....**38** B1
Mursley MK17 ....**67** B3
Newport Pagnell MK16 ..**22** B4
Oving HP22 ....**86** B4
Padbury MK18 ....**53** B1
Potterspury NN12 ......**18** C2
Princes Risborough HP27 **139** A2
Sarratt WD3 ....**156** C2
Slough SL2,SL3 ....**206** B4
Soulbury LU7 ....**69** C1
South Heath HP16 ....**152** A4
Stoke Bruerne NN12 .....**9** A4
Stoke Goldington MK16 ..**12** A4
Stoke Poges SL2 ......**198** C1
Thornborough MK18 ....**54** A4
Tingewick MK18 ....**51** A4
Uxbridge UB8 ....**201** A2
Walter's Ash HP14 ....**161** C3
Walton MK7 ....**47** C3
Wendover HP22 ......**131** B2
Weston Turville HP22 ..**116** C1
Whaddon MK17 ....**45** A1
Whitchurch HP22 ......**87** A3
Wicken MK19 ....**31** A2
Yardley Hastings NN7 ....**1** A4
Church Lees MK14 ......**21** B1
Church Pas MK16 ......**22** B2
Church Path
Lane End HP14 ....**171** A2
Maidenhead SL6 ......**203** B2
Prestwood HP16 .....**151** B3
Stokenchurch HP14 ...**158** B3
Church Piece HP18 ....**112** A1
Church Rd
Aspley Heath MK17 .....**49** A2
Bow Brickhill MK17 .....**48** B1
Brackley NN13 ....**38** A4
Chinnor OX39 ....**147** B3
Cookham SL7 ....**195** A3
Farnham Common SL2 .**198** B1
Ickford HP18 ....**123** C2
Iver Heath SL0 ....**200** B2
Ivinghoe LU7 ....**105** C3
Lane End HP14 ....**171** A2
Leighton Buzzard LU7 ...**80** C3
Lewknor OX49 ....**157** A4
Little Gaddesden HP4 ..**121** B4
Little Marlow SL8 .....**184** B3
Maidenhead SL6 ......**203** A3
Old Windsor SL4 ......**211** A1
Pitstone LU7 ....**105** C3
Seer Green HP9 ......**176** B2
Sherington MK16 ......**13** C1
Slapton LU7 ....**91** B3
South Harefield UB9 ..**190** B4
Stoke Hammond MK17 ..**69** B4
Thame OX9 ....**125** C1
Totternhoe LU6 ....**93** A3
Tylers Green HP10 ...**174** C4
Uxbridge UB8 ....**201** B1
West Drayton UB7 ....**208** C2
Church Row SL3 ......**199** B4
Church Sq
High Wycombe HP13 ...**173** A4
Leighton Buzzard LU7 ...**80** C3
Church St
Amersham HP7 ....**165** A4
Aspley Guise MK17 .....**49** C3
8 Aylesbury HP20 ....**115** B4
Bovingdon HP3 ....**146** A2
Brill HP18 ....**110** A4
Buckingham MK18 .....**52** B4
Burnham SL1 ....**197** B1
Chesham HP5 ....**154** A4
Gawcott MK18 ....**52** A2
Henley-on-T RG9 .....**191** B1
High Wycombe HP11,
HP14 ....**173** A4
Little Horwood MK17 ...**55** A4
Maids Moreton MK18 ...**41** C2
Marsh Gibbon OX27 ....**71** C2
Milton Keynes, Fenny Stratford
MK2 ....**47** C1
Milton Keynes, New Bradwell
MK13 ....**33** C4
Milton Keynes, Stony Stratford
MK11 ....**32** B3
Milton Keynes, Wolverton
MK12 ....**33** B4
North Marston MK18 ...**76** A1
Olney MK46 ....**7** A2
Princes Risborough HP27 **139** A2
Quainton HP22 ....**85** A3
Slough, Chalvey SL1 ...**205** B2
Slough, Upton Park SL1 .**205** C2
South Heath HP16 ....**152** A4
Stokenchurch HP14 ...**158** A3

Church St continued
Twyford MK18 ....**62** B1
16 Windsor SL4 ......**210** B3
Wing LU7 ....**79** C1
Wingrave HP22 ....**89** A1
Winslow MK17 ....**65** C2
Church Terr Turvey MK43 ..**8** C3
Windsor SL4 ....**209** C2
Church View
Brackley NN13 ....**38** A4
Halton HP22 ....**117** B1
Long Marston HP23 ...**104** C1
Newport Pagnell MK16 ..**22** B2
1 Slough SL1 ....**206** A2
Steeple Claydon MK18 ..**63** C1
Church View Ct LU7 .....**80** C3
Church Views SL6 .....**202** C4
Church Way
East Claydon MK18 .....**74** C4
Stone HP17 ....**114** B3
Church Wlk
Milton Keynes MK3 .....**57** C4
North Crawley MK16 ....**24** A3
Weston Turville HP22 ..**116** C1
Winslow MK17 ....**65** C2
Church Yd HP23 ......**119** A2
Churchfields Mews SL2 .**206** A4
Churchfield Rd SL9 ....**177** B1
Churchill Ave HP21 ....**115** B3
Churchill Cl HP10 .....**185** A4
Churchill Ct 6 HP21 ...**115** C4
Churchill Dr
Beaconsfield HP9 .....**175** B3
Marlow SL7 ....**183** C2
Churchill Ho HP21 .....**115** B3
Churchill Rd SL3 ......**206** C1
Churchmead Sch SL3 ..**211** A4
Churchmere Wlk HP21 .**115** B3
Churchside HP15 .....**163** B4
Churchway HP17 ......**127** A3
Chyne The SL9 ....**188** C3
Cinnamon Gr MK7 ......**48** A3
Cippenham Cl SL1 .....**204** C3
Cippenham Inf Sch SL1 **204** B3
Cippenham La SL1 ....**205** A2
Cippenham Mid Sch
SL1 ....**204** C3
City Rd HP14 ....**159** B3
Clailey Ct MK11 ....**32** C3
Claires Court Sch SL6 ..**196** A1
Clammas Way UB8 ....**208** B4
Clapham Pl MK13 ......**34** B1
Clappers Mdw SL6 ....**196** B1
Clappins La HP14 .....**161** B4
Clapton App HP10 ....**185** B4
Clare Dr SL2 ....**198** A4
Clare Pk HP7 ....**164** C3
Clare Rd Maidenhead SL6 **202** B3
Prestwood HP16 .....**151** B3
Slough SL6 ....**204** B4
Stanwell TW19 ......**213** C1
Clarefield Cl SL6 ......**195** A1
Clarefield Dr SL6 .....**195** A1
Claremont SL3 ....**212** B3
Claremont Ave MK11 ...**32** C2
Claremont Ct HP21 ....**115** C3
Claremont Gdns SL7 ..**183** C1
Claremont Rd
Marlow SL7 ....**183** C1
Windsor SL4 ....**210** B3
Clarence Cres SL4 ....**210** B3
Clarence Ct
16 High Wycombe HP13 .**173** A4
Maidenhead SL6 ......**202** C4
Windsor SL4 ....**210** A3
Clarence Rd
Berkhamsted HP4 .....**135** C3
Henley-on-T RG9 .....**191** B1
Milton Keynes MK11 ...**32** C2
Windsor SL4 ....**210** A3
Clarendon Ct SL2 .....**206** A3
Clarendon Dr
Milton Keynes MK8 .....**33** C1
Thame OX9 ....**126** A1
Clarendon Rd
High Wycombe HP13 ...**173** C3
Prestwood HP16 .....**151** A3
Claridge Dr MK10 ......**36** A1
Clarke Ct HP20 ......**101** C1
Clarke Dr HP13 ......**174** A3
Clarke Rd MK1 ....**47** B2
Clarke Wlk 2 HP20 ...**101** C1
Clarke's Spring HP23 ..**119** C3
Clarkes Dr UB8 ......**208** C4
Clarkes Field Cl HP18 .**110** A4
Clarks Cotts HP16 ...**151** C1
Classon Cl UB7 ......**208** C2
Clauds Cl HP15 ......**163** A3
Claverton Ct HP3 .....**146** A2
Clay Acre HP5 ....**144** B1
Clay Cl HP10 ....**185** A4
Clay Hill MK8 ....**33** C1
Clay La
Marlow Bottom SL7 ...**172** A1
Wendover HP22 ......**131** B2
Claycots Inf & Jun Schs
SL2 ....**198** A1
Claycutters MK18 ......**66** A2
Claydon Cl HP21 .....**115** B3
Claydon Ct SL6 ......**172** C2
Claydon End SL9 .....**188** C2
Claydon Ho★ MK18 ....**74** B4
Claydon La SL9 ......**188** C2
Claydon Path HP21 ...**115** C2
Claydons Pl HP27 ....**138** B4
Clayfield Rd HP22 ....**131** B4
Clayfields HP10 ......**163** B1

Clayhall La SL4 ......**210** C1
Clayhill
Marlow Bottom SL7 ...**172** A1
Wigginton HP23 ......**133** C4
Claymoor Pk SL7 .....**172** A1
Clays La MK17 ....**55** C1
Clays The HP17 ......**127** A4
Clayton Ct SL3 ......**207** A2
Clayton Gate MK14 ....**35** A4
Clayton Way UB8 .....**201** B1
Clayton Wlk HP7 .....**166** B4
Claytons Comb Sch SL8 **185** A3
Claytons Mdw SL8 ...**185** A1
Clearbrook Cl HP13 ...**174** A2
Cleares Pasture SL1 ...**197** A1
Cleavers OX39 ....**147** A3
Cleavers Ave MK14 ....**34** C2
Cleeve Cres MK3 ......**47** A1
Clegg Sq MK5 ....**46** A3
Cleland Rd SL9 ......**177** B1
Clement Pl 8 HP23 ...**119** A2
Clementi Ave HP15 ...**163** B4
Clements Cl 16 SL1 ...**206** A2
Clements La OX27 .....**71** C1
Clements Rd
Chorleywood WD3 ....**167** B2
Henley-on-T RG9 .....**191** B2
Clerkenwell Cotts HP17 **126** C3
Clerkenwell Pl MK6 ....**35** A2
Cleve Ct SL4 ....**209** C2
Clevehurst Cl SL2 ....**199** A3
Cleveland MK13 ....**34** A3
Cleveland Cl
Maidenhead SL6 ......**203** A3
Wooburn Green HP10 ..**185** C4
Cleveland Dr LU7 ......**80** B4
Cleveland Pk
Aylesbury HP20 ......**101** C2
Stanwell TW19 ......**213** C5
Cleveland Pl 25 HP20 .**101** C2
Cleveland Rd
Aylesbury HP20 ......**101** C2
Uxbridge UB8 ....**201** B1
Clewer Ave SL4 ......**210** A3
Clewer Ct Rd SL4 .....**210** A4
Clewer Fields SL4 ....**210** B3
Clewer Green CE Sch
SL4 ....**210** A3
Clewer Hill Rd SL4 ....**209** C2
Clewer New Town SL4 .**210** A3
Clewer Pk SL4 ....**210** A4
Clifden Rd HP18 ......**123** B3
Clifford Ave MK2 ......**58** B4
Clifford Rd HP27 .....**139** A2
Cliffords Way SL8 ....**185** A3
Clifton Cl SL6 ....**203** A2
Clifton Ct
High Wycombe HP11 ..**172** C2
Olney MK46 ....**7** A2
8 Stanwell TW19 ....**213** C1
Clifton Gn HP19 ......**101** A1
Clifton Lawns HP6 ....**154** B2
Clifton Lodge Eton SL4 .**205** A1
14 Slough SL1 ....**206** A2
Clifton Rd
Amersham HP6 ......**154** B2
Newton Blossomville MK43 .**7** A2
18 Slough SL1 ....**206** A2
Clifton Rise SL4 ......**209** B3
Cline Ct MK8 ....**45** C3
Clinkard Pl MK14 .....**171** A2
Clinton Cres HP21 ....**116** A4
Clive Ct SL1 ....**205** B2
Cliveden★ SL6 ....**196** C4
Cliveden Mead SL6 ...**196** B1
Cliveden Office Village
HP12 ....**172** C2
Cliveden Rd SL6 ......**196** C2
Clivemont Rd SL6 ....**202** C4
Clock Ho The MK17 ....**59** B3
Clockhouse Mews WD3 **167** C3
Cloebury Paddock MK15 **35** B2
Cloister Garth HP4 ....**135** B2
Cloisters The
High Wycombe HP13 ...**162** B1
Slough SL1 ....**205** B2
Clonmel Way SL1 ....**197** A1
Close The Akeley MK18 ..**42** A4
Ashendon HP18 ....**97** C1
Bierton HP18 ....**102** A2
Bourne End SL8 .....**185** A3
Great Horwood MK17 ...**55** A2
Hardwick HP22 ....**87** A2
Iver Heath SL0 ....**200** B2
Milton Keynes, Bradwell
MK13 ....**34** A2
Milton Keynes, The Green
MK6 ....**47** B4
Olney MK46 ....**6** A1
Ravenstone MK46 ......**5** C1
Slough SL3 ....**204** B3
Closes The HP17 .....**127** A4
Cloudberry MK7 ......**48** A3
Cloutsham Cl MK4 .....**46** B2
Clover Cl MK5 ....**46** A4
Clover End MK18 ......**52** B4
Clover La HP21 ......**115** C3
Club Cotts MK17 ......**49** A2
Cluny Ct MK7 ....**48** B3
Clyde Pl MK3 ....**46** C1
Clydesdale Pl MK14 ...**34** C2
Coach Ho The
High Wycombe HP11 ..**174** A2
Wooburn Green HP10 ..**185** C3
Coach Ride SL2 ......**183** B2
Coachmaker Ct MK14 ..**34** C3
Coachman's Lodge 30
SL4 ....**210** B3

Chi – Col **221**

Coalmans Way SL1 ...**204** A4
Coat Wicks HP9 ......**176** B2
Coates La HP13 ......**162** A1
Cobb Cl SL3 ....**211** B3
Cobb Hall Rd MK17 ....**57** B2
Cobb Rd HP4 ....**134** C2
Cobbetts Mount MK18 ..**63** B1
Cobbetts Ride HP23 ..**118** C2
Cobblers Cl SL2 .....**198** A2
Cobblers Wick HP22 ...**89** A2
Cobblershill La
Prestwood HP16,HP22 ..**141** A2
Wendover HP16,HP22 ..**141** A2
Cobbs Gdn MK46 ....**6** C2
Cobden Cl UB8 ......**201** B2
Coberley Cl MK15 ......**35** A3
Cobham Cl
Buckingham MK18 .....**41** B1
Slough SL1 ....**204** C3
Cochran Cl MK8 ....**45** C4
Cochrane Ho UB8 ....**201** B2
Cock Gr HP4 ....**134** B2
Cock La HP10,HP13 ...**174** A3
Cockerell Gr MK5 ......**46** B3
Cockett Rd SL3 ......**206** C2
Cockpit Cl HP15 .....**151** C1
Cockpit Rd HP15 .....**162** B4
Coddimoor La MK17 ...**56** B4
Codmore Cres HP5 ...**144** C1
Codmore Cross HP5 ..**144** B1
Codmore Wood Rd HP5 **155** B3
Coe Spur SL1 ....**205** A2
Coffee Hall Rdbt MK6 ...**47** A3
Cofferidge Cl MK11 ....**32** B3
Coftards SL2 ....**206** B4
Cogan Ct MK8 ....**45** C4
Cogdells Cl HP5 ......**143** A2
Cogdells La HP5 ......**143** A2
Coggeshall Gr MK7 ....**48** B4
Coin Cl MK10 ....**35** C2
Coke's Farm La HP8 ...**166** A3
Coke's La Amersham HP8 **166** A3
Little Chalfont HP8 ....**166** A3
Cokers Ct 3 SL8 ....**185** A2
Colborne Rd HP13 ....**173** B4
Cold Grove Cotts SL6 .**196** C1
Cold Harbour
CE Comb Sch MK3 .....**46** C2
Coldeaton La MK4 .....**46** A2
Coldharbour Way MK19 **115** A4
Coldmoorholme La SL8 **184** C2
Coldmoreham Yd HP7 ..**165** A4
Cole Rd SL6 ....**115** B3
Coleheath Bottom HP27 **150** B3
Colenorton Cres SL4 ..**204** C1
Coleridge Cl
Milton Keynes MK3 .....**58** A4
Newport Pagnell MK16 ..**21** C2
Coleridge Cres SL3 ...**212** C3
Coleridge Way UB7 ...**208** C1
Coles Hill HP18 ......**111** A4
Colesbourne Dr MK15 ..**35** A3
Coleshill CE Inf Sch
HP7 ....**164** C2
Coleshill La HP7 .....**164** B1
Coleshill Pl MK13 ......**34** B2
Colet Rd HP22 ......**131** B3
Coleville Rd HP11 ....**172** C3
Colgrain St MK9 ....**35** A2
Colham Ave UB7 .....**208** C3
Colham Mill Rd UB7 ..**208** B3
Colham Rd UB8 ......**201** C3
Colin Way SL1 ....**205** A2
Colinswood Rd
Beaconsfield SL2 .....**187** A1
Farnham Common SL2 ..**187** A1
Hedgerley SL2 ....**187** A1
College Ave
Maidenhead SL6 ......**202** C4
Slough SL1 ....**205** C2
College Cl OX33 ......**122** B1
College Cres
Oakley HP18 ....**109** C2
Windsor SL4 ....**210** A3
College Glen SL6 ....**202** B4
College Lake
Wildlife Ctr★ HP23 ...**105** B1
College Rd
Aston Clinton HP22 ...**117** B4
Cranfield MK43 ....**24** C1
Maidenhead SL6 ......**202** C4
Slough SL1 ....**204** C3
College Rise SL6 ....**202** B4
Colley Hill MK13 ......**34** A2
Colley Hill La SL2 ....**187** C1
Colley Ho UB8 ......**201** B2
Colley Land WD3 ....**167** B3
Collier Cl SL6 ....**195** C1
Collings Wlk HP16 ...**151** B3
Collingwood Cl HP13 ..**174** A3
Collins Ho 2 HP11 ...**173** A4
Collins Wlk MK16 .....**22** B2
Collinswood Rd 1 SL2 .**198** B4
Collum Green Rd
Farnham Common SL2 ..**187** C1
Stoke Poges SL2 .....**187** C1
Collyer Rd HP14 .....**158** C2
Coln Cl SL6 ....**202** C4
Coln Trad Est SL3,
TW6 ....**212** C1
Colnbrook By-Pass SL3,
TW6 ....**212** B4
Colnbrook CE Comb Sch
SL3 ....**212** B4
Colnbrook Ct SL3 ....**212** C3

Coldnale Rd SL3 ......212 C3
Colne MK6 ....47 B3
Colne Ave UB7 ....208 B2
Colne Bank SL3 ......212 B2
Colne Orch SL0 ......207 C3
Colne Park Cvn Site
UB7 ....208 B1
Colne Rd HP13 ....173 C4
Colne Reach TW19 ....212 C1
Colne Valley Park
Visitor Ctr★ UB9 ...190 A1
Colnedale Rd UB8 ....201 B4
Colonial Rd SL1 .....206 A2
Colonnade SL6 ....203 A4
Colsons Way MK46 ......6 C3
Colston Bassett MK4 ..46 B1
Coltman Ave HP18 ....125 B3
Colts Holm Rd MK12 ...33 B4
Coltsfoot Dr UB8 ....208 C4
Coltsfoot Pl MK14 ....34 B2
Columbia Pl MK9 .....35 A2
Columbine Rd HP15 ...162 C3
Colville Ct HP16 .....152 A4
Combe Martin MK4 ....46 B2
Combe Rise HP12 .....172 A4
Combermere Cl SL4 ...210 A3
Comerford Way MK18 ...66 A3
Comfrey Cl MK7 ....48 A3
Comfrey The **2** HP20 ...101 C4
Common Field HP23 ...119 B1
Common Gate Rd WD3 .167 C2
Common La Eton SL4 ..205 B1
Hedgerley SL1 ....186 B1
Milton Keynes, Bradwell
MK13 ....34 A2
Milton Keynes, Loughton
MK5 ....46 B4
Common Rd
Chorleywood WD3 ....167 B3
Dagnall LU6 ....107 C2
Dorney SL4 ....204 B1
Eton SL4 ....205 A1
Flackwell Heath HP10 .185 A4
Great Kingshill HP15 .151 B1
Slough SL3 ....207 A1
Common Side HP13 ....161 C2
Common St MK46 ....5 B1
Common The
Berkhamsted HP4 .....135 C3
Chipperfield WD4 ....156 C4
Flackwell Heath HP10 .185 A4
Great Kingshill HP15 .151 B1
Holmer Green HP15 ...163 B4
Common Wood SL2 ....198 B4
Common Wood La
HP10 ....163 C1
Como Rd HP20 ....116 A4
Comp Gate LU6 ....92 C3
Comp The LU6 ....92 C3
Compass Point HP4 ...134 C3
Compton Ct
Moulsoe MK16 ....36 B4
Slough SL1 ....204 C4
Compton Dr SL6 .....202 A4
Compton Rd HP22 ....131 B3
Concorde Cl UB10 ....201 C2
Concorde Rd SL6 .....202 B2
Concorde Way SL1 ....205 B2
Concourse The **7** MK2 ..58 B4
Concra Pk MK17 ......49 B2
Condor Cl MK6 ....47 A4
Conegar Ct SL1 ......205 C3
Conegra Ct **22** HP13 ...173 A4
Conegra Rd HP13 .....173 B4
Coneygere MK46 ....7 A2
Conifer Rise HP12 ...172 C3
Conifers The SL6 ....202 A4
Conigre OX39 ....147 A3
Coningsby Cl SL6 ....202 B2
Coningsby Ct HP13 ...173 A4
Coningsby Rd HP13 ...162 A1
Coniston Cres SL1 ...204 B4
Coniston Gn HP20 ....101 B2
Coniston Rd LU7 ......80 C4
Coniston Way MK2 ....58 B3
Conkers SL6 ....203 A4
Connaught Cl SL6 ....195 C1
Connaught Gdns HP4 ..134 C4
Connaught Rd
Aylesbury HP20 ......116 B4
Slough SL1 ....206 A2
Conniburrow Bvd
MK14 ....34 C2
Conniston Cl SL7 ....183 A1
Conought Ho RG9 ....191 C2
Consort Way UB9 ....189 C3
Constable Cl MK14 ...34 A4
Constable Pl HP19 ...100 C1
Constable's Croft OX25 .94 C4
Constantine Pl UB10 .201 C2
Constantine Way MK13 .33 C3
Convent Rd SL4 .....210 A3
Conway Cl
Aylesbury HP21 .....115 C4
Loudwater HP10 .....174 B1
Milton Keynes MK3 ...57 C4
Conway Cres MK3 ....57 C4
Conway Ct SL9 ......189 A2
Conway Ho HP13 .....173 C4
Conway Rd SL6 ......204 A4
Cook Cl MK7 ....48 A2
Cook's Mdw LU6 ......92 C3
Cookfield Cl LU6 ....93 C4
Cookham Ct HP6 ....154 C1

Cookham Dean Bottom La
SL7 ....195 B4
Cookham Dean
CE Prim Sch SL7 ....195 A4
Cookham Lodge **15** SL6 202 C3
Cookham Rd SL6 ....195 C2
Cookham Rise Prim Sch
SL8 ....195 C3
Cookham Sta SL8 ....195 C4
Cooks Cl MK17 ....9 C4
Cooks La MK17 ....67 C3
Cookshall La HP12 ...161 A1
Coombe Ave
Berkhamsted HP4 ....134 C3
Hughenden Valley HP14 162 A3
Coombe Hill Ct SL4 ..209 B2
Coombe La HP16 .....161 C3
Coombe Vale SL9 ....188 C2
Cooper Rd RG9 ......191 B2
Cooper Way
3 Berkhamsted HP4 ...135 B2
Slough SL1 ....205 A2
Cooper's Court Rd HP14 158 B3
Cooper's Yd HP20 ....101 B1
Coopers Cl MK16 .....22 B2
Coopers Mews MK14 ...34 C3
Coopers Row SL0 ....200 B1
Coots Cl MK18 ....52 C4
Cope Ct SL6 ....202 B4
Copeland Cl MK7 .....48 B3
Copes Haven MK5 ....46 A2
Copes Rd HP15 ......151 C1
Copes Shroves HP15 ..162 C3
Copmans Wick WD3 ...167 B2
Copners Dr HP15 ....163 B3
Copners Way HP15 ...163 B3
Copper Beech Cl
Felden HP3 ....146 C4
Windsor SL4 ....209 B3
Copper Ridge SL9 ...177 C3
Copperfield Mid Sch
MK6 ....47 A3
Copperfield Terr SL2 ..206 A3
Copperfields
Beaconsfield HP9 ...175 C3
High Wycombe HP12 ..161 A1
Copperkins Gr HP6 ...154 A2
Copperkins La HP6 ...154 A2
Coppermill La UB9,WD3 178 C2
Coppermill Rd TW19 ..212 A1
Coppice Cl HP20 .....102 A1
Coppice Farm Rd HP18 163 B1
Coppice The
Great Kingshill HP15 ..151 C1
High Wycombe HP12 ..172 A2
6 Seer Green HP9 ....176 B2
Walter's Ash HP14 ...161 A4
West Drayton UB7 ...208 C4
Wigginton HP23 .....119 B1
Coppice Way
Aylesbury HP20 .....102 A1
Hedgerley SL2 ......187 B1
Coppidwell Dr HP21 ..116 A3
Coppin La MK13 ......34 A2
Coppinger Ct UB7 ...208 C2
Coppins Cl HP4 .....134 C2
Coppins La SL0 .....207 C3
Copse Cl Marlow SL7 .183 B1
Slough SL1 ....204 C1
West Drayton UB7 ...208 B2
Copse Gate MK18 .....66 A2
Copse La HP9 ....176 C2
Copse The
Amersham HP7 ......154 C1
Beaconsfield HP9 ...175 B2
Copse Way HP5 .....144 A2
Copse Wood SL0 ....200 B2
Copthall Cl SL9 ....177 C2
Copthall Cnr SL9 ....177 C2
Copthall Ho SL6 .....203 A4
Copthall La SL9 .....177 C2
Copthorn Cl SL6 .....202 A2
Copthorne Pl MK7 ....48 A4
Copyground Ct HP12 ..172 C4
Copyground La HP12 ..172 C4
Coral Cl LU6 ....92 C3
Coram Ct HP4 ....135 B2
Corbet Ride LU7 .....80 C4
Corbet Sq LU7 ....80 B4
Corbett Cl MK15 .....35 B4
Cordwainer Cl MK14 ..34 C3
Cordwallis Est SL6 ...202 C4
Cordwallis Pk SL6 ...195 C1
Cordwallis Rd SL6 ...202 C4
Cordwallis St SL6 ...202 C4
Cores End Rd SL8 ...185 A2
Corfe Cl HP21 ......116 A3
Corfe Cres MK3 .....57 C4
Corfe Gdns SL1 .....205 A3
Corfe Pl SL6 ....202 B4
Coriander Ct MK7 ....48 A3
Corin Cl MK2 ....58 B3
Corin Way MK2 ......58 B3
Corinium Ind Est HP6 154 C1
Corn Hill MK8 ....33 C1
Cornbrook Rd HP21 ..115 B3
Cornbury Cres MK15 ..35 C3
Corncrake **18** HP20 ...101 C4
Cornel Cl HP15 ......163 A2
Cornel Ho **1** SL4 ...210 B2
Cornelia Cl MK2 .....58 B3
Cornerways HP27 ....150 B3
Cornfield Cl UB8 ...201 B2
Cornfield Cres HP4 ..134 B4

Cornflower Pl MK18 ...52 B4
Cornhill Cty Fst Sch MK6 47 A3
Cornwall Ave SL2 ...198 B1
Cornwall Cl Eton SL4 .204 C1
Maidenhead SL6 ....195 C1
Cornwall Ct UB8 ....201 B3
Cornwall Gr MK3 .....46 C1
Cornwall Ho UB8 ....201 B3
Cornwall Lodge **11** SL6 .202 C3
Cornwall Rd UB8 ....201 B3
Cornwalls Ctr The MK18 .41 B1
Cornwalls Mdw MK18 ..41 B1
Cornwell Rd SL4 ....211 A1
Coronation Ave SL3 ..206 C4
Coronation Cotts MK18 .41 C4
Coronation Cres HP14 171 B3
Coronation Pl MK18 ...63 B1
Coronation Rd
Cranfield MK43 ......25 A1
High Wycombe HP12 ..172 B2
Milton Keynes MK11 ..32 C3
Coronation Villas HP13 .115 C4
Corporation St HP13 .173 A4
Corrid Ind Pk HP19 ..101 A1
Corrigan Cl MK3 .....58 A4
Corsham Ct **4** MK8 ..33 C1
Cosgrove Leisure Pk★
MK19 ....19 C1
Cosgrove Rd MK19 ...32 B4
Cosgrove Village
Prim Sch MK19 .....19 C1
Costers Cotts SL8 ...185 A1
Costins Wlk **7** HP4 ..135 B2
Cotes Way LU7 ......79 C2
Cotman Cl MK12 .....33 A3
Cotswold Cl
Maidenhead SL6 ....203 A3
Slough SL1 ....205 A2
Uxbridge UB8 ....201 B2
Cotswold Ct **1** HP12 ..172 C4
Cotswold Dr LU7 ....80 B4
Cotswold Gn HP20 ...101 C1
Cotswold Way HP13 ..172 C4
Cottage Comm MK5 ...46 A4
Cottage Farm Waye
HP27 ....150 B2
Cottage Grounds HP17 114 B3
Cottage Park Rd SL2 .187 B1
Cottages The
Hyde Heath HP7 .....153 A1
Ickenham UB10 .....190 C1
Syresham NN13 ......27 B3
Cottesbrooke Cl SL3 .212 B3
Cottesloe Cl LU7 ....79 C2
Cottesloe Ct MK11 ...32 C3
Cottesloe Rd HP21 ...115 C2
Cottesloe Sch The LU7 .79 C1
Cottingham Gr MK3 ..58 A4
Cottisford Cres MK14 .21 C1
Cottland Clay HP17 ..127 A4
Cotts The HP18 .....125 B3
Coulson Ave MK8 .....45 B3
Coulson Ct HP16 ....151 B3
Coulson Way SL1 ....204 A4
Council Hos LU7 ....92 A1
Countisbury HP4 ....146 B1
Country Life Ho SL3 ..211 A4
County Rd NN13 ......38 A3
Cours La Ville SL1 MK18 .65 C2
Court Cl Aylesbury HP21 .115 C4
High Wycombe HP13 ..161 B1
Maidenhead SL6 ....203 B1
Princes Risborough HP27 139 A2
Court Cnr MK46 ......6 C2
Court Cres SL1 .....205 B4
Court Dr Maidenhead SL6 196 B2
Uxbridge UB10 .....201 C2
Court Farm Rd HP11 ..205 A3
Court Farm Ind Est
TW19 ....213 C1
Court La Burnham SL1 .197 B4
Dorney SL4 ....204 A2
Court Lawns HP10 ...163 B1
Court Rd Cranfield MK43 .25 A1
Maidenhead SL6 ....196 B2
Court The MK17 .....37 B2
Courteneys Lodge MK4 .46 C2
Courtfield Dr SL6 ...202 B3
Courtfield Gdns UB9 .190 A1
Courthouse★ HP18 ..125 B4
Courthouse Cl MK18 ..65 C3
Courthouse Jun Sch
SL6 ....202 A4
Courthouse Mews MK16 .22 B2
Courthouse Rd SL6 ..202 B4
Courtlands
Leighton Buzzard LU7 .80 C3
14 Maidenhead SL6 ..202 C3
Courtlands Ave SL3 ..206 B1
Courtmoor Cl HP27 ..139 B3
Courtneidge Cl LU7 ..78 C4
Courtyard Arts Ctr★
MK14 ....21 C1
Courtyard Cl HP6 ...154 B1
Courtyard The
Aylesbury HP19 ....101 B1
Bourne End SL8 ....185 A2
6 Marlow SL7 ......183 B1
Cousins Cl UB7 .....208 C3
Cousins Dr HP20 ....101 C1
Cousins Piece HP18 ..112 A1
Coventon Rd HP19 ...101 B1
Coverack Pl MK4 .....57 A4
Coverdale MK13 ......34 B3
Coverdale Way SL2 ..197 C1
Covert Rd HP4 ......134 B3
Cow La Edlesborough LU6 .92 C2
Gawcott MK18 ....51 C2

Cow La continued
Tring HP23 ....119 B2
Cowdray Cl MK15 ....35 B2
Cowleaze OX39 .....147 A3
Cowley Bsns Pk UB8 .201 B1
Cowley Cl HP22 .....102 A2
Cowley Cotts HP7 ...164 B2
Cowley Cres HP7 ....208 B4
Cowley Inf Sch UB8 ..208 B4
Cowley Mill Rd UB8 ..201 A2
Cowley Mill Trad Est
UB8 ....201 A2
Cowley Rd UB8 .....201 A2
Cowper & Newton Mus
The★ MK46 ....6 C2
Cowper Cl MK16 .....22 C4
Cowper Rd
Berkhamsted HP4 ...135 A2
Chesham HP5 ......144 A1
Slough SL2 ....198 A1
Cowper St MK46 .....7 A3
Cowpers Orch MK46 ...6 A1
Cowslip Cl UB10 ....201 C3
Cowslip Rd HP15 ....162 C3
Cox Green La SL6 ...202 B2
Cox Green Rd SL6 ...202 B2
Cox Green Sch SL6 ..202 A2
Coxborrow Cl SL8 ...195 C4
Coxfield Cl HP14 ....158 C3
Coxwell Cl MK18 .....41 C1
Crab Tree Cl
Beaconsfield HP9 ...175 A1
Olney MK46 ....6 C3
Crabbe Cres HP5 ...144 A1
Crabs Gr HP22 ......86 C4
Crabtree Cotts HP27 .139 A1
Crabtree La HP17 ....49 B4
Crabtree Rd HP17 ...127 C4
Craddocks Cl MK13 ..34 A2
Cradley Wlk HP20 ...101 C2
Craigleith Ct HP9 ...175 C3
Craigmore Ave MK3 ..57 C4
Craigwell Ave HP21 ..116 B4
Cranberry Cl MK7 ...48 A3
Cranborne Ave MK4 ..45 C4
Cranbourne Ave SL4 .209 C3
Cranbourne Cl SL1 ..205 B3
Cranbourne Rd SL1 ..205 B3
Cranbrook MK17 .....49 A3
Cranbrook Dr SL6 ...195 B1
Crane Cl MK5 ....34 A1
Crane Way MK43 ....25 B1
Cranes Cl MK43 .....8 C3
Cranesbill Pl MK14 ..34 C2
Cranfield Con Ctr MK43 .24 C1
Cranfield Lower Sch
MK43 ....25 A1
Cranfield Rd
Astwood MK16 ......16 A1
Cranfield MK43 .....25 C2
Moulsoe MK16 ......36 C4
Salford MK17,MK43 ...37 B3
Wavendon MK17 .....49 A4
Cranfield Tech Pk MK43 .37 B4
Cranfield Univ MK43 .24 C1
Craufurd Cl SL6 ....202 C4
Craufurd Rise SL6 ...202 C4
Craven The MK13 ....34 B2
Crawley Rd
Cranfield MK43 .....25 A2
Woburn MK17 ....60 C4
Crawley's La HP23 ...133 C4
Crawshays SL6 .....203 A4
Crayle St SL2 ....198 A1
Creden Cl SL6 ......195 B1
Creed St MK12 ......33 B4
Creighton Rd HP18 ..83 C1
Crendon Rd HP18 ...112 A1
Crendon St HP13 ...173 A3
Crendon Way HP18 ..125 C2
Crenwell Cl MK5 .....46 A2
Crescent Cotts HP18 ..83 A3
Crescent Dale SL6 ..202 C4
Crescent Dr SL6 ....202 C4
Crescent The
Cranfield MK43 .....24 C1
Haversham MK19 ....20 C1
High Wycombe HP13 ..173 C4
Maidenhead SL6 ....202 C4
Marsworth HP23 ....105 A1
Milton Keynes, Fenny Stratford
MK2 ....47 B1
Milton Keynes, Giffard Park
MK14 ....21 C1
Pitstone LU7 ....105 B2
Princes Risborough HP27 139 B2
Slough SL1 ....205 C2
Crescent Villas **5** SL4 .210 B3
Creslow Ct MK11 ....32 C3
Creslow Way HP17 ..114 A3
Cress Rd SL1 ....205 A2
Cressex Bsns Pk HP12 172 B2
Cressex Com Sch HP12 172 B2
Cressex Ent Ctr HP12 .172 C3
Cressex Rd HP12 ...172 B2
Cressey Ave MK5 ....46 A2
Cressington Ct **2** SL8 .185 A2
Cressington Pl SL8 ..185 A2
Cresswell Rd HP5 ...154 B3
Cresswell Row SL7 ..183 B1
Cresswell Way HP15 .163 B4
Cresswells Mead SL6 .203 B1
Crest Rd HP11 ......172 B2
Crest The HP14 .....159 C4
Creswick Mdw HP21 ..116 A3
Crew Curve HP4 .....134 C4
Cricket Field Rd UB8 .201 B2

Cricket Green Rdbt MK9 .35 A2
Cricket Ground HP14 .158 B3
Cricketers Row MK14 ..66 A2
Cricketfield Rd UB7 ..208 B2
Cricklebeck MK13 ....34 A3
Crimp Hill SL4 ......211 A1
Crisp Rd RG9 ....191 B2
Crispin Cl HP9 ......175 B2
Crispin Field LU7 ...105 A2
Crispin Rd MK13 .....34 A2
Crispin Way
Farnham Common SL2 ..198 B4
High Wycombe HP11 ..173 A2
Criss Gr SL9 ....177 B1
Crocketts La HP16 ...142 B3
Crocus Dr HP21 .....115 A3
Croft Cnr SL4 ......211 A1
Croft Ct **10** HP21 ...115 C4
Croft Ctyd HP17 ....126 C3
Croft Gn LU6 ....93 C4
Croft Mdws LU7 ....105 A4
Croft Rd Aylesbury HP21 .115 C4
Gerrards Cross SL9 ..177 C1
Croft The
Haddenham HP17 ...126 C3
Maidenhead SL6 ....202 B3
Marlow SL7 ....184 A2
Crofters SL4 ....211 A1
Crofters Cl TW19 ...213 B1
Crofthill Rd SL2 ....198 A1
Crofton Ho HP11 ...174 A2
Crofts End MK16 ....14 A1
Crofts La MK17 .....57 B1
Croftwood HP13 ....173 C4
Cromarty Ct MK3 ...46 C2
Cromer Cl HP4 .....121 C2
Cromer Ct SL1 .....205 C4
Cromhamstone HP17 ..114 B3
Cromwell Ave
Aylesbury HP19 ....101 B1
Newport Pagnell MK16 ..22 A2
Thame OX9 ....126 A1
Cromwell Cl HP8 ...177 B4
Cromwell Ct MK18 ..41 C1
Cromwell Dr SL1 ...205 C4
Cromwell Gdns SL7 .183 C1
Cromwell Ho
Chesham HP5 ......144 A1
Uxbridge UB8 ......201 B1
Cromwell Rd
High Wycombe HP13 ..173 C4
Maidenhead SL6 ....202 B4
Marlow SL7 ....183 C1
Cropredy Ct MK18 ..41 C1
Cropton Rise MK4 ...46 A1
Cropwell Bishop MK4 .46 B1
Crosby Cl HP9 ......186 C4
Crosby Ct MK8 ......45 C3
Crosland Rd HP21 ...116 A3
Cross Ct HP13 .....161 B1
Cross End MK17 .....48 C3
Cross La
Beaconsfield HP9 ...186 C1
Tingewick MK18 ....105 B4
Weston Underwood MK46 ..6 A1
Cross Lanes
Bledlow HP27 ....138 C3
Chalfont St Peter SL9 .177 C3
Cross Lanes Cl SL9 ..177 C3
Cross Mdw HP5 ....143 A2
Cross Oak SL4 ......210 A3
Cross Oak Rd HP4 ..135 A2
Cross Rd
High Wycombe HP12 ..172 B2
Uxbridge UB8 ......201 B3
Cross St
Newport Pagnell MK16 ..22 B2
Uxbridge UB8 ......201 B3
Cross Tree Rd MK19 ..31 C1
Crossfield Cl HP4 ...134 C2
Crossfield Ho SL9 ...188 C4
Crossfield Rd HP27 ..139 B2
Crosshills MK11 .....32 B2
Crosslands MK14 ....34 C4
Crossleys HP8 ......177 B4
Crossway HP5 ......144 C1
Crossway The UB10 .201 C2
Crossways
Beaconsfield HP9 ...175 C1
Berkhamsted HP4 ...134 C2
High Wycombe HP12 ..172 B2
Crossways St **34** SL4 .210 B3
Crosthwaite Way SL1 .204 B4
Crow La MK17 ......49 A4
Crow Piece La SL2 ..197 C2
Crowborough La MK7 ..48 A4
Crowbrook Rd HP27 ..139 B3
Crown Bsns Est HP5 ..144 C1
Crown Cl SL3 ......212 B4
Crown Cotts Botley HP5 155 A4
Windsor SL4 ....210 B2
Crown Ct HP14 ....161 A1
Crown La Burnham SL2 198 A2
5 High Wycombe HP11 173 A3
Maidenhead SL6 ...203 A4
Marlow SL7 ....183 B1
Tylers Green HP10 ..174 C4
Crown Leys HP20 ...101 C1
Crown Mdw SL3 ...212 A4
Crown Rd SL7 .....183 B1
Crown Rose Ct HP23 ..119 A2
Crown Way UB7 ...208 C4
Crown Wlk
Milton Keynes MK9 ..34 C4
Uxbridge UB8 ......201 B3
Crownhill Rdbt MK8 ..45 C4
Crowther Ct MK5 ...46 B3
Croxley Ct **4** LU7 ...80 C4

Croxley Rise SL6 . . . . .202 B3
Croydon Cl MK4 . . . . .46 B2
Cruickshank Gr MK8 . . . .45 C4
Crummock Cl SL1 . . . . . . .204 B4
Crummock Pl MK2 . . . . . . .58 B3
Crusader Est HP12 . . . . . .172 B3
Crutches La HP9 . . . . .176 C2
Cryers Hill La HP15 . . . . . .162 B3
Cryers Hill Rd HP15 . . . . .162 B3
Cuba Cotts SL6 . . . . .196 A2
Cubb Field HP19 . . . . .115 A4
Cublington Rd HP22 . . . . . .88 B3
Cuddington CE Sch
  HP18 . . . . .112 C2
Cuddington Ct HP18 . . . . .112 C2
Cuddington Hill HP18 . . . .112 C2
Cuddington Rd HP17,
  HP18 . . . . .113 C2
Cudsdens Ct HP16 . . . . . .152 B4
Cuff La MK17 . . . . .59 B1
Culbertson La MK13 . . . . .33 C3
Culham Dr SL6 . . . . .195 C1
Cullen Pl MK2 . . . . .58 B3
Cullen's Pass SL6 . . . . . . .202 C3
Culley Way SL6 . . . . .202 A2
Cullum Rd HP12 . . . . .172 B2
Culmstock Cl MK4 . . . . . . .46 B1
Culrain Pl MK12 . . . . .33 B2
Culross Gr MK10 . . . . .36 A1
Culvers Croft HP9 . . . . . . .176 B3
Culvert La UB8 . . . . .201 A2
Culverton Hill HP27 . . . . .139 A2
Culverton La HP27 . . . . . .139 A1
Cumberland Ave SL2 . . . .198 B1
Cumberland Cl
  Aylesbury HP21 . . . . . . .116 A4
  Little Chalfont HP7 . . . . .166 A4
Cumbrae Cl SL2 . . . . .206 A3
Cumbria Cl
  Maidenhead SL6 . . . . . .202 B2
  Milton Keynes MK3 . . . . .46 C1
Cumbrian Way
  High Wycombe HP13 . . . .172 C4
  Uxbridge UB8 . . . . .201 B3
Curfew Yd The [12] SL4 . . . .205 C2
Curlew HP20 . . . . .101 C2
Curlew Cl
  Berkhamsted HP4 . . . . . .135 B2
  High Wycombe HP13 . . . .161 B1
Curls La SL6 . . . . .202 C2
Curls Rd SL6 . . . . .202 B2
Curran Cl UB8 . . . . .201 B1
Currier Dr MK14 . . . . .34 C3
Curriers La SL1 . . . . .197 B4
Cursley Path HP15 . . . . . .115 A4
Curtis Cotts HP5 . . . . . . .144 C4
Curtis Croft MK5 . . . . .46 A2
Curtis Way HP4 . . . . .135 B2
Curzon Ave
  Beaconsfield HP9 . . . . . .175 B2
  Tylers Green HP15 . . . . .163 B1
Curzon CE Comb Sch
  HP7 . . . . .164 A3
Curzon Cl HP15 . . . . .163 B1
Curzon Gate Ct HP14 . . . .158 C3
Curzon Mall [18] SL1 . . . . .205 C2
Curzon Pl MK7 . . . . .48 C2
Cutler's Ct [9] HP12 . . . . .172 C4
Cutlers Mews MK14 . . . . . .34 C3
Cuttle Brook Gdns OX9 . . .125 C1
Cyclamen Pl HP21 . . . . . .115 A3
Cypress MK16 . . . . .22 A2
Cypress Ho SL3 . . . . .207 A1
Cypress Wlk HP15 . . . . . .163 A2

D

Dacre Rd HP22 . . . . .131 C4
Dadbrook HP18 . . . . .112 C1
Dadbrook Cl HP18 . . . . . .112 C1
Dadfield Cl HP18 . . . . . . .112 C1
Dag La MK16 . . . . .12 A4
Dagmar Rd SL4 . . . . .210 B3
Dagnall Cres UB8 . . . . . . .208 B4
Dagnall Rd Eaton Bray LU6 93 B1
  Olney MK46 . . . . .6 C2
Dagnall Sch HP4 . . . . . . .107 B3
Dair House Sch SL2 . . . . .198 B2
Dairy La RG9 . . . . .192 A4
Dairymede HP27 . . . . . . .150 B2
Daisy Cotts HP14 . . . . . . .171 A2
Dale Cl NN13 . . . . .38 A4
Dale Ct SL1 . . . . .205 B2
Dale Side SL9 . . . . .188 C1
Dalesford Rd HP21 . . . . . .116 A2
Dalgin Pl MK9 . . . . .35 A2
Dalston Cl HP20 . . . . .101 C1
Dalton Gate MK10 . . . . . . .35 C2
Dalvina Pl MK12 . . . . .33 B2
Daly Way HP20 . . . . .116 A4
Damask Ct HP23 . . . . . . .119 B2
Damson Gr SL1 . . . . .205 B2
Dancers End La HP22,
  HP23 . . . . .118 B1
Dandridge Cl SL3 . . . . . . .206 B1
Dandridge Dr SL8 . . . . . .185 B2
Dane Cl HP7 . . . . .165 C3
Dane Ct HP21 . . . . .115 B2
Dane Rd MK1 . . . . .47 C1
Danes Ct SL6 . . . . .202 B4
Danes Gdns SL8 . . . . . . .195 C3
Danesfield Sch SL7 . . . . .193 C4
Daneswood MK17 . . . . . . .49 A1
Daniels Welch MK6 . . . . . .47 A3
Dansbrook Cl MK4 . . . . . . .46 B2
Dansteed Way MK8,MK13,
  MK14,MK15 . . . . .34 B2

Danvers Croft HP23 . . . . .119 B3
Darby Cl MK5 . . . . .46 A3
Darby Lodge HP13 . . . . . .174 A4
Darin Ct MK8 . . . . .45 C4
Dark La Chearsley HP18 . . .112 A1
  Oving HP22 . . . . .86 B4
  Wingrave HP22 . . . . .89 B1
Darley Cl HP21 . . . . .116 A3
Darley Gate MK14 . . . . . . .35 A3
Darley's Cl SL6 . . . . .83 A3
Darling's La SL6 . . . . .194 C1
Darlington Cl HP6 . . . . . . .154 B1
Darnel Cl MK6 . . . . .47 A3
Darr's La HP4 . . . . .134 B3
Darrell Cl SL3 . . . . .206 C1
Darsham Wlk HP5 . . . . . . .154 C1
Dart Cl Aylesbury HP21 . . .115 B3
  Newport Pagnell MK16 . . .22 B2
  Slough SL3 . . . . .212 A4
Dartmouth Cl SL1 . . . . . .205 C2
Dartmouth Rd MK46 . . . . . .6 C2
Darvell Dr HP5 . . . . .144 A4
Darvill Rd HP17 . . . . .114 A3
Darvill's La SL1 . . . . .205 B2
Darvills Mdw HP15 . . . . . .163 B4
Darwin Rd SL3 . . . . .206 C2
Dashfield Gr HP15 . . . . . . .162 C3
Dashwood Ave HP12 . . . . .172 B4
Dashwood Cl SL3 . . . . . . .206 B1
Datchet Pl SL3 . . . . .211 A3
Datchet Rd Datchet SL3 . . .205 C1
  Eton SL3 . . . . .205 C1
  Horton SL3 . . . . .211 C2
  Old Windsor SL4 . . . . . .211 A2
  Windsor SL4 . . . . .210 B4
Datchet St Mary's
  CE Prim Sch SL3 . . . . . .211 A3
Datchet Sta SL3 . . . . .211 A3
Daubeney Gate MK5 . . . . . .45 C3
Davenies Sch HP9 . . . . . .175 C1
Davenport Lea MK7 . . . . . .48 C3
Davenport Rd HP12 . . . . . .172 B2
Daventry Cl SL3 . . . . .212 C3
David Cl HP21 . . . . .116 A2
David Rd SL3 . . . . .212 C3
Davies Cl HP20 . . . . .115 B4
Davies Ct HP12 . . . . .172 B3
Davies Way HP10 . . . . . . .174 B1
Davis Cl SL7 . . . . .183 C1
Davis Rd [18] HP4 . . . . . . .135 B2
Davy Ave MK5 . . . . .46 B3
Dawe's Cl UB10 . . . . .201 C2
Dawe's Rd UB10 . . . . .201 C2
Dawes Cl HP5 . . . . .154 A4
Dawes East Rd SL1 . . . . .197 B4
Dawes La WD3 . . . . .156 C2
Dawes Moor Cl SL2 . . . . .206 B4
Dawley Ride SL3 . . . . .212 C3
Dawn Redwood Cl SL3 . . .212 A2
Dawney Dr HP19 . . . . . . .101 B2
Daws Cl SL0 . . . . .207 C4
Daws Hill La HP11 . . . . . .173 C2
Daws Lea HP11 . . . . .173 C2
Dawson Cl SL4 . . . . .210 A3
Dawson Rd MK1 . . . . .47 B2
Daylesford Cts MK15 . . . . . .35 A3
De Clare Ct MK18 . . . . . . .41 C1
De Havilland Dr HP5 . . . . .162 C1
De Havilland Way TW19 . . .213 A4
De Montfort Univ MK7 . . . . .48 A4
Deacon Cl HP12 . . . . .172 A2
Deacon Cl SL4 . . . . .209 B4
Deacon Pl MK10 . . . . .35 C2
Deadhearn La HP8 . . . . . .166 C1
Deal Ave SL1 . . . . .204 C4
Dean Cl Aylesbury HP21 . . .116 A3
  High Wycombe HP12 . . . .172 C3
  Uxbridge UB10 . . . . . . .201 C3
  Windsor SL4 . . . . .209 B2
Dean Farm La LU7 . . . . . . .69 C2
Dean Field HP3 . . . . .146 A4
Dean La SL7 . . . . .195 B4
Dean Rd LU7 . . . . .68 C1
Dean St SL7 . . . . .183 C1
Dean The HP22 . . . . .89 C2
Dean Way
  Aston Clinton HP22 . . . . .117 C2
  Chalfont St Giles HP8 . . .177 A4
  Holmer Green HP15 . . . .163 A3
Dean Wood Rd HP9 . . . . .176 B1
Dean's Cloisters SL4 . . . . .210 A4
Dean's Rd MK12 . . . . .33 B4
Deanacre Cl SL9 . . . . . . .177 C2
Deancroft Rd SL9 . . . . . . .177 C2
Deanfield HP14 . . . . .160 A4
Deanfield Ave RG9 . . . . . .191 B4
Deanfield Cl
  Bledlow Ridge HP14 . . . .149 B1
  Marlow SL7 . . . . .183 B2
Deanfield Rd RG9 . . . . . . .191 B1
Deangarden Rise HP11 . . .173 C2
Deans Cl Amersham HP6 . . .154 C1
  Stoke Poges SL2 . . . . . .199 A2
  Tring HP23 . . . . .119 A2
Deans Furlong HP23 . . . . .119 A2
Deans Lawn HP4 . . . . .135 B2
Deans Mdw HP4 . . . . .107 B3
Deansfield Cl SL6 . . . . . . .195 B1
Deanshanger Prim Sch
  MK19 . . . . .31 C2
Deanshanger Rd
  Old Stratford MK19 . . . . . .32 A3
  Wicken MK19 . . . . .31 A2
Deansway HP5 . . . . .144 A4
Dearing Cl [12] HP20 . . . . .101 C1
Deben Ct MK16 . . . . .22 C2
Decies Way SL2 . . . . .199 A2
Dedmere Ct SL7 . . . . .183 C1

Dedmere Rd SL7 . . . . .183 C1
Dedmere Rise SL7 . . . . . .183 C1
Dedworth Dr SL4 . . . . . . .209 C3
Dedworth Green Fst Sch
  SL4 . . . . .209 C3
Dedworth Manor SL4 . . . .209 C3
Dedworth Mid Sch SL4 . . .209 B3
Dedworth Rd SL4 . . . . . . .209 B3
Deeds Gr HP12 . . . . .172 C3
Deena Cl SL1 . . . . .204 C3
Deep Acres HP6 . . . . .154 A2
Deep Field SL3 . . . . .211 A3
Deep Mill La HP16 . . . . . .152 B2
Deepdale MK13 . . . . .34 B3
Deer Park Wlk HP5 . . . . . .144 C2
Deer Wlk MK9 . . . . .34 C2
Deerfern Cl MK18 . . . . . . .21 C1
Deerfield Cl MK18 . . . . . . .52 C4
Deermead HP16 . . . . .152 A2
Deerswood SL6 . . . . .196 A1
Deethe Cl MK17 . . . . .49 A3
Delafield Cl HP14 . . . . . . .158 C2
Delaford Cl SL0 . . . . .207 C4
Delaford Ho UB7 . . . . . . .208 B3
Delahay Rise HP4 . . . . . . .135 A3
Delamere Cl HP20 . . . . . .101 C1
Delamere Gdns LU7 . . . . . .80 B4
Delaware Dr MK15 . . . . . . .35 A2
Delius Ct MK7 . . . . .48 B2
Dell Cl SL2 . . . . .198 A3
Dell Field HP5 . . . . .151 B3
Dell Lees HP9 . . . . .176 B2
Dell Rd Berkhamsted HP4 . .134 B4
  West Drayton UB7 . . . . . .208 C2
Dell The Aylesbury HP20 . .102 A1
  Chalfont St Peter SL9 . . .177 C2
  Maidenhead SL6 . . . . . .202 A1
  Tylers Green HP10 . . . . .163 B1
  Uxbridge UB8 . . . . .201 B1
Dellfield HP5 . . . . .144 A1
Dellfield Ave HP4 . . . . . . .135 A3
Dellfield Cl HP4 . . . . .135 A3
Dellfield Cres UB8 . . . . . .201 B1
Dellfield Par UB8 . . . . . . .201 B1
Dells MK6 . . . . .6 C2
Dellside UB9 . . . . .190 B3
Delmeade Rd HP5 . . . . . .154 A4
Deltic Ave MK13 . . . . .34 A1
Demoram Cl MK18 . . . . . . .65 C2
Denbigh East Ind Est
  MK1 . . . . .47 B1
Denbigh Hall MK3 . . . . . . .46 C2
Denbigh Hall Dr MK3 . . . . .46 C2
Denbigh Rd
  Milton Keynes MK1 . . . . .47 A1
  Thame OX9 . . . . .126 A1
Denbigh Sch MK5 . . . . . . .46 A3
Denbigh Way MK2 . . . . . . .47 B1
Denbigh West Ind Est
  MK1 . . . . .47 A1
Denby Wlk HP20 . . . . .116 A4
Denchworth Ct [2] MK4 . . . .46 B1
Dene Cl Winslow MK18 . . . .66 A2
  Woburn Sands MK17 . . . .49 B2
Dene The MK18 . . . . .63 B2
Denewood HP13 . . . . .173 C4
Denham Ave UB9 . . . . . . .189 C2
Denham Cl Denham UB9 . . .190 A1
  Maidenhead SL6 . . . . . .202 B3
  Milton Keynes MK3 . . . . .57 B4
Denham Court Dr UB9 . . . .190 A1
Denham Ctry Pk★ UB9 . . .190 A1
Denham Golf Club Sta
  UB9 . . . . .189 B2
Denham Green Cl UB9 . . . .190 A2
Denham Green La UB9 . . . .189 C2
Denham La SL9 . . . . .178 A1
Denham Lodge UB9 . . . . .201 B3
Denham Rd
  Iver Heath SL0 . . . . .200 C3
  Lane End HP14 . . . . . . .171 B3
Denham Sta SL0 . . . . .190 A2
Denham View MK18 . . . . . .75 C3
Denham Village Inf Sch
  UB9 . . . . .189 C1
Denham Way
  Denham UB9 . . . . .190 A1
  Maple Cross WD3 . . . . . .178 C2
Denham Wlk SL9 . . . . . . .177 C2
Denison Ct MK7 . . . . .48 B3
Denmark St
  High Wycombe HP11 . . . .173 A4
  Maidenhead SL6 . . . . . .202 C4
  Milton Keynes MK2 . . . . .58 C4
Denmead MK8 . . . . .33 C1
Denmead Cl SL9 . . . . .188 C2
Dennis Cl
  Aston Clinton HP22 . . . . .117 C2
  Drayton Beauchamp HP22 118 A2
Dennis Way SL1 . . . . .204 B3
Denniston Ho HP12 . . . . . .172 B4
Denny Rd SL3 . . . . .206 C1
Denny's La HP4 . . . . .134 C1
Denton Ct SL7 . . . . .183 C1
Depot Rd SL6 . . . . .203 A3
Derby Rd UB8 . . . . .201 B2
Dere Pl MK2 . . . . .58 C2
Derehams Ave HP10 . . . . .174 B2
Derehams La HP10 . . . . . .174 B2
Derek Rd SL6 . . . . .203 B4
Deri Dene Cl [2] TW19 . . . .213 A4
Derwent Cl
  Little Chalfont HP7 . . . . .166 A4
  Newport Pagnell MK16 . . .22 B2
Derwent Dr
  Maidenhead SL6 . . . . . .202 B4
  Milton Keynes MK3 . . . . .57 C4
  Slough SL1 . . . . .204 B4

Derwent Rd LU7 . . . . .80 A2
Desborough Ave HP11 . . . .172 C3
Desborough Cres SL6 . . . .202 B3
Desborough Gn [1] HP20 101 B1
Desborough Ho [20]
  HP13 . . . . .173 A4
Desborough Ind Pk
  HP12 . . . . .172 C4
Desborough Park Rd
  HP12 . . . . .172 C4
Desborough Rd HP11 . . . .172 C3
Desborough Sch SL6 . . . .202 C3
Desborough St HP11 . . . .172 C4
Deseronto Wharf
  (Ind Est) SL3 . . . . .206 C2
Develin Cl MK14 . . . . .34 C4
Devereux Pl HP19 . . . . . .101 A1
Devereux Rd SL4 . . . . . . .210 B3
Deverill Rd HP21 . . . . .115 B2
Deverills Way SL3 . . . . . . .207 B1
Devon Ave SL1 . . . . .205 B4
Devon Cl MK3 . . . . .46 C1
Devon Rd HP19 . . . . .101 A2
Devon Way UB10 . . . . . . .201 C2
Devonshire Ave HP6 . . . . .154 A1
Devonshire Cl
  Amersham HP6 . . . . .154 B1
  Farnham Common SL2 . . .198 A2
Devonshire Gn SL2 . . . . . .198 A2
Devonshire Lodge [10]
  SL6 . . . . .202 C3
Dexter Ave MK6 . . . . .46 C4
Dexter Ho MK6 . . . . .46 C4
Dhoon Rise SL6 . . . . .202 C3
Diamond Rd SL1 . . . . . . .206 A2
Diana Cl SL3 . . . . .206 C4
Diane Cl HP21 . . . . .116 A2
Diane Wlk HP21 . . . . .116 A2
Dickens Cl MK43 . . . . .3 C3
Dickens Dr MK19 . . . . .32 A3
Dickens Rd MK12 . . . . .33 B4
Dickens Spinney MK46 . . . .6 C2
Dickens Way HP19 . . . . . .100 C1
Dicks Way HP19 . . . . .100 C1
Diddington Cl MK2 . . . . . . .58 B2
Digby Cl OX9 . . . . .126 A1
Dilwyn Ct [4] HP12 . . . . . .172 C4
Dingle Dell SL4 . . . . .70 C1
Dingleberry MK46 . . . . .6 C2
Dinmore HP3 . . . . .145 C2
Dinton CE Fst Sch HP17 113 C2
Disraeli Cres HP13 . . . . . .161 C1
Disraeli Ct SL3 . . . . .212 A4
Disraeli Cty Comb Sch
  High Wycombe HP12 . . . .172 C4
  High Wycombe HP13 . . . .173 A4
Disraeli Pk HP9 . . . . .175 B2
Ditchingham Cl HP19 . . . .115 A4
Ditton Park Rd SL3 . . . . . .211 C4
Ditton Rd Datchet SL3 . . . .211 B4
  Slough SL3 . . . . .211 C4
Dixie Cl HP20 . . . . .116 A4
Dixie La MK7 . . . . .48 B3
Dixon Cl HP21 . . . . .115 A3
Dobbins La HP22 . . . . . . .131 A3
Dobson's La RG9 . . . . . . .191 B4
Doctors' Common Rd
  HP4 . . . . .135 A2
Dodds La HP8 . . . . .177 A4
Doddsfield Rd SL2 . . . . . .198 A1
Dodkin MK6 . . . . .47 A3
Dodman Gn MK4 . . . . .57 A4
Dog Kennel La WD3 . . . . .167 C3
Doggett St LU7 . . . . .80 C2
Doggetts Farm Rd UB9 . . .189 B2
Doggetts Wood Cl HP8 . . .166 B3
Doggetts Wood La HP8 . . .166 B3
Dolben Ct MK15 . . . . .35 B4
Dolesden La HP14 . . . . . . .169 B1
Dollicott HP17 . . . . .126 C4
Dolphin Ct
  High Wycombe HP11 . . . .174 A2
  Slough SL1 . . . . .206 A2
Dolphin Pl HP21 . . . . .115 C3
Dolphin Rd SL1 . . . . .206 A2
Dolphin Sq [3] HP23 . . . . .119 A2
Don The MK3 . . . . .46 B1
Donkey Dr SL8 . . . . .185 A2
Donkey La
  Bourne End SL8 . . . . . . .185 A2
  Tring HP23 . . . . .118 C2
Donnay Cl SL3 . . . . .188 B3
Donnington MK13 . . . . . . .34 A3
Donnington Gdns SL6 . . . .195 C3
Donnybrook Ho [3]
  HP13 . . . . .173 B4
Doon Way MK2 . . . . .58 B3
Dorchester Ave MK3 . . . . .47 A1
Dorchester Cl
  Maidenhead SL6 . . . . . .195 A1
  Stoke Mandeville HP22 . .116 A1
Dorchester Ho SL9 . . . . . .188 C2
Doreen Cl MK2 . . . . .58 B4
Dorking Pl MK5 . . . . .46 C4
Dormans Cl MK10 . . . . . . .36 A1
Dormer Ave LU7 . . . . .79 C2
Dormer Ct [1] HP21 . . . . . .115 A3
Dormer Ct [4] HP20 . . . . . .101 C1
Dormer La HP15 . . . . .163 A4
Dornels SL2 . . . . .206 B4
Dorney Comb Sch SL6 . . .203 C2
Dorney Ct★ SL4 . . . . .204 A2
Dorney End HP5 . . . . .144 A1
Dorney Hill S HP9 . . . . . . .187 A2
Dorney Lake Park
  Nature Reserve★ SL4 . . .209 A4
Dorney Lake Pk★ SL4 . . . .209 A4

Dorney Lake Rowing Ctr★
  SL4 . . . . .204 A1
Dorney Pl MK13 . . . . .34 B2
Dorney Reach Rd SL6 . . . .203 C2
Dorney Wood Rd SL1 . . . .197 B3
Dorrells Rd HP27 . . . . . . .138 C4
Dorrien's Croft HP4 . . . . . .134 C4
Dorset Cl
  Berkhamsted HP4 . . . . . .134 C3
  Milton Keynes MK3 . . . . .46 C1
Dorset Lodge [9] SL6 . . . .202 C3
Dorset Pl HP21 . . . . .116 B3
Dorset Rd SL4 . . . . .210 B3
Dorset Way UB10 . . . . . . .201 C2
Dorton Cl MK8 . . . . .33 C1
Dorton Rd HP18 . . . . .111 A2
Douglas Ct SL7 . . . . .184 A2
Douglas Gdns HP4 . . . . . .135 A3
Douglas La TW19 . . . . . . .211 C1
Douglas Pl MK6 . . . . .46 C4
Douglas Rd
  Aylesbury HP20 . . . . . . .102 A1
  Slough SL2 . . . . .205 B4
  Stanwell TW19 . . . . .213 B1
Doune Ho MK3 . . . . .46 C1
Dove Acre HP20 . . . . .101 C2
Dove Ct Aylesbury HP21 . . .115 B3
  Buckingham MK18 . . . . . .52 C4
  Newport Pagnell MK16 . . .22 B2
Dove Ct HP9 . . . . .175 B2
Dove Ho HP20 . . . . .101 C2
Dove House Cl
  Edlesborough LU6 . . . . . .92 C2
  Winslow MK18 . . . . .66 A2
Dove House Cres SL2 . . . .197 C1
Dove Pk WD3 . . . . .167 A2
Dove St LU7 . . . . .78 C4
Dovecot Rd MK13 . . . . . . .173 A4
Dovecote
  Haddenham HP17 . . . . . .126 C3
  Newport Pagnell MK16 . . .22 B2
Dovecote Cft MK14 . . . . . .21 C1
Dovecote Ct
  Haddenham HP17 . . . . . .126 C3
  Princes Risborough HP27 .139 B3
Dovehouse Ct [8] HP13 . . .173 A4
Doveleat OX39 . . . . .147 B4
Dover Gate MK5 . . . . .57 C4
Dover Hedge HP21 . . . . . .116 B3
Dover Rd SL1 . . . . .204 C4
Dovetail Cl HP21 . . . . .172 B4
Dowding Rd UB10 . . . . . . .201 C3
Dower Cl HP9 . . . . .175 B3
Dower Pk SL4 . . . . .209 A4
Down Pl SL4 . . . . .209 A4
Downdean MK6 . . . . .47 A4
Downer Cl MK18 . . . . .52 C4
Downer Dr WD3 . . . . .156 C2
Downham Rd MK17 . . . . . .49 B2
Downings Path SL2 . . . . . .197 C1
Downings Wood WD3 . . . . .178 B3
Downland MK8 . . . . .33 C1
Downley Ave MK13 . . . . . .34 B2
Downley Ct HP13 . . . . . . .161 B1
Downley Rd HP14 . . . . . . .161 A1
Downley Sch The
  High Wycombe HP13 . . . .161 B1
  High Wycombe HP13 . . . .161 B1
Downs Barn Fst Sch
  MK14 . . . . .34 C3
Downs Pk HP13 . . . . .161 C1
Downs Rd SL3 . . . . .206 B3
Downs View MK17 . . . . . . .48 B1
Dr Challoner's Gram Sch
  (Boys) HP6 . . . . .154 B1
Dr Challoner's High Sch
  HP7 . . . . .166 A4
Dragon Tail HP17 . . . . . . .127 A3
Drake Ave SL3 . . . . .206 B3
Drake Cl HP21 . . . . .115 A3
Drake's Rd HP17 . . . . .165 C4
Drakeloe Cl MK17 . . . . . . .60 C4
Drakes Dr HP18 . . . . .125 C3
Drakes Farm HP18 . . . . . .125 C3
Drakes Mews MK8 . . . . . . .45 C4
Drakewell Rd MK17 . . . . . .48 B1
Drayton Ct UB7 . . . . .208 C1
Drayton Gdns UB7 . . . . . .208 C2
Drayton Park Comb Sch
  MK2 . . . . .58 B3
Drayton Parslow
  Village Sch MK17 . . . . . .68 C2
Drayton Rd
  Aylesbury HP20 . . . . . . .101 B1
  Milton Keynes MK2,MK3,
    MK17 . . . . .58 B3
  Newton Longville MK17 . . .57 B1
Dresser Rd HP16 . . . . . . .151 B3
Drew Mdw SL2 . . . . .198 B4
Drews Pk HP9 . . . . .175 B3
Drey The SL9 . . . . .177 C2
Drift Rd SL4 . . . . .209 A1
Drift Way SL3 . . . . .212 B4
Drive The Amersham HP7 . 154 B1
  Bourne End SL8 . . . . . . .184 C2
  Chalfont St Peter SL9 . . .177 C2
  Cranfield MK43 . . . . .24 B1
  Datchet SL3 . . . . .211 A3
  Ickenham UB10 . . . . . . .190 C1
  Ivinghoe LU7 . . . . .92 A1
  Slough SL3 . . . . .206 C2
  Wraysbury TW19 . . . . . .211 B1
Dropmore Inf Sch SL1 . . . .186 B1
Dropmore Rd SL1 . . . . . . .197 B3

Drovers Croft MK12 33 A2
Drovers La HP14 169 A1
Drovers Way
Dunstable LU6 93 C4
Newton Longville MK17 57 B1
Seer Green HP9 176 B2
Druce End NN12 18 C3
Druids Wlk OX39 147 B3
Drummond Ho 4 SL4 210 B2
Drummond Ride HP23 119 A3
Drummound Way MK15 35 B4
Drydell La HP5 153 C4
Dryden Cl
6 Aylesbury HP20 101 C1
Newport Pagnell MK16 22 A2
Du Pre Wlk HP10 185 B2
Duchess Gr MK7 48 B4
Duchess St SL1 204 C3
Duck End MK17 59 B1
Duck La Ludgershall HP18 96 B4
Woburn MK17 60 C4
Duck Lake MK18 41 C2
Duck Lake Cl MK18 41 C2
Duck Sq OX39 147 B3
Duckmore La HP23 118 C1
Dudley Cl MK18 76 A1
Dudley Ct SL1 206 A2
Dudley Hill MK5 46 A3
Dudley La RG9 181 A3
Dudswell La HP4 134 B4
Duffield La SL2 198 C3
Duffield Pk SL2 199 A1
Duke St Aspley Guise MK17 49 B2
Eton SL4 210 B4
Henley-on-T RG9 191 C1
High Wycombe HP13 173 B3
Princes Risborough HP27 139 A2
Dukes Cl
Gerrards Cross SL9 188 B2
Shabbington HP18 124 B1
Dukes Dr MK2 47 B1
Dukes La SL9 188 C2
Dukes Piece MK18 52 C4
Dukes Pl SL7 183 B1
Dukes Ride
Gerrards Cross SL9 188 C2
Ickenham UB10 201 C4
Leighton Buzzard LU7 70 C2
Dukes Valley SL9 188 A1
Dukes Way
Berkhamsted HP4 135 A3
Uxbridge UB8 201 B2
Dukes Wood Ave SL9 188 C2
Dukes Wood Dr SL9 188 B2
Dulverton Ct LU7 80 B4
Dulverton Dr MK4 46 B2
Dulwich Cl MK16 22 B1
Dumfries Cl MK3 46 C2
Dunbar Cl
Milton Keynes MK3 57 B4
Slough SL2 206 A3
Dunbar Dr OX9 126 A1
Duncan Gr MK5 45 C3
Duncan Rd MK43 24 C1
Duncannon Cres SL4 209 B2
Dunchurch Dale MK7 48 A3
Duncombe Cl HP6 154 C1
Duncombe Rd HP4 134 C3
Duncombe St MK2 58 B4
Duncroft SL4 209 C2
Dundale Jun Mix Inf Sch
HP23 119 A3
Dundale Rd HP23 119 A2
Dundee Rd SL1 205 A4
Dungrovehill La SL7 194 B2
Dunholme End SL6 202 B2
Dunkeld Ho HP11 174 A2
Dunkery Beacon MK4 46 B2
Dunny La WD4 156 C4
Dunsby Rd MK6 47 A2
Dunsham La HP20 101 C1
Dunsley Pl HP23 119 A2
Dunsmore Ave HP27 139 B3
Dunsmore Ride HP27 139 B3
Dunstable Downs★ LU6 93 C2
Dunstable Ho 11 SL7 183 C1
Dunstable Rd
Dagnall HP4 107 B4
Eaton Bray LU6 93 A3
Totternhoe LU6 93 B4
Dunster Ct MK4 46 C2
Dunster Gdns SL1 205 A3
Dunston Hill HP23 119 A2
Dunthorne Way MK8 45 B3
Dunton Rd LU7 78 B3
Dunvedin Pl MK12 33 B2
Dunvegan Cl MK2 58 B2
Dunwood Ct SL6 202 B3
Dunwood Rise HP13 162 A1
Duparc Cl MK7 48 B3
Dupre Cl SL1 204 C2
Dupre Cres HP9 176 A1
Durgate MK7 48 A4
Durham Ave SL1 205 A4
Durley Hollow HP13 162 A1
Durlston End MK4 57 A4
Durrans Ct MK2 47 C1
Durrans Ho MK2 47 C1
Durrants La HP4 134 C3
Durrants Path HP5 144 A2
Durrants Rd HP4 134 C3
Durrell Cl LU7 80 C4
Dutch Barn Cl TW19 213 B1
Dutton Way SL0 207 C4
Dyers Mews MK14 34 C3
Dyers Rd LU6 92 B4
Dyersdale MK13 34 B3
Dyson Cl SL4 210 A2

E

Eagle Wlk MK9 34 C2
Eagles Rd HP20 116 A4
Eaglestone Rdbt MK6 47 A4
Ealing Chase MK10 47 C4
Eames Cl HP20 101 C2
Earl Cl HP13 162 A1
Earl Howe Rd HP15 163 B3
Earls Cl MK2 58 B4
Earls La SL1 204 C3
Earls Willow MK13 34 A4
Earlsfield SL6 203 B1
Earlswood Cl HP21 116 A3
Easby Gr MK10 36 A1
Easington La HP18 111 A1
East Berkshire Coll
Maidenhead SL6 202 B3
Slough SL3 207 A2
Windsor SL4 210 B3
East Burnham Cotts
SL2 198 A2
East Burnham La SL2 198 A2
East Chapel MK4 57 A4
East Claydon Rd MK18 65 B1
East Claydon Sch MK18 74 C4
East Comm SL9 188 C3
East Cres SL4 209 C3
East Dales MK13 34 B3
East Dr
High Wycombe HP13 173 C4
Stoke Poges SL2 198 C1
East End HP22 87 B1
East Hills MK43 25 A1
East La MK7 47 C4
East Paddock SL7 194 C3
East Rd Cranfield MK43 24 C1
Maidenhead SL6 202 C4
West Drayton UB7 208 C1
East Richardson St
HP11 172 C4
East Ridge SL8 185 A2
East Spur MK7 47 C4
East St Adstock MK18 53 C1
Chesham HP5 154 A4
Olney MK46 7 A2
East View OX25 81 A2
East Way HP9 175 A1
East Wlk N MK9 34 C1
East Wlk S MK9 34 C1
Eastbourne Rd SL1 205 A4
Eastbridge SL2 206 A3
Eastbrook Cl OX25 95 C4
Eastbury Ct MK4 46 B1
Eastcote Rd HP21 116 A2
Eastcroft SL2 198 A1
Eastergate HP9 175 B2
Eastern Dene HP15 163 A3
Eastern Dr SL8 185 B2
Eastern St HP20 101 C1
Eastfield Cl 5 SL1 206 A2
Eastfield Cres NN12 18 C3
Eastfield Dr MK19 11 A2
Eastfield Rd
Aylesbury HP20 116 A4
Burnham SL1 204 A4
Princes Risborough HP27 139 B2
Eastlands HP27 149 C3
Eastnor HP3 146 A2
Easton St HP11 173 A3
Easton Terr HP13 173 B3
Eastwick Cres WD3 178 C4
Eastwood Ct 1 SL7 183 C2
Eastwood Rd HP14 158 C2
Eaton Ave
High Wycombe HP12 172 B4
Milton Keynes MK2 58 B4
Eaton Bray
Com Lower Sch LU6 92 C3
Eaton Bray Rd
Edlesborough LU6 92 B3
Totternhoe LU6 92 C4
Eaton Mill Cty Comb Sch
MK2 58 B3
Eaton Pk LU6 92 C3
Eaton Pl HP12 172 B4
Eaton Rd HP21 115 B4
Eatongate Cl LU6 92 C3
Ebble Cl HP21 115 B2
Ebbsgrove MK5 34 A1
Ebenezer Ho HP10 174 B1
Ebsworth Cl SL6 196 B2
Eddington Ct MK4 46 B1
Eddy St HP4 135 A3
Eden Cl Slough SL3 207 A1
Stoke Mandeville HP21 115 B2
Eden Wlk MK3 46 C1
Edgar Rd UB7 208 C3
Edgar Wallace Pl SL8 185 A3
Edge Hill Ct MK18 41 C1
Edgecombe Rd HP21 116 A3
Edgecote MK8 46 A4
Edgecote Ho 18 HP13 173 A4
Edgecott Rd HP18 82 C4
Edgehill OX9 125 C1
Edgewood HP11 173 B3
Edinburgh Ave SL1 205 A4
Edinburgh Dr UB9 189 C3
Edinburgh Gdns SL4 210 B3
Edinburgh Ho MK3 57 B4
Edinburgh Pl HP21 115 B3
Edinburgh Rd
Maidenhead SL6 195 C1
Edinburgh Rd *continued*
Marlow SL7 183 C2
Edison Rd HP19 100 C1
Edison Sq MK5 46 B3
Edith Bell Ho SL9 177 C2
Edith Rd SL6 202 A4
Edlesborough Sch LU6 92 C2
Edlyn Cl HP4 134 C3
Edmonds Cl MK18 41 C1
Edmonds Rd HP14 171 A2
Edmonds Sh Ctr HP14 171 A2
Edmund Ct
Beaconsfield HP9 186 A4
Milton Keynes MK5 45 C4
Edmunds Cl HP12 172 B3
Edmunds Gdns HP12 172 B3
Edmunds Way SL2 206 A4
Edrich Ave MK6 46 C4
Edward Cl HP21 116 A2
Edward Wlk HP21 116 A2
Edwards Ct SL1 205 C2
Edwin Allman Pl HP15 162 C1
Edwin Cl MK17 48 B1
Edy Ct MK5 34 A1
Eelbrook Ave MK13 34 B1
Eeles Cl HP19 100 C2
Egerton Cl NN13 38 A4
Egerton Gate MK5 46 A2
Egerton Rd
Berkhamsted HP4 135 A3
Slough SL2 197 C1
Egerton-Rothesay
Lower Sch HP4 135 A2
Egerton-Rothesay Mid
& Upper Sch HP4 134 C2
Eghams Cl HP9 175 B2
Eghams Ct SL8 185 A2
Eghams Wood Rd HP9 175 B2
Egmont Ave MK11 32 C3
Egremont Gdns SL1 205 A3
Egypt La SL2 187 A1
Egypt Way HP19 115 A4
Egypt Wood Cotts SL2 187 A1
Eider Cl MK18 52 C4
Eight Acres Burnham SL1 197 A1
Tring HP23 119 A2
Elangeni Jun Sch HP6 154 C2
Elbow Mdw SL3 212 C3
Elder Cl Loudwater HP11 174 A2
West Drayton UB7 208 C3
Elder Gate
Milton Keynes, Rooksley
MK9 34 B1
Milton Keynes, Winterhill
MK9 46 B4
Elder Way HP15 163 A2
Elderdene OX39 147 B4
Elderfield Rd SL2 198 C3
Eldridge La HP17 130 B2
Eleanor Cl MK17 60 C4
Eleanor Gdns HP21 115 C3
Eleanor Rd SL9 177 B1
Eleanor Wlk MK17 60 C4
Elfords MK6 47 A3
Elgar Gr MK7 48 B2
Elgin Ho SL3 212 C3
Elgiva La HP5 154 A4
Elham Way HP21 116 A2
Eliot Cl Aylesbury HP19 100 C1
Newport Pagnell MK16 21 C3
Eliot Dr SL7 183 C2
Elizabeth Ave HP6 166 B4
Elizabeth Cl
Aylesbury HP21 116 A2
Cookham SL8 195 C4
Elizabeth Ct
High Wycombe HP13 173 B3
3 High Wycombe,
Wycombe Marsh HP13 173 C3
9 Slough SL1 206 A2
33 Windsor SL4 210 B3
Elizabeth Dr HP23 119 A3
Elizabeth Rd Marlow SL7 183 C2
Stokenchurch HP14 158 C2
Elizabeth Way SL2 198 C2
Elkins Rd SL2 187 C1
Ellen Pl HP21 115 B3
Ellen Rd HP21 115 B3
Ellen Wlk HP21 115 A3
Ellenstow MK13 34 A2
Ellerburn Pl MK4 46 A2
Ellery Rise HP14 170 C1
Ellesborough Gr MK8 33 B2
Ellesborough Rd
Ellesborough HP17 130 A1
Great Kimble HP17 129 C1
Wendover HP22 131 A2
Ellesmere Cl LU6 93 B3
Ellesmere Rd HP4 135 B2
Elliman Ave SL2 205 C3
Ellington Ct SL6 203 B4
Ellington Gdns SL6 203 B4
Ellington Pk SL6 195 C1
Ellington Prim Sch SL6 195 C1
Ellington Rd SL6 203 B4
Elliots Cl UB8 208 B4
Elliott Ho 3 HP11 172 C4
Ellis Ave
Chalfont St Peter SL9 177 C1
Slough SL1 205 C2
Ellis Way HP14 171 A2
Ellisgill Ct MK13 34 A2
Ellison Cl SL4 209 C2
Ellison Ho 24 SL4 210 B3
Ellsworth Rd HP11 172 C2
Ellwood Terr WD3 167 B2
Ellwood Ho 1 SL9 177 C1
Ellwood Rd HP9 175 A1
Ellwood Rise HP8 177 B4
Elm Brook Cl HP18 112 B1
Elm Cl Amersham HP6 154 B1
Chinnor OX39 147 B3
Ellesborough HP17 130 B2
Farnham Common SL2 198 B3
Hazelmere HP15 163 A2
Newton Longville MK17 57 B1
Weston Turville HP22 116 C1
Elm Croft SL3 211 B3
Elm Ct HP17 130 B2
Elm Dr Chinnor OX39 147 B3
Deanshanger MK19 31 B3
Elm Farm Rd HP21 116 A3
Elm Gn HP21 115 B4
Elm Gr Berkhamsted HP4 135 B2
Maidenhead SL6 202 C4
West Drayton UB8 208 C3
Woburn Sands MK17 49 A2
Elm La SL8 184 C3
Elm Lawn Cl UB8 201 C3
Elm Rd
High Wycombe HP12 172 B2
Princes Risborough HP27 139 A2
Tylers Green HP10 174 B4
Windsor SL4 210 A2
Elm St MK18 52 B4
Elm Tree Cotts HP7 164 B1
Elm Tree Wlk
Chorleywood WD3 167 C3
Tring HP23 119 A3
Elm Trees HP18 125 A4
Elmar Gn SL2 198 A1
Elmdale Gdns HP27 139 A2
Elmers Cl MK19 44 A3
Elmers Mdw MK18 76 A1
Elmers Pk MK3 58 A4
Elmfield Cl NN12 18 B2
Elmfields Gate MK18 66 A2
Elmhurst HP16 152 A4
Elmhurst Cl
High Wycombe HP13 162 B1
Milton Keynes MK4 46 C2
Elmhurst Ct SL3 207 A2
Elmhurst Inf Sch HP20 101 C1
Elmhurst Jun Sch HP20 101 C1
Elmhurst Rd
Aylesbury HP20 101 C1
Slough SL3 207 A2
Elmlea Dr MK46 6 C2
Elmridge Ct MK4 46 B1
Elms Dr SL8 185 B2
Elms Rd SL9 177 C2
Elms The
Leighton Buzzard LU7 80 C4
Milton Keynes MK3 57 C4
Preston Bissett MK18 51 A1
Elmshott Cl HP10 163 A1
Elmshott La SL1 204 C3
Elmside MK18 66 A2
Elmslie Ct SL6 202 C4
Elmtree Ct HP16 152 A4
Elmtree Gn HP16 152 A4
Elmtree Hill HP5 144 A1
Elmtree Sch HP5 144 A1
Elmwood
Maidenhead SL6 196 A2
Turvey MK43 8 C3
Elmwood Cl HP18 109 B3
Elmwood Pk SL9 188 C2
Elmwood Rd SL2 206 A3
Elora Rd HP13 173 C4
Elruge Cl UB7 208 B2
Elsmore Cl HP21 116 A2
Eltham Ave SL1 204 C2
Elthorne Rd UB8 201 B2
Elthorne Way MK16 22 B1
Elton MK6 47 B4
Elton Dr SL6 202 B4
Elwes Rd HP14 171 B2
Ely Ave SL1 205 B4
Ely Cl HP7 165 C4
Ely Ho HP13 173 C4
Ember Path HP21 115 B2
Ember Rd SL3 207 A2
Emberton Ctry Pk★ MK46 6 C1
Emberton Ctry Pk
Visitors Ctr★ MK46 6 C1
Emberton Fst Sch MK46 13 C4
Emberton Gdns MK11 32 C3
Embleton Way MK18 52 B4
Emerald Cl MK18 74 C4
Emerald Ct SL1 205 C2
Emerald Gate MK15 35 C3
Emerson Ct HP10 185 C3
Emerson Valley Mid Sch
MK4 46 B1
Emerton Ct HP4 134 C4
Emerton Garth HP4 134 C4
Emlyns Bldgs SL4 210 B4
Emma Rothschild Ct
HP23 119 A3
Emmett Cl MK4 46 B1
Emperor Cl HP4 134 C4
Empingham Cl MK2 58 B2
Empstead Ct RG9 191 B1
Enborne Cl HP21 115 B2
Enfield Chase MK14 34 B3
Enfield Cl UB8 201 B2
Engaine Dr MK5 45 C4
English Gdns TW19 211 B1
Enmore Gate MK9 35 A2
Enmore Rdbt MK9 35 A2
Ennell Gr MK2 58 B3
Ennerdale Cl MK2 58 B3
Ennerdale Cres SL1 204 B4
Ensbury Path HP20 101 C1
Enstone Rd UB10 190 C1
Enterprise La MK9 35 A2
Epsom Cl LU7 80 B3
Epsom Gr MK3 57 B3
Eriboll Cl LU7 80 A3
Erica Cl SL1 204 C3
Erica Rd MK12 33 C2
Eridge Gn MK7 48 A4
Errington Dr SL4 210 A3
Esk Way MK3 46 C1
Eskdale Ave HP5 144 B1
Eskdale Gdns SL6 203 A1
Eskdale Lodge HP6 154 B1
Eskdale Rd
Stoke Mandeville HP22 116 A1
Uxbridge UB8 201 A2
Essenden Ct MK11 32 C3
Essex Ave SL2 205 B4
Essex Cl MK3 46 C1
Essex Ho 6 HP20 101 B1
Essex Pl HP19 101 A2
Essex Rd HP5 144 B1
Estcourt Dr HP15 162 C3
Eston Ct MK13 34 A3
Estover Way OX39 147 A3
Etheridge Ave MK10 48 B4
Ethorpe MK8 33 C1
Ethorpe Cl SL9 188 C3
Ethorpe Cres SL9 188 C3
Eton Cl SL3 211 A4
Eton Coll SL4 210 B4
Eton Cres MK12 33 B3
Eton Ct SL4 210 B4
Eton End PNEU Sch
SL3 211 A4
Eton Pl SL7 183 B1
Eton Porny CE Fst Sch
SL4 210 B4
Eton Rd SL3 211 A4
Eton Sq SL4 210 B4
Eton Wick CE Fst Sch
SL4 205 A1
Eton Wick Rd SL4 205 A1
Eton Wlk 20 SL1 205 C2
Eunice Gr HP5 154 B4
Europa Ho SL9 188 C3
Evans Cl Aylesbury HP21 116 A2
Chearsley HP18 112 A1
Evans Gate MK6 46 C4
Evans Way HP23 119 A2
Evelyn Cl LU7 79 C1
Evelyn Pl MK13 34 A4
Evelyns Cl UB8 208 C4
Evelyns Com Sch UB8 208 C4
Evenlode SL6 202 C4
Evenlode Cl HP21 115 B3
Evenlode Rd SL8 185 A2
Everard Ave SL1 205 C2
Everest Cl HP13 173 B3
Everest Rd HP13 173 C3
Everglade MK6 47 A4
Everley Cl MK4 46 B2
Evesham Gn HP19 101 B2
Evett Cl HP20 101 C1
Evreham Rd SL0 207 C4
Exchange St HP20 115 C4
Exebridge MK4 46 B2
Exmoor Gate MK4 46 C1
Eyethrope Rd HP17 114 B3
Eynsford Terr UB7 208 C4
Eynsham Ct MK15 35 B1
Eyre Gn SL2 198 A1

F

Factory Yd HP9 175 C1
Fadmoor Pl 3 MK4 46 A2
Fagnall La HP7 164 B1
Fair Acres HP16 151 B3
Fair Leas HP5 144 A1
Fair Mdw MK18 66 A2
Fair Mile Aylesbury HP21 116 A4
Henley-on-T RG9 191 B2
Fair Ridge HP11 172 C2
Fair View Cotts
Chalfont St Peter SL9 177 C2
Cookham SL8 195 C4
Fairacre SL6 202 B3
Fairacres Ind Est SL4 209 B3
Faircroft SL2 198 A1
Fairfax MK13 34 B3
Fairfax Cres HP20 101 C1
Fairfax Mews HP7 165 A4
Fairfield App TW19 211 B1
Fairfield Ave
Datchet SL3 211 B4
Farnham Common SL2 198 A2
Fairfield Cl Datchet SL3 211 B4
Olney MK46 7 A2
Fairfield Rd
Burnham SL1 197 B1
Paulerspury NN12 17 A4
Uxbridge UB8 201 B3
West Drayton UB7 208 C3
Wraysbury TW19 211 B1
Fairfields HP15 151 C1
Fairford Cres MK15 35 A3
Fairford Leys Way HP19 115 A4
Fairford Rd SL6 202 C4
Fairhaven SL9 177 B1
Fairlawn Pk SL4 209 C2
Fairlea SL6 202 A2
Fairlie Rd SL1 205 A4
Fairlight Ave SL4 210 B3
Fairlight Dr UB8 201 B3
Fairmile Ct RG9 191 B2
Fairthorn Cl HP23 118 C2
Fairview La HP10 174 A1

Fairview Rd
Burnham SL6 . . . . .204 A4
Slough SL2 . . . . .197 C1
Fairway HP27 . . . . .139 A2
Fairway Ave UB7 . . . . .208 B3
Fairway Cl UB7 . . . . .208 B3
Fairway The
Burnham SL1 . . . . .197 B2
Flackwell Heath HP10 . . . .185 B4
Maidenhead SL6 . . . . .202 A2
Uxbridge UB10 . . . . .201 C2
Fairways MK8 . . . . .33 B1
Fairways Rdbt MK8 . . . . . . .33 B1
Faith Terr MK1 . . . . .11 A1
Faithfull Cl HP17 . . . . .114 C1
Falaise MK15 . . . . .35 A3
Falcon Ave MK6 . . . . .35 A1
Falcon Dr TW19 . . . . .213 C1
Falcon Ridge HP4 . . . . . . .135 B2
Falcon Rise HP13 . . . . . . .161 B1
Falcon The HP20 . . . . .101 C2
Falconhurst Comb Sch
MK6 . . . . .47 A4
Falcons Croft HP10 . . . . . .185 C4
Falkland Ho SL6 . . . . .202 C4
Falklands Cl MK18 . . . . . . .63 B1
Fall Cl HP19 . . . . .101 B2
Falling La UB7 . . . . .208 C3
Fallow Field HP15 . . . . . . .163 A4
Fallows The SL6 . . . . .196 A1
Falmouth Pl MK6 . . . . .34 C1
Falmouth Rd SL1 . . . . .205 A4
Fane Way SL6 . . . . .202 B3
Fantail La HP23 . . . . .118 C2
Far Furlong Cl HP21 . . . . . .115 B2
Faraday Cl SL2 . . . . .205 A4
Faraday Dr MK5 . . . . .46 B3
Faraday Rd
Aylesbury HP19 . . . . .101 A1
Slough SL2 . . . . .205 A4
Farinton MK8 . . . . .33 C1
Farjeon Ct MK7 . . . . .48 B2
Farm Cl
High Wycombe HP13 . . . . .174 A4
Ickford HP18 . . . . .123 C2
Little Chalfont HP6 . . . . . . .166 A4
Maidenhead SL6 . . . . .203 B1
Maidenhead, Highway SL6 . .203 B1
Stewkley LU7 . . . . .78 C4
Farm Cres SL2 . . . . .206 A4
Farm Dr SL4 . . . . .211 A1
Farm Gr HP9 . . . . .175 B3
Farm La HP9 . . . . .176 B2
Farm Lea HP10 . . . . .185 C4
Farm Pl
Berkhamsted HP4 . . . . . . .134 C3
Chinnor OX39 . . . . .137 C1
Farm Rd Bourne End SL8 . .184 C2
Brackley NN13 . . . . .38 A3
Burnham SL6 . . . . .204 A3
Chorleywood WD3 . . . . . . .167 A3
Maidenhead SL6 . . . . .202 A4
Farm Way TW19 . . . . .212 C1
Farm Yd SL4 . . . . .210 B4
Farmborough MK6 . . . . . . .47 A4
Farmborough Ct HP20 . . . .102 A1
Farmers Cl SL6 . . . . .202 A2
Farmers Way
Maidenhead SL6 . . . . .202 A2
Seer Green HP9 . . . . .176 B2
Farmburn Ave SL1 . . . . . . .205 A3
Farndale Gdns HP15 . . . . .163 A3
Farnell Ct MK5 . . . . .46 B4
Farnham Cl HP3 . . . . .146 A2
Farnham Common Ho 3
SL2 . . . . .198 A4
Farnham Common
Inf Sch SL2 . . . . .198 A4
Farnham Common
Jun Sch SL2 . . . . .198 B4
Farnham Ct MK8 . . . . .33 C1
Farnham La SL2 . . . . .198 A2
Farnham Park La SL2 . . . . .198 B2
Farnham Rd SL1,SL2 . . . . .205 B4
Farnley Rd HP20 . . . . .101 C1
Farrer Cl NN13 . . . . .26 B2
Farrer Theatre SL4 . . . . . . .205 B1
Farrier Ct 12 SL8 . . . . . . .185 A2
Farrier Pl MK14 . . . . .35 A3
Farriers Cl HP3 . . . . .146 A2
Farthing Gr MK6 . . . . .47 B3
Farthing Green La SL2 . . . .199 A2
Farthingales The SL6 . . . . .203 A4
Farthings The HP6 . . . . . . .154 A2
Fassets Rd HP10 . . . . .174 A1
Faulkner Way HP11 . . . . . .161 B2
Faulkner's Way LU7 . . . . . . .80 C4
Favell Dr MK4 . . . . .46 C2
Faversham Cl HP23 . . . . . .119 A2
Fawcett Rd SL4 . . . . .209 C2
Fawley Bottom La RG9 . . . .180 A1
Fawley Cl SL6 . . . . .195 B1
Fawley Ct★ RG9 . . . . .191 C2
Fawsley Cl HP23 . . . . .212 C4
Featherbed La HP15 . . . . . .163 B4
Fedden Ho MK43 . . . . .24 B2
Fegans Ct MK11 . . . . .32 B3
Felbridge MK7 . . . . .48 A4
Felden La HP3 . . . . .146 C4
Fells Cl HP18 . . . . .125 B3
Fellstead Ct SL6 . . . . .202 B3
Fences La MK16 . . . . .13 A1
Fennels Farm Rd HP10 . . . .174 A1
Fennels Rd HP11 . . . . .174 A2
Fennels Way HP10 . . . . . . .174 A1
Fennemore Cl HP18 . . . . . .109 B2

Fennings The HP6 . . . . . . .154 B2
Fenny Rd MK17 . . . . .69 C4
Fenny Stratford Sta MK1 . .47 C4
Fennymere MK8 . . . . .33 B1
Fenton Ct MK8 . . . . .45 C4
Fern Ct HP4 . . . . .135 A2
Fern Dr SL6 . . . . .204 A4
Fern Gr MK2 . . . . .58 B3
Fern La Haddenham HP17 . .127 A3
Little Marlow SL8 . . . . .184 C3
Fern Wlk HP15 . . . . .163 A2
Fernan Dell MK8 . . . . .45 B4
Fernborough Haven 4
MK4 . . . . .46 B1
Ferndale MK6 . . . . .35 A1
Ferndale Cl HP14 . . . . .158 C2
Ferndale Cres UB8 . . . . . . .201 B1
Ferne Furlong MK46 . . . . . . .6 C3
Fernes Cl UB8 . . . . .208 B4
Fernhill Cl OX9 . . . . .136 A3
Fernhurst Cl HP9 . . . . .175 C1
Fernie Fields HP12 . . . . . . .172 B2
Fernlea Cl HP10 . . . . .174 A1
Fernley Ct SL6 . . . . .195 B1
Ferns The HP9 . . . . .175 C1
Fernside
Great Kingshill HP15 . . . . . .151 C1
Hazelmere HP15 . . . . .163 A3
Fernsleigh Cl SL9 . . . . . . .177 C2
Fernwood Ind Sch MK17 . .49 A1
Ferrers Ave UB7 . . . . .208 B2
Ferrers Cl SL1 . . . . .204 C3
Ferry End SL6 . . . . .203 B2
Ferry La Bourne End SL8 . .185 A1
Cookham SL6 . . . . .196 A4
Hambleden RG9 . . . . .192 B3
Medmenham SL7 . . . . .193 A3
Ferry Rd SL6 . . . . .203 B2
Festival Cotts SL3 . . . . . . .212 B4
Field Cl Aylesbury HP20 . . .102 A1
Chesham HP5 . . . . .144 C2
Ickford HP18 . . . . .124 A2
Sherington MK16 . . . . .14 A1
Field End HP18 . . . . .125 C3
Field End HP23 . . . . .119 B1
Field Hurst SL3 . . . . .206 C1
Field La MK13 . . . . .33 A4
Field Rd Denham UB9 . . . . .189 C1
High Wycombe HP12 . . . . .172 A3
Murcott OX5 . . . . .94 A3
Field Way
Aylesbury HP20 . . . . .102 A1
Bovingdon HP3 . . . . .146 A3
Gerrards Cross SL9 . . . . . .177 B2
Uxbridge UB8 . . . . .201 B1
Field Wlk MK9 . . . . .34 C2
Fieldfare HP20 . . . . .101 C2
Fieldhead Gdns SL8 . . . . . .185 A2
Fieldhouse Ct HP13 . . . . . .161 A3
Fieldhouse Ind Est SL7 . . .183 C1
Fieldhouse La SL7 . . . . . . .183 C1
Fieldhouse Way SL7 . . . . . .183 C1
Fielding Gdns SL3 . . . . . . .206 B2
Fielding Rd SL6 . . . . .202 A4
Fields End HP23 . . . . .119 A3
Fields The SL1 . . . . .205 B2
Fieldway Amersham HP7 . . .165 A3
Berkhamsted HP4 . . . . . . .135 C1
Wigginton HP23 . . . . .119 B1
Fifth St HP11 . . . . .173 B2
Filey Spur SL1 . . . . .205 A3
Filmer Rd SL4 . . . . .209 B3
Finch Cl MK10 . . . . .35 C2
Finch Cres LU7 . . . . .80 C3
Finch Ct SL6 . . . . .202 B3
Finch End HP10 . . . . .174 B4
Finch Gn WD3 . . . . .167 C3
Finch La Amersham HP7 . . .166 A4
Beaconsfield HP9 . . . . .175 B3
Little Chalfont HP6 . . . . . . .166 A4
Finch Rd HP4 . . . . .135 A2
Findlay Way MK2 . . . . .58 B4
Fineleigh Ct SL1 . . . . .205 B3
Fingest La Frieth HP14 . . . .170 C2
Lane End HP14 . . . . .170 B1
Fingle Dr MK13 . . . . .33 C4
Finians Cl UB10 . . . . .201 C1
Finings Rd HP14 . . . . .171 A2
Finley Ho RG9 . . . . .191 C2
Finmere CE Prim Sch
MK18 . . . . .50 B3
Finmere Cres HP21 . . . . . .116 B3
Fir Tree Ave SL2 . . . . .198 C1
Fir Tree Cotts HP14 . . . . . .161 A4
Fircroft Cl SL2 . . . . .199 A3
Fire La MK17 . . . . .57 B2
Firs Ave SL4 . . . . .209 C2
Firs Cl Hazelmere HP15 . . .163 A1
High Wycombe HP13 . . . . .173 C4
Iver Heath SL0 . . . . .200 B2
Lane End HP14 . . . . .171 B3
Whitchurch HP22 . . . . .87 A3
Firs Ct Amersham HP6 . . . .154 B1
Bierton HP22 . . . . .102 A2
Firs Dr SL3 . . . . .206 C3
Firs End SL9 . . . . .188 B4
Firs Rise HP16 . . . . .151 C4
Firs The Bierton HP22 . . . .102 A2
Brill HP18 . . . . .110 A4
Maidenhead SL6 . . . . .202 C4
Uxbridge UB8 . . . . .201 B1
Wigginton HP23 . . . . .119 B1
Firs View Rd HP15 . . . . . . .163 A1
Firs Wlk HP15 . . . . .163 A1
First Ave Amersham HP7 . . .165 B4
Marlow SL7 . . . . .184 A1
Milton Keynes MK1 . . . . . . .47 B1
First Cres SL1 . . . . .205 B4

First St HP11 . . . . .173 B2
Firview Cl SL7 . . . . .183 C1
Fish Ponds La OX9 . . . . . . .125 C1
Fisherman's Way SL8 . . . . .185 A2
Fishermans Cl MK46 . . . . . . .6 C2
Fishermans Retreat
SL7 . . . . .183 C1
Fishermead Bvd MK6 . . . . .35 A1
Fishers Field MK18 . . . . . . .52 B4
Fishery Rd SL6 . . . . .203 B3
Fishguard Spur SL1 . . . . . .206 A2
Fishweir LU7 . . . . .68 B1
Fitzgeralds Way HP12 . . . . .172 A4
Fitzhamon Ct SL1 . . . . .33 A3
Five Acre Wood HP12 . . . . .172 B3
Five Acres Chesham HP5 . .154 B3
Wooburn Green HP10 . . . . .185 C4
Five Points SL0 . . . . .200 B2
Flaggs Mdw MK46 . . . . .6 C2
Flambard Cl MK15 . . . . . . .35 A4
Flamborough Spur SL1 . . . .206 A2
Flamingo Zoo Pk★ MK46 . .6 A2
Flaunden Bottom HP5,
HP3 . . . . .155 C2
Flaunden Hill HP3 . . . . . . .156 A3
Flaunden La HP3 . . . . .146 B2
Flavius Gate NN13 . . . . . . .38 C2
Flaxbourne Ct MK7 . . . . . . .48 B4
Flaxen Field HP22 . . . . . . .116 C1
Flaxley Gate MK10 . . . . . . .36 A1
Fledgeling Wlk MK10 . . . . .35 C2
Fleet Cl Buckingham MK18 . .41 C1
Walter's Ash HP14 . . . . . . .161 C4
Fleet St HP20 . . . . .101 B1
Fleet The MK6 . . . . .35 A1
Fleetbrook Ho SL3 . . . . . . .211 B3
Fleetwood Cl HP8 . . . . . . .177 A1
Fleetwood Ct 7 TW19 . . . .213 C1
Fleetwood Rd SL2 . . . . . . .205 C3
Fleetwood Way 7 OX9 . . . .125 C1
Fleming Dr MK7 . . . . .47 A3
Fleming Way HP12 . . . . . . .172 B3
Fletcher Cl HP19 . . . . .100 C2
Fletchers Mews MK14 . . . .34 C4
Flint Hollow OX39 . . . . . . .147 A3
Flint St HP17 . . . . .127 A3
Flint Way HP16 . . . . .151 B4
Flintergill Ct MK13 . . . . . . .34 A2
Flintlock Ct TW19 . . . . . . .213 A2
Flitcroft Lea HP18 . . . . . . .173 A4
Flitton Ct MK11 . . . . .32 C3
Flora Thompson Dr
MK16 . . . . .21 A2
Florence Ave SL6 . . . . .203 A4
Florence Ct HP19 . . . . .101 B1
Florence Way UB8 . . . . . . .201 B3
Florida St HP11 . . . . .173 B2
Florin Cl MK15 . . . . .35 A4
Flowers Bottom La
HP27 . . . . .150 A2
Fog Cotts HP23 . . . . .120 A3
Folding Ct LU7 . . . . .78 C4
Foley Cl HP9 . . . . .175 B2
Foliejohn Way SL6 . . . . . . .202 A1
Folkestone Ct SL3 . . . . . . .207 A1
Follet Ct SL4 . . . . .211 A1
Folly La Hartwell NN7 . . . . .10 B4
North Crawley MK16 . . . . . .24 A3
Folly Rd MK19 . . . . .31 B2
Fontwell Cl SL6 . . . . .202 A4
Fontwell Dr MK3 . . . . .57 B3
Forches Cl MK4 . . . . .46 B1
Ford End UB9 . . . . .189 C1
Ford La SL0 . . . . .208 A4
Ford St Buckingham MK18 . .52 B4
High Wycombe HP11 . . . . .173 C2
Ford Way HP13 . . . . .161 C2
Ford's Cl HP14 . . . . .159 C4
Fordcombe Lea MK4 . . . . . .48 A4
Forelands Way HP5 . . . . . .154 B4
Forest Cl
Princes Risborough HP27 . .139 A2
Wendover HP22 . . . . .131 A2
Forest Point HP13 . . . . . . .173 C3
Forest Rd Hanslope MK19 . .10 C3
Piddington (Northants) NN7 . .4 A4
Windsor SL4 . . . . .209 C3
Forest Rise MK6 . . . . .47 A4
Forest Way HP13 . . . . .174 A4
Foresters
Beacon's Bottom HP14 . . . .159 B3
Chinnor OX39 . . . . .147 A3
Oakley HP18 . . . . .109 B3
Forfar Dr MK3 . . . . .46 C1
Forge Cl Ashendon HP18 . . .97 C1
Holmer Green HP15 . . . . . .163 B3
Horton-cum-S OX33 . . . . . .108 A3
Marsh Gibbon OX27 . . . . . .71 C2
Oakley HP18 . . . . .109 B2
Steeple Claydon MK18 . . . .63 C1
Forge Dr SL2 . . . . .198 B3
Forge End HP7 . . . . .165 A4
Forge Rd HP14 . . . . .161 B4
Forge The MK46 . . . . .13 C4
Forgetts Rd HP14 . . . . .171 B2
Forlease Cl SL6 . . . . .203 A3
Forlease Dr SL6 . . . . .203 A3
Forlease Rd SL6 . . . . .203 A3
Formby Cl
Milton Keynes MK3 . . . . . . .57 B4
Slough SL3 . . . . .207 B1
Forrabury Ave MK13 . . . . . .34 B2
Fort End HP17 . . . . .127 A3
Fortescue Dr MK5 . . . . .46 A3
Fortuna Ct MK7 . . . . .48 B3
Forty Gn HP27 . . . . .137 C2
Forty Green Dr SL7 . . . . . .183 A1
Forty Green Rd HP9 . . . . . .175 B2

Foscote Rd MK18 . . . . .41 C2
Foscott Way MK18 . . . . . . .41 C2
Fossey Cl MK5 . . . . .45 C2
Foster Ave SL4 . . . . .209 C2
Foster Cl HP20 . . . . .101 C2
Fosters La MK13 . . . . .34 A3
Lacey Green HP27 . . . . . . .149 B3
Fosters Path SL2 . . . . .197 C1
Fotherby Ct SL6 . . . . .203 A3
Fotheringay Gdns SL1 . . . .205 A3
Fotherley Rd WD3 . . . . . . .178 A4
Founders Dr UB9 . . . . .189 C3
Founders Mews MK4 . . . . . .34 C3
Foundry La Horton SL3 . . . .212 A2
Fountain Gdns SL4 . . . . . . .210 B2
Fountaine Cl MK14 . . . . . . .34 C4
Four Ashes Rd HP15 . . . . . .162 B3
Fourdrinier Ct HP11 . . . . . .174 A2
Fourth Ave SL7 . . . . .184 A1
Fourth St HP11 . . . . .173 B2
Fowler Ave MK14 . . . . .34 B4
Fowler Rd HP19 . . . . .115 A4
Fowlers Farm Rd HP14 . . . .158 C2
Fox Cover OX39 . . . . .147 B3
Fox Field HP15 . . . . .162 C3
Fox La HP15 . . . . .163 A3
Fox Milne Rdbt MK10 . . . . .35 C2
Fox Way
Holmer Green HP15 . . . . . .163 A3
Slough SL3 . . . . .206 B1
Wigginton HP23 . . . . .119 C2
Fox Way MK18 . . . . .52 C4
Foxborough Cl SL3 . . . . . . .207 A1
Foxborough Ct SL6 . . . . . . .202 C2
Foxborough Prim Sch
SL3 . . . . .207 A3
Foxcovert Rd MK5 . . . . .45 C2
Foxdell Way SL9 . . . . .177 C3
Foxes Piece SL7 . . . . .183 C2
Foxes Piece Sch SL7 . . . . .183 C2
Foxgate MK16 . . . . .22 A2
Foxglove HP21 . . . . .115 A3
Foxglove Cl MK18 . . . . . . .52 B4
Foxglove Ct MK16 . . . . .21 C2
Foxherne SL3 . . . . .206 B2
Foxhill MK46 . . . . .6 C3
Foxhill Cl HP13 . . . . .162 A1
Foxhollow Dr SL2 . . . . .198 B4
Foxhunter Dr MK14 . . . . . . .34 C3
Foxleigh HP11 . . . . .173 A2
Foxmoor Ct UB9 . . . . .190 A3
Foxton MK6 . . . . .47 B3
Fraderica Cotts MK16 . . . . .22 B2
Framers Ct HP14 . . . . .171 A2
Framewood Manor SL2 . . . .199 B3
Framewood Rd SL2,SL3 . . .199 B3
Framlingham Ct MK5 . . . . .46 A4
Frampton Ct UB9 . . . . .189 C3
France Furlong MK14 . . . . .34 C4
Frances Ave SL6 . . . . .196 B1
Frances Rd SL4 . . . . .210 B3
Frances St HP5 . . . . .144 B1
Franchise St 3 HP5 . . . . . .144 B1
Francis Ct MK5 . . . . .46 A3
Francis Edmonds
Comb Sch HP14 . . . . .171 A2
Francis Way SL1 . . . . .204 B3
Frank Atter Croft MK12 . . . .33 B3
Frank Howe Ct MK6 . . . . . .35 A1
Frank Lunnon Cl SL8 . . . . .185 B2
Frank Sutton Way SL1 . . . .205 B3
Franklin Ave SL2 . . . . .205 A4
Franklin Cl Dunstable LU6 . .93 C4
High Wycombe HP13 . . . . .162 C3
Haddenham HP17 . . . . . . .127 A4
Franklins Croft MK12 . . . . .33 B3
Franklyn Cres SL4 . . . . . . .209 B2
Frankston Ave MK11 . . . . . .32 C3
Frankswood Ave UB7 . . . . .208 C4
Frascati Way SL6 . . . . .202 C4
Fraser Rd HP22 . . . . .172 B3
Fraucup Cl HP17 . . . . .128 C4
Fraunchies Ct SL1 . . . . . . .205 C3
Fray's Ct UB8 . . . . .201 B3
Fray's Waye UB8 . . . . .201 B2
Frays Ave UB7 . . . . .208 B2
Frays Cl UB7 . . . . .208 B2
Frayslea UB8 . . . . .201 B2
Frederick Pl HP11 . . . . . . .174 A2
Frederick St HP18 . . . . .99 A4
Fredericks Ct HP9 . . . . . . .186 A4
Freeman Cl MK12 . . . . .33 A3
Freeman Ct HP5 . . . . .144 B1
Freemans Cl SL2 . . . . .199 A3
Freemans Gdns MK46 . . . . . .7 A2
Fremantle Rd
Aylesbury HP21 . . . . .115 C3
High Wycombe HP13 . . . . .162 C3
Frenchum Gdns SL1 . . . . . .204 C3
Frensham Dr MK2 . . . . .58 B4
Frensham Wlk SL2 . . . . . . .198 B3
Friarage Rd HP20 . . . . .115 B4
Friars Field HP4 . . . . .134 C4
Friars Furlong HP18 . . . . . .125 A4
Friars Gdns HP14 . . . . .162 A4
Friars Sq 17 HP20 . . . . . . .115 B4
Friars Wlk
Prestwood HP16 . . . . .151 B3
Tring HP23 . . . . .119 A3
Friarscroft Way HP20 . . . . .115 B4
Friary Gdns HP14 . . . . .162 A4
Friary Rd TW19 . . . . .211 B4
Friary The SL4 . . . . .211 B1
Friday Ct OX9 . . . . .125 C1

Fai – Gai 225

Friday St
Henley-on-T RG9 . . . . .191 C1
Leighton Buzzard LU7 . . . . .80 C4
Frieth CE Comb Sch
HP14 . . . . .170 C1
Frieth Rd Marlow SL7 . . . . .182 C3
Marlow Bottom SL7 . . . . . .182 C3
Frithe The SL2 . . . . .206 A4
Frith Hill HP16 . . . . .152 A4
Frithsden Copse HP4 . . . . .135 C4
Frithwood Cres MK7 . . . . . .48 A4
Frog La HP18 . . . . .112 C2
Froggy La UB9 . . . . .189 B1
Frogmill SL7 . . . . .193 B2
Frogmill Ct SL7 . . . . .193 B2
Frogmoor HP13 . . . . .173 A4
Frogmore Cl
Hughenden Valley HP14 . . .162 A4
Slough SL1 . . . . .205 A2
Frogmore Flats SL4 . . . . . .210 C3
Frogmore St HP23 . . . . . . .119 A2
Frome Cl HP21 . . . . .115 C3
Fromer Rd HP10 . . . . .185 B2
Frost Ho 19 HP4 . . . . .135 B2
Froxfield Ct MK4 . . . . .46 B1
Fryday St MK6 . . . . .46 C4
Fryer Cl HP5 . . . . .154 B3
Fryers Ct HP12 . . . . .172 B4
Fryers La HP12 . . . . .172 B4
Frymley Hill HP12 . . . . .172 B4
Fulbrook Mid Sch MK17 . . .49 A3
Fullbrook Cl SL6 . . . . .203 A4
Fuller's Cl HP5 . . . . .154 A3
Fullers Hill Chesham HP5 . .154 A3
Chesham HP5,HP6 . . . . . .154 A3
Fullers Yd SL6 . . . . .196 A1
Fulmar Pl 9 HP21 . . . . . . .101 C2
Fulmer Chase SL3 . . . . . . .199 B4
Fulmer Common Rd
SL3 . . . . .199 C3
Fulmer Dr SL9 . . . . .188 B1
Fulmer Inf Sch SL3 . . . . . .199 C4
Fulmer Rd SL9 . . . . .188 C1
Fulmer St MK4,MK5,MK8 . .45 C3
Fulmer Way SL9 . . . . .188 C3
Fulwell Cl MK14 . . . . .34 C4
Fulwell Rd Finmere MK18 . .50 B4
Westbury NN13 . . . . .39 A2
Fulwood Ct TW19 . . . . .213 C1
Fulwoods Dr MK6 . . . . .47 A4
Furlong Cl SL8 . . . . .185 A2
Furlong Cres HP17 . . . . . . .115 A1
Furlong La LU6 . . . . .93 B4
Furlong Rd SL8 . . . . .185 A2
Furlong The 15 HP23 . . . . .119 A2
Furness SL4 . . . . .209 B3
Furness Pl 8 SL4 . . . . .209 B3
Furness Row 9 SL4 . . . . . .209 B3
Furness Sq 6 SL4 . . . . . . .209 B3
Furness Way SL4 . . . . .209 B3
Furness Wlk 7 SL4 . . . . . . .209 B3
Furnival Ave SL2 . . . . .205 A4
Furrow Cl HP21 . . . . .115 B2
Furrow Way SL6 . . . . .202 A2
Furrows The UB9 . . . . .190 B3
Furtho Ct MK19 . . . . .32 A4
Furtho La NN12 . . . . .18 C2
Fury Ct MK8 . . . . .45 C4
Furze Down Sch MK18 . . . .65 C2
Furze La MK18 . . . . .65 C3
Furze Platt Halt SL6 . . . . . .195 C1
Furze Platt Inf Sch SL6 . . . .195 B1
Furze Platt Jun Sch
SL6 . . . . .195 B1
Furze Platt Rd SL6 . . . . . . .195 A1
Furze Platt Senior Sch
SL6 . . . . .195 B1
Furze Rd SL6 . . . . .195 B1
Furze View WD3 . . . . .167 B2
Furze Way MK2 . . . . .33 B3
Furzefield Rd HP9 . . . . . . .175 B1
Furzeham Rd UB7 . . . . . . .208 C2
Furzen Cl SL2 . . . . .198 A1
Furzton Rdbt MK4 . . . . .46 B2
Fyfield Barrow MK7 . . . . . .48 B3
Fyne Dr LU7 . . . . .80 B4

G

Gable Thorne MK7 . . . . . . .48 B3
Gables Cl
Chalfont St Peter SL9 . . . . .177 C3
Datchet SL3 . . . . .211 A4
Maidenhead SL6 . . . . .203 A4
Wendover HP22 . . . . .131 A2
Gables Dr HP14 . . . . .149 B1
Gables Mdw HP15 . . . . . . .163 B3
Gables The
Haddenham HP17 . . . . . . .127 A3
Leighton Buzzard LU7 . . . . .80 C3
Gabriel Cl MK7 . . . . .48 B3
Gaddesden Cres MK7 . . . . .48 B3
Gadge Cl OX9 . . . . .125 C1
Gadsden Cl MK43 . . . . .25 B2
Gadsden Ct MK17 . . . . .69 C4
Gage Cl SL6 . . . . .202 C2
Gainsborough SL6 . . . . . . .195 C3
Gainsborough Dr SL6 . . . . .202 B2
Gainsborough Hill RG9 . . . .191 B3
Gainsborough Pl HP10 . . . .100 C3
Gainsborough Rd
Aylesbury HP21 . . . . .115 C2
Henley-on-T RG9 . . . . .191 B1

Gairloch Ave MK2 ....58 A4
Galahad Cl SL1 ....205 A2
Gallagher Cl MK8 ....45 C4
Galley Hill MK11 ....32 C3
Galley La
  Great Brickhill MK17 ....59 A4
  Little Brickhill MK17 ....59 A2
Galleymead Rd SL3 ....212 C4
Galloway HP19 ....101 A2
Galloway Chase SL2 ....206 A3
Galloway Cl MK3 ....46 C1
Gallows La HP12 ....172 B4
Gallys Rd SL4 ....209 B3
Galsworthy Pl HP19 ....100 C1
Galvin Rd SL1 ....205 B3
Gamnel Terr HP23 ....119 A3
Gandon Vale HP13 ....173 A4
Ganton Cl MK3 ....46 B1
Garamonde Dr MK8 ....33 C1
Garbo Cl MK8 ....45 B4
Garden Cl Halton HP22 ....131 B4
  Maidenhead SL6 ....202 A3
Garden Cotts SL3 ....212 B4
Garden Ct HP11 ....174 A2
Garden Field La HP4 ....135 C1
Garden Mews SL1 ....205 C3
Garden Reach HP8 ....166 B3
Gardener Wlk HP15 ....163 B3
Gardens Cl HP14 ....158 C2
Gardens The MK18 ....53 C1
Gardiner Ct MK13 ....33 C3
Gardner Cl
  Aylesbury HP19 ....101 A2
  Great Kingshill HP15 ....151 B1
Gardner Ho SL6 ....195 C1
Gardner Rd SL6 ....195 C1
Gardner's Cl LU6 ....93 C4
Garfield Pl 28 SL4 ....210 B3
Garland Ct MK8 ....45 C4
Garland Way HP22 ....117 C3
Garners Cl SL9 ....177 C2
Garners End SL9 ....177 C2
Garners Rd SL9 ....177 C2
Garnet Cl SL1 ....205 A2
Garnet Ct SL7 ....183 B1
Garrard Rd SL2 ....197 C1
Garratts Way HP13 ....173 A4
Garraways MK6 ....47 A3
Garrett Cl HP5 ....154 B3
Garrick Wlk MK9 ....34 C2
Garron Cl HP21 ....115 B2
Garrowmore Gr MK2 ....58 B3
Garry Cl MK2 ....58 B3
Garson Gr HP5 ....144 A1
Garston MK8 ....33 C1
Garth The HP16 ....152 A4
Garthwaite Cres MK5 ....46 A2
Garvin Ave HP9 ....175 C1
Gas La SL6 ....203 A2
Gascon's Gr SL2 ....198 A1
Gaskin Ct MK14 ....35 A3
Gatcombe MK8 ....33 C1
Gate Cotts WD3 ....167 B3
Gatehouse Cl
  Aylesbury HP19 ....101 A2
  Windsor SL4 ....210 A2
Gatehouse Rd HP19 ....101 B1
Gatehouse Sch
  (Boarding) MK14 ....34 B4
Gatehouse Way HP19 ....101 A1
Gatensbury Pl HP27 ....139 A2
Gatesdene Cl HP4 ....121 B4
Gateway Sch HP16 ....152 A4
Gatewick Cl SL1 ....205 C3
Gatewick La MK7 ....48 A2
Gatting Way UB8 ....201 C3
Gatward Ave SL6 ....202 A2
Gaveston Dr HP4 ....135 A3
Gaveston Rd SL2 ....197 C1
Gaviots Cl SL9 ....188 C2
Gaviots Gn SL9 ....188 C2
Gaviots Way SL9 ....188 C2
Gawcott Fields MK18 ....52 A4
Gawcott Inf Sch MK18 ....51 C2
Gawcott Rd MK18 ....52 A4
Gawdrey Cl HP5 ....154 B3
Gayhurst Rd HP13 ....173 C4
Gayton Cl HP6 ....154 C2
Gees Farm Cl NN7 ....1 A3
Gell Cl UB10 ....190 C1
George Cl SL7 ....183 C2
George Ct HP18 ....83 A3
George Green Rd SL3 ....206 C4
George Inn Pl MK16 ....12 A3
George Lee Ct HP14 ....160 B1
George Rd HP14 ....158 C3
George St
  14 Aylesbury HP20 ....115 B4
  Berkhamsted HP4 ....135 B2
  5 Chesham HP5 ....144 B1
  High Wycombe HP11 ....172 C4
  Milton Keynes MK2 ....47 C1
  Uxbridge UB8 ....201 B3
  Wing LU7 ....79 C1
  Woburn MK17 ....60 C4
George V Pl SL4 ....210 B4
George Yd MK11 ....32 B3
George's Hill HP15 ....162 C3
Georges Dr HP10 ....185 B4
Georgian Cl UB10 ....201 C4
Geralds Ct HP13 ....162 B1
Geralds Rd HP13 ....162 B1
Gerard Cl MK13 ....34 A4
Germain St HP5 ....154 A4

Germains Cl HP5 ....154 A4
Germander Park Fst Sch
  MK14 ....34 B2
Germander Pl MK14 ....34 B2
Gerrards Cross CE
  Comb Sch The SL9 ....188 C2
Gerrards Cross Rd SL2 ....199 A4
Gerrards Cross Sta SL9 ....188 C3
Gershwin Ct MK7 ....48 B2
Gervaise Cl SL1 ....204 C3
Gib La HP22 ....102 B2
Gibbings Cl MK18 ....76 A2
Gibbs Cl HP13 ....172 C4
Gibbs Ho HP11 ....173 C2
Gibbwin MK14 ....34 C4
Gibraltar La SL7 ....184 B1
Gibson Cl SL3 ....206 C1
Gibson La HP17 ....127 A3
Gibson Pl TW19 ....213 B1
Gibson Rd
  High Wycombe HP12 ....172 A2
  Ickenham UB10 ....201 C4
Gibsons Gn MK13 ....34 B2
Giffard Park Comb Sch
  MK14 ....22 A1
Giffard Park Rdbt MK14 ....21 C2
Giffard Rd MK2 ....58 B3
Giffard Way HP18 ....125 B4
Gifford Gate MK14 ....34 C4
Gifford Pl MK18 ....41 C1
Gilbert Cl MK3 ....58 A4
Gilbert Ho 7 HP11 ....172 C4
Gilbert Scott Rd MK18 ....41 B1
Gilbert Way HP4 ....135 A2
Gilbert's Hill HP23 ....132 C2
Gilbey Wlk HP10 ....185 B2
Gilders Mews MK14 ....34 C3
Giles Gate HP16 ....151 A3
Gillamoor Cl 2 MK4 ....46 A2
Gilletts La HP12 ....161 B1
Gillfield Cl HP11 ....172 C2
Gilliat Rd SL1 ....205 C3
Gilliat's Gn WD3 ....167 B3
Gilliatt Cl SL0 ....207 C4
Gilman Cres SL4 ....209 B2
Gilmore Ct HP13 ....173 A4
Gilmore Rd HP20 ....101 C2
Gilpin Way MK46 ....7 A2
Gilpin's Ride HP4 ....135 B3
Gingers Cl HP22 ....117 C3
Gipsy La LU7 ....91 B4
Gisburn Ct MK13 ....34 A3
Glade Ho 3 SL7 ....183 C1
Glade Rd SL7 ....183 C1
Glade The
  Gerrards Cross SL9 ....188 B1
  Tylers Green HP10 ....163 B1
Glade View HP12 ....172 A2
Gladstone Cl MK16 ....22 B2
Gladstone Ind Est SL6 ....202 C4
Gladstone Rd HP5 ....144 B1
Gladstone Rise HP13 ....173 C3
Gladstone Way SL1 ....205 A3
Glaisyer Way SL0 ....200 B2
Glamis Ct HP13 ....173 A4
Glamis Ho MK5 ....57 C4
Glamorgan Cl MK3 ....46 C1
Glanmor Rd SL2 ....206 A3
Glasgow Rd SL1 ....205 A4
Glassmill Ho 4 HP4 ....135 B2
Glastonbury Cl MK3 ....47 A1
Glastonbury Thorn
  Fst Sch MK5 ....46 A3
Glaven Rd HP21 ....115 B2
Glazier Dr MK14 ....34 C3
Glebe Cl Dorney SL6 ....203 C2
  Gerrards Cross SL9 ....177 B2
  Holmer Green HP15 ....163 A4
  Maids Moreton MK18 ....41 C2
  Milton Keynes MK5 ....46 A4
  Pitstone LU7 ....105 B3
Glebe Cotts HP14 ....169 B4
Glebe Dr NN13 ....38 A4
Glebe Ho SL9 ....177 B2
Glebe House Dr MK13 ....39 C3
Glebe La MK19 ....10 C3
Glebe Rd
  Deanshanger MK19 ....31 C3
  Gerrards Cross SL9 ....177 B1
  Maidenhead SL6 ....203 A3
  Old Windsor SL4 ....211 A1
  Uxbridge UB8 ....201 B2
Glebe Rdbt MK9 ....35 A2
Glebe Terr MK18 ....41 C2
Glebe The Lavendon MK46 ....7 C4
  Lewknor OX49 ....157 A4
  Prestwood HP16 ....151 B4
  Stone HP17 ....114 B3
  Walter's Ash HP14 ....161 B3
  West Drayton UB7 ....208 C1
  Weston Turville HP22 ....116 C1
Glebe Way HP6 ....154 B2
Glebelands HP10 ....174 B4
Glebelands Cl HP16 ....151 C2
Gledfield Pl MK12 ....33 B2
Gleeman Cl MK12 ....33 A3
Glen The SL3 ....206 B1
Glenavon Gdns SL3 ....206 B2
Gleneagles Cl
  Milton Keynes MK3 ....57 B4
  Stanwell TW19 ....213 B1
Glenfield Ct HP21 ....116 A3
Glenham Rd OX9 ....126 A3
Glenhaven Dr TW19 ....213 A1
Glenister Rd
  Chesham HP5 ....144 B2
  High Wycombe HP12 ....172 A2
Glenisters Rd HP13 ....173 A4

Glenmore Cl HP10 ....174 A1
Glenmore Ho HP11 ....174 A2
Glentworth Pl SL1 ....205 B3
Glenwater Ho HP15 ....163 A3
Glenwoods MK6 ....22 B2
Glimbers Gr OX39 ....147 B3
Globe La LU7 ....70 C1
Globeside Bsns Pk SL7 ....183 C1
Glory Cl HP10 ....185 C4
Glory Hill La HP9 ....185 C4
Glory Mill La HP10 ....185 C4
Gloucester Ave SL1 ....205 B4
Gloucester Ct UB9 ....190 A2
Gloucester Pl SL4 ....210 B3
Gloucester Rd
  Maidenhead SL6 ....195 C1
  Milton Keynes MK12 ....33 B3
Glovers Ct 17 HP20 ....101 C1
Glovers La MK13 ....34 A2
Glyn Sq MK12 ....33 B3
Glyn St MK13 ....34 A4
Glynswood
  Chalfont St Peter SL9 ....177 C2
  Chinnor OX39 ....147 B3
  High Wycombe HP13 ....162 A1
Glynswood Rd MK18 ....41 B1
Glynwood Ho SL6 ....203 A4
Goathland Croft 2 MK4 ....46 A1
Goddards Croft MK12 ....33 B3
Goddington Rd SL8 ....185 A3
Godfreys Cl HP18 ....96 A1
Godolphin Inf Sch SL1 ....205 B4
Godolphin Jun Sch SL1 ....205 B4
Godolphin Rd
  Seer Green HP9 ....176 B2
  Slough SL1 ....205 B3
Godrevy Gr MK4 ....57 A4
Godstowe Prep Sch
  HP13 ....173 A4
Godwin Cl MK7 ....48 B4
Gogh Rd HP19 ....100 C1
Gold Crest 8 HP20 ....101 C2
Gold Hill E SL9 ....177 B1
Gold Hill N SL9 ....177 B1
Gold Hill W SL9 ....177 B1
Gold Oak Wlk MK9 ....34 C2
Gold St MK19 ....11 A1
Golden Ball La SL6 ....195 A2
Golden Dr MK6 ....47 A4
Golden Hills OX39 ....147 B3
Golden Miller Ct LU7 ....79 C1
Golden Oak SL2 ....198 B3
Golden Riddy LU7 ....80 C1
Golder's Ct HP18 ....123 C2
Goldfield Inf Sch HP23 ....118 C2
Goldfield Rd HP23 ....118 C2
Goldilocks MK7 ....48 A3
Goldlake Ct UB9 ....189 C2
Goldmark Cl MK7 ....48 B3
Goldsmith Dr MK16 ....21 C2
Goldsworthy Way SL1 ....204 B4
Golspie Croft MK12 ....33 B2
Gomm Pl HP13 ....174 A2
Gomm Rd HP13 ....174 A2
Gomm's Wood HP9 ....175 C4
Gomms Wood Cl HP9 ....175 A2
Good Intent LU6 ....92 C2
Goodacres La HP27 ....149 C3
Goodman Gdns MK6 ....47 B4
Goodman Pk SL2 ....206 B3
Goodwick Gr MK4 ....57 A4
Goodwin Mdws HP10 ....185 C3
Goodwin Rd
  Aylesbury HP19 ....115 A2
  Slough SL2 ....197 C1
Goodwin Villas SL1 ....204 C3
Goodwins Mead LU7 ....105 A4
Goodwood MK8 ....45 C4
Goodwood Rise SL7 ....183 B4
Goose Acre Botley HP5 ....145 A1
  Cheddington LU7 ....105 A4
Goose Gn SL2 ....198 A2
Goosemere MK19 ....31 C2
Goosen Gn HP21 ....116 B3
Goran Ave MK11 ....32 C2
Gorman Pl MK2 ....58 C2
Gorrell Cl MK18 ....51 B2
Gorricks MK11 ....32 B2
Gorse Meade SL1 ....205 A3
Gorse Rd SL8 ....195 C4
Gorse Wlk
  Hazlemere HP15 ....163 A2
  West Drayton UB7 ....208 C4
Goslar Way SL4 ....210 A3
Gosling Gn SL3 ....206 C2
Gosling Gr HP13 ....161 B1
Gosling Rd SL3 ....206 C2
Goslington MK1 ....47 B1
Goss Ave HP18 ....99 A3
Gossage Rd UB10 ....201 C3
Gossmore Cl SL7 ....183 C1
Gossmore La SL7 ....183 C1
Gossmore Wlk SL7 ....183 C1

Gossom's End HP4 ....135 A3
Gossoms Ryde HP4 ....135 A3
Goswell Hill SL4 ....210 B3
Goswell Rd SL4 ....210 B3
Governors Ave UB9 ....189 C3
Governors Cl HP6 ....154 C1
Gower Ho HP6 ....154 C2
Gowers Field HP20 ....101 B1
Gowers The HP6 ....154 C1
Gowers Yd MK19 ....32 A4
Goya Pl HP20 ....100 C1
Grace Ave MK6 ....46 C4
Grace Ct SL1 ....205 B3
Graces Cl MK43 ....25 B2
Graces Maltings 7
  HP23 ....119 A2
Graeme Ave HP16 ....151 B3
Graemesdyke Rd HP4 ....135 A2
Grafham HP14 ....35 A3
Grafton Cl
  Maidenhead SL6 ....195 C1
  Potterspury NN12 ....18 C2
  Slough SL3 ....206 C4
Grafton Ct NN7 ....4 A4
Grafton Gate MK9 ....34 B1
Grafton Ho OX39 ....147 B4
Grafton Orch OX39 ....147 B4
Grafton Pk MK9 ....34 B1
Grafton St
  High Wycombe HP12 ....172 B4
  Milton Keynes, Bradwell
  MK13 ....34 A2
  Milton Keynes, Winterhill
  MK6 ....46 C4
Graham Cl SL6 ....202 B3
Graham Dr HP12 ....172 A3
Graham Ho SL8 ....195 C4
Grainge Chase MK17 ....55 A2
Grampian Gate MK6 ....46 C4
Grampian Way SL3 ....207 B4
Gramwell MK5 ....45 C4
Granborough Rd
  North Marston MK18 ....76 A1
  Winslow MK18 ....65 C1
Granby Cl MK1 ....47 A2
Granby Ind Est MK1 ....47 A2
Granby Rdbt MK1 ....47 A2
Grand Union Office Pk
  The UB8 ....208 B4
Grandison Ho RG9 ....191 C2
Granes End MK14 ....34 C4
Grange Cl
  Gerrards Cross SL9 ....177 C1
  Leighton Buzzard LU7 ....80 B3
  Maids Moreton MK18 ....41 C2
  Twyford MK18 ....62 B1
  Wraysbury TW19 ....211 C1
Grange Cotts HP16 ....152 A2
Grange Dr HP10 ....185 B2
Grange Farm Rd HP14 ....159 A4
Grange Farm Rdbt MK8 ....45 B4
Grange Fields SL9 ....177 C1
Grange Gdns
  Farnham Common SL2 ....198 B4
  Wendover HP22 ....131 A3
Grange La SL8 ....195 C4
Grange Rd Cookham SL8 ....195 C4
  Gerrards Cross SL9 ....177 C1
  Hazlemere HP15 ....162 C2
  Hazlemere, Widmer End
  HP15 ....162 C1
  Henley-on-T RG9 ....191 C1
  Milton Keynes MK3 ....57 C4
  Pitstone LU7 ....105 B3
  Tring HP23 ....119 B2
  Wilstone HP23 ....104 B1
Grange Sch The HP21 ....115 C3
Grange The Burnham SL1 ....197 B1
  Old Windsor SL4 ....211 A1
Grange Way SL0 ....207 C4
Grangelands Nature
  Reserve* HP27 ....139 C3
Grangers Croft MK12 ....33 B2
Grangewood SL3 ....206 B4
Grant Ave SL1 ....205 C4
Grant Ho 6 SL8 ....185 A2
Grantham Ct MK5 ....46 B3
Grantham Mews HP4 ....135 B2
Granville Ave SL2 ....205 B4
Granville Dene HP3 ....146 A3
Granville Pl 4 HP20 ....115 B4
Granville Rd HP4 ....134 C3
Granville Sq MK15 ....35 A4
Granville St 3 HP20 ....115 B4
Grapevine Cl HP11 ....173 C2
Grasholm Way SL3 ....207 B1
Grasmere
  Aylesbury HP21 ....116 A3
  Windsor SL4 ....209 C4
Grasmere Ave SL2 ....206 A3
Grasmere Par SL2 ....206 A3
Grasmere Way
  Leighton Buzzard LU7 ....80 B4
  Milton Keynes MK2 ....58 B3
Grass Hays HP21 ....116 A3
Grasscroft MK4 ....46 C2
Grassingham End
  SL9 ....177 C2
Grassingham Rd SL9 ....177 C2
Grassington MK13 ....34 A3
Grasslands HP20 ....102 A1
Grassy La SL6 ....202 A3
Grattan Ct SL7 ....184 A2
Gratton Dr SL4 ....209 C2

Gravel Hill
  Chalfont St Peter SL9 ....177 C2
  Henley-on-T RG9 ....191 B1
  Uxbridge UB8 ....201 B4
Gravel Path HP4 ....135 C3
Gravel Wlk MK46 ....13 C4
Graveney Pl MK6 ....35 A1
Gray's La HP14 ....169 B4
Gray's Mon* SL2 ....198 C1
Gray's Pl SL2 ....205 C3
Gray's Rd Slough SL1 ....205 C3
  Uxbridge UB10 ....201 C3
Grayburn Cl HP8 ....177 A4
Grayling Cl SL7 ....194 B4
Grayling Ct HP4 ....134 C3
Grays Cl NN12 ....17 B4
Grays La
  High Wycombe HP13 ....161 B1
  Paulerspury NN12 ....17 B4
  Yardley Gobion NN12 ....18 C3
Grays Park Rd SL2 ....199 A1
Grays Wlk HP5 ....144 A1
Great Benty UB7 ....208 A1
Great Brickhill La MK17 ....59 B3
Great Denson MK6 ....47 A4
Great Ground MK14 ....34 C4
Great Hill Cres SL6 ....202 B3
Great Hivings HP5 ....144 A2
Great Horwood
  CE Comb Sch MK17 ....55 A2
Great Horwood Rd MK17,
  MK18 ....65 C4
Great Kimble CE Sch
  HP17 ....129 C1
Great Kingshill
  CE Comb Sch HP15 ....162 B3
Great La HP22 ....102 A2
Great Linch MK10 ....36 A1
Great Linford Comb Sch
  MK14 ....34 C4
Great Linford Lakes
  Wildfowl Ctr* MK14 ....21 B1
Great Marlow Sch SL7 ....183 C2
Great Meadow Way
  HP19 ....115 A4
Great Missenden
  CE Comb Sch HP16 ....152 A4
Great Missenden Sta
  HP16 ....152 A4
Great Monks St
  Milton Keynes, Wolverton
  MK12 ....33 B3
  Milton Keynes, Wymbush
  MK8 ....33 C1
Great Slade MK18 ....52 B3
Great Stone HP18 ....112 C2
Great Western St 18
  HP20 ....115 B4
Greatchesters MK13 ....33 C3
Greatheed Dell MK7 ....48 B2
Greaves Rd HP13 ....173 B3
Grebe Cl HP20 ....101 C2
Grecian St HP20 ....116 A4
Green Acre HP21 ....116 A4
Green Acres Cl HP22 ....86 C4
Green Cl Burnham SL1 ....204 A4
  High Wycombe HP13 ....173 C4
  Maidenhead SL6 ....195 C1
Green Common La HP9,
  HP10 ....186 B2
Green Cres HP10 ....185 B4
Green Dragon La HP10 ....185 A4
Green East Rd HP9 ....176 C2
Green End
  Aylesbury HP20 ....115 B4
  Granborough MK18 ....76 A4
  Great Brickhill MK17 ....59 B1
Green End La MK19 ....11 A2
Green End Rd HP14 ....159 C3
Green End St HP22 ....117 C3
Green Farm Rd MK16 ....22 B2
Green Hill HP13 ....162 A1
Green Hill Cl HP13 ....162 B1
Green Hill Gate HP13 ....162 A1
Green La
  Amersham HP6 ....154 C1
  Aspley Guise MK17 ....49 C2
  Bledlow Ridge HP14 ....159 B3
  Bovingdon HP3 ....146 A2
  Burnham SL1 ....197 B2
  Datchet SL3 ....211 A3
  Eaton Bray LU6 ....92 B4
  Farnham Common SL2 ....198 A3
  Ivinghoe LU7 ....105 C3
  Latimer HP5 ....155 C3
  Longwick HP27 ....128 A1
  Maidenhead SL6 ....203 A3
  Milton Keynes MK12 ....33 B3
  Prestwood HP16 ....151 C3
  Stokenchurch HP14 ....158 B3
  Upper Arncott OX25 ....94 C4
  Windsor SL4 ....210 A3
Green Lane Cl HP6 ....154 B2
Green Lane Ct SL1 ....197 B1
Green Lane Rdbt MK9 ....35 C2
Green Leys
  High Wycombe HP13 ....161 B1
  Maidenhead SL6 ....195 C1
Green North Rd HP9 ....176 C2
Green Park Comb Sch
  MK16 ....22 A2
Green Park Dr MK16 ....22 B2
Green Pk HP16 ....151 B3
Green Rd HP13 ....162 B1
Green St
  Chorleywood WD3 ....167 B3
  Hazlemere HP15 ....162 C2
  High Wycombe HP11 ....172 C4

Green Street Cty Fst Sch HP11 172 C4
Green The
Amersham HP7 154 B1
Aston Abbots HP22 88 B3
Burnham SL1 197 A1
Chalfont St Giles HP8 177 B4
Chearsley HP18 112 A1
Cheddington LU7 105 A4
Cosgrove MK19 19 C1
Cranfield MK43 24 C1
Cuddington HP18 112 C2
Datchet SL3 211 A4
Deanshanger MK19 31 C2
Edlesborough LU6 92 C2
Great Horwood MK17 55 A2
Hanslope MK19 11 A1
Horton-cum-S OX33 108 A3
Hyde Heath HP6 153 B3
Longwick HP27 138 B3
Mentmore LU7 90 B2
Milton Keynes, Loughton MK5 46 A4
Milton Keynes, The Green MK6 47 B4
Newport Pagnell MK16 22 B2
Paulerspury NN12 17 A4
Pitstone LU7 105 B2
Quainton HP22 85 A3
Slough SL1,SL3 205 B2
Stoke Hammond MK17 69 C4
Thornborough MK18 54 A4
Turvey MK43 8 C3
West Drayton UB7 208 B2
Wooburn Green HP10 185 C3
Wraysbury TW19 211 C1
Green Tiles UB9 189 C2
Green Tiles La UB9 189 C3
Green Verges SL7 183 C2
Green View HP20 102 A1
Green View Cl HP3 146 A1
Green Way MK17 57 B2
Green West Rd HP9 176 C2
Greenacre SL4 209 C3
Greenacres LU7 105 B2
Greenacres Ave UB10 190 C1
Greenacres La HP10 163 A1
Greenacres The HP13 162 B1
Greenbury Cl WD3 167 B3
Greendale Mews SL2 206 A3
Greene Field Rd HP4 135 B2
Greene Wlk HP4 135 B2
Greenes Ct HP4 135 B3
Greenfern Ave SL1 204 B4
Greenfield End SL9 177 C2
Greenfield Rd MK16 22 A2
Greenfields Adstock MK18 53 C1
Maidenhead SL6 203 A3
Upper Arncott OX25 94 B4
Greenhill Cl MK5 46 A4
Greenlands
Flackwell Heath HP10 185 A4
Lacey Green HP27 149 B3
Greenlands Cl MK16 22 A2
Greenlands Ct SL6 202 A4
Greenlands La HP16 151 A4
Greenlaw Pl MK3 47 A2
Greenleaf Ct SL3 211 A4
Greenleas Lower Sch LU7 80 B4
Greenleys Fst Sch MK12 33 B3
Greenleys La MK12 33 B2
Greenleys Mid Sch MK12 33 B3
Greenock Rd SL1 205 A4
Greenridge HP10 174 A4
Greens Keep HP17 126 C3
Greens The HP22 89 A1
Greenside
Bourne End SL8 185 A3
Prestwood HP16 151 B3
Slough SL2 205 A4
Greenside Hill MK4 46 A1
Greenway
Berkhamsted HP4 135 A2
Burnham SL1 197 A1
Chesham HP5 144 A2
Great Horwood MK17 55 A1
Haddenham HP17 126 C3
[4] Thame OX9 125 C1
Greenway Ct [19] HP13 173 A4
Greenway Cty Prim Sch HP4 135 A2
Greenway Fst Sch HP4 134 C2
Greenway Par HP5 144 A2
Greenway Sch HP5 144 A2
Greenway The
Gerrards Cross SL9 188 B4
High Wycombe HP13 173 A4
Slough SL1 204 B3
Tring HP23 118 C3
Tylers Green HP10 163 A1
Uxbridge UB8 201 B2
Greenway Wlk MK18 41 C1
Greenways
Bow Brickhill MK17 48 B1
Eaton Bray LU6 92 B4
Greenways Dr SL6 202 A4
Greenwich Gdns MK16 22 B1
Greenwood HP14 150 A1
Greenwood Ave OX39 147 B3
Greenwood Cl
Amersham HP6 154 C1
[5] Seer Green HP9 176 B2
Greenwood Mdw OX39 147 B3
Greenwood Pl MK18 63 B2
Greenwood The HP22 117 B3
Greenyard The NN7 1 A4
Greetham Rd HP21 116 B3
Gregories Dr MK7 48 B3
Gregories Farm La HP9 175 B1
Gregories Rd HP9 175 B2
Gregory Dr SL4 211 A1
Gregory Rd SL2 187 B1
Grenadine Way HP23 119 A3
Grendon Rd Edgcott HP18 72 C1
Grendon Underwood HP18 83 B2
Grendon Underwood Comb Sch HP18 83 A3
Grendon Way HP22 102 A2
Grenfell Ave
High Wycombe HP12 172 B4
Maidenhead SL6 202 C3
Grenfell Pl SL6 202 C3
Grenfell Rd
Beaconsfield HP9 175 C2
Maidenhead SL6 202 C3
Grenville Ave HP22 131 A4
Grenville Cl SL1 197 A2
Grenville Comb Sch MK18 52 B4
Grenville Ct WD3 167 B3
Grenville Gn HP21 115 B2
Grenville Rd
Aylesbury HP21 115 B3
Buckingham MK18 41 B1
Grenville Way OX9 126 A1
Gresham Ct HP4 135 A2
Gresham Rd SL1 205 A4
Greyhound La
Thame OX9 125 C1
Winslow MK18 66 A2
Greys Hill RG9 191 B1
Greys Rd RG9 191 B1
Greys The MK6 47 B4
Greystoke Cl HP4 135 A2
Greystoke Rd SL2 204 C4
Greystonley [1] MK4 46 B1
Griffin Cl
Maidenhead SL6 202 C3
Slough SL1 205 B2
Griffin Ind Mall HP19 101 A1
Griffin La HP19 101 A1
Griffith Gate MK10 36 A2
Griffith Gate Rdbt MK10 36 A1
Griffith Ho HP10 174 B1
Griffiths Acre HP17 114 C3
Griffiths Yd HP5 144 A1
Griffon Cl MK6 47 A4
Grigby Rise MK6 47 A4
Griggs Orch MK16 14 A1
Grimbold Ct MK15 35 B4
Grimmer Cl HP19 100 C2
Grimms Hill HP16 151 C4
Grimms Mdw HP14 150 A1
Grimsdell's La HP6 154 B1
Grimsdyke Rd HP23 119 B1
Gringer Hill SL6 202 C4
Grizedale MK13 34 A3
Groom Rd HP16 151 B3
Groombridge MK7 48 A4
Grooms Cotts HP5 145 A1
Grooms Ct HP11 174 A2
Groomsby Dr LU7 105 C3
Grosmont Cl [1] MK4 46 A1
Grosvenor Cl SL0 200 B1
Grosvenor Ct SL1 205 C4
Grosvenor Dr SL6 203 B4
Groundsel Cl MK7 48 A3
Grove Ash MK1 47 B2
Grove Cl
Gerrards Cross SL9 177 B1
[7] Slough SL1 206 A2
Grove Ct
Beaconsfield HP9 175 B1
Bierton HP22 102 B3
Maidenhead SL6 202 B4
Turvey MK43 8 C3
Grove End SL9 177 B1
Grove Gdns HP23 119 A3
Grove Hill SL9 177 B2
Grove Ind Sch The MK5 46 B4
Grove La
Ashley Green HP5 145 B3
Gerrards Cross SL9 177 B1
Great Kimble HP17 129 C1
Uxbridge UB8 201 C1
Grove Pk HP23 119 B3
Grove Rd Amersham HP6 154 C1
Beaconsfield HP9 175 C1
Burnham SL1 197 C2
Hazlemere HP15 162 C2
Henley-on-T RG9 191 C1
High Wycombe HP12 172 B4
Maidenhead SL6 202 C4
Tring HP23 119 B3
Turvey MK43 8 C3
Uxbridge UB8 201 B3
Windsor SL4 210 B3
Grove Road Prim Sch HP23 119 B3
Grove The
Amersham HP6 154 B2
Latimer HP5 155 B2
Medmenham SL7 193 C3
Milton Keynes, Bradwell MK13 34 A2
Milton Keynes, Rickley Park MK3 58 A4
Newport Pagnell MK16 22 A2
Slough SL1 206 A2
Tring HP23 119 B3
Waddesdon HP18 99 A3
Grove Way
Chorleywood WD3 167 A2
Uxbridge UB8 201 B3
Waddesdon HP18 99 A3
Grovelands HP11 173 A3
Grovers Ct HP27 139 A1
Groves Cl SL8 185 B2
Groves Rd HP22 131 C4
Groves Way SL8 195 C3
Grovesbrook MK17 48 B1
Groveway MK6,MK7 47 B3
Grovewood Cl WD3 167 A2
Grubbins La HP27 150 A3
Grubwood La SL7 195 A4
Grundy Ho UB8 201 B2
Gryms Dyke HP16 151 B3
Guards Club Rd SL6 203 B4
Guards Rd SL4 209 B3
Guards Wlk [1] SL4 209 B3
Guernsey Cl HP19 101 A2
Guest Gdns MK13 34 A4
Guildford Cl MK18 52 A2
Guillemot Way HP20 101 C2
Guinea Orch MK46 6 C2
Guinions Rd HP13 173 C3
Guise Ct MK17 49 C2
Gull Way [12] HP20 101 C2
Gulliver's Land★ MK15 35 B2
Gun La MK16 14 A1
Gundale Ct MK4 46 A1
Gunmaker Ct MK14 34 C3
Gunthorpe Rd SL7 184 A2
Gunver La MK4 57 A4
Gurnard Cl UB7 208 B3
Gurnards Ave MK6 35 A1
Gurnells Rd HP9 176 B3
Gurney Cl
[11] Aylesbury HP20 101 C1
Beaconsfield HP9 175 B1
Milton Keynes MK5 46 A4
Gurney Ct LU6 92 C3
Gurneys Mdw HP15 163 B4
Guttmann Rd HP21 115 C3
Gwendale SL6 195 B1
Gweneth Ct SL7 183 B2
Gwent Cl SL6 202 A2
Gwynant Ct MK2 58 B2
Gwynne Cl Tring HP23 119 A3
Windsor SL4 209 C3
Gynant Rd HP13 173 C3
Gyosei Int Sch UK The MK15 35 B3
Gypsy La
Aspley Guise MK17 49 C2
High Wycombe HP11 173 B3
Marlow SL7 183 C2
Stoke Poges SL2 187 C1

H

Haberley Mead MK13 34 A2
Hackett Pl MK16 24 A3
Haddenham & Thame Parkway Sta HP17 126 C3
Haddenham Aerodrome Bsns Pk HP17 126 C4
Haddenham Inf Sch HP17 127 A3
Haddenham Jun Sch HP17 127 A3
Haddenham St Mary's CE Sch HP17 127 A2
Haddington Cl
Milton Keynes MK3 46 C1
Wendover HP22 131 B3
Haddington Way HP20 102 A1
Haddon MK8 45 C4
Haddon Rd
Chorleywood WD3 167 B2
Maidenhead SL6 202 B3
Hadfield Rd TW19 213 B1
Hadland Cl HP3 146 A2
Hadley Ct SL3 212 C3
Hadley Pl MK13 34 B2
Hadlow Ct SL1 205 B3
Hadrians Dr MK13 34 A3
Hadrians Gate NN13 38 A4
Hag Hill La SL6 204 A4
Hag Hill Rise SL6 204 A4
Haglis Dr HP22 131 A3
Haig Dr SL1 205 A2
Hailey Cft OX39 147 A3
Hailey Ct SL6 202 C3
Haileybury Ct SL4 210 A2
Hainault Ave MK14 22 A1
Haines Cl HP19 100 C1
Haines Rd HP15 162 C3
Haithwaite MK8 33 B1
Haldene MK8 33 C1
Hale SL4 209 C3
Hale Ave MK11 32 C3
Hale La HP22 131 C2
Hale Leys Ctr HP20 115 B4
Hale Rd HP22 131 B2
Hale St HP20 115 C4
Hales Croft HP21 116 A2
Halfacre Hill SL9 177 C1
Halfway Hos SL6 195 C2
Halfway House La HP5 153 C4
Halifax Cl SL6 202 A4
Halifax Ho HP7 166 B4
Halifax Rd
Heronsgate WD3 167 B1
High Wycombe HP12 172 B3
Maidenhead SL6 202 A4
Halifax Way SL6 202 A4
Halings La UB9 189 C4
Halkingcroft SL3 206 B2
Hall Cl
High Wycombe HP13 173 C3
Maids Moreton MK18 41 C2
Hall Cl *continued*
Old Stratford MK19 32 A3
Hall Cotts HP18 82 C4
Hall Ct SL3 211 A4
Hall La MK16 23 B4
Hall Mdw SL1 197 A2
Hall Park Gate HP4 135 C2
Hall Park Hill HP4 135 C2
Hall Pk HP4 135 C2
Halldore Hill SL8 195 C4
Halls Cnr HP10 174 A1
Halswell Pl MK10 36 A2
Halton Comb Sch HP22 131 B4
Halton La Halton HP22 131 A4
Wendover HP22 131 A4
Halton Wood Forest Wlks★ HP23 132 A3
Halton Wood Rd HP22 131 B3
Haltonchesters MK13 33 C3
Haly Cl MK13 34 A2
Ham Island SL4 211 B2
Ham La SL4 211 B2
Hamberlins La HP4, HP23 134 A4
Hamble Dr HP21 115 B3
Hambleden Mill RG9 192 B4
Hambleden Pl RG9 192 B3
Hambleden Rise RG9 192 B4
Hambleden Wlk SL6 195 C1
Hambledon Cl HP21 116 A3
Hambleton Gr MK4 46 A1
Hambling Pl LU6 93 C4
Hamburg Croft MK5 46 A2
Hambye Cl HP27 149 C2
Hamer Cl HP3 146 A2
Hamfield Cotts SL8 195 C4
Hamilton Ave RG9 191 C1
Hamilton Cl HP4 107 B3
Hamilton Ct
Aylesbury HP19 101 B1
High Wycombe HP13 173 A4
Hamilton Gdns SL1 197 A1
Hamilton La MK3 57 B3
Hamilton Mead HP3 146 A2
Hamilton Pk SL6 202 A3
Hamilton Pl SL9 188 C3
Hamilton Prim Sch HP13 173 A4
Hamilton Prim Sch (Annexe) HP13 173 A4
Hamilton Rd
Berkhamsted HP4 135 A2
High Wycombe HP13 162 B1
Slough SL1 205 A4
Thame OX9 126 A1
Uxbridge UB8 201 B1
Hamlins MK6 47 A3
Hammersley La HP10, HP13 174 A3
Hammerwood Gate MK7 48 A4
Hammond Cres MK15 35 A3
Hammond End SL2 198 A4
Hampden Ave HP5 144 A1
Hampden Cl
Aylesbury HP21 115 B3
Stoke Poges SL2 199 A1
Hampden Gdns HP21 115 B3
Hampden Hall Coll HP22 116 B2
Hampden Hill
Beaconsfield HP9 175 A1
Charndon OX27 72 C3
Hampden Ho HP13 173 C3
Hampden Rd
Aylesbury HP21 115 B3
Gerrards Cross SL9 177 B1
High Wycombe HP13 173 A4
Hughenden Valley HP16 151 A2
Lacey Green HP27 150 B3
Maidenhead SL6 202 A4
Prestwood HP16 151 A2
Slough SL3 206 C2
Stoke Mandeville HP22 116 A1
Wendover HP22 131 B3
Hampshire Ave SL1 205 B4
Hampshire Ct MK3 46 C1
Hampshire Lodge [8] SL6 202 C3
Hampson Cl MK13 34 A3
Hampstead Gate MK13 34 B2
Hampton MK8 46 A4
Hampton Cl HP22 116 A1
Hampton Ho SL3 212 B4
Hanbury Cl SL1 204 A4
Handel Mead MK7 48 C3
Handley Page Cl MK43 24 C2
Handy Cross HP11 172 C2
Hangar Rd UB9 189 C4
Hanging Croft Cl HP13 173 C3
Hangings La HP16 151 A3
Hanley Cl SL4 209 B3
Hanmer Rd MK6 47 C3
Hannah Ball Inf Sch HP13 173 B4
Hannon Rd HP21 115 B3
Hanover Cl
Aylesbury HP19 101 A1
Slough SL1 206 A2
Windsor SL4 209 C3
Hanover Ct
[7] Aylesbury HP21 115 C4
Hazelmere HP15 163 A2
Leighton Buzzard LU7 80 B4
Milton Keynes MK14 34 B4
Hanover Mead SL6 203 B2
Hanover Way SL4 209 C3
Hanscomb Cl MK15 35 B1
Hansen Croft MK5 46 A3
Hanslope Comb Sch MK19 11 A2
Hanslope Rd MK19 19 C3
Hanson Cl UB7 208 C2
Hanson Way HP21 116 A2
Harborne Ct MK8 33 B1
Harborough Cl SL1 204 B3
Harbourne Cl HP21 115 B2
Harby Cl MK4 46 B1
Harcourt
Milton Keynes MK13 34 A2
Wraysbury TW19 211 C1
Harcourt Cl Dorney SL6 203 C2
Henley-on-T RG9 191 B1
Leighton Buzzard LU7 80 C4
Harcourt Gn HP19 101 A1
Harcourt Rd Dorney SL6 203 C2
Stokenchurch HP14 158 C2
Tring HP23 119 B2
Windsor SL4 209 C3
Hardenwaye HP13 162 C1
Harding Rd
Chesham HP5 144 B1
Milton Keynes Village MK10 48 B4
Hardings Cl SL0 200 B1
Hardings Row SL0 200 B1
Hardmead Rd MK43 8 A2
Hardwick Cl SL6 202 A4
Hardwick Mews MK17 49 A2
Hardwick Pl MK17 49 A2
Hardwick Rd MK17 49 A2
Hardwicke Gdns HP6 154 C1
Hardy Cl Aylesbury HP21 115 C4
Slough SL1 205 A3
Hare Cl MK18 52 C4
Hare La HP16 152 A2
Hare Lane End HP16 152 A2
Hare Shoots SL6 202 C3
Harebell Cl MK7 48 A3
Harebell Wlk HP15 162 C3
Hareden Croft MK4 46 A1
Harefield Rd
Maidenhead SL6 202 A4
Uxbridge UB8 201 B3
Harehatch La SL1,SL2 186 C2
Harescombe Ct HP9 175 B2
Haresfoot Jun Sch HP4 135 A1
Harewood Pl SL1 206 A2
Harewood Rd HP8 166 B3
Hargrave Rd SL6 202 B4
Hargreaves Nook MK14 22 A1
Harkness Cl MK2 58 B3
Harkness Rd SL1 204 A4
Harlans Cl MK6 47 A4
Harlech Ho [5] HP13 173 C4
Harlech Pl MK3 57 C4
Harlequin Pl MK5 45 C2
Harlestone Ct MK14 22 A1
Harley Ct SL1 205 B2
Harleyford La SL7 194 A4
Harling Rd LU6 93 A2
Harlow Rd HP11,HP13 173 B3
Harman Wlk HP12 172 B2
Harmondsworth La UB7 213 C4
Harmondsworth Prim Sch UB7 213 B4
Harmondsworth Rd UB7 208 C1
Harnett Dr MK12 32 C3
Harper Cl OX25 94 B4
Harpers La MK14 34 C4
Harrier Cl HP20 101 C2
Harrier Ct MK6 47 A4
Harrier Dr MK6 47 A4
Harries Cl HP5 144 A1
Harries Way HP15 163 A3
Harriet Walker Way WD3 167 C1
Harrington Cl SL4 209 C2
Harris Cl HP18 110 A4
Harris Ct [8] HP20 101 C1
Harris Gdns SL1 205 B2
Harris Rd HP14 171 A3
Harrison Cl MK5 46 B3
Harrison Pl [5] OX9 125 C1
Harrison Way SL1 204 B3
Harroell HP18 125 B3
Harrogate Ct SL3 207 A1
Harrold Lower Sch MK43 3 C3
Harrold Priory Mid Sch MK43 3 C3
Harrold Rd MK46 8 A4
Harrow Cl
Aylesbury HP21 115 C2
Maidenhead SL6 195 C1
Harrow La SL6 195 C1
Harrow Mkt The SL3 207 A2
Harrow Rd SL3 206 C2
Harrow Yd
[9] Tring HP23 119 A2
Tring HP23 119 A2
Harrowden MK13 34 A4
Hart Moor Cl HP14 158 C2
Hart St RG9 191 C1
Hartdames MK5 46 A2
Hartfield Cl MK7 48 A4
Hartington Gr MK4 46 A2
Hartland Ave MK4 46 A1
Hartland Cl SL1 205 B3
Hartley MK14 34 C4
Hartley Cl SL3 199 B2
Hartley Copse SL4 211 A1
Hartley Ct SL9 188 C3
Harts Rd HP17 127 A3
Hartwell Cl HP10 163 B1

Hartwell Dr HP9 175 B2
Hartwell End HP21 115 A4
Hartwell Rd Ashton NN7 9 C4
Hanslope MK19 10 C3
Hartwort Cl MK7 48 A3
Harvard Cl MK14 21 C1
Harvest Bank HP6 153 B2
Harvest Hill SL8,HP10 185 B1
Harvest Hill Rd SL6 202 C2
Harvester Cl MK12 33 A3
Harvey Orch HP9 175 B2
Harvey Rd
Aylesbury HP21 115 C3
Dunstable LU6 93 B4
Slough SL3 207 A2
Harvil Rd UB9,UB10 190 C2
Harwich Rd SL1 205 A4
Harwood Dr UB10 201 C2
Harwood Rd SL7 183 B1
Harwood St MK13 34 A4
Hasgill Ct MK13 34 A2
Haslemere Rd SL4 210 A3
Haslow Ct MK8 33 C2
Hasting Cl SL6 203 B1
Hastings MK11 32 C3
Hastings Mdw SL2 199 A2
Hastoe Cross HP23 133 A4
Hastoe Farm HP23 132 C4
Hastoe Hill
Buckland Common HP23 132 C4
Hastoe HP23 119 A1
Hastoe La HP23 119 A1
Hastoe Pk HP20 101 C1
Hastoe Row HP23 133 A4
Hatch La
Radnage HP14 160 A2
Harmondsworth UB7 213 B4
Windsor SL4 210 A3
Hatch The SL4 209 B4
Hatches La HP15,HP16 162 A4
Hatchet Leys La
MK18 53 C4
Hatchgate Gdns SL1 197 B1
Hatchlands MK8 33 C1
Hatfield Cl SL6 202 B3
Hatfield Rd SL1 206 A2
Hathaway Ct MK8 45 C4
Hatter's La HP13 173 C3
Hatter's Lane Sch The
HP13 173 C4
Hatton MK6 47 B3
Hatton Ave SL2 198 B1
Hatton Ct SL4 210 B3
Hatton Gr UB7 208 B2
Hauksbee Gdns MK5 46 B3
Havelock Cres SL6 202 A4
Havelock Ct HP20 101 B1
Havelock Rd SL6 202 A4
Havelock St HP20 101 B1
Haven Of Rest SL6 203 A4
Haven Shaw Cl HP21 116 A3
Havenfield Ct 23 HP13 173 A4
Havenfield Rd HP12 172 B2
Haversham Fst Sch
MK19 20 C1
Haversham Rd MK19 20 B1
Haw La HP14 149 A1
Hawfinch 17 HP20 101 C2
Hawker Ct SL3 207 A2
Hawkhurst Gate MK7,
MK10 47 C4
Hawkins Cl MK11 32 B3
Hawkins Way HP3 146 A3
Hawkmoor Cl MK6 47 A4
Hawkridge MK4 46 C2
Hawks Hill SL8 185 B1
Hawkshill Dr HP1 146 C4
Hawkshill Rd SL2 198 A1
Hawkslade Furlong
HP21 115 B2
Hawksmoor Cl HP13 173 A4
Hawkswood MK46 6 C3
Hawkswood La SL9 199 C4
Hawkwell Dr HP23 119 B2
Hawkwell Est MK19 32 A4
Hawleys La HP22 87 A3
Hawridge & Cholesbury
CE Comb Sch HP5 133 C1
Hawridge La
Chartridge HP5 143 C4
Cholesbury HP5 143 C4
Hawridge Vale HP5 133 C1
Hawthorn Ave MK2 58 C4
Hawthorn Cl
Aylesbury HP20 101 C1
Iver Heath SL0 200 B1
Turvey MK43 8 C3
Hawthorn Cres HP15 163 A1
Hawthorn Dr UB9 201 B3
Hawthorn Gdns SL6 202 C3
Hawthorn La SL2 198 A3
Hawthorn Pl HP10 174 B4
Hawthorn Rd HP27 139 B2
Hawthorn Way
Chesham HP5 144 B1
Wing LU7 79 C2
Hawthorn Wlk HP15 163 A1
Hawthorne Cl
Leighton Buzzard LU7 80 C4
Marlow SL7 183 C2
Hawthorne Cres
Slough SL1 205 C4
West Drayton UB7 208 C2
Hawthorne Gdns HP10 174 A1
Hawthorne Rd HP13 174 A3
Hawthorns The
Berkhamsted HP4 135 A3
Cranfield MK43 25 A1
Felden HP3 146 C4
Flackwell Heath HP10 185 A4
Little Chalfont HP8 166 B4
Maple Cross WD3 178 B3
Poyle SL3 212 C3
Princes Risborough HP27 139 B3
Wooburn Green HP10 185 C3
Hawtrey Cl SL1 206 A2
Hawtrey Rd SL4 210 B3
Hay Barn Bsns Pk The
HP22 88 B3
Hay La SL3 199 B4
Hayden Ho 12 HP11 172 C4
Haydock Cl MK3 57 B3
Haydon Abbey Sch
HP19 101 B1
Haydon Ct SL6 202 C3
Haydon Rd HP19 101 B1
Hayes Pl SL7 183 B1
Hayes Rd MK19 31 C3
Hayfield Dr HP15 163 A1
Hayles Field HP14 170 C1
Haymaker Cl UB10 201 C3
Haymill Rd SL1,SL2 197 B1
Haynes Cl
Bow Brickhill MK17 48 B1
Slough SL3 206 C1
Haynes Ho HP12 172 A2
Haynes Mead HP4 135 A3
Hayse Hill SL4 209 B3
Haystacks The HP13 173 A4
Haythorp Cl MK15 35 A3
Hayward Pl SL8 185 B1
Haywards Cl RG9 191 B1
Haywards Croft MK12 33 A3
Haywards Mead SL4 204 C1
Haywood Pk
Chorleywood WD3 167 C2
Stewkley LU7 68 B2
Haywood Way HP19 100 C2
Haywoods Dr HP3 146 C4
Hazel Ave HP21 116 A4
Hazel Cl SL7 183 B3
Hazel Ct WD3 178 C3
Hazel Gr MK2 58 B4
Hazel Rd HP4 135 B2
Hazelbury Rd HP13 173 B3
Hazelcroft Cl UB10 201 C3
Hazeldene HP22 131 B2
Hazele Mere Ct HP15 163 A2
Hazelhurst 7 MK4 46 A1
Hazelhurst Dr HP21 116 A3
Hazelhurst Rd SL1 197 B2
Hazell Cl SL6 202 C4
Hazell Pk HP7 165 B4
Hazell Rd HP16 151 B3
Hazell Way SL2 198 C3
Hazelmere Rd SL2 206 A3
Hazelwood MK14 34 C4
Hazelwood Cl HP5 144 B1
Hazely HP23 119 B2
Hazlemere CE Comb Sch
HP15 162 C2
Hazlemere Rd HP10 163 B1
Hazlemere View HP15 163 A3
Hazlerig Cl HP21 115 C3
Hazley Wlk MK18 41 C1
Headington Cl SL6 202 A4
Headington Rd SL6 202 A4
Headland Cl HP16 152 A4
Healey Ave HP13 173 B4
Heaney Cl MK16 22 A3
Hearn Cl HP10 162 C1
Hearn's Mdw HP9 176 B2
Hearne Ct HP8 177 A4
Hearne Dr SL6 203 A1
Hearne Pl MK6 46 C4
Hearne's Cl HP9 176 B3
Heath Cl Aylesbury HP21 116 A3
Holmer Green HP15 163 A3
Stanwell TW19 213 B1
Woburn Sands MK17 49 B2
Heath Ct
Leighton Buzzard LU7 70 C2
Uxbridge UB8 201 C3
Heath End Cl HP15 151 C1
Heath End Rd
Flackwell Heath HP10 173 B1
Great Kingshill HP15,HP16 151 C1
Little Kingshill HP16 151 C1
Little Marlow HP10 173 B1
Heath La MK17 49 A1
Heath Lawn HP10 173 C1
Heath Rd
Beaconsfield HP9 185 C4
Great Brickhill MK17 59 C1
Hyde Heath HP6 153 B3
Heath The LU7 70 C2
Heath Way SL0 200 B2
Heathacre SL3 212 C3
Heathcote SL6 203 A1
Heathcote Ct 2 SL4 210 B2
Heathcote Way UB7 208 B3
Heathcroft MK14 34 C4
Heather Cl UB8 208 C4
Heather La UB7 208 C4
Heather Mead LU6 92 C3
Heather Wlk
Aylesbury HP21 115 A3
Hazelmere HP15 163 A2
Heatherden Gn SL0 200 B2
Heatherside Gdns SL2 187 B1
Heatherton House Sch
HP6 154 B2
Heatherton Pk HP6 154 A2
Heathfield MK12 33 C2
Heathfield Rd
High Wycombe HP12 172 A4
Taplow SL1 186 A1
Heathlands Dr SL6 202 A3
Heathrow Bvd UB7 213 C4
Heathrow Cl UB7 213 A3
Heathrow Prim Sch
UB7 213 C4
Heavens Lea SL8 185 B1
Hedge Lea HP10 185 B4
Hedgerley OX39 147 A3
Hedgerley Hill SL2 187 B1
Hedgerley La
Beaconsfield HP9 186 C4
Gerrards Cross SL2,SL9 188 A2
Hedgerley HP9,SL2 187 B3
Hedgerows The MK4 46 C2
Hedges Ct MK5 46 A3
Hedingham Ct MK5 46 A3
Hedingham Mews SL6 202 B4
Hedley Cl HP22 118 A2
Hedley Rd HP10 185 A4
Hedley View HP10 174 B1
Hedsor Hill SL8 185 B1
Hedsor La
Bourne End HP10,SL1 185 C1
Taplow SL1 186 A1
Hedsor Rd SL8 185 A1
Hedsor View Cotts SL8 195 C4
Heelands Fst Sch MK13 34 A2
Heights The SL7 194 A4
Hele Ct MK7 48 A2
Helen Cotts SL4 209 B3
Helena Rd SL4 210 B3
Helford Cl HP21 115 B2
Helford Pl MK6 35 A1
Hellfires Caves★ HP14 160 C1
Hellyer Way SL8 185 B2
Helston La SL4 210 A3
Helston Pl 5 MK6 34 C1
Hemel Hempstead Rd
HP4 107 C1
Hemingway Rd HP19 100 C1
Hemming Way SL2 198 A1
Hemmings The HP4 134 C2
Hemmingway Cl MK16 21 C3
Hemp Hill HP19 115 A4
Hemp La HP23 119 C1
Hempson Ave SL3 206 B2
Hempstead Rd HP3 146 A3
Hemsdale SL6 195 A1
Hemwood Rd SL4 209 B2
Hencroft St N SL1 205 C2
Hencroft St S SL1 205 C2
Henders MK11 32 C3
Hendon Way TW19 213 B1
Hendons Way SL6 203 A1
Hendrix Dr MK8 45 B4
Hengistbury La
Milton Keynes MK4 45 C1
Milton Keynes MK4 46 A1
Henley Coll The
(Deanfield Bldgs) RG9 191 B1
Henley Coll The (Rotherfield
Bldgs) RG9 191 B1
Henley Coll The
(Southfield Bldgs) RG9 191 B1
Henley Lodge 12 SL6 202 C3
Henley Rd
Bisham SL6,SL7 194 A1
Hurley RG9,SL7 193 B2
Marlow SL7 194 A4
Slough SL1 204 C4
Henley-on-Thames Sta
RG9 191 C1
Hennerton Way HP13 173 C3
Henrietta Rd OX9 126 A1
Henry Rd Aylesbury HP20 116 A4
Slough SL1 205 B2
Henry St HP23 119 A2
Hensman Gate MK10 35 C2
Henson Cl MK43 24 C2
Hepleswell MK8 33 C1
Hepplewhite Cl HP13 173 B4
Herbert Rd HP13 174 A4
Herberts Hole HP16 142 C1
Hercies Rd UB10 201 C3
Herd's Hill MK18 64 A2
Herdman Cl MK12 33 A3
Hereford Ho HP13 173 C4
Hereford Way HP19 101 A2
Heritage Cl UB8 201 B1
Heritage House Sch
HP5 144 B1
Heritage Wlk WD3 167 C3
Herman Terr HP12 172 B4
Hermitage Cl SL3 206 B2
Hermitage La SL4 210 A2
Hermitage Prim Sch
UB8 201 B3
Hermitage The
Great Missenden HP16 152 A4
Uxbridge UB8 201 B3
Heron Cl Aylesbury HP20 116 B4
Uxbridge UB8 201 B3
Heron Dr SL3 207 A1
Heron The HP20 101 C2
Herons Elm HP4 134 C4
Herons Pl
Maidenhead SL6 196 B2
Marlow SL7 183 C2
Heronsgate Dr WD3 167 A2
Heronsgate Mid Sch
MK7 48 A3
Heronshaw Fst Sch MK7 48 A3
Herriot Cl MK16 22 A3
Herschel Gram Sch SL1 205 B4
Herschel St SL1 205 C2
Herston Cl HP21 116 A3
Hertford Pl MK3 46 C1
Hervines Ct HP6 154 B1
Hervines Rd HP6 154 B1
Hesketh Rd NN12 18 C3
Het's Orch HP27 149 C3
Hetherington Cl SL2 197 C1
Hetherington Way
UB10 201 C4
Hetton Cl MK13 34 B2
Heusden Way SL9 188 C2
Hever Cl SL6 202 B3
Hewgate Ct RG9 191 C1
Hexham Gdns MK3 57 B3
Heybridge Cres MK7 48 A2
Heydon Ct MK13 34 A4
Heyer Cl LU7,HP23 105 B1
Heynes Gn SL6 202 A2
Heythrop Dr UB10 201 C4
Heywood Ave SL6 202 A1
Heywood Court Cl SL6 202 A1
Heywood Gdns SL6 202 A1
Hibbert Rd SL6 203 A2
Hibbert's Alley 26 SL4 210 B3
Hibberts Way SL9 188 C3
Hickmans Cl MK18 51 A3
Hickox Ct HP10 185 C4
Hicks Farm Rise HP13 173 C4
Hide The MK6 47 B3
Higgs Ct MK5 46 A4
High Ash CE Comb Sch
MK17 59 B1
High Beeches
Gerrards Cross SL9 188 B1
High Wycombe HP12 172 B3
High Bois La HP6 154 B2
High Coppice HP7 165 B4
High Halden MK7 48 A4
High Heavens Wood
SL7 183 B4
High Land Cl HP18 96 A1
High March Sch HP9 175 B2
High Moors HP22 131 A4
High Park Dr MK12 33 A3
High Rd Cookham SL8 195 C3
Soulbury LU7 69 C1
Uxbridge UB7,UB8 208 B4
High St Amersham HP7 165 A4
Aylesbury HP20 115 C4
Berkhamsted HP4 134 C3
Bovingdon HP3 146 A2
Brill HP18 110 A4
Buckingham MK18 41 B1
Burnham SL1 197 B1
Chalfont St Giles HP8 177 B4
Cheddington LU7 105 A4
Chesham HP5 154 A4
Chinnor OX39 147 A2
Chinnor OX39 147 B4
Colnbrook SL3 212 B4
Cookham SL8 196 A4
Cranfield MK43 25 A1
Cublington LU7 78 A1
Datchet SL3 211 A3
Deanshanger MK19 31 C2
Dinton HP17 113 C1
Eaton Bray LU6 92 C3
Edlesborough LU6 92 C2
Emberton MK46 13 C4
Eton SL4 210 B4
Gerrards Cross SL9 177 C1
Great Horwood MK17 55 A2
Haddenham HP17 126 C3
Hanslope MK19 11 A1
Harmondsworth UB7 213 B4
Harrold MK43 3 C3
Haversham MK19 21 A2
High Wycombe HP11 173 A3
High Wycombe, Downley
HP13 161 B2
Iver SL0 207 C4
Ivinghoe LU7 105 C3
Lane End HP14 171 A2
Lavendon MK46 7 C4
Leighton Buzzard LU7 80 C3
Lewknor OX49 157 A4
Long Crendon HP18 125 B3
Ludgershall HP18 96 A4
Maidenhead SL6 203 B2
Marlow SL7 183 C1
Milton Keynes, Great Linford
MK14 21 C1
Milton Keynes, New Bradwell
MK13 33 C4
Nash MK17 44 B1
Newport Pagnell MK16 22 B2
North Crawley MK16 24 A3
North Marston MK18 76 A1
Olney MK46 6 C2
Paulerspury NN12 17 B4
Potterspury NN12 18 B2
Prestwood HP16 151 B3
Princes Risborough HP27 139 A2
Sherington MK16 13 C1
Slough, Langley SL3 207 A1
Slough, Upton SL1,SL3 205 C2
South Heath HP16 152 A4
Stanwell TW19 213 B1
Stoke Goldington MK16 12 A3
Syresham NN13 27 A4
Taplow SL6 196 C1
Thame OX9 125 C1
Thornborough MK18 54 A4
Tring HP23 119 A2
Turvey MK43 8 C3
Uxbridge UB8 201 B3
Uxbridge, Cowley UB8 201 B1
High St *continued*
Waddesdon HP18 99 A3
Weedon HP22 87 B1
Wendover HP22 131 A2
West Drayton UB7 208 C3
Westcott HP18 98 A4
Weston Underwood MK46 6 A1
Whaddon MK17 45 A1
Whitchurch HP22 87 A3
Windsor SL4 210 B3
Wing LU7 79 C1
Wing, Burcott LU7 79 B2
Winslow MK18 65 C2
Woburn MK17 60 C4
Woburn Sands MK17 49 A2
Wraysbury TW19 211 C1
Yardley Gobion NN12 18 C3
Yardley Hastings NN7 1 A3
High St Mall 1 SL6 202 C4
High St N LU7 68 B1
High St S Olney MK46 6 C2
Stewkley LU7 78 C4
High St The MK8 33 B1
High Town Rd SL6 202 C4
High Trees MK6 47 A4
High View
Chalfont St Giles HP8 177 B4
Deanshanger MK19 31 C3
High View Cl HP10 183 B4
High Wycombe
CE Comb Sch HP11 173 A3
High Wycombe Sta
HP13 173 A4
Higham Cross Rd MK19 10 C2
Higham Mead HP5 144 B1
Higham Rd HP5 144 B1
Highbeeches Cl SL7 183 B4
Highbridge Ind Est UB8 201 B3
Highbridge Rd HP21 115 C4
Highbridge Wlk 3
HP21 115 C4
Highbury La MK9 35 A2
Highcroft Cl NN12 18 C3
Highfield
Chalfont St Giles HP8 177 B4
Long Crendon HP18 125 B4
Highfield Ave HP12 172 A3
Highfield Cl
Amersham HP6 154 B1
Milton Keynes MK3 47 A1
Newport Pagnell MK16 22 C2
Highfield Ct
Burnham SL2 198 A2
Hazelmere HP15 163 A2
Highfield Dr UB10 190 C1
Highfield La SL6 202 A2
Highfield Pk SL7 183 A1
Highfield Rd
Berkhamsted HP4 135 B2
Bourne End SL8 185 A2
Chesham HP5 144 A1
Flackwell Heath HP10 185 A4
Maidenhead SL6 202 A4
Princes Risborough HP27 139 B2
Tring HP23 118 C2
Wigginton HP23 119 B1
Windsor SL4 209 C2
Winslow MK18 65 C3
Highfield Sch SL6 202 C4
Highfield Way
Hazelmere HP15 163 A2
Yardley Hastings NN7 1 A3
Highgate Over MK7 48 A3
Highgrove Hill MK8 45 C4
Highgrove Pk SL6 202 C4
Highland Cl MK3 46 C2
Highland Rd HP7 165 B4
Highlands
Flackwell Heath HP10 185 A4
High Wycombe HP13 174 A3
Highlands Cl SL9 177 C2
Highlands End SL9 177 C2
Highlands La SL9 177 C2
Highlands Rd
Buckingham MK18 41 C1
Seer Green HP9 176 B3
Highlands The SL2 198 A4
Highlea Ave HP10 185 A4
Highmoor HP7 165 B4
Highmore Cotts HP7 152 C2
Highover Pk HP7 165 B4
Highveer Croft MK4 46 A1
Highway MK17 68 B3
Highway Ave SL6 202 A3
Highway Ct
Beaconsfield HP9 175 B2
Chesham HP5 144 B1
Highway Rd SL6 202 A3
Highway The HP9 175 B1
Highwood Ave HP12 172 A3
Highwood Bottom
HP27 150 A3
Highwood Cres HP12 172 A3
Highwoods Cl SL7 183 B4
Highwoods Dr SL7 183 B4
Highworth Cl HP13 162 C1
Highworth Comb Sch
HP13 162 C1
Hikers Way HP18 125 C2
Hilbury Cl HP6 154 B2
Hilda Wharf HP20 115 C4
Hildreth Rd HP16 151 B3
Hilgrove Ho SL6 195 B1
Hiljon Cres SL9 177 C1
Hill Ave Amersham HP6 154 B1
Hazelmere HP15 163 A3
Hill Cl HP10 185 C4
Hill Cotts HP18 97 C1

Hill Farm MK18 .... 76 A1
Hill Farm App HP10 .... 185 C4
Hill Farm Ct OX39 .... 147 B3
Hill Farm La
Chalfont St Giles HP8 .... 166 A1
Little Horwood MK17 .... 55 C1
Hill Farm Rd
Chalfont St Peter SL9 .... 177 C2
Chesham HP5 .... 154 B3
Marlow Bottom SL7 .... 183 C3
Taplow SL6 .... 196 C1
Hill Farm Way HP15 .... 163 A1
Hill Gr SL9 .... 177 C1
Hill House Cl SL9 .... 177 C2
Hill Mdw HP7 .... 164 C2
Hill Mead HP4 .... 135 A2
Hill Pl SL2 .... 198 A3
Hill Rd Chinnor OX39 .... 147 B3
Lewknor OX49 .... 157 A4
Lewknor OX49,HP14 .... 157 B3
Hill Rise SL9 .... 177 B1
Hill Rise Cres SL9 .... 177 C1
Hill Side LU7 .... 104 C4
Hill St HP13 .... 174 A3
Hill The Coleshill HP7 .... 164 B2
Syresham NN13 .... 27 A4
Hill Top Dr SL7 .... 183 A1
Hill Top La OX39 .... 147 C2
Hill View
Berkhamsted HP4 .... 135 A3
Great Kimble HP17 .... 129 B1
Newport Pagnell MK16 .... 22 A2
Oakley HP18 .... 109 B3
Hill View Rd TW19 .... 211 B1
Hill Waye SL9 .... 188 C2
Hillary Cl Aylesbury HP21 116 A3
High Wycombe HP13 .... 173 C3
Hillary Rd
High Wycombe HP13 .... 173 C3
Slough SL3 .... 206 C2
Hillbottom Rd HP12 .... 172 A4
Hillcrest MK43 .... 25 B1
Hillcrest Ave SL8 .... 195 C3
Hillcrest Cl MK5 .... 46 A3
Hillcrest Ct HP6 .... 154 B1
Hillcrest Rise MK18 .... 52 C3
Hillcrest Way MK18 .... 52 C3
Hillcrest Waye SL9 .... 188 C3
Hillcroft Rd
Chesham HP5 .... 144 B1
Tylers Green HP10 .... 163 B1
Hillersdon SL2 .... 206 A4
Hillersdon Chase MK17 .... 69 B4
Hillesden Hamlet MK18 .... 51 C1
Hillesden Way MK18 .... 41 C1
Hillfield Cl HP13 .... 161 C1
Hillfield Rd SL9 .... 177 C2
Hillfield Sq SL9 .... 177 C2
Hilliard Dr MK13 .... 34 A2
Hilliards Rd UB8 .... 208 B4
Hillier Rd HP21 .... 115 B2
Hillingdon Hill UB10 .... 201 C1
Hillingdon Hospl UB8 .... 208 C4
Hillingdon Rd UB10 .... 201 C2
Hillington Cl HP19 .... 115 A4
Hillman Cl UB8 .... 201 C4
Hillmead Ct SL6 .... 203 C4
Hillrise SL3 .... 212 A4
Hills Cl MK14 .... 34 C4
Hills La SL7 .... 195 B4
Hillside Amersham HP7 .... 165 C4
Chesham HP5 .... 144 A2
Gawcott MK18 .... 51 C2
High Wycombe HP13 .... 173 B4
Maidenhead SL6 .... 202 B3
Slough SL1 .... 205 C2
South Harefield UB9 .... 190 B3
Tingewick MK18 .... 51 A3
Hillside Cl
Chalfont St Giles HP8 .... 177 A4
Chalfont St Peter SL9 .... 177 C2
Upper Arncott OX25 .... 94 C4
Hillside Cotts HP18 .... 112 C1
Hillside Gdns
Berkhamsted HP4 .... 135 B2
High Wycombe HP13 .... 173 B4
Hillside Rd
Chorleywood WD3 .... 167 B2
Marlow SL7 .... 183 C2
Tylers Green HP10 .... 163 A1
Hilltop HP18 .... 125 B3
Hilltop Ave MK18 .... 41 C1
Hilltop Fst Sch SL4 .... 209 C2
Hilltop Rd HP4 .... 135 B2
Hillview
Bledlow Ridge HP14 .... 149 B1
Sherington MK16 .... 14 A1
Hillview Rd HP13 .... 173 B4
Hillway Amersham HP7 .... 165 A3
Woburn Sands MK17 .... 49 A3
Hillwerke OX39 .... 147 B3
Hillyer Ct MK6 .... 35 B1
Hilperton Rd 3 SL1 .... 205 C2
Hilton Ave HP20 .... 101 C1
Hilton Cl UB8 .... 201 A2
Himley Gn LU7 .... 80 B3
Hindemith Gdns MK7 .... 48 B3
Hindhead Knoll MK7 .... 48 A3
Hinkley Cl UB9 .... 190 B4
Hinksey Cl SL3 .... 207 A2
Hinton Cl HP13 .... 162 A1
Hinton Ct MK3 .... 46 C1
Hinton Rd Slough SL1 .... 204 C3
Uxbridge UB8 .... 201 B2
Hipwell Ct MK46 .... 6 C2
Hitcham Ho SL1 .... 197 A1
Hitcham La Burnham SL1 197 A1
Taplow SL6 .... 196 C1
Hitcham Rd SL1,SL6 .... 204 A4
Hither Mdw SL9 .... 177 C1
Hithercroft Rd HP13 .... 161 C1
Hithermoor Rd TW19 .... 213 A1
Hiving's Hill HP5 .... 144 A1
Hivings Pk HP5 .... 144 A2
HM Prison (Bullingdon)
OX25,HP18 .... 95 A4
HM Prison (The Mount)
HP3 .... 145 C2
HM Young Offender Inst
(Grendon) HP18 .... 73 A1
HM Young Offender Inst
(Winnamore Wood
Camp) SL7 .... 182 B4
Hoathly Mews MK7 .... 48 A4
Hobart Cl HP13 .... 162 C1
Hobart Cotts HP16 .... 150 B4
Hobart Cres MK15 .... 35 A4
Hobart Ct SL7 .... 184 A2
Hobart Rd HP13 .... 162 B1
Hobarts Dr UB9 .... 189 C3
Hobbis Dr SL6 .... 202 A3
Hobbs Rd HP14 .... 171 B2
Hobsons Wlk HP23 .... 118 C3
Hockett La Bisham SL7 .... 195 A3
Cookham SL7 .... 195 A3
Hockley La SL2 .... 199 A3
Hockliffe Brae MK7 .... 48 A3
Hodder La MK4 .... 46 B1
Hodds Wood Rd HP5 .... 154 B3
Hodge Lea La MK12 .... 33 B2
Hodgemoor View HP8 .... 177 A4
Hodgemore Ct MK14 .... 21 C1
Hoe Mdw HP9 .... 175 B2
Hog Hall La HP4 .... 107 A3
Hog La Ashley Green HP5 144 B4
Berkhamsted HP4 .... 134 B1
Hogarth Cl SL1 .... 204 C3
Hogarths Ct 9 MK8 .... 33 C1
Hogback Wood Rd HP9 175 A2
Hogfair La SL1 .... 197 B1
Hogg La HP15 .... 163 B3
Hoggshill Rd HP16 .... 152 A3
Hogshaw Rd MK18 .... 75 C3
Hogtrough La HP22 .... 131 B1
Holborn Cres MK4 .... 57 A4
Holdom Ave MK1 .... 47 B1
Holes La MK46 .... 6 C2
Holiday La MK19 .... 10 C2
Holland Cl Chinnor OX39 .147 B4
Wendover HP22 .... 131 A2
Holland Rd
Aylesbury HP19 .... 101 A1
Marlow SL7 .... 183 C2
Holland Way MK16 .... 22 B2
Hollandridge La OX49 .... 168 B2
Holliday Cl MK8 .... 45 C4
Holliday St HP4 .... 135 B2
Hollies The
Beaconsfield HP9 .... 175 C2
Bovingdon HP3 .... 146 A1
Leighton Buzzard LU7 .... 80 C4
Tring HP23 .... 119 A2
Wigginton HP23 .... 119 B1
Hollin La MK12 .... 33 C2
Hollingdon Rd LU7 .... 69 B2
Hollington HP18 .... 125 A4
Hollinwell Cl 8 MK3 .... 46 B1
Hollis Rd HP13 .... 173 C4
Hollister Chase MK5 .... 46 A2
Hollow Hill End MK18 .... 75 C4
Hollow Hill La SL0 .... 207 B3
Hollow Rise HP13 .... 162 A1
Hollow Way HP5 .... 143 C1
Hollow Way La
Amersham HP5,HP6 .... 154 C2
Chesham HP6 .... 154 C2
Hollow Wood MK46 .... 6 C2
Holloway Cl UB7 .... 208 C1
Holloway Dr MK18 .... 41 C1
Holloway La
Chenies WD3 .... 156 B1
Ibstone HP14 .... 169 B2
West Drayton UB7 .... 208 C1
Holloway The
Drayton Beauchamp HP22,
HP23 .... 118 B2
Princes Risborough HP27 .139 B3
Holly Cl
Farnham Common SL2 .... 198 B4
Milton Keynes MK8 .... 45 C3
Holly Cres SL4 .... 209 B3
Holly Dr Aylesbury HP21 .115 C3
Berkhamsted HP4 .... 135 B2
Maidenhead SL6 .... 202 C4
Windsor SL4 .... 210 C1
Holly End HP14 .... 161 B4
Holly Gdns UB7 .... 208 C2
Holly Green La HP27 .... 138 A2
Holly Hedges La HP3 .... 156 B4
Holly Pl HP11 .... 174 A2
Holly Tree Cl HP5 .... 155 A4
Holly Tree La HP18 .... 112 C2
Holly Wlk MK17 .... 49 A1
Hollyberry Gr HP15 .... 163 B4
Hollybush Cnr SL2 .... 187 B1
Hollybush Hill SL2 .... 199 A3
Hollybush La
Amersham HP6 .... 154 B2
Cookham SL7 .... 195 A3
Denham UB9 .... 200 C4
Iver SL0,SL3 .... 207 A4
Hollybush Rd HP5 .... 144 A2
Hollybush Row HP23 .... 133 B4
Hollyfield HP23 .... 119 B3
Hollyfield Cl HP23 .... 119 B3
Hollytree Cl SL9 .... 177 C3
Holm Gate MK5 .... 46 A4
Holman St HP19 .... 101 B1
Holmanleaze SL6 .... 203 A4
Holmdale SL2 .... 206 B3
Holmer Green Inf Sch
HP15 .... 163 A4
Holmer Green Jun Sch
HP15 .... 163 B4
Holmer Green Rd HP15 .163 A2
Holmer Green Upper Sch
HP15 .... 163 A4
Holmer Pl HP15 .... 163 B4
Holmers Ct HP12 .... 172 A2
Holmers Farm Way
High Wycombe HP12 .... 172 B2
Little Marlow HP12 .... 172 B2
Marlow Bottom HP12 .... 172 B2
Holmers La HP12 .... 172 B2
Holmewood MK4 .... 46 C2
Holmfield Cl MK6 .... 47 B3
Holmlea Rd SL3 .... 211 B3
Holmlea Wlk SL3 .... 211 B3
Holmoak Wlk HP15 .... 163 A2
Holmsdale Cl SL0 .... 207 C4
Holmwood Cl SL6 .... 202 A3
Holmwood Fst Sch MK8 .33 C1
Holne Chase
Cty Comb Sch MK3 .... 58 A4
Holst Cres MK7 .... 48 B2
Holt Gr MK5 .... 46 A4
Holt The MK18 .... 52 C4
Holton Hill MK4 .... 46 B1
Holton Rd MK18 .... 41 B1
Holts Gn MK17 .... 59 B1
Holtspur Ave HP10 .... 185 C4
Holtspur Cl HP9 .... 186 A4
Holtspur Comb Sch
HP9 .... 175 A1
Holtspur La HP10 .... 185 C3
Holtspur Par HP9 .... 186 A4
Holtspur Top La HP9 .... 175 A1
Holtspur Way HP9 .... 175 A1
Holy Family RC Sch The
SL3 .... 206 C1
Holy Thorn La MK5 .... 45 C3
Holy Thorne La MK5 .... 46 A3
Holy Trinity CE Prim Sch
SL8 .... 196 A4
Holy Trinity CE Sch SL7 .183 B2
Holyhead Cres MK4 .... 57 B4
Holyport Rd SL6 .... 203 A1
Holyrood MK8 .... 45 C4
Holywell Gdns HP13 .... 173 C4
Holywell Mid Sch MK43 .25 A1
Holywell Pl MK6 .... 35 B1
Holywell Rd MK43 .... 25 B1
Home Cl
Milton Keynes MK3 .... 47 A1
Shabbington HP18 .... 124 B2
Weston Turville HP22 .... 116 C1
Home Farm MK17 .... 57 B2
Home Farm Ct
Bovingdon HP3 .... 145 C1
Emberton MK46 .... 13 C4
Home Farm La MK17 .... 59 B1
Home Farm Rd HP4 .... 134 B4
Home Farm Way SL3 .... 199 B2
Home Field
Aylesbury HP19 .... 115 A4
Bow Brickhill MK7 .... 48 A2
Home Mdw SL2 .... 198 B2
Home Meadow Dr HP10 185 A4
Home Way WD3 .... 167 C1
Home Wood SL7 .... 193 C3
Homefarm Ct HP8 .... 177 A4
Homefield HP3 .... 146 A2
Homefield Cl HP14 .... 158 C2
Homefield Rd WD3 .... 167 B3
Homeground MK18 .... 52 C3
Homelands Gdns HP15 .162 B4
Homelands Way RG9 .... 191 B4
Homer Fst Sch SL4 .... 209 B3
Homeridings Ho MK13 .... 34 A2
Homers Rd SL4 .... 209 B3
Homeside Cl SL6 .... 195 C1
Homestall MK18 .... 52 B3
Homestall Cl MK5 .... 46 A4
Homestead Cl HP17 .... 114 A2
Homestead Rd SL6 .... 202 B2
Homestead The
Great Kingshill HP15 .... 151 B1
Little Marlow HP12 .... 172 B2
Milton Keynes MK5 .... 46 A3
1 Thame OX9 .... 125 C1
Homestead Way NN12 .... 18 C2
Homeward Ct MK5 .... 46 A4
Homewood SL3 .... 206 B4
Homewood Ct WD3 .... 167 C3
Homstead Pl HP19 .... 115 A4
Hondur Cl HP20 .... 102 A1
Honey Banks HP22 .... 131 B2
Honey Hill Emberton MK46 13 C4
Uxbridge UB10 .... 201 C3
Honey Hill Dr MK19 .... 31 C3
Honey La SL7,RG10 .... 193 C1
Honey Way HP14 .... 161 A4
Honeycroft Hill UB10 .... 201 C3
Honeypot Cl MK13 .... 34 A2
Honeysuckle Cl SL0 .... 207 B4
Honeysuckle Ct SL3 .... 212 B4
Honeysuckle Fld HP5 .... 144 B1
Honeysuckle Rd HP15 .... 162 C4
Honeywick La LU6 .... 92 C4
Honiton Ct MK7 .... 48 B4
Honor End La HP16 .... 151 A4
Honor Rd HP16 .... 151 B3
Honorwood Cl HP16 .... 151 A3
Honours Mead HP1 .... 146 A2
Hoods Farm Cl HP22 .... 102 B2
Hooke The MK15 .... 35 B4
Hooper Gate MK15 .... 35 B4
Hop Gdns RG9 .... 191 B1
Hopcraft Cl OX25 .... 94 C4
Hopkins Cl MK10 .... 36 A1
Hopkins Ct HP20 .... 101 C1
Hoppers Mdw MK5 .... 46 A4
Hoppers Way HP15 .... 162 B4
Hopton Rd OX9 .... 126 A1
Hordern Cl HP17 .... 126 C3
Horn La MK11 .... 32 B3
Horn St MK18 .... 65 C2
Hornbeam MK16 .... 22 A2
Hornbeam Cl HP12 .... 172 A2
Hornbeam Gdns 2 SL1 .206 A2
Hornbeam Wlk HP15 .... 163 A2
Hornbill Cl UB8 .... 208 B4
Hornby Chase MK4 .... 46 A1
Horners Croft MK12 .... 33 B3
Hornhill Rd WD3 .... 178 B3
Horns La
High Wycombe HP12 .... 172 A2
Princes Risborough HP27 .139 A2
Horse Hill HP5 .... 155 B4
Horsefair Gn MK11 .... 32 B3
Horseguards Dr SL6 .... 203 A4
Horsemoor Cl SL3 .... 207 A1
Horsemoor La HP7 .... 164 B1
Horsenden La HP27 .... 138 C1
Horsenden Rd HP13 .... 173 C3
Horsepond MK17 .... 59 B1
Horseshoe Cl LU7 .... 105 A4
Horseshoe Cloisters 13
SL4 .... 210 B3
Horseshoe Cres HP9 .... 175 C1
Horseshoe Hill SL1 .... 197 B4
Horseshoe Rd HP14 .... 159 B4
Horsetone Cotts HP17 .... 129 B1
Horsleys WD3 .... 178 B3
Horton Bridge Rd UB7 .208 C3
Horton Cl
Aylesbury HP19 .... 115 A4
Maidenhead SL6 .... 196 B1
West Drayton UB7 .... 208 C3
Horton Depot SL3 .... 212 B2
Horton Gate MK14 .... 21 C1
Horton Gdns SL3 .... 211 C2
Horton Grange SL6 .... 196 B1
Horton Ind Pk UB7 .... 208 C3
Horton Par UB7 .... 208 C3
Horton Rd Datchet SL3 .211 B3
Horton SL3 .... 212 A3
Ivinghoe LU7 .... 91 A1
Slapton LU7 .... 91 B3
Stanwell TW19 .... 213 A1
West Drayton UB7 .... 208 C3
Horton Road Ind Est
UB7 .... 208 C3
Horton Trad Est SL3 .... 212 A2
Hortonsfield Rd NN12 .... 18 C3
Horwood Ct MK1 .... 47 B1
Hospital Circular Rd
HP22 .... 131 B3
Hospital Hill HP5 .... 154 B4
Hospital Rdbt MK6 .... 47 A3
Hotch Croft MK43 .... 25 B2
Hotley Bottom La HP16 .151 B4
Houghton Ct MK8 .... 45 C4
Housman Cl MK16 .... 22 A3
Houston Ct 36 SL4 .... 210 B3
How's Cl UB8 .... 201 B2
How's Rd UB8 .... 201 B2
Howard Agne Cl HP1 .... 146 A2
Howard Ave
Aylesbury HP21 .... 116 A3
Slough SL2 .... 205 C4
Howard Cres HP9 .... 176 B3
Howard Ct 10 SL8 .... 185 A2
Howard Est The HP5 .... 144 B1
Howard Mews SL3 .... 212 A4
Howard Rd
Chesham HP5 .... 144 A2
Seer Green HP9 .... 176 B3
Howard Way MK16 .... 23 A2
Howards Thicket SL9 .... 188 B1
Howards Wood Dr SL9 .188 B1
Howarth Rd SL6 .... 203 A3
Howe Dr HP9 .... 175 C3
Howe Hill La HP15 .... 163 A4
Howe Rock Pl MK4 .... 46 A1
Howell Hill Cl LU7 .... 90 B3
Howland Pl MK17 .... 60 C4
Howletts Cl HP19 .... 115 A4
Hoylake Cl
Milton Keynes MK3 .... 57 B4
Slough SL1 .... 204 C2
Hoyton Gate MK8 .... 45 B3
HRH Princess Christians
Hospl SL4 .... 210 B3
Hubbard Cl MK18 .... 41 C1
Hubbards Ct WD3 .... 167 B2
Hubbards Rd WD3 .... 167 B2
Hubert Day Cl HP9 .... 175 B2
Hubert Rd SL3 .... 206 B2
Huckleberry Cl MK7 .... 48 A3
Hudnall La HP4 .... 121 C4
Hudson La MK8 .... 45 B4
Hudsons Ave UB9 .... 189 C3
Hughenden Ave HP13 .... 173 A4
Hughenden Ct UB8 .... 201 B1
Hughenden Gn HP21 .... 115 C2
Hughenden Inf Sch
HP14 .... 162 A4
Hughenden Manor★
HP14 .... 162 A2
Hughenden Rd
High Wycombe HP13 .... 162 A1
Hughenden Rd *continued*
Slough SL1 .... 205 B4
Hughendon Cl SL6 .... 202 B3
Hulbert End HP21 .... 116 B3
Hulcombe Wlk HP20 .... 101 C1
Hull Cl Aylesbury HP21 .... 115 C3
Slough SL1 .... 205 B2
Hulton Dr MK46 .... 13 C4
Humber Cl UB7 .... 208 B3
Humber Dr HP21 .... 115 B3
Humber Way
Milton Keynes MK3 .... 46 C1
Slough SL3 .... 207 A1
Hundred Acres La HP7 .165 B4
Hungerford Ave SL2 .... 205 C4
Hungerford Dr SL6 .... 195 C2
Hungerford Ho 6 MK4 .... 46 B1
Hunsdon Cl MK14 .... 34 B3
Hunstanton Cl SL3 .... 212 B4
Hunstanton Way MK3 .... 57 B4
Hunt Rd HP13 .... 173 C3
Hunt's La SL6 .... 196 C2
Hunter Ct SL1 .... 204 B4
Hunter Dr MK2 .... 58 B3
Hunter St MK18 .... 52 B4
Huntercombe Cl SL6 .... 204 B4
Huntercombe La N SL1 .204 B4
Huntercombe La S SL6 .204 B3
Hunters Cl
Bovingdon HP3 .... 146 A1
Chesham HP5 .... 144 A1
Tring HP23 .... 119 A3
Hunters Hill HP13 .... 173 C3
Hunters Mews SL4 .... 210 B3
Hunters Pk HP4 .... 135 C3
Hunters Point OX39 .... 147 B3
Hunters Reach MK13 .... 34 A2
Hunters Way SL1 .... 204 C2
Huntingbrooke MK8 .... 45 C4
Huntingdon Cres MK3 .... 57 B3
Huntington Pl SL3 .... 207 A2
Huntley Cl HP13 .... 162 B1
Hunts Hill La HP14 .... 161 C3
Huntsman Gr MK14 .... 22 A1
Huntsmans Cl HP4 .... 107 B3
Huntswood La SL6 .... 196 C2
Hurley Croft MK10 .... 36 A1
Hurley High St SL7 .... 193 C2
Hurley La SL7 .... 194 A2
Hurlstone Gr MK4 .... 46 B2
Hurricane Way SL3 .... 207 A1
Hurst Rd SL1 .... 204 B4
Hurstfield Dr SL6 .... 204 A4
Hurstleigh WD3 .... 167 B2
Hurworth Ave SL3 .... 206 B2
Hutchings Cl MK5 .... 46 A4
Hutchings Rd HP9 .... 175 B3
Hutton Ave MK6 .... 34 C1
Hutton Way MK17 .... 49 A3
Huxley Cl
Newport Pagnell MK16 .... 21 C2
Uxbridge UB8 .... 201 B1
Huxtable Gdns SL6 .... 203 C1
Hyacinth Dr UB10 .... 201 C3
Hychenden Cl HP14 .... 161 C3
Hyde Cl MK16 .... 22 B1
Hyde Gn
Beaconsfield HP9 .... 175 C2
Marlow SL7 .... 183 C1
Hyde Heath Inf Sch
HP6 .... 153 B3
Hyde Heath Rd HP6 .... 153 A3
Hyde La Bovingdon HP3 .146 A2
South Heath HP16 .... 152 C3
Hyde Mdws HP3 .... 146 A2
Hyde The HP22 .... 116 C1
Hyland Ho 19 SL8 .... 185 A2
Hylle Cl SL4 .... 209 C3
Hylton Rd HP12 .... 172 B4
Hyrons Cl HP6 .... 154 C1
Hyrons Ct HP6 .... 154 C1
Hyrons La HP6 .... 154 B1
Hythe The MK8 .... 33 C2

I

Ibotson Ct SL3 .... 212 C3
Ibstone Ave MK13 .... 34 B2
Ibstone CE Sch HP14 .... 169 B3
Ibstone Rd HP14 .... 158 B2
Ickford Comb Sch HP18 124 A2
Ickford Rd
Shabbington HP18 .... 124 B1
Worminghall HP18 .... 123 C3
Icknield Cl Chinnor OX39 147 A2
Wendover HP22 .... 131 B3
Icknield Cotts HP17 .... 129 C1
Icknield Gn HP23 .... 119 A3
Icknield Jun Sch HP27 .139 A3
Icknield Line★ OX39 .... 147 C3
Icknield Way
Eaton Bray LU6 .... 93 B2
Tring HP23 .... 118 C2
Icknield Way Farm Cotts
LU6 .... 93 B2
Iffley Cl UB8 .... 201 B3
Ilchester Cl SL6 .... 202 B3
Ilex Cl HP15 .... 163 A2
Ilex Ct HP4 .... 135 A2
Illingworth SL4 .... 209 C2
Illingworth Pl MK6 .... 46 C4
Imperial Ct
Henley-on-T RG9 .... 191 C1
Windsor SL4 .... 210 A2

Imperial Rd SL4 210 A3
In The Ray SL6 203 A4
Independent Bsns Pk HP14 158 B3
India Rd SL1 206 A2
Ingleglen SL2 198 A4
Ingleside SL3 212 C3
Ingleton Cl MK13 34 B2
Ingram Ave HP21 116 B3
Inkerman Dr HP15 163 A3
Inkerman Rd SL4 204 C1
Inkerman Terr HP5 154 B3
Inn Farm Ct MK16 22 B4
Innholder Ct MK14 34 C3
Innings Gate HP14 170 C1
Inniscrown Ho SL3 211 A4
Institute Rd Marlow SL7 183 C1
Taplow SL6 203 C4
Taplow SL6 203 C4
Intalbury Ave HP19 101 A1
Inverness Cl MK3 46 C1
Inwood Cl SL7 195 A3
Iona Cres SL1 204 C4
Ipswich Rd SL1 205 A4
Ireland Cl MK7 48 B2
Ireton Ct OX9 125 C1
Iris Cl HP21 115 A3
Ironmonger Ct MK14 34 C3
Irvine Dr HP22 116 A1
Irvine Ho SL4 209 C3
Irving Cres LU7 105 A4
Irving Dale MK7 48 C3
Isaacson Dr MK7 48 B3
Isambard Cl UB8 201 B1
Isis Cl HP21 115 B2
Isis Way SL8 185 A2
Isis Wlk MK3 46 C1
Island Ho UB7 213 A3
Island The MK18 63 B1
Islet Park Dr SL6 196 B2
Islet Park Ho SL6 196 B2
Islet Pk SL6 196 B2
Islet Rd SL6 196 B2
Isling Brook MK5 46 A2
Ivanhoe Cl UB8 208 B4
Iver Heath Cty Mid Sch SL0 200 B2
Iver Heath Jun Sch SL0 200 B1
Iver La SL0 208 A4
Iver Lodge SL0 207 C4
Iver Sta SL0 207 C2
Iver Village Inf Sch SL0 207 C4
Iver Village Jun Sch The SL0 207 C4
Iverdale Cl SL0 207 B3
Ives Rd SL3 207 A2
Ivester Ct LU7 80 C3
Ivinghoe View HP20 102 A1
Ivinghoe Way LU6 92 C1
Ivinghoe YH★ LU7 105 C3
Ivins Rd HP9 175 A1
Ivy Cl Longwick HP27 138 C3
Newport Pagnell MK16 22 C2
Ivy Cotts HP8 177 A4
Ivy Cres SL1 204 C3
Ivy House La HP4 135 C3
Ivy La Bierton HP22 102 B1
Great Brickhill MK17 70 B4
Newton Longville MK17 57 B2
Stewkley LU7 68 C1
Wing LU7 79 B2
Ivy Pl HP14 171 B3
Ivybridge Cl UB8 201 C1
Ivyhill Ct HP27 139 A2

J

Jack's La MK43 8 C3
Jacks Cl MK46 7 C4
Jackson Cl UB10 201 C3
Jackson Ct HP15 163 A2
Jackson Ind Est SL8 185 A1
Jackson Rd
Aylesbury HP19 101 A2
Uxbridge UB10 201 C3
Jacksons Cl LU6 92 C2
Jacob Cl SL4 209 C3
Jacobs Cl MK14 34 B4
Jakeman Way HP21 115 A3
Jakes Ho SL6 203 A4
Jamaica MK6 47 A3
James Cl
Hazelmere HP15 163 A3
Marlow SL7 183 C2
James Elliman Prim Sch SL2 205 C4
James Martin Cl UB9 190 A3
James Rd HP14 171 A2
James St SL4 210 B3
James Way MK1 47 A1
Jane Cl HP21 116 A2
Jansel Sq HP21 116 A3
Japonica La MK15 35 B3
Jardine Cotts SL2 199 A4
Jarman Cl MK18 52 C4
Jarratt Ho SL4 210 A2
Jarry Ct SL7 183 C2
Jarvis Cl HP21 116 A3
Jasmine Cl HP21 116 A2
Jasmine Cres HP27 139 A2
Jason Ho HP12 172 C2
Jasons Hill HP5 145 A1
Jeeves Cl MK6 47 B4
Jefferies Rd HP17 114 A3
Jefferson Cl SL3 207 A1
Jeffrey Wlk HP19 115 A4
Jeffries Ct SL8 185 A1
Jellicoe Cl SL1 205 A2
Jenkins Cl MK5 45 C3
Jenkins Ct HP22 89 B2
Jenkins La HP23 132 C2
Jenna Way MK16 23 A2
Jenner Rd HP21 115 C3
Jennery La SL1 197 B1
Jennings MK14 34 B4
Jennings Field HP10 185 B4
Jennings Wharf SL4 210 B4
Jerome Cl SL7 183 C2
Jersey Rd MK12 33 B3
Jesse's La HP18 125 B3
Job's La SL7 195 A4
John Colet Sch HP22 131 B3
John Hall Way HP11 172 B2
John Hampden Gram Sch (Boys) HP11 172 C2
John Hampden Sch The HP22 131 A3
John Hampden Way HP16 151 A4
John Hellins Prim Sch NN12 18 B2
John Taylor Ct SL1 205 B3
John Watson Sch OX33 122 A1
Johns La HP5 134 C1
Johnson Rd HP14 171 A3
Johnsons Field MK46 6 C2
Johnston Pl MK6 46 C4
Joiner's Cl Botley HP5 145 A1
Chalfont St Peter SL9 177 C2
Joiner's La SL9 177 C2
Joiners Way
Chalfont St Peter SL9 177 C2
Lavendon MK46 7 C4
Jonathan Ct SL6 202 C4
Jonathans MK6 47 A3
Jones Way SL2 187 B1
Jordan YH★ HP9 176 C2
Jordans Fst Sch HP9 176 C2
Jordans La HP9 176 C2
Jordans Way HP9 176 C2
Joules Ct MK5 46 B3
Jourdelay's Pas SL4 210 B4
Journeys End SL2 205 C4
Jubilee Rd
High Wycombe HP11 172 C4
High Wycombe, Downley HP13 161 C1
Stokenchurch HP14 158 C2
Jubilee Terr MK11 32 C3
Judge's La LU7 80 C3
Judy's Pas SL4 205 B1
Juniper Cl HP15 163 A2
Juniper Ct SL1 206 A2
Juniper Dr
High Wycombe HP12 172 B3
Maidenhead SL6 203 A4
Juniper Gdns MK7 48 A4
Juniper Hill Comb Sch HP10 185 A4
Juniper La HP10 185 B4
Juniper Rd SL7 183 B3
Jupiter Hts UB10 201 C2
Juson's Glebe HP22 131 B3
Jutland Ho SL4 209 C3

K

Kalman Gdns MK7 48 B3
Kaplan Cl MK5 46 A3
Katherine Cl
Tylers Green HP10 174 B4
Walton MK7 48 A2
Katrine Pl MK2 58 B3
Kaybridge Cl HP13 173 C3
Kaywood Cl SL3 206 B2
Keach Cl MK18 66 A3
Keasden Ct MK4 46 A1
Keaton Cl MK8 45 B4
Keats Cl
High Wycombe HP11 172 C3
Newport Pagnell MK16 22 A2
Keats La SL4 210 B4
Keats Way
Milton Keynes MK3 57 C4
West Drayton UB7 208 C1
Keble Cl HP19 115 A4
Keble Rd SL6 202 C4
Keel Dr SL1 205 B2
Keeler Cl SL4 209 C2
Keen Cl HP19 115 A4
Keen's Cl HP13 162 C1
Keens La OX39 147 B3
Keensacre SL0 200 B2
Keep Hill Dr HP11 173 B2
Keep Hill Rd HP11 173 B3
Keeper's Cl LU7 105 A4
Keepers Farm Cl SL4 209 C3
Keepers La HP6 153 B2
Keinches La HP22 87 A3
Keith Park Rd UB10 201 C3
Kellan Dr MK6 35 A1
Keller Cl MK11 33 A1
Kelpatrick Rd SL1 204 B4
Kelsey Cl SL6 202 B2
Kelso Cl MK3 57 B3
Kelvin Cl HP13 172 C4
Kelvin Dr MK5 46 B3
Kemble Ct MK15 35 A3
Kempe Cl SL3 207 B1
Kemps Piece HP17 127 A3
Kempson Cl HP19 101 A1
Kempton Gdns MK3 57 B3
Kemsley Chase SL2 198 B2
Kenchester MK13 33 C3
Kendal Cl
Aylesbury HP21 116 A3
Slough SL2 206 A3
Kendal Dr SL2 206 A3
Kendal Gdns LU7 80 B4
Kendalls Cl HP13 173 C3
Kendrick Rd SL3 206 A2
Kenilworth Cl SL1 205 C2
Kenilworth Dr
Aylesbury HP19 101 B1
Milton Keynes MK3 57 C4
Kenneally SL4 209 B3
Kenneally Cl 11 SL4 209 B3
Kenneally Pl 12 SL4 209 B3
Kenneally Row 13 SL4 209 B3
Kenneally Wlk 10 SL4 209 B3
Kennedy Ave HP11 173 A2
Kennedy Cl
Farnham Common SL2 198 B3
Maidenhead SL6 202 B3
Marlow SL7 183 C2
Kennedy Ct 5 LU7 80 C4
Kennedy Ho SL1 204 B3
Kennel La SL7 195 B4
Kennet Cl
Aylesbury HP21 115 B2
High Wycombe HP13 162 B1
Kennet Dr MK3 57 C4
Kennet Pl MK3 57 C4
Kennet Rd SL6 202 C4
Kennett Rd
Bourne End SL8 185 A2
Slough SL3 207 A2
Kennington Cl MK16 22 B2
Kennish Cl MK18 65 C2
Kensington Dr MK8 33 C1
Kensington Pl MK46 6 C3
Kent Ave SL1 205 B4
Kent Cl UB8 201 B3
Kent Lodge 6 SL6 202 C3
Kent Way SL6 195 C1
Kentmere Rd HP21 116 A4
Kenton Cl SL7 183 C1
Kenton Ct HP19 101 B1
Kenton's La SL4 209 C3
Kents Hill Fst Sch MK7 48 A4
Kents Hill Rdbt MK10 47 C4
Kents Rd MK14 34 B4
Kenway Dr HP7 166 A4
Kenwell Ct MK15 35 B2
Kenwood Cl SL6 202 A4
Kenwood Dr WD3 178 C4
Kenwood Gate MK6 35 A1
Keppel Ave MK19 20 B1
Keppel St SL4 210 B3
Kepwick MK8 33 C1
Kercroft MK8 33 C1
Kernow Cres MK6 35 A1
Kerria Pl MK3 47 A2
Kerry Cl HP19 101 A2
Kersey MK14 34 B4
Kesters Rd HP5 154 B4
Kestrel Cl
17 Berkhamsted HP4 135 B2
High Wycombe HP13 161 B1
Kestrel Dr HP15 163 A3
Kestrel Path SL2 197 C1
Kestrel Way
Aylesbury HP20 101 C2
Buckingham MK18 52 C4
Keswick Ct SL2 205 C3
Keswick Rd MK19 11 A1
Ketchmere Cl HP18 125 B3
Ketelbey Nook MK7 48 C3
Ketton Cl MK15 35 B4
Kew Ct MK8 33 C1
Kew Gr HP11 173 A2
Keyes Way MK18 41 C1
Keynes Cl MK16 22 C2
Keys Pl SL6 202 C3
Khasiaberry MK7 48 A3
Kidd Cl MK8 45 C3
Kidderminster Rd SL2 198 A1
Kidwells Cl SL6 202 C4
Kidwells Park Dr SL6 202 C4
Kildonan Pl MK12 33 B2
Kilfillan Gdns HP4 135 A2
Kilfillan Pk HP4 135 A2
Kilkenny Ho MK4 45 C1
Killarney Dr SL6 202 C4
Kiln Ave HP6 155 B1
Kiln Cl HP16 151 B4
Kiln Croft Cl SL7 184 A2
Kiln Ct HP9 186 A4
Kiln Farm Ind Est MK11 33 A2
Kiln Farm Rdbt MK11 33 A2
Kiln Fields SL6,SL8 185 C1
Kiln La Botley HP5 155 A4
Bourne End SL8,HP10 185 B2
Hedgerley SL2 187 B2
Lacey Green HP27 149 C3
Kiln Pl SL6 195 A2
Kiln Pond La HP13 161 B2
Kiln Rd HP16 151 A4
Kiln The HP5 144 B1
Kilner Rd HP21 115 C3
Kilnwood HP14 150 A1
Kilpin Gn MK16 24 A3
Kilwinning Dr MK10 35 C1
Kimbells Cl HP18 124 B1
Kimber Cl SL4 210 A2
Kimber's La SL6 202 C2
Kimberley Cl SL3 206 C1
Kimbers Dr SL1 197 B1
Kimble Ct HP22 129 C2
Kimblewick Rd HP17 129 B3
Kimbolton Ct MK14 35 A4
Kincardine Dr MK3 46 C2
Kindermann Ct MK5 46 A3
Kindleton MK14 34 C4
Kinellan Ct HP9 175 B2
King Charles Cl MK18 41 C1
King Edward Ave HP21 116 A4
King Edward Ct 15 SL4 210 B3
King Edward St
Milton Keynes MK13 33 C4
Slough SL1 205 B2
King Edward VII Ave SL4 210 C4
King Edward VII Hospl SL4 210 B2
King George Cres MK11 32 C3
King George V Rd HP6 154 B1
King John's Cl TW19 211 B1
King St Chesham HP5 154 A4
Lane End HP14 160 B1
Maidenhead SL6 202 C3
Milton Keynes MK11 32 C3
Tring HP23 119 A2
King Stable St SL4 210 B4
King's Gr SL6 202 C3
King's La
Great Missenden HP16 141 B1
Lee Common HP16,HP22 141 C4
South Heath HP16 152 C4
Wendover HP16 141 B1
King's Rd Aylesbury HP21 115 C4
Henley-on-T RG9 191 B1
High Wycombe HP11 173 C2
Slough SL1 205 C2
Uxbridge UB8 201 B2
Windsor SL4 210 B2
King's Road Ho 29 SL4 210 B3
King's Terr SL3 212 A4
King's Wood Inf Sch HP13 173 C4
King's Wood Jun Sch HP13 173 C4
Kingfisher HP20 101 C2
Kingfisher Cl HP16 151 B3
Kingfisher Ct
3 High Wycombe HP11 173 A3
Slough SL2 198 A1
Kingfisher Ctr The MK16 22 B1
Kingfisher Ho HP11 174 A2
Kingfisher Rd MK18 52 C4
Kinghorn La SL6 195 B2
Kinghorn Pk SL6 195 B2
Kings Cl
Beaconsfield HP9 186 A4
Chalfont St Giles HP8 177 B4
Henley-on-T RG9 191 B1
Worminghall HP18 123 B3
Kings Ct HP4 135 B3
Kings Farm Rd WD3 167 B2
Kings Head Par HP22 131 A2
Kings La SL7 195 A4
Kings Lodge HP6 154 B1
Kings Mdw HP22 102 B2
Kings Mead LU6 92 C2
Kings Oak Cl HP27 139 B3
Kings Rd
Berkhamsted HP4 135 A2
Chalfont St Giles HP8 177 B4
West Drayton UB7 208 C2
Kings Ride HP10 163 A1
Kings Sq HP11 173 C2
Kings St LU7 78 C4
Kings Wlk
Henley-on-T RG9 191 B1
4 Maidenhead SL6 202 C4
Kings Wood SL7 193 B4
Kingsbridge MK4 46 B1
Kingsbrook Sch MK19 31 C2
Kingsbury HP20 115 B4
Kingsbury Dr SL4 211 A1
Kingscote Sch SL9 188 C4
Kingsdale Rd HP4 135 A2
Kingsey Rd OX9 126 B1
Kingsfield SL4 209 B3
Kingsfold MK13 34 A4
Kingsgate HP19 115 A4
Kingshill Dr MK19 31 C3
Kingshill Rd
Great Kingshill HP13,HP15 162 B2
High Wycombe HP13, HP15 162 B2
Kingshill Way HP4 135 A1
Kingsland Rd HP21 116 A2
Kingsley Cl MK16 21 C2
Kingsley Cres HP11 172 C3
Kingsley Dr SL7 183 B3
Kingsley Path SL2 197 B1
Kingsley Wlk HP23 119 A2
Kingsmead HP27 139 A3
Kingsmead Ho SL1 205 B3
Kingsmead Office Campus HP11 174 A2
Kingsmead Rd
High Wycombe HP11 173 C2
Loudwater HP11 174 A2
Kingsmead Rdbt MK4 56 C4
Kingsoe Leys MK10 36 A1
Kingston Ave
Milton Keynes MK11 32 C3
West Drayton UB7 208 C3
Kingston Hill OX39,HP14 158 A4
Kingston La
Uxbridge UB8 201 C1
West Drayton UB7 208 C2
Kingston Rd HP13 162 B1
Kingston Rdbt MK10 36 B1
Kingsway
Farnham Common SL2 198 B3
Gerrards Cross SL9 188 C4
Iver SL0 207 C4
Kingswood Ave HP10 174 A4
Kingswood Creek TW19 211 B1
Kingswood Ct SL6 202 C3
Kingswood Ho SL2 205 B4
Kingswood La HP18 96 C3
Kingswood Par SL7 183 B3
Kingswood Pl HP13 162 C1
Kingswood Rd HP10 163 A1
Kingswood View HP13 162 C1
Kinloch Pl MK2 58 C3
Kinnaird Cl SL1 204 B4
Kinnear Cl MK8 45 C4
Kinross Dr MK3 46 C1
Kinson Gn HP20 101 C2
Kipling Ct SL4 210 A3
Kipling Dr MK16 21 C2
Kipling Rd MK3 58 A4
Kippell Hill MK46 6 C3
Kirby Est UB7 208 B3
Kirke Cl MK5 46 A3
Kirkeby Cl MK14 34 B3
Kirkham Ct MK5 46 B4
Kirkstall Pl MK6 46 B4
Kirkwall Spur SL1 205 C4
Kirtle Rd HP5 144 B1
Kirtlington MK15 35 A3
Kitchener Rd HP11 172 C4
Kite Field HP4 134 C4
Kite Hill MK6 47 A4
Kite Wood Rd HP10 163 A1
Kitelee Cl MK19 11 A2
Kitsbury Ct HP4 135 A2
Kitsbury Rd HP4 135 A2
Kitsbury Terr HP4 135 A2
Kittiwake HP20 101 C2
Klee Cl HP22 85 A3
Klondyke SL7 183 B1
Knapp Gate MK5 45 C4
Knaves Beech HP10 174 B1
Knaves Beech Bsns Ctr HP10 174 B1
Knaves Beech Ind Est HP10 174 B1
Knaves Beech Way HP10 174 B1
Knaves Hill LU7 80 B4
Knaves Hollow HP10 174 B1
Knebworth Gate MK14 22 A1
Knighton Way La UB9 201 A3
Knights Cl Eaton Bray LU6 92 C3
Great Brickhill MK17 59 B1
Windsor SL4 209 B3
Knights Ct LU6 92 C3
Knights Hill HP12 172 C3
Knights Pl 35 SL4 210 B3
Knights Templar Way HP11 173 A2
Knoll Cl MK16 13 C1
Knoll The MK17 49 A1
Knolls Cl HP22 89 A2
Knolton Way SL2 206 B4
Knottocks Cl HP9 175 B3
Knottocks Dr HP9 175 B3
Knottocks End HP9 175 B3
Knowl Gate MK5 46 B4
Knowland Way UB9 189 C3
Knowles Cl UB7 208 C3
Knowles Cty Fst Sch MK2 58 B4
Knowles Cty Mid Sch MK2 58 B4
Knowles Gn MK2 58 B4
Knowlhill Rdbt MK5 46 B3
Knowsley Cl SL6 195 A1
Knox Bridge MK7 48 A4
Kola Ho SL2 206 A3
Kop Hill Rd HP27 139 B2
Krohn Cl MK18 52 C4
Krypton Cl MK5 46 B3
Kynaston Ave HP21 115 C2
Kynaston Sch HP21 115 C2

L

La Roche Cl SL3 206 B2
Laburnham Cotts LU7 69 C2
Laburnham Rd SL6 202 C3
Laburnum Ave UB7 208 C3
Laburnum Cl SL7 183 C2
Laburnum Gr
Milton Keynes MK2 58 C4
Slough SL3 212 A4
Laburnum Rd HP12 172 B3
Lace Mews MK46 7 A2
Lacemakers
Chinnor OX39 147 B3
Long Crendon HP18 125 B4
Lacey Dr HP14 161 B4
Lacey Green Windmill★ HP27 149 B3
Laceys Dr HP15 163 A3
Lacy Dr MK15 35 A4
Ladbroke Cl HP20 101 C1
Ladbroke Rd SL1 205 B2
Lady Verney Cl HP13 173 A4
Lady Yorke Pk SL0 200 C3
Ladybridge Terr MK43 8 C3
Ladyday Pl SL1 205 B3
Ladymead Cl MK17 56 A4
Ladysmith Rd LU7 105 C3
Ladywalk WD3 178 C3
Laggan Ct MK2 58 B2
Laggan Rd SL6 195 C1

Laggan Sq SL6 ....195 C1
Lagger Cl HP8 ....177 A4
Lagger The HP8 ....177 A4
Lagonda Cl MK16 ....22 C2
Laidon Cl MK2 ....58 B2
Lake Ave SL1 ....205 B3
Lake Cl MK18 ....66 A3
Lake End Ct SL6 ....204 A4
Lake End Rd SL4,SL6 ....204 A3
Lake View SL6 ....196 A1
Lake's Cotts LU7 ....90 B4
Laker Ct MK6 ....46 C4
Lakes La
  Beaconsfield HP9 ....186 C4
  Newport Pagnell MK16 ....22 A3
Lakes The SL7 ....194 A3
Lakeside Aylesbury HP20 .101 C2
  Maidenhead SL6 ....196 A1
  Tring HP23 ....119 A3
Lakeside Dr SL2 ....198 C2
Lakeside Est SL3 ....212 C4
Lakeside Rd SL3 ....212 C4
Lamb Cl MK16 ....22 A2
Lamb La MK7 ....48 B4
Lambe Rd HP22 ....131 B3
Lamberhurst Gr MK7 ....48 A4
Lambert Ave SL3 ....206 C2
Lambert Wlk OX9 ....125 C1
Lamberts Croft MK17 ....33 B3
Lambourn Ct MK4 ....46 B1
Lambourne Ave HP21 .115 B2
Lambourne Ct
  Maidenhead SL6 ....203 B4
  Uxbridge UB8 ....201 A1
Lambourne Dr SL6 ....202 B2
Lambridge La RG9 ....191 B2
Lambridge Wood Rd
  RG9 ....191 A2
Lambscroft Way SL9 .177 C1
Lambtons Way MK18 .....66 A3
Lamesley Ho SL6 ....202 B4
Lammas MK6 ....47 A4
Lammas Ave 32 SL4 .210 B3
Lammas Ct SL4 ....210 B3
Lammas La HP21 ....112 A1
Lammas Path HP18 ....112 A1
Lammas Rd
  Cheddington LU7 ....105 A4
  Slough SL1 ....204 B4
Lammas Way
  Lane End HP14 ....171 A2
  Loudwater HP10 ....174 B1
Lampitts Cross MK6 ....47 A3
Lamport Ct MK8 ....46 A4
Lamva Ct MK11 ....32 C3
Lancaster Ave SL2 ....198 B1
Lancaster Cl TW19 ....213 C1
Lancaster Ct HP12 ....172 B2
Lancaster Dr HP3 ....145 C2
Lancaster Gate MK3 ....57 C4
Lancaster Rd
  Aylesbury HP21 ....116 A3
  High Wycombe HP12 .172 C2
  Maidenhead SL6 ....202 A4
  Uxbridge UB8 ....201 B3
Lancaster Ride HP10 .174 A4
Lancastria Mews SL6 .202 B4
Lance Way HP13 ....174 A3
Lancelot Cl SL1 ....205 A2
Lanchester Rd MK43 ....24 B1
Lancot Ave LU6 ....93 C4
Lancot Dr LU6 ....93 C4
Lancot Lower Com Sch
  LU6 ....93 C4
Lancotbury Cl LU6 ....93 A4
Lancresse Cl UB8 ....201 A1
Lander Rd HP10 ....100 C2
Landrace Ct MK5 ....45 C2
Lands The LU7 ....79 C2
Landsborough Gate
  MK15 ....35 B4
Lane End HP4 ....134 C2
Lane End Rd HP12 ....172 A3
Lane The
  Grafton Regis NN12 ....9 B1
  Mursley MK17 ....67 B3
Lane Wood Cl HP7 ....165 C4
Lanercost Cres MK10 ....36 A1
Lanfranc Gdns HP15 ....35 A4
Langcliffe Dr MK13 ....34 B3
Langdale Cl
  Maidenhead SL6 ....203 B4
  Milton Keynes MK2 ....58 B2
Langdale Ho HP11 ....174 A2
Langdon Ave HP21 ....116 A3
Langdon St HP23 ....119 A2
Langerstone La MK4 ....46 A1
Langland Comb Sch MK6 47 B3
Langland Ho MK6 ....47 B3
Langlands MK46 ....7 C4
Langley Broom SL3 .206 C1
Langley Bsns Ctr SL3 .207 A2
Langley Bsns Pk SL3 .207 C2
Langley Cl MK18 ....65 C2
Langley Cnr SL3 ....199 C3
Langley Gram Sch SL3 206 C1
Langley Manor Sch The
  SL3 ....206 C1
Langley Park Ctry Pk*
  SL0,SL3 ....200 A1
Langley Park Rd SL0 .207 B4
Langley Rd SL3 ....206 C2
Langley Sta SL3 ....207 B4
Langley Way SL7 ....183 B1
Langleywood Sch SL3 .206 C2

Langston Ct HP12 ....172 B4
Langstone Cl HP20 ....101 C2
Langton Cl 28 HP20 ....101 C2
Langton Cl
  Maidenhead SL6 ....202 B4
  Slough SL1 ....204 B3
Langton Dr MK8 ....33 C2
Langton's Mdw SL2 .198 B3
Lanner Wlk MK6 ....47 A4
Lanrick Copse HP4 .135 C3
Lansdell Ave HP12 ....172 A4
Lansdown Rd SL1 ....177 B1
Lansdowne Ave SL1 .205 C3
Lansdowne Ct SL1 ....205 C3
Lansdowne
  Cty Comb Sch HP12 .172 B2
Lansdowne Rd
  Aylesbury HP20 ....101 B1
  Chesham HP5 ....144 B1
Lansdowne Way HP11 .172 C2
Lantern Way UB7 ....208 C2
Lanterns Wlk SL6 ....203 A4
Lanthorn Cl MK14 ....34 C3
Lappetts La HP16 ....152 C4
Larch Cl Aylesbury HP20 .102 A1
  Slough SL2 ....205 A4
  Tylers Green HP10 .163 B1
Larch Gr MK2 ....58 C4
Larch Rise HP4 ....135 A3
Larches The
  Berkhamsted HP4 ....134 B3
  Holmer Green HP15 .163 B4
  Little Chalfont HP6 .155 A1
Larchfield Prim Sch
  SL6 ....202 B2
Larchfield Rd SL6 ....202 C3
Larchlands The HP10 .163 B4
Larchmoor Pk SL2 .199 A4
Larchwood HP16 ....152 A4
Lark Cl MK18 ....52 C4
Lark Rise HP15 ....163 A3
Lark Vale HP20 ....101 C2
Larkfield Cl HP13 ....162 C1
Larkin Cl MK18 ....22 C1
Larkings La SL2 ....199 A2
Larks Rise HP5 ....154 B3
Larkspur Ave MK14 ....34 C3
Larkspur Way HP15 .162 C3
Larvic Rd HP21 ....115 B3
Larwood Pl MK6 ....34 C1
Lasborough Rd MK10 ...36 B1
Lascelles Cl MK5 ....35 A4
Lascelles Ho 15 SL1 .206 A2
Lascelles Rd SL3 ....206 A2
Laser Cl MK5 ....46 B3
Lashlake Rd OX9 ....125 C1
Lassell Gdns SL6 ....203 A4
Lastingham Gr MK4 ....46 A1
Latchmoor Ave SL9 .188 B4
Latchmoor Gr SL9 .188 B4
Latchmoor Way SL9 .188 B4
Latimer Latimer HP5 .155 C1
  Milton Keynes MK11 .....32 C2
Latimer Ct HP6 ....166 B4
Latimer Ct HP20 ....116 A4
Latimer Rd HP5 ....155 B1
Latimer Way HP9 ....175 B3
Laud's Cl RG9 ....191 B1
Launceston Ct MK5 ....46 B3
Launde MK10 ....36 A1
Laurel Ave SL3 ....206 C2
Laurel Bank HP3 ....146 C4
Laurel Cl
  Lacey Green HP27 ....150 B2
  Milton Keynes MK8 .....45 B4
  Poyle SL3 ....212 C4
  Prestwood HP16 ....150 B2
Laurel Ct Amersham HP6 .154 B2
  Iver Heath SL0 ....200 B3
Laurel Dr
  Loudwater HP11 ....174 A2
  Walter's Ash HP14 .161 B4
Laurel La UB7 ....208 C1
Laurel Rd SL6 ....177 B1
Laurel Way 9 HP21 .115 C3
Laurels Rd SL0 ....200 B2
Laurels The
  High Wycombe HP12 .172 B2
  Milton Keynes MK1 .....47 B1
Laurence Cl SL7 ....183 B1
Lautrec Way HP19 ....100 C1
Lautree Gdns SL8 ....195 C4
Lavender Cl HP21 ....115 A3
Lavender Gr MK7 ....48 A3
Lavender Rd UB8 ....208 C4
Lavender Way HP15 .162 C3
Lavender Wlk HP21 ....115 A3
Lavendon Comb Sch
  MK46 ....7 C4
Lavendon Rd MK46 ....7 A3
Lawford Ave WD3 ....167 B2
Lawkland SL2 ....198 B1
Lawn Ave UB7 ....208 B2
Lawn Cl SL3 ....211 B4
Lawn Hill HP18 ....73 A4
Lawn House La HP18 ....72 C1
Lawn Rd UB8 ....201 B3
Lawn The SL3 ....211 B3
Lawns The Brill HP18 ....96 A1
  Tylers Green HP10 .163 A1
Lawnsmead Gdns MK16 .22 B3
Lawrence Cl SL4 ....210 B3
Lawrence Gr HP16 ....151 B3
Lawrence Way SL1 .204 B4
Lawrence Wlk MK16 ....21 C1
Lawson Pl MK5 ....46 A3

Lawsone Rise HP13 ....162 A1
Laxton Gn SL6 ....202 B2
Lay Rd HP19 ....101 A1
Layer's Ave SL9 ....177 B1
Layter's Ave S SL9 ....177 B1
Layter's Cl SL9 ....177 B1
Layter's End SL9 ....177 A1
Layters Green La SL9 .177 A1
Layters Way SL9 ....188 B3
Lea Cl SL7 ....183 B3
Lea Ct HP7 ....165 C4
Lea Inf Sch SL2 ....206 A3
Lea Jun Sch SL2 ....206 A3
Lea La HP18 ....125 C2
Leach Rd HP21 ....115 B4
Leachcroft SL9 ....177 A1
Leacroft Cl UB7 ....208 C3
Leacroft Rd SL0 ....207 C4
Leadenhall Rdbt MK6 ....46 A4
Leaders Cl HP22 ....89 C2
Leafield Rise MK8 ....33 B1
Leafy La HP27 ....118 C1
Leaholme Gdns SL1 .204 B4
Leapingwell La MK18 .....66 A3
Leary Cres MK16 ....22 C2
Leas Cl HP13 ....173 C4
Leas Dr SL0 ....207 C4
Leaside MK16 ....12 A3
Leasowe Pl MK13 ....34 B2
Leather La HP22 ....142 A2
Leaver Rd RG9 ....191 B1
Leckhampstead Rd
  Akeley MK18 ....42 A4
  Wicken MK19 ....31 A2
Ledborough Gate HP9 .175 C2
Ledborough La HP9 ....175 C2
Ledborough Wood HP9 .175 C2
Ledburn Gr LU7 ....80 C3
Ledbury MK14 ....21 C1
Ledeview Ct HP11 ....174 A2
Ledger's Rd SL1 ....205 B2
Lee Common CE Sch
  HP16 ....142 B3
Lee Cres HP17 ....114 B3
Lee Farm Cl HP5 ....145 A1
Lee Ho 2 MK2 ....58 B4
Lee La SL6 ....194 C1
Lee Rd Aylesbury HP21 .115 B3
  Bledlow Ridge HP27 .148 C3
  Quainton HP22 ....85 A3
Leeches Way LU7 ....105 A4
Leeds Rd SL1 ....205 C3
Lees Cl SL6 ....202 A3
Lees Gdns SL6 ....202 A3
Lees Wlk SL7 ....183 B1
Leeson Gdns SL4 ....204 C1
Legoland Windsor*
  SL4 ....209 B1
Leicester Ct RG9 ....191 B2
Leigh Hill MK4 ....46 B1
Leigh Pk SL3 ....211 A4
Leigh Rd SL1 ....205 A3
Leigh Sq SL4 ....209 B3
Leigh St HP11 ....172 C4
Leighton Buzzard Sta
  LU7 ....80 C4
Leighton Gdns SL6 .196 A1
Leighton Ho 5 SL7 .183 C1
Leighton Mid Sch LU7 .80 C3
Leighton Rd
  Edlesborough LU6 ....92 B2
  Leighton Buzzard LU7 .80 C4
  Soulbury LU7 ....70 A1
  Stoke Hammond MK17 ...69 C4
  Wing LU7 ....80 A2
  Wingrave HP22 ....89 B2
Leighton St MK17 ....60 C3
Leiston Spur SL1 ....205 C4
Leisure Plaza MK9 ....46 B4
Leith Cl SL1 ....206 A3
Leith Rd HP19 ....115 A4
Lembrook Wlk HP21 ....115 A4
Lennox Dr MK8 ....45 C4
Lennox Rd MK2 ....58 B4
Lent Gn SL1 ....197 A1
Lent Green La SL1 ....197 A1
Lent Rise Comb Sch
  SL1 ....204 A4
Lent Rise Rd SL1 ....197 A1
Lenthall Cl MK13 ....34 A2
Leon Ave MK2 ....58 B4
Leon Sch MK2 ....58 B3
Leonards Cl HP12 ....172 C1
Leopard Dr MK15 ....35 A4
Leopold Mall 12 SL1 .205 C2
Leopold Rd LU7 ....80 B4
Lerwick Dr SL1 ....205 C4
Lester Cl MK7 ....48 B4
Lester Gr HP15 ....163 A2
Lesters Rd SL7 ....195 B3
Letchfield HP5 ....155 A4
Letter Box La HP27 .139 C2
Leven Cl
  Leighton Buzzard LU7 ....80 A4
  Milton Keynes MK2 ....58 B2
Leverkus Ct OX39 ....147 B3
Leverkus Ho OX39 ....147 B3
Levings Cl HP19 ....101 A2
Lewes Cl SL1 ....205 B2
Lewes Ho MK3 ....57 B4
Lewins Farm Ct 4 SL1 .204 C3
Lewins Rd SL9 ....188 B4
Lewins Way SL1 ....204 B4
Lewis Cl MK16 ....21 C1
Lewis La SL9 ....177 C1

Lewknor CE Sch OX49 .157 A4
Lewknor Cl OX49 ....157 A4
Lexham Gdns MK4 ....46 B1
Lexington Ave SL6 .202 B3
Ley Hill Rd HP3 ....145 C1
Ley Hill Sch HP5 ....145 A1
Leybourne Gdns OX39 .147 B4
Leyburne Cl LU7 ....90 B4
Leyfield Rd HP21 ....115 C3
Leyland Pl 3 MK6 ....34 C1
Leylands La TW19 ....212 A1
Leys Cl MK5 ....46 A4
Leys La MK18 ....62 A4
Leys Rd MK5 ....46 A4
Leys The Amersham HP6 .154 A2
  Buckingham MK18 ....41 C2
  Halton HP22 ....117 B1
  Tring HP23 ....119 A2
  Woburn Sands MK17 .....49 A2
  Yardley Hastings NN7 ....1 A3
Leys View MK16 ....13 C1
Leywood Cl HP7 ....165 C4
Libra Ho HP10 ....185 A4
Lichfield Down MK7 ....48 A3
Lichfield Ho HP21 ....115 C4
Liddall Way UB7 ....208 C3
Liddel SL4 ....209 B3
Liddell Pl SL4 ....209 B2
Liddell Sq 14 SL4 ....209 B3
Liddell Way SL4 ....209 B2
Liffre Dr HP22 ....131 A3
Lightfoot Ct MK7 ....47 C3
Lightlands La SL8 .195 C3
Ligo Ave HP22 ....116 B2
Lilac Cl MK17 ....57 B2
Lilac Ct SL2 ....197 C1
Lilac Pl UB7 ....208 C3
Lilies The HP22 ....87 B1
Lilleshall Ave MK10 ....35 C1
Lilley Way SL1 ....204 C3
Lillibrooke Cres SL6 .202 B2
Lilly Bottom La HP27 .150 A4
Lilly Hill MK46 ....6 C3
Lillyfee Farm La HP10 .186 A3
Lily Dr UB7 ....208 B1
Lily's Wlk HP11 ....173 A3
Limbaud Cl MK7 ....48 A3
Lime Ave
  Buckingham MK18 ....52 C4
  High Wycombe HP11 .173 B4
  West Drayton UB8 ....208 C3
Lime Cl Hazelmere HP15 .163 A2
  Newport Pagnell MK16 ....22 C4
Lime Gr Chinnor OX39 .147 B3
  Leighton Buzzard LU7 ....80 C4
  Woburn Sands MK17 .....49 A2
Lime Rd
  Princes Risborough HP27 .139 A2
  Yardley Gobion NN12 ....18 C3
Lime St MK46 ....6 C3
Lime Tree Cl HP15 .162 B4
Lime Tree Wlk HP7 .165 C4
Lime Wlk
  Maidenhead SL6 ....202 A4
  New Denham UB9 ....201 B3
Limerick La MK9 ....35 A2
Limes Ave HP21 ....116 A4
Limes The
  Amersham HP6 ....154 A2
  Milton Keynes, Fenny Stratford
  MK2 ....58 C4
  Milton Keynes, Stony Stratford
  MK11 ....32 C3
Limes Way HP18 ....124 B1
Limmer La HP12 ....172 A2
Limmers Mead HP15 .162 B4
Linceslade Gr MK5 ....46 A4
Linchfield HP13 ....173 C4
Linchfield Rd SL3 ....211 B4
Lincoln MK14 ....34 B4
Lincoln Cl HP22 ....116 A1
Lincoln Ct
  Berkhamsted HP4 ....135 A2
  22 Slough SL1 ....205 C2
Lincoln Park Bsns Ctr
  HP12 ....172 B2
Lincoln Pk
  Amersham HP7 ....165 C4
  Brackley NN13 ....38 C2
Lincoln Rd
  Chalfont St Peter SL9 .177 C1
  High Wycombe HP12 .172 C3
  Maidenhead SL6 ....202 A4
Lincoln Way SL1 ....204 B3
Lincolns The HP16 ....152 A2
Lincombe Slade LU7 ....80 C4
Lincroft MK43 ....25 A1
Linden SL3 ....207 A4
Linden Ave SL6 ....195 C4
Linden Ct HP12 ....172 B3
Linden Dr
  Chalfont St Peter SL9 .177 C1
  Farnham Common SL2 .198 B2
Linden End HP21 ....115 C3
Linden Gr MK14 ....34 C4
Linden Lea HP22 ....131 A3
Linden Way MK17 ....128 A4
Linden Wlk HP15 .163 A2
Lindens The HP5 ....146 C4
Lindisfarne Dr MK10 ....36 A1
Lindlay Ave HP12 ....172 C4
Lindsay Ct TW19 ....213 B1
Lindsey Rd UB9 ....190 A4
Lines Hill HP22 ....88 A2
Lines Rd HP14 ....171 A3

Lines The HP22 ....88 B2
Linfields HP7 ....166 B4
Linford Ave MK16 ....22 A2
Linford La
  Milton Keynes, Willen MK15 .35 B4
  Milton Keynes, Woolstone
  MK15 ....35 B2
Linford Lakes (Nature
  Reserve)* MK14 ....21 C1
Lingfield MK12 ....33 C2
Lingfield Cl HP13 ....174 A1
Lingholm Cl SL6 ....202 B3
Linington Ave HP5 .145 A1
Link Cl HP12 ....172 B3
Link Rd Datchet SL3 .211 B1
  High Wycombe HP12 .172 B3
  South Heath HP16 ....152 A2
Link The Hazelmere HP15 .163 A3
  Slough SL2 ....206 A4
Link Way UB9 ....190 A3
Links App HP10 ....185 A4
Links Rd HP10 ....185 A4
Links Way HP10 ....185 A4
Linkswood Rd SL1 .197 B2
Linnet Cl HP22 ....172 A2
Linnet Dr HP18 ....98 B3
Linney Ct MK4 ....46 A1
Linslade Lower Sch LU7 .80 B4
Linslade Mid Sch LU7 .80 C3
Linslade Rd LU7 ....70 C2
Lintlaw Pl MK3 ....47 A2
Linton Cl MK13 ....34 B2
Lintott Ct TW19 ....213 B1
Linx The MK3 ....47 A1
Lionel Ave HP22 ....131 A3
Lionel Ct HP22 ....131 A3
Lipscomb La MK5 ....46 A4
Lipscombe Dr MK18 ....41 C1
Lisburn Path 1 HP20 .101 C1
Lisle Rd HP13 ....162 A1
Lisleys Field HP15 ....162 B4
Lismore Pk SL2 ....205 C4
Lissel Rd MK6 ....47 C3
Lisset Rd SL6 ....203 A3
Lister Gn HP21 ....115 C3
Liston Ct 4 SL7 ....183 B1
Liston Rd SL7 ....183 B1
Litcham Spur SL1 ....205 B4
Little Balmer MK18 ....52 C3
Little Benty UB7 ....208 B1
Little Boltons 7 SL7 .183 C1
Little Bridge Rd HP4 .135 B2
Little Britain HP18 ....99 A4
Little Buntings SL4 .209 C2
Little Chalfont Com Sch
  HP6 ....166 C4
Little Chartridge Ct
  HP5 ....144 A1
Little Cl Aylesbury HP20 .101 B1
  High Wycombe HP12 .172 C2
Little Dunmow MK10 ....36 A1
Little Gaddesden CE Sch
  HP4 ....121 B4
Little Gaddesden Ho
  HP4 ....121 B4
Little Greencroft HP5 .144 A2
Little Habton 3 MK4 ....46 A1
Little Ham La HP27 .139 A3
Little Hame MK10 ....35 C2
Little Hampden Cl HP22 131 A2
Little Hill WD3 ....167 B2
Little Hivings HP5 .144 A2
Little Hollis HP16 ....151 C4
Little Hoo HP23 ....118 C2
Little Horwood Manor
  MK17 ....55 C2
Little Horwood Rd
  Great Horwood MK17 ....55 B2
  Little Horwood MK17 ....55 B2
Little Hundridge La
  HP16 ....153 A4
Little Kimble Sta HP17 .129 C1
Little Kingshill
  Comb Sch HP16 ....152 A1
Little La
  Lacey Green HP27 ....149 B2
  Yardley Hastings NN7 ....1 A4
Little Linford La MK16,
  MK19 ....21 C2
Little London
  Deanshanger MK19 ....31 C2
  Whitchurch HP22 ....87 A3
Little London Gn HP18 .109 C3
Little Marlow CE Sch
  SL8 ....184 B3
Little Marlow Rd SL7 .183 C2
Little Marsh Rd OX27 .72 A2
Little Mdw MK5 ....46 B4
Little Missenden CE Sch
  HP7 ....153 A1
Little Mollards HP22 ....89 A2
Little Orchard Cl HP27 .138 C3
Little Orchards HP20 .101 C2
Little Pk Bovingdon HP3 .146 C4
  Princes Risborough HP27 .139 B2
Little Reeves Ave HP7 .165 A4
Little Shardeloes HP7 .165 A4
Little Spinney MK43 ....25 B2
Little Spring HP5 ....144 A2
Little St NN7 ....1 A3
Little Stanton MK14 ....34 B3
Little Stocking MK5 ....46 A2
Little Sutton La SL3 .207 B1
Little Tring Rd HP22 .118 C3

Little Twye Rd HP23 ....132 C2
Little Windmill Hill
WD4 ....156 C4
Little Woodlands SL4 ..209 C2
Littlebrook Ave SL2 ....204 C4
Littlecote MK8 ....34 A1
Littledown Cotts SL1 ...205 C3
Littledown Rd SL1 ......205 C3
Littledown Sch SL1 .....205 C3
Littlefield Ct UB7 ......213 B4
Littlemarsh MK7 ....48 A3
Littlemere MK8 ....33 B1
Littleport Spur SL1 ....205 C4
Littlewood HP14 ....158 C3
Littleworth LU7 ....79 C2
Littleworth Rd
Hedgerley SL1 ....186 B1
High Wycombe HP13 ...161 C1
Litton Ct HP10 ....174 A1
Liverpool Rd SL1 ....205 A4
Liverpool Victoria Ho 10
HP13 ....173 A4
Livesey Hill MK5 ....46 A3
Livingstone Dr MK15 .....35 B3
Lloyds MK6 ....47 A4
Loakes Ho HP11 ....173 A3
Loakes Rd HP11 ....173 A3
Lochinvar Ct SL1 ....205 A2
Lochnell Rd HP4 ....134 C3
Lochy Dr MK7 ....80 B4
Lock Ave SL6 ....196 B4
Lock Bridge Rd SL8 ....185 A2
Lock La Cosgrove MK19 ..19 C1
Maidenhead SL6 ....202 B2
Lock Mead SL6 ....196 B1
Lock Path SL4 ....209 B4
Lock Rd SL7 ....183 C1
Lock View La MK1 ....47 C1
Lockbridge Ct SL6 .....203 B4
Locke Cl HP19 ....101 A1
Locke Gdns SL3 ....206 B2
Locke Rd MK2 ....58 B4
Lockets Cl SL4 ....209 B3
Locksley Ct 28 SL1 ....205 C2
Lockton MK4 ....46 A2
Lockview Cotts MK1 ......47 C1
Lodden Cl HP21 ....115 B2
Loddon Dr SL6 ....202 B4
Loddon Rd SL8 ....185 A2
Loddon Spur SL1 ....205 C4
Lodge Cl
Cheddington LU7 ......105 A4
Marlow SL7 ....183 C1
Padbury MK18 ....53 B1
Slough SL1 ....205 B2
Uxbridge UB8 ....201 B1
Lodge Farm MK19 ....20 B2
Lodge Farm Ct MK19 .....19 C3
Lodge Gate MK14 ....34 C4
Lodge La
Little Chalfont HP8 ...166 C3
Prestwood HP16 ....151 B3
Stoke Hammond MK17 ...69 C4
Lodge The SL2 ....206 A4
Lodge Way SL4 ....209 C2
Lodgings of the Military
Knights 14 SL4 ....210 B3
Lodore Gn UB10 ....190 C1
Logan Rock MK4 ....57 A4
Lollards Cl HP6 ....154 B1
Lombardy Dr HP4 ....135 B2
Lomond Dr
Leighton Buzzard LU7 ..80 B4
Milton Keynes MK2 .....58 B2
London Central American
High Sch HP11 ....173 A2
London Ct HP21 ....115 C4
London End
Beaconsfield HP9 .....175 C1
Newton Longville MK17 .57 B2
Woburn MK17 ....60 C3
London End La MK17 ....48 B1
London Rd
Beaconsfield HP9 .....187 A4
Berkhamsted HP4 .....135 C2
Buckingham MK18 ......52 C3
Chalfont St Giles HP8 .177 B4
Datchet SL3 ....211 B4
Drayton Beauchamp HP22 118 A2
Felden HP1 ....146 C4
Great Haseley OX9 ....136 A2
Great Missenden HP16 .152 A3
High Wycombe HP11 ...173 A3
Little Kingshill HP16 .152 A3
Milton Keynes MK5 ....46 A4
Milton Keynes Village MK10 36 A3
Newport Pagnell MK16 .22 C1
Old Stratford MK19 ....32 B4
Slough SL3 ....206 C1
Tring HP23 ....119 B2
Wendover HP22 ....141 B3
Wheatley OX33 ....122 A1
London Rd E HP7 ....165 C3
London Rd W HP7 ......165 C4
Londrina Ct 9 HP4 .....135 B2
Londrina Terr 10 HP4 ..135 B2
Long Ayers MK7 ....48 A2
Long Cl SL2 ....198 A3
Long Close Sch SL3 ....206 C4
Long Crendon Ind Est
HP18 ....125 C3
Long Crendon Rd HP18 .124 B2
Long Crendon Sch
HP18 ....125 B4

Long Croft Rd WD3 .....178 B3
Long Dr SL1 ....197 B1
Long Furlong
Haddenham HP17 ......126 C3
Stone HP17 ....114 A3
Long Furlong Dr SL2 ...197 C1
Long Gr HP9 ....176 B2
Long Hale LU7 ....105 B2
Long La Bovingdon HP3 155 C4
Cookham SL7 ....195 B3
Heronsgate WD3 .....167 B1
Olney MK46 ....6 C2
Long Ley LU7 ....105 A4
Long Leys HP19 ....115 A4
Long Lional HP20 ......115 B3
Long Mdw
Aylesbury HP21 ....116 A3
Chesham HP5 ....144 B3
Long Meadow CH HP27 .139 B3
Long Orchard Dr HP10 .174 B4
Long Park Cl HP6 ......154 B2
Long Park Way HP6 ....154 B2
Long Pk HP6 ....154 B2
Long Plough HP22 .....117 B3
Long Readings La SL2 .198 A1
Long Ride HP27 ....139 B2
Long Row
Leckhampstead MK18 ...30 C1
Prestwood HP16 ......151 B3
Long Street Rd MK19 ...11 A2
Long View HP4 ....135 A3
Long Walk The ★ SL4 ..210 C2
Long Wall HP17 ....126 C3
Long Wlk HP8 ....166 C3
Long Wood Dr HP9 ....176 C2
Longbottom La HP9 ...176 B2
Longbournes MK43 ....25 B1
Longbridge Cl HP23 ...119 A3
Longbridge Way UB8 ..201 A2
Longcroft HP22 ....117 C3
Longcroft Ave HP22 ...131 B3
Longcroft La HP3 .....146 B3
Longcross MK15 ....35 A3
Longdown Hill HP27 ...139 C3
Longfellow MK16 ....22 A2
Longfield Hedgerley SL2 187 B1
Little Kingshill HP16 ..152 A2
Longfield Dr HP6 .....154 A1
Longfield Gdns HP23 ..118 C2
Longfield Rd
Chesham HP5 ....143 C1
Tring HP23 ....118 C2
Longfoot La NN12 ......17 B4
Longford Rdbt UB7 ....213 A4
Longhedge MK7 ....48 A1
Longland Way HP17 ...172 B3
Longlands Ct MK18 .....66 A3
Longlands Wlk MK18 ...66 A3
Longleat Ct 7 MK8 .....33 C1
Longleat Gdns SL6 ....202 B3
Longlees SW3 ....178 B3
Longmead SL4 ....209 C3
Longmead La SL1 .....197 B3
Longmead Prim Sch
UB7 ....208 C1
Longmire MK46 ....7 C4
Longmore Cl WD3 .....178 C3
Longpeak Cl MK4 ....46 A1
Longridge Scout Boating
Activity Ctr SL7 .....194 C4
Longstone Rd SL0 ....200 B2
Longview HP9 ....185 C4
Longville MK12 ....33 A4
Longwick CE Comb Sch
HP27 ....138 B3
Longwick Rd
Longwick HP27 ....139 A3
Princes Risborough HP27 139 A3
Longwood La HP7 .....165 B4
Longworth Dr SL6 .....196 B1
Lonsdale Cl SL6 ......196 A1
Lonsdale Way SL6 ....203 B1
Look Ahead SL1 ....205 C2
Loosen Dr SL4 ....202 A2
Loosley Hill HP27 .....149 B3
Lord Grey Sch MK3 ....46 C1
Lord Knyvett Cl TW19 .213 C1
Lord Knyvetts Ct TW19 213 C1
Lord Raglan Ho SL4 ...210 A4
Lords Cl MK2 ....47 B1
Lordsmead MK43 ......25 B1
Loriner Pl MK14 ....35 A3
Loring Rd
Berkhamsted HP4 .....135 B2
Dunstable LU6 ....93 C4
Windsor SL4 ....209 C3
Lorne Cl SL1 ....205 A2
Lorraine Rd HP13 .....173 C4
Losely Ct MK8 ....33 C1
Losfield Rd SL4 ......209 C3
Lossie Dr SL0 ....207 A3
Lothersdale MK13 .....34 A3
Lothian Cl MK3 ....46 C1
Lott Mdw HP21 ....115 B2
Lott Wlk HP21 ....115 B2
Louches La HP14 ......161 C3
Loudhams Rd HP7 .....166 B4
Loudhams Wood La
HP8 ....166 B4
Loudwater Comb Sch
HP11 ....174 A1
Loughton Manor
First Sch MK5 ....46 A4

Loughton Middle Sch
MK5 ....46 A4
Loughton Rd MK13 ....34 A2
Loughton Rdbt MK8 ...45 C4
Louisa Cotts 13 HP23 .119 A2
Louise Wlk HP3 ....146 A2
Lovat Mid Sch MK16 ...22 B2
Lovat St MK16 ....22 B2
Lovatt Dr MK3 ....57 C4
Love Green La SL0 ....207 C4
Love Hill La SL3 ......207 A3
Love Row MK17 ....68 B3
Lovegrove Dr SL2 .....197 C1
Lovejoy La SL4 ....209 B3
Lovel End SL9 ....177 B2
Lovel Mead SL9 ......177 B2
Lovel Rd SL9 ....177 B1
Lovelace Cl SL7 ....193 C2
Lovett Gdns SL6 ......196 B3
Lovett Rd UB9 ....190 B4
Lovetts End LU7 ......78 C4
Lovibonds Ave UB7 ...208 C4
Lowbrook Cl HP21 ....116 A2
Lowbrook Dr SL6 .....202 A2
Lowbrook Prim Sch
SL6 ....202 A2
Lowdell Cl UB7 ....208 C4
Lowdon Cl HP11 ......173 B2
Lower Ash Yd MK17 ...67 C4
Lower Boynton Rd SL6 202 C1
Lower Britwell Rd SL2 .197 B1
Lower Church St
Cuddington HP18 .....112 C2
Stokenchurch HP14 ..158 C3
Lower Cippenham La
SL1 ....204 C3
Lower Cl HP19 ....115 A4
Lower Cookham Rd SL6 196 B1
Lower Dr HP9 ....175 B3
Lower Eighth St MK9 ..34 C1
Lower End Ashendon HP18 97 C1
Piddington OX25 ......95 C4
Thornborough MK18 ...53 C4
Wingrave HP22 ....89 A1
Lower End Rd MK17 ...49 A4
Lower Farm Cl HP18 ..124 B2
Lower Farm Gate HP17 114 A2
Lower Fourth St MK9 ..34 B1
Lower Furney Cl HP13 173 B4
Lower Gn
Cuddington HP18 .....112 C2
Westcott HP18 ....98 B4
Weston Turville HP22 .115 C2
Lower Green La HP18 .112 B1
Lower Hammersley La
HP13 ....174 A2
Lower Icknield Way
Aston Clinton HP22 ...117 C2
Chinnor OX39 ....147 B4
Drayton Beauchamp HP22,
HP23 ....118 A4
Great Kimble HP17 ...129 B1
Princes Risborough HP27 138 B2
Lower King's Rd HP4 .135 B3
Lower Lees Rd SL2 ...198 A1
Lower Lodge La HP15 .163 A3
Lower Mead SL0 ......200 B3
Lower Ninth St MK9 ..34 C1
Lower Pound La SL7 ..183 B1
Lower Rd Blackthorn OX25 81 A4
Chinnor OX39 ....147 B4
Chorleywood WD3 ...167 B3
Cookham SL8 ....195 C4
Denham Green UB9 ..189 B2
Gerrards Cross SL9 ..188 C4
Hardwick HP22 ....87 A2
Lacey Green HP27 ...149 B3
Stoke Mandeville HP21,
HP22 ....115 C2
Lower Ridge SL8 .....185 A2
Lower Riding HP9 ....175 A1
Lower Second St MK9 .34 B1
Lower St
Paulerspury NN12 ....17 A4
Quainton HP22 ....85 A3
Lower Stonehayes MK14 34 C4
Lower Tenth St MK9 ...34 C1
Lower Third St MK9 ...34 B1
Lower Twelfth St MK9 .34 C1
Lower Ventnor Cotts
SL7 ....195 B4
Lower Way
Great Brickhill MK17 ..59 B1
Padbury MK18 ....53 B1
Lower Wharf MK18 ....41 C1
Lowes Cl HP14 ....158 B3
Lowestoft Dr SL1 .....204 B4
Lowfield Cl HP15 .....163 A4
Lowfield Way HP15 ...163 A2
Lowick Pl 4 MK4 .....46 A1
Lowland Rd MK4 ......57 A4
Lowlands Cres HP15 .151 B1
Lowlands Dr TW19 ...213 B1
Lowman Way HP21 ...115 B2
Lowndes Ave HP5 ....144 A1
Lowndes Way MK18 ..66 A3
Lownes Gr MK5 ....45 C4
Loxbeare Dr MK4 .....46 B2
Loxboro Hill HP14 ....160 B2
Loxley Rd HP4 ....134 C4
Loxwood Cl HP3 .....146 C4
Loyne Cl LU7 ....80 A4
Lucas Pl MK6 ....47 B4
Luccombe MK4 ....46 B2
Lucky La or Cock La
HP20 ....101 B1
Lucy La MK5 ....46 A4

Ludgate
Milton Keynes MK6 ....46 C4
Tring HP23 ....118 C2
Ludgershall Rd OX25 ..95 C4
Ludlow Cl MK3 ....57 C4
Ludlow Ho SL6 ....202 C3
Ludlow Mews HP11 ...174 A2
Ludlow Pl HP20 ......116 A4
Ludlow Rd SL6 ....202 C3
Luff Cl SL4 ....209 C2
Lufford Pk MK14 ......34 C4
Luke Ho MK10 ....35 C2
Luker Ave RG9 ....191 B3
Lukes La HP23 ....104 B2
Lukes Lea HP23 ......105 A1
Lullingstone Dr MK13 .33 C3
Lumber La NN12 ......17 A4
Lundholme MK13 .....34 A3
Lundy Ct SL1 ....204 C3
Lupin Cl UB7 ....208 B1
Lupin Ct HP21 ....115 A3
Lupin Wlk HP21 ......115 A3
Lutman La SL6 ....195 C1
Lutyens Gr MK7 ....48 B3
Luxborough Gr MK4 ..46 B2
Lychgate Cotts HP3 ..146 A2
Lycrome La HP5 .....144 C2
Lycrome Rd HP5 .....144 C2
Lyde End HP27 ....138 A1
Lydford Ave SL2 .....205 B4
Lydiard MK8 ....33 C1
Lydiard Cl HP21 .....116 A2
Lydsey Cl SL2 ....198 A1
Lye Green Rd HP5 ...144 C1
Lye The HP4 ....121 B3
Lyell Pl E SL4 ....209 B2
Lyell Pl W SL4 ......209 B2
Lyell Rd SL4 ....209 B3
Lyell Wlk E SL4 .....209 B3
Lyell Wlk W SL4 ....209 B2
Lyme Ave HP4 ....134 B4
Lymington Pl MK8 ...201 B3
Lynch Cl UB8 ....201 B3
Lynch Hill Comb Sch
SL2 ....197 C1
Lynch Hill La SL2 ...197 C1
Lynch The UB8 ......201 B3
Lyndhurst Ave SL3 ..195 C3
Lyndhurst Cl HP13 ..161 B1
Lyndhurst Rd HP5 ...144 A1
Lyndon Cl HP16 .....151 B4
Lyndon Gdns HP13 ..173 C4
Lyndwood Dr SL4 ...211 A1
Lyneham Par SL4 ....211 A2
Lyneham Gdns SL6 ..195 A1
Lynher Cl HP21 .....115 B2
Lynmouth Cres MK4 ..46 B2
Lynott Cl MK8 ....45 C3
Lynton Gn SL6 ......202 C4
Lynton Rd HP5 ......144 B2
Lynwood Ave SL3 ...206 A4
Lynwood Rd HP21 ...116 A3
Lyon Rd MK1 ....47 A4
Lysander Cl HP11 ...146 A2
Lysander Mead SL6 .203 B4

M

Macdonald Cl HP6 ...154 B2
Mackenzie Mall 10 SL1 .205 C2
Mackenzie St 9 SL1 .205 C2
Maclaren Ct MK6 ....46 C4
Madeira Wlk SL4 ....210 B3
Madeley Cl HP6 .....154 B2
Madeley Rd HP21 ...115 C3
Magdalen Cl
Milton Keynes MK11 ..32 B3
Syresham NN13 ......27 B4
Magdalen Ho MK11 ...32 B3
Magenta Cl MK2 .....58 B3
Magnolia Dene HP15 .162 C1
Magnolia Gdns SL3 ..206 B2
Magnolia St UB7 .....208 B1
Magpie Cl
Flackwell Heath HP10 174 A1
Milton Keynes MK5 ...46 A2
Magpie La Coleshill HP7 165 C4
Flackwell Heath HP10 174 A1
Loudwater HP11,HP13 .174 A1
Magpie Way Slough SL2 197 C1
Winslow MK18 ......66 A3
Mahler Cl MK7 ....48 B3
Mahoney Ct HP11 ...172 C4
Maidenhead Ave MK13 34 B2
Maidenhead Coll
for Girls SL6 ....202 C4
Maidenhead Court Pk
SL6 ....196 B4
Maidenhead Rd
Cookham SL8 ....195 C3
Oakley Green SL4 ...209 C4
Windsor SL4 ....209 C4
Maidenhead Sta SL6 .202 C3
Maids Moreton CE Sch
MK18 ....41 C2
Maidstone Rd MK10 ..36 B1
Main Dr
Gerrards Cross SL9 ..188 B3
Iver SL0 ....207 C2
Main Par WD3 ....167 B2
Main Rd Astwood MK16 16 A2
Drayton Parslow MK17 68 A3
Lacey Green HP27 ...149 C2
Syresham NN13 ......27 B4
Waddesdon HP18 ....99 A1
Walter's Ash HP14 ...161 B4
Main Rd N HP4 ......107 A3
Main Rd S HP4 ......107 B2

Main St Adstock MK18 .53 C1
Ashendon HP18 ......97 C1
Beachampton MK19 ..44 A3
Buckingham MK18 ...41 C2
Chackmore MK18 .....41 A2
Charndon OX27 ......72 C3
Cosgrove MK19 ......19 C1
Gawcott MK18 ....51 C2
Grendon Underwood HP18 83 A1
Mursley MK17 ....67 B3
Padbury MK18 ....53 C1
Preston Bissett MK18 .62 A4
Shalstone MK18 .....39 C3
Tingewick MK18 .....51 A3
Turweston NN13 .....38 B4
Twyford MK18 ....62 B1
Westbury NN13 ......39 A2
Weston Turville HP22 .116 C1
Maitland Dr HP13 ....173 A4
Maitland Rd HP22 ...131 B3
Major's Farm Rd SL3 .211 B4
Malbons St MK6 .....46 C4
Malborough Ho HP4 ..135 A2
Malborough Way NN12 .18 C3
Malcolm Rd UB10 ...201 C4
Malden Cl HP6 ......154 C1
Malders La Cookham SL6 195 B2
Maidenhead SL6 ....195 B2
Malet Cl HP14 ....158 C3
Malins Gate MK14 ...34 C4
Malkin Dr HP9 ......175 B2
Mallard Cl HP20 .....101 C2
Mallard Croft HP17 .127 A4
Mallard Dr
Buckingham MK18 ...52 C4
Slough SL1 ....204 C3
Mallard Ho HP11 ....173 B3
Mallets End HP22 ....85 A2
Malletts Cl MK11 ....32 C3
Mallow Gate MK14 ..34 C2
Mallow Pk SL6 ......195 B1
Malmers Well Rd HP13 173 A4
Malpas Rd SL6 ......206 A3
Malt La NN13 ....27 A4
Malthouse Sq
Beaconsfield HP9 ....186 C4
Princes Risborough HP27 139 A2
Malthouse Way 9 SL7 183 B1
Malting Cl MK18 ......12 A3
Malting La Aldbury HP23 120 B3
Dagnall HP4 ....107 B3
Maltings Cl
Cranfield MK43 ......25 A1
Stewkley LU7 ....78 C4
Maltings The
Chackmore MK18 ....41 A2
Olney MK46 ....7 A2
Tingewick MK18 .....51 A3
Maltmans Green Sch
for Girls SL9 ....188 B4
Maltmans La SL9 ....188 B4
Malton Ave SL1 ......205 A3
Malton Cl MK10 .....35 C1
Malvern Cl HP13 ....172 C4
Malvern Ct SL3 ......212 A4
Malvern Dr
Leighton Buzzard LU7 .80 B4
Milton Keynes MK11 ..32 C2
Malvern Rd
Aylesbury HP20 .....116 B4
Maidenhead SL6 ....195 B1
Malyns Cl OX39 .....147 B4
Manchester Terr HP14 171 A2
Mandela Ct UB8 .....208 A4
Mandelyns HP4 .....134 C4
Mandeville Dr MK10 ..36 B3
Mandeville Mews HP21 115 C2
Mandeville Rd
Aylesbury HP21 .....115 C3
Prestwood HP16 ....151 A4
Mandeville Upper Sch
HP21 ....115 B2
Manfield Cl SL2 .....198 A1
Manifold La MK4,MK5 .46 A2
Manor Cl
Berkhamsted HP4 ...135 B2
Cosgrove MK19 .....19 C1
Hanslope MK19 .....11 A1
Milton Keynes MK10 ..35 C2
Salford MK17 ....37 B2
Stoke Hammond MK17 .69 C4
Tylers Green HP10 ..163 A4
Manor Cotts
Chorleywood WD3 ..167 A2
Milton Keynes MK12 .33 A4
Manor Court Yd
High Wycombe HP13 .162 A1
Waterperry OX33 ...123 A1
Manor Cres
Seer Green HP9 ....176 B3
Wendover HP22 ....131 B3
Manor Ct
Leighton Buzzard LU7 .70 C2
Marlow SL7 ....183 C1
Slough, Cippenham SL1 .204 C3
28 Slough, Upton Park
SL1 ....205 C2
Twyford MK18 ....62 B1
Manor Ctyd MK16 ...13 C1
Manor Dr Amersham HP6 154 A2
Aylesbury HP20 .....101 C1
Haversham MK19 ...20 C1
Stewkley LU7 ....78 C4
Manor Farm Cl
Soulbury LU7 ....69 C1
Stone HP17 ....114 B3
Weston Turville HP22 .116 C1
Windsor SL4 ....209 C2

Manor Farm Comm Inf Sch
HP15 . . . .**163** A1
Manor Farm Comm Jun Sch
HP15 . . . .**163** A1
Manor Farm Cotts SL4 . .**211** A1
Manor Farm Ho SL4 . . . .**209** C2
Manor Farm La LU7 . . . . . .**90** B4
Manor Farm Way 4
HP9 . . . .**176** B2
Manor Gdns
Grendon Underwood HP18 . .**83** A3
High Wycombe HP13 . . . . .**162** A1
Maids Moreton HP22 . . . . . .**41** C1
Wooburn Green HP10 . . . .**185** C4
Manor House Cl HP20 . . .**101** C1
Manor House Hospl
HP20 . . . .**101** C1
Manor House La SL3 . . . .**211** A3
Manor La
Gerrards Cross SL9 . . . . . .**188** B2
Maidenhead SL6 . . . .**202** C2
Manor Park Ave HP27 . . .**139** A2
Manor Pk MK18 . . . .**41** C1
Manor Pound Rd LU7 . . .**105** A4
Manor Rd Akeley MK18 . . .**41** C4
Aylesbury HP20 . . . .**101** C1
Bierton HP22 . . . .**102** B4
Cheddington LU7 . . . .**104** C4
Chesham HP5 . . . .**144** A1
Chinnor OX9 . . . .**137** A3
Maidenhead SL6 . . . .**202** C2
Milton Keynes, Bletchley
MK2 . . . .**58** C4
Milton Keynes, Wolverton
MK12 . . . .**33** A4
Newport Pagnell MK16 . . . .**22** A2
Newton Longville MK17 . . . .**57** B2
Oakley HP18 . . . .**109** B3
Oving HP22 . . . .**86** B4
Princes Risborough HP27 . .**139** A1
Seer Green HP9 . . . .**176** B3
Tring HP23 . . . .**119** A3
Tylers Green HP10 . . . . . .**163** A1
Wendover HP22 . . . .**131** B3
Windsor SL4 . . . .**209** C3
Manor St
Berkhamsted HP4 . . . .**135** B2
Buckingham MK18 . . . .**52** B4
Manor View HP15 . . . . . .**163** A1
Manor View Ho HP13 . . .**161** C1
Manor Way
Chesham HP5 . . . .**144** B1
Coleshill HP7 . . . .**164** C2
Yardley Gobion NN12 . . . . .**18** C3
Manor Waye UB8 . . . . . .**201** B2
Manorfields Rd MK19 . . . .**32** A3
Mansard Cl 11 HP23 . . . .**119** A2
Manse MK11 . . . .**32** B3
Mansefield Cl HP5 . . . . . .**144** B1
Mansel Cl Cosgrove MK19 . .**19** C1
Slough SL2 . . . .**206** A4
Mansell Cl
Milton Keynes MK5 . . . .**46** A3
Windsor SL4 . . . .**209** C4
Manshead Cl MK11 . . . . . .**32** C3
Mansion Dr HP23 . . . . . .**119** A2
Mansion Hill HP22 . . . . . .**131** C4
Mansion La Harrold MK43 . . . .**3** C1
Iver SL0 . . . .**207** B3
Mansion The HP4 . . . . . .**135** C2
Manton Rd LU6 . . . .**93** B3
Maple Ave UB8 . . . .**208** C2
Maple Cl
Hazelmere HP15 . . . .**163** A2
High Wycombe HP12 . . . . .**172** A4
Maidenhead SL6 . . . .**202** B3
Maple Cres SL2 . . . .**206** A3
Maple Cross JMI Sch
WD3 . . . .**178** C3
Maple Ct
Gerrards Cross SL9 . . . . . .**188** B2
Marlow SL7 . . . .**183** C2
Windsor SL4 . . . .**210** B2
Maple Gr
Milton Keynes MK2 . . . .**58** C4
Woburn Sands MK17 . . . . . .**49** C4
Maple Leys MK18 . . . .**63** C2
Maple Lodge Cl WD3 . . . .**178** C3
Maple Pl UB7 . . . .**208** C4
Maple Rise SL7 . . . .**183** C2
Mapledean MK12 . . . .**33** C2
Mapledurham MK4 . . . .**48** A2
Mapledurham Wlk SL6 . . .**195** C4
Maplefield La HP8 . . . . . .**166** A3
Maples The
16 Bourne End SL8 . . . . .**185** A2
Wendover HP22 . . . .**131** B3
Maplewood Gdns HP9 . . .**175** A1
Maplewood Sch HP12 . . .**172** B2
Maplin Pk SL3 . . . .**207** A2
Mapridge Green La
HP16 . . . .**141** B1
Marand Ct HP21 . . . .**115** C4
Marbeck Cl SL4 . . . .**209** B3
March Edge MK18 . . . .**41** C1
March Mdw MK7 . . . .**48** B4
March Pl HP19 . . . .**115** C4
Marchant Ct SL7 . . . .**184** A2
Marcia Ct SL1 . . . .**204** C3
Mardle Rd LU7 . . . .**80** C3
Mare Leys MK18 . . . .**52** C4
Maree Cl
Leighton Buzzard LU7 . . . . .**80** B4
Milton Keynes MK2 . . . .**58** C3
Marefield Rd SL7 . . . .**183** B1
Marescroft Rd SL2 . . . . . .**197** C4
Margam Cres MK10 . . . . . .**36** A1

Margaret Ct 5 HP13 . . . .**173** C3
Margaret Powell Sq MK9 . .**34** C2
Margaret Smyth Ho
SL9 . . . .**188** C3
Marie Cl OX27 . . . .**71** C4
Marigold Pl MK14 . . . .**34** C2
Marigold Wlk HP15 . . . . .**162** C4
Marina Dr Dunstable LU6 . .**93** C4
Milton Keynes MK12 . . . . . .**33** B4
Marina Way Iver SL0 . . . .**208** A3
Slough SL1 . . . .**204** B3
Marish Ct SL3 . . . .**207** A2
Marish Cty Fst Sch SL3 . .**207** A2
Marish Jun Sch SL3 . . . . .**207** A2
Marish La UB9 . . . .**189** B4
Marish Wharf (Ind Est)
SL3 . . . .**206** C2
Marjoram Pl MK14 . . . .**34** C2
Mark Dr SL9 . . . .**177** B3
Markenfield Pl MK4 . . . . . .**45** C1
Market Hill
Milton Keynes MK6 . . . .**47** A4
Whitchurch HP22 . . . .**86** C3
Market Ho 8 SL9 . . . .**177** B1
Market La SL3 . . . .**207** B2
Market Par HP15 . . . .**163** A2
Market Pl Colnbrook SL3 . .**212** B4
Gerrards Cross SL9 . . . . . .**177** B1
Henley-on-T RG9 . . . .**191** B1
Olney MK46 . . . .**6** C2
Woburn MK17 . . . .**60** C4
Market Sq
Amersham HP7 . . . .**165** A4
Aylesbury HP20 . . . .**115** B4
Chesham HP5 . . . .**154** B4
Hanslope MK19 . . . .**11** A1
Marlow SL7 . . . .**183** B1
Milton Keynes MK11 . . . . . .**32** B3
Princes Risborough HP27 . .**139** A2
Uxbridge UB8 . . . .**201** B3
Winslow MK18 . . . .**65** C2
Market St
15 Aylesbury HP20 . . . . . .**115** B4
Maidenhead SL6 . . . .**202** C4
19 Windsor SL4 . . . .**210** B3
Markham Pl HP19 . . . . . .**115** A4
Markhams Cl MK18 . . . . . .**52** B4
Marks Orch MK18 . . . .**75** C4
Marlborough Cl SL6 . . . . .**202** A3
Marlborough Ct SL1 . . . . .**204** C4
Marlborough Gate MK9 . . .**34** C2
Marlborough Ho 5 SL6 .**202** C3
Marlborough Rd
Aylesbury HP21 . . . .**115** C2
Maidenhead SL6 . . . .**202** A3
Slough SL3 . . . .**206** C1
Marlborough St MK14 . . . .**34** C2
Marlborough Trad Est
HP11 . . . .**172** C4
Marley Gr MK8 . . . .**45** C4
Marlin Cl HP4 . . . .**134** C3
Marlin Copse HP4 . . . . . .**135** A2
Marlin Ct SL7 . . . .**183** B1
Marlin Hill HP23 . . . .**133** A4
Marlins Cl WD3 . . . .**167** C4
Marlins End HP4 . . . .**134** C2
Marlow Bottom SL7 . . . . .**183** B4
Marlow Bridge La SL7 . . .**194** C4
Marlow Com Hospl SL7 . .**183** C1
Marlow Comm SL7 . . . . . .**182** C2
Marlow Dr MK16 . . . .**22** A2
Marlow Hill HP11 . . . .**173** A3
Marlow Inf Sch SL7 . . . . .**183** B2
Marlow Lodge 13 SL6 . . .**202** C3
Marlow Mill SL7 . . . .**183** C1
Marlow Rd
Beacon's Bottom HP14 . . . .**170** A4
Bisham SL6,SL7 . . . .**194** C2
Henley-on-T RG9 . . . .**191** C2
High Wycombe HP11 . . . . .**172** C2
Lane End HP14,SL7 . . . . . .**171** C1
Little Marlow SL7,SL8 . . . .**184** B3
Maidenhead SL6 . . . .**202** C4
Marlow Sta SL7 . . . .**183** C1
Marmion Rd RG9 . . . .**191** C1
Marquis Ct MK17 . . . .**60** C4
Marram Cl MK6 . . . .**47** A3
Marriott Terr WD3 . . . . . .**167** C3
Marriotts Ave HP16 . . . . .**142** C4
Marriotts Cl HP17 . . . .**126** C3
Marriotts La HP17 . . . .**126** C3
Marriotts Way HP17 . . . . .**126** C3
Marrod's Bottom HP7,
HP9 . . . .**175** B4
Marron La MK18 . . . .**33** B3
Marroway
Stoke Mandeville HP22 . . . .**116** B1
Weston Turville HP22 . . . . .**116** B1
Marsh Ct HP11 . . . .**173** C2
Marsh Dr MK14 . . . .**21** C1
Marsh End Rd MK16 . . . . .**22** B2
Marsh Gibbon CE Sch
OX27 . . . .**71** C2
Marsh Gibbon Rd HP18 . . .**82** C3
Marsh La
Stoke Mandeville HP22 . . . .**129** C4
Taplow SL6 . . . .**203** C3
Marsh Sch HP11 . . . .**173** C2
Marshall Court Ind Est
MK1 . . . .**47** A1
Marshalls La MK15 . . . . . .**35** B1
Marshalls Lea HP22 . . . . .**102** B2
Marsham Cl HP21 . . . .**116** A2
Marsham La SL9 . . . .**188** C3

Marsham Lodge SL9 . . . .**188** C3
Marsham Way SL9 . . . . . .**188** C3
Marshaw Pl 3 MK4 . . . . . .**46** B1
Marshcroft La HP23 . . . . .**119** B3
Marshfield SL3 . . . .**211** B3
Marshgate Trad Est
SL6 . . . .**204** A4
Marshworth MK6 . . . .**47** B3
Marston Cl HP5 . . . .**144** A2
Marston Ct HP23 . . . .**104** A2
Marston Hill
Cranfield MK43 . . . .**25** C1
Oving HP22,MK18 . . . .**86** B4
Marston Rd
Granborough MK18 . . . .**75** C2
Thame OX9 . . . .**126** A1
Marstonfields Rd MK18 . . .**76** A1
Marsworth CE Inf Sch
HP23 . . . .**105** A1
Marsworth Rd LU7 . . . . . .**105** A2
Marsworth Resr (Nature
Reserve)★ HP23 . . . . . .**119** A4
Martin Cl
Buckingham MK18 . . . .**52** C1
Milton Keynes MK14 . . . . . .**34** C3
Uxbridge UB10 . . . .**201** C2
Windsor SL4 . . . .**209** B3
Martin Dell Cotts HP16 .**142** C2
Martin Rd
Maidenhead SL6 . . . .**202** C4
Slough SL1 . . . .**205** C2
Martin's Plain SL2 . . . . . .**198** C2
Martindale SL0 . . . .**200** B1
Martingale Pl MK14 . . . . . .**34** C3
Martins Dr The LU7 . . . . . .**80** C4
Martinsend La HP16 . . . . .**151** C4
Martyrs Ct HP7 . . . .**165** B4
Marunden Gn SL2 . . . . . .**197** C1
Marwood Cl MK4 . . . .**46** B2
Mary Bassett Lower Sch
LU7 . . . .**80** C4
Mary Cross Cl HP23 . . . . .**119** B1
Mary Macmanus Dr
MK18 . . . .**41** B1
Mary Morgan Ct SL2 . . .**205** B4
Mary Towerton Sch The
HP14 . . . .**159** B2
Marygold Wlk HP6 . . . . . .**166** B4
Maryland Coll MK17 . . . . . .**60** C3
Maryland Rd MK15 . . . . . .**35** A4
Maryot Cl MK15 . . . .**13** C1
Marys Mead HP16 . . . . . .**163** A3
Maryside SL3 . . . .**206** C2
Mascoll Path SL2 . . . .**197** C1
Masefield Cl MK16 . . . . . .**22** A2
Masefield Gr MK3 . . . .**58** A4
Maslin Dr MK6 . . . .**47** A3
Mason MK14 . . . .**34** B4
Mason's Ct
Aylesbury HP19 . . . .**115** A4
Chinnor OX39 . . . .**147** B3
Henley-on-T RG9 . . . .**191** C1
Masons Cl HP16 . . . .**151** B3
Masons Ct HP5 . . . .**144** B1
Masons Rd SL1 . . . .**204** C3
Masons Yd HP4 . . . .**135** B2
Massie Cl MK15 . . . .**35** A3
Mathieson Rd MK13 . . . . .**34** A3
Mathisen Way SL3 . . . . . .**212** C3
Matilda Gdns MK5 . . . .**46** A3
Matlock Rd HP20 . . . .**101** C1
Matson Dr RG9 . . . .**191** C1
Matthew Ct MK5 . . . .**46** A3
Matthews Cl 18 HP20 . . . .**101** C1
Maud Jane's Cl LU7 . . . . .**105** C3
Maude Ct HP9 . . . .**176** A1
Maude Rd HP9 . . . .**176** A1
Maudsley Cl MK5 . . . .**46** B3
Mauduit Rd MK19 . . . .**11** A2
Maulden Gdns MK14 . . . . .**35** A4
Maurice Mount HP15 . . . . .**162** C3
Mavoncliff Dr MK4 . . . .**57** A4
Maxham MK5 . . . .**46** A2
Maxwell Cl SL6 . . . .**197** B1
Maxwell Dr HP15 . . . .**163** A4
Maxwell Rd
Beaconsfield HP9 . . . .**175** C2
West Drayton UB7 . . . .**208** C1
May Cl LU6 . . . .**92** C4
May Rd MK43 . . . .**8** C3
May Tree Cl SL7 . . . .**183** B3
Maybach Ct MK5 . . . .**46** A3
Maybrook Gdns HP13 . . . .**173** B4
Maybury Cl SL1 . . . .**204** B4
Maybush Gdns HP16 . . . . .**151** B3
Maybush Wlk MK46 . . . .**6** C3
Mayditch Pl MK13 . . . .**34** B2
Mayer Gdns MK5 . . . .**46** B3
Mayfield Ave SL9 . . . .**188** C3
Mayfield Rd HP10 . . . .**185** C3
Mayflower Ct HP17 . . . . . .**114** C3
Mayflower Way
Beaconsfield HP9 . . . .**186** A4
Farnham Common SL2 . . . .**198** B4
Maygoods Cl UB8 . . . .**208** B4
Maygoods Gn UB8 . . . . . .**208** B4
Maygoods La UB8 . . . .**208** B4
Maygoods View UB8 . . . . .**208** B4
Mayhall La HP6 . . . .**154** A2
Mayhew Cres HP13 . . . . . .**173** B4
Maylands Dr UB8 . . . .**201** B3
Maynard Cl MK13 . . . .**34** A2
Maynard Ct SL4 . . . .**210** A3
Maypole Rd SL6 . . . .**204** A4
Mays Way NN12 . . . .**18** B2
McConnell Dr MK12 . . . . . .**33** C3
McDougall Rd 8 HP4 . . . .**135** B2
McEwen Ride HP22 . . . . . .**117** B1

McKay Trad Est SL3 . . . .**212** C3
McKenzie Cl MK18 . . . .**66** A3
McLernon Way MK18 . . . . .**66** A3
Mead Acre HP27 . . . .**139** A3
Mead Ave SL3 . . . .**207** A2
Mead Cl Denham UB9 . . . .**190** A1
7 Marlow SL7 . . . .**183** B1
Princes Risborough HP27 . .**139** A2
Slough SL3 . . . .**207** A2
Mead Haze SL6 . . . .**196** B1
Mead Ho SL0 . . . .**200** B1
Mead Pk HP15 . . . .**163** B4
Mead Platt HP14 . . . .**158** B3
Mead Rd UB8 . . . .**201** B3
Mead St HP13 . . . .**174** A2
Mead The
Beaconsfield HP9 . . . .**175** C1
Soulbury LU7 . . . .**69** C2
Mead Way
High Wycombe HP11 . . . . .**173** C2
Slough SL1 . . . .**204** B4
Mead Wlk SL3 . . . .**207** A2
Meades La HP5 . . . .**154** A4
Meadfield Ave SL3 . . . . . .**207** A2
Meadfield Rd SL3 . . . .**207** A2
Meadfurlong Comb Sch
MK6 . . . .**34** C1
Meadow Bank SL8 . . . . . .**185** A4
Meadow Cl
Aylesbury HP20 . . . .**102** A1
Berkhamsted HP4 . . . .**135** A1
Chesham HP5 . . . .**144** A2
Cublington LU7 . . . .**78** B1
High Wycombe HP11 . . . . .**173** C2
Marlow SL7 . . . .**183** C1
Oakley HP18 . . . .**109** B2
Old Windsor SL4 . . . .**211** A1
Tring HP23 . . . .**119** A2
Meadow Cott La HP7 . . . .**164** C2
Meadow Cotts
Beaconsfield HP9 . . . .**175** C1
Little Kingshill HP16 . . . . . .**152** A2
Meadow Dr
Amersham HP6 . . . .**154** C1
Longwick HP27 . . . .**138** B3
Meadow Gate
Padbury MK18 . . . .**53** A1
Prestwood HP16 . . . .**151** B2
Meadow Gdns MK18 . . . . .**52** C3
Meadow La
Beaconsfield HP9 . . . .**175** C1
Eton SL4 . . . .**210** B4
Long Crendon HP18 . . . . .**125** C2
Milton Keynes Village MK10 .**36** A2
Pitstone LU7 . . . .**105** C2
South Heath HP16 . . . .**152** C4
Meadow Pk HP22 . . . .**116** B1
Meadow Rd
Berkhamsted HP4 . . . .**135** A3
Chinnor OX39 . . . .**147** B3
Henley-on-T RG9 . . . .**191** C1
Slough SL3 . . . .**206** C2
Meadow Rise HP27 . . . . . .**149** C3
Meadow Row MK18 . . . . . .**41** B1
Meadow Sch UB8 . . . .**208** C4
Meadow View
Aspley Guise MK17 . . . .**49** B3
Chalfont St Giles HP8 . . . .**177** A4
Long Crendon HP18 . . . . .**125** C2
Marlow Bottom SL7 . . . . . .**183** C3
Pottersbury NN12 . . . .**18** B2
Stanwell TW19 . . . .**213** A1
Uxbridge UB8 . . . .**208** B4
Meadow Way
Aylesbury HP20 . . . .**102** A1
Dorney SL6 . . . .**203** C2
Felden HP3 . . . .**146** C4
Hyde Heath HP6 . . . .**153** B2
Old Windsor SL4 . . . .**211** A1
3 Thame OX9 . . . .**125** C1
Wing LU7 . . . .**79** C2
Meadow Wlk
Bourne End SL8 . . . .**185** A3
Buckingham MK18 . . . .**41** B1
Tylers Green HP10 . . . . . .**163** B1
Meadoway
Steeple Claydon MK18 . . . . .**63** C2
Stone HP17 . . . .**114** C3
Meadowbank Cl HP18 . . . .**125** C3
Meadowbrook HP23 . . . . .**119** A3
Meadowbrook Cl SL3 . . . .**212** C3
Meadowcroft
Aylesbury HP19 . . . .**101** A2
Berkhamsted HP4 . . . .**134** C2
Gerrards Cross SL9 . . . . . .**177** B1
Meadowlea Cl UB7 . . . . . .**213** A3
Meadows Comb Sch The
HP10 . . . .**185** C4
Meadows The
Amersham HP7 . . . .**154** C1
Flackwell Heath HP10 . . . .**185** A4
Whitchurch HP22 . . . .**86** C4
Meadowside HP9 . . . .**176** C2
Meadowsweet MK7 . . . . . .**48** A3
Meadowvew TW19 . . . . . .**212** C1
Meads Cl MK13 . . . .**34** A4
Meads The
Berkhamsted HP4 . . . .**134** C3
Eaton Bray LU6 . . . .**92** C3
Tring HP23 . . . .**119** A2
Uxbridge UB8 . . . .**201** C1
4 Windsor SL4 . . . .**210** A3
Meadway
Berkhamsted HP4 . . . .**135** A3
Buckingham MK18 . . . .**52** B2
Dunstable LU6 . . . .**93** C4
Oving HP22 . . . .**76** C1
Meadway Ct LU6 . . . .**93** C4

Meadway The MK5 . . . . . .**46** A4
Meare Est HP10 . . . .**185** C4
Meavy Cl HP13 . . . .**174** A2
Medale Rd MK6 . . . .**47** A3
Medallion Pl SL6 . . . .**203** A4
Medbourne Rdbt MK8 . . . .**45** C3
Medeswell MK6 . . . .**46** C2
Medhurst MK8 . . . .**33** C1
Medland MK6 . . . .**47** B4
Medley Cl LU6 . . . .**92** C3
Medman Cl UB8 . . . .**201** B2
Medway Cl MK16 . . . .**22** C2
Meeting Oak La MK18 . . . .**66** A3
Megdale Pl HP20 . . . .**101** B1
Melbourne Ave SL1 . . . . .**205** B4
Melbourne Cl HP21 . . . . . .**115** C3
Melbourne Rd HP13 . . . . .**173** C3
Melbourne Terr MK13 . . . . .**34** A4
Meldon Rise MK5 . . . .**46** A4
Melford Gn HP19 . . . .**101** B2
Melfort Dr
Leighton Buzzard LU7 . . . . .**80** A3
Milton Keynes MK2 . . . .**58** B3
Melick Rd MK6 . . . .**47** A2
Mellish Ct MK3 . . . .**47** A1
Mellstock Rd MK21 . . . . . .**115** C3
Melrose Ave MK3 . . . .**47** A2
Melrose Ct HP13 . . . .**162** A1
Melrose Wlk MK21 . . . . . .**115** C3
Melton MK14 . . . .**34** B4
Melton Ct Dunstable LU6 . .**93** C4
Maidenhead SL6 . . . .**202** A3
Mendelssohn Gr MK7 . . . . .**48** B2
Mendip Cl SL3 . . . .**207** A1
Mendip Way HP13 . . . . . .**172** C4
Mendy St HP11 . . . .**173** A4
Menmarsh Rd HP18 . . . . .**123** C3
Menteith MK2 . . . .**58** B3
Mentmore★ LU7 . . . .**90** B2
Mentmore Cl HP12 . . . . . .**172** A3
Mentmore Crossroads
LU7 . . . .**89** C3
Mentmore Cl MK8 . . . .**45** C4
Mentmore Gdns LU7 . . . . .**80** C3
Mentmore Gn HP21 . . . . .**115** C2
Mentmore Rd
Cheddington LU7 . . . .**104** C4
High Wycombe HP12 . . . . .**172** A3
Leighton Buzzard LU7 . . . . .**80** C3
Mentmore View HP23 . . . .**118** C3
Mentone Ave MK17 . . . . . .**49** B2
Menzies Cl MK5 . . . .**46** A2
Mercer Wlk UB8 . . . .**201** B4
Mercers Dr MK13 . . . .**34** A3
Mercers Mdw MK22 . . . . .**131** A3
Merchant La
Cranfield MK43 . . . .**25** A1
Cranfield, Wharley End
MK43 . . . .**24** C1
Mercia Rd SL6 . . . .**202** B2
Mercian Way SL1 . . . .**204** B3
Mercury Gr MK8 . . . .**45** C4
Mere Cl SL7 . . . .**183** C1
Mere Rd Finmere MK18 . . .**50** B3
Slough SL1 . . . .**205** C2
Merebrook First Sch
MK4 . . . .**46** B2
Meredith Dr HP19 . . . .**100** C1
Meriland Ct MK2 . . . .**58** C2
Merlebank HP5 . . . .**154** B4
Merlewood Cl HP11 . . . . .**173** A2
Merlewood Dr MK5 . . . .**45** C4
Merlin Cl SL6 . . . .**202** A4
Merlin Ctr HP19 . . . .**101** B1
Merlin Wlk MK6 . . . .**47** A4
Merling Croft HP4 . . . .**134** C4
Merrivale Mews UB7 . . . . .**208** B3
Merry Down HP3 . . . .**161** B1
Merryfields UB8 . . . .**201** B2
Mersey Cl MK3 . . . .**46** C1
Mersey Way MK3 . . . .**46** C1
Merthen Gr MK4 . . . .**57** A4
Merton Cl SL6 . . . .**202** B2
Merton Dr MK6 . . . .**47** A2
Merton Rd
Princes Risborough HP27 . .**139** A1
Slough SL1 . . . .**206** A2
Merwin Way SL4 . . . .**209** B2
Messenger Cl HP21 . . . . .**116** A3
Metcalfe Gr MK14 . . . .**22** A1
Michael Rd SL6 . . . .**202** B3
Michigan Dr
Milton Keynes MK15 . . . . . .**35** A4
Newport Pagnell MK15 . . . .**22** C3
Micholls Ave SL9 . . . .**177** C3
Micklefield Rd HP13 . . . . .**174** A4
Mickleton MK15 . . . .**35** A3
Mid Cross La SL9 . . . .**177** C3
Midas Ind Est UB8 . . . . . .**201** A2
Midcot Way HP4 . . . .**134** C3
Midcroft SL2 . . . .**198** A1
Middle Cres UB8 . . . .**189** B2
Middle Dr HP9 . . . .**175** B3
Middle Field HP22 . . . . . .**116** C2
Middle Gn SL3 . . . .**206** C3
Middle La HP3 . . . .**146** A1
Middle Mdw HP8 . . . .**177** B4
Middle Rd
Aylesbury HP21 . . . .**116** A4
Berkhamsted HP4 . . . .**135** A2
Denham Green UB9 . . . . . .**189** B2
Middle Slade MK18 . . . . . .**52** C3
Middle Way OX39 . . . .**147** A3
Middle Wlk SL1 . . . .**197** B1

Middlebrook Rd HP13 ....161 C1
Middlefield Cl MK18 ....41 C1
Middlegreen Rd SL3 ...206 B3
Middlegreen Trad Est
  SL3 ....206 B2
Middlesex Dr MK3 .....46 C1
Middleton MK14 ....34 C4
Middleway The HP12 ..172 B3
Midhurst Cl HP21 ......116 A3
Midland Rd MK46 ....7 A3
Midsummer Arc MK9 ...34 C2
Midsummer Bvd MK9 ...34 C1
Midsummer Rdbt MK9 ..34 B1
Miersfield HP11 ....172 B2
Mikern Cl MK2 ....58 B4
Milburn Ave MK6 ....46 C4
Milburn Dr UB7 ....208 C3
Mildenhall Rd SL1 ....205 C4
Mile Elm **3** SL7 ....183 C2
Milebush LU7 ....80 B4
Milecastle MK13 ....34 A3
Miles Cl Aylesbury HP21 .116 A4
  Milton Keynes MK14 ...22 A2
Miles End HP21 ....115 A3
Milesmere MK8 ....33 B1
Milestone Cl HP14 ....158 C3
Milfoil Ave MK14 ......34 C2
Milford Ave MK11 ......32 C2
Milford Ct **10** SL1 ..206 A2
Milk Hall Barns HP5 ..154 C3
Mill Ave UB8 ....201 B2
Mill Bridge Pl UB8 ...201 B2
Mill Cl Chesham HP5 ..154 C3
  West Drayton UB7 ....208 B2
  Wingrave HP22 ....89 A3
Mill Ct Horton SL3 ...212 B2
  Milton Keynes MK12 ...33 A3
  Waddesdon HP18 ....99 A4
  West Drayton UB7 ....208 B2
Mill End RG9 ....192 B4
Mill End Cl LU6 ....92 C2
Mill End Rd HP12 .....172 B4
Mill Gdns HP23 ....119 A2
Mill Gn MK43 ....8 B3
Mill Ho
  Buckingham MK18 ......52 B4
  West Drayton UB7 ....208 B3
Mill La Amersham HP7 .165 A4
  Aspley Guise MK17 ....49 B3
  Beaconsfield HP9 ....175 C1
  Brackley NN13 ....38 A3
  Buckingham MK18 ......52 B4
  Chalfont St Giles HP8 .177 A4
  Chinnor OX39 ....147 A4
  Cookham SL6 ....196 B4
  Gerrards Cross SL9 ..188 C3
  Great Brickhill MK17 ..58 C1
  Haddenham OX9 ....126 A4
  Horton SL3 ....212 A2
  Horton-cum-S OX33 ...108 A3
  Hurley SL7 ....193 C2
  Milton Keynes, Bradville
    MK13 ....34 A4
  Milton Keynes, Stony Stratford
    MK11 ....32 B3
  Milton Keynes, Woolstone
    MK15 ....35 B2
  Princes Risborough MK27 .139 A3
  Salford MK17 ....37 B2
  South Heath HP16 ....152 B4
  Stokenchurch HP14 ...158 B3
  Taplow SL6 ....203 B4
  Turvey MK43 ....8 B3
  Twyford MK18 ....62 B1
  Upper Arncott OX25 ...94 C4
  Westbury NN13 ....39 A2
  Weston Turville HP22 .117 A1
  Windsor SL4 ....210 A4
  Wingrave HP22 ....89 B1
Mill Lane Cty Prim Sch
  OX39 ....147 A4
Mill Mdw HP19 ....115 A4
Mill Mead HP22 ....131 A3
Mill Pl SL3 ....211 B3
Mill Rd Cranfield MK43 ..25 B1
  2 Leighton Buzzard LU7 ..80 C4
  Marlow SL7 ....183 C1
  Milton Keynes MK2 ....58 C4
  Oakley HP18 ....109 B2
  Slapton LU7 ....91 B4
  Stokenchurch HP14 ...158 B3
  West Drayton UB7 ....208 B2
  Whitfield NN13 ....26 C2
Mill Sq MK12 ....33 A3
Mill St Aylesbury HP20 .101 C1
  Berkhamsted HP4 .....135 B4
  Colnbrook SL3 ....212 B4
  High Wycombe HP11 ..172 C4
  Newport Pagnell MK16 ..22 B3
  Slough SL2,SL3 ......205 C3
Mill Terr MK12 ....33 A3
Mill Twr LU6 ....92 C3
Mill View Rd HP23 ....118 C2
Mill W SL2 ....205 C3
Mill Way
  Aspley Guise MK17 ....49 B3
  Aylesbury HP20 ......115 B4
  Rickmansworth WD3 ..167 C1
Millards Rd MK43 ......25 B1
Millbank
  Leighton Buzzard LU7 ..80 C4
  Marlow SL7 ....183 C1
Millbank Ho HP7 ...... A4
Millboard Rd SL8 .....185 C4
Millbrook Cl HP12 ....172 B4

Millbrook Comb Sch
  HP12 ....172 B4
Millbrook Way SL3 ....212 C3
Milldun Way HP12 .....172 B3
Millennium Cl UB8 ....201 B2
Millennium Point HP19 .101 A1
Miller Pl SL9 ....188 B3
Miller's La SL4 ......211 A1
Millers Cl HP18 ....82 C3
Millers Turn OX39 ....147 A3
Millers Way
  Aylesbury HP19 ......115 A4
  Milton Keynes MK11,MK12,
    MK13 ....33 B3
Millfield HP4 ....135 B3
Millfield Ave OX27 ....71 C2
Millfield Cl Cranfield MK43 25 A1
  Marsh Gibbon OX27 ...71 C2
Millfields HP5 ....154 B3
Millhayes MK14 ....34 C4
Millholm Rise MK6 .....47 C3
Milliners The **16** HP20 .101 C1
Millington Gate MK15 ..35 B4
Millshot Dr HP7 ......165 B4
Millside SL8 ....185 B2
Millstream HP22 ......116 C1
Millstream La SL1 ....204 C3
Millstream Way
  Leighton Buzzard LU7 ..80 C4
  Wooburn Green HP10 ..185 C4
Milner Rd SL1 ....204 A4
Milton Ave SL9 ....188 C3
Milton Cl
  Henley-on-T RG9 .....191 B1
  Horton SL3 ....212 A2
Milton Dr MK16 ....22 C2
Milton Fields HP8 ....177 A4
Milton Gdns MK27 .....139 A1
Milton Gr MK3 ....57 C4
Milton Hill HP8 ......177 A4
Milton Keynes Central Sta
  MK9 ....34 B1
Milton Keynes Coll MK6 .46 C4
Milton Keynes Coll
  (Bletchley Ctr) MK3 ..58 A4
Milton Keynes Coll
  (Wolverton Ctr) MK12 .33 A3
Milton Keynes
  General Hospl MK6 ....47 A4
Milton Keynes Mus★
  MK12 ....33 B3
Milton Keynes Prep Sch
  MK3 ....57 B4
Milton Keynes Recycling
  Factory★ MK12 ......33 B3
Milton Lawns HP6 ....154 B2
Milton Rd
  Aston Clinton HP22 ..117 C3
  Aylesbury HP21 ......115 C3
  Chesham HP5 ....144 A1
  Milton Keynes MK15 ...35 B4
  Slough SL2 ....198 B1
  Walton MK7 ....47 C2
Milton Way UB7 ....208 C1
Milton's Cottage (Mus)★
  HP8 ....177 A4
Milverton Ct SL6 .....202 A2
Mimosa Ct HP21 ....115 A3
Mina Ave SL3 ....206 B2
Mineral La HP5 ....154 B4
Minerva Cl TW19 .....213 A1
Minerva Gdns MK7 .....48 B4
Minerva Way HP9 .....176 A1
Ministry Wharf HP14 .149 B1
Minniecroft Rd SL1 ..197 A1
Minshull Cl MK18 ......41 B1
Minster Way SL3 .....206 C2
Minstrel Ct MK13 .....34 A4
Minton Cl MK14 ....22 A1
Minton Rise SL6 .....204 A4
Mirador Cres SL2 ....206 A3
Mirrie La UB9 ....189 B3
Misbourne Ave
  Chalfont St Peter SL9 .177 C3
  High Wycombe HP13 ..173 C3
Misbourne Cl
  Chalfont St Peter SL9 .177 C3
  Stoke Mandeville HP22 .115 B2
Misbourne Ct SL3 ....207 A1
Misbourne Dr HP16 ..152 A3
Misbourne Ho HP8 ...166 B1
Misbourne Mdws UB9 .189 B2
Misbourne Sch The
  HP16 ....152 A3
Misbourne Vale SL9 ..177 B3
Missenden Cl MK18 ...65 C2
Missenden Gdns SL1 .204 A4
Missenden Rd
  Chesham HP5 ....154 A1
  Ellesborough HP17 ...118 B2
  Great Kingshill HP15,HP16 .151 B1
  Winslow MK18 ....65 C2
Miswell La HP23 .....118 C2
Mitcham Pl MK13 ......34 B2
Mitcham Wlk HP19 ....101 A1
Mitchell Cl
  Bovingdon HP3 ......145 C4
  Slough SL1 ....205 A2
  Thame OX9 ....125 C1
Mitchell Rd MK43 .....24 C1
Mitchell Wlk HP6 ....154 C1
Mithras Gdns MK7 .....48 B4
Mitre Cl MK18 ....52 B4
Mitre St MK18 ....52 B4
Moat Cl Prestwood HP16 .151 B3
  Wendover HP22 ....131 A4
Moat Dr Prestwood HP16 .151 B4
  Slough SL2 ....206 B4

Moat End HP22 ....102 A2
Moat La
  Aston Abbots HP22 ....88 B2
  Marsh Gibbon OX27 ...71 C1
  Prestwood HP16 ......151 B4
  Wingrave HP22 ....89 A1
Moat Pl UB9 ....201 A4
Mobwell Terr HP16 ...152 A4
Model Row HP22 ......117 C3
Moeran Cl MK7 ....48 B3
Moffy Hill SL6 ....195 C1
Mole Run HP13 ....161 B1
Molyns Ho RG9 ....191 C2
Molyns Mews **7** SL1 .204 C3
Monellan Gr MK7 ......48 A2
Monet Pl HP19 ....100 C1
Money La UB7 ....208 B2
Monkey Island La SL3 .203 C1
Monks Hollow SL7 ....183 C3
Monks Path HP19 .....115 A4
Monks Rd SL4 ....209 B4
Monks Risborough
  CE Comb Sch HP27 ..139 B3
Monks Risborough Sta
  HP27 ....139 A3
Monks Way
  Harmondsworth UB7 ..213 C4
  Milton Keynes MK12,MK13,
    MK14,MK15,MK16 .....34 B3
Monksfield Way SL2 ..198 A1
Monkston Rdbt MK10 ..36 A1
Monkswood Ct **6** SL3 ..183 C1
Monkton Waye MK27 ..150 B3
Monmouth Cl HP19 ...101 A1
Monmouth Gr MK4 .....45 C1
Monro Ave MK8 ....45 C4
Montabaur Rd NN13 ...38 A4
Montagu Dr MK6 ....47 A4
Montagu Rd SL3 ......211 A3
Montague Rd
  Aylesbury HP21 ......115 B4
  Berkhamsted HP4 .....135 A2
  Slough SL1 ....205 C3
  Uxbridge UB8 ....201 B3
Montem Cty Mid Sch
  SL1 ....205 A2
Montem Infs Sch SL1 .205 A2
Montem La SL1 ....205 B2
Montford Mews HP13,
  HP15 ....162 C1
Montgomerie Cl HP4 ..135 A3
Montgomery Cres MK13 .35 A4
Montgomery Pl SL2 ..206 B4
Montpelier Ct SL4 ...210 B3
Montrose Ave
  Datchet SL3 ....211 B4
  Slough SL1 ....205 A4
Montrose Dr SL6 .....202 A3
Montrose Way SL3 ...211 B4
Monument La SL3 ....177 C3
Monycrower Dr SL6 ..202 C4
Moon St MK12 ....33 B4
Moor End Eaton Bray LU6 .92 C3
  Maidenhead SL6 .....203 B1
Moor End Cl LU6 ......92 C2
Moor End La LU6 ......92 C3
Moor Furlong SL1 ....204 C3
Moor La
  Harmondsworth UB7 ..213 B4
  High Wycombe HP13 ..161 B2
  Maidenhead SL6 .....195 C1
  Sarratt WD3 ....156 C2
Moor Pk Halton HP22 .131 A4
  Milton Keynes MK3 ...57 B4
Moor Rd HP5 ....154 B3
Moor Rdbt UB7 ....213 A4
Moor The SL8 ....184 B2
Moor's Farm Cotts HP5 145 A1
Moorbridge Rd SL6 ..203 A4
Moorcroft Sch UB7 ..208 C3
Moore Cl SL1 ....205 A2
Moore Rd HP4 ....134 C3
Moorend La Thame OX9 .125 C1
  Thame OX9 ....126 A1
Moorend Rd NN12 .....18 C3
Moores Hill MK46 ......6 C3
Moores La SL4 ....204 C1
Moorfield MK17 ....57 B2
Moorfield Rd
  Denham Green UB9 ..190 A3
  Uxbridge UB8 ....208 A4
Moorfield Terr SL6 ..203 A4
Moorfoot MK11 ....33 A2
Moorgate MK6 ....46 C4
Moorhall Rd UB9 .....190 A3
Moorhen Ct **20** HP20 .101 C2
Moorhen Way MK18 ...52 C4
Moorhills Cres LU7 ...79 C2
Moorhills Rd LU7 .....79 C2
Moorings The MK18 ...52 B4
Moorland Cty Fst Sch
  MK6 ....47 A3
Moorland Rd UB7 ....213 B4
Moorlands LU7 ....79 C2
Moorlands Rd LU7 ....79 C2
Moorside HP10 ....185 C4
Moorside Cl SL6 .....195 C1
Moorstown Ct **7** SL1 .205 C2
Mop End La HP7 ......164 A4
Morar Cl LU7 ....80 B4
Moray Dr SL2 ....206 A4
Moray Pl MK3 ....46 C1
Mordaunt Cl MK43 .....8 C2
Mordaunts St MK15 ...35 B1
More Ave HP21 ....115 B4
Moreau Wlk SL3 .....206 C4
Morebath Gr MK4 .....46 B2
Morefields HP23 ....119 A3

Moreland Ave SL3 ....212 B4
Moreland Dr SL9 .....188 C2
Morello Dr SL3 ......206 C3
Moreton Cl MK18 ......41 C1
Moreton La HP17 .....115 A4
Moreton Rd MK18 .....41 B1
Moreton Way SL1 ....204 B3
Morland Dr MK8 ....45 B3
Morley Cl SL3 ....206 C2
Morley Cres MK7 ......48 B2
Morrell Cl MK5 ....46 A3
Morrice Cl SL3 ......207 A1
Morris Cl SL3 ....177 C1
Morris Ct Aylesbury HP21 115 B2
  Windsor SL4 ....209 C3
Morris Pl **1** SL7 ...183 B1
Morris Wlk MK16 ......22 A1
Morrison Ct MK8 ......45 C3
Mortain Cl MK7 ....48 A2
Mortain Dr HP4 ......134 C3
Morten Gdns UB9 ....190 A2
Mortens Wood HP7 ...165 C4
Mortimer Hill HP23 ..119 A2
Mortimer Rd SL3 ....206 B2
Mortimer Rise HP23 .119 A2
Morton Cl
  North Marston MK18 ..76 A1
  Pitstone LU7 ....105 B2
Morton King Cl HP18 .124 B2
Mortons Fork MK13 ...33 C3
Moseley Rd HP14 ....161 B4
Moses Plat La HP27 .150 A3
Moss Ct **2** HP9 ...176 B2
Mossdale MK13 ....34 A3
Mossway HP9 ....175 B3
Mossy Vale SL6 .....195 B1
Moundsfield Way SL1 .204 C2
Mount Ave MK1 ....47 C2
Mount Cl
  Aston Clinton HP22 ..117 C2
  Farnham Common SL2 .198 B4
  High Wycombe HP12 ..172 C3
Mount Farm Ind Est MK1 .47 B2
Mount Farm Rdbt MK1 ..47 B2
Mount Hill La SL9 ...188 A1
Mount La UB9 ....189 B1
Mount Nugent HP5 ...144 A2
Mount Pleasant
  Aspley Guise MK17 ...49 C2
  Aylesbury HP19 ......101 B1
  Lane End HP14 ......171 A4
  Milton Keynes MK17 ..47 B2
  Soulbury LU7 ....69 C2
  Steeple Claydon MK18 .63 C1
  Stoke Goldington MK46,
    MK16 ....12 A4
  Stoke Hammond MK17 ..69 C4
  Whitchurch HP22 .....86 C4
  Yardley Gobion NN12 .18 C3
Mount Pleasant Cl MK18 .52 B4
Mount Pleasant Cotts **18**
  SL8 ....185 A2
Mount St HP20 ....115 B4
Mount The
  Aspley Guise MK17 ...49 B2
  Milton Keynes MK46 ..47 C2
Mount View RG9 .....191 B1
Mount View Ct RG9 ..191 B1
Mount Way HP27 .....139 A2
Mountain Ash SL7 ...183 B3
Mountbatten Cl **3** SL6 .202 A2
Mountbatten Sq **4** SL4 .210 B3
Mounthill Ave MK19 ..32 A4
Mountsfield Cl
  Newport Pagnell MK16 .22 B2
  Stanwell TW19 ....213 A1
Mow Mead MK46 ....6 C3
Mowbray Dr LU7 ......80 B4
Mowbray Rd HP20 ...101 B1
Mowhills MK43 ....3 C3
Moyleen Rise SL7 ...183 B1
Mozart Cl MK7 ....48 B2
Muddiford La MK4 .....46 B2
Muirfield Dr MK3 .....46 B1
Mulberry Cl
  Amersham HP7 ....165 C4
  Tring HP23 ....119 A3
Mulberry Ct HP15 ....163 B4
Mulberry Dr SL3 ....206 C1
Mulberry Wlk SL6 ...202 B4
Mullen Ave MK14 .....34 C2
Mullins Way HP19 ...100 C1
Mullion Pl MK6 ....35 A1
Mumfords La SL9 ....188 A4
Munces Rd SL7 ......183 B3
Munday's Farm HP21 .116 B4
Mundaydean La SL7 ..183 A2
Mundesley Spur SL1 .205 C4
Murcott Rd OX25 .....94 B3
Murray Rd HP4 ......135 A3
Murrey Cl MK5 ....46 A3
Murrin Rd SL6 ......202 B4
Mursley CE Sch MK17 .67 B3
Mursley Rd
  Little Horwood MK17 ..55 C1
  Mursley MK17 ....67 A2
Mus of Eton Life The★
  SL4 ....210 B4
Museum Ct **12** HP23 .119 A2
Musgrave Rd OX39 ...147 B4
Musgrave Wlk HP14 ..158 C3
Musgrove Ph MK5 .....46 A3
Myddleton Rd UB8 ...201 B4
Mylne Cl HP13 ......172 C4
Mynchen Cl HP9 .....175 B3
Mynchen End HP9 ...175 B3

Mynchen Rd HP9 .....175 B3
Myrke The SL3 ......205 C1
Myrtle Bank MK12 ....33 C3
Myrtle Cl Poyle SL3 .212 C3
  Uxbridge UB8 ....208 C4
  West Drayton UB7 ..208 C2
Myrtle Cres SL2 ....205 C3

N

Nag's Head La
  Great Kingshill HP16 .152 A2
  Little Kingshill HP16 .152 A2
Nailzee Cl SL9 ......188 C2
Nairdwood Cl HP16 ..151 C2
Nairdwood La HP16 ..151 B3
Nairdwood Way HP16 .151 C2
Nairn Ct MK3 ....46 C1
Naisby Dr MK17 ....59 B1
Nalders Rd HP5 .....144 B1
Nan Aires HP22 ....89 A2
Nancy Hall Ct HP12 .172 B2
Naphill & Walters Ash
  Comb Sch HP14 .....150 A1
Naphill Pl MK13 ......34 B2
Napier Cl UB7 ......208 C2
Napier Rd
  Harmondsworth TW6 .213 B3
  Maidenhead SL6 ....202 A3
Napier St MK2 ....58 B4
Nappin Cl HP19 .....101 A2
Nappins Cl HP18 ....125 B3
Narberth Dr HP20 ...116 A4
Narcot La
  Chalfont St Giles HP8 .177 A3
  Gerrards Cross HP8 ..177 A3
Narcot Rd HP8 ......177 A4
Narcot Way HP8 .....177 A3
Narrow La HP13 .....161 C2
Narrow Path MK17 ...49 A2
Naseby Cl
  Newport Pagnell MK16 .22 A2
  Thame OX9 ....126 A1
Naseby Ct
  Buckingham MK18 ....41 C1
  Milton Keynes MK13 ..34 A3
Nash Cl HP21 ....116 A2
Nash Croft MK4 ......57 A4
Nash Lee End HP22 .130 C4
Nash Lee La HP22 ...130 C3
Nash Lee Rd HP17,HP22 .130 B3
Nash Pl HP10 ....163 A1
Nash Rd
  Great Horwood MK17 ..55 A2
  Slough SL3 ....207 A1
  Thornborough MK18 ..54 A4
  Whaddon MK17 ....45 A1
Nashdom La SL1 ....197 A3
Nashleigh Hill HP5 ..144 B2
Nashs Farm HP22 .....88 B2
Nathanial Cl MK5 .....46 A3
Nathaniel Wlk HP23 .119 A1
National Badminton Ctr
  MK8 ....34 A1
National Bowl The MK6 .46 C3
National Film
  & Television Sch HP9 .175 C1
National Hockey Stad
  MK9 ....34 B1
Natwoke Cl HP9 .....175 B3
Neal Cl SL9 ....189 A2
Neale Cl HP12 ......172 B2
Neapland MK6 ....47 A3
Near Town MK46 ....7 A3
Near Town Gdns MK46 .7 A2
Nearton End MK17 ....67 A2
Neath Cres MK3 ......47 A1
Neath Hill Rdbt MK15 .35 A3
Needham Cl SL4 ....209 C3
Needlemakers HP18 .125 B4
Neilson Ct MK7 ......48 B3
Nelson Cl Coleshill HP7 .164 B2
  High Wycombe HP13 ..173 C3
  Milton Keynes MK8 ...45 C4
  Slough SL3 ....206 B1
Nelson Ct MK18 ......52 B4
Nelson Rd Dagnall HP4 .107 B3
  Harmondsworth TW6 .213 C3
  Windsor SL4 ....209 C2
Nelson St MK18 ......52 B4
Nelson Terr HP20 ...115 B4
Nene Cl Aylesbury HP21 .115 B2
  Newport Pagnell MK16 .22 B2
Nene Dr MK3 ....57 C4
Neptune Way MK2 ...204 C2
Ness Way MK2 ....58 B4
Nether Cl NN13 ......38 A4
Nether Gr MK5 ....46 A2
Netherby Cl HP23 ...119 B3
Nethercote La OX49 .157 A4
Netherfield Rdbt MK6 .47 B4
Netherwood Rd HP9 .175 B3
Netley Ct MK10 ......36 A1
Nettlecombe MK4 ....46 B2
Nettleden Rd HP4 ...121 C2
Nettleton Rd UB10 ..201 C4
Neve Ho SL6 ....202 C4
Nevill Cl MK19 ....11 A1
Neville Cl SL2 ......198 C3
Neville Ct SL1 ......197 B1
Nevis Cl LU7 ....80 B4
Nevis Gr MK2 ....58 C2
New Chilterns HP7 ..165 C4
New Cl RG9 ....192 A4
New Ct
  High Wycombe HP13 ..173 B3

New Ct continued
Marlow SL7 . . . . .183 B1
New Dr HP13 . . . . .173 C4
New Footpath HP5 . . . .154 A4
New Garden Dr UB7 . . .208 C2
New Inn La MK18 . . . . . .51 C2
New Mdw HP21 . . . . . .116 B4
New Mill Terr HP23 . . . .119 A3
New Par
Chorleywood WD3 . . . . .167 B3
West Drayton UB7 . . . . .208 B4
New Peachey La UB8 . . .208 B4
New Pond Rd HP15 . . . .163 B4
New Provident Pl 5
HP4 . . . . .135 C2
New Rd Amersham HP6 .154 C1
Aston Clinton HP22 . . . .117 C3
Aylesbury HP22 . . . . . .116 C3
Berkhamsted HP4 . . . . .135 B3
Berkhamsted, Northchurch
HP4 . . . . .134 C4
Bourne End SL8 . . . . . .185 A2
Castlethorpe MK19 . . . . .19 C3
Chipperfield WD4 . . . . .146 C1
Coleshill HP7 . . . . . . .164 C2
Cookham SL8 . . . . . . .195 C4
Datchet SL3 . . . . .211 C3
Dinton HP17 . . . . .113 C1
Drayton Parslow MK17 . . .68 B3
Great Kingshill HP15 . . .162 B4
Harrold MK43 . . . . .3 C3
High Wycombe HP12 . . . .172 B3
Hurley SL7 . . . . .193 C2
Lacey Green HP27 . . . . .149 C2
Lane End HP14 . . . . . . .170 C3
Leighton Buzzard LU7 . . . .80 C4
Little Chalfont HP8 . . . .166 C3
Little Kingshill HP16 . . . .152 A2
Marlow Bottom SL7 . . . .183 A2
Prestwood HP16 . . . . . .151 B3
Princes Risborough HP27 .139 B2
Sarratt WD3 . . . . .156 C1
Slough SL3 . . . . .207 A2
Stokenchurch HP14 . . . .158 C2
Tring HP23 . . . . .119 A3
Tylers Green HP10 . . . . .163 B1
Walter's Ash HP14,HP27 . .150 A1
Weedon HP22 . . . . . . .101 A4
Wilstone HP23 . . . . . . .118 B4
New Road Cl HP12 . . . .172 B3
New Road Gdns HP12 . .172 B3
New Row MK46 . . . . . . .7 C4
New Sq SL1 . . . . .205 C2
New St Aylesbury HP20 .101 B1
Berkhamsted HP4 . . . . .135 B2
Cheddington LU7 . . . . . .104 C4
Henley-on-T RG9 . . . . .191 C1
Milton Keynes MK11 . . . . .32 B3
Tingewick MK18 . . . . . . .51 A3
Waddesdon HP18 . . . . . .99 A4
New Windsor St UB8 . . .201 B2
New Zealand Gdns LU7 . .79 C1
Newark Ct MK7 . . . . . . .48 A2
Newbarn La HP9 . . . . . .176 C3
Newberry Cres SL4 . . . .209 B3
Newbery Way SL1 . . . . .205 B2
Newbolt Cl
Newport Pagnell MK16 . . .21 C3
Paulerspury NN12 . . . . . .17 A4
Newbridge Oval MK4 . . . .46 A2
Newbury Ct MK3 . . . . . . .57 B3
Newbury Dr SL6 . . . . . .203 A3
Newbury Rd TW6,UB7 . . .213 C3
Newby Pl MK4 . . . . .46 A1
Newchurch Rd SL2 . . . .204 C4
Newcombe Rise UB7 . . .208 C4
Newcourt UB8 . . . . . . .208 B4
Newcroft Cl UB8 . . . . . .208 C4
Newell Cl HP21 . . . . . . .116 A3
Newells Hedge LU7 . . . .105 B3
Newfield Gdns SL7 . . . .183 C2
Newfield Rd SL7 . . . . . .183 C2
Newfield Way SL7 . . . . .183 C1
Newground Rd HP23 . . . .120 A2
Newhall Cl HP3 . . . . . . .146 A2
Newhaven Spur SL2 . . . .198 A1
Newhouse Rd HP3 . . . . .146 A3
Newland Ho UB8 . . . . . .201 B2
Newlands Dr
Maidenhead SL6 . . . . . .202 A4
Poyle SL3 . . . . .212 C2
Newlands Girls Sch SL6 .202 A4
Newlyn Pl MK6 . . . . .35 A1
Newmans Cl MK14 . . . . . .21 C1
Newmans Ctyd MK17 . . . .68 B3
Newmarket Ct MK10 . . . . .36 B1
Newmer Rd HP12 . . . . . .172 A2
Newport Pagnell Rd
MK43 . . . . .16 B2
Newport Rd
Astwood MK16 . . . . . . .15 B1
Emberton MK46 . . . . . . .13 C4
Hanslope MK19 . . . . . . .11 A1
Milton Keynes Village MK10 .36 B1
Milton Keynes, New Bradwell
MK13 . . . . .34 A4
Milton Keynes, Oakgrove
MK15,MK17,MK6 . . . . . .35 B1
Milton Keynes, Willen MK15 .35 B4
Milton Keynes, Woolstone
MK15 . . . . .35 B3
Moulsoe MK16 . . . . .36 B4
Slough SL2 . . . . .197 C1
Wavendon MK17 . . . . . . .48 C4
Woburn MK17 . . . . .60 C4
Newton Blossomville
CE Fst Sch MK43 . . . . . .8 A2
Newton Cl SL3 . . . . . . .206 C4

Newton Ct SL4 . . . . . . .211 A1
Newton La SL4 . . . . . . .211 A1
Newton Longville CE
Comb Prim Sch MK17 . . . .57 B2
Newton Rd
Drayton Parslow MK17 . . .68 B4
Milton Keynes MK17,MK3 . .57 C3
Stoke Hammond MK17 . . . .69 B4
Turvey MK43 . . . . .8 C3
Newton Side Orch SL4 . .211 A1
Newton St MK46 . . . . . . .7 A2
Newtonside SL4 . . . . . .211 A1
Newtown Rd Marlow SL7 .183 C2
New Denham UB9 . . . . .201 A3
Newville HP22 . . . . .87 B1
Newyears Green La
UB9 . . . . .190 C3
Neyland Dr HP19 . . . . . .101 B2
Nicholas Gdns
High Wycombe HP13 . . . .173 B4
Slough SL1 . . . . .204 C3
Nicholas Mead MK14 . . . .34 C4
Nicholls SL4 . . . . .209 B3
Nicholls Wlk SL4 . . . . . .209 B2
Nicholsons Ctr **5** SL6 . .202 C4
Nicholsons La SL6 . . . . .202 C4
Nickson Ct HP15 . . . . . .163 A2
Nicol Cl SL9 . . . . .177 B1
Nicol End SL9 . . . . .177 B1
Nicol Rd SL9 . . . . .177 B1
Nigel Ct NN13 . . . . .38 A3
Nightingale Cl
Hazlemere HP15 . . . . . .163 A3
Steeple Claydon MK18 . . .63 C1
Nightingale Cres MK13 . . .34 A4
Nightingale Ho HP11 . . . .174 A2
Nightingale La SL6 . . . . .195 B2
Nightingale Lodge HP4 .135 A2
Nightingale Pk SL2 . . . . .197 C3
Nightingale Pl
Buckingham MK18 . . . . . .41 C1
Cookham SL8 . . . . . . .195 C4
Nightingale Rd
Aylesbury HP21 . . . . . .115 C3
Chesham HP5 . . . . . . .144 A1
Wendover HP22 . . . . . .131 A3
Nightingale Way UB9 . . .189 C3
Nightingale Wlk SL4 . . . .210 B2
Nightingales Cnr HP7 . . .166 B4
Nightingales Ct HP8 . . . .166 B4
Nightingales La
Chalfont St Giles HP8 . . .166 B2
Little Chalfont HP8 . . . . .166 B2
Nijinsky Ho UB8 . . . . . .201 B2
Nine Acres SL1 . . . . . . .204 C3
Nine Elms Ave UB8 . . . .208 B4
Nine Elms Cl UB8 . . . . . .208 B4
Nine Stiles Cl UB9 . . . . .201 A3
Ninnings Rd SL9 . . . . . .177 C2
Ninnings Way SL9 . . . . .177 C2
Nixey Cl SL1 . . . . .206 A2
Nixons Cl MK6 . . . . .46 C3
Noble Cl MK15 . . . . .35 A4
Noon Layer Dr MK10 . . . .35 C2
Norbrek MK8 . . . . .33 C1
Norcotts Kiln Cotts HP18 .96 A1
Norden Cl SL6 . . . . .202 B2
Norden Mdws SL6 . . . . .202 B3
Norden Rd SL6 . . . . . . .202 B3
Norelands Dr SL1 . . . . . .197 B2
Norfolk Ave SL1 . . . . . . .205 B4
Norfolk Park Cotts SL6 . .202 C4
Norfolk Rd
Maidenhead SL6 . . . . . .202 C4
Turvey MK43 . . . . .8 C3
Uxbridge UB8 . . . . . . .201 B3
Norfolk Terr HP20 . . . . . .101 C1
Norgrove Pk SL9 . . . . . .188 C4
Norjo-An Villas HP5 . . . .154 B3
Norland Dr HP10 . . . . . .185 B4
Norman Ave RG9 . . . . . .191 C1
Normandy Dr HP4 . . . . . .135 A3
Normandy Way MK3 . . . . .46 C1
Normans Cl UB8 . . . . . .208 C4
Normans Ct 2 HP13 . . . .173 C3
Normans The SL2 . . . . .206 A4
Normill Terr HP22 . . . . . .117 A3
Norreys Dr SL6 . . . . . . .202 B2
Norrington MK8 . . . . .33 C1
Norris Ho SL6 . . . . .202 C4
Norris Rd OX25 . . . . . . .94 C4
North Bridge Rd HP4 . . . .135 A3
North Burnham Cl SL1 . . .197 A2
North Cl
Drayton Parslow MK17 . . .68 B4
Medmenham SL7 . . . . . .193 B4
Windsor SL4 . . . . .209 C3
North Common Rd UB8 .201 C4
North Cotts SL2 . . . . . . .198 B1
North Crawley CE Fst Sch
MK16 . . . . .24 A3
North Crawley Rd
Moulsoe MK16 . . . . . . .23 B2
Newport Pagnell MK16 . . .23 B2
North Crawley MK16 . . . .23 B2
North Croft Winslow MK18 .66 A2
Wooburn Green HP10 . . . .185 C3
North Dr Aylesbury HP21 .115 C3
Beaconsfield HP9 . . . . . .186 A4
High Wycombe HP13 . . . .173 C4
North Eastern Rd HP19 . .101 B1
North Eighth St MK9 . . . . .34 C2
North Elder Rdbt MK9 . . . .34 B1
North Eleventh St MK9 . . .34 C2
North End Rd
Quainton HP22 . . . . . . .85 A3

North End Rd continued
Steeple Claydon MK18 . . .63 B2
North Fifth St MK9 . . . . . .34 B1
North Fourteenth St
MK9 . . . . .34 C2
North Fourth St MK9 . . . . .34 B1
North Gate MK2 . . . . . . .47 B1
North Gn
3 Maidenhead SL6 . . . .195 C1
Slough SL1 . . . . .205 C2
North Hill Brill HP18 . . . . .96 A1
Dadford MK18 . . . . .28 B1
North La
Chorleywood WD3 . . . . .167 C4
Walton MK7 . . . . .47 C4
North Lee La HP22 . . . . .129 C4
North Links Rd HP10 . . . .174 A1
North Marston CE Sch
MK18 . . . . .76 A1
North Marston La HP22 . . .86 C4
North Mill Rd HP27 . . . . .138 A3
North Ninth St MK9 . . . . .34 C2
North Orbital Rd
Denham Green UB9 . . . .189 C4
Maple Cross WD3 . . . . .178 C2
North Overgate Rdbt
MK15 . . . . .35 A3
North Pk
Gerrards Cross SL9 . . . . .188 C4
Iver SL0,SL3 . . . . .207 B2
Tylers Green HP10 . . . . .174 B4
North Ridge MK6 . . . . . . .35 A1
North Row Fulmer SL3 . . .199 C4
Milton Keynes MK9 . . . . .34 C2
North Second St MK9 . . . .34 B1
North Seventh St MK9 . . . .34 B1
North Sixth St MK9 . . . . . .34 B1
North Skeldon Rdbt MK9 .35 A2
North Sq MK16 . . . . .22 B3
North St
Castlethorpe MK19 . . . . .19 C3
Milton Keynes, Bradville
MK13 . . . . .34 A4
Milton Keynes,
Fenny Stratford MK2 . . . .47 B1
Thame OX9 . . . . .125 C1
North Star La SL6 . . . . . .202 B3
North Tenth St MK9 . . . . .34 C2
North Third St MK9 . . . . .34 B1
North Thirteenth St MK9 .34 C2
North Town Cl **1** SL6 . . . .195 C1
North Town Mead **4**
SL6 . . . . .195 C1
North Town Moor SL6 . . .195 C1
North Town Rd SL6 . . . . .195 C1
North Twelfth St MK9 . . . .34 C2
North View HP22 . . . . . . .87 A2
North Way
Deanshanger MK19 . . . . .31 C3
Pottersbury NN12 . . . . . .18 C1
Uxbridge UB10 . . . . . . .201 C3
Northall Cl LU6 . . . . .92 B3
Northall Rd LU6 . . . . .92 B3
Northampton Ave SL1 . . .205 B4
Northampton Rd
Brackley NN13 . . . . . . .26 A1
Cosgrove MK19 . . . . . . .19 B1
Grafton Regis NN12 . . . . .9 B2
Lathbury MK16 . . . . . . .22 B3
Lavendon MK46 . . . . . . .7 C4
Yardley Hastings NN7 . . . .1 A3
Northborough Rd SL2 . . .198 A1
Northburgh MK7 . . . . . . .47 C4
Northchurch La HP5 . . . .134 B1
Northcliffe LU6 . . . . .92 C3
Northcroft
Milton Keynes MK5 . . . . .46 B3
Slough SL2 . . . . .198 A1
Weedon HP22 . . . . .87 B1
Northdean **5** SL6 . . . . . .195 C1
Northdown Rd SL9 . . . . .177 C2
Northend HP16 . . . . .5 C2
Northend Cl HP10 . . . . . .185 B4
Northend Sq MK18 . . . . . .41 B1
Northern Hts SL2 . . . . . .185 A3
Northern Perimeter Rd
(W) TW6 . . . . .213 B3
Northern Rd
Aylesbury HP19 . . . . . .101 B1
Slough SL2 . . . . .198 A1
Northern Woods HP10 . . .185 B4
Northfield Ct RG9 . . . . . .191 B3
Northfield Dr MK15 . . . . . .35 C3
Northfield End RG9 . . . . .191 B3
Northfield Rd
Aylesbury HP20 . . . . . .116 A4
Eton SL4 . . . . .204 C1
Maidenhead SL6 . . . . . .195 C1
Princes Risborough HP27 .139 B2
Tring HP23 . . . . .119 C4
Northfield Rdbt MK18 . . . .36 A3
Northlands Rd MK18 . . . . .53 C2
Northleigh MK4 . . . . .46 B1
Northmead Rd SL2 . . . . .204 C4
Northmill HP27 . . . . .138 C2
Northmoor Rd TW6 . . . . .213 C3
Northumberland Ave
HP21 . . . . .116 A3
Northumberland Cl
TW19 . . . . .213 C1
Northumbria Rd SL6 . . . .202 A2
Northwich MK6 . . . . .47 B4
Northwood Rd TW6 . . . . .213 C3
Nortoft Rd SL9 . . . . .177 C2

Norton Leys MK7 . . . . . . .48 A2
Norton Rd MK18 . . . . . . .201 B1
Norton's Pl MK18 . . . . . . .52 B4
Nortons The MK7 . . . . . . .48 A2
Norvic Rd HP23 . . . . . . .105 A1
Norway Dr SL2 . . . . .206 A4
Norwich Ho
High Wycombe HP13 . . . .173 C4
Maidenhead SL6 . . . . . .202 C4
Norwood Cl HP20 . . . . . .101 C1
Norwood Ct HP7 . . . . . . .165 A4
Norwood La
Newport Pagnell MK16 . . .22 B2
Uxbridge SL0 . . . . .200 B1
Norwood Rd HP10 . . . . . .174 A1
Nottingham Gr MK3 . . . . .46 C1
Nottingham Ho **3** HP13 .173 C4
Nottingham Rd WD3 . . . .167 B1
Nova Lodge MK4 . . . . . . .46 A1
Novello Croft MK7 . . . . . .48 B2
Nugent Cl SL7 . . . . .183 C2
Nugent Ct HP5 . . . . .144 A2
Nuneham Gr MK4 . . . . . . .45 C2
Nup End Cl HP22 . . . . . . .89 A2
Nup End La HP22 . . . . . . .89 A2
Nurseries The LU6 . . . . . .92 C3
Nursery Cl
Amersham HP7 . . . . . . .165 C4
Aylesbury HP21 . . . . . .115 B3
Tylers Green HP10 . . . . .174 B4
Nursery Ct HP12 . . . . . . .172 B3
Nursery Dr HP14 . . . . . . .171 A3
Nursery Gdns
Milton Keynes MK13 . . . . .34 A2
Tring HP23 . . . . .119 A2
Nursery La Slough SL3 . . .206 B3
Tylers Green HP10 . . . . .174 B4
Nursery Rd SL6 . . . . . . .204 A3
Nursery Way TW19 . . . . .211 B1
Nursery Waye UB8 . . . . .201 B2
Nursery Wlk SL7 . . . . . . .183 A1
Nutfield La HP11 . . . . . . .172 C4
Nuthatch **19** HP20 . . . . . .101 C2
Nutkin Wlk UB10 . . . . . . .201 C3
Nutkins Way HP5 . . . . . .144 B1
Nutmeg Cl MK7 . . . . .48 A3
Nye Way HP3 . . . . .146 A2

O

O'Grady Way HP19 . . . . .101 A2
Oak Barn Cl MK43 . . . . . .25 A1
Oak Cres HP12 . . . . .172 B2
Oak Ct MK9 . . . . .34 C1
Oak Dr HP4 . . . . .135 B2
Oak End Dr SL0 . . . . . . .200 B2
Oak End Way
Chinnor OX39 . . . . . . .147 B3
Gerrards Cross SL9 . . . . .188 C3
Oak Farm
Rare Breeds Pk★ HP22 116 B4
Oak Field HP5 . . . . .144 A1
Oak Green Sch HP21 . . . .115 B4
Oak La
Buckland Common HP23,
HP5 . . . . .133 A1
Windsor SL4 . . . . .210 A1
Oak Rd HP27 . . . . .139 B2
Oak St HP11 . . . . .173 B2
Oak Stubbs La SL6 . . . . .203 C2
Oak Tree Ave SL7 . . . . . .183 B2
Oak Tree Cl SL7 . . . . . . .183 B2
Oak Tree Cotts HP18 . . . .83 A3
Oak Tree Dr HP14 . . . . . .171 A3
Oak Tree Rd SL7 . . . . . . .183 B2
Oak View HP15 . . . . . . .162 B4
Oak Way MK18 . . . . .66 A2
Oakdene HP9 . . . . .175 C2
Oakdown Cres MK46 . . . . .6 C2
Oaken Gr SL6 . . . . .195 B4
Oaken Head MK4 . . . . . . .46 B1
Oakengrove HP16 . . . . . .151 B3
Oakengrove Cl HP15 . . . .163 B3
Oakengrove La HP15 . . . .163 A2
Oakengrove Rd HP15 . . . .163 B3
Oakeshott Ave HP14 . . . .161 B3
Oakfield WD3 . . . . .167 C1
Oakfield Ave SL1 . . . . . .205 A3
Oakfield Cl HP6 . . . . .154 B1
Oakfield Cnr HP6 . . . . . .154 B1
Oakfield Fst Sch SL4 . . . .210 A3
Oakfield Rd
Aylesbury HP20 . . . . . .116 A4
Bourne End SL8 . . . . . .185 A2
Oakgrove Rdbt MK10 . . . .35 C1
Oakhill Cl
Maple Cross WD3 . . . . .178 A3
Milton Keynes MK5 . . . . .45 C3
Oakhill Rd
Maple Cross WD3 . . . . .178 B3
Milton Keynes MK5 . . . . .45 B3
Oakhill Rdbt MK5 . . . . . . .45 B3
Oakhurst SL6 . . . . .196 A2
Oakington Ave HP6 . . . . .166 C4
Oakland Way HP10 . . . . .174 A1
Oaklands HP4 . . . . .135 A2
Oaklawn HP23 . . . . .119 A2
Oakley HP10 . . . . .185 C4
Oakley CE Comb Sch
HP18 . . . . .109 B2
Oakley Cres SL1 . . . . . .205 C4
Oakley Gdns MK15 . . . . . .35 A3
Oakley Green Rd SL4 . . . .209 A3
Oakley La OX39 . . . . . . .147 A3
Oakley Rd Chinnor OX39 .147 B3
Horton-cum-S OX33 . . . .108 A3

Oakridge MK4 . . . . .46 C2
Oakridge Ct HP12 . . . . . .172 B3
Oakridge Rd HP11 . . . . . .172 C4
Oakridge Sch HP12 . . . . .172 C4
Oaks Rd TW19 . . . . .213 A1
Oaks The MK4 . . . . .135 A2
Oakside UB9 . . . . .201 A3
Oaktree Cl HP10 . . . . . . .163 A1
Oaktree Ct MK15 . . . . . . .35 B4
Oakview HP6 . . . . .153 B2
Oakway HP6 . . . . .154 A2
Oakwell Cl LU6 . . . . .93 C4
Oakwood
Berkhamsted HP4 . . . . .134 C2
Flackwell Heath HP10 . . . .174 A1
Oakwood Dr MK2 . . . . . . .58 C4
Oatlands Dr SL1 . . . . . . .205 B4
Oban Ct SL1 . . . . .205 B2
Ockwells Rd SL6 . . . . . .202 B1
Octagon Arc **9** HP11 . . . .173 A4
Octagon Par **6** HP11 . . . .173 A4
Octavian Dr MK13 . . . . . .33 C3
Octavian Way NN13 . . . . .38 A3
Oddley La HP27 . . . . . . .148 B4
Odds Farm Pk★ HP10 . . .186 A2
Oddy Hill HP23 . . . . .119 B1
Odell Cl MK6 . . . . .47 B4
Odencroft Rd SL2 . . . . . .198 A1
Odney La SL8 . . . . .196 A4
Offas La MK18 . . . . .66 A3
Ogilvie Rd HP12 . . . . . . .172 C4
Okeford Cl HP23 . . . . . . .118 C2
Okeford Dr HP23 . . . . . . .118 C2
Okeley La HP23 . . . . . . .118 C2
Old Amersham Rd SL9 . . .189 A2
Old Bakery The HP14 . . . .171 A2
Old Barn Cl MK18 . . . . . .52 A2
Old Brewery Cl HP21 . . . .115 C4
Old Burrs HP21 . . . . .115 B2
Old Chapel Cl HP17 . . . . .129 C2
Old Coach Dr HP11 . . . . .174 A2
Old Court Cl SL6 . . . . . . .202 A2
Old Crown SL1 . . . . .205 C2
Old Dashwood Hill
HP14 . . . . .159 C1
Old Dean HP3 . . . . .146 A2
Old End MK18 . . . . .53 A1
Old English Cl MK17 . . . . .44 B1
Old Farm LU7 . . . . .105 B2
Old Farm Cl
Beaconsfield HP9 . . . . .175 B3
Worminghall HP18 . . . . .123 B3
Old Farm Rd
High Wycombe HP13 . . . .161 C1
West Drayton UB7 . . . . .208 B2
Old Ferry Dr TW19 . . . . . .211 B1
Old Field Cl HP6 . . . . . . .166 C4
Old Fives Ct SL1 . . . . . . .197 A1
Old Forge Cl
Maidenhead SL6 . . . . . .203 A2
Tingewick MK18 . . . . . . .51 A3
Old Forge Gdns HP22 . . .102 A2
Old Forge Rd HP10 . . . . .174 B1
Old Forge The HP23 . . . .104 A2
Old Gaol Mus★ MK18 . . . .41 B1
Old Garden Ctr The
HP27 . . . . .139 A2
Old Groveway MK6 . . . . . .47 B3
Old Hardenwaye HP13 . . .162 C1
Old Horns La HP13 . . . . . .172 A2
Old House Ct SL3 . . . . . .206 B4
Old Kiln Rd
Flackwell Heath HP10 . . . .185 A4
Tylers Green HP10 . . . . .163 B1
Old Linslade Rd LU7 . . . . .70 C2
Old Lodge Dr HP9 . . . . . .175 C1
Old Maltings The **2**
OX9 . . . . .125 C1
Old Manor Cl
Princes Risborough HP27 .139 B4
Whaddon MK17 . . . . . . .45 A1
Old Manor Ct LU7 . . . . . .78 C4
Old Marsh La
Dorney SL6 . . . . .203 C2
Taplow SL6 . . . . .203 C2
Old Mead SL9 . . . . .177 C2
Old Mill Cl HP17 . . . . . . .127 A3
Old Mill Furlong MK18 . . . .66 C2
Old Mill Gdns **12** HP4 . . .135 B2
Old Mill La
Maidenhead SL6 . . . . . .203 B2
Uxbridge UB8 . . . . . . .208 B2
Old Mill Rd UB9 . . . . . . .190 A1
Old Moor La HP10 . . . . . .185 C4
Old Nursery Ct SL2 . . . . .187 B1
Old Oak Gdns HP4 . . . . .134 C4
Old Orch OX39 . . . . .137 C1
Old Orchard Mews **14**
HP4 . . . . .135 B2
Old Orchards HP22 . . . . .102 A2
Old Oxford Rd HP14 . . . . .160 B1
Old Palace Ct SL3 . . . . . .212 B3
Old Plough Ct HP18 . . . . .112 A1
Old Post Office La **10**
SL6 . . . . .202 C2
Old Rd LU7 . . . . .80 C4
Old Rectory La UB9 . . . . .189 C2
Old Risborough Rd
HP22 . . . . .130 A4
Old Sax La HP5 . . . . . . .143 B2
Old School Cl
Halton HP22 . . . . .117 B1
Stokenchurch HP14 . . . .158 C2
Old School Cotts HP5 . . .145 B3

Old School Ct
Buckingham MK18 . . . . .52 B4
Eaton Bray LU6 . . . . .92 C3
Old School La MK17 . . . . . .69 C4
Old School La The MK18 . .63 B2
Old School Rd UB8 . . . . . .201 C1
Old School The HP10 . . . .185 B4
Old Shire La WD3,HP8 . .167 A2
Old Slade La SL0 . . . . . . .207 C1
Old Stable Yd The
MK18 . . . . .65 C2
Old Station Way HP10 . .185 C3
Old Stoke Rd HP21 . . . . . .115 B3
Old Stratford Prim Sch
MK19 . . . . .32 A3
Old Tan Yard Cl MK18 . . . .65 C2
Old Town NN13 . . . . .38 A4
Old Town Cl HP9 . . . . . . .175 C1
Old Town Farm HP16 . . . .152 A4
Old Uxbridge Rd WD3 . . .178 C2
Old Vicarage Way HP10 . .185 B2
Old Watery La HP10 . . . . .185 C4
Old Windmill Way HP18 . .125 B4
Old Wolverton Rd MK12 . .33 B4
Oldacres SL6 . . . . .203 A4
Oldbrook Bvd MK6 . . . . . .46 C4
Oldbrook Fst Sch MK6 . .46 C4
Oldbury Gr HP18 . . . . .175 B3
Olde Bell Cl MK17 . . . . . . .69 C4
Olde Bell La MK6 . . . . .46 A4
Oldershaw Mews SL6 . . . .202 A4
Oldfield Prim Sch SL6 . .203 A3
Oldfield Rd SL6 . . . . .203 A4
Oldfield Rd Ind Est SL6 .203 A4
Oldhams Mdw 10 HP20 . .101 C1
Oldhouse Cl HP11 . . . . . . .172 C2
Oldway La SL1 . . . . .204 B3
Oliffe Cl HP20 . . . . .101 B2
Oliffe Way HP20 . . . . .101 B2
Oliver Rd MK2 . . . . .58 A4
Oliver's Paddock SL7 . . .183 B3
Olivier Way HP20 . . . . . . .116 A4
Olleberrie La WD4 . . . . . .156 B4
Olney Fst Sch MK46 . . . . .6 C2
Olney Mid Sch MK46 . . . .6 C3
Olney Rd Emberton MK46 . .13 C4
Lavendon MK46 . . . . .7 C4
One Pin La SL2 . . . . .187 B1
One Tree La HP9 . . . . .175 C2
Onslow Cl MK7 . . . . .48 A2
Onslow Dr OX9 . . . . .126 A1
Onslow Gdns HP13 . . . . . .173 C4
Opal Ct SL3 . . . . .199 B1
Opal Dr MK15 . . . . .35 C2
Open University (Walton
Hall) The MK7 . . . . .47 C4
Opendale Rd SL1 . . . . . . .204 A4
Orbell Ct HP27 . . . . .139 C2
Orbison Ct MK8 . . . . .45 B4
Orchard Ave
Berkhamsted HP4 . . . . . . .135 A2
Slough SL1 . . . . .204 B4
Windsor SL4 . . . . .210 A3
Orchard Cl
27 Aylesbury HP20 . . . . . .101 C2
Beaconsfield HP9 . . . . . . .175 B2
Chorleywood WD3 . . . . . . .167 B3
Cranfield MK43 . . . . .25 A1
Henley-on-T RG9 . . . . .191 C1
Hughenden Valley HP14 . . .162 A4
Longwick HP27 . . . . .138 B4
Maidenhead SL6 . . . . .203 A2
Milton Keynes MK3 . . . . . . .57 C4
New Denham UB9 . . . . . . .201 A3
Newton Longville MK17 . . .57 B2
Oakley HP18 . . . . .109 B2
Stoke Mandeville HP22 . . .116 A1
Waddesdon HP18 . . . . .99 A4
Wendover HP22 . . . . .131 A3
Wingrave HP22 . . . . .89 A2
Yardley Gobion NN12 . . . . .18 C3
Orchard Ct
Bovingdon HP3 . . . . .146 A2
Harmondsworth TW6 . . . . .213 B4
Seer Green HP9 . . . . .176 B3
Orchard Dr
Aston Clinton HP22 . . . . . .117 C2
Chorleywood WD3 . . . . . . .167 B3
Hazelmere HP15 . . . . .163 A2
Leighton Buzzard LU7 . . . . .80 B3
Uxbridge UB8 . . . . .201 B1
Wooburn Green HP10 . . . .185 B2
Orchard End
Edlesborough LU6 . . . . .92 C2
Hazelmere HP15 . . . . .163 A3
Orchard End Ave HP7 . . .165 C4
Orchard Gate SL2 . . . . . . .198 A4
Orchard Gr
Flackwell Heath HP10 . . . .185 A4
Gerrards Cross SL9 . . . . . .177 B1
Maidenhead SL6 . . . . .202 B4
Orchard Ho 8 SL8 . . . . . .185 A2
Orchard La
Amersham HP6 . . . . .154 B1
Harrold MK43 . . . . .3 C4
Prestwood HP16 . . . . .151 B3
Stewkley LU7 . . . . .78 C4
Orchard Lodge 9 SL1 . . .204 C3
Orchard Mews 3 HP9 . . .176 B2
Orchard Mill SL8 . . . . . . .185 A1
Orchard Pk HP15 . . . . . . .163 B4
Orchard Pl
Princes Risborough HP27 . .139 B3
Uxbridge UB8 . . . . .201 B3
Westbury NN13 . . . . .39 A2

Orchard Rd
Beaconsfield HP9 . . . . . . .175 C1
Chalfont St Giles HP8 . . . .177 B4
High Wycombe HP13 . . . . .174 A2
Old Windsor SL4 . . . . .211 A1
Seer Green HP9 . . . . .176 B3
Orchard Rise
Aston Clinton HP22 . . . . . .117 C3
Flackwell Heath HP10 . . . .185 A4
Halton HP22 . . . . .131 B4
Hazelmere HP15 . . . . .163 A3
Marlow SL7 . . . . .183 C2
Pottersbury NN12 . . . . .18 B2
Walter's Ash HP14 . . . . . . .161 C3
Orchard View UB8 . . . . . .201 B1
Orchard Way
Aylesbury HP20 . . . . .101 C1
Bovingdon HP3 . . . . .146 A2
Chinnor OX39 . . . . .147 B3
Cranfield MK43 . . . . .25 A1
East Claydon MK18 . . . . . . .74 C3
Eaton Bray LU6 . . . . .92 C3
Holmer Green HP15 . . . . . .163 B3
North Crawley MK16 . . . . . .24 A3
Pitstone LU7 . . . . .105 C2
Slough SL3 . . . . .206 C3
Stoke Goldington MK16 . . . .12 A4
Wing LU7 . . . . .79 C1
Orchard Waye UB8 . . . . . .201 B2
Orchard Wlk MK46 . . . . . . .7 C4
Orchards The
Eaton Bray LU6 . . . . .92 C4
Little Kingshill HP16 . . . . .152 A1
Tring HP23 . . . . .118 C2
Orchardville SL1 . . . . . . .197 A1
Orchehill Ave SL9 . . . . . .188 B4
Orchehill Ct SL9 . . . . . . .188 C3
Orchehill Rise SL9 . . . . . .188 C3
Oregano Cl UB7 . . . . .208 C3
Orford Ct MK5 . . . . .46 A3
Orkney Cl
Milton Keynes MK3 . . . . . . .46 C1
Stewkley LU7 . . . . .78 C4
Orkney Ct SL6 . . . . .196 C3
Ormesby Cl HP21 . . . . . . .116 A3
Ormond Rd OX9 . . . . .126 A1
Ormonde MK14 . . . . .34 B4
Ormsgill Ct MK13 . . . . . . .34 A3
Orne Gdns MK15 . . . . .35 A4
Orpington Gr MK5 . . . . . . .46 A2
Ortensia Dr MK7 . . . . .48 C4
Orwell Cl Aylesbury HP21 .115 B2
Newport Pagnell MK16 . . . .21 C3
Windsor SL4 . . . . .210 B2
Orwell Dr
Aylesbury HP21 . . . . .115 B2
Stoke Mandeville HP21 . . .115 B2
Osborn Rd UB8 . . . . .201 B1
Osborn's Ct MK46 . . . . .6 C2
Osborne Mews SL4 . . . . .210 B3
Osborne Rd SL4 . . . . .210 B2
Osborne St
Milton Keynes MK2 . . . . . . .58 B4
Slough SL1 . . . . .205 C2
Osborne Way HP23 . . . . . .119 B1
Osbourne Ct SL4 . . . . . . .210 B3
Osbourne St MK12 . . . . . .33 B3
Osier La MK5 . . . . .46 A2
Osier Way HP20 . . . . .115 C4
Osmington Pl HP23 . . . . . .118 C2
Osney Rd SL6 . . . . .195 C1
Osprey Cl
Aylesbury HP20 . . . . .101 C1
Slough SL3 . . . . .206 C2
Osprey The HP20 . . . . . . .101 C2
Osprey Wlk
Aylesbury HP20 . . . . .101 C1
Buckingham MK18 . . . . . . .52 C4
Ostler Gate SL6 . . . . .195 B1
Ostlers Ct HP11 . . . . .174 A2
Ostlers La MK11 . . . . .32 B3
Otter Cl MK3 . . . . .46 B1
Otterfield Rd UB7 . . . . . . .208 C3
Otters Brook MK18 . . . . . .52 C4
Otway Cl HP21 . . . . .115 C2
Oulton Cl HP21 . . . . .116 A3
Our Lady of Peace
RC Inf Sch SL1 . . . . .204 A4
Our Lady of Peace
RC Md Sch SL1 . . . . .204 B4
Our Lady's RC Sch
HP6 . . . . .154 A2
Ousebank St MK16 . . . . . .22 B3
Ousebank Way MK11 . . . . .32 B3
Ousedale Comb Sch
MK16 . . . . .22 A2
Ouseley Rd TW19 . . . . . . .211 B1
Outfield Rd SL9 . . . . .177 B2
Outlook Dr HP8 . . . . .177 B4
Ouzel Cl MK3 . . . . .46 C1
Oval The MK6 . . . . .46 C4
Oval Way SL9 . . . . .188 C4
Over Hampden HP16 . . . .151 B4
Over The Misbourne Rd
SL9,UB9 . . . . .189 A3
Overdale Rd HP5 . . . . .144 C1
Overdales HP15 . . . . .162 C2
Overend Cl MK13 . . . . .34 C2
Overgate MK9 . . . . .35 A2
Overhills MK46 . . . . .6 C2
Overn Ave MK18 . . . . .41 B1
Overn Cl MK18 . . . . .41 B1
Overn Cres MK18 . . . . .41 B1
Overshot Ho HP10 . . . . . .174 B1
Oversley Ct MK14 . . . . . . .22 A1
Overstone Cl LU7 . . . . .79 C1
Overstone Comb Sch
LU7 . . . . .79 C1

Overstrand HP22 . . . . .117 C3
Overstreet MK14,MK15 . . . .35 A3
Overton Dr OX9 . . . . .126 A1
Oville Ct MK5 . . . . .46 A3
Oving Rd HP22 . . . . .86 C4
Ovitts Cl MK18 . . . . .66 A3
Owl Cl 18 HP20 . . . . .101 C2
Owlsears Cl HP9 . . . . .175 B2
Oxendon Ct LU7 . . . . .70 C1
Oxfield Cl HP4 . . . . .135 A2
Oxford Ave Burnham SL1 .197 A2
Slough SL1 . . . . .204 C4
Oxford Gdns UB9 . . . . . . .190 A1
Oxford Rd Denham UB9 . .189 B1
Gerrards Cross SL9 . . . . . .188 B3
High Wycombe HP11 . . . . .173 A4
Lane End HP14 . . . . .160 B1
Marlow SL7 . . . . .183 B1
New Denham UB9 . . . . . . .201 A3
Oakley HP18 . . . . .109 B3
Stokenchurch HP14 . . . . . .158 B3
Stone HP17 . . . . .114 B3
Thame OX9 . . . . .125 C1
Windsor SL4 . . . . .210 B3
Oxford Rd E SL4 . . . . .210 B3
Oxford St
4 High Wycombe HP11 . . .173 A4
Lee Common HP16 . . . . . .142 B3
Milton Keynes,
Fenny Stratford MK2 . . . . .58 B4
Milton Keynes,
Stony Stratford MK11 . . . . .32 B3
Milton Keynes, Wolverton
MK12 . . . . .33 B3
Oxley Park Rdbt MK5 . . . . .45 C2
Oxleys MK46 . . . . .6 C2
Oxman La MK12 . . . . .33 A3
Oxwich Gr MK4 . . . . .57 A4

P

Pack & Prime La RG9 . . . .191 B1
Packet Boat La UB8 . . . . .208 B4
Packhorse Rd SL9 . . . . . .188 C3
Padbury CE Sch MK18 . . .53 B1
Padbury Oaks UB7 . . . . . .213 A3
Padcroft Rd UB7 . . . . .208 B3
Paddock Cl SL6 . . . . .202 A1
Paddock Cotts SL6 . . . . . .202 A1
Paddock The
Aylesbury HP21 . . . . .116 B4
Chalfont St Peter SL9 . . . .177 C3
Datchet SL3 . . . . .211 A3
Emberton MK46 . . . . .13 C4
Maidenhead SL6 . . . . .195 B1
Paddock Way MK2 . . . . . . .47 B1
Paddocks End 1 HP9 . . . .176 B2
Paddocks Hospl The
HP27 . . . . .139 B2
Paddocks The
Chorleywood WD3 . . . . . . .167 C3
Flackwell Heath HP10 . . . .185 A4
Haddenham HP17 . . . . . . .127 A3
High Wycombe HP12 . . . . .172 A2
Leighton Buzzard LU7 . . . . .80 C4
Prestwood HP16 . . . . .151 B3
Steeple Claydon MK18 . . . .63 C2
Wendover HP22 . . . . .131 A3
Padstow Ave MK6 . . . . .34 C1
Padstow Cl
Aylesbury HP20 . . . . .101 C1
Slough SL3 . . . . .206 C2
Page Hill Ave MK18 . . . . . .41 C1
Page Hill Inf Sch MK18 . .41 C1
Pages Croft HP4 . . . . .135 A3
Pages La UB8 . . . . .201 B3
Pages Wharf SL6 . . . . . . .203 B4
Paget Cl SL7 . . . . .183 C2
Paget Ct UB7 . . . . .208 C2
Paget Dr SL6 . . . . .202 A2
Paget Rd SL3 . . . . .206 C1
Pagg's Ct MK16 . . . . .22 B2
Pagoda Rdbt MK15 . . . . . . .35 B3
Pagoda The SL6 . . . . .196 A1
Paines Orch LU7 . . . . .105 A4
Palace Cl SL1 . . . . .204 C3
Palace Sq MK6 . . . . .46 C4
Palliser Rd HP8 . . . . .177 A4
Palmer Ave
Aylesbury HP19 . . . . .115 B4
Upper Arncott OX25 . . . . . .94 C4
Palmer's Moor La SL0 . . .201 A1
Palmers Cl SL6 . . . . .202 A2
Palmers Moor MK18 . . . . .54 A4
Palmers Rd MK46 . . . . .7 A2
Palmerston Ave SL3 . . . . .206 A2
Pankridge Dr HP16 . . . . . .151 B4
Panleigh Cotts HP14 . . . .171 A2
Pannier Pl MK14 . . . . .35 A3
Pantile Row SL3 . . . . .207 A1
Pantile Wlk UB8 . . . . .201 B3
Paprika Ct MK7 . . . . .48 A3
Par The SL2 . . . . .198 B3
Parade Ct 7 SL8 . . . . . . .185 A2
Parade The
Bourne End SL8 . . . . .185 A2
High Wycombe HP11 . . . . .172 C3
Uxbridge UB8 . . . . .208 B4
Windsor SL4 . . . . .209 B3
Paradise MK17 . . . . .57 B2
Paradise Mews RG9 . . . . .191 B1
Paradise Rd RG9 . . . . .191 B1
Parchment Cl HP6 . . . . . . .154 C1
Parish La SL2 . . . . .187 B1
Parish Piece HP15 . . . . . .163 B4

Park Ave
Newport Pagnell MK16 . . . .22 A2
Totternhoe LU6 . . . . .93 A4
Wraysbury TW19 . . . . .211 B3
Park Cl Cosgrove MK19 . . . .19 C1
Hoggeston MK18 . . . . .77 C3
Lane End HP14 . . . . .171 B3
Windsor SL4 . . . . .210 B3
Park Cnr SL4 . . . . .209 C2
Park Crescent Sch
HP12 . . . . .172 B2
Park Ct SL8 . . . . .201 B2
Park Farm Rd HP12 . . . . . .161 A1
Park Farm Way HP14 . . . . .171 B3
Park Gate LU7 . . . . .79 C1
Park Gdns MK3 . . . . .47 A1
Park Gr HP8 . . . . .166 B3
Park Hill OX33 . . . . .122 A1
Park Ho
Berkhamsted HP4 . . . . . . .135 A3
Maidenhead SL6 . . . . .202 C3
Park La Beaconsfield HP9 .175 C1
Burnham SL1 . . . . .197 C4
Eaton Bray LU6 . . . . .92 B3
Hazelmere HP15 . . . . .163 A2
Horton SL3 . . . . .212 A2
Lane End HP14 . . . . .171 B3
Paulerspury NN12 . . . . .17 A4
Slough SL3 . . . . .206 A2
Stokenchurch HP14 . . . . . .158 C3
Stonor RG9 . . . . .179 B3
Park Lawn SL2 . . . . .198 B1
Park Mdw HP27 . . . . .139 A2
Park Parade Ctr The
HP15 . . . . .163 B3
Park Pl Amersham HP6 . . .154 C1
Seer Green HP9 . . . . .176 B3
Park Rd Amersham HP6 . .154 C1
Chesham HP5 . . . . .154 A4
Farnham Common SL2 . . .198 C2
Granborough MK18 . . . . . . .75 C3
Grendon Underwood HP18 .82 C4
Hartwell NN7 . . . . .10 B4
Henley-on-T RG9 . . . . .191 C1
Milton Keynes MK11 . . . . . .32 B3
Sherington MK16 . . . . .14 A1
Stanwell TW19 . . . . .213 B1
Tring HP23 . . . . .118 C1
Uxbridge UB8 . . . . .201 C3
Winslow MK18 . . . . .65 C3
Park Rd E UB10 . . . . .201 B2
Park Rd S MK18 . . . . .65 C2
Park Rise HP4 . . . . .134 C3
Park Sch HP20 . . . . .101 C1
Park St Aylesbury HP20 . .115 C4
Berkhamsted HP4 . . . . . . .135 A3
High Wycombe HP11 . . . . .173 B3
Maidenhead SL6 . . . . .202 C4
Poyle SL3 . . . . .212 C4
Princes Risborough HP27 . .139 A2
Slough SL1,SL3 . . . . .205 C2
Tring HP23 . . . . .119 A2
Windsor SL4 . . . . .210 B3
Woburn MK17 . . . . .60 C4
Park Street Ind Est
HP20 . . . . .115 C4
Park View
Newport Pagnell MK16 . . . .22 B2
West Drayton UB7 . . . . . . .208 C3
Park View Ct
Berkhamsted HP4 . . . . . . .135 A2
High Wycombe HP12 . . . . .172 B4
13 Leighton Buzzard LU7 . .80 C4
Park View Rd
Berkhamsted HP4 . . . . . . .135 A2
Uxbridge UB8 . . . . .208 C4
Parker Cl MK13 . . . . .34 A3
Parker Knoll Way HP13 . .173 A4
Parker Wlk HP19 . . . . .101 C3
Parkfield WD3 . . . . .167 C3
Parkgate SL1 . . . . .197 B1
Parkland Ave SL3 . . . . . . .206 B1
Parklands MK14 . . . . .21 B1
Parkside
Gerrards Cross SL9 . . . . . .188 C4
Henley-on-T RG9 . . . . .191 B1
Maidenhead SL6 . . . . .195 B1
Milton Keynes MK4 . . . . . . .46 C2
Walter's Ash HP14 . . . . . . .150 A1
Parkside Wlk SL1 . . . . . . .206 A2
Parkview
Flackwell Heath HP10 . . . .185 A4
Maidenhead SL6 . . . . .202 C4
Parkview Chase SL1 . . . . .204 C4
Parkway
Bow Brickhill MK17 . . . . . . .48 B1
Marlow SL7 . . . . .184 A2
Woburn Sands MK17 . . . . .49 A3
Parkway The SL0 . . . . . . .200 B2
Parkwood HP14 . . . . .150 A1
Parlaunt Park Comb Sch
SL3 . . . . .207 A2
Parlaunt Rd SL3 . . . . .207 A1
Parliament Cl HP16 . . . . . .151 A4
Parliament La SL1 . . . . . . .196 C3
Parliament Rd OX9 . . . . . .125 C1
Parmiter Ct HP19 . . . . .115 A4
Parmoor La HP14 . . . . .170 C1
Parneleys MK10 . . . . .35 C2
Parrishs Piece HP22 . . . . .87 C4
Parrock La MK10 . . . . .36 A1
Parrott Cl HP21 . . . . .115 A3
Parrott's La HP23 . . . . .133 C2
Parrs Rd HP14 . . . . .158 C2
Parry Cotts SL4 . . . . .177 C2

Parry Gn S SL3 . . . . .207 A1
Parry Green N SL3 . . . . . .206 C1
Parsley Cl
Aston Clinton HP22 . . . . . .117 B3
Walton MK7 . . . . .48 A3
Parslow Cl HP21 . . . . .115 B2
Parslow Ct HP21 . . . . .115 B2
Parson's Fee HP20 . . . . . .115 C4
Parson's Wood La SL2 . . .198 A3
Parsonage Cl
High Wycombe HP13 . . . . .173 B3
1 Tring HP23 . . . . .119 A2
Parsonage Ct 2 HP23 . . . .119 A2
Parsonage Farm HP22 . . .89 A2
Parsonage Gdns SL7 . . . .183 C1
Parsonage La
Farnham Common SL2 . . .198 B3
Windsor SL4 . . . . .210 A3
Parsonage Pl
Amersham HP7 . . . . .165 B4
Tring HP23 . . . . .119 A2
Parsonage Rd HP8 . . . . . .177 A4
Parsons Cl Stewkley LU7 . .78 C4
Winslow MK18 . . . . .65 C2
Parsons Cres MK5 . . . . . . .46 B3
Parsons La HP22 . . . . .102 A2
Parsons Wlk HP15 . . . . . . .163 B3
Parton Cl HP22 . . . . .131 A3
Parton Rd HP20 . . . . .116 A4
Partridge Cl
Buckingham MK18 . . . . . . .52 C4
Chesham HP5 . . . . .144 C2
Partridge Mead SL6 . . . . .195 C1
Partridge Piece MK43 . . . .25 B2
Partridge Way
15 Aylesbury HP20 . . . . . .101 C2
High Wycombe HP13 . . . . .161 B1
Pascomb Rd LU6 . . . . .93 C4
Passalewe La MK7 . . . . . . .48 B4
Passmore MK6 . . . . .47 B3
Pastern Pl MK14 . . . . .35 A3
Pastures The
Aylesbury HP20 . . . . .102 A1
Edlesborough LU6 . . . . .92 C2
High Wycombe HP15 . . . . .161 C1
Patch Cl UB10 . . . . .201 C2
Patches Field SL7 . . . . . . .183 C3
Paterson Rd HP21 . . . . . . .115 B3
Patricia Cl SL1 . . . . .204 C3
Patrick Haugh Rd OX25 . .94 C4
Patrick Way HP21 . . . . . . .116 A2
Patrick's La MK19 . . . . .31 C2
Patrington Cl UB8 . . . . . . .201 B1
Patriot Dr MK13 . . . . .34 A1
Patrons Dr UB9 . . . . .189 C3
Patterson Rd HP5 . . . . . . .144 A3
Pattison La MK15 . . . . .35 B2
Paul's Row 4 HP11 . . . . . .173 A3
Paulerspury CE Sch
NN12 . . . . .17 A4
Pauls Hill HP10 . . . . .174 C3
Pavers Ct HP21 . . . . .115 B2
Pavilion Cl HP20 . . . . .116 A4
Pavilion Way HP6 . . . . .166 B4
Pavilions The UB8 . . . . . .201 B3
Paxton Ave SL1 . . . . .205 B2
Paxton Cl MK46 . . . . .6 C2
Paxton Cres MK5 . . . . .46 A3
Paxton Rd HP4 . . . . .135 B2
Paynes Dr MK5 . . . . .46 A4
Paynes Field Cl HP4 . . . . .134 B3
Pea La HP4 . . . . .134 B4
Peace La SL8 . . . . .195 C3
Peach Mdws HP22 . . . . . . .131 A4
Peach Tree Ave UB7 . . . . .208 C4
Peachey Cl UB8 . . . . .208 B4
Peachey La UB8 . . . . .208 B4
Peacock Hay MK4 . . . . .46 B1
Peacock Rd SL7 . . . . .184 A2
Peacocks Cl HP4 . . . . .134 C4
Pear Tree Ave UB8 . . . . . .208 C4
Pear Tree Cl
Amersham HP7 . . . . .165 C4
Seer Green HP9 . . . . .176 B2
Pear Tree Ct HP15 . . . . . . .163 B4
Pearce Cl
Aylesbury HP21 . . . . .115 C2
Maidenhead SL6 . . . . .195 C1
Pearce Dr SL8 . . . . .195 C3
Pearce Rd Chesham HP5 . .144 A1
Maidenhead SL6 . . . . .195 C1
Pearces Orch RG9 . . . . . .191 B1
Pearl Gdns SL1 . . . . .205 A3
Pearse Gr MK7 . . . . .48 A2
Pearson Ct HP19 . . . . .115 A3
Peartree Cl SL1 . . . . .204 C3
Peartrees UB7 . . . . .208 B3
Peascod Pl 22 SL4 . . . . . .210 B3
Peascod St SL4 . . . . .210 B3
Peascroft HP18 . . . . .109 A3
Pebble Brook Sch HP21 .115 B4
Pebble La
Aylesbury HP20 . . . . .115 C4
Brackley NN13 . . . . .38 A4
Pebblemoor LU6 . . . . .92 C2
Peckover Ct 8 MK8 . . . . . .33 C1
Pednor Bottom HP5 . . . . .143 A2
Pednor Rd HP5 . . . . .143 C1
Pednormead End HP5 . . .154 A4
Peebles Pl MK3 . . . . .46 C2
Peel Cl SL4 . . . . .210 A2
Peel Ct
Princes Risborough HP27 . .139 C2
Slough SL1 . . . . .205 A4
Peel Rd MK12 . . . . .33 B3
Peel Way UB8 . . . . .208 C4
Peerless Dr UB9 . . . . .190 B4

Peers Dr MK17 ....49 C2
Peers La MK5 ....46 A3
Peggs La HP22 ....117 C3
Pelham Ct SL6 ....202 C4
Pelham Pl MK14 ....34 C3
Pelham Rd OX9 ....126 A1
Pelton Ct MK5 ....46 B3
Pemberton Cl HP21 ....115 C3
Pemberton Rd SL2 ....197 C1
Pembridge Chase HP3 ....146 A2
Pembridge Cl HP3 ....146 A2
Pembridge Rd HP3 ....146 A2
Pembroke Rd HP20 ....101 C1
Pencarrow Pl MK6 ....35 A1
Pendeen Ct SL1 ....205 A3
Penfold HP22 ....116 C1
Penfold Cotts HP15 ....163 B4
Penfold La
  Holmer Green HP7,HP15 ....152 C1
  Hyde Heath HP7,HP15 ....152 C1
Pengelly Ct MK6 ....35 A1
Penhale Cl MK4 ....57 A4
Penina CI MK3 ....46 B1
Penington Rd HP9 ....186 A4
Penlee Rise MK4 ....57 A4
Penley CI OX39 ....147 A3
Penling Cl SL8 ....195 C3
Penmon CI MK10 ....35 C1
Penn Ave HP5 ....144 A1
Penn Cl
  Chorleywood WD3 ....167 B2
  Uxbridge UB8 ....201 B1
Penn Ct **8** SL7 ....183 C1
Penn Dr UB9 ....189 C3
Penn Gaskell La SL9 ....177 C3
Penn Gn HP9 ....175 B2
Penn Haven SL9 ....188 B2
Penn Mdw SL2 ....198 C2
Penn Rd Aylesbury HP21 ....115 B4
  Beaconsfield HP9 ....175 B3
  Chorleywood WD3 ....167 C1
  Datchet SL3 ....211 B3
  Gerrards Cross SL9 ....177 B1
  Hazelmere HP15 ....163 B4
  Milton Keynes MK2 ....58 C4
  Slough SL2 ....198 B1
Penn Sch HP10 ....174 B4
Penn Way WD3 ....167 B2
Penn Wood View HP7 ....164 A2
Pennefather Ct **8** HP21 115 C4
Pennine Rd SL2 ....205 A4
Pennings The HP22 ....131 A3
Pennington Pl OX9 ....126 A1
Pennington Rd
  Gerrards Cross SL9 ....177 B2
  High Wycombe HP13 ....173 C3
Penningtons The HP6 ....154 C1
Pennycress Way MK16 ....21 C2
Pennylets Gn SL2 ....199 A3
Pennyroyal MK7 ....48 A4
Penrith Cl UB8 ....201 B3
Penrith Way HP21 ....116 A4
Penryn Ave MK6 ....35 A1
Penshurst Cl SL9 ....177 B1
Penshurst Rd SL6 ....202 B3
Pentewan Gate MK6 ....34 C1
Pentland Rd
  Aylesbury HP21 ....115 C3
  Slough SL2 ....205 A4
Pentlands MK11 ....32 C2
Pentlands Ct **1** HP11 ....174 A2
Pentlands The HP13 ....174 A2
Penwith Fst Sch MK6 ....34 C1
Penwood Ct SL6 ....202 A4
Penwood La SL7 ....183 B1
Penyston Rd SL6 ....202 B4
Penzance Spur SL2 ....198 A1
Peplow Cl UB7 ....208 B3
Peppard Mdw HP16 ....151 B3
Pepper Hill Fst Sch
  MK13 ....34 A4
Peppet's Gn HP5 ....143 B4
Peppiatts The LU6 ....92 A3
Pepys Cl SL3 ....212 A4
Pepys Dr HP16 ....151 B3
Perch Cl SL7 ....194 B4
Percheron Pl MK14 ....34 C3
Percy Pl SL3 ....211 A3
Percy Terr HP8 ....177 A4
Peregrine HP20 ....101 C2
Peregrine Bsns Pk
  HP13 ....174 A2
Peregrine Ct MK6 ....47 A4
Perks La HP16 ....151 B2
Permayne MK13 ....34 A4
Perracombe MK4 ....46 C2
Perran Ave MK6 ....35 A1
Perrin Springs La HP14 170 C1
Perry Hill HP18 ....73 A1
Perry Ho SL1 ....197 A1
Perry La HP27 ....138 C1
Perry Mead LU6 ....92 A3
Perry Oaks Dr TW6,UB7 .213 B3
Perry St HP22 ....131 A3
Perrycroft SL4 ....209 C2
Perryfields Way SL1 ....197 A1
Perryman Way SL2 ....197 C1
Perrys The HP22 ....131 A3
Pershore Croft MK10 ....36 A1
Perth Ave SL1 ....205 A4
Perth Cl MK3 ....46 C1
Perth Rd HP13 ....173 B4
Perth Trad Est SL1 ....205 A4
Peter's Cl HP16 ....151 B3
Peter's Pl HP4 ....134 C3

Peterborough Ave **2**
  HP13 ....173 B4
Peterborough Gate MK15 35 B3
Peterhead Mews SL3 .207 A1
Peterhill Cl SL9 ....177 C3
Peterley HP16 ....151 C2
Peterley Ave HP16 ....151 C2
Peters La HP27 ....139 C2
Petersfield HP22 ....116 B2
Petersfield Ave SL2 ....206 A3
Petersham CI MK16 ....22 B1
Pettifer Way HP12 ....172 B3
Pettingrew Cl MK7 ....48 A3
Petty Pl SL6 ....202 B2
Petworth MK8 ....33 C1
Petworth Ct SL4 ....210 A3
Petworth Ho **4** MK8 ....33 C1
Pevensey Cl
  Aylesbury HP21 ....116 A3
  Milton Keynes MK3 .....57 C4
Pevensey Rd SL2 ....205 A4
Peverel Dr MK1 ....47 A2
Peveril Cl HP21 ....116 A3
Pevers La MK46 ....6 A1
Pheasant Cl
  Berkhamsted HP4 ....135 B2
  Tring HP23 ....119 A3
Pheasant Dr HP13 ....161 B1
Pheasant Hill HP8 ....177 B4
Pheasant Rise HP5 ....154 B3
Pheasant Wlk HP27 ....177 C3
Pheasants Croft SL6 ....202 A2
Pheasants Dr HP15 ....163 A3
Pheasants Ridge SL7 ...183 B4
Philbye Mews SL1 ....204 C2
Philip Dr HP10 ....185 B4
Philip Rd HP13 ....173 B4
Philips Rd HP19 ....115 A4
Phillip Ct HP15 ....46 A3
Phillimore Cl MK15 ....35 A4
Philpots Cl UB7 ....208 B3
Philps Cl HP14 ....171 B2
Phipps Cl
  Aylesbury HP20 ....102 A1
  Maidenhead SL6 ....202 A1
Phipps Rd SL1 ....204 C4
Phoebe La HP4 ....48 C3
Phoebe's Orch MK17 .....69 C4
Phoenix Bsns Ctr HP5 ..144 A1
Phoenix Ct SL6 ....202 B2
Phoenix Dr MK6 ....46 C4
Phygtle The SL9 ....177 C2
Phyllis Ct Dr RG9 ....191 C2
Picasso Pl HP19 ....100 C1
Pickering Dr MK4 ....46 A1
Pickford Dr SL3 ....206 C3
Pickings Piece SL3 ....212 A3
Pickwick Terr SL2 ....206 A3
Picton St MK4 ....45 C1
Picts La HP27 ....139 A1
Piddington La HP14 ....171 A4
Piddington Rd HP18 ....96 A4
Field Heath House sch
  UB8 ....201 C1
Pield Heath Rd UB8 .....201 C1
Pierson Rd SL4 ....209 B3
Pigeon Farm Rd HP14 .158 C3
Piggott's Hill HP14 ....150 C1
Piggotts End HP7 ....165 A4
Piggotts Orch HP7 ....165 A4
Pightle Cres MK18 ....41 B1
Pightle The
  Buckingham MK18 ....41 B1
  Maids Moreton MK18 .....41 C2
  Oving HP22 ....86 B4
  Pitstone LU7 ....105 B2
Pigott Dr MK5 ....46 A3
Pigott Orch HP22 ....85 A3
Pike Cl Marlow SL7 ....194 B4
  Uxbridge UB10 ....201 C2
Pilch La HP17 ....54 B2
Pilgrim St MK9 ....35 A2
Pilgrims Ct HP27 ....139 A3
Pilot Trad Est HP12 .....172 C4
Pimms Cl HP13 ....174 A3
Pimms Gr HP13 ....174 A3
Pimpernel Gr MK7 ....48 A3
Pinchfield WD3 ....178 B3
Pinders Croft MK12 ....33 A3
Pine Chase HP12 ....172 A2
Pine Cl
  Berkhamsted HP4 ....135 A2
  Hazelmere HP15 ....163 A2
  Maidenhead SL6 ....202 A4
Pine Crest Mews LU7 ....80 C3
Pine Gr MK17 ....49 A3
Pine Hill HP15 ....162 C2
Pine Rd LU6 ....106 C4
Pine Trees Dr UB10 .....201 C4
Pine Wlk
  Berkhamsted HP4 ....134 B4
  Hazelmere HP15 ....163 A2
Pineapple Rd HP7 ....165 C4
Pinecroft SL7 ....183 B2
Pineham Rdbt MK15 ......35 C3
Pinels Way HP11 ....172 C2
Piner Cotts SL4 ....209 C2
Pines Cl Amersham HP6 .154 C1
  Little Kingshill HP16 ....152 A2
Pines The Felden HP3 ...146 A4
  Tylers Green HP10 ....163 A1
Pinetree Cl SL9 ....177 B2
Pinewood Ave UB8 .....208 C4
Pinewood Cl
  Gerrards Cross SL9 .....188 C2
  Iver Heath SL0 ....200 B3
Pinewood Dr MK2 ....58 C4

Pinewood Film Studios
  SL0 ....200 A3
Pinewood Gn SL0 ....200 B3
Pinewood Mews TW19 .213 B1
Pinewood Rd
  High Wycombe HP12 ....172 B4
  Iver Heath SL0 ....200 A3
Pinfold MK7 ....48 A3
Pinglestone Cl UB7 ......213 C4
Pinions Rd HP13 ....173 C3
Pink Hill HP27 ....149 C4
Pink La SL1 ....197 A2
Pink Rd HP27 ....149 C4
Pinkard Ct MK6 ....47 B4
Pinkneys Dr SL6 ....195 A1
Pinkneys Rd SL6 ....202 A4
Pinks Cl MK5 ....46 B4
Pinkworthy MK4 ....46 B2
Pinn Ct SL1 ....208 B4
Pinstone Way SL9 ....189 A1
Pintail Cl HP20 ....101 C2
Pipard MK14 ....34 C2
Pipers Cl SL1 ....197 B1
Pipers Corner Sch
  HP15 ....162 A4
Pipers Croft LU6 ....93 C4
Pipers Ct SL1 ....197 B1
Pipers La HP15 ....162 B4
Pipit Gdns **7** HP20 ....101 C2
Pipit Wlk **6** HP20 ....101 C2
Pippins Cl UB7 ....208 B3
Pippins Sch SL3 ....212 C3
Pippins The SL3 ....206 C3
Pipston Gn MK7 ....48 A4
Pistone Windmill★ LU7 105 C2
Pitch Pond Cl HP9 ....175 B3
Pitch The HP14 ....159 B2
Pitchcott Rd HP22 ....86 A3
Pitcher La MK5 ....46 A4
Pitcher Wlk HP19 ....115 A4
Pitchford Ave MK18 ....41 C1
Pitchford Wlk MK18 ....41 C1
Pitfield MK11 ....33 A2
Pitt Gn MK18 ....41 C1
Pitters Piece HP18 ....125 A4
Pitts Rd SL1 ....205 B3
Place Farm Ho HP27 .....139 A3
Place Farm Way HP27 ...139 A3
Plackett Way SL1 ....204 B3
Plaines Cl SL1 ....204 C3
Plaiters Cl HP23 ....119 A2
Plantain Ct MK7 ....48 A3
Plantation Pl MK5 ....46 A4
Plantation Rd
  Amersham HP6 ....154 C1
  High Wycombe HP13 ....174 A4
  Leighton Buzzard LU7 ....70 C2
Platt The HP7 ....165 A4
Playing Field Rd NN13 ...39 A2
Pleasant Cotts SL0 ......200 A4
Pleasant Pl WD3 ....178 C2
Pleasaunce The HP22 ...117 C3
Pleshey Cl MK5 ....46 A3
Plested Ct HP22 ....116 B1
Plomer Green Ave
  HP13 ....161 B1
Plomer Green La HP13 .161 B2
Plomer Hill HP13 ....161 B1
Plough Cl HP21 ....115 C2
Plough La Sarratt WD3 ..156 C3
  Stoke Poges SL2 ....199 A2
Ploughlees La SL1 ....205 C3
Ploughley Rd OX25 ....94 C4
Plover Cl
  16 Berkhamsted HP4 ...135 B2
  Buckingham MK18 ....52 C4
  Newport Pagnell MK16 ...22 C2
Plover The **4** HP20 .....101 C2
Plover Wlk **3** HP20 .....101 C2
Plowman Cl MK12 ....33 A3
Plum Park La NN12 ....17 B4
Plumer Rd HP11 ....172 C4
Plumstead Ave MK13 .....34 B2
Pluto Cl SL1 ....204 C2
Plym Cl HP21 ....115 B3
Plymouth Gr MK4 ....46 A1
Plymouth Rd SL1 ....204 A1
Pocock Ave UB7 ....208 C2
Pococks La SL4 ....205 C1
Poets Chase HP21 ....115 C3
Points The SL6 ....202 A2
Poles Hill Chesham HP5 .144 A1
  Sarratt WD3 ....156 C3
Police Ho's SL9 ....189 A1
Polidoris La HP15 ....163 B4
Polish Ave HP22 ....131 C2
Pollard Ave UB9 ....189 C3
Pollard Cl SL4 ....211 A1
Pollards WD3 ....178 B3
Pollys Yd MK14 ....22 B3
Pollywick Rd HP23 ....119 B1
Polmartin Ct MK6 ....35 A1
Polruan Pl MK6 ....35 A1
Polygon Bsns Ctr SL3 ..212 C3
Pomander Cres MK7 .....48 A4
Pomeroy Cl HP7 ....165 B4
Pond App HP15 ....163 B4
Pond Cl Coleshill HP7 ....164 B2
  Newton Longville MK17 ...57 B1
  Tring HP23 ....119 A2
Pond Cotts HP14 ....171 A2
Pond La SL3 ....177 A1
Pond Park Rd HP5 ....144 A1
Pondgate MK7 ....48 A4
Pondwicks HP7 ....165 A4
Pool La SL1 ....205 C3
Poolmans Rd SL4 ....209 B2
Pope Way HP21 ....115 C2

Popes Acre HP17 ....126 C3
Popes Cl Amersham HP6 .154 C1
  Colnbrook SL3 ....212 B3
Popes La SL7 ....195 B4
Poplar Ave
  Amersham HP7 ....165 C4
  West Drayton UB7 ....208 C3
Poplar Cl Aylesbury HP20 102 A1
  Milton Keynes MK6 ....47 C3
  Poyle SL3 ....212 C3
Poplar Ho SL3 ....206 C1
Poplar Rd
  Aylesbury HP20 ....102 A1
  New Denham UB9 ....201 B3
Poplars Cl HP17 ....114 B3
Poplars Gr SL6 ....196 A1
Poplars Rd MK18 ....52 B4
Poplars The HP22 ....131 B3
Poppy Rd HP27 ....139 A1
Popular Cl HP5 ....144 B2
Porlock La MK4 ....46 B2
Port Field Farm MK16 ....21 C3
Portal Cl UB10 ....201 C3
Portal Rd HP22 ....131 B4
Portchester Ct **1** MK8 ..33 C1
Porter's Cl MK19 ....31 C2
Porters Way UB7 ....208 C2
Portfield Cl MK18 ....52 C4
Portfield Way MK18 ....52 C4
Portfields Comb Sch
  MK16 ....22 A3
Portfields Rd MK16 ....22 A2
Porthcawl Gn MK4 ....57 B4
Porthleven Pl MK6 ....35 A1
Porthmellin Cl MK4 ....57 A4
Portishead Dr MK4 ....45 C1
Portland Bsns Ctr SL3 ..211 A3
Portland Ct SL1 ....197 B1
Portland Dr MK15 ....35 B4
Portland Gdns SL7 ....183 B1
Portland Ho HP13 ....173 B4
Portlands Alley SL7 ......183 B1
Portlands Mews **7** SL7 .183 B1
Portlock Rd SL6 ....202 B4
Portmarnock Cl MK3 ......57 B4
Portnall Pl MK43 ....25 A1
Portobello Cl HP5 ....144 A1
Portrush Cl MK3 ....57 B4
Portsmouth Ct SL1 ......205 C3
Portway
  Milton Keynes MK15,MK9 .35 B3
  North Marston MK18 ......76 A1
  Stone HP17 ....114 C2
Portway Dr HP12 ....161 A1
Portway Rd MK18 ....62 B2
Post Mdw SL0 ....200 B1
Post Office Cotts SL2 ...199 A3
Post Office La
  Beaconsfield HP9 ....175 B2
  Slough SL3 ....206 B4
  Whitchurch HP22 ....87 A3
Potash La HP23 ....104 A3
Potkiln La HP9 ....176 B1
Potter Row HP16 ....142 B3
Potters Cl HP18 ....151 A4
Potters Cross SL0 ....200 C1
Potters Cross Cres
  HP13 ....162 C1
Potters La MK11 ....33 A2
Potterspury Lodge Sch
  NN12 ....18 A3
Pottery Cl HP19 ....115 A4
Potts Pl **5** SL7 ....183 B1
Poulcott TW19 ....211 C1
Pound Cl
  Steeple Claydon MK18 ...63 B2
  Wicken MK19 ....31 A2
Pound Cres SL7 ....183 B1
Pound Hill MK17 ....59 B1
Pound La
  Little Marlow SL8 ....184 B2
  Marlow SL7 ....183 B1
  North Crawley MK16 ......24 A4
  Preston Bissett MK18 ....62 A4
Pound St HP22 ....131 B2
Pound The Cookham SL8 .195 C4
  Syresham NN13 ....27 A4
Poundfield La SL8 ....195 C4
Poundfield Rd NN12 .....18 C1
Pounds MK43 ....25 A1
Powis Cl SL6 ....202 B4
Powis La MK4 ....45 C1
Powney Rd SL6 ....202 B4
Poyle 14 Trad Est SL3 ..212 C2
Poyle La SL1 ....197 A2
Poyle New Cotts SL3 ...212 C3
Poyle Rd SL3 ....212 C3
Poyle Tech Ctr The SL3 .212 C3
Poynings SL0 ....207 C1
Pratt Ho HP6 ....154 C1
Prebendal Ave HP21 .....115 B4
Prebendal Ct **9** HP20 ..115 B3
Prebendal Ct **1** HP20 ..115 B4
Precedent Dr MK13 ....34 A2
Precincts The SL1 ....197 B1
Prentice Gr MK5 ....46 A2
Prescott Rd SL3 ....212 C3
Prescotts The UB9 ....189 C2
Presley Way MK8 ....45 C4
Press Rd UB8 ....201 B3
Preston Ct MK15 ....35 A4
Preston Hill **7** HP5 .....144 B1
Preston Rd SL2 ....206 B3
Prestwick Ct MK3 ....57 B4
Prestwold Ho HP11 ......115 A4
Prestwold Way HP19 ....115 A4
Prestwood SL2 ....206 A4

Prestwood Cl HP12 .....172 B4
Prestwood Inf Sch
  HP16 ....151 B4
Prestwood Jun Sch
  HP16 ....151 B3
Prestwood Lodge Sch
  HP16 ....151 B3
Prestwood Pl HP16 ......151 B3
Pretoria Rd HP13 ....173 B4
Priestend OX9 ....125 C1
Primatt Cres MK5 ....46 A3
Primrose Cotts HP14 ...150 A3
Primrose Ct HP21 ....115 A3
Primrose Dr
  Aylesbury HP21 ....115 A3
  West Drayton UB7 ....208 B1
Primrose Gn HP15 ....162 C3
Primrose Hill HP15 ......162 C4
Primrose Terr HP18 .....110 A4
Primrose Way MK18 .....52 B4
Prince Andrew Cl SL6 ..196 A1
Prince Andrew Rd SL6 .196 A1
Prince Consort Cotts
  SL4 ....210 B3
Prince Edward St HP4 ..135 B2
Prince Philip Ave MK43 ..24 B1
Prince's Rd HP21 ....115 C4
Princes Ct
  Berkhamsted HP4 ....135 A3
  Chilton HP18 ....111 A2
  Eton SL4 ....204 C1
Princes Ct
  Leighton Buzzard LU7 ....80 C4
  Wooburn Green SL8 .....185 B2
Princes Est HP27 ....138 C2
Princes La HP16 ....142 B3
Princes Pl HP27 ....139 A1
Princes Rd SL8 ....185 B2
Princes Risborough Sch
  HP27 ....139 B1
Princes Risborough Sta
  ....138 C1
Princes St
  Lane End HP14 ....160 A1
  Slough SL1 ....206 A2
Princes Way MK2 ....58 A4
Princes Way Rdbt MK2 ..58 A4
Princess Ave SL4 ....210 A2
Princess Margaret Hospl
  The SL4 ....210 B3
Princess Dr HP12 ....161 A1
Princess St SL6 ....202 C3
Printers End HP19 ....101 A1
Prior Gr HP5 ....144 B1
Priors Cl Maidenhead SL6 203 A1
  4 Slough SL1 ....206 A2
Priors Pk MK4 ....46 B1
Priors Rd SL4 ....209 B2
Priors Way SL6 ....203 A1
Priors Way Ind Est SL6 .203 A1
Priory Ave
  High Wycombe HP13 ....173 A4
  South Harefield UB9 ....190 B4
Priory Cl Aylesbury HP19 .101 A1
  Denham UB9 ....190 A1
  Horton-cum-S OX33 ....108 A3
  Newport Pagnell MK16 ...22 C2
  South Harefield UB9 ....190 B4
Priory Cotts UB9 ....190 B4
Priory Cres HP19 ....101 B1
Priory Ct **15** HP4 ....135 B2
Priory Farm Cotts OX27 .71 C1
Priory Gdns
  Berkhamsted HP4 ....135 B2
  South Harefield UB9 ....190 B4
Priory Rd
  Gerrards Cross SL9 .....188 B3
  High Wycombe HP13 ....173 A4
  Slough SL1 ....204 B4
Priory Sch SL1 ....204 B4
Priory St MK16 ....22 C2
Priory Way Datchet SL3 .211 A4
  Gerrards Cross SL9 .....188 B3
  Harmondsworth UB7 ....213 C4
Pritchard Ct MK14 ....34 C4
Progress Bsns Ctr SL1 .204 B4
Progress Rd HP12 ....172 A4
Proiry Common Fst Sch
  MK13 ....34 A2
Promenade SL4 ....210 B4
Prospect Cl MK17 ....68 B3
Prospect Cotts HP14 ...161 B4
Prospect Ct HP14 ....171 A3
Prospect Pl
  Castlethorpe MK19 ....19 C3
  Hurley SL7 ....193 C2
  3 Windsor SL4 ....210 B2
  Wing LU7 ....79 C1
Prospect Rd Marlow SL7 .183 B1
  Milton Keynes MK11 ......32 B3
Protheroe Field MK7 .....48 B2
Providence Pl
  11 Maidenhead SL6 ...202 C4
  Milton Keynes MK13 .....34 A2
Providence Rd UB7 .....208 C3
Prudential Bldgs **8**
  SL1 ....205 C2
Pudseys Cl SL7 ....195 A3
Puers Field HP9 ....176 C2
Puers La HP9 ....176 C2
Puffin Way HP20 ....101 C2
Pulborough Cl MK3 ....46 B1
Pulford Rd LU7 ....80 C3
Pullfields HP5 ....144 A1
Pulpit Cl HP5 ....144 A4
Pulpit La HP22 ....76 B1

Pump La N SL7 183 C3
Pump La S SL7 184 A2
Pump Mdw HP16 152 A4
Pumpkin Hill SL1 197 C3
Pumpus Gn MK18 66 A2
Punch Bowl La HP5 154 B4
Purbeck MK14 34 B3
Purbeck Cl HP21 116 A3
Purcel Dr MK16 22 B2
Purse La MK16 11 C4
Purssell Cl SL6 202 A2
Purssell Pl HP27 139 A3
Purssells Mdw HP14 161 B4
Purton Ct SL2 198 B3
Purton La SL2 198 B3
Pury Rd Alderton NN12 9 A1
Paulerspury NN12 17 B4
Pusey Way HP14 171 B3
Putlowes Dr HP18 100 B2
Putman Ho MK5 46 B3
Putman Pl RG9 191 C1
Putnams Dr HP22 117 B3
Puxley Rd MK19 31 B3
Pyebush La HP9 187 A4
Pyghtle The Olney MK46 6 C2
Turvey MK43 8 C3
Pyghtles The HP22 85 A3
Pykes Gr MK8 33 B2
Pym Wlk OX9 125 C1
Pymcombe Cl HP27 139 A3
Pynefield Ho WD3 167 C1
Pyxe Ct MK7 48 A2

Q

Quadrangle The HP13 173 C4
Quadrans Cl MK15 35 A4
Quadrant The
High Wycombe HP13 162 C1
Maidenhead SL6 203 A3
Quainton CE Comb Sch HP22 85 A3
Quainton Rd
North Marston MK18 76 A1
Waddesdon HP18 99 A4
Quaker Mede HP17 127 A3
Quaker's Mead HP22 116 C2
Quantock Cl SL3 207 A1
Quantock Cres MK4 46 B1
Quarrendon Ave HP19 101 A1
Quarrendon Rd HP7 165 C4
Quarrendon Upper Sch HP19 101 B1
Quarry Cl HP18 125 B4
Quarry Green Cl MK19 31 A2
Quarry Wood Rd SL7 195 A4
Quarrydale Dr SL7 183 C1
Quaves Rd SL3 206 B2
Quebec Rd HP13 173 C3
Queen Alexandra Rd HP11 173 A3
Queen Anne Royal Free CE Fst Sch The SL4 210 B2
Queen Anne St MK13 33 C4
Queen Anne's Ct 10 SL4 210 B3
Queen Anne's Rd SL4 210 B2
Queen Catherine Rd MK18 63 C1
Queen Charlotte St 20 SL4 210 B3
Queen Cl RG9 191 C1
Queen Eleanor St MK11 32 C3
Queen Mother's Dr UB9 189 C3
Queen Sq 7 HP11 173 A4
Queen St Aylesbury HP20 116 A4
Henley-on-T RG9 191 C1
High Wycombe HP13 173 B4
Lane End HP14 160 A1
Leighton Buzzard LU7 80 C4
Maidenhead SL6 202 C4
Milton Keynes MK11 32 C3
Pitstone LU7 105 B2
Tring HP23 119 A2
Waddesdon HP18 98 C3
Queen Victoria Rd 6 HP11 173 A3
Queen's Acre SL4 210 B2
Queen's Cl SL4 211 A1
Queen's Ct SL1 205 C3
Queen's Dr The WD3 167 C1
Queen's Gate SL4 210 B2
Queen's La 8 SL6 202 C4
Queen's Pk HP21 115 C4
Queen's Rd
Datchet SL3 211 A4
Marlow SL7 183 B1
Slough SL1 205 C3
Uxbridge UB8 201 B1
Windsor SL4 210 B3
Queen's Terr 5 SL4 210 B2
Queen's Way MK3 58 B4
Queens Acre HP13 173 B3
Queens Acre Ho 6 SL4 210 B2
Queens Ave MK16 22 B2
Queens Cl OX9 125 C1
Queens Ct HP13 173 B3
Queens Mead HP21 116 B4
Queens Rd
Berkhamsted HP4 135 A3
1 Chesham HP5 144 B1
Eton SL4 204 C1
High Wycombe HP13 173 B3
Princes Risborough HP27 139 B2
West Drayton UB7 208 C2
Queens Wlk Mall 3 SL6 202 C4
Queensgate HP19 115 A4
Queensmead SL3 211 A3
Queensmead Ho HP10 174 B1
Queensmead Rd HP10 174 B1
Queensmere Rd 11 SL1 206 A2
Queensway
Hazelmere HP15 163 A2
Maidenhead SL6 195 C1
Milton Keynes MK2 58 B4
Queensway The SL9 188 B4
Quickberry Pl HP7 165 B4
Quickley Brow WD3 167 A2
Quickley La WD3 167 B2
Quickley Rise WD3 167 A2
Quill Hall La HP6 154 C1
Quilter Mdw MK7 48 B3
Quilters Way HP22 130 B4
Quinbrookes SL2 206 B4
Quince Cl MK7 48 A3
Quinton Dr MK13 34 A2
Quoiting Sq SL7 183 B1
Quoitings Dr SL7 183 B1

R

Raans Rd Amersham HP6 154 C1
Little Chalfont HP6 154 C1
Rabans Cl HP19 100 C1
Rabans La HP19 100 C1
Rabbs Farm Prim Sch UB7 208 C3
Rachels Way HP5 154 B3
Rackstraw Gr MK7 48 B3
Radcliffe Sch The MK12 33 A3
Radcliffe St
Milton Keynes MK12 33 B3
Milton Keynes MK12 33 B4
Radclive Rd MK18 51 C3
Radcot Ave SL3 207 A2
Radcot Cl SL6 195 C2
Radman Gr MK12 33 A3
Radnage CE Inf Sch HP14 159 B3
Radnage Common Rd HP14 159 B3
Radnage La HP14 148 B1
Radnor Cl RG9 191 C1
Radnor End HP20 101 C1
Radnor Way SL3 206 C1
Radworthy MK4 46 B2
Raeside Cl HP9 176 B3
Ragmans Cl HP10 183 B4
Ragmans La HP10 172 B1
Ragnall's La OX33 108 A3
Ragstone Rd SL1 205 C2
Ragstones HP10 174 A1
Railway Cotts
Steeple Claydon MK18 64 A1
Wigginton HP23 119 C3
Railway St 2 HP20 115 C4
Railway Terr SL2 205 C3
Rainborough Gdns HP20 101 C1
Rainbow Dr MK6 46 C4
Rainsborough MK14 35 A4
Rainsborough Chase SL6 202 A2
Rake Way HP21 115 B2
Raleigh Cl SL1 205 A3
Ralphs Retreat HP15 162 C2
Ram Alley MK16 12 A3
Rambler Cl SL6 204 A4
Rambler La SL3 206 B2
Ramsay Cl MK13 34 A2
Ramsay View HP15 163 A2
Ramsey Ct SL2 197 B1
Ramsgill Ct MK13 34 B3
Ramsons Ave MK14 34 C2
Ramsthorn Gr MK7 48 A3
Ramworth Way HP21 116 A3
Randall Cl SL3 206 C1
Randall Ct SL4 211 A1
Randolph Cl MK13 34 A3
Randolph Rd SL3 206 C2
Ranelagh Gdns MK16 22 B1
Rangers Ct MK8 33 C1
Rannal Dr OX39 147 B3
Rannoch Cl MK2 58 B3
Rannock Gdns LU7 80 B4
Ranston Cl UB9 189 C3
Rashleigh Pl MK6 46 C4
Ratcliffe Cl UB8 201 B1
Rathbone Cl MK8 45 C4
Ravel Cl MK7 48 B3
Raven Cl 11 HP20 101 C2
Raven Cres HP18 98 B3
Raven Rd HP14 158 C2
Ravens Ct HP4 135 C3
Ravens Field SL3 206 B2
Ravens La HP4 135 B2
Ravens Wharf HP4 135 B2
Ravensbourne Pl MK6 35 A1
Ravensbourne Rd HP21 115 B2
Ravenscar Ct MK4 46 B1
Ravenscourt SL7 184 A2
Ravenscroft Rd RG9 191 B1
Ravenshoe Cl SL8 185 A2
Ravensmead
Chalfont St Peter SL9 177 C3
Chinnor OX39 147 B3
Ravenstone Mill Rd MK46 12 C4
Ravensworth Rd SL2 198 A1
Ravigill Pl MK12 33 B2
Rawcliffe Ho SL6 203 A3
Rawlings La HP9 176 B4
Rawlins Rd MK13 34 A2
Ray Dr SL6 203 A4
Ray Ho 5 SL8 185 A2
Ray Lea Cl SL6 203 A4
Ray Lea Rd SL6 203 A4
Ray Lodge SL6 203 A4
Ray Lodge Mews SL6 203 A4
Ray Mdw SL6 196 A1
Ray Mead Ct SL6 196 B1
Ray Mead Rd SL6 203 B4
Ray Mill Rd E SL6 196 A1
Ray Mill Rd W SL6 203 A4
Ray Park Ave SL6 203 A4
Ray Park La SL6 203 A4
Ray Park Rd SL6 203 A4
Ray St SL6 203 A4
Ray's Hill HP5 133 B1
Rayfield SL6 203 A4
Raylands Mead SL9 188 B3
Rayleigh Cl MK5 46 A3
Raylens HP12 172 A3
Raymond Cl SL3 212 C3
Raymond Rd
Maidenhead SL6 202 B4
Slough SL3 207 A2
Rayners Ave HP10 174 A2
Rayners Cl Colnbrook SL3 212 B4
Loudwater HP10 174 B2
Rays Ave SL4 209 C4
Rays La HP10 163 B1
Razzaq HP12 172 C4
Read Dr HP22 102 B2
Reade Ct SL2 198 B3
Reading Cl HP19 101 A2
Reading Rd RG9 191 C1
Readings The WD3 167 C3
Reads La LU7 78 B1
Recreation Rd SL8 185 A2
Rectory Ave HP13 173 B4
Rectory Cl
Farnham Common SL2 198 B1
Marsh Gibbon OX27 71 C2
Slapton LU7 91 B3
Windsor SL4 210 A3
Rectory Ct
8 High Wycombe HP13 173 C3
Lewknor OX49 157 A4
Rectory Dr HP18 99 A3
Rectory Fields MK15 35 B2
Rectory Gdns HP8 177 A4
Rectory Hill HP6,HP7 165 A4
Rectory La
Amersham HP7 165 A4
Berkhamsted HP4 135 B2
Bix RG9 179 B1
Yardley Hastings NN7 1 A4
Rectory Mdw OX39 147 B4
Rectory Orch MK46 7 C4
Rectory Rd SL6 196 C1
Rectory Terr SL2 198 B2
Red Cottage Mews SL3 206 B2
Red Ct SL1 205 C3
Red House Cl
Beaconsfield HP9 175 A2
Newton Longville MK17 57 B2
Red Leaf Cl SL3 206 C3
Red Leys UB10 201 C3
Red Lion Cl MK43 25 A1
Red Lion Cotts SL2 199 A1
Red Lion Dr HP14 158 B3
Red Lion St HP5 154 B4
Red Lion Way HP10 185 C3
Red Lodge Gdns HP4 135 A2
Redbourne Ct MK11 32 C3
Redbridge MK14 34 B4
Redcliffe Wlk HP19 101 A1
Redcote Manor MK7 48 A2
Redding Dr HP6 154 A1
Redding Gr MK8 45 C3
Reddings Cl HP22 131 A3
Reddington Dr SL3 206 C1
Redfern Cl UB8 201 B2
Redfield Cl LU6 93 C4
Redford Rd SL4 209 B3
Redford Way UB8 201 B3
Redgrave Pl SL7 183 C1
Redhill UB9 189 B2
Redhouse Cl HP11 172 C2
Redhuish Cl MK4 46 B2
Redland Cl MK18 63 B1
Redland Dr MK5 46 B4
Redland Way HP21 116 A3
Redman Rd HP12 172 A2
Redriff Cl SL6 202 B3
Redshaw Cl MK18 41 C1
Redshots Cl SL7 183 C2
Redvers Gate MK15 35 A4
Redway Sch The MK6 47 B3
Redwing HP20 101 C2
Redwood SL1 197 A2
Redwood Cl
Hazelmere HP15 163 A2
Wing LU7 79 C1
Redwood Dr
Aylesbury HP21 115 C4
Wing LU7 79 C1
Redwood Gate MK5 46 B2
Redwood Gdns SL1 205 B3
Redwood Glade LU7 70 C2
Redwoods The SL4 210 B2
Reed Cl SL0 207 C4
Reeves Croft MK12 33 B2
Reform Rd SL6 203 A4
Regal Ct
Maidenhead SL6 203 A1
17 Tring HP23 119 A2
Regency Ct HP21 116 A4
Regent Ct
9 Maidenhead SL6 202 C4
Slough SL1 205 C4
Windsor SL4 210 B3
Regent Ho HP27 139 A2
Regent Rd HP21 116 A4
Regent St MK2 58 B4
Regius Ct HP10 174 B4
Reid Ave SL6 202 C3
Reliance La MK9 35 A2
Rembrandt End HP19 100 C1
Remenham Church La RG9 192 A2
Remenham La RG9 191 C2
Remenham Row RG9 191 C1
Remenham Terr RG9 192 B1
Remus Gate NN13 38 A3
Rendlesham MK15 35 B2
Rendlesham Way WD3 167 B2
Renfrew Way MK3 46 C2
Rennie Cl HP13 161 C1
Repton Cl SL6 202 B2
Repton Pl HP7 166 A4
Retreat La HP14 148 B1
Retreat The
Little Chalfont HP6 166 C4
Milton Keynes MK11 32 B3
Princes Risborough HP27 139 A2
Revel Rd HP10 185 B4
Revesby Cl SL6 202 B2
Reyners Gn HP16 152 A2
Reynold Dr HP20 102 A1
Reynolds Cl
Cranfield MK43 24 C2
High Wycombe HP13 173 C4
Reynolds Rd HP9 175 B2
Reynolds Wlk HP5 144 A2
Rhodes Pl MK6 46 C4
Rhondda Cl MK1 47 C1
Rhoscolyn Dr MK4 57 B4
Rhuddlan Cl MK5 45 C4
Rhymer Cl MK19 10 C2
Ribble Cl MK16 22 C2
Ribble Cres MK3 57 B4
Ribstone Rd SL6 202 A2
Ricardo Rd SL4 211 A1
Richard Gdns HP13 173 C4
Richards Way SL1 205 A3
Richardson Pl 2 MK6 34 C1
Richborough MK13 34 A3
Richings Way SL0 207 C2
Richmond Cl
Amersham HP6 154 C1
Milton Keynes MK3 46 B1
Richmond Cres SL1 206 A3
Richmond Ct HP13 173 B4
Richmond Rd HP20 116 B4
Richmond Way MK16 22 B2
Rick Yd The MK16 13 C1
Rickard Cl
Stoke Mandeville HP21 115 B2
West Drayton UB7 208 B2
Rickford's Hill HP20 115 B4
Rickley La MK3 58 A4
Rickley Mid Sch MK3 57 C4
Rickman Wlk HP19 115 A4
Rickman's La SL2 198 C3
Rickmansworth La SL9 177 C2
Rickmansworth Rd
Amersham HP6 154 B1
Chorleywood WD3 167 C3
Rickyard Cl
Milton Keynes MK13 34 A2
Whitchurch HP22 87 A4
Rickyard Gr HP18 83 A3
Rickyard The MK46 7 B2
Riders The LU6 93 A3
Riders Way OX39 147 B3
Ridge Cl Lane End HP14 171 B2
Stoke Mandeville HP21 115 B2
Ridge Ct SL4 210 B2
Ridge Side HP14 160 A4
Ridge View HP23 119 B3
Ridge Way
High Wycombe HP13 162 B1
Iver SL0 207 C3
Ridgebank SL1 204 C3
Ridgemount End SL9 177 C3
Ridgeway
Berkhamsted HP4 134 C2
Milton Keynes, Stony Stratford MK11 32 C2
Milton Keynes, Wolverton Mill MK17 33 A3
Wing LU7 79 C2
Ridgeway Cl
Chesham HP5 144 A2
Marlow SL7 183 C2
Ridgeway Cotts MK17 67 A2
Ridgeway Ct 18 HP20 101 C1
Ridgeway Meads HP27 138 A1
Ridgeway Rd HP5 144 A2
Ridgeway The
Amersham HP7 165 C4
Gerrards Cross SL9 188 C4
Marlow SL7 183 C2
Ridgeway Trad Est The SL0 207 C3
Ridgmont MK19 31 C3
Ridgmont Cl MK19 31 C3
Ridgway MK17 49 A3
Riding Court Rd SL3 211 B4
Riding Ct SL3 211 B4
Riding La HP9,HP10 174 C2
Riding The MK19 31 C3
Ridings Cotts HP15 163 B3
Ridings The
Amersham HP6 154 B2
Ridings The *continued*
Iver SL0 207 C1
Latimer HP5 155 B2
Maidenhead SL6 202 A4
Ridings Way LU7 78 A1
Rigby Lodge SL1 205 C4
Rignall Rd HP16 151 C4
Riley Cl HP20 115 B4
Riley Rd SL7 183 B1
Rillington Gdns MK4 46 A2
Rimmington Way HP19 101 A1
Rimsdale Ct MK2 58 B2
Ring Rd HP10 173 C1
Ring Rd E MK7 47 C4
Ring Rd N MK7 47 C4
Ring Rd W MK7 47 C4
Ringshall Dr HP4 121 A4
Ringshall Rd HP4 107 A2
Ringstead Way HP21 116 A3
Ripley Cl
High Wycombe HP13 173 A4
Slough SL3 206 C1
Ripon Ho HP21 115 C3
Ripon St 8 HP20 101 B1
Risborough Rd
Great Kimble HP17 129 C1
Maidenhead SL6 202 C4
Stoke Mandeville HP17, HP22 130 A4
Rise The Amersham HP7 165 B4
Gawcott MK18 51 C2
Hazelmere HP15 163 A3
Loudwater HP13 174 A2
Uxbridge UB10 201 C2
Riseley Rd SL6 202 B4
Risings The HP13 162 A1
River & Rowing Mus RG9 191 C1
River Cl MK16 22 B2
River Ct SL6 203 B4
River Gdns SL6 203 B2
River Park Ind Est HP4 135 A3
River Rd SL6 203 B3
River Side MK16 22 B2
River Side Cotts HP10 185 C4
River St SL4 210 B4
River View HP10 185 A4
River Wlk UB9 201 B4
Riverbank The SL4 210 A4
Rivercrest Rd MK19 32 A3
Rivermead Ct SL7 194 C4
Riverpark Dr SL7 183 C1
Rivers Edge HP11 174 A2
Rivers Fst Sch MK3 46 C1
Riversdale SL8 185 A1
Riversdale Cotts SL8 185 A1
Riversdale Ct SL8 185 A1
Riverside Bsns Ctr 11 HP11 172 C4
Riverside Cotts UB7 208 B1
Riverside Fst Sch MK16 22 B2
Riverside Gdns HP4 135 A3
Riverside Mews MK18 52 B4
Riverside Pl TW19 213 C1
Riverside Rd TW19 213 B1
Riverside Way UB8 201 A2
Riverside Wlk SL4 210 B4
Riverswood Gdns HP11 174 A2
Riverwood Ave SL7 184 A1
Riverwoods Dr SL7 184 A1
Rivets Cl HP21 115 C3
Rivetts Cl MK46 6 C2
Rixband Cl MK7 48 A2
Rixman Cl SL6 202 B3
Rixon Cl SL3 206 C4
Rixons Mdw HP19 115 A4
Roade Hill NN7 9 C4
Robert Rd SL2 187 B1
Robert's Dr HP19 101 B1
Roberts Cl
Deanshanger MK19 31 C2
Stanwell TW19 213 B1
West Drayton UB7 208 C3
Roberts La SL9 178 A3
Roberts Rd
Haddenham HP17 127 A3
High Wycombe HP13 173 A4
Roberts Ride HP15 163 A3
Roberts Way HP21 115 A3
Roberts Wood Dr SL9 177 C3
Robertson Cl MK5 45 C4
Robertson Cnr LU6 93 C2
Robertson Rd 6 HP4 135 B2
Robertswood Comb Sch SL9 177 C2
Robeson Pl MK8 45 C4
Robin Cl Aylesbury HP20 101 C2
Buckingham MK18 52 C4
Great Kingshill HP15 151 B1
Robin Hill HP4 135 B2
Robin Ho HP11 174 A2
Robin Hood Cl SL1 204 C3
Robin Par 5 SL2 198 B4
Robin Willis Way SL4 211 A1
Robins Cl
Little Marlow HP12 172 B2
Uxbridge UB8 208 B4
Robins Hill MK6 47 A3
Robins Orch SL9 177 C2
Robins Platt OX39 147 A3
Robinson Cl HP19 100 C2
Robinson Rd HP13 174 A2
Robinswood Cl
Beaconsfield HP9 175 B3
Leighton Buzzard LU7 70 C1
Robinwood Gr UB8 201 C1
Roblin Cl HP21 115 C2
Robson Cl SL9 177 C3

Robson Ct HP16 ....152 A4
Roche Gdns MK3 ......58 A4
Rochester Ct MK5 .....46 A3
Rochester Mews LU7 ...80 C3
Rochester Pl HP19 .....115 A4
Rochford Way SL6 .....204 A4
Rochfords MK6 ....46 C3
Rochfords Gdns SL2 ...206 B3
Rock Cl LU7 ....80 B3
Rock La LU7 ....80 B4
Rockall Ct SL3 ....207 A2
Rockingham Cl
 Pitstone LU7 ....105 B2
 Uxbridge UB8 ....201 B2
Rockingham Dr MK14 ...34 C3
Rockingham Par UB8 ...201 B3
Rockingham Pl HP9 ....175 C1
Rockingham Rd UB8 ....201 B2
Rockingham Wharf
 UB8 ....201 A2
Rockleigh Ct 14 LU7 ...80 C4
Rockspray Gr MK7 .....48 A3
Rodney Way SL3 ....212 C3
Rodwell Gdns MK7 .....48 B2
Rodwell Rd MK19 ......20 B1
Rodwell Yd 6 HP23 ....119 A2
Roebuck Ave HP13 .....173 C3
Roebuck Gn SL1 ....204 C3
Roebuck Way MK5 .....46 B3
Roeburn Cres MK4 .....46 B1
Rogers Croft MK6 ......47 B4
Rogers La SL2 ....198 C2
Roker Park Ave UB10 ..201 C4
Rokesby Rd SL2 ....197 C1
Rolfe Cl HP9 ....175 C1
Rolvenden Gr MK7 .....48 A4
Roman Lea SL8 ....195 C4
Roman Way
 Aylesbury HP19 ....115 A4
 Bourne End SL8 ....185 A2
 Brackley NN13 ....38 A4
Romans Field Sch MK3 .46 C1
Romar Ct MK1 ....47 B1
Romney Ct 11 SL7 .....183 C1
Romney Lock Rd SL4 ...210 B4
Romney Rd HP21 ......115 C2
Romsey Cl SL3 ....206 C2
Romsey Dr SL2 ....187 B1
Romsey Way HP11 .....173 A2
Romulus Way NN13 ....38 A3
Ronald Rd HP9 ....175 C1
Ronaldsay Spur SL1 ...205 C4
Rook Rd HP10 ....185 B2
Rook Tree Farm Ind Est
 MK17 ....37 C2
Rook Wood Way HP16 ..152 A3
Rookery Ct SL7 ....183 B1
Rookery Mdw HP15 ....163 B4
Rookery Way MK18 ....63 C2
Rooks Terr UB7 ....208 C2
Rooksley Rdbt MK13 ...34 A2
Ropa Ct 12 LU7 ....80 C4
Rosary The HP15 ......163 B4
Rose Ave Aylesbury HP19 .115 A4
 Hazelmere HP15 ......163 A1
Rose Cnr HP14 ....158 C3
Rose Cotts SL6 ....202 B2
Rose Ct Chesham HP5 .154 B3
 Eaton Bray LU6 ....92 B3
Rose Dr HP5 ....154 B4
Rose Hill SL1 ....197 A3
Rose Ind Est
 18 Bourne End SL8 ...185 A2
 Marlow Bottom SL7 ...183 B3
Rose La RG9 ....193 A1
Rose Wlk SL2 ....205 A4
Roseary Cl UB7 ....208 C1
Rosebank Cl SL8 .....195 C4
Rosebank Cotts HP10 .174 A3
Rosebarn La HP23 .....104 B1
Rosebay Ct MK7 ......48 A3
Rosebery Ave
 High Wycombe HP13 ..173 C3
 Leighton Buzzard LU7 .80 C4
Rosebery Ct 9 LU7 ....80 C4
Rosebery Mews LU7 ...90 B2
Rosebery Rd HP22 ....117 C3
Rosebery Way HP23 ...119 A3
Rosecomb Pl MK5 .....46 A2
Rosehill HP4 ....135 A2
Rosehill Cres MK18 ...62 B1
Rosehill Ct SL1 ....206 A2
Roseleigh Cl SL6 .....202 A4
Rosemary Cl HP12 ....161 A1
Rosemary Ct
 High Wycombe HP12 ..161 A1
 Walton MK7 ....48 A3
Rosemary La HP17 ....127 A4
Rosemead HP22 ......117 C1
Rosemullion Ave MK4 .57 A4
Rosery The SL8 ....185 A4
Roses Cl LU7 ....78 A1
Roses La SL4 ....209 B3
Rosetree Cl HP16 .....151 B3
Rosewood Gdns HP12 .172 B2
Rosewood Way SL2 ...198 B4
Rosken Gr MK15 ......35 B4
Roslyn Ct MK15 ....35 B4
Ross Rd Aston Abbotts HP22 .88 B3
 Maidenhead SL6 ......202 C2
Ross Way MK3 ....46 C1
Rossal Pl MK12 ....33 C3
Rossendale MK14 .....34 B4
Rossetti Pl HP15 ......163 B4
Rossini Pl MK7 ....48 B3
Rossiter Cl SL3 ....206 C1
Rossway La HP23 .....134 A4
Rostrevor Gdns SL0 ..200 B2
Rostherpe MK14 .....35 A4

Rothesay Cl HP20 .....101 C1
Rothesay Ct HP4 ......135 A2
Rothschild Ave HP22 ..117 C3
Rothschild Rd
 Leighton Buzzard LU7 .80 C4
 Wing LU7 ....79 C1
Rotten Row MK17 .....59 B1
Roughwood La HP8 ...166 C2
Round Hill HP17 ......114 B3
Round Wood Rd HP6 ..154 C1
Roundhead Dr OX9 ...125 C1
Roundheads End HP9 .175 A2
Roundlands HP27 .....149 C3
Roundwood Rd HP12 .172 B4
Rouse Ct SL9 ....188 C3
Roveley Ct MK11 ......32 C3
Row The Cholesbury HP5 .133 B1
 Coleshill HP7 ....164 B2
 Lane End HP14 ....171 A2
Rowan Ave HP13 ......173 B4
Rowan Cl Aylesbury HP21 .115 C2
 Beaconsfield HP9 .....175 A1
 Hazelmere HP15 .....163 A2
Rowan Dr MK19 ....20 B1
Rowan Ho 1 SL8 .....185 A2
Rowan Pl HP6 ....154 C1
Rowan Rd UB7 ....208 B1
Rowan Way SL2 ......205 A4
Rowanhurst Dr SL2 ..198 B4
Rowans The SL9 ......188 B4
Rowborough Rd HP22 .131 B3
Rowland Cl SL4 ......209 B2
Rowland Ho HP9 .....175 C1
Rowland Way HP19 ...115 A4
Rowlands Cl MK2 .....58 C4
Rowle Cl MK14 ....34 C4
Rowley Furrows LU7 ..80 B4
Rowley Rd Iver Heath SL3 .199 B3
 Stoke Poges SL3 .....199 B2
Rowlheys Pl UB7 .....208 C2
Rowliff Rd HP12 ......172 B3
Rowsham Dell MK14 ..21 C3
Roxburgh Way MK3 ..46 C2
Roxhill Rd MK43 .....25 C2
Roxwell Cl SL1 ....204 C3
Roxwell Path 5 HP20 .101 C1
Royal Buckinghamshire
 Hospl HP19 ....101 B1
Royal Cl UB7,UB8 ....208 C4
Royal Cotts SL7 ......195 B4
Royal Ct SL7 ....120 A3
Royal Free Ct 25 SL4 .210 B3
Royal Gram Sch The
 HP13 ....162 B1
Royal La UB7 ....208 C4
Royal Latin Sch MK18 .52 B4
Royal Mans RG9 .....191 C1
Royal Mead HP21 ....130 B3
Royal Windsor
 Race Course SL4 .....209 C4
Royce Cl LU6 ....93 C4
Royce Rd MK43 ......24 B2
Royle Cl SL9 ....177 C2
Royston Way SL1 ....204 B4
Rubbra Cl MK7 ....48 B3
Rubens Cl HP19 ......100 C1
Ruby Cl SL1 ....205 A2
Ruckles Way HP7 ....165 B4
Rudchesters MK13 ...33 C3
Ruddlesway SL4 .....209 B3
Rudds Cl MK18 ......66 A3
Rudds La HP17 ......127 A4
Rudsworth Cl SL3 ...212 B4
Ruffle Cl SL3 ....208 C2
Rugwood Rd HP10 ..173 C1
Rumptons Paddock
 HP18 ....82 C3
Run Furrow HP17 ....127 A4
Runford Ct MK5 .....46 B3
Runnymede MK14 ...21 C1
Runrig Hill HP6 ......154 C2
Rupert Ave HP12 ....172 C2
Rupert Ct RG9 ....191 C2
Rupert House Sch RG9 .191 C1
Rupert Way OX9 ....126 A1
Rupert's La 6 RG9 ..191 C2
Rural Bygones Mus★
 LU7 ....105 B2
Ruscombe Gdns SL3 .211 A4
Rushall Rd OX9 .....126 A1
Rushbeds Wood
 Nature Reserve★ HP18 .96 B2
Rushbrooke Cl HP13 .162 C1
Rushburn HP10 .....185 C3
Rushendon Furlong
 LU7 ....105 B2
Rushes Mead UB8 ...201 B2
Rushes The
 Maidenhead SL6 ....203 A3
 Marlow SL7 ....194 B4
Rushington Ave SL6 .202 C3
Rushmere Cl MK17 ..48 B1
Rushmere La HP5 ...145 A2
Rushmere Ret Pk MK1 .47 B1
Rushmoor Ave HP15 .163 A2
Rushton Ct MK8 .....45 C4
Ruskin Ct MK16 .....22 B1
Ruskin Way HP20 ...101 C3
Rusland Cir MK4 ....46 B1
Russell Ave HP21 ...115 B3
Russell Cl
 Little Chalfont HP6 ..166 B4
 Tylers Green HP10 ..163 A1
Russell Ct
 Aylesbury HP21 ....115 A3
 Chesham HP5 ......144 B1
 Maidenhead SL6 ...202 C4

Russell Ct continued
 Walter's Ash HP14 ...161 B4
 Wendover HP22 .....131 A3
Russell Cty Prim Sch
 WD3 ....167 A3
Russell Dr TW19 ....213 B1
Russell Fst Sch MK11 .32 B3
Russell Ho 4 SL8 ...185 A1
Russell Sch The WD3 .167 A3
Russell St
 Milton Keynes MK11 ..32 B3
 Windsor SL4 ....210 B3
 Woburn Sands MK17 .49 A2
Russet Cl TW19 .....212 C1
Russet Rd SL6 ......202 B2
Russets The SL9 ....177 B1
Russett Hill SL9 ....188 C4
Rustlings Gate HP14 .171 B3
Rutherford Cl
 Uxbridge UB8 ....201 C1
 Windsor SL4 ....209 C2
Rutherford Gate MK5 .46 B3
Rutherford Rd HP21 .115 C2
Ruthven Ct MK2 ....58 B2
Rutland Ave
 High Wycombe HP12 .172 B3
 Slough SL1 ....205 B4
Rutland Ct 2 HP11 ..173 A3
Rutland Gate SL6 ...202 B3
Rutland Pl SL6 .....202 B3
Rutland Rd SL6 ....202 B3
Rutland St HP11 ...173 A3
Ryans Mount SL7 ..183 B1
Rycote La OX9 .....136 B3
Rycotewood Coll OX9 .125 C1
Rycroft Milton Keynes MK4 .46 C2
 Windsor SL4 ....209 C2
Rydal Way
 High Wycombe HP12 .172 A3
 Milton Keynes MK2 ..58 B3
Ryder Cl HP3 ....146 A2
Ryding The MK5 ....46 A2
Rydings SL4 ....209 C2
Rye Cl Aylesbury HP21 .115 B2
 Maidenhead SL6 ...202 A2
Rye Ct 8 SL1 ......206 A2
Rye The LU6,LU7 ..92 A4
Rye View HP13 ....173 B4
Ryeland MK11 ....32 C3
Ryeland Cl UB7 ...208 C4
Rylstone Cl
 Maidenhead SL6 ..202 B2
 Milton Keynes MK13 .34 A2
Ryman Ct WD3 ...167 B2
Rymill Cl HP3 .....146 A2
Ryton Pl MK4 ....46 B2
Ryvers End SL3 ..206 C2
Ryvers Prim Sch SL3 .206 B2
Ryvers Rd SL3 ...206 C2

S

Sabina Cl HP12 ......172 C3
Sacred Heart
 RC Prim Sch The RG9 .191 B1
Saddington MK6 .....47 B3
Saddlers Gn MK17 ...49 A3
Saddlers Pl MK14 ...35 A3
Sadlers Mews SL6 ..203 A4
Saffron Cl SL3 ......211 A3
Saffron Ct HP13 ....173 B3
Saffron Rd HP13 ...173 B3
Saffron Rise LU6 ...92 C3
Saffron St MK2 ....58 B4
Saham Croft Cl MK18 .65 C2
Sailing Club SL8 ...185 A2
St Adrian's Cl SL6 .202 A2
St Aidan's Cl MK3 ..57 C3
St Alban's Rd MK18 .65 C2
St Alban's St SL4 ...210 B3
St Albans Cl 17 SL4 .210 B3
St Andrew's Ave SL4 .209 C3
St Andrew's CE Inf Sch
 OX39 ....147 B4
St Andrew's CE Prim Sch
 Chinnor OX39 ......147 B4
 Uxbridge UB8 ......201 B2
St Andrew's Cl
 High Wycombe HP13 .162 C1
 Old Windsor SL4 ...211 A1
 Wraysbury TW19 ...211 C1
St Andrew's Cres SL4 .209 C3
St Andrew's Rd
 Chinnor OX39 ......147 B3
 Milton Keynes MK3 .57 C4
 Uxbridge UB10 .....201 C3
St Andrew's Way SL1 .204 B3
St Andrews Cotts 1
 SL4 ....210 A3
St Andrews Ct
 Colnbrook SL3 .....212 B4
 21 Slough SL1 ......205 B3
St Andrews Ho OX39 .147 B3
St Andrews Rd RG9 .191 C1
St Andrews Way Ind Est
 HP19 ....101 B1
St Ann's HP10 .....174 B1
St Ann's Ct HP10 ..174 B1
St Anne's Cl
 Henley-on-T RG9 ..191 B1
 Wendover HP22 ...131 A3
St Anne's Rd
 Aylesbury HP19 ...115 A4
 South Harefield UB9 .190 B4

St Anthony's Cl HP19 .115 A4
St Anthony's Ct HP9 .186 B4
St Anthony's Pl MK4 .57 A4
St Anthony's
 RC Prim Sch SL2 ..198 A1
St Augustine's
 RC Prim Sch SL2 ..173 A2
St Bartholomew's
 CE Sch HP23 ....119 B1
St Bartholomews MK10 .36 A1
St Bees MK10 ......36 A1
St Bernard's
 Convent Sch SL3 ..206 A4
St Bernard's Prep Sch
 SL1 ....206 A2
St Bernard's RC Sch
 HP11 ....173 A2
St Bernards Ct HP13 .173 B3
St Bernards Rd SL3 .206 B2
St Birinus HP10 ....174 A1
St Botolphs MK10 ..36 A1
St Brides Cl MK6 ...35 B1
St Catherine's Ave MK3 .57 B3
St Catherine's Ct HP19 .115 A4
St Catherine's
 RC Prim Sch UB7 ..208 B2
St Catherines Ct 3 SL4 .210 A3
St Chad's Rd SL6 ..202 A2
St Christopher Rd UB8 .208 B4
St Christopher's Cl
 HP16 ....152 A2
St Christophers Ct WD3 .167 B3
St Clement Cl UB8 .208 B4
St Clement Danes Sch
 WD3 ....167 A4
St Clement's Dr MK3 .57 B3
St Columba's Cl SL6 .202 A2
St David Cl UB8 ....208 B4
St David's Cl
 Iver Heath SL0 .....200 B2
 Maidenhead SL6 ...202 A2
St David's Ct MK10 .38 A1
St David's Par SL0 .200 B2
St David's Rd MK3 .57 C3
St Dunstans MK6 ..47 B4
St Edmund Campion
 RC Prim Sch SL6 ..202 A3
St Edmund's Cl HP19 .115 A4
St Edmunds HP4 ...135 B2
St Edward's RC Fst Sch
 SL4 ....210 A3
St Edward's RC Jun Sch
 HP21 ....116 A4
St Edward's Royal Free
 Ecumenical Mid Sch
 SL4 ....210 A3
St Edwards Ct MK14 .34 C4
St Elmo Cl SL2 ....198 B1
St Elmo Cres SL2 ..198 B1
St Ethelbert's
 RC Comb Sch SL2 .206 A4
St Faith's Cl MK17 ..57 B2
St Francis de Sales
 Prep Sch HP23 ....118 C2
St Francis Rd
 Beacon's Bottom HP14 .159 B2
 Denham Green UB9 .189 C3
St George's CE Inf Sch
 HP7 ....165 C4
St George's Cl
 High Wycombe HP13 .173 B4
 Windsor SL4 ....209 C3
St George's Cres SL1 .204 B3
St George's Dr UB10 .190 C1
St George's Rd MK3 .57 C3
St George's Sch SL4 .210 B4
St Georges Ct HP11 .172 B4
St Georges Ind Est HP7 .165 C4
St Georges Way MK12 .33 B3
St Giles Mews MK11 .32 B3
St Giles St MK13 ...33 C4
St Govans Cl MK4 ..57 A4
St Helen Cl UB8 ...208 B4
St Helens Gn MK10 .47 C4
St Hilda's Ct HP19 .115 A4
St Hilda's Way MK10 .174 A1
St Huberts Cl SL9 ..188 C1
St Huberts Cotts SL9 .188 C2
St Huberts La SL9 ..188 C1
St Hugh's Ave HP13 .173 C3
St Hugh's Ct MK4 ..158 C2
St Hugh's Pl HP14 ..158 C2
St Ives Cres MK4 ..57 A4
St Ives Rd SL6 .....203 A4
St James Cl MK19 ..11 A1
St James Ctyd 4 SL7 .183 C1
St James Pl SL1 ...204 B4
St James St MK13 .33 C4
St James Way HP22 .102 A2
St James Wlk SL0 .207 C2
St John Cl MK16 ..22 B2
St John's Ave HP10 .174 A4
St John's CE Comb Sch
 HP27 ....149 C2
St John's Cl UB8 ..201 A2
St John's La MK19 .31 A2
St John's Rd
 Hazelmere HP15 ..162 C1
 Milton Keynes MK3 .57 C3
 Uxbridge UB8 .....201 A2
St John's St HP20 .101 C1
St John's Terr MK16 .22 B1
St John's Well Ct HP4 .135 C2
St John's Well La HP4 .135 C2
St Johns Cl HP10 .163 A1
St Johns Cres MK12 .33 B3
St Johns Dr Stone HP17 .114 A3
 Windsor SL4 ....210 A3

St Johns Rd Slough SL2 .206 A3
 Tylers Green HP10 .163 A1
 Windsor SL4 ......210 A3
St Joseph's
 RC Comb Sch SL9 .188 B4
St Joseph's RC High Sch
 SL2 ....206 A4
St Joseph's RC Inf Sch
 HP21 ....116 A4
St Josephs Cl MK46 ..6 C2
St Katherine's Way HP4 .134 C4
St Laurence CE Jun Sch
 UB8 ....208 A4
St Laurence Cl UB8 .208 B4
St Laurence Rd MK18 .65 C2
St Laurence Way SL1 .206 A2
St Lawrence Cl HP3 .146 A2
St Lawrence View MK13 .34 A2
St Leger Ct MK14 ..34 C4
St Leger Dr MK14 ..34 C4
St Leonard's Ave 31 SL4 .210 B4
St Leonard's Rd
 Oakley Green SL4 ..209 A4
 Windsor SL4 ......210 B2
St Leonard's Way LU6 .92 C1
St Leonards Hill SL4 .209 A2
St Leonards Rd HP6 .154 C2
St Leonards Wlk SL0 .207 C2
St Louis RC Comb Sch
 HP20 ....101 C1
St Luke Cl UB8 ...208 B4
St Luke's CE Prim Sch
 SL6 ....202 C4
St Luke's Rd
 Maidenhead SL6 ..202 C4
 Old Windsor SL4 ..211 A1
 Uxbridge UB10 ....201 C3
St Margaret Ct MK2 .58 C4
St Margaret's Cl
 Berkhamsted HP4 .135 B2
 Iver Heath SL0 ...200 B2
 Tylers Green HP10 .174 A1
St Margaret's Gate SL0 .200 B2
St Margaret's Rd SL6 .202 A4
St Margarets Cl MK16 .22 C2
St Margarets Ct SL0 .200 B2
St Margarets Gr HP15 .151 C1
St Mark's Cres SL6 .202 A4
St Mark's Hospl SL6 .202 C4
St Mark's Pl SL4 ..210 B3
St Mark's Rd
 Aylesbury HP21 ...115 B4
 Henley-on-T RG9 ..191 C1
 Maidenhead SL6 ..202 C4
 Windsor SL4 ......210 B3
St Martin Cl UB8 ..208 B4
St Martin's Cl UB7 .208 B2
St Martin's Rd UB7 .208 B2
St Martin's St MK2 .58 C4
St Mary & All Saints
 CE Comb Sch HP9 .175 C2
St Mary & St Giles
 CE Mid Sch MK11 .32 C3
St Mary Magdalene
 RC Comb Sch MK12 .33 A3
St Mary St
 High Wycombe HP11 .173 A3
 Milton Keynes MK13 .33 C4
St Mary's Ave
 Berkhamsted HP4 .134 B3
 Milton Keynes MK3 .57 C4
 Milton Keynes, Stony Stratford
 MK11 ....32 C3
St Mary's CE Fst Sch
 HP4 ....134 B3
St Mary's CE Prim Sch
 SL1 ....206 A3
St Mary's Cl
 Amersham HP7 ...165 A4
 Aylesbury HP20 ..115 A4
St Mary's Cl
 Maidenhead SL6 ..203 A4
 South Harefield UB9 .190 A4
 Wavendon MK17 ..48 C4
St Mary's Glebe LU6 .92 C1
St Mary's Ind Day Sch
 for Girls SL9 ......188 C1
St Mary's La HP16 .142 B3
St Mary's RC Prim Sch
 Maidenhead SL6 ..195 C1
 Uxbridge UB8 .....201 B2
St Mary's Rd
 Denham Green UB9 .189 C3
 Slough SL3 ....206 A3
 South Harefield UB9 .190 A4
St Mary's Row 5 HP20 .115 A4
St Mary's Sq 2 HP20 .115 B4
St Mary's Way
 Chesham HP5 ....154 A4
 Gerrards Cross SL9 .177 B1
 Leighton Buzzard LU7 .80 C4
St Mary's Wlk 12 SL6 .202 C4
St Marys
 East Claydon MK18 .74 C4
 Mursley MK17 ....67 B3
St Marys Ct MK18 .51 A4
St Marys Rd MK18 .74 C4
St Matthew Cl UB8 .208 B4
St Matthew's
 CE Prim Sch UB7 .208 C2
St Matthews Ct MK3 .57 C3
St Michael's
 CE Comb Sch LU7 .68 C1
St Michael's Cl HP22 .117 B1
St Michael's Ct SL2 .197 B1

240 St M – Sil

St Michael's Gn HP9 .....175 C2
St Michael's Way MK18 ..63 C2
St Michaels Cl
  Edgcott HP18 ....72 C1
  Halton HP22 ....131 B4
  Stewkley LU7 ....68 C1
St Michaels Ct NN7 .....9 C4
St Michaels Dr MK7 .....47 C4
St Monica's RC Comb Sch
  MK14 ....34 C3
St Nicholas CE Comb Sch
  SL6 ....196 C1
St Nicholas Cl
  Cublington LU7 ....78 A1
  Little Chalfont HP7 ..166 A4
  Uxbridge UB8 ....208 B4
St Patrick's Cl SL6 ....202 A2
St Patrick's Way MK3 ...57 C3
St Paul Cl UB8 ....208 B4
St Paul's CE Comb Sch
  HP10 ....185 B2
St Paul's Ct SL6 ......202 C3
St Paul's Rd SL6 ......57 C3
St Pauls Ave SL2 ......206 A3
St Pauls Ct MK11 ......32 B3
St Pauls RC Sch 46 C4
St Pauls Yd MK16 ......22 B2
St Peter St SL7 ....183 C1
St Peter's Ave HP19 ...101 B2
St Peter's CE Comb Sch
  SL1 ....197 A1
St Peter's CE Mid Sch
  SL4 ....210 C1
St Peter's Cl
  Burnham SL1 ....197 A1
  Old Windsor SL4 .....211 A1
St Peter's Ct 2 SL9 ..177 C1
St Peter's Hill HP23 ..119 C2
St Peter's RC Prim Sch
  SL7 ....183 B2
St Peter's Rd
  Brackley NN13 ....38 A4
  Maidenhead SL6 .....195 B1
  Uxbridge UB8 ....208 B4
St Peters Cl
  Lacey Green HP27 ....150 B2
  Loudwater HP11 .....174 A4
St Peters Gate NN13 ...38 A4
St Peters Way
  Chorleywood WD3 ....167 A3
  Milton Keynes MK13 ..34 A4
St Pirans Ind Day Sch
  SL6 ....195 C1
St Rumbold's La MK18 ..52 B4
St Stephen's Rd UB7 ...208 B3
St Stephens Dr MK15 ...35 A4
St Teresa's Cl HP27 ...139 A2
St Teresa's Sch HP27 ..139 A2
St Thomas Aquinas RC
  Comb Prim Sch MK3 ..57 C4
St Thomas Ct MK4 .....45 C1
St Thomas More
  RC Prim Sch HP4 ....135 A2
St Thomas Wlk SL3 ....212 B4
St Tiggywinkles
  Wildlife Hospl★ HP17 .127 A2
St Vincents MK7 ....49 C2
Salcey Forest Trail
  (Rose Copse)★ MK16 ..4 B1
Salden Cl
  Drayton Parslow MK17 .68 B3
  Milton Keynes MK5 ...46 A3
Salford Rd MK17 ....49 B4
Salisbury Ave SL2 .....205 B4
Salisbury Cl
  Amersham HP7 ....165 C4
  Princes Risborough HP27 .139 A2
Salisbury Ct SL6 ......202 C3
Salisbury Gr MK14 .....21 C1
Salisbury Mews SL2 ....198 B1
Salisbury Rd
  High Wycombe HP13 ...162 B1
  Uxbridge UB8 ....201 A2
Salmons La HP16 ......151 B3
Salt Hill Ave SL1 ....205 B3
Salt Hill Cl UB8 .....201 C4
Salt Hill Dr SL1 .....205 B3
Salt Hill Mans SL1 ...205 B3
Salt Hill Way SL1 ....205 B3
Saltash Cl HP13 .....174 A2
Salter's Cl HP4 .....134 C3
Salters Cl SL6 ......203 A4
Salters La HP18 .....96 B4
Salters Mews MK14 ...34 C3
Salters Rd SL6 ......203 A4
Salters Row HP10 ....186 A2
Salton Link MK4 .....46 A1
Saltwood Ave MK4 ....45 C1
Samphire Ct MK7 .....48 A3
Sampsons Gn SL2 .....197 C1
Sampsons Hill HP7 ...164 C1
San Remo Rd MK17 ...49 C2
Sanctuary Rd HP15 ...163 A3
Sandage Rd HP14 ....171 A3
Sandal Ct MK5 ......46 A3
Sandbrier Cl MK7 ...48 A3
Sandbrook La HP23 ..104 B1
Sandels Way HP9 ....175 B2
Sandelswood End HP9 .175 B3
Sanders La NN12 ....18 B2
Sanderson Rd UB8 ...201 B3
Sandford Gdns HP11 .173 A2
Sandhill Rd MK18 ...74 C4
Sandhill Way HP19 ..115 A4
Sandholme MK18 ....63 C2

Sandhurst Dr MK18 ...52 B4
Sandisplatt Rd SL6 ..202 A3
Sandlers End SL2 ....198 A1
Sandon Cl HP23 .....118 C2
Sandown Ct MK3 ....57 B3
Sandown Rd SL2 ....204 C4
Sandpiper 1 HP20 ...101 C2
Sandpit Hill MK18 ...50 C3
Sandpit Hill Cotts HP23 133 A2
Sandpit La MK7 .....138 A2
Sandpits La HP10 ...174 B4
Sandringham Ct
  15 High Wycombe HP13 .173 A4
  Newport Pagnell MK16 .22 A2
  Slough SL1 ....204 B4
Sandringham Pl MK2 ..58 B3
Sandringham Rd
  Maidenhead SL6 ....195 C1
  Stanwell TW6 ......213 C1
Sands Farm Dr SL1 ..197 B1
Sands Ind Est HP12 ..172 A4
Sandwell Ct MK8 ....33 B1
Sandy Cl
  Buckingham MK18 ...52 C4
  Milton Keynes MK14 .34 B4
Sandy Cl
  Aspley Heath MK17 ..49 A1
  Leighton Buzzard LU7 .70 C2
  Long Crendon HP18 ..125 A3
Sandy Mead SL9 ....203 B1
Sandy Rise SL9 .....177 C1
Sandycroft Rd HP6 ..155 B1
Sandygate Cl SL7 ...183 B2
Sandygate Rd SL7 ...183 B2
Sandywell Dr MK15 ..35 A3
Santen Gr MK2 .....58 B2
Sargeants Cl UB8 ...201 B1
Sarum Complex UB8 .201 A2
Satis Ho SL3 ......211 B4
Saunders Ct MK7 ...48 B3
Saunders Ct 1 HP13 .173 C1
Saunders End HP6 ..153 B3
Saunders Pl HP19 ..115 A4
Saunders Rd UB10 ..201 C3
Saunders Wood Copse
  HP14 ....158 C2
Saunderton Sta HP14 .149 B1
Saunderton Vale HP14 .149 B1
Savay Cl UB9 ......190 A2
Savay La UB9 ......190 A2
Savernake Rd HP19 ..101 B2
Savill Way SL7 ....183 C1
Savoy Cres MK9 ....34 C2
Sawmill Rd MK27 ...138 B4
Sawpit Hill MK15 ..163 A4
Sawyer's Cl SL4 ...209 C4
Sawyers Cl SL6 ....202 A1
Sawyers Cres SL4 ..202 A1
Saxeways Bsns Ctr HP5 143 C2
Saxhorn Rd HP14 ...171 B2
Saxon Cl Amersham HP6 .154 B1
  Dunstable LU6 .....93 C4
  Slough SL3 ....206 C2
  Uxbridge UB8 ......208 C4
Saxon Ct
  High Wycombe HP12 ..172 B4
  Stanwell TW19 .....213 A1
Saxon Gdns SL6 ....196 B1
Saxon Lodge 10 SL1 .204 C3
Saxon St
  Milton Keynes MK3 ..58 B4
  Milton Keynes, Ashland MK1,
    MK2, MK6 ....47 B2
  Milton Keynes, Leadenhall
    MK13, MK14, MK4, MK6 ..34 B3
Saxon Way
  Harmondsworth UB7 ..213 B4
  Old Windsor SL4 ...211 A1
Saye & Sele Cl HP18 ..82 C3
Sayers Gdns HP4 ...135 A3
Sayward Cl HP5 ....144 B1
Scafell Rd SL2 ....204 C4
Scarborough Way SL1 ..205 A2
Scardale MK18 .....34 B3
Scarlett Ave HP22 ..131 C3
Scatterdells La WD4 .146 C1
Scatterill Cl MK13 ..34 A2
Scholars Way HP6 ..154 C1
Scholars Wlk SL9 ..177 C2
School Cl
  Great Kingshill HP15 .162 B3
  High Wycombe HP11 ..173 A2
  High Wycombe, Downley
    HP13 ....161 B1
  Holmer Green HP15 ..163 B4
  Ickford HP18 ......124 A2
School Dr MK17 ....57 B2
School End MK17 ...54 C2
School Hill
  Charndon MK18 ....73 A3
  North Marston MK18 .76 A1
School Ho TW19 ...213 B1
School La
  Amersham HP7 ....165 A4
  Buckingham MK18 ..52 B4
  Castlethorpe MK19 ..19 C3
  Chalfont St Giles HP8 .177 A4
  Chearsley HP18 ...112 A1
  Cookham SL8 .....196 A4
  Cookham, Cookham Dean
    SL7 ....195 A4
  Dinton HP17 ......113 C1
  Eaton Bray LU6 ...92 C3
  Gerrards Cross SL9 .177 C3
  Ibstone HP14 .....169 C2
  Little Marlow SL8 ..184 B3
  Maidenhead SL6 ...195 C1
  Medmenham SL7 ...193 A3

School La continued
  Milton Keynes MK5 ...46 A4
  Oakley HP18 ....109 B3
  Preston Bissett MK18 .62 A4
  Seer Green HP9 ....176 B2
  Shabbington HP18 ..124 B3
  Sherington MK16 ...14 A1
  Stoke Poges SL2 ...199 A1
  Twyford MK18 .....62 B1
  Tylers Green HP7 ..164 A3
  Waddesdon HP18 ..99 A3
  Waddesdon, Upper Winchendon
    HP18 ....99 A1
  Weston Turville HP22 .116 C1
  Yardley Gobion NN12 .18 C3
School Rd
  Harmondsworth UB7 .213 B4
  Tylers Green HP10 ..174 B4
  Wooburn Green HP10 .185 C3
School St MK13 ....33 C4
School The HP23 ...118 B4
School Way HP11 ...174 A1
Schorne La MK18 ..76 A1
Schumann Cl MK7 ..48 B2
Scotch Firs MK7 ..48 B3
Scotlands Dr SL2 ..198 A3
Scotney Gdns MK3 .57 C4
Scotsgrove Cotts OX9 .126 A2
Scotswood Cl HP9 ..175 B3
Scott Cl
  Farnham Common SL2 .198 B4
  West Drayton UB7 ..208 C1
Scott Dr MK16 .....22 A3
Scott End HP19 ....100 C1
Scott Evans Ct MK18 .66 A3
Scotts Cl
  Marsh Gibbon OX27 .72 A2
  Stoke Hammond MK17 .69 C4
Scotts Cnr NN13 ...39 A2
Scotts Farm Cl MK18 .41 C2
Scotts Cl Adstock MK18 .53 C1
  Buckingham MK18 ..41 C2
  Marsh Gibbon OX27 .71 C1
Scriven Ct MK15 ...35 C4
Scriveners La NN12 .17 A4
Scrubb's La HP14 ..160 A4
Seacourt Rd SL3 ..207 A1
Seaford Rd TW6 ...213 B1
Seagrave Ct MK7 ..48 A2
Seagrave Rd HP9 ..175 B2
Sears The LU6 ....92 A3
Seaton Dr HP21 ...115 A4
Secklow Gate MK9 .34 C2
Second Ave MK1 ...47 B1
Second Cres SL1 ..205 B4
Second St HP11 ...173 B2
Sedgemere Dr OX9 .126 A1
Sedgemoor Gr HP10 .185 A4
Sedgmoor Gdns HP10 .185 A4
Sedgmoor La HP10 .185 A4
Sedgmoor Rd HP10 .185 A4
Sedley Gr UB9 ....190 B4
Sedrup La HP17 ...114 C2
Seeleys Cl HP9 ...175 B2
Seeleys Ct HP9 ...175 B2
Seeleys La HP9 ...175 B2
Seeleys Rd HP9 ...175 B2
Seer Green & Jordans
  Sta HP9 ....175 C1
Seer Green
  CE Comb Sch HP9 .176 B2
Seer Green La HP9 .176 C2
Seer Mead HP9 ...176 B2
Sefton Cl SL2 ....198 C2
Sefton Paddock SL2 .199 A3
Sefton Park Cotts SL2 .199 A2
Sefton Way UB8 ..208 A4
Selbourne Ave MK3 .57 C4
Selby Gr MK5 .....46 A3
Selkirk Ave HP19 ..101 B1
Selkirk Gr MK3 ...46 C1
Selwood Cl TW19 ..213 A1
Selwood Gdns TW19 .213 B1
Selwood Way HP13 .161 C1
Selworthy MK4 ....46 B2
Selwyn Cl SL4 ....209 C3
Selwyn Ct HP21 ...116 A3
Selwyn Pl 2 SL1 ..204 C3
September Ct UB10 .201 B2
Serjeants Gn MK14 .34 C3
Serles Cl MK6 ....47 A3
Sermed Ct SL2 ...206 B3
Serpentine Ct MK2 .58 B3
Servite Ho SL6 ...203 A4
Seven Acre Ho HP10 .174 B1
Seven Acres HP18 .125 A4
Sevenhills Rd SL0 .200 B3
Severalls Ave HP5 .144 B1
Severn Cres SL3 ..212 A4
Severn Dr MK16 ...22 C2
Severn Ho HP11 ...173 C4
Severn Way MK3 ..46 C1
Sewell Cl HP19 ...100 C1
Seymour Cl
  Flackwell Heath HP10 .173 C1
  Maidenhead SL6 ...202 A2
Seymour Court La SL7 .183 A3
Seymour Court Rd SL7 .183 B2
Seymour Ct HP4 ..134 C3
Seymour Ho
  High Wycombe HP12 ..172 C2
  Slough SL3 ......206 C2
Seymour Park Rd SL7 .183 B2
Seymour Plain SL7 .183 B3
Seymour Rd
  Berkhamsted HP4 ..134 C3
  Chalfont St Giles HP8 .177 B3

Seymour Rd continued
  Slough SL1 ....205 B2
Shackleton Ct 6 TW19 .213 C1
Shackleton Pl MK6 ...34 C1
Shackleton Rd
  High Wycombe HP12 ..172 C3
  Slough SL1 ....205 B2
Shaftesbury Cres MK3 .47 A1
Shaftesbury Ct
  Maidenhead SL6 ...202 C3
  6 Slough SL1 .....205 C2
Shaftesbury Ho HP21 .116 B4
Shaftesbury St HP11 .172 C4
Shaftsbury St SL8 ..65 C3
Shaggy Calf La SL2 .206 A3
Shakespear Cl MK16 .22 A3
Shakespeare Orch HP18 .82 C2
Shakespeare Way HP20 116 A4
Shallowford Cl MK4 .46 B2
Shamrock Ct MK7 ...48 A3
Shannon Ct
  Chesham HP5 .....144 B1
  Milton Keynes MK14 .35 A3
Shantock Hall La HP3 .145 C1
Shantock La HP3 ..145 C1
Shantung Pl HP5 ..154 B3
Sharkham Ct MK4 ..46 A1
Sharman Wlk MK13 .34 A2
Sharney Ave SL3 ..207 A2
Sharp Cl HP21 ....115 C3
Sharp's Cl HP18 ..99 A3
Sharrow Vale HP12 .172 C4
Shaw Cl Aylesbury HP20 .116 A4
  Newport Pagnell MK16 .22 A3
Shaw Ct Old Windsor SL4 .211 A1
  Stoke Mandeville HP21 .115 C2
Shaw The SL8 ....195 C3
Shawfield Ct UB7 ..208 C2
Shaws Cl HP16 ...151 B3
Shearmans MK11 ..33 A2
Sheehy Way SL2 ..206 A3
Sheelin Gr MK2 ..58 B2
Sheep St MK18 ...66 A2
Sheepcoat Cl MK5 .46 A3
Sheepcote Cl HP9 .175 B2
Sheepcote Dell Rd HP7,
  HP16 ....163 C4
Sheepcote Gdns UB9 .190 A3
Sheepcote La SL1, HP10 .186 A1
Sheepcote Rd Eton SL4 .205 A1
  Windsor SL4 .....209 C3
Sheepfold La HP7 .165 B4
Sheephouse Rd SL6 .196 A1
Sheepridge La HP10, SL8 184 C4
Sheerstock HP17 ..126 C3
Sheerwater HP20 ..101 C2
Sheet St SL4 .....210 B3
Sheet Street Rd SL4 .210 B1
Sheffield Dr HP21 .115 C3
Sheffield Rd SL1 ..205 B4
Shelburne Ct HP21 .172 C2
Shelburne Cty Fst Sch
  HP12 ....172 B2
Shelburne Rd HP12 .172 C2
Sheldon Cl MK8 ...33 C1
Sheldon Rd HP18 ..124 A2
Shelduck Cl 21 HP20 .101 C2
Shelley Cl
  Medmenham SL7 ..193 B4
  Newport Pagnell MK16 .22 A2
  Slough SL3 ......206 C1
  Wooburn Green HP10 .185 C4
Shelley Dr MK3 ...57 C4
Shelley Rd Chesham HP5 144 A1
  High Wycombe HP11 .172 C3
  12 Marlow SL7 ...183 C2
Shellfield Cl TW19 .213 A1
Shelsmore MK14 ..35 A4
Shelton Ct Slough SL3 .206 B2
  Woburn Sands MK17 .49 A2
Sheney Rd MK3 ..57 C4
Shenley Brook End Sch
  MK3 ....47 A1
Shenley Brooke End Sch
  MK5 ....46 A3
Shenley Rd
  Milton Keynes MK5 ..46 A3
  Milton Keynes, Bletchley
    MK3 ....46 C1
  Whaddon MK17 ...56 B4
Shenley Rdbt MK5 .46 A3
Shenstone Dr SL1 .197 B1
Shenstone Hill HP4 .135 C3
Shepherd Dr HP20 .102 A1
Shepherd's La WD3 .167 C1
Shepherds MK11 ..33 A2
Shepherds Cl
  Beaconsfield HP9 .175 C1
  Hurley SL7 ......193 C2
  Uxbridge UB8 ....201 B1
Shepherds Ct SL4 .209 C3
Shepherds Fold HP15 .163 B4
Shepherds Gate HP16 .152 A1
Shepherds La
  Beaconsfield HP9 .175 C1
  Hazlemere HP15 ..162 C3
  Hurley SL7 ......193 C2
Shepherds Row MK18 .66 A2
Shepherds Way HP5 .154 B3
Shepherdswell Fst Sch
  MK6 ....35 A1
Sheppards Cl MK16 .22 B2
Shepperds Cl MK18 .76 A1
Shepperds Gn MK5 .45 C3
Shepperton Cl MK19 .19 C2
Sheraton Dr HP13 .162 B1
Sheraton Ho WD3 .167 B3
Sherborne Dr SL3 .212 C3

Sherborne Ct SL6 ..202 C3
Sherbourne Dr
  Bow Brickhill MK7 ..48 A2
  Maidenhead SL6 ..202 B2
  Windsor SL4 .....209 C2
Sherbourne Wlk SL2 .198 B4
Shereway HP19 ...115 A4
Shergold Way SL8 .195 C3
Sheridan Cl HP21 .115 C3
Sheridan Ct
  Maidenhead SL6 ..203 A4
  1 Slough SL1 ....204 C3
Sheriff Cl HP19 ..115 A4
Sherington CE Fst Sch
  MK16 ....14 A1
Sherington Rd
  Lathbury MK16 ...22 C4
  Sherington MK16 ..22 C4
Sherman Rd SL1 ..205 C4
Shernfold MK7 ...48 A4
Sherriff Cotts HP18 .99 A4
Sherwood Cl SL3 ..206 C2
Sherwood Ct
  Colnbrook SL3 ...212 B4
  Slough SL3 ......206 C1
Sherwood Dr
  Maidenhead SL6 ..202 A3
  Milton Keynes MK1, MK2,
    MK3 ....47 A1
Shields Ct HP10 ..163 A1
Shifford Cres SL6 .195 C2
Shilling Cl MK15 ..35 A4
Shillingridge Pk SL7 .182 C3
Shinfield Cl HP18 ..63 B1
Ship Hill SL1, HP9 .186 C2
Ship Rd LU7 .....80 C3
Ship St HP11 ....173 A4
Shiplake Ho SL8 ..185 A2
Shipley Rd MK16 ..22 A3
Shipman Ct MK15 ..35 A4
Shipton Hill MK13 ..34 A3
Shipton Rd UB8 ..201 C4
Shire Ct MK14 ...35 A3
Shire La
  Chalfont St Peter SL9 .178 A3
  Cholesbury HP23 ..133 A2
  Chorleywood WD3 .167 B2
  North Crawley MK16 .24 C2
Shires Bsns Pk The
  NN13 ....38 A3
Shires Rd SL4 ...209 C3
Shirley Ave SL6 ..202 B3
Shirley Moor MK7 ..48 A4
Shirley Rd SL6 ...202 B3
Shirwell Cres MK4 .46 B3
Shogmoor La HP14 .170 B1
Sholto Rd TW19 ..213 C1
Shootacre Cnr HP27 .149 A4
Shootacre La HP27 .149 A4
Shootersway HP4 .134 C2
Shootersway La HP4 .134 C2
Shootersway Pk HP4 .134 C2
Shop La NN7 ....1 A3
Shoppenhanger's Rd
  SL6 ....202 C2
Shorediche Cl UB10 .190 C1
Shoreham Rd (E) TW6 .213 C1
Shoreham Rd (W) TW6 .213 C1
Shoreham Rise SL2 .197 B1
Shorham Rise MK8 ..33 C1
Short Ditch HP17 ..127 A4
Short Hale LU7 ...105 B1
Short Massey MK46 ..6 C3
Short Rd TW6 ....213 C1
Short St HP11 ....172 C4
Shortborough Ave
  HP27 ....139 A3
Shortfern SL2 ....206 B4
Shortway Amersham HP6 154 B1
  Chesham HP5 .....144 A1
Shotfield Rd HP14 .171 B2
Shothanger Way HP3 .146 B3
Shouler Cl MK5 ...46 A3
Shrewsbury Cl MK10 .36 A1
Shrimpton Cl HP9 .175 B3
Shrimpton Rd
  Beaconsfield HP9 .175 B3
  High Wycombe HP12 .172 A2
Shrubbery Rd HP13 .173 A4
Shrublands Ave HP4 .135 A2
Shrublands Rd HP4 .135 A3
Shucklow Hill MK17 .55 C2
Shugars Gn HP23 ..119 A3
Shupp's La HP18 ..112 A1
Shutlanger Rd NN12 .9 A4
Shuttleworth Gr MK7 .48 B3
Sibleys Rise HP16 .152 B4
Side Rd UB9 .....189 B2
Sidings Ind Est The
  NN13 ....38 A4
Sidlow Ct MK11 ...32 C2
Sidney Cl UB8 ....201 B3
Sidney Rd SL4 ...209 B2
Sidney Terr HP22 .131 A3
Silbury Arc MK9 ..34 C2
Silbury Bvd MK9 ..34 B1
Silbury Rdbt MK9 ..34 B1
Silchester Ho SL6 .203 A4
Silchester House Sch
  SL6 ....203 B4
Silco Dr SL6 ....202 C3
Silicon Ct MK5 ...46 B3
Silk Mill Way HP23 .119 A3
Silk St HP18 .....99 A3
Sillswood MK46 ..6 C2
Silsden Cres HP8 .177 B4
Silver Birch Cl UB10 .201 C4
Silver Birch Dr HP27 .149 C3

Silver Cl SL6 202 A3
Silver End MK46 7 A2
Silver Hill HP8 177 A4
Silver St
16 Aylesbury HP20 115 B4
Cublington LU7 78 A1
Milton Keynes MK11 32 B3
Newport Pagnell MK16 22 B2
Silverbirches La MK17 49 A1
Silverdale Cl
5 Aylesbury HP20 101 B1
Tylers Green HP10 163 A1
Silvermead HP18 123 B3
Silverstone Motor Racing Circuit★ MK18 28 C4
Silvertrees Dr SL6 202 A3
Silverweed Ct MK7 48 A3
Simatt Ho HP10 174 B1
Simdims MK43 25 A1
Simmons Cl SL3 207 A1
Simmons Ct
Aylesbury HP21 115 C2
High Wycombe HP12 172 C4
Simmons Rd RG9 191 B2
Simmons Way
Lane End HP14 171 B2
Thame OX9 125 C1
Simms Croft MK10 36 A1
Simnel MK6 47 A3
Simon Dean HP3 146 A2
Simons Lea MK13 34 A2
Simonsbath MK4 46 B1
Simpson Cl SL6 203 A4
Simpson Cty Comb Sch MK6 47 B3
Simpson Dr MK6 47 C3
Simpson Pl HP21 115 C3
Simpson Rd MK1,MK2, MK6,MK7 47 C2
Sinclair Ct MK1 47 A2
Sinclair Rd SL4 210 B2
Singer La RG9 191 C1
Singleborough La MK17 54 C2
Singleton Dr MK8 45 B3
Singleton Way HP19 115 A4
Singret Pl UB8 201 B1
Sion Terr MK18 51 A3
Sipson Rd UB7 208 C2
Sipthorp Cl MK7 48 B3
Sir Frank Markham Com Sch MK6 47 A4
Sir Henry Floyd Gram Sch HP21 115 B4
Sir Sydney Camm Ho SL4 210 A3
Sir William Borlase's Gram Sch SL7 183 B1
Sir William Ramsay Sch HP15 163 A2
Sitwell Cl MK16 21 C3
Six Cotts MK18 29 C3
Sixth St HP11 173 B2
Sixty Acres Rd HP16 151 B3
Skeats Wharf MK15 35 A4
Skeldon Gate MK9 35 A2
Skeldon Rdbt MK9 35 A2
Skelton Cl HP9 186 A4
Skene Cl MK2 58 B2
Skerries Ct SL3 207 A1
Skimmers Cl HP15 163 B3
Skimmers End HP15 163 B3
Skimmers Field HP15 163 B3
Skippon Way 6 OX9 125 C1
Skipton Cl MK15 35 B3
Skittle Gn HP27 138 A1
Skydmore Path SL2 197 C1
Skylark Rd UB9 189 B2
Skyport Dr UB7 213 B4
Skyway 14 Trad Est SL3 212 C2
Slad La HP27 149 C2
Slade Hill HP19 115 A4
Slade La MK11 33 A2
Slade Oak La UB9 189 B3
Slade Rd HP14 158 C2
Slade The MK17 57 B2
Slapton La LU6 91 C3
Slated Row MK12 33 A4
Slated Row Sch MK12 33 A4
Slater St HP13 173 B3
Slattenham Cl HP19 115 A4
Slave Hill HP17 126 C3
Slayter Rd HP14 171 B2
Slickett's La LU6 92 C2
Slipe The LU7 105 A4
Slough & Eton CE Sch SL1 205 B2
Slough Gram Sch SL3 206 A2
Slough Mus★ SL1 206 A2
Slough Rd Datchet SL3 211 A4
Iver Heath SL0 200 C2
Slough SL3 205 C1
Slough Sta SL1 205 C3
Slough Trad Est SL1 205 A4
Sly Cnr HP16 142 C2
Smabridge Wlk MK15 35 B4
Small Cres MK18 52 C4
Smalldean La HP14, HP27 149 C1
Smarden Bell MK7 48 A4
Smeaton Cl
Aylesbury HP19 100 C1
Milton Keynes MK14 22 A1
Smewin Ct HP11 172 C4
Smith Cl HP20 116 A4
Smith's La SL4 209 C3
Smithergill Ct MK13 34 B3
Smithfield End MK17 66 C2
Smithfield Rd SL6 202 A2
Smithsons Pl MK9 35 A2
Snaith Cres MK5 46 A4
Snakeley Cl HP10 174 B1
Snape Spur SL1 205 C4
Snells Wood Ct HP7 166 B4
Snelshall St MK4 56 C4
Snowball Hill SL6 202 A1
Snowberry Cl MK12 33 B3
Snowden Cl SL4 209 B2
Snowdon Dr MK6 46 B4
Snowdrop Way HP15 162 C4
Snowhill Cotts HP5 144 C4
Snowshill Ct MK14 21 C1
Soane Wlk HP13 173 A4
Soho Cres HP10 185 B2
Soho Mills Ind Est HP10 185 B2
Sokeman Cl MK12 33 A3
Solar Ct MK14 21 C1
Solesbridge Cl WD3 167 C3
Solesbridge La WD3 167 C3
Solters Cl HP18 96 B4
Somerford Cl SL6 203 A4
Somerford Pl HP9 175 B2
Somers Lees HP19 115 A4
Somersby Cres SL6 202 C2
Somerset Cl MK3 46 C1
Somerset Lodge 3 SL6 202 C3
Somerset Way SL0 207 C2
Somerville Rd SL4 205 B1
Somerville Way HP19 115 A4
Sorrell Dr MK16 21 C2
Soskin Dr MK14 34 B3
Sospel Ct SL2 198 B2
Soulbury Rd
Leighton Buzzard LU7 80 B4
Stewkley LU7 68 C1
Wing LU7 79 B2
South Bank Rd HP4 134 C3
South Cl Medmenham SL7 193 B4
Slough SL1 204 B3
West Drayton UB7 208 C2
South Common Rd UB8 201 C3
South Cott Dr WD3 167 C2
South Cott Gdns WD3 167 C2
South Dr
Beaconsfield HP9 186 A4
High Wycombe HP13 173 B4
South Eighth St MK9 34 C1
South End HP17 126 C3
South End La LU6 92 A2
South Enmore Rdbt MK6 35 A2
South Field Cl SL4 204 B2
South Fifth St MK9 34 C1
South Fourth St MK9 34 B1
South Gn SL1 205 C3
South Hills HP18 96 A1
South Ho MK1 47 B2
South La LU7 78 C4
South Lawne MK3 57 C4
South Maundin HP14 162 A4
South Meadow La SL4 210 B4
South Ninth St MK9 34 C1
South Overgate Rdbt MK6 35 A2
South Park Ave WD3 167 C2
South Park Cres SL9 188 C4
South Park Dr SL9 188 C4
South Park Gdns HP4 135 A3
South Park View SL9 188 C4
South Path SL4 210 B3
South Pk SL9 188 C3
South Pl SL7 183 C1
South Rd Amersham HP6 154 B2
Chorleywood WD3 167 B2
Maidenhead SL6 202 C3
West Drayton UB7 208 C2
South Row Fulmer SL3 199 C4
Milton Keynes MK9 34 C1
South Saxon Rdbt MK9 34 C1
South Second St MK9 34 B1
South Seventh St MK9 34 C1
South Side SL9 188 B4
South Sixth St MK9 34 C1
South St
Castlethorpe MK19 19 C3
Wendover HP22 131 A2
South Tenth St MK9 34 C1
South Terr MK2 58 B4
South Vale NN7 1 A3
South View Cookham SL8 195 C4
High Wycombe HP13 161 B1
Slough SL4 205 A1
Wooburn Green HP10 185 B4
South View Rd SL9 188 B4
South Way HP9 186 A4
Southampton Rd TW6 213 C1
Southbourne 1 HP13 173 B4
Southbourne Dr SL8 185 A2
Southbridge Gr MK7 48 A4
Southcliffe Dr SL9 177 C3
Southcote Way HP10 163 A1
Southcott Lower Sch LU7 80 B4
Southcott Village LU7 80 B3
Southcourt Ave LU7 80 B3
Southcourt Ho LU7 80 B4
Southcourt Inf Sch HP21 115 B3
Southcourt Rd LU7 80 B4
Southcroft SL2 198 A1
Southern Cotts TW19 213 A1
Southern Perimeter Rd TW6,TW19 213 B1
Southern Rd
Aylesbury HP19 101 B1
Thame OX9 125 C1
Southern Way MK12 33 B3
Southfield Cl MK15 35 C4
Southfield Cotts HP17 130 B2
Southfield Dr HP15 163 A3
Southfield Gdns SL1 204 A4
Southfield Rd
Aylesbury HP20 116 A4
Flackwell Heath HP10 174 A1
High Wycombe HP13 161 B1
Princes Risborough HP27 139 B2
Southgate Ho SL6 202 C4
Southlea Rd SL3 211 A3
Southview Rd SL7 183 C2
Southwick Ct MK8 45 C4
Southwold Cl HP21 116 A3
Southwold Spur SL3 207 B2
Southwood Gdns SL8 195 C3
Southwood Mid Sch MK14 34 C3
Southwood Rd SL8 195 C3
Sovereign Cl MK18 75 C4
Sovereign Ct
Aylesbury HP19 101 B1
High Wycombe HP13 173 B3
Sovereign Dr MK15 35 A4
Sovereign Lodge MK15 35 A4
Spa Cl HP18 110 A4
Spackmans Way SL1 205 B2
Spade Oak Farm SL8 184 C2
Spade Oak Mdw SL8 184 C2
Spark Way MK16 21 C3
Sparrow Cl HP20 101 C2
Sparsholt Cl 5 MK4 46 B1
Spearing Rd HP12 172 B3
Spearmint Cl MK7 48 A3
Specklands MK5 46 A4
Speedbird Way UB7 213 A4
Speedwell Pl MK14 34 C2
Speen CE Fst Sch HP27 150 A2
Speen Rd HP14,HP16, HP27 150 B1
Speldhurst Ct MK7 48 A4
Spencer MK14 34 B4
Spencer Cl UB8 201 B1
Spencer Gdns OX27 72 C3
Spencer Rd SL3 206 C2
Spencer St MK13 33 C4
Spencers Cl SL6 202 B4
Spencers La SL8 195 C3
Spencers Rd SL6 202 B4
Spenlows Rd MK3 47 A2
Spens SL6 202 C4
Spenser Ho HP21 115 C3
Spenser Rd HP21 115 C3
Sperling Rd SL6 195 C1
Spickett's La HP18 113 A2
Spier's La OX27 71 C1
Spiert The HP17 114 B3
Spindle Cl HP15 163 A2
Spindle Ct HP12 172 C4
Spinfield La SL7 183 A1
Spinfield La W SL7 183 B1
Spinfield Mount SL7 183 A1
Spinfield Pk SL7 183 B1
Spinfield Sch SL7 183 A1
Spinners Wlk
Marlow SL7 183 B1
Windsor SL4 210 B3
Spinney SL1 205 A3
Spinney Bglws LU7 91 B3
Spinney Cl
Steeple Claydon MK18 63 C1
West Drayton UB7 208 C3
Spinney Cres LU6 93 C4
Spinney Hill Rd MK46 6 C2
Spinney La MK17 49 C2
Spinney The
Beaconsfield HP9 175 C1
Berkhamsted HP4 134 C2
Chesham HP5 144 B1
High Wycombe HP11 173 A2
Holmer Green HP15 163 B4
Milton Keynes MK13 34 A2
Winslow MK18 66 A3
Spinneys The HP13 174 A4
Spire View TW19 213 B1
Spittal St SL7 183 B1
Spoondell LU6 93 C4
Spoonley Wood MK13 33 C3
Sportsman Cl MK18 63 B2
Spout La TW19 213 A2
Spout La N TW19 213 A2
Sprigs Holly La HP14 159 A4
Spring Cl
Great Horwood MK17 55 A1
High Wycombe HP13 173 C4
Latimer HP5 155 B2
Maidenhead SL6 195 C1
Spring Coppice HP14 171 C3
Spring Coppice La HP27,HP16 150 B3
Spring Field Rd HP4 135 A3
Spring Gardens Rd 4 HP13 173 C3
Spring Gdns
Bourne End SL8 185 A2
Marlow SL7 183 C2
Newport Pagnell MK16 22 B2
Wooburn Green HP10 185 C4
Spring Gr MK17 49 A3
Spring Hill SL6 202 C2
Spring Ho SL7 183 C1
Spring La Alderton NN12 9 A1
Clifton Reynes MK46 7 B2
Cookham SL7 195 B3
Farnham Common SL2 198 B3
Flackwell Heath HP10, HP11 173 C2
Great Horwood MK17 55 A1
Olney MK46 6 C2
Spring La *continued*
Slough SL1 204 C3
Spring Mdw HP18 97 A1
Spring Valley Dr HP14 162 A4
Springate Field SL3 206 C2
Springbank Ct MK16 12 A4
Springett Pl HP6 154 C1
Springfield Olney MK46 6 C2
Slough SL1 206 A2
Springfield Bvd MK6 35 A1
Springfield Cl
Aylesbury HP21 115 B4
Chesham HP5 154 B4
Windsor SL4 210 A3
Springfield Ct
15 Leighton Buzzard LU7 80 C4
Maidenhead SL6 203 A4
Milton Keynes MK6 35 A1
Springfield Gdns
Chinnor OX39 147 B4
Deanshanger MK19 31 C2
Springfield Mid Sch MK6 35 A1
Springfield Pk SL6 203 B1
Springfield Rd
Eaton Bray LU6 93 B3
Leighton Buzzard LU7 80 B4
Slough SL3 212 A4
Stokenchurch HP14 158 C2
Windsor SL4 210 A3
Springfield Rdbt MK6 35 A1
Springfield Way MK43 25 B1
Springfields
Amersham HP6 154 B1
Padbury MK18 53 B1
Tylers Green HP10 163 B1
Springfields Cl MK18 53 B1
Springfields Ct MK18 53 B1
Springhill (HM Prison) HP18 73 A1
Springhill Rd HP18 83 A4
Springs Cl HP17 130 A1
Springs La HP17 130 A2
Springside 16 LU7 80 C4
Springwater Mill HP11 173 C2
Springwood HP27 150 B2
Spruce Ct 24 SL1 205 C2
Spruce Dene HP15 162 C1
Spur The SL1 204 B4
Spurgrove La HP14 170 C1
Spurlands End Rd HP15 162 C4
Spurt St HP18 112 C2
Square Close Cotts HP14 169 C2
Square The Akeley MK18 41 C4
Aspley Guise MK17 49 C2
Brill HP18 110 A4
Harmondsworth UB7 213 A3
Long Crendon HP18 125 B3
Milton Keynes MK12 33 B3
Preston Bissett MK18 62 A4
South Heath HP16 152 A4
Waddesdon HP18 99 A3
Yardley Hastings NN7 1 A3
Squires Cl MK6 47 A3
Squirrel La HP12 172 B3
Squirrel Rise SL7 183 B3
Squirrels Way MK18 52 C4
St-Cloud Way SL6 203 A4
Stable Cl MK18 50 B4
Stable Cotts SL7 194 B3
Stable La HP9 176 B2
Stable Rd HP22 131 C4
Stablebridge Rd HP22 117 C2
Stables Ct SL7 183 A1
Stacey Ave MK12 33 B3
Stacey Bushes Trad Ctr MK12 33 C2
Stacey Ho HP12 172 C2
Stacey's Ct HP8 177 B4
Staddle Stones HP27 139 A2
Stafferton Way SL6 203 A3
Stafford Ave SL2 198 B1
Stafford Cl SL6 204 A4
Stafford Gr MK5 46 A3
Stag Ct WD3 167 B3
Stag La Berkhamsted HP4 135 A3
Chorleywood WD3 167 B2
Great Kingshill HP15 151 B1
Stagshaw Gr 5 MK4 46 A1
Stainby Cl UB7 208 C2
Stainton Dr MK13 34 B2
Stamford Ave MK6 35 A1
Stamford Rd SL6 202 B3
Stanbridge Cl HP17 127 A4
Stanbridge Ct MK11 32 C3
Stanbridge Rd HP17 127 A3
Stanbrook Pl MK10 36 A1
Standfield Cl HP19 115 A4
Standing Way MK10,MK4, MK6 47 B4
Standring Pl HP20 101 C1
Stanhope Cl HP22 131 A4
Stanhope Heath TW19 213 B1
Stanhope Rd
Aylesbury HP20 116 A4
Slough SL1 204 B4
Stanhope Way TW19 213 B1
Stanier Rise HP4 134 C4
Stanier Sq 6 MK2 58 B4
Stanley Ave HP5 154 A4
Stanley Cl Marlow SL7 183 C2
Uxbridge UB8 201 B2
Stanley Cotts SL2 205 C3
Stanley Ct MK46 6 C2
Stanley Gdns HP23 118 C2
Stanley Green E SL3 206 C1
Stanley Green W SL3 206 C1
Stanley Hill HP7 165 C4
Stanley Hill Ave HP7 165 C4
Stanley Ho SL4 211 A1
Stanley Rd HP12 172 B4
Stanmore Gdns MK16 22 A1
Stanstead Pl HP7 165 B4
Stansted Rd TW6 213 C1
Stanton Ave MK13 34 A3
Stanton Gate MK14 34 B4
Stanton Mid Sch MK13 34 A4
Stanton Way SL3 206 C1
Stantonbury Campus MK14 34 B4
Stanway Cl MK15 35 A3
Stanwell Cl TW19 213 B1
Stanwell Gdns TW19 213 B1
Stanwell Moor Rd TW6, TW19,UB7 213 A2
Stanwell Rd SL3 212 B2
Staple Hall Rd MK1 47 C1
Stapleton Cl SL7 183 C2
Stars La HP17 113 C1
Startins La SL7 195 B4
Starveall Cl UB7 208 C2
Starwood Ct SL3 206 B2
Staters Pound MK15 35 A4
Statham Pl MK6 46 C4
Station App
Amersham HP6 154 B1
Chorleywood WD3 167 B3
Denham Green UB9 189 B2
Gerrards Cross SL9 188 C3
Little Chalfont HP7 166 B4
Maidenhead SL6 202 C3
Marlow SL7 183 C1
South Heath HP16 152 A4
Wendover HP22 131 A2
West Drayton UB7 208 C3
Station Cotts
Denham UB9 190 A2
Denham Green UB9 189 C2
Station Hill SL8 195 C4
Station Par
Beaconsfield HP9 175 B2
Cookham SL8 195 C3
Denham Green UB9 190 A2
Station Rd Aldbury HP23 120 A3
Amersham HP6,HP7 165 B4
Beaconsfield HP9 175 C1
Berkhamsted HP4 135 B2
Blackthorn OX25 81 A2
Bourne End SL8 185 A2
Bow Brickhill MK17 48 B1
Buckingham MK18 52 B4
Castlethorpe MK19 19 C3
Chesham HP5 154 B4
Chinnor OX39 147 B3
Cookham SL8 195 C4
Gerrards Cross SL9 188 C3
Great Kimble HP17 129 C1
Haddenham HP17 126 C3
Henley-on-T RG9 191 C1
High Wycombe HP13 173 B3
Ivinghoe LU7 105 C3
Leighton Buzzard LU7 80 C4
Long Marston HP23 104 A2
Loudwater HP10 174 B1
Marlow SL7 183 C1
Marsh Gibbon OX27 71 C2
Mentmore LU7 91 A1
Mursley MK17 67 A4
Newport Pagnell MK16 22 B2
Padbury MK18 53 A1
Princes Risborough HP27 139 A1
Quainton HP22 85 A2
Slough SL1 204 C4
Slough, Langley SL3 207 A2
Stoke Mandeville HP22 116 A1
Taplow SL6 203 C4
Tring HP23 119 B2
Uxbridge UB8 201 B1
West Drayton UB7 208 C2
Winslow MK18 66 A3
Woburn Sands MK17 49 A3
Wraysbury TW19 212 A1
Station Rise SL7 183 C1
Station St HP20 115 C4
Station Terr
Buckingham MK18 52 B4
Milton Keynes MK14 21 C1
Station Way HP20 115 B4
Staunton Ho MK17 60 C4
Staunton Rd SL2 205 B4
Staveley Cl HP21 116 B3
Stavordale MK10 36 A1
Stayning La MK14 34 C3
Steeple Cl MK4 57 A4
Steinbeck Cres MK4 56 C4
Stephenson Cl
Aylesbury HP19 115 A4
High Wycombe HP13 161 C1
Leighton Buzzard LU7 80 C3
Stephenson Ct 19 SL1 205 C2
Stephenson Dr SL4 210 A4
Stepnells HP23 105 A1
Steppingstones LU6 93 C4
Stevens Cl
Holmer Green HP15 163 A4
Prestwood HP16 151 B3
Stevens Field MK7 48 B3
Stevens Ho HP7 165 A4
Stevenson Rd SL2 187 B1
Stewart Ave SL1 205 C4
Stewarts Dr SL2 198 A4
Stewarts Way SL7 183 B4
Stewkley La MK17 67 C2

Stewkley Rd
Cublington LU7 78 B1
Soulbury LU7 69 B1
Wing LU7 79 A2
Stile Mdw HP9 175 C2
Stile Rd SL3 206 B2
Stilebrook Rd MK46 6 C3
Stilwell Dr UB8 201 C1
Stirling Ave HP20 101 C1
Stirling Cl
Milton Keynes MK15 35 A3
Uxbridge UB8 201 B1
Windsor SL4 209 B3
Stirling Gr SL6 202 A4
Stirling Ho
2 High Wycombe HP13 173 C4
Milton Keynes MK3 57 B4
Stirling Rd
High Wycombe HP12 172 B3
Slough SL1 205 A4
Stanwell TW6 213 C1
Stock Field Cl HP15 163 A2
Stock La MK17 45 A1
Stockdale MK13 34 B3
Stockdales Rd SL4 204 C1
Stocken Cl MK46 6 C2
Stockgrove Ctry Pk★ LU7 70 C4
Stockhall Cres LU7 69 B4
Stocking Green Cl MK19 11 A2
Stocking La HP14 161 C4
Stocklake
Aylesbury HP20 101 C1
Bierton HP20 101 C1
Stocklands Way HP16 151 B3
Stockleys La MK18 51 A3
Stockport Rd WD3 167 B1
Stocks Cl MK18 65 C2
Stocks Rd HP23 120 B4
Stocks The MK19 19 C1
Stockway HP22 87 B1
Stockwell HP17 127 A3
Stockwell Furlong HP17 127 A3
Stockwell La
Longwick HP27 139 A4
Wavendon MK17 48 B4
Stockwells SL6 196 B1
Stoke Bruerne CE Prim Sch NN12 9 A4
Stoke Common Rd SL2, SL3 199 A4
Stoke Court Dr SL2 198 C2
Stoke Farm La HP21 115 C2
Stoke Gdns SL1 205 C3
Stoke Gn SL2 199 A1
Stoke Goldington CE Fst Sch MK16 12 A3
Stoke La MK17 59 B1
Stoke Leys Sch HP21 115 C2
Stoke Mandeville Comb Sch HP22 116 A1
Stoke Mandeville Hospl HP21 115 C2
Stoke Mandeville Sta HP22 116 A1
Stoke Park Ave SL2 198 B1
Stoke Poges La SL1 205 C4
Stoke Poges Sch
Stoke Poges SL2 198 C3
Stoke Poges SL2 199 A3
Stoke Rd Ashton NN7 9 C4
Aylesbury HP21 115 C3
Leighton Buzzard LU7 70 B1
Milton Keynes MK2 58 C3
Newton Longville MK17 57 C2
Slough SL2 205 C4
Stoke View SL1 205 C3
Stoke Wood SL2 198 C4
Stokenchurch Inf Sch HP14 158 C2
Stokenchurch Jun Sch HP14 158 C3
Stokenchurch Pl MK13 34 B2
Stokes Croft HP17 127 A4
Stokes End HP17 127 A4
Stokes La HP17 127 A4
Stokesay SL2 205 C3
Stokesley Rise HP10 185 C4
Stolford Rise MK4 46 A1
Stomp Rd SL1 204 A4
Stompits Rd SL6 203 B1
Stone CE Comb Sch HP17 114 B3
Stone Cl UB7 208 C3
Stone Croft HP17 114 B3
Stone Ct MK46 13 C4
Stone Hill MK8 33 B1
Stone House La SL8 184 B1
Stone Pit Cl MK46 6 C2
Stone View HP22 86 B4
Stonebridge Field SL4 205 A1
Stonebridge Rd HP19 101 A2
Stonebridge Rdbt MK13 33 C4
Stonechat HP20 101 C2
Stonecroft HP6 153 B2
Stonecroft Ave SL0 207 C4
Stonecrop Pl MK14 34 C2
Stonefield Pk SL6 202 B4
Stonefield Rd HP14 161 B4
Stonegate MK13 34 A3
Stonehaven Rd HP19 101 A1
Stoneleigh Ct MK4 45 C1
Stonepitts Pk HP18 111 A2
Stones Row HP11 173 C2
Stones Way MK17 68 B3
Stoney Cl HP4 134 C3
Stoney Croft HP23 120 B3
Stoney Dean Sch HP7 165 C4
Stoney Gr HP5 144 B1
Stoney La
Berkhamsted HP1 146 A4
Bovingdon HP3 146 B3
Burnham SL2 198 A2
Chipperfield WD4 146 C1
Stoney Meade SL1 205 A3
Stoney Ware SL7 194 C4
Stoney Ware Cl SL7 194 B4
Stoneyfield SL9 188 B2
Stonor Ct MK8 45 C4
Stonor Ho★ OX49 180 A4
Stony Hill NN12 17 B3
Stony La Chenies HP6 155 C1
Little Chalfont HP6 166 C4
Little Kingshill HP16 152 B2
Stony Stratford Nature Reserve★ MK11,MK19 32 B4
Stookslade HP22 89 A2
Stopps Orch HP27 139 B3
Stork Cl 10 HP20 101 C2
Stornaway Rd SL3 207 B1
Stotfold Ct MK11 32 C2
Stour Cl Aylesbury HP21 115 B2
Milton Keynes MK3 57 C4
Newport Pagnell MK16 22 C2
Slough SL1 205 A2
Stourhead Gate MK4 45 C1
Stovell Rd SL4 210 A4
Stowe Ave MK18 41 A2
Stowe Cl MK18 41 B1
Stowe Ct MK14 34 B4
Stowe Landscape Gdns★ MK18 40 C4
Stowe Rd SL1 204 C3
Stowe Rise MK18 41 B1
Stowe Sch MK18 40 C4
Stowe View MK18 51 A4
Straight Bit HP10 185 A4
Straight Rd SL4 211 A1
Strand The HP22 85 A3
Strande La SL8 195 C3
Strande View Wlk SL8 195 C3
Strangers La MK18 51 A3
Strangford Dr MK2 58 B2
Stranraer Gdns SL1 205 C3
Stranraer Rd TW19 213 C1
Stranraer Way 1 TW19 213 C1
Stratfield Ct
Maidenhead SL6 203 A4
Milton Keynes MK8 33 C1
Stratfield Rd SL1 206 A2
Stratford Arc MK11 32 B3
Stratford Ave UB10 201 C2
Stratford Cl SL2 197 B1
Stratford Dr
Aylesbury HP21 115 A3
Wooburn Green HP10 185 B2
Stratford Gdns SL6 202 B2
Stratford Rd
Buckingham MK18 41 C1
Cosgrove MK19 19 B1
Maids Moreton MK18 42 B1
Milton Keynes MK12,MK19 33 B4
Nash MK17 44 B1
Whaddon MK17 45 A1
Stratfords Way HP17 127 A3
Strathcona Cl HP10 185 B4
Strathcona Way HP10 185 B4
Strathnaver Pl MK12 33 B2
Stratton Chase Dr HP8 177 A4
Stratton Gn HP21 116 A3
Stratton Rd
Beaconsfield HP9 175 A1
Princes Risborough HP27 139 A2
Strauss Gr MK7 48 B2
Strawberry Cl HP16 151 B3
Straws Hadley Ct HP22 89 A1
Streamside SL1 204 C3
Streamside Wlk HP21 115 B3
Streatham Pl MK13 34 B1
Stretton Cl HP10 174 B4
Stretton Pl HP6 154 C1
Stringers Cotts 3 SL9 177 B1
Stringfellow Cl MK43 24 C1
Stroma Ct SL1 204 B3
Stroud Cl SL4 209 B2
Strudwick Dr MK6 46 C4
Stuart Cl
Milton Keynes MK2 47 B1
Windsor SL4 209 C3
Stuart Ct HP6 154 B1
Stuart Rd HP13 173 B3
Stuart Way Thame OX9 126 A1
Windsor SL4 209 C3
Stubble Hill HP19 115 A4
Stubbles La SL7 195 A3
Stubbs End Cl HP6 154 C1
Stubbs Wood HP6 154 C2
Stuchbury Cl HP19 115 A4
Studdridge Ct HP14 158 B2
Studham La HP4 107 B2
Studland Cl HP21 116 A3
Studley Knapp MK7 48 A3
Studridge La HP27 150 A2
Sturges Cl MK7 48 A3
Stylecroft Rd HP8 177 B4
Styles Cl OX27 71 C1
Styles Ct HP18 99 A4
Sudgrove Ho MK15 35 A3
Suffield Rd HP11 172 C4
Suffolk Cl
Milton Keynes MK3 46 C1
Slough SL1 204 C4
Suffolk Ct
Maidenhead SL6 202 C4
Marsh Gibbon OX27 71 C2
Suffolk Rd SL6 202 B2
Sulby Cl HP21 115 B3
Sulgrave Cres HP23 119 B3
Sulgrave Ct MK8 45 C4
Sullivan Cres MK7 48 B3
Sultan Croft MK5 46 A2
Sumburgh Way SL1 205 C4
Summerfield Comb Sch MK13 34 B2
Summergill Ct MK13 34 B3
Summerhayes MK14 34 C4
Summerhouse La UB7 213 B4
Summerlea SL1 205 A3
Summerleaze Rd SL6 196 A1
Summerleys LU6 92 C2
Summerleys Rd HP27 138 C2
Summers Rd SL1 197 B1
Summerson Rd MK6 46 C3
Summit Ctr UB7 213 B4
Sumner Ct MK5 46 A4
Sun Cl SL4 210 B4
Sun Cres HP18 109 B3
Sun La SL6 202 C4
Sun Pas 25 SL4 210 B3
Sunbury Cl MK13 34 A3
Sunbury Ct SL4 210 B4
Sunbury Rd SL4 210 B4
Sunderland Ct
Milton Keynes MK4 45 C1
11 Stanwell TW19 213 C1
Sunderland Rd SL6 202 A4
Sunningdale Cl HP12 172 A3
Sunningdale Way MK3 57 B4
Sunny Bank
Cheddington LU7 104 C4
Hazlemere HP15 162 C3
Sunny Croft HP13 161 B1
Sunny View NN7 1 A3
Sunnybank SL7 183 B2
Sunnybrook Cl HP22 117 B3
Sunnyhill Rd WD3 178 B2
Sunnymeads Sta TW19 211 C2
Sunnymede Ave HP5 144 C2
Sunnymede Cotts SL6 196 A1
Sunnyside Rd HP5 144 B1
Sunray Ave UB7 208 B2
Sunridge Cl MK16 22 B2
Sunrise Parkway MK14 34 C3
Sunset Cl MK2 58 B4
Sunset Wlk MK9 34 C1
Sunters End HP12 172 A4
Sunters Wood Cl HP12 172 A3
Surly Hall Wlk SL4 209 C3
Surrey Ave SL2 198 B1
Surrey Pl
Milton Keynes MK3 46 C1
Tring HP23 119 A2
Surrey Rd MK3 46 C1
Sussex Cl
Aylesbury HP19 101 A2
Chalfont St Giles HP8 177 A4
High Wycombe HP13 162 B1
Slough SL1 206 A2
Sussex Ho SL2 198 B3
Sussex Keep 18 SL1 206 A2
Sussex Lodge 7 SL6 202 C3
Sussex Pl SL1 206 A2
Sussex Rd MK3 46 C1
Sussex Way UB9 189 C3
Sutcliffe Ave MK6 34 C1
Sutherland Gr MK3 46 C2
Sutherland Grange SL4 209 B4
Sutherland Wlk HP21 115 C3
Sutleye Ct MK5 46 A3
Sutton Ave SL3 206 B2
Sutton Cl Cookham SL8 196 A4
Maidenhead SL6 202 B3
Tring HP23 119 A3
Sutton Ct MK4 46 B1
Sutton La SL3 207 B1
Sutton Pl SL3 212 A4
Sutton Rd SL8 196 A3
Swabey Rd SL3 207 A1
Swains Cl UB7 208 C2
Swains La HP10 174 A1
Swains Mkt HP10 174 A1
Swakeleys Rd UB10 201 C4
Swale Rd HP21 115 B3
Swallow Cl MK18 52 C4
Swallow Dr HP15 163 A3
Swallow Ho SL7 184 A1
Swallow La HP22 116 A1
Swallow St Iver SL0 207 B4
Iver Heath SL0 200 B1
Swallowdale SL0 200 B1
Swallowfield MK8 33 C1
Swallowfield Lower Sch MK17 49 A3
Swallowsprings LU6 93 C1
Swan Cl Aylesbury HP20 101 C2
Buckingham MK18 52 C4
Chesham HP5 144 A2
Ivinghoe LU7 92 A1
Whitchurch HP22 87 A3
Swan Cotts HP17 129 B1
Swan Ct
Chorleywood WD3 167 B3
Leighton Buzzard LU7 80 C3
Olney MK46 7 A2
West Drayton UB7 208 B2
Swan Hill HP18 112 C2
Swan Hill Cotts HP18 112 C2
Swan La OX27 72 A2
Swan Mews HP22 131 A3
Swan Rd Iver SL0 207 C4
Swan Rd *continued*
West Drayton UB7 208 B2
Swan Terr
Milton Keynes MK11 32 B3
Windsor SL4 210 A4
Swan Wharf UB8 201 B2
Swan's Way MK18 75 B1
Swanbourne CE Sch MK17 67 A2
Swanbourne House Sch MK17 66 C2
Swanbourne Rd MK17 67 B2
Swann Rd HP22 131 B4
Swansons LU6 92 C2
Swayne Rise MK10 36 A1
Sweetcroft La UB10 201 C3
Sweetlands Cnr MK7 48 A4
Swift Cl Aylesbury HP20 101 C2
Newport Pagnell MK16 22 A3
Swift Ho SL7 184 A1
Swimbridge La MK4 46 B2
Swinden Ct MK13 34 A2
Swinfens Yd MK11 32 B3
Swing Gate La HP4 135 B1
Swing Gate Sch HP4 135 B2
Swinnerton Ho RG9 191 C2
Switchback Cl SL6 195 B1
Switchback Rd SL6 195 C2
Switchback Rd N
Cookham SL6 195 C2
Maidenhead SL6 195 C2
Switchback Rd S SL6 195 B1
Switchback The SL6 195 B1
Sycamore Ave MK2 58 C4
Sycamore Cl
Amersham HP6 154 B1
14 Bourne End SL8 185 A2
Buckingham MK18 52 C4
Chalfont St Giles HP8 177 A4
Long Crendon HP18 125 B3
Maidenhead SL6 202 B2
Stewkley LU7 68 B1
West Drayton UB7 208 C3
Sycamore Cnr HP6 154 B1
Sycamore Ct
Aylesbury HP19 101 B1
High Wycombe HP12 172 B2
Windsor SL4 210 B2
Sycamore Dene HP5 144 B2
Sycamore Dr
Marlow Bottom SL7 183 B3
Tring HP23 119 A2
Sycamore Ho
Amersham HP6 154 B1
Princes Risborough HP27 139 A2
Sycamore Leys MK18 63 C2
Sycamore Pl HP6 154 B1
Sycamore Rd
Amersham HP6 154 B1
Chalfont St Giles HP8 177 A4
High Wycombe HP12 172 B2
Sycamore Rise
Berkhamsted HP4 135 B2
Chalfont St Giles HP8 177 A4
Sycamore Way HP15 163 A2
Sycamore Wlk SL3 206 C4
Sycamores The HP3 146 C4
Sydney Gr SL1 205 B4
Syke Cluan SL0 207 C2
Syke Ings SL0 207 C2
Sykes Croft MK4 46 B1
Sykes Rd SL1 205 A4
Sylvana Cl UB10 201 C2
Sylvester Rd SL6 195 C1
Sylvia Cl HP16 152 A2
Symington Ct MK5 46 A3
Syon Gdns MK16 22 B1
Syresham CE Prim Sch NN13 27 B4

T

Tabard Gdns MK16 22 B1
Tachbrook Rd UB8 201 B2
Tacknell Dr MK5 46 A2
Tacks La HP17 126 C3
Tadmarton MK15 35 A3
Tadmere MK8 33 B1
Talbot Ave
High Wycombe HP13 161 B1
Slough SL3 206 C2
Talbot Ct
Milton Keynes MK15 35 B1
Windsor SL4 210 A2
Talbot Pl SL3 211 B3
Talbot Rd HP22 117 C3
Talbots Dr SL6 202 A3
Talbots Hyde MK46 6 C2
Tall Oaks HP6 154 B1
Tall Pines LU7 70 C1
Tall Trees SL3 212 C3
Talland Ave MK6 34 C1
Tallis La MK7 48 B3
Tamar Cl Aylesbury HP21 115 B2
Loudwater HP13 174 A2
Tamar Ho
High Wycombe HP13 173 C4
Milton Keynes MK3 46 C1
Tamar Way SL3 207 A1
Tamarisk Ct MK7 48 A3
Tamarisk Way SL1 205 A3
Tamworth Stubb MK7 48 A3
Tancred Rd HP13 162 A1
Tandra MK6 47 A3
Tandys Cl MK43 8 C3
Tanfield La MK10 36 A2
Tangier Ct SL4 210 B4
Tangier La SL4 210 B4
Tank House Rd MK18 66 A3
Tanners Dr MK14 22 A1
Tannery Rd HP13 174 A2
Tansman La MK7 48 B3
Tapestries The SL4 211 A1
Taplin Way HP10 163 B1
Taplow Common Rd
Burnham SL1 197 A2
Taplow SL1 197 A2
Taplow Rd SL6 204 A4
Taplow Sta SL6 203 C4
Tapping Rd HP14 171 B3
Taranis Cl MK7 48 B4
Tarbay La SL4 209 A3
Tarbert Cl MK2 58 B3
Tarmac Way UB7 213 A4
Tarnbrook Cl 6 MK4 46 A1
Tarragon Cl MK7 48 A3
Task The MK46 7 A2
Taskers Ho LU6 92 C2
Taskers Row LU6 92 C2
Tatchbrook Cl SL6 203 A4
Tate Rd SL9 177 C3
Tathams La MK17 67 A2
Tatling Gr MK7 48 A3
Tattam Cl MK15 35 B1
Tattenhoe La MK3 57 C4
Tattenhoe St MK5 45 C2
Tattershall Cl MK5 46 A3
Tattlers Hill HP22 89 A2
Taunton Deane MK4 46 B1
Taurus Cl MK18 63 B1
Tavelhurst MK8 33 C1
Taverner Cl MK7 48 B3
Tavistock Cl
Maidenhead SL6 202 A4
Woburn Sands MK17 49 A3
Tavistock Rd UB7 208 B3
Tavistock St MK2 47 B1
Tavistock Wlk HP20 101 C1
Tay Rd MK3 46 C1
Taylor Rd HP21 115 B3
Taylor's La HP23 132 B2
Taylor's Ride LU7 70 C1
Taylors Cl SL7 183 C1
Taylors Ct SL6 202 A4
Taylors Mews MK14 34 C3
Taylors Rd HP5 144 B1
Taylors Turn HP13 161 B2
Taymouth Pl MK9 35 A2
Teal Ho HP11 173 B3
Teale Cl OX25 94 C4
Teasel Ave MK14 34 C3
Tedder Cl UB10 201 C3
Tedder Rd HP22 131 B3
Tees Way MK3 46 B1
Teesdale Rd SL2 204 C4
Teign Cl MK16 22 B2
Teikyo Sch (UK) SL2 199 B3
Telford Cl HP19 100 C1
Telford Dr SL1 205 A2
Telford Way
High Wycombe HP13 162 A1
Milton Keynes MK14 22 A1
Telston Cl SL8 185 A3
Temperance Terr MK11 32 B3
Templars Pl 9 SL7 183 C1
Temple MK14 34 B4
Temple Cl
Buckingham MK18 41 C1
Milton Keynes MK3 57 B4
Temple End HP13 173 A4
Temple Ho RG9 191 C2
Temple La SL7 194 B3
Temple Mill Cotts SL7 194 B3
Temple Mill Island SL7 194 B3
Temple Orch HP13 173 A4
Temple Pk SL7 193 C2
Temple Rd SL4 210 B3
Temple Sq 13 HP20 115 B4
Temple St
Aylesbury HP20 115 B4
Brill HP18 96 A1
High Wycombe HP11 173 A4
Temple Way SL2 198 B4
Templecroft Terr HP17 114 A2
Templewood HP14 150 A1
Templewood Gate SL2 198 B4
Templewood La SL2 198 B4
Tene Acres MK5 45 C3
Tennis La MK18 66 A2
Tennyson Dr MK16 22 A2
Tennyson Gr MK3 57 C4
Tennyson Rd
Aylesbury HP21 115 C3
High Wycombe HP11 173 A3
Tennyson Way SL2 197 C1
Tenterden Cres MK7 48 A4
Tenzing Dr HP13 173 C3
Terrace The
Aspley Guise MK17 49 C3
Maidenhead SL6 203 B2
10 Tring HP23 119 A2
Terrent Ct SL4 210 A3
Terrington Hill SL7 183 A1
Terry Dr HP19 101 B2
Terry Orch HP13 173 B4
Terry Pl UB8 208 B4
Terry Rd HP13 173 B4
Terry's La SL8 195 C4
Terryfield Rd HP13 173 C3
Tess Rd HP21 115 B3
Testwood Rd SL4 209 B3
Tetherdown HP16 151 B3
Tewkesbury La MK10 35 C1
Tews End La NN12 17 A4
Thackeray End HP19 100 C1

Thame Ho 12 HP13 .....173 A4
Thame Rd
  Aylesbury HP21 ....115 A4
  Blackthorn OX25 ....81 A2
  Brill HP18 ....110 A4
  Chilton HP18 ....111 A2
  Chinnor OX39 ....147 A4
  Haddenham HP17 ......126 B3
  Long Crendon HP18,OX9 .125 B2
  Longwick HP27 ....138 B3
  Oakley HP18 ....109 C3
  Piddington OX25,HP18 ..95 B3
Thame Rd S HP21 ......115 A3
Thames Ave SL4 ....210 B4
Thames Cl
  Bourne End SL8 ....185 A2
  Milton Keynes MK3 .....57 C4
Thames Cres SL6 ......196 A1
Thames Dr MK16 ....22 C2
Thames Ho RG9 ....191 C2
Thames Mead SL4 ......209 C3
Thames Rd SL3 ....207 A2
Thames Reach SL7 .....193 B3
Thames Side
  Henley-on-T RG9 .....191 C1
  Windsor SL4 ....210 B4
Thames St SL4 ....210 B4
Thames Valley Nuffield
  Hospl The SL3 ....199 B2
Thames Valley Univ
  SL1 ....205 C3
Thamesbourne Mews 11
  SL8 ....185 A2
Thamesfield Gdns SL7 .183 C1
Thane Ct MK14 ....34 B4
Thanstead Copse HP10 .174 B1
Thanstead Ct HP10 ....174 B1
Thatcher Cl HP18 .....208 C2
Thatchers Dr SL6 .....202 A3
Theatre Wlk MK9 ....34 C2
Thellusson Way WD3 ..167 C1
Theydon Ave MK17 .....49 A2
Thicket The
  Tylers Green HP10 ....163 A1
  West Drayton UB7 ....208 C4
Third Ave Marlow SL7 .183 C1
  Milton Keynes MK1 .....47 A1
Third Cres SL1 ....205 B4
Third St HP11 ....173 A2
Thirkleby Cl SL1 .....205 B3
Thirlby La MK5 ....46 A3
Thirlmere Ave
  Milton Keynes MK2 .....58 B3
  Slough SL1 ....204 B4
Thirsk Gdns MK3 ....57 B3
Thistle Ct HP21 ......115 B3
Thomas Bourne Ho 1
  HP4 ....135 B2
Thomas Coram Sch The
  HP4 ....135 B1
Thomas Ct
  Berkhamsted HP4 .....134 C3
  Maidenhead SL6 ......202 A1
Thomas Dr MK16 ....22 A3
Thomas Harding
  Jun Sch HP5 ....154 A4
Thomas Hickman Sch
  HP19 ....101 A1
Thomas Rd HP10 ......185 B4
Thompkins La SL2 .....198 A3
Thompson Cl SL3 .....207 A1
Thompson Rd UB10 ....201 C3
Thompson St MK13 .....34 A4
Thomson Wlk HP21 ....115 A3
Thorn Dr SL3 ....206 C4
Thornaby Pl HP10 ....185 C4
Thornbank St TW19 ...213 A1
Thornborough Inf Sch
  MK18 ....54 A4
Thornborough Rd MK17 .55 B4
Thornbridge Rd SL0 ...200 B2
Thorncliffe MK8 ......33 B1
Thorndike SL2 ....205 A4
Thorne Rd HP14 ......171 B2
Thorne Way
  Aylesbury HP20 ......101 C1
  Drayton Beauchamp HP22 118 A2
Thorney La N SL0 .....207 C3
Thorney La S SL0 .....207 C3
Thorney Mill La SL0 ..208 A2
Thorney Mill Rd SL0,
  UB7 ....208 A2
Thorneycroft La MK15 ..35 A3
Thornhill MK18 ....54 A4
Thornhill Cl HP7 .....165 A4
Thornhill Rd UB10 ....201 C4
Thornlea Croft MK46 ...6 C2
Thornley Croft MK4 ....46 B1
Thorns Cl HP27 ....139 B3
Thornton Ave UB7 ....208 C2
Thornton Cl UB7 .....208 C2
Thornton Coll Convent
  of Jesus & Mary MK17 .43 B3
Thornton Cres HP22 ..131 A4
Thornton Rd MK17 .....44 A1
Thorntree Dr HP23 ...118 C2
Thorpe Cl HP21 ......116 A2
Thorpe House Prep Sch
  SL9 ....188 C4
Thorwold Pl MK5 ......46 A4
Thrasher Rd HP21 ....115 B3
Three Close La HP4 ...135 B2
Three Gables HP9 ....175 C1
Three Households HP8 .176 C3
Three Oaks Cl UB10 ..190 C4
Three Points La MK18 ..74 A4
Thresher Gr MK12 .....33 A3

Thrift La SL6 ....202 B1
Thrift View MK43 ......25 B1
Thrupp Cl MK19 ....20 A3
Thrush Cl
  14 Aylesbury HP20 ...101 C2
  High Wycombe HP12 ..172 B2
Thurlby Way SL6 .....202 B3
Thurley Cotts SL2 ....199 A2
Thurne Cl MK16 ....22 C2
Thursby Cl MK15 ......35 B4
Thurston Rd SL1 .....205 C4
Thyme Cl MK16 ....21 C3
Tibbys La HP18 ......112 C2
Ticehurst Cl MK7 .....48 A4
Tichborne WD3 ......178 B3
Tickford Arc MK16 ....22 C2
Tickford St MK16 .....22 C2
Tidbury Cl MK17 ......49 A2
Tierney Ct 10 SL7 ...183 C1
Tiffany Cl MK2 ....58 B3
Tilbrook Ind Est MK7 .48 A2
Tilbrook Rdbt MK7 ....48 A1
Tilbury Wlk SL3 .....207 A2
Tilburywood Cl HP13 ..161 B1
Tilebarn Cl RG9 .....191 B1
Tilecotes Cl SL7 ....183 B1
Tilehouse Comb Sch
  UB9 ....189 C3
Tilehouse La UB9 ....189 C3
Tilehouse Way UB9 ...189 C2
Tilers Rd MK11 ....33 A1
Tilling Cres HP13 ....174 A4
Tilman Cl MK12 ....33 B3
Tilstone Ave SL4 ....204 C1
Tilstone Cl SL4 .....204 C1
Tilsworth Rd HP9 ....175 B1
Timber La MK17 ....60 C4
Timber Way OX39 ....147 B3
Timbers Wlk SL6 .....202 A3
Timberscombe MK4 ....46 B2
Timbold Dr MK7 ....48 A4
Timor Ct MK11 ....32 B3
Timpson La MK46 ......7 A2
Timpsons Row MK46 ...7 A2
Tindal Rd HP20 ......101 C1
Tingewick Inf Sch MK18 .51 B3
Tingewick Rd
  Buckingham MK18 .....52 A4
  Tingewick MK18 ......51 C4
Tingewick Road Ind Est
  MK18 ....52 A4
Tinkers Dr MK18 ......65 C2
Tinkers La
  Berkhamsted HP23 ...134 A3
  Windsor SL4 ....209 B3
Tinkers Wood Rd HP13 .161 C1
Tintagel Ct MK6 ......47 A4
Tintagel Ho SL1 .....205 B3
Tintern Cl SL1 ......205 B2
Tinterne Cl HP21 ....116 B3
Tippet Cl MK7 ....48 B2
Tiree Ho SL2 ....205 A4
Titchmarsh Ct MK6 ...46 C4
Tithe Barn Dr SL6 ...203 C1
Tithe Cl SL6 ....203 B1
Tithe Ct SL3 ....207 A1
Tithe La TW19 ....212 A1
Titmus Rd HP22 ......131 C4
Tiverton Cres HP19 ..101 B2
Tockley Rd SL1 ......197 A1
Todd Cl Aylesbury HP21 115 A3
  Holmer Green HP15 ..163 A3
Tolcarne Ave MK6 .....35 A1
Tollcarne SL6 ....202 A3
Tollgate Cl WD3 .....167 C3
Tolman Ct HP21 ......115 A3
Tomkins Cl MK6 ....46 A2
Tomkins La OX27 ......71 C1
Toms Hill Cl HP23 ...120 B3
Toms Hill Rd HP23 ...120 B3
Toms Turn HP15 .....162 C3
Tongwell La MK16 ....35 B4
Tongwell St
  Milton Keynes MK15 ..35 C4
  Milton Keynes Village MK7 .48 A4
  Walton MK7 ....48 B3
Toot Hill Cl MK5 .....46 A4
Top Angel MK18 ....52 B3
Top Farm Cl HP9 ....175 A1
Top Mdw MK7 ....48 A2
Top Pk SL9 ....188 B3
Top Station Rd NN13 ..38 A4
Topaz Cl SL1 ....205 B3
Topland Rd SL9 ......177 B2
Topping La UB8 ......201 B1
Torbay HP22 ....85 A2
Tornay Ct LU7 ....91 B3
Torquay Spur SL2 ....198 A1
Torre Cl MK3 ....47 A1
Torridge Rd
  Aylesbury HP21 ......115 B2
  Slough SL3 ....212 A4
Torridon Ct MK2 ......58 B2
Torrington Rd HP4 ...135 A2
Tortoiseshell Way HP4 .134 C3
Torwood Cl HP4 .....134 C2
Totteridge Ave HP13 .173 B3
Totteridge Dr HP13 ..162 C1
Totteridge La HP13 ..162 C1
Totteridge Par HP13 .173 C4
Totteridge Rd HP13 ..173 B3
Totternhoe Knolls Nature
  Reserve* LU6 ....93 A4

Totternhoe Lower Com Sch
  LU6 ....93 A4
Totternhoe Rd
  Dunstable LU6 ....93 C4
  Eaton Bray LU6 ....92 B4
Towan Ave MK6 ....35 A1
Towcester Dr NN12 ....18 A2
Towcester Rd
  Buckingham MK18 .....41 C2
  Old Stratford MK19 ...32 A4
Tower Cl
  Berkhamsted HP4 .....135 A2
  Emberton MK16 ....13 B3
  Flackwell Heath HP10 .185 B4
Tower Ct MK14 ....34 C3
Tower Dr MK14 ....34 C4
Tower Hill WD4 ......146 C1
Tower Ho Iver SL0 ...207 C4
  4 Slough SL1 ....205 C2
Tower Rd HP7 ....165 C2
Tower St HP13 ....162 B1
Towergate Cl UB8 ....201 C4
Toweridge La
  High Wycombe HP12 ..172 B4
  High Wycombe, Towerage
  HP14 ....160 C1
Towers Lea HP13 ....173 B4
Towersey Way HP21 ..115 A4
Town Bridge Ct HP5 .154 A4
Town MK18 ....50 B3
Town End Cres MK16 ..12 A3
Town End Rd HP14 ...159 B4
Town Farm LU7 ......105 A4
Town Field La HP8 ..177 B4
Town La Stanwell TW19 .213 B1
  Wooburn Green HP10 .185 B2
Town Sq 15 SL1 .....205 C2
Townfield HP5 ....154 B4
Townfield Rd 5 HP13 .173 B4
Townlands Hospl RG9 .191 B1
Townsend
  Marsh Gibbon OX27 ...71 C1
  Quainton HP22 ....85 A3
Townsend Cotts MK17 ..55 A2
Townsend Gr MK13 ...34 A4
Townsend La OX27 ....71 C1
Townsend Piece HP19 .101 B1
Townsend Rd HP5 ....144 B1
Townside
  Edlesborough LU6 ....92 C2
  Haddenham HP17 ....126 C3
Tozer Wlk SL4 ......209 B2
Trafalgar Ave MK3 ...46 C1
Trafford Cl HP16 ....152 A4
Trafford Rd HP16 ....152 A4
Tramhill HP18 ....96 A1
Tranlands Brigg MK13 .34 A2
Trapp's Ct HP5 ......154 B3
Trapp's La HP5 ......154 B3
Travell Ct MK13 .....34 A2
Travic Rd SL2 ....197 C1
Travis Ct MK13 .....34 A2
Travis Gr MK3 ......58 A4
Travistock Mews HP12 .172 C4
Treacher's Cl HP5 ...154 A4
Treadaway Bsns Ctr
  HP10 ....174 B1
Treadaway Hill
  Flackwell Heath HP10 .174 A1
  Loudwater HP10 .....174 A1
Treadaway Rd HP10 ..174 A1
Treborough MK4 ......46 B1
Tredington Gr MK7 ..48 A2
Treehanger Cl HP23 .119 A2
Trees Ave HP14 .....162 A3
Trees Rd Bourne End SL8 .185 A2
  Hughenden Valley HP14 .162 A3
Treeside Cl UB7 ....208 B1
Treesmill Dr SL6 ...202 B2
Trelawney Ave SL3 ..206 C2
Tremayne Ct MK6 ....47 A4
Trenchard Ave HP22 .131 B3
Trenches La SL3 ....207 A3
Trengothal Ct NN13 .26 B2
Trent Dr MK16 ....22 B2
Trent Rd
  Milton Keynes MK3 ..46 C1
  Slough SL3 ....212 A4
Trent Villas Est SL3 .211 A3
Trentishoe Cres MK4 .46 B2
Tresco Rd HP4 .....134 C3
Tresham Ct MK5 .....46 A4
Tressel The SL6 ....202 B3
Trevelyan Mid Sch SL4 .210 A3
Trevelyan Way HP4 ..135 A3
Treves Gn HP21 ....115 C3
Trevithick La MK5 ...46 A3
Trevone Cl MK46 ....47 A4
Trevor Ct TW19 ....213 A1
Trevose Ho SL2 ....198 A1
Trewarden Ave SL0 .200 B2
Triangle Bsns Pk HP22 .130 B4
Trident Ind Est SL3 .212 C2
Tring Bsns Ctr HP23 .118 C2
Tring Ford Rd HP23 .119 A4
Tring Hill HP23 ....118 B2
Tring Rd
  Aylesbury HP20 ....116 A2
  Berkhamsted HP4 ...134 B4
  Dunstable LU6 ....93 C4
  Edlesborough LU6 ..106 C4
  Long Marston HP23 .104 A2
  Wendover HP22 .....131 B3
  Wingrave HP22 ......89 B1
Tring Sch HP23 ....119 A2
Tring Sta HP23 ....120 A3
Trinity Ave SL7 ....183 B2

Trinity CE Prim Sch
  RG9 ....191 B1
Trinity Cl
  Old Stratford MK19 ...32 A4
  Stanwell TW19 ......213 B1
Trinity Ct HP5 ......154 B4
Trinity Ho SL8 ......195 C3
Trinity Pl SL4 ......210 B3
Trinity Rd
  Hazlemere HP15 .....162 C2
  Marlow SL7 ....183 B1
  Milton Keynes MK12 ..33 A4
Trinity St Stephens
  CE Fst Sch SL4 ....210 A3
Tripps Hill Cl HP8 ..177 A4
Trispen Ct MK6 .....47 A4
Trooper Rd HP23 ...120 B3
Trout Cl SL7 ....194 B4
Trout La UB7 ....208 B3
Trout Rd UB7 ......208 B3
Troutbeck MK6 ......47 B4
Troutbeck Cl SL2 ..206 A3
Trubys Gdn MK6 ....47 A4
Trueman Pl MK6 ....46 C4
Truesdale Dr UB9 ..190 B4
Trumper Way
  Slough SL1 ....204 C3
  Uxbridge UB8 ....201 B2
Trumpton La MK7 ...48 B4
Trunk Furlong Est MK17 .49 B3
Truro Cl SL6 ....202 A4
Trust Cotts HP4 ...107 A1
Trustees Way HP8 ..189 C3
Tubwell Rd SL2 ....199 A2
Tucker Cl HP13 ....173 B4
Tuckers Dr HP5 ....163 B4
Tudeley Hale MK7 ..48 A4
Tudor Dr
  Amersham HP6 .....154 B1
  Lane End HP14 .....160 B1
  10 Leighton Buzzard LU7 .80 C4
  Maidenhead SL6 ....196 B1
  3 Stanwell TW19 ..213 C1
Tudor Dr HP10 .....185 B4
Tudor Gdns
  Milton Keynes MK11 .32 C2
  Slough SL1 ....204 B4
Tudor Mill HP10 ...185 C3
Tudor Orch HP4 ....134 C3
Tudor Pk HP6 ......154 B1
Tudor Rd HP15 ....163 B2
Tudor Way SL4 ....209 B2
Tuffnell Cl HP15 ...35 C4
Tulip Way UB7 ....208 B1
Tulkers Cl MK16 ...151 B3
Tulla Ct MK2 ....58 B2
Tummell Way MK2 ..58 B3
Tunbridge Gr MK7 ..48 A4
Tunmers Ct 1 SL9 ..177 B1
Tunmers End SL9 ..177 B1
Tunmers Ho 2 SL9 .177 B1
Tuns La Henley-on-T RG9 .191 C1
  Slough SL1 ....205 B2
Turks Head Ct SL4 .210 B4
Turnberry Cl MK3 ..57 B4
Turner Cl HP20 ....101 C2
Turner Rd SL3 ....206 B2
Turner Wlk 24 HP20 .101 C2
Turners Dr HP13 ...173 C4
Turners Field HP13 .161 C2
Turners Mews MK14 .34 C3
Turners Pl HP15 ...163 B3
Turners Wlk 4 HP5 .144 B1
Turners Wood Dr HP8 .177 B4
Turneys Dr MK12 ...33 A3
Turneys Orch WD3 .167 B2
Turnfields HP18 ...124 A2
Turnfurlong HP21 ..115 C4
Turnfurlong Inf Sch
  HP21 ....116 A3
Turnfurlong Jun Sch
  HP21 ....116 A3
Turnfurlong La HP21 .115 A4
Turnham Way HP19 .115 A4
Turnip Cl HP18 ....112 A1
Turnmill Ave MK6 ..35 A1
Turnmill Ct MK6 ...35 A1
Turnoak Pk SL4 ...209 C2
Turnpike End HP21 .115 C3
Turnpike La UB10 ..201 C1
Turnpike Rd HP12 ..172 B2
Turnpike The HP18 .109 B3
Turnpike Way HP12 .172 B2
Turnstone Way HP20 .101 C2
Turpins Gn SL6 ...202 A3
Turpyn Ct MK6 .....47 B4
Turton Way SL1 ...205 B2
Turvey Cl HP22 ...117 C3
Turvey Lower Sch MK43 .8 C3
Turvey Mill MK43 ...8 C3
Turvey Rd Astwood MK16 .15 C3
  Carlton MK43 ....3 C1
Turville Rd HP21 ..116 B3
Turweston Rd NN13 .26 A1
Tweed Cl HP4 .....135 A3
Tweed Dr MK3 .....46 B1
Tweed Rd SL3 .....212 A4
Tweedale Cl MK17 .67 B4
Tweenways HP5 ...144 C1
Twelve Leys HP22 ..89 A2
Twinches La SL1 ..205 A3
Twinflower MK7 ....48 A3
Twist The HP23 ...119 B1
Twitchell La HP22 .117 C3
Twitchell Rd HP16 .152 A4
Twitchell's La MK4 .176 C3
Twitchen La MK4 ...46 B2
Two Dells La HP5 .145 A2
Two Gates La HP5 .143 B4

Two Mile Ash Mid Sch
  MK8 ....33 C1
Two Mile Dr SL1 ...204 C2
Twyford CE Sch MK18 .62 B1
Twyford La MK7 ....48 B3
Twynham Rd SL6 ...202 A4
Tyburn Ave MK6 ....35 A1
Tyle Pl SL4 ....211 A1
Tylers Cres HP15 ..163 A1
Tylers Gn MK13 ....34 B2
Tylers Green Fst Sch
  HP10 ....174 B4
Tylers Green Mid Sch
  HP10 ....174 B4
Tylers Hill Rd HP5 .154 C4
Tylers Rd HP15 ...163 A1
Tylsworth Cl HP6 ..154 B1
Tyne Rd HP21 .....115 B2
Tyne Sq MK3 ......46 B1
Tyneham Cl HP21 ..116 A2
Tyrell Cl MK18 ....52 B4
Tyrell Gdns SL4 ..209 C2
Tyrells Gdns MK17 .69 C4
Tyrells Rd MK17 ..69 C4
Tyrill MK14 ....34 B4
Tyson Pl MK6 .....46 C4
Tythe Cl LU7 .....78 C4
Tythe Gdns LU7 ...78 C4
Tythe Mews LU6 ...92 C2
Tyzack Rd HP13 ..162 C1

U

Ufton Court Yd SL8 .185 A2
Ufton Ct SL8 ......185 A2
Ullswater Cl SL1 ..204 B4
Ullswater Dr LU7 ..80 B4
Ulverscroft MK10 ..36 A4
Ulyett Pl MK6 .....46 C4
Umberville Way SL2 .197 C1
Underhill Cl SL6 ..202 C3
Underwood Cotts HP7 .164 B1
Underwood Pl MK6 .46 C4
Underwood Rd HP13 .173 B4
Union Bldgs UB8 ..201 A1
Union Bsns Pk UB8 .201 A1
Union Ct 11 HP4 ..135 B2
Union St
  High Wycombe HP11 .173 A4
  Newport Pagnell MK16 .22 B4
Univ of Buckingham
  Buckingham MK18 ...52 B4
  Buckingham MK18 ...52 C4
University Way
  Cranfield MK43 .....24 B1
  Salford MK43 ....37 B4
Up Corner Cl HP8 ..177 A4
Upcroft SL4 ......210 A2
Upland Ave HP5 ...144 A2
Uplands SL7 ......183 B3
Uplands Cl
  Gerrards Cross SL9 .188 C2
  High Wycombe HP13 .173 C4
Uplands Ct HP15 ..144 B1
Uplands The SL9 ..188 C1
Upper Abbotts Hill
  HP19 ....115 A4
Upper Ashlyns Rd HP4 .135 A2
Upper Belmont Rd HP5 .144 A2
Upper Bourne End La
  HP1 ....146 A4
Upper Bray Rd SL6 .203 B2
Upper Church St HP12 .112 C2
Upper Coombe LU7 .80 C4
Upper Dr HP9 .....175 B3
Upper Fifth St MK9 .34 B1
Upper Fourth St MK9 .34 B1
Upper George St HP5 .144 B1
Upper Gladstone Rd 2
  HP5 ....144 B1
Upper Hall Pk HP4 .135 C1
Upper Hollis HP16 .151 C4
Upper Hundreds Way
  HP20 ....115 C4
Upper Icknield Way
  Aston Clinton HP22 .117 C1
  Drayton Beauchamp HP22 117 C1
  Halton HP22 ....117 C1
  Pitstone LU7 ......105 C1
  Princes Risborough HP27 149 A4
  Princes Risborough,
  Whiteleaf HP27 ....139 B3
Upper Lees Rd SL2 .198 A3
Upper Lodge La HP15 .162 C3
Upper Mdw HP5 ...144 A1
Upper Rd UB9 ....189 B2
Upper Riding HP9 ..175 A1
Upper Second St MK9 .34 B1
Upper St Quainton HP22 .85 A3
  Tingewick MK18 ....51 A3
Upper Stonehayes MK14 .34 C4
Upper Third St MK9 .34 B1
Upper Ventnor Cotts
  SL7 ....195 B4
Upper Way MK17 ..59 B1
Upton Cl
  Henley-on-T RG9 ...191 C1
  29 Slough SL1 .....205 C2
Upton Court Rd SL3 .206 A1
Upton Gr MK5 .....46 B2
Upton Hospl SL1 ..205 C2
Upton House Sch SL4 .210 B3
Upton Lea Par SL2 .206 A3
Upton Pk SL1 .....205 C2

Upton Rd Dinton HP17 . . . . .**114** A2
Slough SL1 . . . .**206** A2
Upton Terr HP17 . . . .**114** A2
Upway SL9 . . . .**177** C1
Uxbridge Coll UB8 . . . . . .**201** C3
Uxbridge High Sch UB8 .**201** B2
Uxbridge Ind Est UB8 . . .**201** A2
Uxbridge Rd
Slough SL1,SL2,SL3 . . . . .**206** B3
Uxbridge UB10 . . . .**201** C1
Uxbridge Sta UB8 . . . . . .**201** B3

V

Vache La
Chalfont St Giles HP8 . . . .**177** B4
Milton Keynes MK5 . . . . . .**45** C3
Vale Cl SL9 . . . .**177** B1
Vale Ct MK43 . . . .**25** B1
Vale Gr SL1 . . . .**205** C2
Vale Ho HP19 . . . .**115** B4
Vale Park Dr HP20 . . . .**115** C4
Chesham HP5 . . . .**144** B2
Windsor SL4 . . . .**209** C3
Vale Rise HP5 . . . .**144** B2
Vale Rise The, Peveral F
HP17 . . . .**114** C2
Vale The SL9 . . . .**177** B1
Valens Cl MK8 . . . .**45** C4
Valentine Cl MK8 . . . .**45** C4
Valentine Way HP8 . . . .**177** B4
Valerian Pl MK16 . . . .**21** C2
Valley Cl NN13 . . . .**38** A4
Valley Cres NN13 . . . .**38** A4
Valley Ctr The HP13 . . . . .**173** B3
Valley End SL3 . . . .**199** B1
Valley Rd
Berkhamsted HP4 . . . .**134** C3
Brackley NN13 . . . .**38** A4
Buckingham MK18 . . . .**52** C4
Finmere MK18 . . . .**50** B3
Henley-on-T RG9 . . . .**191** B1
Hughenden Valley HP14,
HP15 . . . .**162** A3
Uxbridge UB10 . . . .**201** C2
Valley Rise NN13 . . . .**38** A4
Valley View HP5 . . . .**144** A1
Valley Way SL9 . . . .**188** B3
Valpy Cl HP23 . . . .**119** B1
Van Der Bilt Ct MK13 . . . . .**33** C3
Van Diemens Cl OX39 . . .**147** B4
Vandyke Cl MK17 . . . .**49** A3
Vane Rd OX9 . . . .**126** A1
Vanguard Cl HP12 . . . .**172** B4
Vanguard Ho 5 TW19 . . .**213** C1
Vansittart Est SL4 . . . .**210** B3
Vansittart Rd
Bisham SL7 . . . .**194** C4
Windsor SL4 . . . .**210** A3
Vantage Cl MK16 . . . .**22** C2
Vantage Rd SL1 . . . .**205** A3
Vanwall Bsns Pk SL6 . . . .**202** B3
Vanwall Rd SL6 . . . .**202** B2
Varnell Terr RG9 . . . .**181** B1
Vaughan Copse SL4 . . . . .**205** B1
Vaughan Gdns SL4 . . . . . .**204** C1
Vaughan Way SL2 . . . .**197** C1
Vauxhall MK13 . . . .**34** A3
Vellan Ave MK6 . . . .**35** A1
Venables La MK15 . . . .**35** A4
Venetian Ct MK7 . . . .**48** B4
Ventfield Cl OX33 . . . .**108** A3
Venus Hill HP3 . . . .**156** A4
Verbena Cl UB7 . . . .**208** B1
Verdi Cl MK7 . . . .**48** B3
Verdon Ct SL2 . . . .**198** A1
Verdon Dr MK15 . . . .**35** A4
Verity Pl MK6 . . . .**34** C1
Verley Cl MK6 . . . .**47** B4
Vermont Pl MK15 . . . .**22** C1
Vermont Rd SL2 . . . .**197** C1
Verney Ave HP12 . . . .**172** B2
Verney Avenue Sch
HP12 . . . .**172** C2
Verney Cl
Berkhamsted HP4 . . . .**134** C3
Buckingham MK18 . . . .**41** B1
Marlow SL7 . . . .**183** B1
Tring HP23 . . . .**119** B3
Verney Farm Cl MK18 . . . .**74** C4
Verney Rd Slough SL3 . . . .**207** A1
Winslow MK18 . . . .**65** C2
Verney Wlk HP21 . . . .**115** B3
Verona UB8 . . . .**208** B4
Verwood Rd HP20 . . . .**101** C1
Veryan Pl MK6 . . . .**35** A1
Vicarage Cl
Cookham SL8 . . . .**196** A4
Seer Green HP9 . . . .**176** B2
Steeple Claydon MK18 . . . .**63** B1
Wendover HP22 . . . .**131** A3
Yardley Gobion NN12 . . . . .**18** C3
Vicarage Dr SL6 . . . .**203** B2
Vicarage Flats SL4 . . . . . .**210** B4
Vicarage Gdns
Leighton Buzzard LU7 . . . . .**80** C3
Marsworth HP23 . . . .**105** A1
Milton Keynes MK13 . . . . . .**34** C2
Vicarage La
Bovingdon HP3 . . . .**146** A2
Ivinghoe LU7 . . . .**105** C3

Vicarage La continued
Piddington OX25 . . . .**95** C3
Steeple Claydon MK18 . . . .**63** B1
Wing LU7 . . . .**79** C1
Vicarage Rd
Aylesbury HP21 . . . .**115** B3
Henley-on-T RG9 . . . .**191** C1
Leighton Buzzard LU7 . . . . .**80** C3
Maidenhead SL6 . . . .**202** C4
Marsworth HP23 . . . .**105** A1
Milton Keynes, Bradwell
MK13 . . . .**34** A2
Milton Keynes, Fenny Stratford
MK2 . . . .**58** C4
Milton Keynes, Stony Stratford
MK11 . . . .**32** B3
Pitstone LU7 . . . .**105** B2
Whaddon MK17 . . . .**56** A4
Wigginton HP23 . . . .**119** B1
Winslow MK18 . . . .**65** C2
Vicarage St MK17 . . . .**49** B2
Vicarage Way
Colnbrook SL3 . . . .**212** B3
Gerrards Cross SL9 . . . . . .**188** C3
Vicarage Wlk
Maidenhead SL6 . . . .**203** B2
Milton Keynes MK13 . . . . . .**32** B3
Vickers Ct 9 TW19 . . . . .**213** C1
Vickery Way HP21 . . . .**115** C3
Victor Cl SL6 . . . .**202** A4
Victor Rd SL4 . . . .**210** B2
Victoria CE Fst Sch MK4 .**135** B2
Victoria CE Sch HP4 . . . .**135** A3
Victoria Cres SL3 . . . .**208** A3
Victoria Ct
Henley-on-T RG9 . . . .**191** C1
2 High Wycombe HP11 . . .**172** C4
2 Marlow SL7 . . . .**183** C1
Slough SL1 . . . .**205** C3
Victoria Gdns
High Wycombe HP11 . . . . .**172** C2
Marlow SL7 . . . .**183** C1
Victoria Ho SL4 . . . .**211** A1
Victoria Rd
Berkhamsted HP4 . . . .**135** B2
Chesham HP5 . . . .**144** B1
Eton SL4 . . . .**204** C1
Farnham Common SL2 . . . .**198** B3
Leighton Buzzard LU7 . . . . .**80** C3
Marlow SL7 . . . .**183** C1
Milton Keynes MK2 . . . .**47** C1
Slough SL2 . . . .**206** A3
Uxbridge UB8 . . . .**201** B3
Victoria Row MK18 . . . .**52** B4
Victoria St
Aylesbury HP20 . . . .**115** C4
High Wycombe HP11 . . . . .**172** C4
Milton Keynes MK12 . . . . . .**33** B3
16 Slough SL1 . . . .**205** C2
Windsor SL4 . . . .**210** B3
Victory Ct MK1 . . . .**47** A1
Victory Rd
Berkhamsted HP4 . . . .**135** A3
Steeple Claydon MK18 . . . .**63** B1
Wendover HP22 . . . .**131** A3
Vienna Ave MK13 . . . .**33** C3
Villa Pk MK17 . . . .**37** C4
Village Cl MK16 . . . .**13** C1
Village La SL2 . . . .**187** B2
Village Rd Coleshill HP7 . .**164** C2
Denham UB9 . . . .**190** A2
Dorney SL4 . . . .**204** A2
Village Sh Ctr The 11
SL1 . . . .**205** C2
Village Way HP7 . . . .**166** B4
Villier St UB8 . . . .**201** B2
Villiers Bldgs 6 HP20 . . .**115** B4
Villiers Cl MK18 . . . .**41** C1
Villiers Ct SL4 . . . .**210** A4
Villiers Rd SL2 . . . .**205** B4
Vimy Rd LU7 . . . .**80** C4
Vincent Ave MK8 . . . .**45** C4
Vincent Cl HP19 . . . .**101** C1
Vincent Dr UB10 . . . .**201** C1
Vincents Way HP14 . . . . . .**161** B3
Vine Cl Hazelmere HP15 . .**163** A2
Stanwell TW19 . . . .**213** A1
Vine Ct SL2 . . . .**199** A3
Vine Gr UB10 . . . .**201** C3
Vine Rd SL2 . . . .**198** C3
Vine St UB8 . . . .**201** B2
Vine The HP18 . . . .**124** B2
Vinetrees HP22 . . . .**131** A2
Vineyard Dr SL8 . . . .**185** A3
Vineyards The HP27 . . . . .**138** A1
Vinio House Sch HP12 . . .**172** B2
Vinlake Ave UB10 . . . .**190** C1
Vintners Mews MK14 . . . .**34** C4
Violet Ave UB8 . . . .**208** C4
Violet Cl HP27 . . . .**149** B3
Violets Cl MK16 . . . .**24** A3
Virginia MK6 . . . .**47** A4
Virginia Gdns HP14 . . . . .**159** C4
Viscount Cl 14 HP20 . . . .**101** C1
Viscount Ct 40 SL4 . . . . .**210** A4
Viscount Trad Est SL3 . . .**212** C2
Viscount Way MK2 . . . .**47** B1
Vivien Cl SL8 . . . .**195** C3
Vyne Cres MK8 . . . .**33** C1
Vyners Sch UB10 . . . .**201** C4

W

Waborne Rd SL8 . . . .**185** A2
Waddesden Village
Prim Sch HP18 . . . .**99** A3
Waddesdon CE Sch HP18 .**99** A3

Waddesdon Gn HP21 . . . .**115** C2
Waddesdon Hill HP18 . . . .**99** B2
Waddesdon Manor (NT) ★
HP18 . . . .**98** C3
Wade Dr SL1 . . . .**205** A3
Wadesmill La
Bow Brickhill MK7 . . . .**48** A2
Walton MK7 . . . .**48** A2
Wadhurst La
Milton Keynes Village MK10 .**36** A1
Milton Keynes Village, Kents Hill
MK7 . . . .**48** A4
Wagner Cl MK7 . . . .**48** B2
Waine Cl MK18 . . . .**52** B4
Wainers Croft MK12 . . . . . .**33** A2
Wainwrights HP18 . . . .**125** B3
Waivers Way HP21 . . . .**116** A3
Wakefield Cl MK14 . . . .**34** C4
Wakefield Cres SL2 . . . . . .**198** C3
Wakelins End SL8 . . . .**195** C4
Wakeman Rd SL8 . . . .**185** A2
Walbank Br MK5 . . . .**46** A2
Walbrook Ave MK6 . . . .**35** A2
Waldeck Rd SL6 . . . .**203** A4
Waldens Cl SL8 . . . .**185** A2
Walducks Cl LU7 . . . .**78** C4
Walford Rd UB8 . . . .**201** B2
Walgrave Dr MK13 . . . .**34** A2
Walk House MK43 . . . .**25** A1
Walk The Eton SL4 . . . .**205** A1
Winslow MK18 . . . .**65** C2
Walk Wood Rise HP9 . . . . .**186** B4
Walker Rd SL6 . . . .**203** A4
Walkers Rd HP27 . . . .**138** B4
Walkham Cl HP13 . . . .**174** A2
Walkhampton Ave MK13 . .**34** B2
Walkwood End HP9 . . . . . .**175** B1
Wallace Cl Marlow SL7 . . .**183** C2
Uxbridge UB10 . . . .**201** C2
Wallace Dr LU6 . . . .**92** C3
Wallace End HP21 . . . .**116** A3
Wallace Mews LU6 . . . .**92** C3
Wallace St MK13 . . . .**33** C4
Wallace Wlk SL4 . . . .**205** C1
Wallbridge Cl HP19 . . . . . .**115** A4
Waller Rd HP9 . . . .**175** C1
Wallinger Dr MK5 . . . .**46** A2
Wallingford Cl MK13 . . . . . .**34** A3
Wallingford Gdns HP11 . .**173** A2
Wallingford Rd UB8 . . . . . .**201** A1
Wallington Rd HP5 . . . .**144** C1
Wallis Ct SL1 . . . .**206** A2
Wallmead Gdns MK5 . . . . . .**46** A4
Walney Pl MK4 . . . .**45** C1
Walnut Cl
Long Crendon HP18 . . . . .**125** B4
Newport Pagnell MK16 . . . .**22** A2
South Heath HP16 . . . .**152** A4
Stoke Mandeville HP22 . . .**116** B1
Walnut Cres HP27 . . . .**138** B4
Walnut Dr
Maids Moreton MK18 . . . . . .**41** C2
Milton Keynes MK2 . . . .**58** C4
Wendover HP22 . . . .**131** A3
Walnut Gr HP10 . . . .**185** C2
Walnut Tree Cl
Bourne End SL8 . . . .**185** A1
High Wycombe HP12 . . . . .**172** B4
Walnut Tree Ct HP22 . . . . .**116** B2
Walnut Tree Ho HP11 . . . .**174** B2
Walnut Tree La HP7 . . . . .**138** B3
Walnut Tree Rdbt MK7 . . . .**48** A4
Walnut Way
Bourne End SL8 . . . .**185** A1
Hyde Heath HP6 . . . .**153** B2
Walnuts Sch The MK6 . . . .**47** C3
Walpole Rd SL1 . . . .**204** B4
Walsh's Manor MK14 . . . . .**34** B4
Walsingham Gate HP11 .**173** A2
Walter Rostholld
Zoological Mus ★ HP23 .**119** A2
Waltham Dr MK10 . . . .**36** A1
Walton Cl HP13 . . . .**162** C1
Walton Court Ctr HP21 . . .**115** B3
Walton Dene HP21 . . . .**115** C4
Walton Dr
High Wycombe HP13 . . . . .**162** C1
Walton MK7 . . . .**47** C3
Walton End MK7 . . . .**48** B3
Walton Gdns MK18 . . . .**41** C1
Walton Gn HP21 . . . .**115** C1
Walton Gr HP21 . . . .**115** C4
Walton Heath MK3 . . . .**57** B4
Walton La SL2 . . . .**197** C2
Walton Park Rdbt MK7 . . . .**48** A2
Walton Pl HP22 . . . .**116** C2
Walton Rd
Aylesbury HP21 . . . .**115** C4
Bow Brickhill MK7 . . . .**48** A2
Milton Keynes Village MK10 .**36** A1
Walton MK7 . . . .**48** A4
Wavendon MK10,MK17 . . . .**48** A4
Walton St HP20,HP21 . . . .**115** C4
Walton Way HP21 . . . .**116** A4
Wandlebury MK14 . . . .**35** A4
Wandsworth Pl MK13 . . . . .**34** B2
Wannions Cl HP5 . . . .**145** A1
Wantage Cl LU7 . . . .**79** C2
Wantage Cres LU7 . . . .**79** C2
Wappenham Rd NN13 . . . . .**27** A4
Wapping HP18 . . . .**125** B3
Wapseys La SL2 . . . .**187** C2
Ward Cl SL0 . . . .**207** C4
Ward Gdns SL1 . . . .**204** C3
Ward Pl HP7 . . . .**165** A4
Ward Rd Brackley NN13 . . . .**38** A3
Milton Keynes MK1 . . . .**47** C2
Ward Royal 6 SL4 . . . . . .**210** B3

Ward Royal Par 3 SL4 . .**210** B3
Wardes Cl HP16 . . . .**151** B3
Wardle Pl MK6 . . . .**46** C4
Wardrobes La HP27 . . . . .**149** B4
Wardstone End MK4 . . . . . .**46** A1
Ware Leys Cl OX27 . . . .**71** C2
Wargrave Rd RG9 . . . .**191** C1
Warmington Gdns MK15 . .**35** A3
Warmstone Cl HP18 . . . . . .**99** A3
Warmstone La HP18 . . . . . .**99** A3
Warneford Ave HP22 . . . . .**131** B3
Warner Cl SL1 . . . .**204** C3
Warners Cl MK17 . . . .**59** B1
Warners Hill SL7 . . . .**195** B4
Warners Rd MK17 . . . .**57** B2
Warren Bank MK6 . . . .**47** C3
Warren Cl
Buckingham MK18 . . . .**52** C4
Slough SL3 . . . .**206** C2
Stone HP17 . . . .**114** A3
Warren Ct
Farnham Common SL2 . . . .**198** B4
Little Horwood MK17 . . . . . .**55** C3
Warren Field SL0 . . . .**200** B2
Warren Ho HP19 . . . .**101** A1
Warren Rd
Ickenham UB10 . . . .**201** C4
Little Horwood MK17 . . . . . .**55** C3
Yardley Gobion NN12 . . . . .**18** C3
Warren The
Chalfont St Peter SL9 . . . .**177** C2
Chartridge HP5 . . . .**143** C2
Hazelmere HP15 . . . .**163** A3
Warren Wood Dr HP11 . . .**173** A2
Warren Yd MK12 . . . .**33** A3
Warrendene Rd HP14 . . . .**162** A4
Warrender Rd HP5 . . . .**144** C1
Warrington Ave SL1 . . . . .**205** B4
Warrington Rd Olney MK46 .**7** A4
Warrington MK46 . . . .**7** A4
Warwick Ave
High Wycombe HP12 . . . . .**172** A3
Slough SL3 . . . .**198** B1
Warwick Cl
Aston Clinton HP22 . . . . . .**117** C3
Maidenhead SL6 . . . .**202** A2
Warwick Ct
Beaconsfield HP9 . . . .**175** B2
Chorleywood WD3 . . . . . .**167** C3
37 Windsor SL4 . . . .**210** B3
Warwick Dr LU7 . . . .**79** C2
Warwick Ho 7 HP13 . . . . .**173** C4
Warwick Pl
Milton Keynes MK3 . . . .**57** C4
Uxbridge UB8 . . . .**201** B3
Warwick Rd
Beaconsfield HP9 . . . .**175** B2
Hanslope MK19 . . . .**11** A2
Milton Keynes MK3 . . . .**57** C4
Pitstone LU7 . . . .**105** B1
West Drayton UB7 . . . . . .**208** C3
Wash Hill HP10 . . . .**185** C2
Wash Hill Lea HP10 . . . . . .**185** C2
Washfield MK4 . . . .**46** B2
Washingleys MK43 . . . .**25** B1
Washington Ct SL7 . . . . . .**184** C2
Washington Dr
Slough SL1 . . . .**204** B3
Windsor SL4 . . . .**209** C2
Washington Row HP7 . . . .**165** B4
Wastel MK6 . . . .**47** A3
Watchcroft Dr MK18 . . . . . .**41** C1
Watchet Cl MK4 . . . .**46** B2
Watchet La
Holmer Green HP16 . . . . . .**152** B1
Little Kingshill HP16 . . . . . .**152** B1
Water Cl MK19 . . . .**32** A4
Water Eaton Rd MK2,MK3 .**58** B4
Water End Rd HP14 . . . . . .**159** B3
Water Gdns The HP15 . . . .**162** C1
Water La
Berkhamsted HP4 . . . .**135** B2
Bovingdon HP3 . . . .**146** A1
Brackley NN13 . . . .**38** A4
Chesham HP5 . . . .**154** A4
Dinton HP17 . . . .**128** A4
Lacey Green HP27 . . . . . .**150** B2
Leighton Buzzard LU7 . . . . .**80** C4
Sherington MK16 . . . .**13** C1
Water Mdw HP5 . . . .**154** A4
Water Meadow Way
HP22 . . . .**131** A3
Water Stratford Rd
Tingewick MK18 . . . .**51** A4
Water Stratford MK18 . . . . .**40** A1
Waterbeach Rd SL1 . . . . .**205** B4
Waterfield WD3 . . . .**167** B4
Waterford Ho UB7 . . . .**208** B2
Waterglades The HP9 . . . .**175** B3
Waterhall Comb Sch
MK2 . . . .**58** B2
Waterhouse Cl MK16 . . . . .**22** B2
Waterlily 5 HP20 . . . .**101** C2
Waterloo Ct MK3 . . . .**46** C1
Waterloo Rd
Leighton Buzzard LU7 . . . . .**80** C3
Uxbridge UB8 . . . .**201** B2
Waterlow Cl MK16 . . . .**22** C1
Waterman Ct 5 SL1 . . . . .**204** C3
Watermead HP20 . . . .**101** C2
Watermead Slopes
& Sails ★ HP19 . . . .**101** B2
Watermeadow HP20 . . . . .**101** C2
Watermill Way HP22 . . . . .**116** C1
Waterperry OX33 . . . .**123** A1
Waterperry Gdns ★
OX33 . . . .**123** A1

Waterperry Rd HP18 . . .**123** B3
Waterside
Berkhamsted HP4 . . . .**135** B2
Chesham HP5 . . . .**154** B3
Edlesborough LU6 . . . .**92** C2
Milton Keynes MK6 . . . .**47** B4
Uxbridge UB8 . . . .**208** B4
Wooburn Green HP10 . . . .**185** C4
Waterside Comb Sch
HP5 . . . .**154** B3
Waterside Ct HP5 . . . .**154** B4
Waterside Dr SL3 . . . .**207** A2
Waterside Lodge SL6 . . . .**203** B4
Waterslade Pens HP17 . . .**126** C3
Watersmeet Cl MK4 . . . . . .**46** B2
Watery La
Beachampton MK19 . . . . . .**44** A3
Brackley NN13 . . . .**38** A4
Frieth HP14 . . . .**170** A1
Marsworth HP23 . . . .**104** C1
Wooburn Green HP10 . . . .**185** C4
Watling St
Bow Brickhill MK17 . . . .**58** C4
Milton Keynes MK19 . . . . . .**33** A1
Potterspury NN12 . . . .**18** B2
Watling Terr MK2 . . . .**47** C1
Watling Way Fst Sch
MK11 . . . .**32** C2
Watling Way Mid Sch
MK11 . . . .**32** C2
Watlington Ct HP16 . . . . . .**152** B4
Watlington Rd OX49 . . . . .**157** A4
Watten Ct MK2 . . . .**58** C2
Wattleton Rd HP9 . . . .**175** C1
Watts Cl MK19 . . . .**11** A2
Watts Gn HP18 . . . .**112** A1
Wavell Cl MK15 . . . .**35** A4
Wavell Gdns SL2 . . . .**197** C1
Wavell Rd
Beaconsfield HP9 . . . .**176** A1
Maidenhead SL6 . . . .**202** A3
Wavendon Fields MK17 . . .**48** C3
Wavendon Fst Sch MK17 .**48** C4
Wavendon Gate Com Sch
MK7 . . . .**48** B2
Wavendon House Dr
MK17 . . . .**49** A4
Wavendon Rd MK17 . . . . . .**37** B1
Waveney Cl MK16 . . . .**22** C2
Waverley Rd SL1 . . . .**205** B4
Waverley Wlk HP20 . . . . . .**101** B4
Waxwing Cl HP20 . . . .**101** C2
Wayfarers Pk HP4 . . . .**134** C2
Waylands TW19 . . . .**211** C1
Wayside
High Wycombe HP13 . . . . .**173** B4
Lacey Green HP27 . . . . . .**150** B2
Wayside Ct HP6 . . . .**154** B1
Wayside Gdns SL9 . . . . . .**188** B2
Wayside Mews SL6 . . . . . .**202** C4
Wealdstone Pl MK6 . . . . . .**35** A1
Weasel La MK3 . . . .**57** B3
Weatherby LU6 . . . .**93** C4
Weathercock Cl MK17 . . . .**49** A3
Weathercock Gdns
HP15 . . . .**163** B4
Weathercock La MK17 . . . .**49** B2
Weavers End MK19 . . . .**11** A1
Weavers Hill MK11 . . . .**33** A2
Weavers Rd HP23 . . . .**118** C2
Webb Cl Chesham HP5 . . . .**144** A1
Slough SL3 . . . .**206** B1
Webber Heath MK7 . . . .**48** B2
Webbs Home Cl MK10 . . . .**36** A1
Webbs Mdw MK19 . . . .**115** A4
Webster Cl
Maidenhead SL6 . . . .**202** A3
Thame OX9 . . . .**125** C1
Webster Rd HP21 . . . .**116** A3
Websters Mdw MK4 . . . . . .**46** B1
Wedgewood Ave MK14 . . . .**22** A4
Wedgewood Dr HP14 . . . .**162** A3
Weedon Cl SL9 . . . .**177** A1
Weedon Hill HP6 . . . .**153** B2
Weedon La HP6 . . . .**154** A2
Weedon Rd HP19 . . . .**101** B4
Weekes Dr SL1 . . . .**205** A2
Weill Rd HP21 . . . .**116** A2
Weir La Blackthorn OX25 . . .**81** A2
East Claydon MK18 . . . .**74** C3
Whitchurch HP22 . . . .**86** C3
Weirside Gdns UB7 . . . . . .**208** B3
Welbeck Ave HP21 . . . . . .**116** B3
Welbeck Cl MK10 . . . .**35** C1
Welbeck Rd SL6 . . . .**202** B3
Welburn Gr MK4 . . . .**46** A1
Welby Cl SL6 . . . .**202** A2
Welden SL2 . . . .**206** B4
Welders La
Chalfont St Giles SL9 . . . .**177** A2
Gerrards Cross SL9 . . . . . .**177** A2
Seer Green SL9 . . . .**177** A2
Welford Way HP18 . . . .**112** C2
Well Head Rd LU6 . . . .**93** B3
Well La LU7 . . . .**79** C1
Well St MK18 . . . .**52** B4
Welland Cl SL3 . . . .**212** A4
Welland Dr MK16 . . . .**22** C2
Welland Ho MK3 . . . .**57** C4
Welland Rd HP21 . . . .**115** B3
Wellank SL6 . . . .**196** C1
Wellbrook Mews 4
HP23 . . . .**119** A2
Wellcroft LU7 . . . .**105** C3
Wellcroft Rd SL1 . . . .**205** A3
Weller Cl HP6 . . . .**154** C1
Weller Ct LU6 . . . .**93** B4
Welles Rd HP13 . . . .**173** C4

Wellesbourne Gdns HP13 162 B1
Wellesley Ave SL0 207 C2
Wellesley Ct SL0 207 C2
Wellesley Ho SL4 210 A3
Wellesley Path SL1 206 A2
Wellesley Rd SL1 206 A2
Welley Ave TW19 211 C2
Welley Rd TW19 211 C1
Wellfield HP15 163 A2
Wellfield Ct MK15 35 B4
Wellfield Rd HP14 171 A4
Wellhayes MK14 34 C4
Wellhouse Rd SL6 195 C1
Wellhouse Way HP14 161 C3
Wellingborough Rd MK46 6 C3
Wellington Ave HP27 139 A2
Wellington Pl
Aylesbury HP21 115 C2
Milton Keynes MK3 58 A4
Wellington Rd
Aylesbury HP21 115 C2
High Wycombe HP12 172 C3
Maidenhead SL6 202 B4
Uxbridge UB8 201 B2
Wellington St SL1 206 A2
Wells Cl SL4 210 A4
Wellsmead Fst Sch MK3 46 C1
Wellsmead Mid Sch MK3 46 C1
Welsh La MK18 40 B3
Welton Rd HP21 116 A4
Wendover CE Jun Sch HP22 131 A3
Wendover House Sch HP22 131 B2
Wendover Hts HP22 131 B3
Wendover Rd
Aylesbury HP21,HP22 116 B2
Bourne End SL8 185 A3
Burnham SL1 204 A4
Ellesborough HP17 130 B2
Stoke Mandeville HP22 116 B2
Wendover St HP11 172 C4
Wendover Sta HP22 131 A2
Wendover Way
Aylesbury HP21 115 C3
High Wycombe HP11 173 A3
Wendover Wood Forest Wlks★ HP23 131 C3
Wenlack Cl UB9 190 A1
Wenning La MK4 46 A1
Wentworth Ave SL2 198 A1
Wentworth Cl HP13 173 B4
Wentworth Cres SL6 202 B3
Wentworth Way MK3 57 B4
Wenwell Cl HP22 118 A2
Werner Ct HP21 115 C2
Werner Terr MK18 73 A3
Werth Dr MK17 49 A1
Wescott Way UB8 201 B2
Wesley Cl HP20 102 A1
Wesley Dene 11 HP13 173 A4
Wesley Hill HP5 144 A1
Wessex Ct
4 Stanwell TW19 213 C1
27 Windsor SL4 210 B3
Wessex Inf Sch SL6 202 A2
Wessex Jun Sch SL6 202 A2
Wessex Rd
Bourne End SL8 185 A1
Harmondsworth TW6,UB7 213 C2
Wessex Road Ind Est SL8 185 A1
Wessex Way SL6 202 A2
Wessons Hill SL7 195 B4
West Acres HP7 165 B4
West Ave HP10 163 B1
West Cl SL7 193 B4
West Comm SL9 188 B3
West Common Cl SL9 188 C3
West Common Rd UB8 201 B3
West Cres SL4 209 C3
West Ct
High Wycombe HP13 161 B2
Maidenhead SL6 203 B2
West Dales MK13 34 B3
West Dean SL6 202 C4
West Dr HP13 173 B4
West Drayton Park Ave UB7 208 C2
West Drayton Prim Sch UB7 208 C2
West Drayton Sta UB7 208 C3
West Edge OX27 71 C1
West End HP22 116 C1
West End Cl MK18 63 B1
West End Ct SL2 198 C2
West End La SL2 198 C2
West End Pl HP22 116 C1
West End Rd
Cheddington LU7 104 C4
High Wycombe HP11 172 C4
West End St HP11 172 C4
West Farm Way MK46 13 C4
West Furlong MK18 53 A1
West Hill MK17 49 B2
West Hyde La SL9 178 A2
West La Bledlow HP27 138 A1
Emberton MK46 13 C4
Henley-on-T RG9 191 B1
West Leith HP23 118 C1
West Mead SL6 195 C1
West Pas 14 HP23 119 A2
West Point SL1 204 B3
West Rd
Berkhamsted HP4 135 A3
Cranfield MK43 24 B1
Maidenhead SL6 202 C4
West Rd *continued*
West Drayton UB7 208 C2
Woburn Sands MK17 49 A3
West Richardson St HP11 172 C4
West Ridge SL8 185 A2
West Side Rise MK46 6 C2
West Sq SL0 207 C4
West St Adstock MK18 53 C1
Aylesbury HP19 101 B1
Buckingham MK18 41 B1
Dunstable LU6 93 C4
Henley-on-T RG9 191 B1
Leighton Buzzard LU7 80 C4
Maidenhead SL6 202 C4
Marlow SL7 183 B1
Olney MK46 6 C2
Steeple Claydon MK18 63 B1
West View Chesham HP5 144 B1
Hardwick HP22 87 A2
West Way HP9 174 C1
West Waye HP13 162 B1
West Well Cl MK18 51 A3
West Well La MK18 51 A3
West Wlk MK9 34 C1
West Wycombe Comb Sch HP14 160 C1
West Wycombe Hill Rd HP14 160 C1
West Wycombe Pk★ HP14 160 C1
West Wycombe Rd HP12 161 B1
West Yard Ind Est HP14 160 B4
Westanley Ave HP7 165 B4
Westborne Ct MK13 34 A3
Westborough Ct SL6 202 B3
Westborough Rd SL6 202 B3
Westbourne St HP11 172 C4
Westbrook SL6 203 C1
Westbrook End MK17 57 B2
Westbrook Hay Prep Sch HP1 146 B4
Westbury Cl MK16 22 A2
Westbury Ho 4 HP20 101 B1
Westbury La MK16 22 A3
Westbury Terr OX27 71 C1
Westcliffe MK8 33 B1
Westcoign Ho SL6 203 A4
Westcott CE Sch HP18 98 A4
Westcroft Slough SL2 198 A1
Tring HP23 119 A2
Westcroft Rdbt MK4 46 A1
Westcroft Stables★ HP27 150 A2
Westdean La HP5 143 B2
Westdown Gdns LU6 93 C4
Western Ave
Buckingham MK18 41 B1
New Denham UB9 201 B4
Uxbridge UB8 201 B3
Western Dene HP15 163 A3
Western Dr
Hanslope MK19 11 A2
Wooburn Green HP10 185 C3
Western House Inf Sch SL1 204 C3
Western La MK18 65 C2
Western Perimeter Rd TW6,TW19,UB7 213 A3
Western Perimeter Road Rdbt TW19 213 B1
Western Rd
Great Horwood MK17 55 A2
Milton Keynes, Fenny Stratford MK2 47 B1
Milton Keynes, Wolverton MK12 33 B3
Tring HP23 118 C2
Westfield
Hyde Heath HP6 153 B2
Stoke Mandeville HP21 115 C2
Westfield Ave MK19 31 B3
Westfield Bglws SL7 192 C3
Westfield Cotts SL7 192 C3
Westfield Fst Sch HP4 134 C3
Westfield Rd
Beaconsfield HP9 175 B1
Berkhamsted HP4 134 C3
Dunstable LU6 93 C4
Maidenhead SL6 202 A4
Milton Keynes MK2 58 B4
Pitstone LU7 105 B2
Slough SL2 198 A1
Wheatley OX33 122 A1
Westfield Sch SL8 185 A2
Westfield Wlk HP12 172 B3
Westfields
Buckingham MK18 52 B4
Princes Risborough HP27 139 B2
Westgate Cres SL1 204 C3
Westgate Ct HP13 174 A2
Westgate Sch SL1 205 A3
Westhill MK14 34 B4
Westhorpe Rd SL7 183 C2
Westland Cl TW19 213 C1
Westlands Ave SL1 204 B4
Westlands Cl SL1 204 B4
Westlands Rd HP27 149 C3
Westlington La HP17 113 C1
Westlington Lea HP17 113 C1
Westmead
Princes Risborough HP27 139 A3
Windsor SL4 210 A2
Westminster Cl
Brackley NN13 38 A4
High Wycombe HP11 173 A2
Westminster Cres NN13 38 A4
Westminster Dr
Aylesbury HP21 115 C3
Milton Keynes MK3 47 A1
Westmorland Ave HP21 116 A3
Westmorland Rd SL6 202 B3
Westmount Ave HP7 165 B4
Weston Ct HP22 117 B3
Weston Gdns HP23 119 A2
Weston La OX9 136 C4
Weston Rd
Aston Clinton HP22 117 B3
Lewknor OX49 157 A4
Olney MK46 6 C2
Ravenstone MK46 5 C1
Slough SL1 204 C4
Weston Underwood MK46 6 C2
Weston Turville CE Sch HP22 116 C2
Weston Way HP22 116 A1
Westover Ct HP13 161 B1
Westover Rd HP13 161 B1
Westpits MK46 13 C4
Westrick Wlk HP16 151 B3
Westside 8 LU7 80 C4
Westside La MK16 12 A3
Westwood HP12 172 A2
Westwood Cl
Little Chalfont HP6 166 B4
Milton Keynes MK8 45 C4
Westwood Dr HP6 166 B4
Westwood Gn SL8 195 C3
Westwood Rd SL7 183 B1
Westwood Wlk 7 HP20 101 C1
Wetherburn Ct 5 MK2 58 B4
Wetherby Gdns MK3 57 B3
Wethered Dr SL1 204 A4
Wethered Pk SL7 183 B1
Wethered Rd SL7 183 B1
Wexford Ct SL6 203 A4
Wexham Court Prim Sch SL2 206 B4
Wexham Park Hospl SL3 199 B1
Wexham Park La
Iver Heath SL3 199 B1
Stoke Poges SL3 199 B1
Wexham Pl SL2 199 A3
Wexham Rd SL1,SL2 206 A3
Wexham Sch SL2 206 B4
Wexham St SL3 199 A2
Wexham Woods SL3 206 B4
Wey La HP5 154 A4
Whadden Rd MK4,MK5 45 C1
Whaddon CE Sch MK17 56 A4
Whaddon Chase HP19 101 B1
Whaddon Rd
Milton Keynes MK5 46 A2
Mursley MK17 56 B2
Nash MK17 44 B1
Newport Pagnell MK16 22 A2
Newton Longville MK17 57 B2
Whaddon Way MK3 46 C1
Whales La OX27 71 C1
Whalley Dr MK3 47 A1
Wharf Cl
Old Stratford MK19 32 A4
Wendover HP22 131 A3
Wharf Ct UB8 201 B1
Wharf La
Berkhamsted HP4 134 B4
Bourne End SL8 185 A2
Henley-on-T RG9 191 C1
Old Stratford MK19 32 B4
Wharf Rd HP22 131 A3
Wharf The
Milton Keynes MK2 58 C3
Milton Keynes, Giffard Park MK14 21 C1
Wharf View MK18 41 C1
Wharf Way HP22 118 A2
Wharfside MK2 47 C1
Wharfside Pl MK18 41 C1
Wharton Ho 3 HP20 101 B1
Whatmore Cl TW19 213 A1
Wheat Cl HP21 115 C2
Wheatbutts The SL4 204 C1
Wheatcroft Cl MK6 47 A3
Wheatfield Cl SL6 202 A2
Wheathouse Copse MK17 55 A2
Wheatlands Rd SL3 206 B2
Wheatley Campus (Brookes Univ) OX33 122 B1
Wheatley Cl MK4 46 B1
Wheatley Park Sch OX33 122 A1
Wheatley Way SL9 177 C2
Wheatsheaf Par SL4 211 A1
Wheeler Ave HP10 174 B4
Wheeler Cl HP20 116 A4
Wheeler Rd OX39 147 B3
Wheelers Flats HP10 174 B4
Wheelers La MK13 34 A3
Wheelers Orch SL9 177 C2
Wheelers Pk HP13 173 B4
Wheelers Yd HP16 152 A4
Wheelwright Mews MK14 34 C3
Wheelwright Rd HP27 138 B4
Wheelwrights HP22 116 C1
Wheelwrights Pl SL3 212 B4
Wheelwrights Way MK19 32 A4
Wheelwrights Yd HP22 85 A3
Whetstone Cl MK13 34 A2
Whichcote Gdns HP5 154 B3
Whichert Cl HP9 175 B3
Whichford MK14 22 A1
Whielden Cl HP7 165 A4
Whielden Gn HP7 165 A4
Whielden La
Amersham HP7 165 A3
Coleshill HP7 164 C3
Whielden St HP7 165 A4
Whinchat HP20 101 C2
Whincup Cl HP11 172 C2
Whinneys Rd HP10 174 B2
Whipass Hill HP9 176 A3
Whipsnade Rd LU6 93 C3
Whipsnade Tree Cathedral★ LU6 93 C1
Whipsnade Wild Animal Pk★ HP4 107 C4
Whitby Cl MK3 47 A1
Whitby Rd SL1 205 B3
Whitchurch Cl
Maidenhead SL6 195 C2
Westcott HP18 98 A4
Whitchurch Comb Sch HP22 86 C4
Whitchurch La HP22 86 B4
Whitchurch Rd LU7 78 A1
White Alder MK12 33 C3
White Cl
High Wycombe HP13 161 B1
Slough SL1 205 B3
White Cotts MK18 29 B2
White Cres HP22 131 B4
White Hart HP18 96 A4
White Hart Cl HP8 177 A4
White Hart Field HP22 85 A2
White Hart La HP17 127 A3
White Hart Mdw HP9 175 C1
White Hart Rd
2 Maidenhead SL6 202 C4
Slough SL1 205 B2
White Hart St 8 HP11 173 A4
White Hermitage SL4 211 B1
White Hill
Ashley Green HP4,HP5 145 B4
Beaconsfield HP9,HP10 185 C4
Chesham HP5 144 B1
High Wycombe HP13 162 A1
Remenham Hill RG9 192 A1
White Hill Cl
Chesham HP5 144 B1
Marlow Bottom SL7 183 B3
White Horse Dr MK4 46 B1
White Horse La HP22 87 A3
White Horse Rd SL4 209 B3
White House Cl SL9 177 C2
White Lilies Island SL4 210 A4
White Lion Cl HP7 166 A4
White Lion Rd
Amersham HP7 166 A4
Little Chalfont HP7 166 A4
White Lodge Cl SL7 183 B3
White Paddock SL6 202 A1
White Rock SL6 196 A1
White Spire Sch MK3 46 C1
White View 26 HP20 101 C2
Whiteacres Dr SL6 203 A1
Whitebaker Ct MK14 34 C3
Whitecross Rd HP17 126 C3
Whitefield La HP16 152 A3
Whiteford Rd SL2 205 C4
Whitegate Ct MK6 47 A3
Whitehall SL6 196 A1
Whitehall Ave MK10 36 B1
Whitehall Cl UB8 201 B2
Whitehall Inf Sch UB8 201 B2
Whitehall Jun Sch UB8 201 B2
Whitehall La TW19 212 A1
Whitehall Rd UB8 201 B2
Whitehall St 7 HP20 101 B1
Whitehaven SL1 205 C3
Whitehead Way HP21 115 C3
Whitehill
Berkhamsted HP4 135 B3
Olney MK46 6 C3
Whitehill Ct HP4 135 B3
Whitehill La LU7 105 B1
Whitehorns MK16 22 A2
Whitehorse Yd MK11 32 B3
Whitehouse Cl HP9 174 C1
Whitehouse La HP10 174 C1
Whitehouse Way
Iver Heath SL0 200 B1
Slough SL3 206 B2
Whitelands Ave WD3 167 A3
Whitelands Rd HP12 172 B4
Whitelands Way HP12 172 B4
Whiteleaf Way HP27 139 B3
Whiteley SL4 209 C4
Whiteley Cres MK3 57 C3
Whitelock Ho RG9 191 C2
Whitepit La HP10 185 B4
Whites Cl MK18 63 B2
Whites La SL3 211 A4
Whitethorn Ave UB7 208 C3
Whitethorn Cl HP22 130 A4
Whitethorn Pl UB7 208 C3
Whitewood Rd HP4 135 A2
Whitfield Rd HP14 162 A3
Whitfield Way WD3 167 C1
Whitley Cl TW19 213 C1
Whitley Ct HP21 115 C2
Whitmees Cl MK46 6 C2
Whitsun Pasture MK15 35 A4
Whittaker Rd SL2 197 C1
Whittenham Cl SL2 206 A3
Whittle Parkway SL1 204 B4
Whitton Way MK16 22 B2
Whitworth La MK5 46 A4
Whurley Way SL6 195 C1
Whybrow Gdns HP4 135 C3
Whyteladyes La SL8 195 C3
Whytingham Rd HP23 119 B2
Wick Rd HP23 133 B4
Wicken Park Rd MK19 31 A1
Wicken Rd MK18 30 C1
Wickets The SL6 202 B4
Wickstead Ave MK8 45 B3
Widbrook Rd SL6 196 A2
Widdenton View HP14 171 B3
Widecroft Rd SL0 207 C4
Widewater Pl UB9 190 B3
Widgeon Ho HP11 173 B3
Widmer End Comb Sch HP15 162 C3
Widmere Field HP16 151 B3
Widmere La SL7 183 A4
Widmore Cl HP5 143 C3
Widnell La OX25 95 B4
Wigan's La HP27 148 B3
Wiggington Bottom HP23 133 C4
Wiggington Ho SL4 210 B4
Wigmore Ct HP19 101 A1
Wigmore Rd HP19 101 A1
Wigwell Gdns MK17 55 A1
Wilberforce Mews 13 SL6 202 C4
Wildacre Rd MK5 46 A2
Wilderness The HP4 135 B2
Wildgreen N SL3 207 A1
Wildgreen S SL3 207 A1
Wildwood Ct WD3 167 C3
Wilford Cl MK15 35 B1
Wilford Rd SL3 206 C1
Wilfrids Wood Cl SL8 185 A3
Willen Comb Sch MK15 35 B4
Willen La MK14 34 C4
Willen Park Ave MK15 35 A4
Willen Rd MK16 22 B2
Willets Rise MK5 46 A3
Willetts La UB9 200 C4
Willey Ct MK11 32 C2
William Bandy Cl LU7 79 C2
William Burt Cl HP22 116 C1
William Durrant Sch The HP5 144 A2
William Ellis Cl SL4 211 A1
William Harding Cl HP21 115 C4
William Harding Comb Sch HP21 116 A3
William Hartley Yd SL3 199 A1
William Hill Dr HP22 102 B2
William Ho 7 HP13 173 C3
William Moulder Ct HP5 144 A2
William Penn Sch The SL2 198 B1
William St
Berkhamsted HP4 135 B2
Slough SL1 205 C3
Windsor SL4 210 B3
William Sutton Ho MK5 46 A3
Williams Circ MK7 48 A2
Williams Cl
Aylesbury HP19 101 B1
Hanslope MK19 10 C2
Williams Way HP27 138 B3
Williiam Smith Cl MK15 35 B2
Willis Rd HP17 127 A3
Willoners SL2 205 A4
Willoughby Rd SL3 207 A2
Willoughby's Wlk HP13 161 B1
Willow Ave
High Wycombe HP12 172 A2
New Denham UB9 201 B3
West Drayton UB8 208 C3
Willow Bank SL7 183 B3
Willow Chase HP15 162 C2
Willow Cl Colnbrook SL3 212 B4
Flackwell Heath HP10 185 B3
Moulsoe MK16 36 B4
Willow Cres E UB9 201 B4
Willow Cres W UB9 201 B4
Willow Ct
Aylesbury HP19 101 A1
High Wycombe HP11 173 C2
Walter's Ash HP14 161 B4
Willow Dr
Buckingham MK18 52 C4
Maidenhead SL6 203 A1
Willow End HP22 116 C1
Willow Gr
Old Stratford MK19 32 A3
Windsor SL4 210 A2
Willow Herb HP20 101 C2
Willow La HP7 165 C3
Willow Par SL3 207 A2
Willow Pk SL2 199 A3
Willow Pl SL4 210 B4
Willow Rd
Aylesbury HP19 101 B1
Brackley NN13 38 A3
Chinnor OX39 147 B3
Great Horwood MK17 55 A2
Poyle SL3 212 C3
Thame OX9 125 C1
Willow Rise HP17 127 A4
Willow Way
Loudwater HP11 174 A1
Milton Keynes MK2 58 B4
Princes Risborough HP27 139 A2
Wing LU7 79 C2
Willow Wlk HP15 163 A2
Willow Wood Cl SL1 197 A2
Willowbank HP22 131 A4

Willowbank Terr [5] HP21 ....115 C4
Willowbrook Slough SL4 .205 B1
Wendover HP22 ....131 A4
Willowford MK13 ....33 C3
Willowmead HP17 ......114 C3
Willowmead Cl [10] SL7 .183 C2
Willowmead Gdns SL7 .183 C2
Willowmead Rd [8] SL7 .183 C2
Willowmead Sq [9] SL7 .183 C2
Willows First Sch The MK6 ....35 A1
Willows Rd SL8 ....185 A2
Willows The
Amersham HP6 ....154 A2
[15] Bourne End SL8 .....185 A2
High Wycombe HP12 ...172 C4
Longwick HP27 ....138 C3
Windsor SL4 ....209 A4
Wilmar Cl UB8 ....201 B3
Wilmin Gr MK5 ....46 A4
Wilmot Rd SL1 ....197 A1
Wilsley Pound MK7 ....48 A4
Wilson Ct MK8 ....45 C4
Wilstone Resr Nature Reserve★ HP23 ......118 B4
Wilton Ave MK3 ....58 A4
Wilton Cl UB7 ....213 B4
Wilton Cres
Beaconsfield HP9 .....175 C2
Windsor SL4 ....209 B2
Wilton Hollow HP9 ...175 C2
Wilton La SL7 ....176 C2
Wilton Rd HP9 ....175 C2
Wiltshire Ave SL2 ....198 B1
Wiltshire Lodge [2] SL6 .202 C3
Wiltshire Rd SL7 .....183 C2
Wimbledon Pl MK13 ...34 B2
Wimblington Dr MK6 ...47 A2
Wimborne Cres MK4 ...45 C1
Wimpole Rd UB7 ......208 B3
Winbury Ct SL6 ....202 C4
Winbury Sch SL6 .....203 A2
Wincanton Hill MK3 ...57 B3
Winch Terr SL4 ....209 B3
Winchbottom La SL7, HP10 ....184 A4
Winchendon Rd HP18 ..112 A1
Winchester Circ MK10 ..36 A1
Winchester Cl
Amersham HP7 ....165 C4
Poyle SL3 ....212 C4
Winchester Ct HP11 ...174 A2
Winchester Dr SL6 ....202 A2
Winchester Ho HP21 ..115 C4
Windemere Dr MK2 ....58 B3
Windermere Cl
Aylesbury HP21 ....116 A3
Chorleywood WD3 ....167 A2
Windermere Gdns LU7 ..80 B4
Windermere Way
Slough SL1 ....204 B4
West Drayton UB7 ....208 C3
Windmill Cl
Aylesbury HP19 ......115 A4
Buckingham MK18 .....41 C1
Ivinghoe LU7 ....105 C3
Windsor SL4 ....210 A3
Windmill Dr HP15 .....162 C3
Windmill Hill
Chipperfield WD4 .....156 C4
Coleshill HP7 ....164 C1
Princes Risborough HP27 .139 A1
Windmill Hill Dr MK3 ...57 A4
Windmill Hill Rdbt MK4 ..46 B1
Windmill La HP15 .....162 C4
Windmill Par HP15 ....162 C4
Windmill Rd
Cookham SL8 ....195 C3
Fulmer SL3 ....199 B4
Gerrards Cross SL9 ...177 B2
Haddenham HP17 .....126 C3
Slough SL1 ....205 B3
Thame OX9 ....126 C1
Windmill St HP18 ......96 A1
Windmill Way
Cranfield MK43 ....25 B2
Tring HP23 ....118 C2
Windmill Wood HP6 ..154 A1
Windrush Ave SL3 ....207 A4
Windrush Cl UB10 ....201 C4
Windrush Ct
Aylesbury HP21 ....115 B2
High Wycombe HP13 ..173 C3
Windrush Dr HP13 ....173 C3
Windrush Ho SL8 .....185 A2
Windrush Way SL6 ....202 C4
Windsor & Eton Central Sta SL4 .....210 B3
Windsor & Eton Riverside Sta SL4 ...210 B4
Windsor Ave
Leighton Buzzard LU7 ..80 C4
Newport Pagnell MK16 ..22 C4
Windsor Boys' Sch The SL4 ....210 A3
Windsor Bsns Ctr The SL4 ....210 B4
Windsor Castle★ SL4 .210 C4
Windsor Cl
Bovingdon HP3 ......146 A2
Burnham SL1 ....197 B1
Windsor Cres HP10 ...174 B1
Windsor Ct HP6 ......154 B1
Windsor Dr HP13 .....162 B1

Windsor End HP9 .....186 C4
Windsor Girls' Sch SL4 .210 A2
Windsor Hill
Princes Risborough HP27 .139 B3
Wooburn Green HP10 .185 C3
Windsor La Burnham SL1 .197 B1
Little Kingshill HP16 ...152 B2
Windsor Rd
Aylesbury HP21 ....116 A4
Chesham HP5 ....144 A2
Datchet SL3 ....211 A4
Gerrards Cross SL9 ...188 B2
Maidenhead SL6 .....203 B1
Oakley Green SL6 ....203 B1
Pitstone LU7 ....105 B2
Slough SL1,SL2,SL3 ..205 C2
Wraysbury TW19 .....211 C1
Windsor Royal Sta [11] SL4 ....210 B3
Windsor St
Milton Keynes MK2 ....58 B4
Milton Keynes, Wolverton MK12 ....33 B3
Uxbridge UB8 ....201 B3
Winemar Cl MK19 ......11 A2
Winfold La MK4 ....46 A1
Wing Cl SL7 ....183 B1
Wing Rd Cublington LU7 .78 B1
Leighton Buzzard LU7 ..80 B3
Stewkley LU7 ....78 C3
Wingate Ave HP13 ....173 C4
Wingate Circ MK7 .....48 A2
Wingate Cl HP13 .....173 C4
Wingate Wlk HP20 ....116 A4
Wingfield Gr MK10 .....36 A1
Wingrave CE Comb Sch HP22 ....89 A2
Wingrave Crossroads HP22 ....88 C2
Wingrave Rd
Aston Abbots HP22 ....88 C2
Long Marston HP23 ...104 B1
Tring HP23 ....119 A3
Winkers Cl SL9 ....177 C1
Winkers La SL9 ......177 C2
Winkfield La SL4 .....209 A1
Winkfield Rd SL4 ....209 C1
Winnock Rd UB7 .....208 B3
Winsford Hill MK4 ....46 C2
Winslow CE Sch MK18 ..66 A3
Winslow Field HP16 ...151 C4
Winslow Gdns HP13 ..174 A4
Winslow Rd
Granborough MK18 ....75 C4
Great Horwood MK17 ..54 C1
Little Horwood MK17 ..55 B4
Nash MK17 ....55 B4
Swanbourne MK17 ....66 C2
Wingrave HP22 ....89 A2
Winstane Cl HP6 .....154 A3
Winstanley La MK5 ....46 B2
Winston Cl SL6 ......202 A1
Winston Gdns HP4 ...134 C3
Winston Ho HP11 ....174 A2
Winter Hill SL7,SL8 ..184 B1
Winter Hill Rd SL7 ...195 A2
Winterburn MK13 ......34 A3
Winters Way HP15 ...163 B4
Winterton Dr HP21 ...115 C2
Wintoun Path SL2 ...197 C1
Winvale SL1 ....205 C2
Winwood Slough SL2 .206 B4
Windsor SL4 ....209 C3
Winwood Dr HP22 ....85 A3
Wise La UB7 ....208 B1
Wisewood Rd MK4 ....45 C2
Wishart Gn MK7 ......48 C3
Wisley Ave MK13 .....34 B2
Wistmans MK4 ....46 B2
Witan Gate MK9 ......34 B1
Witchell HP22 ....131 A2
Witham Ct MK3 ....46 B1
Witham Way HP21 ...115 A2
Witheridge La HP9,HP10 .175 A4
Withey Cl SL4 ....209 C3
Withington MK13 .....34 A3
Withycombe MK4 ....46 C2
Withycroft SL3 ......206 C4
Witney Cl UB10 .....201 C4
Wittington Cotts SL7 .193 B3
Wittmills Oak MK18 ...41 C1
Wivelsfield LU6 ......92 C3
Woad La MK14 ......34 C4
Woburn Ave MK12 ....33 B3
Woburn Golf & Ctry Club The MK17 ....59 C4
Woburn La MK17 .....49 C2
Woburn Lower Sch MK17 ....60 C4
Woburn Rd
Aspley Heath MK17 ...49 B1
Little Brickhill MK17 ...59 C3
Sheeplane MK17 ......60 B1
Woburn Sands Rd MK17 .48 B2
Woburn Sands Sta MK17 .49 A3
Wodehouse Wlk MK16 ..22 A3
Wolf La SL4 ....209 C2
Wolfscote La MK4 ....46 A2
Wolsey Gdns MK13 ...34 A2
Wolstan Cl UB9 .....190 A1
Wolston Mdw MK10 ...35 C2
Wolverton Rd
Castlethorpe MK19 ....20 A3
Milton Keynes, Giffard Park MK14 ....21 C1
Milton Keynes, Wolverton MK12,MK19 ....33 C4
Newport Pagnell MK16 ..22 A4

Wolverton Sta MK19 ...33 C4
Wooburn Common Rd SL1,HP10 ....186 A1
Wooburn Grange HP10 .185 B2
Wooburn Green La HP9 .186 A4
Wooburn Manor Pk HP10 ....185 C3
Wooburn Mews HP10 .185 C3
Wood Cl SL4 ....210 B2
Wood End
Little Horwood MK17 ..55 C1
Nash MK17 ....55 B4
Wood End Cl SL2 ....187 B1
Wood End Fst Sch MK14 .34 B4
Wood End La MK16 ....23 C1
Wood La
Aspley Guise MK17 ....49 B2
Iver SL0 ....207 A4
Milton Keynes MK14 ...34 C4
Pottspury NN12 ......18 C2
Slough SL1,SL2 ......205 A2
South Heath HP16 ...152 C4
Tingewick MK18 ......51 A3
Weston Underwood MK46 ..6 A1
Wood Lane Cl
Flackwell Heath HP10 .173 C1
Iver Heath SL0 ....200 A1
Wood Pond Cl HP9 ...176 B2
Wood Rd MK43 ....3 C4
Wood St
Milton Keynes MK13 ...33 C4
Waddesdon HP18 .....99 A4
Woburn Sands MK17 ..49 A2
Wood Way MK17 .....174 C1
Woodbank HP27 .....149 B3
Woodbank Ave SL9 ..188 B3
Woodbank Dr HP8 ...177 B4
Woodbine Cl HP27 ...138 C3
Woodbine Cotts SL9 .188 B4
Woodbridge Ho SL8 .201 B3
Woodburn Mead HP10 .185 C3
Woodbury Cl SL8 ....185 B2
Woodchester Pk HP9 .175 B3
Woodcock Ave HP14 .161 A4
Woodcote SL6 ....202 B3
Woodcote Gn HP13 ..161 B1
Woodcote Lawns HP5 .144 A2
Woodcroft Rd HP5 ...144 B2
Woodfield HP27 .....149 B3
Woodfield Dr SL6 ...202 A3
Woodfield Pk HP6 ...154 A2
Woodfield Rd HP27 ..139 B2
Woodford Cl HP19 ...115 C4
Woodford Way SL2 ..198 A1
Woodhall Cl UB8 ....201 B4
Woodhill Ave SL9 ...189 A3
Woodhill Ct
Amersham HP6 .....154 B1
Gerrards Cross SL9 ..188 C2
Woodhouse Ct MK14 ..34 B3
Woodhurst Dr UB9 ..189 C3
Woodhurst Rd SL6 ..196 A1
Woodhurst S SL6 ...196 B1
Woodland Ave
Leighton Buzzard LU7 ..70 C4
Slough SL1 ....205 B3
Windsor SL4 ....209 C2
Woodland Cl
High Wycombe HP12 ..172 B3
Marlow SL7 ....183 C2
Tring HP23 ....118 C1
Woodland La WD3 ...167 B3
Woodland Pl WD3 ...167 C3
Woodland Rd WD3 ..178 B3
Woodland View
Chesham HP5 ....154 B3
Milton Keynes MK12 ...33 B3
Woodland Way
Marlow SL7 ....183 C2
Woburn Sands MK17 ..49 A2
Woodlands SL9 .....188 C3
Woodlands Ave HP4 .135 B2
Woodlands Bsns Pk SL6 ....202 A1
Woodlands Cl
Buckingham MK18 ....41 C1
Gerrards Cross SL9 ..189 A3
Holmer Green HP15 ..163 B3
Woodlands Cotts [4] SL2 ....198 B4
Woodlands Cres MK18 ..41 C1
Woodlands Dr
Beaconsfield HP9 ...175 B2
Walter's Ash HP14 ...161 B4
Woodlands Glade
Beaconsfield HP9 ...175 B2
Farnham Common SL2 .187 B1
Woodlands Hill HP9 .186 C3
Woodlands Park Ave SL6 ....202 A1
Woodlands Park Prim Sch SL6 ......202 A1
Woodlands Park Rd SL6 ....202 A2
Woodlands The
Amersham HP6 .....154 B2
Tylers Green HP10 ...162 C4
Woodlands View HP14 .174 A4
Woodlane Gdns HP10 .174 A1
Woodley Cl HP7 .....165 B4
Woodley Headland MK6 .47 B3
Woodley Hill HP5 ...154 B3
Woodman Cl LU7 ....79 C2
Woodmans Cl MK19 ..31 C2
Woodmans Croft HP15 .44 A3
Woodmoor End SL8 .196 A4
Woodpiece Rd OX25 ..94 C4
Woodruff Ave MK14 ..34 C2

Woodrush Cl MK6 ....47 A2
Woods Pl [16] Tring HP23 .119 A2
Wendover HP22 .....131 A2
Woodside
Aspley Guise MK17 ....49 B2
Eaton Bray LU6 ......92 C3
Flackwell Heath HP10 .185 B3
Milton Keynes MK11 ...32 C3
Woodside Ave
Amersham HP6 .....154 B2
Beaconsfield HP9 ...175 B2
Flackwell Heath HP10 .185 B4
Woodside Cl
Beaconsfield HP9 ...175 B2
Gerrards Cross SL9 ..177 C1
Loudwater HP11 ....174 A1
Woodside Hill SL9 ...177 C1
Woodside Jun Sch HP6 .154 C1
Woodside Rd
Amersham HP6 .....154 B1
Beaconsfield HP9 ...175 B2
High Wycombe HP13 .174 A4
Woodside Way
Leighton Buzzard LU7 ..80 B3
Tylers Green HP10 ...174 B4
Woodspring Ct MK10 ..35 C1
Woodstock Ave SL3 .206 B1
Woodstock Cl
Aylesbury HP21 .....116 A3
Maidenhead SL6 ....195 C1
Woodstock Ct MK10 ..34 A4
Woodstock Dr UB10 ..201 C4
Woodview Cl HP12 ...161 A1
Woodview Dr HP27 ..150 B3
Woodville OX39 .....147 B3
Woodville Cres NN12 ..18 C3
Woodward Ho [4] MK2 ..58 C4
Woodward Pl MK8 ...34 A1
Woodway HP27 .....149 B3
Woodways HP17 ....127 A3
Woodwicks WD3 ....178 B3
Woollerton Cres HP22 .131 B3
Woollerton Ct HP27 ..139 A2
Woolmans MK11 .....33 A2
Woolrich Gdns MK12 .32 C3
Wooster Rd HP9 ....175 B2
Wootton Dr HP10 ...185 C4
Wootton Gn OX27 ....72 C3
Wootton La HP17 ...113 C1
Wootton Way SL6 ...202 B3
Worcester Cl
Maidenhead SL6 ....202 B2
Newport Pagnell MK16 ..22 A2
Worcester Gdns SL1 .205 B2
Worcester Rd UB8 ..208 B4
Wordsworth Ave MK16 .22 A2
Wordsworth Dr MK3 .58 A4
Wordsworth Rd
High Wycombe HP11 .173 A3
Slough SL2 ....197 B1
Wordsworth Way UB7 .208 C1
Worlds End La HP22 .130 C4
Worminghall Rd
Ickford HP18 ....123 C2
Oakley HP18 ....109 B2
Worminghall Rd SL1,HP10 ....123 B4
Worple The TW19 ...211 C1
Worrelle Ave MK10 ...36 A2
Worster Rd SL8 ....195 C3
Worthies The HP7 ...165 A4
Worthington Rd LU7 ..93 C4
Wotton End HP18 ....96 B4
Wotton Path HP21 ..115 C2
Wotton Rd HP18 .....97 C1
Wr Twr Cl UB8 .....201 C4
Wray Ct MK4 ....46 A1
Wraysbury Prim Sch TW19 ....211 C1
Wraysbury Sta TW19 .212 A1
Wren Cl MK18 ......52 C4
Wren Ct SL3 ....207 A2
Wren Dr UB7 ....208 B2
Wren Rd HP16 .....151 B3
Wren Vale HP13 ....173 A4
Wren Wlk LU6 ......92 C2
Wrens Pk MK10 .....36 A1
Wrensfield SL7 .....183 B1
Wright SL4 ....209 B3
Wright Sq SL4 .....209 B2
Wright Way SL4 ....209 B2
Wright's Cotts [4] SL9 .177 B1
Wrights Cl HP14 ....171 A3
Wroxton Ct MK4 ....45 C1
Wyatt Cl HP13 ......172 C4
Wyatt Rd SL4 ......209 B2
Wyatt's Rd WD3 ....167 C3
Wychwood HP10 ...152 A2
Wychwood Gdns HP12 .172 B3
Wychwood Rise HP16 .152 A2
Wyclands Ho HP12 ..161 A1
Wycombe Abbey Sch HP11 ....173 A3
Wycombe Chair Mus★ HP13 ....173 A4
Wycombe End HP9 .175 C1
Wycombe General Hospl HP11 ....173 A3
Wycombe High Sch (Girls) HP11 ....172 C2
Wycombe Ind Mall HP11 ....172 C4
Wycombe La HP10 ..185 C4
Wycombe Rd
Beacon's Bottom HP14 .159 B2
Holmer Green HP15 ..163 A3
Lacey Green HP27 ..149 A2

Wycombe Rd continued
Lane End HP14 ....159 C1
Marlow SL7 ....183 C2
Prestwood HP16 ....151 B3
Wycombe View HP10 .174 A1
Milton Keynes MK3 ...46 C1
Wye Cl Aylesbury HP21 .115 B3
Milton Keynes MK3 ...46 C1
Wye Est HP11 ....173 C3
Wye Rd HP10 ....185 B4
Wye Valley Sch The SL8 ....185 A2
Wykeham Gate HP17 .126 C3
Wykeham Rise OX39 .147 B3
Wykeham Way HP17 .126 C3
Wykeridge Cl HP5 ...144 A2
Wylands Rd SL3 ....207 A1
Wylie End MK13 .....34 A4
Wymering Rd HP21 ..116 B3
Wymers Cl SL1 .....197 A2
Wymers Wood Rd SL1 .197 A2
Wymondham MK10 ...36 A1
Wynbury Dr HP13 ...162 C1
Wyndale Cl RG9 ....191 C1
Wyndham Ave HP13 .161 C1
Wyndham Cres SL1 .197 A2
Wyness Ave MK17 ...59 C3
Wynford Gn HP21 ...115 C3
Wyngates LU7 ......80 C3
Wyngrave Pl HP9 ...175 B3
Wynn Gr HP15 ......163 A2
Wynne Jones Ctr HP21 .115 C4
Wynnstay Gdns SL7 .183 C3
Wynnswick Rd HP9 .176 B3
Wynyard Ct MK6 ....46 C4
Wyre Cl HP17 ......127 A3
Wyvern Fst Sch MK12 .33 B3
Wyvern Way UB8 ...201 B2

Y

Yalts Brow MK4 .....46 A1
Yardley Ave LU7 ....105 B2
Yardley Gn HP20 ...101 C1
Yardley Gobion CE Prim Sch NN12 ..18 C3
Yardley Hastings Prim Sch NN7 ....1 A4
Yardley Rd Cosgrove MK19 19 A1
Olney MK46 ....6 C3
Pottspury NN12 ......18 C2
Yarmouth Rd SL1 ...205 B3
Yarrow Pl MK14 .....34 C2
Yarrowside HP7 ....166 A4
Ye Meads SL6 ......203 C3
Yeates Cl Thame OX9 .125 C1
Yeats Cl MK16 ......21 C3
Yeomans Cl NN13 ...38 A4
Yeomans Dr MK14 ...22 A1
Yeovil Fst Ctr SL1 ..204 C4
Yeovil Rd SL1 ......204 C4
Yew Ave UB7 ....208 C3
Yew Tree Cl
Beaconsfield HP9 ...175 C1
Botley HP5 ....145 A1
Eaton Bray LU6 .....92 C3
Ivinghoe LU7 ....105 C3
Maidenhead SL6 ....202 C4
Newton Longville MK17 .57 B2
Stoke Mandeville HP22 .116 A1
Yew Tree Ct MK19 ...11 A1
Yew Tree Dr
Bovingdon HP3 .....146 A2
Hazlemere HP15 ...162 C3
Yew Tree Rd Slough SL1 .206 A2
Uxbridge UB10 .....201 C2
Yew Wlk HP15 .....163 A2
Yiewsley Ct UB7 ...208 C3
Yolsum Cl HP17 ....126 C3
Yonder Slade MK18 ..52 C3
York Ave Slough SL1 .205 B4
Windsor SL4 ....210 A3
York Cl HP7 ....165 C4
York Ct [6] LU7 .....80 C4
York Ho
High Wycombe HP13 .173 C4
Milton Keynes MK3 ...57 C4
York Pl HP21 ....115 C4
York Rd Henley-on-T RG9 .191 B1
Maidenhead SL6 ....203 A4
Marlow SL7 ....183 B1
Milton Keynes MK11 ..32 B3
Uxbridge UB8 ......201 B3
Windsor SL4 ....210 A3
York Way HP12 ....172 C2
Yorke Cl HP22 .....117 C3
Youens Rd HP12 ...172 B3
Young Cl HP21 .....116 A3

Z

Zealand Ave UB7 ...213 B4
Zetland Ct SL6 .....203 A4

NH	NJ	NK		
NN	NO	NP		
NS	NT	NU		
NX	NY	NZ		
SC	SD	SE	TA	
SH	SJ	SK	TF	TG
SN	SO	SP	TL	TM
SS	ST	SU	TQ	TR
SX	SY	SZ	TV	

Any feature in this atlas can be given a unique reference to help you find the same feature on other Ordnance Survey maps of the area, or to help someone else locate you if they do not have a Street Atlas.

The grid squares in this atlas match the Ordnance Survey National Grid and are at 1 kilometre intervals. The small figures at the bottom and sides of every other grid line are the National Grid kilometre values (**00** to **99** km) and are repeated across the country every 100 km (see left).

To give a unique National Grid reference you need to locate where in the country you are. The country is divided into 100 km squares with each square given a unique two-letter reference. Use the administrative map to determine in which 100 km square a particular page of this atlas falls.

The bold letters and numbers between each grid line (**A** to **F**, **1** to **4**) are for use within a specific Street Atlas only, and when used with the page number, are a convenient way of referencing these grid squares.

Example   The railway bridge over DARLEY GREEN RD in grid square A1

Step 1: Identify the two-letter reference, in this example the page is in **SP**

Step 2: Identify the 1 km square in which the railway bridge falls. Use the figures in the southwest corner of this square: Eastings **17**, Northings **74**. This gives a unique reference: **SP 17 74**, accurate to 1 km.

Step 3: To give a more precise reference accurate to 100 m you need to estimate how many tenths along and how many tenths up this 1 km square the feature is. This makes the bridge about **8** tenths along and about **1** tenth up from the southwest corner.

This gives a unique reference: **SP 178 741**, accurate to 100 m.

Eastings (read from left to right along the bottom) come before Northings (read from bottom to top). If you have trouble remembering say to yourself "Along the hall, THEN up the stairs"!

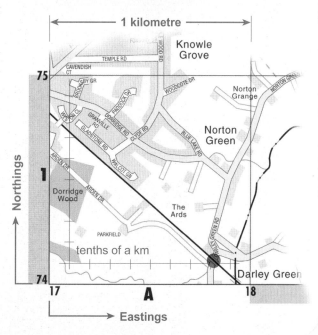